Heinrich Potthoff/Susanne Miller

The Social Democratic Party of Germany

1848–2005

Translated by Martin Kane

Bibliografische Information der Deutschen Bibliothek

Die Deutsche Bibliothek verzeichnet
diese Publikation in der Deutschen Nationalbibliografie;
detaillierte bibliografische Daten sind im Internet
über *http://www.dnb.ddb.de* abrufbar.

ISBN-10: 3-8012-0365-4
ISBN-13: 978-3-8012-0365-8

English Translation © 2006 Verlag J. H. W. Dietz Nachf. GmbH,
Dreizehnmorgenweg 24, 53175 Bonn
Updated version of „Kleine Geschichte der SPD 1848-2002".
© 2002 Verlag J. H. W. Dietz Nachf., Bonn
Jacket Design: Daniela Müller, Bonn
Cover Photo: demonstration by young German workers, around 1907,
Archiv der sozialen Demokratie der Friedrich-Ebert-Stiftung,
Ulrich Baumgarten/vario press
Typesetting: PAPYRUS – Schreib- und Büroservice, Bonn
Printing: Ebner & Spiegel, Ulm
All rights reserved.
Printed in Germany 2006

Please visit our website: *www.dietz-verlag.de*

Preface

German social democracy never regarded itself as a movement focused solely on Germany. Its influence stretched beyond national borders into Europe and the rest of the world. Amongst its sister parties it plays, even today, a significant political and programmatic role. It has been instrumental in shaping the concept of a free democratic socialism, and in smoothing the path to social democracy.

The SPD is a party with tradition which has exercised a vital political role in German history over many decades. At heart, its roots go back to the European revolution of 1848/49. In most other European countries, on the other hand, social democratic or socialist parties did not come into existence until the end of the nineteenth, and beginning of the twentieth century. In many respects, German social democracy served as a model. It was considered to hold strong theoretical principles, was organisationally strong, successful in elections, and played a leading role in the Second International. Founded as a class party of oppressed workers, the SPD has transformed itself in the course of its history into an open, left-wing *Volkspartei* (people's party). It played a decisive part in shaping and driving forward the construction and development of a more socially just society. It has fought more than any other German party for democracy, freedom, and international understanding.

Under Willy Brandt, it won great respect as a party of peace and as the advocate for liberal social movements in Europe and the Third World. As President of the Socialist International he set important guidelines for overcoming eurocentrism and taking a more global perspective. With Gerhard Schröder as Chancellor, the party set Germany on the path to modernisation and raised Germany's profile as a power committed to peace and the avoidance of conflict.

The most recent German edition of this history of German social democracy, which has become a standard work, appeared in 2002. For this updated 8th edition, the second part dealing with the period 1945 to 1982, which was written by Susanne Miller, was completely revised. A new addition was a third section covering the development of the SPD from 1982 to 2002. It dealt with the long years in opposition (1982–1998), the upheaval of 1989/90, and finally the first years of the red-green coalition under Gerhard Schröder (1998–2002). This present English edition takes the history of the German Social Democratic Party up to the federal elections on 18 September 2005, and the loss of the office of Chancellor. The detailed account includes an updated chronological table, informative tables and diagrams, and a selected bibliography.

The revision and expansion of this history of the Social Democratic Party of Germany has been conducted in close consultation with Susanne Miller, whose knowledge and advice have benefited the work at every step. I am deeply grateful for her friendship and assistance. The critical help, scrutiny, and stimulating comments of Dieter Dowe, Bernd Faulenbach, Sabine Lemke, Thomas Meyer, and Peter Munkelt have been invaluable. To them, as well as to colleagues in the *Archiv der sozialen Demokratie* and all those many others who have lent me their support, I owe a great debt of gratitude. Martin Kane (Canterbury, England), who has a sound knowledge of the history of the SPD, has been responsible for translating the German original into English. The publishers J.H.W. Dietz Nachf. and the Friedrich-Ebert-Foundation have given me constant encouragement and backing in the writing of this history of the German Social Democratic Party. To them both, my heartfelt thanks.

Königswinter, October 2005.

Heinrich Potthoff

Contents

Part One
Heinrich Potthoff
Social Democracy from its Beginnings to 1945

Introduction 13

  I. Early Beginnings with the Revolution of 1848/49 18

    1. Political and Social Conditions around the Middle of the Century 18
    2. Theories about Solving the Social Question 20
    3. 1848 and the First Workers' Organisations 24

  II. The Formation of the Social Democratic Workers' Movement 28

    1. Ferdinand Lassalle and the General Association of German Workers 28
    2. The First International 32
    3. The "Eisenachers" 35
    4. Unification in Gotha 38

  III. From the Founding of the Reich to the Lapsing of the Anti-Socialist Law 42

    1. The Paris Commune 42
    2. The Anti-Socialist Law 43
    3. The Political Consequences of Oppression 46

  IV. Between Radical Theory and Reformist Practice: on the Path to the First World War as a Mass Party 50

    1. The Erfurt Programme 50
    2. Economic and Social Change 53
    3. Practical Politics and Theoretical Disputes 57
    4. The Revisionism Dispute and Mass Strike Debate 62

  V. In the First World War 69

    1. Defence of the Fatherland and *"Burgfrieden"* (domestic truce) .. 69

2. Schism in the Party and the Birth of the USPD (Independent Social Democratic Party) 72
  3. The Majority Social Democrats on the Path to Government Responsibility 74

VI. From the Revolution to the Weimar Republic 78

  1. The German Revolution 1918/19 78
  2. A New State on Old Foundations 86
  3. "Versailles" and the Consequences 92

VII. Weimar Democracy 97

  1. Workers' Parties and Trade Unions in the Early Years of the Republic 97
  2. The Kapp Putsch and its Repercussions 102
  3. The Path of Social Democracy from 1920 to 1928 106
  4. The Second Hermann Müller Cabinet 117

VIII. The Destruction of Democracy 120

  1. Factors in the Crisis in State and Society 120
  2. The Social Democrats' Defensive Battle 127

IX. The Struggle for a Better Germany 136

  1. Resisting Totalitarian *Gleichschaltung* (Co-ordination) 136
  2. Resistance in the Labour Movement 139
  3. The Path and Goals of Democratic Socialism in Exile 148

X. The Legacy and the Task Ahead 160

Part Two
Susanne Miller:
The SPD – the People's Party of the Left
Revised Version by Heinrich Potthoff

I. Social Democracy in Postwar Germany 165

  1. Organisational Refoundation 165
  2. Programmatic Political Perspectives 171

    3. Opting for Opposition 179
    4. The Creation of the *Grundgesetz* (Basic Law) 182

II. "Constructive Opposition" 187

    1. The Struggle for a "New National Self-Awareness" 189
    2. Party Reform and the Godesberg Programme 195
    3. A Party in Waiting 202

III. The Social Democrats in Government 209

    1. The SPD in the Grand Coalition 209
    2. Off to Pastures New 213
    3. A Party in Flux 224

IV. The Social-Liberal Coalition in the Shadow of Worldwide Economic Recession 231

    1. Setbacks and Testing Times 232
    2. Renewal of the Mandate 235
    3. New Tasks for the SPD 238
    4. The Federal Elections of 5 October 1980 242

V. Crisis and the End of the Social-Liberal Coalition 244

    1. Discontent and Conflicts in the SPD 244
    2. Genscher's Call for a *Wende* (turnabout) 249
    3. The SPD Munich Party Congress 252
    4. The Collapse of the Social-Liberal Coalition 254

VI. A Balance Sheet for the Social-Liberal Era 258

Part Three
Heinrich Potthoff:
A Party in Transition
Stagnation – Search for Direction – The Responsibility of Government

I. The Predicament in Opposition 271

    1. Adjusting to Opposition 272
    2. Stirring Topics of the Day 278
    3. The Internal Development of the SPD 284

      4. Falling in Step and Hopeful Prospects 291
      5. A New Basic Programme 302

  II. Peaceful Revolution and the Process of Unification 307

      1. From the Citizens' Movement to the SDP/SPD 308
      2. Social Democracy and German Unification 320

  III. The Search for Direction in Unified Germany 331

      1. Elections, Fluctuating Events, and Change 331
      2. The Internal Problems of a Fragmented Party 339
      3. A Short Interregnum 344
      4. Shadows from the Past 349
      5. Fresh Impetus under Lafontaine's Regency 357

  IV. The Schröder Government and the SPD as the Party of
     Government 365

      1. Shaky Beginnings and Consolidation 365
      2. Growing Maturity in the Face of Difficult Challenges 377
      3. Profile and Practice of a Transformed SPD 381
      4. A Provisional Balance Sheet 389

Addendum: The SPD at the Crossroads 397

1. A Laborious Start after Re-election 397
2. The Party and its Development 404
3. In Troubled Waters 411

Chronological Table 425

Statistical Tables and Diagrams 453

Select Bibliography 467

Index 485

Part One

Heinrich Potthoff:

Social Democracy from its Beginnings to 1945

Introduction

In Gerhard Schröder, from 1998 to 2005, Germany once again had an SPD Federal Chancellor. The Social Democratic Party carried the responsibility for policy in a unified Germany as well as for German policy in Europe and the world. The difficult tasks confronting Schröder's government also shaped the face of the party. Social democracy underwent a transformation in this period. Under changed conditions it attempted to define its identity as a party of freedom and social democracy for both the present and the future. The SPD is the oldest German party, with roots going back to the middle of the nineteenth century. There would have been good reasons in 1988 to mark its one hundred and fortieth anniversary; instead, it celebrated the hundred and twenty-five years since its founding. At this point the SPD only existed in the Federal Republic. Then in 1989 brave men and women in the GDR had the courage to set up a social democratic party there. Following the process of German unification Social Democrats on both sides of the border were reunited. Since 27 September 1990 the party can once again rightly call itself the "Social Democratic Party of Germany".

This has been the official designation of the party since 1890. Throughout every period of turmoil, crisis, and fresh beginnings it has remained unchanged. The "Social Democratic Workers Party" founded in 1869 by August Bebel and Wilhelm Liebknecht in Eisenach had already called itself "social democratic". In its programme it declared its belief in "political freedom" as the "indispensable precondition of the economic liberation of the working classes. The social question is therefore inseparable from the political one, its solution conditional on it, and only possible in a democratic state."[1] Even at this point something of central importance was emerging which would remain a defining feature of social democracy: the close association of socialism and democratic freedom. In its Frankfurt Declaration of 3 July 1951, the Socialist International had captured this concept in the memorable words: "There can be no socialism

---

1 Programm der Sozialdemokratischen Arbeiterpartei, Eisenach 1869, published in Dieter Dowe and Kurt Klotzbach (eds), Programmatische Dokumente der deutschen Sozialdemokratie (Bonn 4th rev. edn 2004), pp. 159–163.

without freedom. Socialism can only be brought about by democracy, democracy can only be perfected by socialism."[2]

From the very beginning, the synthesis between socialism and democracy was a vital guideline for the activities of the social democratic workers' movement. Even though, with the adoption in theoretical statements of Marxist analyses and slogans, terms such as "class struggle", "revolution", and "seizing of political power" predominated, this was not seen as clashing with the aim of achieving a free and democratic socialism.

The German Social Democrats totally repudiated Lenin's call for a dictatorship of the proletariat. They were in no doubt that the Russian way was not their own and considered respect for democratic majority decisions, the rule of law, freedom of speech and the individual, civil rights, and respect for human dignity to be the indispensable prerequisites of a just social order. They constituted the self-evident principles which determined how they acted. To clearly distinguish it from communism, socialism put express emphasis on freedom and democracy. The experience of Hitler's fascism and Stalin's terror regime shifted the belief in democracy and freedom even more sharply into focus. Social democracy and democratic socialism became largely overlapping and interchangeable terms.

In the Godesberg Programme of 1959, in which the SPD presented itself as a democratic people's party of the left, central importance was given to the basic principles of "freedom, justice, and solidarity". Explicitly renouncing any claim to "ultimate truths" and insights, the SPD committed itself to the principle of social dynamism, constant struggle and action: "Socialism is a perpetual endeavour to achieve and preserve freedom and justice, and to prove oneself within them". This basic declaration is also fundamental to the Berlin Programme of 1989.

The words "socialism" and "socialist" are barely used today by German Social Democrats. The autocratic rule of Communist Party dictatorships which presented themselves as "real-existing socialism" has continued to inflict discredit on the term socialism. Social democracy never regarded systems such as these as socialist or as representing socialism, since socialism is only conceivable under freedom and democracy. Nevertheless, this abuse of the concept brought democratic socialism itself into disrepute. The Social Democrats and their sister parties in other countries wanted to use this term to reduce their striving for a juster society and a more comprehensive democracy to one common denominator, and in

---

2 In Dowe and Klotzbach (eds), *Programmatische Dokumente (2004)*, pp. 266–275, quotation p. 269.

Poster depicting the "Family Tree of Modern Socialism"

doing this they were going back to their historical roots. After 1800, the term "socialism" had increasingly become part of the political vocabulary. Under the influence of Marxism, one view gained ground which saw it as a system operating in a society freed from exploitation and repression by the socialisation of the means of production. Alongside this understanding of the term, however, there existed other forms and interpretations of it, such as religious, Christian socialism, cooperative socialism, guild socialism, and state socialism.

In a further sense, the terms "socialism" and "socialist" were increasingly used to denote social endeavours which had equality and a new community of solidarity as their guiding principles. In modern times they were increasingly thought of in relation to the workers' movement for emancipation – inasfar as this manifested itself as an independent political and social force – and to its "socialist" ideas which had the aim of changing society. This context can still be traced today as, for instance, in the names of many of the sister parties of social democracy, and in the term "Socialist International". Thus, the term "socialist" was used primarily to distinguish those workers' organisations which were not associated with the Christian or liberal camp. The term "socialist" covers the whole broad spectrum of the movement for social freedom of the "Fourth Estate", with its goal of a new social order of freedom and justice. The struggle to achieve this was a product not least of the state and social order and the economic structure with which the "socialists" were confronted. Moreover, since even within German social democracy in the nineteenth and twentieth centuries the words "socialism" and "socialist" were seldom deployed in a consistent and unambiguous manner, they always have to be understood in their particular context.

The history of the social democratic movement in Germany has to be seen against the background of political, economic, and social developments. It is imperative here, too, to consider the hostile forces it had to confront. Insofar as length permits, this is what this book attempts to do. In presenting the history of the actual party it has been necessary to concentrate on particular areas. It was felt important, however, to focus not only on the great ideas and outstanding political figures. This book is also at pains to depict the situation and concerns of ordinary Social Democrats at grassroots level, as well as the condition of men and women, blue and white-collar workers and members of other social classes, who felt drawn to social democracy. This has only been possible in broad-brush outline. A comprehensive, complete history in several volumes of "Workers and the Workers' Movement in Germany" was not embarked upon in the Federal Republic until the 1980s.[3] In addition to this there are a number of useful reference works and materials,[4] as well as an abundance of substantial monographs and specialised studies.

This short history of the SPD has continued to expand since its first edition. It has been revised, reworked, and updated. It has always aimed to deal with events as close as possible to the present. In the last and seventh edition of 1991 additions were made to the chronological table and documents, the narrative, however, did not go beyond the end of the SPD/FDP coalition.

After losing power in September 1982, the SPD began a difficult and arduous period in opposition. When, in December 1989 in Berlin, they announced their new Basic Programme, eastern Europe and the GDR were already in the grip of complete change. The awakening to freedom and self-determination, democracy and pluralism, and the striving for individual happiness and prosperity heralded a new era for Europe and Germany, and also for social democracy. In this new edition, Part Two, which deals with the period from 1949 to 1982, has been given a particularly thorough reworking since the history of social democracy in unified Germany required an extension of the predominantly Western perspective to include developments in Eastern Germany. Completely new is the Third Part on the development of German social democracy from 1982 up to the present and the SPD government under Gerhard Schröder. For the historian who prefers to maintain a certain distance in time from events, experiencing the present as it happens is certainly fraught with risk. Nevertheless, in the interest of readers who wish to see account taken of most recent events, this risk has been taken.

---

3 See the three volumes by Heinrich August Winkler: Von der Revolution zur Stabilisierung. Arbeiter und Arbeiterbewegung in der Weimarer Republik 1918 bis 1924 (Berlin/Bonn, 2nd edn 1985); Der Schein der Normalität. Arbeiter und Arbeiterbewegung in der Weimarer Republik 1924 bis 1930 (Berlin/Bonn 1985, 2nd edn 1990); Der Weg in die Katastrophe. Arbeiter und Arbeiterbewegung in der Weimarer Republik 1930 bis 1933 (Berlin/Bonn 1987, 2nd edn 1990). See the bibliography for further works on this project by Jürgen Kocka, Gerhard A. Ritter and Klaus Tenfelde, and Michael Schneider. In the 1960s, an eight-volume Geschichte der deutschen Arbeiterbewegung (Berlin 1966) was published in the GDR by the Institut für Marxismus Leninismus beim Zentralkomitee der SED.
4 Particularly worthy of mention is the Lern- und Arbeitsbuch deutsche Arbeiterbewegung. Darstellung – Chroniken – Dokumente, published under the direction of Thomas Meyer, Susanne Miller, and Joachim Rohlfes, 4 vols (Bonn 2nd rev. edn 1988).

I. Early Beginnings with the Revolution of 1848/49

1. Political and Social Conditions around the Middle of the Century

"Freedom, equality, fraternity!", and "Unity makes strong!" – these are the slogans on a red flag carefully preserved in the SPD party archive. At its centre is depicted a handshake amidst a garland of oak leaves, with the words beneath: "23 May 1863, Ferdinand Lassalle".[1] It is the old flag of the General Association of German Workers (ADAV), and the traditional banner of the SPD.

The founding of an independent workers' party in Leipzig on 23 May 1863 is held to mark the birth of German social democracy. From this point on we may speak of an uninterrupted continuity in the socialist, social democratic workers' movement and the party in Germany. It is now an independent political organisation, its democratic and social purpose underpinned by a theory all its own, and whose long road ahead would be accompanied both by great successes as well as setbacks. However, while acknowledging the contribution of great personalities to its historical development, a movement such as social democracy was not created out of nothing by singular acts of individual will. Only under certain favourable political and social preconditions does energetic willpower have a chance of translating itself into action.

The handshake on the flag of the General Association of German Workers is a reminder that already fifteen years beforehand workers' organisations had stepped onto the political stage. The printer Stephan Born's *Arbeiterverbrüderung* (Brotherhood of Workers) began the tradition of this symbol. Under this emblem of solidarity, workers found themselves steadfastly united for the first time in an organisation of their own.

In the same year, just a few months before, the *Communist Manifesto* appeared in February 1848. When Karl Marx and Friedrich Engels spoke of proletarians who "live only as long as they find work" and who "must sell themselves piecemeal, are a commodity, like every other article of commerce",[2] they were thinking primarily of the industrial workforce. In central Europe at the time, this was only a small section of the population. In contrast to England, which was much further advanced, indus-

---

[1] The SPD party archive is to be found today at the Friedrich-Ebert-Stiftung in Bonn.
[2] From The Communist Manifesto. In Karl Marx: Selected Writings, edited by David McLellan (Oxford 1977), p. 226.

trialisation in Germany was still in its infancy. The talk in the *Communist Manifesto* of proletarians who had "nothing to lose but their chains" was applicable nevertheless, in a modified form, to a whole stratum of German society.

It was not industrialisation which had created the misery of a broad, hard-working, but nonetheless starving and possessionless class. This "Fourth Estate", the "proletariat" as the language of the time had it, had already existed previously in other forms. With the dissolution of feudal structures, the right to exercise a trade, and the peasants' liberation in the wake of the Enlightenment and the French Revolution, there was a rapid increase in marriage amongst journeymen and peasants' sons. More suitable nutrition (cultivation of potatoes), increased agricultural production (crop rotation), an improved system of food distribution, the absence of plague and other catastrophes, and the beginnings of hygiene (use of soap) are important causes of the population explosion. This led to what became known as pauperism, the rise of a numerically large underclass which could barely keep itself alive. Statistics show that in the first half of the nineteenth century almost fifty per cent of the population belonged to this "proletariat".[3] It was virtually impossible to find paid work. Particularly bleak was the situation of the weavers and spinners in Silesia, Saxony, and Westphalia whose earnings from outwork lay far below subsistence level. As Gerhart Hauptmann depicted so impressively in *The Weavers*, their rebellion in the 1840s against hunger and exploitation was ruthlessly suppressed by military force.

Factory work on the other hand at least meant work and bread. Despite its severity, it was an anchor of hope to cling to. Before 1850, in Germany the chance of finding work in industry was offered to very few. The Krupp firm, for instance, began in 1811 with seven workers, and had grown to just eighty by 1849. This is when the rapid rise began: by 1857 the work force numbered one thousand. The early beginnings of industrialisation are characterised by a surplus of labour. Unimaginable poverty amongst large sections of the population, alongside the rapidly increasing prosperity of a small band of capitalists, opened up a deep and growing gulf between the haves and the have-nots. A working day in the 1840s of thirteen, fourteen, and even up to seventeen hours under the harshest of conditions, falling wages, and with widespread cheap female and child

---

[3] A detailed description of these circumstances is to be found in Jürgen Kocka, *Weder Stand noch Klasse. Unterschichten um 1800*, and *Arbeitsverhältnisse und Arbeiterexistenzen. Grundlagen der Klassenbildung im 19. Jahrhundert*, both published 1990 in Bonn.

labour, catastrophic living conditions and the lack of any provision in the case of accidents, sickness, or old age, are characteristic of this epoch.

With the break-up of the old, feudal social order and the emergence of early capitalism, society underwent a process of profound transformation. The guiding principle of this so-called "Manchester liberalism" was the survival of the fittest, and could be summarised under the motto: "Make way for the diligent". The bourgeoisie who, as the "Third Estate" in the French Revolution of 1789, had made unmistakable claims to power, were the driving force behind this movement. The old conservative ruling groups in the German states were an obstacle to liberalism on the political level, but in the economic sphere it came fully into its own. Here, even the state showed a liberal face, giving its backing to the forces of economic self-regulation and their inherent dynamism. It was clear where this early capitalism was leading. The powerful – the owners of land, capital, and the centres of production – were able to dictate their own terms to the weak, that is, the propertyless. The state burocracy, which still maintained a certain pre-liberal social concern, would intervene only in the most extreme cases of acute misery. In Prussia in 1828, General Horn, worried about the strength of the army, issued a timely warning. He cautioned against excessive child labour, since "the poor state of health it caused" would lead to a shortfall in recruitment. But it would be eleven years before the enactment of child-protection regulations would forbid the regular employment of children under the age of nine in factories and mines. Inadequate implementation, however, meant that the improvement they brought about was minimal. Nevertheless, Prussia was still ahead of other German states with this child-protection legislation. Bavaria and Baden would follow in 1840, Saxony in 1861, and Württemberg the year after. Such measures, however, were still no more than a drop in the ocean. They continued to fail to take account of the central problem of the social question.

2. Theories about Solving the Social Question

These theories had spread from England, the motherland of industry and capitalism, first to the West European continent and France and Belgium, countries which became pioneers of the new form of production, and also where the first criticisms of the consequences of industrialisation were voiced. The aim was not merely to pillory social conditions, but to elaborate theories and develop models in order to find radical solutions to the problems arising from the change from an agrarian and feudal, to a bourgeois and industrial, economy and society.

The manufacturer Robert Owen attempted to put his ideas on overcoming social injustice in practice, first at the New Lanark mills in Scotland, and then in America in "villages of cooperation", self-supporting communities run on communist principles. Although this initiative in America collapsed, the theory and practice behind it gave great impetus to the later development of social reforms and the cooperatives. Owen became the father of the trade-union and cooperative movement in England. In France, it was chiefly Saint-Simon, who regarded the economy as the driving force of society, and Fourier, who saw the equitable distribution of goods as the solution to all social problems, who drew up models of socialist and communist social systems which were soon to influence criticism of society in Germany. Pierre Joseph Proudhon, with his criticism of capitalist "property as theft", had a more long-term effect. For him, the path to the achievement of a new social order lay via the existing bourgeois state.

The theories of the French socialists spread to Germany, *inter alia*, through the writing of the conservative thinker and sociologist Lorenz von Stein. The writer Georg Büchner, with his rallying cry "Peace to the cottages, war on the palaces!", also contributed to the propagation of early socialist ideas. Of greater influence was the tailor's apprentice Wilhelm Weitling (1808–1871) with his persistent call for the violent overthrow of society. The main support for his views came from amongst German itinerant craftsmen abroad. With his demand for community of property and the abolition of money, the removal of national borders and universal brotherhood, Weitling was aiming for an egalitarian communism, which he also held to be the true goal of Christianity.

It was not until Karl Marx and Friedrich Engels, however, that interpreters of social problems would offer solutions of more than short-term effect. Their ideas would shape and change the world of the nineteenth and twentieth centuries.

Marx and Engels

Karl Marx was born on 5 May 1818 in Trier, the son of a Jewish lawyer. After completing his studies, he worked for a short time as a journalist on the liberal, democratic *Rheinische Zeitung* in Cologne. After six months he moved to Paris. When he was expelled from there, he took up residence in Brussels. Friedrich Engels, born the son of a factory owner in Barmen on 28 November 1820, and who had met Karl Marx in 1844 and would enjoy a life-long friendship with him, also moved there. In Paris and Brussels both friends were in close contact with the so-called "League of the Just". In November 1847 Marx was commissioned by a splinter group of this organisation, which called itself the "League of Communists", to formulate a comprehensive theoretical and practical party programme.

The *Communist Manifesto*, written for a small, radical secret organisation, would make history. The ideas in the *Manifesto* were based on what Karl Marx had been writing since the beginning of the 1840s. Worthy of mention are: *A Critique of Hegel's Doctrine of the State* (1843), *Towards a Critique of Hegel's Philosophy of Right* (1843/44), *The Holy Family* (1844), as well as those manuscripts which were not published until later, *Towards a Critique of National Economy* (1931), and, together with Engels, *The German Ideology* (1932). In addition, Engels's study *The Condition of the Working Class in England* (1845) had gone a long way towards clarifying their point of view. His thesis-like *Principles of Communism* written in 1847 offers a further, useful preliminary work. The *Manifesto of the Communist Party* was published in February 1848. On the eve of the revolution it announced menacingly: "A spectre is haunting Europe – the spectre of Communism".[4]

"The history of all hitherto existing society is the history of class struggles." This sentence from the *Manifesto* sums up the basic idea of the so-called "materialist conception of history". The bourgeoisie, so goes the argument, had brought about, in barely a century of its domination as a class, an unparalleled historical leap forward, and unleashed undreamt-of forces of production. The dynamics of capitalism had swept away old barriers and traditions, and thus laid bare what was at the heart of the nexus between man and man: control of the means of production and property. "Society as a whole is more and more splitting up into great hostile camps, into two great classes directly confronting each other: Bourgeoisie and Proletariat." But the bourgeoisie is "unfit any longer to be the ruling class in society [...] because it is incompetent to ensure an existence to its slave within his slavery." The capitalist mode of production, it is argued, was producing a rapidly growing proletariat which, concentrated in the factories, was being forged into an ever stronger unit. The mode of production, however, as Marx postulated in the preface to *A Critique of Political Economy*, conditions "the social, political, and intellectual life process in general. It is not the consciousness of men that determines their being, but, on the contrary, their social being that determines their consciousness."[5] In tandem with the triumphant onward march of the bourgeoisie and the capitalist mode of production was the shaping of the growing proletariat into a solid revolutionary class con-

---

4 See note 2.
5 See David McLellan (ed.), Karl Marx: Selected Writings (Oxford 1977), p. 389.

scious of its own power. "The development of Modern Industry [...] cuts from under its feet the very foundation on which the bourgeoisie produces and appropriates products. What the bourgeoisie, therefore, produces, above all, is its own grave-diggers. Its fall and the victory of the proletariat are equally inevitable."[6]

Along with prognoses such as these in the *Manifesto* about the seemingly inevitable course of history, were calls for revolutionary action: "The immediate aim of the Communists is the same as that of all the other proletarian parties: formation of the proletariat into a class, overthrow of the bourgeois supremacy, conquest of political power by the proletariat". The Communists "openly declare that their ends can be attained only by the forcible overthrow of all existing social conditions. Let the ruling classes tremble at a Communistic revolution. The proletarians have nothing to lose but their chains. They have a world to win. WORKING MEN OF ALL COUNTRIES, UNITE!"[7]

Both this appeal for violent overthrow, and the thesis about the "inevitable" victory of the proletariat, which Marx reinforced in his great theoretical work *Capital*, have repeatedly preoccupied both politicians and academics, and also advocates of revolution as well as those of evolution. For some, the change from the exploitative system of early capitalism to social democracy was proof that a different path from that marked out by Marx was possible, and could lead to success. For others it was misguided and had led inexorably to a dead end. The obvious contradiction between a development driven by inevitability and the exhortation to take political action, between the freedom to act and being bound by economic and social laws, provoked lively argument about what precisely constituted the central core of Marxist thought. Marx and Engels themselves never expressed an entirely unambiguous view on the problem. One can probably deduce, however, from the unity of theory and practice which determines their thought, that for them socialism is the necessary consequence of the development of society, but that it also requires "the power of the human will impelled by revolutionary awareness".[8]

The final goal of this reshaping of society was for Marx the abolition of "man's estrangement from man" which degraded the proletarian in the capitalist system to a commodity and had led to the "complete loss of the man". The only freedom granted to him by the private ownership of the means of production seemed to him to be the bitter, double free-

6 Ibid., p. 231.
7 Ibid., p. 246.
8 See Helga Grebing, Geschichte der deutschen Arbeiterbewegung. Ein Überblick, dtv, 3rd edn 1972, p. 32.

dom of being able to be "free of the means of production, and free to sell his labour". Communism as positive "abolition of private property" would, on the other hand, create conditions in which man would not only be free *of* something, but be free *to become* something, in other words to realise his full potential. "In place of the old bourgeois society, with its classes and class antagonisms, we shall have an association in which the free development of each is the condition for the free development of all."[9]

3. 1848 and the First Workers' Organisations

With their "philosophy", Marx and Engels achieved, in the long term, what Marx saw as their real task: changing the world. In 1848, however, the claim in the *Manifesto* that, "Communism is already acknowledged by all European Powers to be itself a Power", was more dream than reality. At this time, Marx and Engels, as the latter would later admit, were abandoning themselves to illusionary hopes. Initially, their *Manifesto* reached in Germany only the League of Communists. In contrast to England, there was up until 1848 no trade union or political workers' movement in Germany. In addition to the fact that, in comparison to other Western European countries, industrialisation there began much later, the principal reason for this was a state policy of repression exercised in an age of reaction. Whereas in England the ban on freedom of association was lifted in 1824/5, in Germany it remained in place, and the founding of political organisations was prohibited, until the revolution of 1848. Strict censorship of the press ensured that any expression of libertarian aspirations was stifled wherever possible. Admittedly, there were individual craftsmen's social self-help organisations in the form of friendly societies, but any political activity was only possible abroad, amongst the travelling journeymen.[10] New Germany, Young Germany, the League of Outlaws, and the League of the Just, are the most important organisations worthy of note where apprentices could gather together in discussion groups. Initially, the centres were mainly in France and Switzerland, until after 1840

---

9   See McLellan p. 238. Also Erich Fromm, Das Menschenbild bei Marx (Frankfurt/Main 3rd edn 1969), p. 44.
10 For these early organisational associations, see Ernst Schraepler, Handwerkerbünde und Arbeitervereine 1830–1853 (Berlin and New York 1972). On the development of social democracy in the nineteenth century, see too, Hedwig Wachenheim, Die deutsche Arbeiterbewegung 1844–1914 (Cologne and Opladen 1967), and Thomas Welskopp, Das Banner der Brüderlichkeit. Die deutsche Sozialdemokratie vom Vormärz bis zum Sozialistengesetz (Bonn 2000).

when their focus moved to London. With energetic support from Marx and Engels there finally emerged from the League of the Just, the League of Communists, founded in London in 1847. It lasted little more than three months.

Revolution broke out in February 1848 in France, and would soon spread to Germany. In contrast to France, where the revolution had a powerful admixture of social elements, the wave of revolution was largely a movement for national unity, democratic freedom, parliament, and constitution. For most people, therefore, the goal was achieved with the constituent National Assembly – elected by universal, equal suffrage – in the Paulskirche in Frankfurt. Nevertheless, pinned on it were further hopes of a restructuring of political and social life in Germany. While Marx and Engels were appealing, in the *Neue Rheinische Zeitung* which they edited, to democracy to take over political power and complete the work of the revolution, the first signs were appearing – barely noticed at first – of an emergent workers' movement in Germany.

Apprentices and workers were in the front line on the barricades when, in March 1848, the revolutionary movement in Germany forced absolutism to its knees. The self-confidence this had aroused, along with the newly won freedoms, smoothed the way for the foundation of organisations of the most diverse kind. Along with the beginnings of affiliations resembling trade unions, for which printers and tobacco workers set the tone, workers' education associations founded for the most part by bourgeois democrats sprang up. They were the product of a social welfare mentality which regarded the liberal educational ideal that "education liberates" as the way out of misery.

Of quite different complexion was the printer Stephan Born's "Workers' Brotherhood".[11] At a conference held in Berlin from 23 August to 3 September 1848 attended by representatives of thirty-two workers' associations from throughout Germany, an independent political organisation was founded, the *Allgemeine Deutsche Arbeiterverbrüderung* (General German Workers' Brotherhood) which soon numbered over 230 local associations and district organisations. The "Workers' Brotherhood" was made up largely of journeymen and trained, qualified craftsmen. There was a marked gulf between them and unqualified workers, the navvies, day-labourers, and the so-called lumpenproletariat. The very fact, however, that these qualified craftsmen termed themselves "workers", and began to see themselves as belonging to the "working class", meant the growth of a

---

[11] See Frolinde Balser, Sozial-Demokratie 1848/49–1863. Die erste deutsche Arbeiterorganisation "Allgemeine Arbeiterverbrüderung" nach der Revolution (Stuttgart 1962).

social identity which later gave such a tremendous boost to the rise of the workers' movement.

The watchword of the Workers' Brotherhood, "One for all, all for one", which not by chance would be later adopted by the Free Trade Unions, demonstrates the significance which Stephan Born and his supporters attached to the concept of solidarity. This, for them, was the basis for the emancipation of the working class. Through their own organisations they wanted to become a political and moral force, and push through social reforms in a democratic state system. In a circular of 18 September 1848, their central committee summed up once more their basic policies:

"We workers must help ourselves, this is the principle on which the Berlin congress was based. Its decisions, built on the principle of self-help, now lie ready for the public to judge. Germany's workers must strive to become a moral force within the state, a powerful body which can withstand any storm, which presses forward, ever forward, and in its progress suppresses and sweeps aside everything which stands in the way of a freer and better way of fashioning the world, which embraces everyone who has a heart for the misery of the oppressed and is himself shackled by the power of Capital, whose bodily and spiritual energies are in the service of one of the earth's favoured ones. To everyone who works, or wants to work. ... workers of Germany, we appeal to you once more: Be united, then you will be strong. Shy away from no obstacle. You will conquer them all, but only with your strength united."[12]

Their hopes were directed towards the Paulskirche in Frankfurt, in which the first "Imperial Parliament elected by the people" was sitting. They expected it to engage with their concrete goals: freedom of association, information about employment, public health facilities, sickness insurance, consumer and producers' cooperatives, statutory health and safety at work, and involvement in determining working hours and wages. The attempts, however, by individual Paulskirche deputies to introduce a legally guaranteed minimum wage, social legislation, and a right of codetermination for workers in the production process, foundered on the Liberal parliamentary majority.

The Liberals wanted to create a constitutional German national state with bourgeois civil rights and liberties. They owed the chance to do this to a revolution which they regarded with utter ambivalence. On the one

---

12 Quoted in Max Quarck, Die erste deutsche Arbeiterbewegung. Geschichte der Arbeiterverbrüderung 1848/49. Ein Beitrag zur Theorie und Praxis des Marxismus (Leipzig 1924), p. 369 and p. 371. Reproduced in Die Allgemeine Deutsche Arbeiterverbrüderung 1848–1850, edited and with an introduction by Horst Schlechte (Weimar 1979), pp. 338 ff.

hand, they were opposed to the monarchist conservatives in state and society who had been only temporarily shaken by events, on the other, they were in conflict with the onward march of democratic, republican and social-revolutionary forces.

Not only the expectations of the workers' associations, but also those of the bourgeois radical democrats were dashed by the Paulskirche. Angry masses demonstrated outside the parliament which was protected by soldiers of the Prussian king. The forces of reaction saw that their chance had come to reconquer one lost position after the other. The Austrian monarchy made the first move, followed by the Prussian king. Parliaments were dissolved, and revolts by resolute democrats suppressed by armed force. One by one the workers' associations were banned, and any chance of forming political alliances was rendered impossible. The failure of the 1848/49 revolution had a profound effect on the workers' movement in Germany and its relationship with the bourgeoisie. Large sections of the Liberals became depoliticised, were overcome by resignation, or made accommodation with the ruling powers. It gradually dawned on Marx, as it did on other advocates of the Fourth Estate, that the bourgeoisie had failed in the revolution of 1848, and capitulated in the face of the powers of the monarchical authoritarian state. The social democratic workers' movement, as it would evolve in the sixties, saw itself as the heir to this failed revolution. It took upon itself the dual task of achieving democracy and fighting for the emancipation of the working class. In October 1848, the Democratic Congress, at which Stephan Born, Wilhelm Weitling, and supporters of Karl Marx were represented, had committed itself to the principle "that the solution to social questions is only possible in the social democratic state"[13]. This principle would become one of the political guidelines for German social democracy.

---

13 Quoted from Schraepler, Handwerkerbünde und Arbeitervereine, p. 318.

II. The Formation of the Social Democratic Workers' Movement

1. Ferdinand Lassalle and the General Association of German Workers

In a letter to Jean Baptist von Schweitzer of 13 October 1868 Karl Marx paid homage to the work of Ferdinand Lassalle: "Lassalle – and this remains his immortal service – re-awakened the workers' movement in Germany after its fifteen years of slumber"[1]. The forces of political reaction in the years following the failed revolution of 1848 had been able to suppress, but not kill off, the struggle for freedom, democracy, and equality. The unification movement in Italy, and a brief liberalisation of Prussian policy, stimulated a wave of politicisation. This gave a powerful boost not only to the desire for national unity, but also to the emancipatory aspirations of those classes who had been kept at arm's length from political responsibility. In this situation, the liberal German bourgeoisie once again showed itself to be the eloquent advocate of parliamentarism and democratic rights, freedom, and national unity. In Prussia a struggle arose between parliament and monarch which was decided to the disadvantage of the Liberal Democrats when, in 1862, Bismarck, a superior, energetic opponent, entered the fray.

This constitutional conflict was a key experience for Ferdinand Lassalle. Whereas Marx and Engels in the *Communist Manifesto* had issued a call to "labour everywhere for the union and agreement of the democratic parties of all countries"[2], Lassalle was convinced that the Liberals, and with them the entire bourgeoisie, were not really prepared to fight for democracy. He wrote bitterly to the businessman Lewy in Düsseldorf: "Believe me, I have studied the Progressive Party (the party of the Liberals) here very closely, and their first principle is: 'Anything but revolution from below, rather despotism from above'."[3]

In his view, the bourgeoisie had betrayed the ideals of 1848. Only the Fourth Estate was carrying forward the banner of democracy. "Its cause

---

1 Karl Marx in a letter to Jean Baptiste von Schweitzer, 13.10.1868. In David McLellan (ed.), Karl Marx: Selected Writings (Oxford 1977), p. 586.
2 Ibid., p. 246.
3 Quoted from Willi Eichler, Hundert Jahre Sozialdemokratie (Bielefeld 1963), p. 15. See also Toni Offermann, Arbeiterbewegung und liberales Bürgertum in Deutschland 1850–1863 (Bonn 1979).

is, therefore, in truth the cause of all mankind, its freedom is the freedom of mankind itself, its power is the power of all."[4] There were practical motives for this hostile stance towards the liberal bourgeoisie. The workers whom Lassalle wished to win over were organised, if at all, at this time into workers' and workers' educational organisations. These had been founded by bourgeois democrats. When, at the end of the fifties and beginning of the sixties, the call for freedom and unity began to ring out once more, they began looking for allies amongst the workers. Even though the founding of these associations had a social dimension, there was no question of there being equal representation of workers' interests. Saxony, with its comparatively advanced industrialisation, was a central focus for these workers' associations. A favourable consequence of the lifting of the ban on free association was that these societies were subject to fewer limitations than in the other German states. An increasingly more active minority in the Leipzig educational association was seeking, under the leadership of the shoemaker Vahlteich and the cigar worker Fritsche, to become independent of their bourgeois patrons, and was in favour of directing the association towards political goals. The group formed a "Central Committee to call a German Workers' Congress", and, in February 1863, turned to the writer and early socialist Ferdinand Lassalle to ask him to draw up a draft programme.

Ferdinand Lassalle (1825–1864) had become famous as a result of the long years of litigation he had conducted on behalf of Countess Hatzfeld. In addition to the writing of philosophical works, about which he had corresponded with Marx and Engels, he had also concerned himself with the social problems of the working class. In his writing and speeches from spring 1862 on, he dedicated himself completely to the cause of working people. He expounded his ideas in talks such as "On the particular connection of the present period of history to the idea of the working class" (the *Arbeiterprogramm*, the Workers' Programme) and "Science and the workers", both subsequently published as pamphlets.[5]

In his "Open reply" (1 March 1863)[6] Lassalle revealed his views on ways of improving the political and social lot of the workers to the Leip-

---

4 This from the Arbeiterprogramm. In Ferdinand Lassalle, Gesammelte Reden und Schriften, vol. 2, edited and with an introduction by Eduard Bernstein (Berlin 1919), p. 186f. On Lassalle's and the Social Democratic party's political programmes up to the revisionism debate, see Susanne Miller, Das Problem der Freiheit im Sozialismus. Freiheit, Staat und Revolution in der Programmatik der Sozialdemokratie von Lassalle bis zum Revisionismusstreit (Berlin and Bonn 5th edn 1977).
5 See Lassalle, Gesammelte Reden und Schriften, vol. 2, pp. 165ff., and pp. 242ff.
6 Ferdinand Lassalle, Offenes Antwortschreiben an das Zentralkomitee zur Berufung eines Allgemeinen Deutschen Arbeiter-Congresses zu Leipzig (Zurich 1863).

zig "Committee". His call for the founding of an autonomous workers' party independent of the bourgeoisie met with a positive response. On 23 May 1863 in Leipzig the *Allgemeiner Deutscher Arbeiterverein* (General Association of German Workers) was brought into existence by workers' representatives from eleven different towns, and Lassalle elected as its president. Although, despite Lassalle's tireless efforts, the membership remained initially relatively small (roughly 4,600 by the end of 1864), the Association was a stirring source of encouragement for the workers' sense of their own worth. This finds expression in the celebrated poem which Georg Herwegh penned for the Association:

> Arise, o man of toil!
> Let your arm become a foil!
> All factories will fall still,
> At just one sign of strength and will.
>
> Smash the yoke of tyranny!
> Smash of slave the misery!
> Smash the misery of slave!
> Seize your freedom, bread you crave!

Lassalle had been at the head of the General Association of German Workers for just over a year when he died on 31 August 1864 as the result of a duel over a woman. This brief period, along with the romantic circumstances of his death, were enough to make him an idol in the eyes of many workers. In Jakob Audorf's "Workers' Marseillaise" we find the proud, and resoundingly self-confident lines: "Boldly we follow the path/ Down which Lassalle has led us!".

The direction given by Lassalle had led to the establishment of an independent workers' party based on the staple programmatic slogans of universal suffrage, free and productive association, exploitation and class struggle. He was, however, leading the Association down a blind alley with his notion of the "iron" law of wages, whereby "remuneration is kept to the minimum necessary to sustain the most basic level of human existence and to enable procreation".[7] For him, this thesis was a weapon with which to defeat his main rival, Hermann Schulze-Delitzsch, in the battle to win over the workers.

In keeping with the principles of early liberalism, Schulze-Delitzsch rejected state aid as impermissible intervention, and propagated instead self-help measures in the form of consumer cooperatives, savings banks,

---

7 On this and what follows, see notes 4 and 5.

and friendly societies for the sick and disabled. Lassalle's argument, however, was that under the conditions of capitalism these could offer the workers no long-term improvement to their lot. Only if the workers were to set up their own cooperatives, thereby removing the "divide between wages and entrepreneurial profit" and reaping the full fruits of their labour, could the seemingly insoluble dilemma be resolved. Since the workers were not strong enough to do this of their own accord, the state would have to lend "an encouraging hand" in the form of state credits. Given its impetus by the party of the workers, there would arise from the liberal "nightwatchman's state" a socially responsible state, which would fulfil its real task which was to "facilitate and mediate mankind's great cultural step forward".

In this assessment of the role of the state in the emancipation of the Fourth Estate lay the most important bone of contention with Marx. If Marx regarded the state primarily as the instrument of oppression of the ruling class, Lassalle saw in it a positive form of social organisation. "The purpose of the state", we are told in the *Arbeiterprogramm* (Workers' Programme), "is not merely to protect personal freedom and property [...]; the purpose of the state is rather more by means of this union to enable individuals to achieve goals, and a level of existence such as they could never achieve singly, to empower them to attain a measure of education, power and freedom which would be a sheer impossibility for them as a collection of individuals."[8]

Despite these conflicting conceptions of the state, the differences between them are not easily reduced to a formula as simple as: "the social democratic reformism of Lassalle which affirms the national state, and the international, revolutionary socialism of Marx and Engels."[9] In their analysis of the capitalist system, of the role of the labour force and the workers' movement, and even in the conception of the final goal, they were in widespread agreement. It is no coincidence that Marx should accuse Lassalle of having, in his *Arbeiterprogramm*, plagiarised his ideas.[10] Lassalle considered the "associating with state means", which had been attacked so savagely by Marx and Engels, merely as a practical approach to changing the economic structure. For him too, the prerequisite for a solution to the social question was the abolition of "property and capi-

---

8   Lassalle, Gesammelte Reden und Schriften, vol. 2, p. 197f. There are similar arguments in his 'Die Wissenschaft und die Arbeiter', p. 267.
9   Helga Grebing, Geschichte der deutschen Arbeiterbewegung. Ein Überblick (Munich 3rd edn 1972), p. 57.
10 In a letter to Friedrich Engels of 28.1.1863. In Karl Marx and Friedrich Engels, Collected Works (London 1985), vol. 41, p. 452.

tal".[11] However, in the day-to-day process of political agitation, the revolutionary demands of the General Association of German Workers with its vision of the ultimate goal of socialism, was reduced to the call for universal suffrage and cooperatives. The dualism between radical ideology and reformist practice which was so characteristic of nineteenth-century social democracy was thus already firmly lodged in Lassalle's Association.

2. The First International

Marx and Engels were strongly critical of Lassalle's one-sided attack on the liberal bourgeoisie. According to the tactics proposed by the *Communist Manifesto*, the working class should, in its battle with the forces of reaction, initially make alliance with the democratic elements within the bourgeoisie. According to Marx and Engels, only when certain economic and political conditions were in place could the proletariat come fully into its own. A few years after Lassalle's death, they urged Wilhelm Liebknecht and his fellow socialist August Bebel to break with "petit-bourgeois democracy" and found an independent workers' organisation.

After the collapse of the revolution in June 1849, Marx, together with Engels, his comrade-in-arms, settled in England, where he lived until his death. Along with his intervention in the Cologne Communist trials, and a series of newspaper articles, these years were taken up mainly with academic work. Apart from his analysis of the seizure of power by Napoleon III ("The Eighteenth Brumaire of Louis Bonaparte", 1852), he wrote with the *Grundrisse* to the "Critique of Political Economy" (published in 1938 from Marx's unpublished papers) the first draft of his most important work. Here the central ideas of Capital, the first volume of which appeared in 1867, are worked out: namely, the doctrine of labour as a commodity in the capitalist system and the theory of surplus value. Marx uses the term surplus value to identify the difference between the value of the goods produced by the worker, and the wages which he receives for his labour.

Marx discovered his political platform in the "International Working Men's Association" (First International), at the foundation of which on 28 September 1864 he had initially participated as a spectator.[12] The initia-

11 See Lassalle's letter to Karl Rodbertus of 28.4.1863. In Ferdinand Lassalle, Nachgelassene Briefe und Schriften, edited by Gustav Mayer, vol. 6 (Stuttgart and Berlin 1925), p. 329. For the context, see Miller, Das Problem der Freiheit im Sozialismus, esp. pp. 35 ff.
12 There is a good survey of this in Karl-Ludwig Günsche and Klaus Lantermann, Kleine Geschichte der Internationale (Bonn-Bad Godesberg 1977), pp. 25 ff.

tive came from a group representing English and French workers who had made contact at the World Exhibition of 1862 in London. In the view of the English initiators of the association, cross-border solidarity and international cooperation were the only remedy against oppression of the proletariat and the low wages induced by cheap foreign competition. In September 1864 a group of men from England, France, Italy, and Germany met in London to set up an umbrella organisation for workers' associations throughout the world. Neither differing forms of organisation (parties or trade unions), nor diverse theoretical orientations were to be an obstacle to joining the "International Working Men's Association". Socialist tendencies as disparate as those of the French Proudhonists and the English trade unionists were represented in the IWMA. In addition, national-revolutionary democrats such as the Italian Guiseppe Mazzini and an anarchist wing were also members. The joining in 1868 of the Russian anarchist Michail Bakunin led to stormy internal conflicts which eventually, in 1872, led to a split. In 1876, the International, which in the meantime had moved its location to New York, was dissolved. Although it never became a mass movement, it excited attention far beyond its practical significance. Wherever there were strikes or unrest, the ruling powers saw the International at work. They painted the spectre of a gigantic, revolutionary organisation which was developing secretly into a "second power in the state, into a second government".[13]

At its foundation, in an "inaugural address" penned by Marx, the International called for the setting up of cooperatives and independent workers' parties. At its congress in Geneva in 1866 the Marxist majority within the International declared itself in favour of an independent role for the trade unions in the struggle of wage earners for a new social order. At the same time, and in the face of strong resistance from a powerful minority, it adopted the demand for the introduction of a statutory eight-hour day as part of its programme. The appeal of the IWMA to the international revolutionary solidarity of the working class also met with response in Germany, although its organisational successes remained modest. The membership numbered just 385. However, those workers who were in the process of emancipation found compensation for the social and political isolation into which separation from the bourgeoisie in the 1860s had plunged them in the vision of supra-national solidarity. The "Eisenachers", a new workers' party which was springing up, joined the International Working Men's Association.

---

13 This according to a Viennese public prosecutor. In Julius Braunthal, Geschichte der Internationale, vol. 1 (Berlin and Bonn 2nd edn 1974), p. 121 f.

May Day poster depicting the "Solidarity of Work"

3. The "Eisenachers"

The collapse of the Progressives in the Prussian constitutional conflict, and the successes of Bismarck's "sword strategy" in solving the national question, mercilessly revealed the weaknesses of bourgeois liberalism in the face of the authoritarian state. Not only the inability it had demonstrated in Prussia to institute democracy, but also its contradictory stance on the national question, and its failure *vis-à-vis* the social problems of the Fourth Estate, meant that the politically awakening workers were thrown back on their own resources. Instead of the seemingly most obvious coalition between radical, bourgeois democrats and the workers in the struggle for democracy and social justice, there arose an alliance of interests between the old, agrarian aristocracy and the new ruling class of bourgeois industrialists.

The formation, which began with the General Association of German Workers, of independent, socialistically oriented parties was the logical "response of the German workers' movement to its exclusion from access to equal political rights and economic redistribution in the national state"[14]. The endeavour in 1863 by committed democrats to form a counter-organisation to Lassalle's GAGW by bringing local educational societies together in the Confederation of German Workers' Associations enjoyed only short-term success. With its single-minded concentration on further education it made a big contribution to the later widespread social democratic belief that knowledge was power.

Increasingly in the ascendancy were those forces which were striving for a more effective perception of where the political and social interests of working people lay. An excellent example of this was the development of the young Bebel.

August Bebel (1840–1913), after years as a travelling journeyman, took up residence in Leipzig as a turner, and was active there in the trades' educational association. Initially, Bebel had been opposed to the politicisation of the association, and had even rejected the idea of universal suffrage, believing the workers were not yet ready for it. It was not until his involvement with supporters of Lassalle, whom he had at first accused of waving the flag of Communism with all its terrors, that he was directed towards socialism and, under the influence of Liebknecht, the theories of Marx.[15]

---

14 Wolfgang Schieder, 'Das Scheitern des bürgerlichen Radikalismus und die sozialistische Parteibildung in Deutschland', in Hans Mommsen (ed.), Sozialdemokratie zwischen Klassenbewegung und Volkspartei (Frankfurt/Main 1974), p. 21.
15 See Bebel's autobiography, Aus meinem Leben, vol. 1 (Stuttgart 1910), pp. 50 ff.; Brigitte Seebacher-Brandt, Bebel. Künder und Kärrner im Kaiserreich (Bonn 2nd edn 1990).

Wilhelm Liebknecht (1826–1900), a fighter in the revolution of 1848, had, on its collapse, emigrated to London, where he soon found himself a member of Marx's inner circle. As a convinced supporter of his doctrines, which he nevertheless interpreted in accord with his own political ideas, he returned to Germany in 1862. In Leipzig he got to know Bebel with whom he founded the radical, democratic People's Party of Saxony, and both of them were elected the following year to the North German Reichstag.

In the same year Bebel replaced the Liberal, Dr. Max Hirsch, as the chairman of the League of German Workers' Associations. He immediately began to agitate for the politicisation of the associations. Bebel replaced the liberal ideas which had hitherto predominated with positions much closer to those of the First International. The Associations' conference in Nuremberg in 1868 produced a split between the Liberal Democrats and the followers of a socialist orientation. A majority led by Bebel declared their belief in the principle that the emancipation of the working classes was a battle they had to fight themselves, and resolved to "commit themselves to the efforts of the International Working Mens' Association".[16] The members of the association were simultaneously urged to band together in trade unions, as a way of furthering their economic interests more effectively. The divide in the workers' associations between the bourgeois democrats and the later Social Democrats ran parallel to the split in the People's Party of Saxony and similarly constituted popular parties in other federal states. The decisive initiatives came from Wilhelm Liebknecht and August Bebel who, over the coming decades, would become the outstanding personality in the social democratic movement and be primarily responsible for shaping its image.

On 7 to 9 August 1869 the Social Democratic Workers' Party was founded in Eisenach. In addition to the GAGW there was now a second workers' party in Germany. Their supporters were recruited mainly from the workers' associations in central and southern Germany, former members of the People's Party of Saxony, and discontented elements in the GAGW. In their programme, the Eisenachers called for the abolition of class rule, and the "establishment of a free people's state".[17] Further points in their programme were: a statutory maximum working day, limiting the working hours of women, prohibition of child labour, compul-

---

16 See Hermann Weber, Das Prinzip Links. Eine Dokumentation. Beiträge zur Diskussion des demokratischen Sozialismus in Deutschland 1847–1973 (Hanover 1873), p. 29.
17 See the 'Programm der Sozialdemokratischen Arbeiterpartei, Eisenach 1869'. In Dowe and Klotzbach (eds), Programmatische Dokumente (2004), pp. 159–163.

sory education, an independent judicial system, the replacement of indirect taxes by progressive income and inheritance taxes, referenda, and universal, equal, and direct suffrage. It was only logical that the Eisenachers should stand as candidates in the Reichstag elections and see parliament as a forum for their ideas. The specifically socialist component of their programme was to be found in point ten which called for: "state promotion of the cooperative system and state credits for free production cooperatives with democratic guarantees".

The new party regarded political freedom as the prerequisite for the "economic liberation of the working classes". "The social question is inseparable from the political one, the solution of the one is conditional on the solution of the other, and is only possible in a democratic state." Although the Eisenachers saw themselves expressly as a "branch of the International Working Men's Association", terms such as socialism and communism were double Dutch for many of their supporters. Even leading figures, as Kautsky remarked in retrospect, had, until the end of the seventies, only a superficial knowledge of the teachings of Marx and Engels. What principally motivated working people at this time was the harshness of everyday life, their experience of daily injustice and oppression – which they sought to combat and overcome by working together in solidarity.

The existence of two workers' parties was, therefore, less the result of different theoretical considerations than of actual, day-to-day problems. On the national question, which at that time dominated public discussion, the Eisenachers, following the radical-democratic tradition, advocated a federalist, Pan-German course. They rejected a unification of the Reich from above and by means of Prussian power politics as a unification by force, and without liberty. Lassalle and his supporters, on the other hand, were playing the Prussian card. If Lassalle, in his struggle against his main enemy, the liberal bourgeoisie, was seeking the support of Bismarck, Bebel and his friends were filled with deep distaste for the blood and iron policies of the Prussian Junker. The Eisenachers fought bitterly against the authoritarian organisational structure which Lassalle had brought to the GAGW, and which resembled a kind of plebiscitary rule, and was used as such by his later successor J.B. von Schweitzer. Their party was democratic from the bottom up. Its main support base lay in Saxony. In 1870 its membership numbered roughly 10,000, in 1875 roughly 9,000, whereas the GAGW numbered over 21,000 in 1872, and in 1875 roughly 15,000.

4. Unification in Gotha

In 1873 the in part stormy conflict between the two competing parties slowly began to wane. A personal obstacle was removed with the retirement of the long-term and controversial president of the GAGW, von Schweitzer, and with the founding of the Reich and the consolidation of the Bismarck state, the old differences faded. The Eisenachers had to bury their hopes for Pan-German and democratic unification. But the "Small German" (*kleindeutsch*) Lassalleans, who favoured a Prussian Reich with Austria excluded, also had their expectations dashed: their hope of social concessions from the state proved to be illusory. The policy of state oppression which set in after the founding of the Reich, and in which the public prosecutor Tessendorf was to play a leading role, affected the GAGW and Eisenachers alike, and was therefore conducive to a process of mutual understanding and reconciliation. Not least the emerging economic crisis of 1873 forced both parties to concentrate their attention on the immediate concerns of working people – strikes, wretched living conditions, trade union issues. It was the simple, rank-and-file membership who pressed for a coming together of the two parties.

The unification congress in Gotha from 23 to 27 May 1875 saw a successful conclusion to their demands. The programme of the new Socialist Workers' Party of Germany drawn up there was subject to a devastating attack by Marx in his "Randglossen" (marginal notes), or *Critique of the Gotha Programme*.[18] It has often been claimed that the lack of any Marxist basis to the programme was a result of concessions made to the Lassalleans. It is true that Marx, quite rightly, mocks the Lassallean nonsense about the "iron" law of wages. The other tenet which he pilloried that, compared to the working class, "all other classes were merely a reactionary mass" was factually nonsensical and politically tactless since it made it difficult to form alliances with other party groupings. Nevertheless, this Lassallean dictum gave expression to the elemental outrage of a minority who were held largely in contempt by bourgeois society, and harassed and denigrated by the state. It was from this very process of isolation and criminalisation that the concept of solidarity and class consciousness drew its strength.

In the Gotha Programme, it was basically not a matter of striking a compromise between moderate, state-affirming Lassalleans and the Marxist Eisenachers. Liebknecht's argument, with which he later justified the concealment of the "Randglossen" passed on to him by Marx, that he had

---

18 David McLellan, Karl Marx: Selected Writings (Oxford 1977), pp. 564–570.

Commemorative illustration for the unification party congress of 1875

had to make compromises in the interest of unity, was hardly in accord with the truth. The Lassalleans, who in many respects were much more radical in their demands, would undoubtedly have accepted a more Marxist programme. Tölcke, the GAGW representative, declared that in the interest of unity he would be prepared to accept any programme, even if it were nothing more than "a piece of white paper with a clenched fist on it".[19] In reality, Liebknecht, whom Marx and Engels, despite their irate outbursts at "little Willy's stupidity", had long regarded as their "only reliable link" in Germany,[20] enjoyed a largely free hand in drawing up the programme. Apart from some components of Lassalle's ideological legacy, the draft is therefore mainly a reflection of Liebknecht's ideas. Even though they diverged considerably from the theories of his friends Marx and Engels, they nevertheless met with the unanimous agreement of the congress, particularly after Bebel had withdrawn his misgivings.

In these early years of the workers' movement, there was as yet no solid, self-contained body of theory. It was more a case of programmatic declarations born of the need to give the movement a powerful weapon which would appeal to, and enthuse, its followers. Particularly in the years preceding Gotha, the interest in abstract theory was submerged by the dire troubles arising from the intensification of the social and political conflict. Statutory limitation of working hours and the prohibition of child labour, unrestricted freedom of association and right of assembly, were concrete matters of concern for working people. Alongside these ranked the desire for universal, equal suffrage and political democracy, the call to fight against the rule of the "one reactionary mass", and the declaration of international working-class solidarity.

All bridges to the bourgeois movements for social reform had now been burned.[21] Schulze-Delitzsch's concept of the pure self-help organisation had increasingly lost support. An attempt by democrats in Württemberg to breathe new life into the social question from a liberal perspective quickly failed. There were figures in the Catholic camp – men such as Ketteler, the Bishop of Mainz, and Kolping, the "father of the journeymen" – who recognised the explosive potential of deplorable social conditions, and demanded measures which would remove the worst excesses of early capitalism. Ketteler, however, as did the Protestant Wichern, looked at social problems from the perspective of pastoral care. Kolping's efforts at welfare provision were directed more at apprentices than at workers. By contrast, much greater influence would later be exerted by the Association for Social Policy, a union of committed academics who

---

19 Volksstaat, no. 58, 23.5.1875. See too, Georg Eckert, 'Die Konsolidierung der sozialdemokratischen Arbeiterbewegung zwischen Reichsgründung und Sozialistengesetz', in Hans Mommsen (ed.), Sozialdemokratie, pp. 47 ff.
20 In a letter from Engels to Marx of 7.8.1865. In Karl Marx and Friedrich Engels, Collected Works (London 1987), vol. 42, p. 178.
21 See Carl Jantke, Der Vierte Stand. Die gestaltenden Kräfte der deutschen Arbeiterbewegung im XIX. Jahrhundert (Freiburg 1955).

campaigned to arouse public awareness of the desperate plight of the Fourth Estate and made a decisive contribution to the development later of state social policy. Unlike, however, for instance in England, in Imperial Germany no bridges were constructed between social democracy on the one hand, and Church social politicians and bourgeois social reformers on the other. Two events were to widen the gulf to the point where it would seem unbridgeable: the Paris Commune and the Anti-Socialist Law.

III. From the Founding of the Reich to the Lapsing of the Anti-Socialist Law

1. *The Paris Commune*

The question of war credits which would split the German Social Democrats in the First World War, was already a controversial issue in the Franco-German War of 1870/71. Then, too, the same problem was at issue, whether to wage war out of self-defence. In the Reichstag of the Prussian dominated North German Confederation, Schweitzer from the GAGW and the Eisenacher Fritsche voted in favour of the first bill, while Bebel and Liebknecht abstained. In doing this, they put themselves at odds with majority opinion in the party which maintained that socialists, too, had to stand up as "Germans for Germany". When, however, after the abdication of Napoleon III, fighting continued against the French Republic, the Eisenachers as well as the Lassalleans, turned against further pursuit of the war and the intended annexation of Alsace and Lorraine. Amidst the rising tide of nationalistic passions, a tiny handful raised its voice of opposition and expressed solidarity, not with annexation, but with the insurrection of the Paris Commune on 19 March 1871. Both Eisenachers and Lassalleans welcomed the Paris revolution as the dawning of a new age and protested passionately against the May massacres in which French government troops, with the tacit support of Bismarck, drowned the experiment of a new democracy and social order in a sea of blood. With the Reichstag as his platform, Bebel testified to his high esteem for the Commune, now overthrown, and declared to the deputies that this was only a preliminary skirmish, and that "within a few decades the battle-cry of the Parisian proletariat, 'War on the palaces, peace to the cottages, death to misery and slothful indolence', will be the battle-cry of the entire European proletariat."[1]

Later, during the discussions about the Anti-Socialist Law, Bismarck claimed that this speech had opened his eyes to the subversive threat to the state which social democracy represented, thereby cunningly inflaming the fear of revolution which had increasingly gripped the nobility and bourgeoisie since the Paris Commune. The German Social Democrats' solidarity with the Parisian communards, and Marx's celebration of the

---

[1] Stenographische Berichte über die Verhandlungen im Deutschen Reichstag, 1. Legislaturperiode, p. 921.

Commune constitution as "the political form at last discovered under which to work out the economic emancipation of labour"[2], delivered the arguments with which to continue to castigate the German workers' movement as "the party of moral decadence, of political ill discipline and social discord"[3], as the party of upheaval and violence. The aggressive and often revolutionary language of social democracy had certainly contributed to the enkindling of such fears, but their roots went much deeper. For the ruling classes intent on preserving their privileges, the invocation of the "red menace" served to bind the economically increasingly dominant bourgeoisie to the authoritarian and military state, with its power to guarantee peace and order.

Objectively, the fear of revolution was groundless. Admittedly, with the "myth" of the Commune, German social democracy secured a revolutionary tradition for its theoretical beliefs, in practice, however, and particularly after the experiences of the Commune, the concept of "revolutionary" overthrow of the social order was interpreted as non-violent change. More than ever it staked everything on what, in the view of many Social Democrats, the Paris Commune had lacked: the forging of an effective, disciplined organisation. The Reichstag elected on wide popular franchise delivered a reliable measure of the strength of the movement. From 3.2 per cent (Eisenachers and GAGW) in 1871, over 6.8 per cent for the two parties in the 1874 elections, their share of the vote in 1877, two years after Gotha, rose to 9.1 per cent. Despite state repression and the setting up, on the entrepreneurial side, of counter-organisations (1875, the Central Association of Industrialists), there had been no stopping the movement. It was well on the way to becoming a factor in German domestic affairs when the Anti-Socialist Law gave this development a quite different twist.

2. *The Anti-Socialist Law*

Two attempts on the life of Emperor William I which had nothing to do with the Social Democrats, who decisively rejected terrorist methods, gave Bismarck a welcome pretext to lay before the Reichstag the so-called Anti-Socialist Law. The moment had come for him to move against a further expansion of "the menacing band of robbers with whom we have to share our cities". Fresh Reichstag elections after the second assassination attempt

---

2 In David McLellan (ed.), Karl Marx: Selected Writings (Oxford 1977), p. 544.
3 In this vein, amongst others, Heinrich Treitschke, 'Der Sozialismus und seine Gönner', in Preußische Jahrbücher, 34 (1874), pp. 67 ff. and pp. 248 ff.

brought him the pliable parliament he needed. In spite of an unprecedented campaign against them, the Social Democrats still won 437,000 votes as opposed to 493,000 in 1877. In October 1878 the Reichstag passed by 221 votes to 149 the "law against the dangerous activities of social democracy".[4] Social Democrats, the Catholic Centre Party, and the left-liberal Progressive Party voted against, the conservative parties and the majority of the National Liberals, who had at first rejected emergency legislation, voted in favour.

The Anti-Socialist Law was initially valid for three years. It was extended three times before being finally lifted on 30 September 1890. The Social Democrats, as Bebel characterized their oppressive situation in a letter of 12 December 1878 to his great comrade-in-arms Georg von Vollmar in Bavaria, were now fair game: "For us, justice and the law do not exist"[5].

The Law banned all organisations "whose Social Democratic, Socialist, or Communist endeavours are aimed at overthrowing the existing state and social order", along with associations "in which Social Democratic, Socialist, or Communist endeavours directed towards the overthrow of the existing state and social order manifest themselves in a way which endangers the public peace and particularly the harmony of all classes in society".[6] All meetings and press publications "in which Social Democratic endeavours manifest themselves" were subject to the same judgement. In addition to the threat of imprisonment and fines, the state police were empowered to expel from the locations and districts in question, "persons suspected of being a danger to public safety". The elastic phrasing of the law offered the authorities extensive leeway for interpretation. Not only the party organisations, but also those trade unions close to social democracy were dissolved. Already by November 1878, 153 associations, as well as 175 newspapers and periodicals were prohibited, and 67 Social Democrats were banished from Berlin alone. Altogether, in the twelve years of the Anti-Socialist Law, between eight and nine hundred "suspicious persons", with almost 1500 dependants, were expelled from their homes. In the two years 1878 and 1879 alone, the courts imposed a total of 600 years imprisonment for *lèse majesté* and breaches of this oppressive law, and up until 1888 eight hundred and eighty-one further years. The only legal political activity left to Social Democrats was participation in the Reichstag elections and in individual Landtag elections. These

---

4 Reichs-Gesetzblatt (1878) no. 34, p. 351.
5 Bebel in a letter to Vollmar of 12.12.1878, quoted from Bebel, Aus meinem Leben, vol. 3, p. 28f.
6 See note 4.

demonstrated that all the restrictions and inducements could not, in the long term, stop the movement. After the Anti-Socialist Law had failed to be renewed, Bebel, at the party congress in Halle, proudly took stock:

"In the general election of 1871, 102,000 votes were cast for us. In 1874, 352,000. In 1877, two years after the unification congress of the party which had been split until 1875, 493,000. That was the high point before the *Ausnahmegesetz* (special law). A year later, as a result of the two assassination attempts, the Reichstag was dissolved and a monstrous smear campaign mounted against our party, to which the attempts quite disgracefully had been attributed, and, under the extreme pressure of that, the number of votes in summer 1878 fell from 493,000 to 437,000: we received 56,000 votes less than a year and a half before. Then came the body blow of the special law, but despite this, in the general elections of 1881 which were held under unprecedented conditions, we received 312,000 votes. This is even more to our credit, since, under the state of emergency and the pressure of that time, a large number of constituencies didn't even receive either leaflets or voting papers, because the opposition's printers would not print them for us, and our own printing works had been almost all destroyed, and even where we did have leaflets, they could only be distributed with great difficulty and danger. Then came the elections of 1884. These elections presented a quite different picture. In the meanwhile, the party was much recovered. We had had the party congresses of Wyden and Copenhagen which were a great boost to party confidence. Here and there, there were successful attempts to found new journals, to set up printing works etc., with the result that we gained 550,000 votes this time, 238,000 more than in 1881. Then in 1887 we grew to 763,000, and at the last general election this year (20 February 1890), which is still vivid in everyone's memory, we gained 1,427,000 votes. With this, the party had become the strongest party in Germany."[7]

And so it had, despite Bismarck's policy of "kicks and halfpence"[8]. Even the Prussian Junker at the head of the German Imperial Reich knew that a movement such as social democracy had not arisen from nothing, but had its origins in deplorable social and economic conditions. It was at this point that he inaugurated his social policy, announced in an imperial proclamation of 17 November 1881. In 1883 the Reichstag approved a bill introducing legislation on medical insurance. This was followed in 1884 by an accident insurance act, and in 1889 workers were given a

---

7 Protokoll über die Verhandlungen des Parteitages der Sozialdemokratischen Partei Deutschlands, abgehalten zu Halle a.S. vom 12. bis 18. Oktober 1890 (Berlin 1890 – reprint 1978), p. 32f.
8 This is G.P. Gooch's expression. See G.P. Gooch, Germany (London 1925), p. 35.

graduated pension scheme at seventy, or earlier if disabled. The guiding principle behind this much-vaunted, pioneering social legislation was state welfare thinking, a kind of – as Bismarck characterised it – "further development of the form on which state provision for the poor is based". It is not difficult to detect the deeper motivation behind these initiatives: "If there were no such thing as social democracy, and if there were not a whole host of people who feared it, the moderate progress which we have made hitherto in social reform would not yet have happened."[9] His actions were motivated, "albeit with a tinge of practical Christianity"[10], by tactical political considerations. These acts of state benevolence were designed to cut the ground from beneath the Social Democrats he hated so much, seeking thereby to win over the workers to the existing monarchical and conservative order, in order then to subject them to the tightened rein of a bureaucratic and authoritarian state.

3. The Political Consequences of Oppression

Even with the double strategy of stick and carrot the workers could not be so easily enticed. They wanted equal rights and social justice, not Lady Bountiful gestures. The workers' movement was also concerned to take into democratic self-administration the friendly societies they had in part built up themselves. Workers experienced at first-hand how this selfsame state continued to persecute those suspected of being Social Democrats. Many thought the same way as August Bebel:

"I felt it as a mortal insult that we were expelled like vagabonds and criminals, and snatched away from wife and child without judicial process, and, had I had the power, I would have wreaked revenge. No trial, no sentence, caused me such feelings of hatred and embitterment than those expulsions which continued year upon year until, finally, that law which had become so untenable collapsed, bringing to an end the cruel game with human lives."[11]

The thorn of mistrust and embitterment penetrated deep into the hearts of Social Democratic workers denounced and outlawed as a pestilence on the state. Despite this, the party emphatically rejected the argument for anarchistic underground tactics proposed by the group round Johann Most and Wilhelm Hasselmann, and punished them with expul-

---

9   Speech in the Reichstag of 26.11.1884. In Stenographische Berichte über die Verhandlungen des Reichstags, VI. Legislaturperiode, I. Session 1884/88, vol. 1 (Berlin 1885), p. 25.
10 Grebing, Geschichte der Arbeiterbewegung, p. 75.
11 August Bebel, Aus meinem Leben, vol. 3, p. 183.

sion. The removal of the word "legal" from the Gotha programme as a result of the Wyden congress in Switzerland in 1880 merely expressed the fact that the party wished to continue its work under the illegal circumstances forced on it by the law.

The deeper consequences of the Anti-Socialist Law were to be found on a different plane. Outrage at the present state escalated into a hostility, characterised by mistrust and revulsion, towards the state as such. Who could begrudge the Social Democrats their view of the state as being increasingly nothing more than an instrument of oppression for the ruling classes? Out of the radicalised consciousness of those anathematised by bourgeois society and persecuted by the authorities, there arose the need for an ideological basis for their embitterment capable of administering a savage rebuke to the entire system, and also of holding out the promise of a rosier future. They found support and alleviation of their lot in the teachings of Marx, the main disseminators and popularisers of which were Eduard Bernstein and Karl Kautsky. Decisive in this turning to Marx was not a differentiated understanding of his theories, but a choice of emphasis in the interpretation of them which was determined by a particular state of consciousness. Here was a system, expressed in scholarly terms, but couched in aggressive, revolutionary language which mirrored their own feelings, and which predicted with confidence the inevitable decline of bourgeois class society and the certain victory of the socialist workers' movement.

Despite the radical veneer and the talk of proletarian revolution, "German social democracy", as the long-standing Party Secretary Ignaz Auer put it so precisely, "has never been a party of revolution, nor is it or does it, despite the special Anti-Socialist Law, wish to become so today". He continued:

"The strength of German social democracy lay, and lies, in the fact that it is the representative of the politically thinking worker. [...] If we wish to be a mere sect, then we can grant ourselves the luxury of being, on principle, a party of revolution. If, however, we wish to remain the party of the German workers then, at the forefront of our endeavours must be the desire to bring this about through peaceful – I do not say legal – propaganda, reforms, and revolutions in the political and economic sphere which will be of benefit to working people, and at the same time bring us a stage closer to a socialist state."[12]

Ironically, it was the Anti-Socialist Law, which banned the party, but allowed the participation in elections and parliamentary activity, which

---

12 Quoted in Eduard Bernstein, Ignaz Auer. Eine Gedenkschrift (Berlin 1907), pp. 37ff.

Past – Present – Future

fostered the development of reformist practice. The Social Democratic group in the Reichstag, to whom the leadership of the party was now transferred, visibly gained an importance all its own. Parliament offered a public platform which the Social Democrats rapidly learned to exploit in the advancement of their political programme and particular goals. After the first setbacks, the seemingly unstoppable rise in their vote appeared to demonstrate that, under the circumstances of universal suffrage, the ballot paper was the right and most promising method of successfully gaining power and turning the system upside down. It was none other than Friedrich Engels who, in his preface to Marx's *The Class Struggles in France*, gave backing to this optimism about the ballot box. He noted that with the successful use of the system of universal suffrage by German social democracy, "an entirely new mode of proletarian struggle came into force." The SPD "mass", he went on, "increases uninterruptedly. Its growth proceeds so spontaneously, as irresistibly, and yet at the same time as tranquilly as a natural process".[13] There were, therefore, two contradictory consequences of the Anti-Socialist Law. If it prompted a conscious radicalisation in terms of theory, it nonetheless gave rise to day-to-day methods which were directed towards practical, parliamentary reform work.

---

13 Karl Marx, The Class Struggles in France (1845–1850) (London [The Marxist-Leninist Library] 1936), p. 23 and pp. 28–29.

IV. Between Radical Theory and Reformist Practice: on the Path to the First World War as a Mass Party

1. *The Erfurt Programme*

At its party conference in Erfurt in 1891, German social democracy gave itself a new name, the "Social Democratic Party of Germany", and also adopted a different programme. Eight years after the death of Karl Marx on 14 March 1883, Engels announced triumphantly: "We can declare with satisfaction that Marx's criticism [of the Gotha Programme] has taken full effect."[1] With the "Erfurt programme", Marxism became the official theoretical basis of German social democracy. Without long discussion, the party conference unanimously approved the draft which had been submitted by the party's two leading theoreticians, Kautsky and Bernstein. Dubbed half-mockingly, half-admiringly "younger fathers of the Church", the two authors had striven to mould the "intellectual weaponry from the Marx and Engels' arsenal"[2] into a form suitable for everyday use. What emerged was a double-edged sword.

The Erfurt Programme fell into two clearly different parts: one theoretical, the other political and practical. The critics drew their sustenance not least from the contradictory nature of this bipolarity.

The first, basic part drew in places almost word for word on chapter 24 (section seven) of *Capital*. It did not represent a programme in the true sense of the word, but offered a short analysis of "the economic development of bourgeois society" and the conclusions to be drawn therefrom. It detailed how the gulf between those with and those without property was becoming ever wider, how "the army of superfluous workers" was growing ever larger, and ever more oppressive the misery, the enslavement, the exploitation, ever more fierce the class struggle between bourgeoisie and proletariat:

"Only the transference of capitalist ownership of the means of production – land, pits and mines, raw materials, tools, machines, means of

---

[1] Letter of Friedrich Engels. In Briefe und Auszüge aus Briefen von Joh. Phil. Becker, Jos. Dietzgen, Friedrich Engels, Karl Marx u.a. an F. A. Sorge und andere (Stuttgart 1906), p. 370.
[2] Susanne Miller, 'Zur Rezeption des Marxismus in der deutschen Sozialdemokratie', in Freiheitlicher Sozialismus, edited by Heiner Flohr, Klaus Lompe, Lothar F. Neumann (Bonn-Bad Godesberg 1973), p. 24.

transport – to social ownership, and the transformation of commodity production into socialist production driven by, and for, society, can ensure that the large industrial concern, and the constantly growing profitability of social labour, are transformed, for the hitherto exploited classes, from a source of misery and oppression into a source of the greatest welfare and harmonious perfection for all. This social transformation signifies not only the liberation of the proletariat, but of the whole human race which is suffering under the present-day conditions."

But the working class alone was called upon to fight and win this struggle for liberation: by engaging in the "economic struggle", by obtaining their political rights through sheer persistency, and by seizing political power as the basis for "transferring the means of production into the possession of the community as a whole".[3]

If it seemed, after the first part of the programme, that only the socialisation of the means of production could bring long-term improvements to the workers' situation, the second part made practical demands for democratisation of the state and for the amelioration of the workers' social lot. In addition to the appeal for a system of universal and equal proportional representation for all parliaments, and for the election of state authorities and self-government at all levels, the programme also called *inter alia* for equal standing and the right to vote for women, secularisation of the education system, free legal and medical services, progressive income and wealth taxes, the creation of labour exchanges, freedom of expression and assembly, absolute right of association, "takeover by the Reich of the entire workers' insurance system" with democratic workers' participation, and the "statutory enactment of a maximum eight-hour standard working day". The markedly plebiscitary components of the Gotha, and earlier of the Eisenach programme, were toned down in the Erfurt programme. Instead of "administration of justice by the people", the expression was now "administration of justice by judges elected by the people", and the decision on war or peace was no longer, as in the Gotha programme, to be made by the people, but was now handed over to the "representative body of the people".

Any fundamental statement on the structure of the state was conspicuous by its absence. In his comments on the draft, Engels had noted that if "one wanted to come to identify with socialism", then one would also have to acknowledge that the SPD could only come to power "under

---

3 Protokoll über die Verhandlungen des Parteitages der Sozialdemokratischen Partei Deutschlands abgehalten zu Erfurt vom 14. bis 20. Oktober 1891. In Dowe and Klotzbach (eds), Programmatische Dokumente (2004), pp. 171–175.

some form of democratic republic".[4] There was indeed a huge discrepancy here. It was hardly possible under the conditions of the Imperial Reich to issue an open demand for a democratic republic. This would have been held to be a call to insurrection and offered the state powers a pretext to intervene. Moreover, social democracy at this time also lacked any real understanding of the central intrinsic value and status of a democratic republic. Marx and Engels were not without fault here because they had never described unambiguously the relationship between objectively inevitable development and practical action, between the setting of revolutionary goals and the need to work for reform, and drew attention only to the dissolution of the contradiction in the dialectical unity between theory and practice. In the Erfurt Programme and Kautsky's interpretations of Marx, social democracy adopted from Marx and Engels' teachings their conviction that social development would proceed according to the strict rules of a law of nature. It would culminate in the abolition of class rule and with it the demise of the thus redundant state. Friedrich Engels described this process in the following, celebrated words: "The society which organizes production anew [...] will put the whole state machinery where it will then belong – into the museum of antiquities, next to the spinning wheel and the bronze axe."[5]

With this, socialism would have achieved its aim. But how precisely this goal was to be attained, and how the seizure of state power by the proletariat was to be brought about, what changes to the political and social structure and transitional institutional stages would be required, these could only be read between the lines of the Erfurt Programme. Its very lack of precision gave rise to different points of emphasis. The programme could be used primarily to justify the struggle for democratic freedoms and social reforms. Or the attempt could be made, with reference to the basic section, to press for an intensification of class conflict and social revolution. Despite such divergent tendencies, the activities of the Social Democratic Party were governed by the principle they had firmly anchored in the Erfurt Programme: the commitment to "abolition of class rule and of the classes themselves, and to equal rights and equal obligations for all, regardless of gender and birth", and to the struggle, not only against exploitation of the workers, but also against "every kind of exploitation and oppression, whether it be directed against a class, a party, a sex, or a race."[6]

4 This extract from Engels' criticism of the Erfurt programme is taken from Das Prinzip Links, p. 65.
5 Friedrich Engels, The Origin of the Family, Private Property and the State (London 1972), p. 232.
6 See Dowe and Klotzbach (eds), Programmatische Dokumente (2004), p. 173.

2. Economic and Social Change

In the Reichstag elections of 20 February 1890, the Social Democrats achieved 19.7 per cent of the vote. This result made them the strongest single party in the Imperial Reich. The 1,427,000 voters who had expressed their allegiance to the despised SPD at the ballot box signalised the final breakthrough to becoming a movement with mass support. In a consistent rise in numbers, interrupted only briefly in 1907, the party continued its expansion up until the First World War. From 23.3 per cent in 1893 (1,786,000 voters), to 27.2 per cent in 1898 (2,107,000), 31.7 per cent in 1903 (3,010,000) and 28.9 per cent in 1907 (3,258,000), their share of the vote in 1912 went up to 34.8 per cent (4,250,000) of the electorate.[7] Hundreds of thousands of men and women demonstrated their allegiance to the SPD with their party membership book, even though this frequently brought them difficulty and disadvantage in their work or profession. The first-past-the-post electoral system prevented the number of overall votes cast being reflected in the number of seats gained. The lack of consideration for shifts in population when constituency boundaries were decided at the time of the founding of the Reich favoured the sparsely inhabited agrarian regions over the centres of heavy population. It was not until 1912 that the SPD, with 110 deputies, became the biggest single party in the Reichstag. Despite enjoying an unprecedented boom, the Social Democrats remained essentially a party of tradesmen and industrial workers. They achieved no successes of note amongst agricultural labourers who, under the influence of estate owners, teachers and clergy, for the most part voted conservative. Nor did they manage to make any inroads amongst Catholic workers, where, as before, the Centre Party continued to dominate.

The trade union movement experienced a similarly meteoric growth.[8] Printers and cigar workers, who already in 1848 had banded together to form associations, were also the first to become active again in the sixties. The founding of the Cigar Workers' Organisation in 1865 and the Printers' Association in 1866, as well as the initiatives emanating from the socialist parties, led to the creation of further associations. Their attempt to create a central superstructure in 1878 was thwarted by the Anti-Socialist Law. This was also responsible for the break-up of trade unions close to social democracy which at best could only keep going in disguised form.

---

7 See also tables and diagrams nos 1 and 2.
8 The most recent survey of the history of the trade unions is Michael Schneider's History of the German Trade Unions (Bonn 2005).

Only when the Law lapsed was real trade-union activity once again possible. Differences about the appropriate forms of organisation were, by and large, smoothed over. Already in 1890, with the creation of the General Commission of the Free Trade Unions of Germany, which in 1891 had over 277,000 trade-union members, a flexible administrative structure was in place. After stagnating up until 1895 in a period of economic crisis, numbers began to rise rapidly again. In 1899 the 500,000 threshold was crossed. In 1904 the first million was achieved, 1910 the second million, and finally, before the outbreak of the First World War, their members numbered 2.5 million. In addition to these "Free Trade Unions", as they called themselves, which were closely allied to the Social Democrats, there were also the Christian trade unions, and the unions associated with the Liberals. Both of these catered for small minorities, their high point being reached in 1913 before the war with 340,000, and 105,000 members respectively.

The growth of the social democratic workers' movement took place against the background of vigorous economic expansion. Improvements to the transport system – the driving force behind industrialisation – and the railways with their need for steel, all played a role in this. The network grew from 549 kilometres in 1840, to over 6,044 in 1850, 19,575 in 1870, and to 51,678 in 1900.[9] From the year of the founding of the Reich, when the industrial revolution first became fully up and running, up until 1910, the production of pig iron grew from 1.6 million, to 14.8 million metric tons. Technical innovations – the Bessemer converter (1855/60), the dynamo (1866), chemistry – created the basis for whole new branches of industry. Characteristic of this epoch was the springing up like mushrooms of joint-stock companies, trust companies, cartels, the first large combines, for instance in the electrical industry, big banks such as Deutsche Bank, the Dresdner Bank, as well as the increasingly powerful link-ups between banks and business concerns. Germany was transformed from an agricultural, to an industrial state. The share of agriculture in the gross national product sank from 47 per cent in 1850 to 23 per cent in 1913, while in the same period the contribution of the industrial sector quadrupled, and by the outbreak of the First World War had reached almost 60 per cent. The growth in population (40 million in 1871, 67 million in 1914), and the mass migration from the agrarian regions, led to the concentration of population in the conurbations. The face of Germany, the new economic super power, was determined by the industrial centres on the Rhine and Ruhr rivers, in Saxony and Berlin. In the period between 1887 and 1914

---

9 See Fritz Voigt, Verkehr, vol. II (Berlin 1965), pp. 505, 529, and 537.

"Progress is unstoppable", depicting Progress assailing the bastion of Capitalism

alone, the number of industrial workers doubled. If 65 per cent of the population were still living in villages and small towns in 1871, by 1910 it was only 40 per cent. In the same period, the number of cities with populations of more than 100,000 rose from 5 to 20 per cent. This flight from the land and process of urbanisation led to a loosening of traditional ties, and to a new awareness of community shaped by common living and working conditions.[10] Although productivity rose rapidly, due to technical improvements and increased division of labour, the mass unemployment predicted in the Erfurt Programme and by Marx did not materialise. It in fact sank to a relatively low level, offering workers the prerequisite for a promising outcome to their struggle. Amongst employees who were members of a trade union, the number out of work hovered between 1 and 3 per cent.[11] Since the 1870s, there had been a gradual reduction in working hours to twelve, then, since the 1890s, to eleven and finally approaching ten, albeit that great variations still existed between different industrial branches and concerns.

Wages had shown an upward trend since 1880. What was crucial, was that there was not only an increase in nominal wages, but also, if not always continuously, in real wages. Particularly in the 1880s and the 1890s there was a steep rise which was perhaps more deserving of the title of "real material, social reform"[12] than was Bismarck's system of social security. If, in 1850, a Prussian working household had to spend 58 per cent of its wages on the most basic foodstuffs alone, the figure in 1913 was just 33 per cent.

Nevertheless, although income was still just about sufficient to feed a reasonably sized family without too much difficulty, it was still not enough to sustain a dignified human existence. It was, therefore, an absolute necessity in most working-class households for the wife to work. Living conditions were appalling. For the most part, people lived a rough-and-ready existence in grim back buildings and gloomy, jerry-built tenements. As late as 1895, there were still 25,000 dwellings in Berlin consisting of a single room. Almost 80,000 so-called *Schlafburschen* (lodgers) had just a temporary bed in someone else's lodging, and even this they often had to share, on a shift basis, with other people.

But workers felt oppressed not just by the material worries which, despite many improvements, continued to exist; the roots of their disgruntlement went much deeper. The ostentatious display of their wealth by the rich, continuing political and social discrimination, and above all the widespread lack of justice in the work process, was a constant source of

---

10 For a very detailed account of the situation of the labour force, see Gerhard A. Ritter and Klaus Tenfelde, Arbeiter im Deutschen Kaiserreich (Bonn 1992).
11 See Gerhard Bry, Wages in Germany 1871–1945. A Study by the National Bureau of Economic Research (New York, Princeton 1960), pp. 325 ff.
12 Hans Rosenberg's description, in Große Depression und Bismarckzeit (Berlin 1967), p. 217.

bitterness about "them up there". This was directed as much against the works' foremen, who were despised as slave-drivers, as against capitalists, employers, and entrepreneurs who, apart from honourable exceptions such as Ernst Abbe and Robert Bosch, were for the most part adherents of an inflexible, authoritarian "I'm the master here" philosophy. The industrial magnate Kirdorf delivered an autocratic formulation of their point of view in 1899 on the occasion of the miners' strike: "Neither kaisers nor kings have any say in the factories. There, we alone decide."[13]

Thrown back on their own resources, individual workers were helpless in the face of this brutal exercise of power. Mutual solidarity offered the only chance of defending their own interests. It was precisely as a result of daily experiencing the same as their colleagues that consciousness of belonging to one great, exploited and oppressed working class arose. They saw the Social Democrats as the party which represented their concerns and which was fighting for a better future. In their organisations, and in the trade unions, they found a community of like-minded equals in which the sense of their own impotence could be overcome. The SPD offered both a haven and a home. It made workers aware that their situation was not hopeless, and that the day when exploitation and oppression would end was not a distant dream. Inspired by belief in the approaching victory of social democracy, and the promised socialist society of the future, they felt themselves to be the proud, self-confident pioneers of a new age. A young metal worker articulated these sentiments when he said: "I am not without hope, since anyone as totally convinced about socialism as I am, believes in liberation as much as he would in a new gospel."[14]

3. Practical Politics and Theoretical Disputes

With the collapse of the Anti-Socialist Law and Bismarck's fall from power signalling a shift in course in domestic politics, social democracy was confronted with a changed situation. Nevertheless, there was no halt to discrimination. With harassment from the authorities, *lèse-majesté* trials, and the use of the law of association, the state continued to make things difficult for the SPD and the trade unions. Beyond this, attempts were made

---

[13] See Dieter Schuster, Die deutsche Gewerkschaftsbewegung/DGB (Düsseldorf 4th edn 1973), p. 24. On the attitudes of the well-known industrialists Alfred Krupp and Carl Ferdinand von Stumm-Halberg, see Ernst Schraepler, Quellen zur Geschichte der sozialen Frage in Deutschland, vol. II (Göttingen 1957), pp. 87 ff.

[14] Adolf Levenstein, Die Arbeiterfrage. Mit besonderer Berücksichtigung der sozialpsychologischen Seite des modernen Großbetriebes und der psychologischen Einwirkungen auf den Arbeiter (Munich 1912), p. 314.

from time to time to implement new, more stringent measures in the fight against social democracy. The best-known of these were the so-called "subversion bill" of 1894/95, and the so-called "penal bill" of 1898/99. Both, however, were defeated in the Reichstag. Notwithstanding all these attempts at suppression, after 1890, and in contrast to the previous twelve years, the Social Democrats could finally operate within the law as a political party. This gave a whole new dimension to the question of future political tactics.[15] The opposition movement of the so-called "Young Ones" with their polemics against the "leaders", and revolutionary, in part anti-parliamentary and syndicalist slogans, remained a short-lived, peripheral phenomenon. They appealed in vain to the authority of Engels, who reproached them with being incapable of "seeing the simplest of things with their own eyes", and in "economic and political matters" of "assessing dispassionately neither the gravity of the facts, nor the strength of the forces coming into play".[16]

The emergence of reformism was on a quite different footing from the "Young Ones". According to Kautsky's analysis, it sprang from "a real need": "We have become too big to be able to remain merely a party of demonstration."[17] It was in line with this that in his celebrated "Eldorado speeches" of 1891 (so named after the meeting hall in Munich), Georg von Vollmar, who had been a long-standing member of the radical wing, called for an emphatic policy of reform based on the existing state and social order. Instead of alienating those progressive forces outside their ranks by an unconciliatory stance and revolutionary speeches, social democracy should work with them, thereby making it easier to push ahead with a decisive policy of social and democratic reforms. Under the motto "To those of good will a welcoming hand, to those of bad the fist"[18], Vollmar wanted to speed up the struggle for emancipation by concentrating energies on practical reforms within the framework of the existing state. August Bebel warned the party at this point of the danger of dissi-

---

15 For an overall view, see Gerhard A. Ritter, Die Arbeiterbewegung im Wilhelminischen Reich. Die Sozialdemokratische Partei und die Freien Gewerkschaften 1890–1900 (Berlin Dahlem 1959: 2nd edn 1963), and Hans-Josef Steinberg, Sozialismus und deutsche Sozialdemokratie. Zur Ideologie der Partei vor dem Ersten Weltkrieg (Berlin-Bonn 5th edn 1979).
16 Karl Marx/Friedrich Engels, Werke, vol. 22 (Berlin/GDR), p. 84.
17 In a letter to Eduard Bernstein of 8.12.1896, quoted by Hans-Josef Steinberg, 'Die deutsche Sozialdemokratie nach dem Fall des Sozialistengesetzes. Ideologie und Taktik der sozialistischen Massenpartei im Wilhelminischen Reich', in Hans Mommsen (ed.), Sozialdemokratie, p. 54.
18 Georg von Vollmar, Über die nächsten Aufgaben der deutschen Sozialdemokratie (Munich 1891), p. 54.

pating its efforts in the detail, and, in the process, of losing sight of the ultimate goal. He was convinced the final battle was imminent. In his criticism of Vollmar's initiative, he announced to the delegates at the Erfurt party congress: "It is my conviction that the realisation of our goals is so near, that there are few in this room who will not live to see the day."[19] Although Vollmar's theses were officially rejected at first, they met with increasing resonance. Pre-eminently the product of *Realpolitik*, they overlapped in great measure with the course adopted by the Free Trade Unions, who were fighting for improvements "on the basis of society today"[20] and, like the reformists, did not want to let themselves be forced into an inflexible theoretical programme. The passionate discussions unleashed by Vollmar's initiative should not disguise the fact that day-to-day political work was governed by widespread agreement. The struggle for democratic freedoms and social change, which Marx and Engels had also expressly championed, was laid down in the second part of the Erfurt Programme and also determined the activities of those propagating irreconcilable class struggle and the coming social revolution. Paul Kampffmeyer characterised this attitude as follows:

"Strangely, the split which exists today between the Radicals and the Possibilitists runs right through the heart of the Erfurt Programme, and it runs, almost palpably, through the souls of our most gifted theoreticians and party leaders. On the one hand they heap curse after curse on bourgeois society, and on the other they seek, with ardent endeavour, to tinker about with it."[21]

The basis of this work was to be found in party organisations, parliaments, trade unions, cooperatives, and involvement in social-security and labour-law institutions. The organisational structure of the party was adapted flexibly to meet legal restrictions, thereby also allowing women in most of the states a degree of participation. Not until 1908 did the legislator permit them membership throughout the Reich. After the lifting of the prohibition of association in 1900, the party had, with the statute of 1905, changed its organisational structure from the system of representatives which had predominated hitherto to one of associations with fixed membership contributions. They began at local or constituency level,

---

19 Protokoll über die Verhandlungen des Parteitages der Sozialdemokratischen Partei Deutschlands, abgehalten zu Erfurt vom 14. bis 20. Oktober 1891 (Berlin 1891), p. 172.
20 See the appeal of the General Commission in 1891, quoted in Schuster, Die deutsche Gewerkschaftsbewegung, p. 27.
21 Paul Kampffmeyer, 'Schrittweise Sozialisierung oder gewaltsame Sprengung der kapitalistischen Wirtschaftsordnung', in Sozialistische Monatshefte, no. 10 (1899), p. 466.

The Workers' Movement as an Educational Movement

then were built up through regional, provincial and state associations, culminating at Reich level with the party executive. The upswing in the organisation can be documented in the rise in membership from 384,327 in the period 1905/06, to 1,085,905 in 1913/14.[22] The growth in party bureaucracy with the employment of salaried functionaries was the virtually inevitable concomitant of being a mass party from which advice and help were sought from every quarter. With its advice service, given free of charge by the mostly trade-union maintained workers' secretarial offices, the social democratic movement helped great numbers of people to secure their legal rights, primarily in the area of social security. In addition, there was the intensive educational activity, with hundreds of courses and individual lectures, its own libraries, theatre performances and the creation of the *Freie Volksbühne* (Free Peoples' Theatre), peripatetic teachers and the setting up of a central school for workers' education, and the famous Party School. With all of this, the SPD and the Free Trade Unions were not only delivering the necessary tools for the political and social struggle, but were also a cultural movement in the widest sense of the term.

22 See Dieter Fricke, Zur Organisation und Tätigkeit der deutschen Arbeiterbewegung (1890–1914). Dokumente und Materialien (Leipzig 1962), p. 64 ff.

Much more the focus of public attention, however, was the work in the parliaments. Basic differences over the state and social order, along with the bourgeois parties who for the most part confronted them with a solid bloc of opposition, imposed strict limits on the effectiveness of the Social Democrats in the Reichstag. In very few cases were they able to find allies in the bourgeois camp. In their commitment to greater rights for parliament and more democracy, the SPD were most likely to find support from left-liberal groupings, while in the sphere of social policy there were some bridges to the Catholic Centre Party and its Christian workers' wing. On other decisive issues such as the demand for the statutory introduction of the eight-hour working day, or the abolition of the discriminatory Prussian three-class franchise, it was virtually impotent in the face of a solid bloc of oppositional forces.

Only by means of tactical compromise could the SPD, in borderline cases, exercise direct influence on legislation. In 1894, the parliamentary party voted for the first time for a government bill. This made provision for a reduction in the import duty on wheat, thereby encouraging a drop in the price of food. In 1913, their vote helped bring in new tax laws which finally affected the wealthy, and were necessary because of the rise in military expenditure. With this, Wilhelm Liebknecht's principle of "Not one man, not one penny for this system", which had found tangible expression in the rejection of the domestic budget, had been seriously breached.

In the state parliaments this had happened before, the first time in Hesse and Baden in 1891. In 1894, the Bavarian parliamentary party also voted for the state budget, in contravention of the policy of the party as a whole. In Prussia, with its inegalitarian three-class system which entailed the division of the electorate according to the payment of direct taxes, it was not until 1908 that socialists could enter parliament, thus giving north Germans visible demonstration of their view of the state as the instrument of oppression of the ruling class. In the south German states of Baden, Hesse, Württemberg and Bavaria, however, a more liberal climate prevailed. Through electoral alliances with bourgeois parties, voting for state budgets and parliamentary bills, the SPD here was able to win various socio-political and democratic concessions, such as the replacement of the class-based electoral systems by universal suffrage.

The Social Democrats now gave particular emphasis to work at local level, founding the tradition of community politics which would be intensified after 1945. The institution, in some places, of unemployment benefit, and the setting-up of local labour exchanges, were due not least to their tireless efforts. In 1913, the number of Social Democrats on municipal and district councils was approaching 13,000.[23] Here, and in their work in the administration of industrial insurance, in community employment offices and courts of arbitration, lay one of the roots of the gradual penetration by the Social Democrats of the imperial German state.

Another grew out of the work of the trade unions. With their system of benefit organisations, which had a total expenditure of 389.9 million marks in the years 1891–1914, of which 143.5 million went on strike pay, 89.9 million on unemployment benefit, and 91.0 million on sickness benefit,[24] they offered their members a system of social security which was highly attractive even to those who previously had not been members of a union. Strike funds made it possible to hold out longer when taking industrial action. From the turn of the century the idea of wage agreements, which were initially denigrated as "dozy notions of harmony" and "betrayal of the class struggle", gained momentum. Carl Legien, the chairman of the General Commission of Free Trade Unions, regarded them not only as an effective instrument for improving wages and working conditions, but also as "recognition of workers' right of co-determination in the stipulation of working conditions".[25] Like Legien, most trade-union officials, conditioned by the need to bring about practical improvements, were reformist in inclination. They had little time for speeches about revolutionary theory or abstract theories of any kind, and wanted to avoid at all cost anything which would have jeopardised the unity of their organisation and the socio-political successes it had achieved.

4. The Revisionism Dispute and Mass Strike Debate

Under communism, anyone who harboured doubts about the validity of the "true doctrine" was instantly pilloried as a "revisionist". Being reproached with "revisionism" weighed heavily. It is an old expression. It is associated with Eduard Bernstein who unleashed fierce arguments in the German social democratic movement around the turn of the century with his theories of reform. The reformism of Vollmar and others was directed towards a change of political strategy and goals, without questioning directly the substance of Marxist theory. But in the "reformist debate" the first expressions of doubt about the universal validity of Marxist teaching

---

23 See the detailed statistics in Ritter, Die Arbeiterbewegung im Wilhelminischen Reich, p. 233f.
24 See Paul Umbreit, 25 Jahre deutsche Gewerkschaftsbewegung 1890–1915 (Berlin 1915), especially the illustrated chart on p. 175.
25 Carl Legien, 'Tarifgemeinschaften und gemeinsame Verbände von Arbeitern und Unternehmern', in Sozialistische Monatshefte, no. I (1902), p. 29.

began to be heard. In effect, these arguments are the harbingers of the later revisionism dispute.

It was set in motion by Eduard Bernstein. In a series of articles in *Neue Zeit* (New Age) in 1896/97 dealing with the problems of socialism, and in his book, *Die Voraussetzungen des Sozialismus und die Aufgaben der Sozialdemokratie* (Presuppositions of Socialism and the Tasks for Social Democracy [1899]), he expressed well-founded doubts about whether society was really developing towards a two-class system along the lines predicted by the *Communist Manifesto* and the Erfurt Programme. The middle classes were not disappearing, merely changing their character. The theory of imminent catastrophe, with its prognostications of ever worsening crises and the growing impoverishment of the workers, had also not been borne out. Indeed, quite contrary tendencies could be observed, indicating a process of transformation, and a certain reining-in of unbridled capitalism. Bernstein saw the reasons for this development primarily in the energetic struggle of unionised labour for social betterment and a democratic share in decision-making. For him, therefore, a policy of reform was a way of both changing, and of stabilising, the system.

Social democracy, he maintained, must not allow its policies to be dictated by the prospect of the "great, impending social catastrophe", the ineluctable collapse of capitalism and its inevitable supplanting by socialism. On the contrary, it must revise its radical, revolutionary dogmas and also commit itself, in its theoretical goals, to "what it in reality is today: a party of democratic and social reform"[26]. This is the sense in which he wished the often misinterpreted assertion – "the movement means everything to me, but that which is commonly called the final goal of socialism, nothing"[27] – to be understood.

Bernstein's theses, which were based mainly on his study of industrial development in England, but also on German statistical evidence, unleashed many years of passionate discussion. The condemnation of revisionism at party congresses, for the last time in 1903, and the affirmation of the Marxism transmitted by Kautsky and advocated so passionately by Bebel, did not settle the dispute. Vollmar asserted quite rightly, that, with reference to political practice, he could envisage no situation in which solid fronts of Marxists and revisionists would ever confront each other in the Reichstag. At bottom, the dispute did not revolve around the problem of a policy of reform or not. The controversy turned much more on

26 Eduard Bernstein, Die Voraussetzungen des Sozialismus und die Aufgaben der Sozialdemokratie (Stuttgart 1904, first edition 1899), p. 165.
27 This in a submission to the party congress of 1898. See Wilhelm Mommsen, Deutsche Parteiprogramme (Munich 1960), p. 371.

the concept of legitimate development towards socialism via the necessary transitional stage of a social revolution. For Bernstein, who advocated an ethically grounded socialism, who had "ideals to realise, but not doctrines", this expectation was mere "Utopianism". The concept of revolution was associated for him with direct action and the use of violence. But this meaning of the word "revolution" as deployed in current speech was hardly ever used in the party anymore. Kautsky's remark that the Social Democrats were a "revolutionary party, but not one which made revolutions"[28], was indicative of the complex nature of the term. What emerged as the party's defining characteristics were the winning of political power by the working class, and the radical reshaping of economic structures. The struggle for social reforms could thus merge seamlessly with the concept of revolutionary goals.

The Marxists who dominated the party regarded the successive economic crises since the *Gründerkrach*, the economic crash of 1873, as heralding the collapse of capitalism. August Bebel eloquently proclaimed the belief that one last, severe economic crisis would bring an end to capitalism and lead to the collapse of the existing social order. "Ultimately", he reflected in 1884, "one good push and the whole load of junk will collapse like a pack of cards"[29], ushering in the age of socialism. In his book *Die Frau und der Sozialismus* (Woman under Socialism), the social democratic movement's most widely distributed book, Bebel depicts it in impressive terms. It produces a society with complete freedom and equality, one with all the blessings of cooperative institutions, and in which people can freely develop their creative powers in concord and harmony.

Since its beginnings, social democracy has seen itself as the standard bearer for a new age. Revolutionary theory had a double function in this. Firstly, it was the radical declaration of war on exploitation and the existing class society. Secondly, it represented hope for a future socialist society. From the teachings of Marx and Engels it drew the "scientific" backing for the certainty of being on the side of history, and also the conviction that the great vision of socialism would come about as inevitably as a natural force of nature. This two-fold optimism was the target of the revisionists' doubts. Bebel accused them of robbing the socialist workers' movement of its beliefs and enthusiasm.

28 Karl Kautsky, 'Zur Frage der Revolution', first published in Neue Zeit XIV (1893), no. 1. Thereafter in Karl Kautsky, Der Weg zur Macht (2nd edn 1910, reprint Frankfurt/Main 1972), pp. 154ff.
29 Bebel in a letter to Hermann Schlüter of 24.2.1884, quoted by Hans-Josef Steinberg, 'Die deutsche Sozialdemokratie nach dem Fall des Sozialistengesetzes', in Hans Mommsen (ed.), Sozialdemokratie, p. 57.

Reality put a powerful damper on the conviction about the impending collapse of the bourgeois and capitalist social order, and the unstoppable victory of socialism. The economic upswing which began in 1896 was an astonishing demonstration for the SPD of the ability of capitalism to survive and adapt. The turn of the century was characterised by rising entrepreneurial profits and incipient stagnation in real wages, a standstill in state social policy, and renewed attempts at state repression by means of the so-called Sedition and Penal Bill. Even the great election success of 1912, in which the Social Democrats had come to an arrangement with the left-liberal Progressive Party in the run-off elections, scarcely took them any further forward, and only served to mobilise their opponents. In the so-called "cartel of the creative classes", interest groups from industry, agriculture and middle-class businessmen forged a powerful fighting force against the Social Democrats. The inability which was clearly crystallising at the beginning of the twentieth century to translate the increasing growth in numbers into corresponding political influence, mobilised those forces within the party who were looking for fresh direction. The flaring-up of discussion about the mass political strike was a reaction to the increasingly fraught inner contradictions of the Imperial Reich, and the *cul-de-sac* in which social democracy found itself. The mass strike was initially rejected as unfeasible by Engels and Bebel, as well as by the Second International after its christening in July 1889 in Paris. Nor did a general downing of tools figure in its first May Day proclamation of 1890. The Belgian strikes over the right to vote, the Sedition Bill, the Russian Revolution of 1905, and the fear of reactionary plans for a *coup d'état* to abolish Reichstag electoral law, provoked intense discussion in the party press and at party congresses. This culminated in 1906 in a resolution of the Mannheim party congress to recognise mass withdrawal of labour as an appropriate defensive tactic in the case of an attack on Reichstag electoral law and the right of freedom of association. This signified not only a rejection of any offensive use of strikes, but also implied serious reservations about their defensive use.

The formulation at the party congress took into consideration the views of the trade unions who, at their previous congress in Cologne, had energetically rejected any commitment to the principle of mass strikes. It was resolved in the Mannheim Agreement that any strike action affecting both party and unions could only be decided upon jointly. With this settlement the unions were guaranteed their long-disputed independence from the party, which was forced from now on to agree important political decisions with the General Commission. Alongside the principle, advocated mainly by the unions, of unavoiding unnecessary risks and making the

*Poster entitled "The Voters' Party" depicting
"Red Siegfried" after the election battle of 1912*

strengthening and unity of the organisation their priority, there began to emerge, in the mass strike debate, the outlines of a quite different strategy. A "left wing" formed around Rosa Luxemburg, Franz Mehring and Karl Liebknecht who thought they had found in the revolutionary components of Marxism the answer to the aggravated conflict between the classes, and a pointer to fresh ways ahead. Under the impact of the Russian Revolution of 1905/06, the political mass strike was for them a crucial weapon in mobilising the masses. Out of the spontaneous uprising of the workers, to prevent a war for instance, would develop revolutionary struggles which ultimately would lead to the socialist revolution. The left-wing radicals did not develop a coherent strategy for seizing political power. They sought to arouse the desire of the masses for revolutionary struggle, but were forced to accept that the workers were unlikely to be won over to such a risky course of action.

On one point, their conception corresponded to that of the leading figure on the reformist wing, Ludwig Frank, and even to the views of Bernstein. Frank, a political activist on the right, whom Bebel at times regarded as his "crown prince", wished to use the political mass strike to force through reforms to Prussian electoral law. These initiatives formed part of his strategy of "total mobilisation of the party's forces in the service of the democratisation of Germany" with which he wanted to take the Social Democrats down the path towards becoming a party of consistent democratic and social reform.

None of the two groups pressing for action was successful, neither the one on the left seriously seeking to put revolutionary theory into practice, nor that on the right which wanted to make the policy of democratic and social reform the main guideline for what was said and done.[30] The slogans of the left-wing radicals met with little response amongst the working-class following. Being tied into the practical day-to-day work of the trade unions with their network of support, and state social security which, over time, had taken effect, led to a partial integration of the work force into the existing state. A further contributory factor in this was that the Social Democrats had toiled successfully to build up their own domain of varied organisations, of popular meeting places, their own press, educational establishments, and self-help organisations – all of which they were duly proud. The belief grew amongst a not inconsiderable section of workers that the existing social order was reformable, and that they had more to lose than their chains. If, in spite of these tendencies, revi-

---

30 For the broad picture, see Detlef Lehnert, Reform und Revolution in der Strategiediskussion der klassischen Sozialdemokratie (Bonn 1977).

sionism as a theory did not make its mark, then first and foremost because it could offer no ready substitute for the visionary element which was firmly anchored in the prevailing ideology of Marxism. Despite positive moves to escape the isolation, as in southern Germany, with the successful electoral coalition with the Progressive Party in 1912, and partial cooperation with left-wing Liberals and the Centre Party, the policy lines of revisionist theory were not compatible with the internal situation of the Imperial Reich. The state constitution of the Wilhelminian Reich, the socio-political power structure, and the intransigence of the ruling classes were an obstacle to the consistent, constructive process of participation sought by the revisionists and reformists.

The party continued to be defined by the broad spectrum in the centre which combined the work of practical reform with the belief in popular Marxist theory. It was clear that their ideology was becoming merely one of integration, serving as little more than a safety valve for the aggressions arising from the social and political situation. Although the party strictly rejected the notion of revolution, and pursued a politically unambiguous course of reform, radical vocabulary with its revolutionary pathos continued to be a defining feature of social democracy. It saw social revolution as a process of total economic and political restructuring which would come about without any actual involvement on their part. The consequence of this thinking was the loss of any real will to actively participate, and the anticipation of some great, unforeseen event. What mattered, was to be prepared for this moment, to keep intact the only solid bastion, the organisations, and not to jeopardise their power, or supposed power, by reckless manoeuvres.

When August Bebel died on 13 August 1913, he bequeathed a party all too inadequately equipped for the difficult tasks ahead. As the hard core of those forces pushing for parliamentarism, democratic freedom, and social justice, it had to fend off the attacks of those who wished to block any change to the political and social structure of Imperial Germany. With the electoral successes of the SPD came a hardening of the *Fronde* composed of "Junkers and factory barons", the Prussian-German army, and Pan-Germans of *völkisch* (national) disposition. In imperialism they found an instrument which they could wield successfully, particularly in the Reichstag elections of 1907, in leading the bourgeois masses into battle under the flag of a new ideology against the *vaterlandslose Gesellen* (comrades without a country).

V. In the First World War

1. Defence of the Fatherland and "Burgfrieden" (domestic truce)

On 25 July 1914, as the ever more threatening storm clouds of war gathered, the Social Democratic party executive sounded a warning: "Danger looms. World war threatens! The ruling classes who gag, despise and exploit you in peacetime, want to exploit you now as cannon fodder. Everywhere, we must make ring in the ears of the rulers: We don't want war! Down with war! Long live the international brotherhood of man!"[1]. Just a few days later, one could hear a quite different note from the socialist press: "When the fateful hour strikes, the comrades without a country will do their duty, and will in no way be outdone in this by the patriots."[2] Finally, on 4 August the parliamentary party in the Reichstag, including Karl Liebknecht, voted unanimously for the war credits requested by the government. As their spokesman, the party chairman Hugo Haase declared: "In its hour of danger we will not leave our own fatherland in the lurch."[3]

How could this change of mood and approval of the war credits have come about? This question has always been the subject of great controversy. The verdicts have veered from betrayal and fall from grace, to the statement that the attitude of the Social Democrats was merely rooted in a strong tradition. Holders of the latter view based their argument, *inter alia*, on Marx and Engels's endorsement of defensive war, and August Bebel's declaration that, in the case of a Russian attack, he would "pick up his rifle"[4]. Even the Erfurt Programme had not been pacifist, but demanded "general military training for self-defence" and a "*Volkswehr* (popular militia) instead of a standing army".[5] Opponents of this argument countered by saying this was not a war of defence, but imperialistic

---

1 Appeal of the party executive, in Vorwärts, 25.7.1914.
2 Reader's letter (Friedrich Stampfer) of 31.7.1914 with the article, "To be, or not to be" which appeared in the party press on 2.8.1914.
3 Stenographische Berichte des Deutschen Reichstags, vol. 306, p. 8f.
4 On 7.3.1904 in the Reichstag: Stenographische Berichte, vol. 198, p. 1588. In Summer 1913, a few weeks before his death, he stated in the Reichstag budget commission: "There is not a single person in Germany who would leave his fatherland defenceless in the face of foreign attack. This also holds good, and especially so, for Social Democrats."
5 See Dowe and Klotzbach (eds), Programmatische Dokumente (2004), p. 174.

genocide, and that the Social Democratic leadership had betrayed the Socialist International and the principle of internationalism. With resolutions passed at the congresses of Stuttgart (1907), Copenhagen (1910), and Basel (1912), the socialist parties had committed themselves to "preventing the outbreak of war by means which seemed the most effective, and should they not be able to prevent it, to working to bring it rapidly to an end".[6] This was phrased extremely loosely. Since no concrete measures were agreed, everything remained open.

The parties of the Second International were united in their moral condemnation of the war, and looked for ways to prevent the outbreak of the threatening conflict. August Bebel repeatedly used the forum of the Reichstag and the party congress to express his opposition to warmongering and the race to arms. The well-founded concern that the nationalistic and militaristic *Fronde* in Germany would fan the flames of war was a persistent nightmare for him. It determined the tone of his conversations in Zurich with Consul General Angst who conveyed Bebel's warnings to the British government. At their conference in Basel cathedral in 1912, Europe's leading socialists, August Bebel and Jean Jaurès, Victor Adler and Keir Hardie, Hermann Greulich and Édouard Vaillant, pilloried war as the scourge of humanity. Their warning, directed to the door of their respective governments, that rifle barrels could, should there be a war, be turned on them, revealed itself in August 1914 for what it was: a threatening gesture to intimidate the warmongers, but, when it came down to it, an empty threat.

As long as it only seemed to be a matter of the usual crises in Morocco or the Balkans, the massed battalions of workers demonstrated as one against the war. But at the moment, on 31 July, when regional conflict finally tipped over into full-scale war, the Second International split apart. In Russia and Serbia, where the socialists, brutally repressed and weak in numbers, pursued a path of violent revolution, they turned against war credits. In every other country at war, and in which the workers' movement enjoyed a broad basis of well-organised mass support and had gone down the path of parliamentary, democratic, and social reform, socialists demonstrated their solidarity with the majority of their nation and supported the government. The change in mood amongst the mass of workers on the outbreak of war indicated just how much working people in these countries felt a part of their nation, and the extent to which they had come to identify with the existing state.

---

6 See Julius Braunthal, Geschichte der Internationale, vol. 2 (Hanover 1961), pp. 325, 349 ff., and 370 ff. New edition, Bonn 1978.

Susanne Miller has summed up the situation as follows: "Whichever of the various justifications one chooses to investigate for the war policy inaugurated in August 1914 by the [German] trade-union or party leadership: going along with the general mood of the people; combating Russian tsarism, British imperialism and French claims on Alsace and Lorraine; the hope for improvement in one's personal status through domestic political reforms; concern about the preservation of Social Democrat and trade-union "achievements", as well as the level of assets of its organisations – each individual one of them, and all of them together, point to the fact that the Wilhelminian Reich seemed to the German workers' movement to be the basis, which it wished to preserve, for its work and very existence."[7]

Perhaps August Bebel, in his words to the party congress of 1907, has described this attitude most clearly: "If, one day, we really have to defend the fatherland, then we will be defending it because it is our fatherland, as the soil on which we live, whose language we speak, whose customs are our customs, because we wish to make this, our fatherland, into a land such as exists nowhere else on earth in such perfection and beauty."[8]

On the outbreak of war, the declaration of belief in national defence formulated here took hold, with elemental force, of those masses who only a few days before had been out on the streets demonstrating for peace. It was also welcomed by the overwhelming majority of those Social Democrats who had rejected the approval of the war credits, but had bowed to party discipline in the Reichstag vote. Even Karl Liebknecht did not at first uncompromisingly reject the principle of defending the fatherland. What really mattered to the 14 deputies, amongst them party chairman Hugo Haase, who in the parliamentary party meeting of 3 August 1914 voted against the war credits, were two things: their appraisal of the conflagration as a rapacious, imperialistic war, and their stance towards the government and the bourgeois parties. Their resistance stiffened when the various political and economic power groups committed themselves to a so-called *Burgfrieden*, the maintenance of a domestic political truce for the duration of hostilities. Under the aegis of the *Burgfrieden*, the ma-

---

7 Susanne Miller, 'Die Sozialdemokratie in der Spannung zwischen Oppositionstradition und Regierungsverantwortung in den Anfängen der Weimarer Republik', in Hans Mommsen (ed.), Sozialdemokratie, p. 84. The same author gives a comprehensive account in her book, Burgfrieden und Klassenkampf. Die deutsche Sozialdemokratie im Ersten Weltkrieg (Düsseldorf 1974).
8 Protokoll über die Verhandlungen des Parteitags der Sozialdemokratischen Partei Deutschlands, abgehalten zu Essen a.d. Ruhr vom 15. bis 21. September 1907 (Berlin 1907), p. 255. He expressed similar sentiments on 7.3.1904 in the Reichstag: Stenographische Berichte, vol. 198, p. 1588, and vol. 199, p. 3263.

jority of the party regarded itself as providing support for the Reich government under Chancellor Bethmann Hollweg. It only went on the offensive when it wanted to pillory domestic shortcomings affecting working people in particular, or attacked war goals and attempts to restore the old domestic order which went beyond the government line. This shift towards the government was made easier not least due to the tactical skill and personality of Bethmann Hollweg who avoided openly supporting annexationist and reactionary conservative forces amongst business, military, and party circles. Instead of negotiating firm guarantees of concessions in domestic and foreign policy, the majority of the party were hoping, in exchange for their cooperation, for a "reorientation" of home affairs, above all in the shape of Prussian electoral reform. Up until early 1917, the Chancellor and the left-of-centre bourgeois parties repeatedly succeeded, by promises and outward cooperation, in keeping the Social Democrats committed to government policy.

2. *Schism in the Party and the Birth of the USPD (Independent Social Democratic Party)*

In contrast to the majority of the party, the group of war-credits protesters advocated the retention of the party's traditional oppositional role. There is much to be said for the argument that these differences would not necessarily have led to the split, if the tricky problem had not raised its ugly head again and again with every fresh vote on war credits. Karl Liebknecht was the first to break party ranks, and to vote openly on 2 December 1914 against the second war-credits bill. He was joined by Otto Rühle for the next bill, while other opposition deputies left the plenary chamber before voting began. In December 1915, 20 deputies released a declaration accusing the Reichskanzler of favouring the annexationist lobby, and voted in the Reichstag against the credits. The final break came in March 1916 when the majority of the parliamentary party voted for the emergency budget, while the minority, along with party chairman Haase, rejected it, referring as they did so to the Magdeburg party resolution of 1910. Since they had kept secret their intention of voting against the decision of the parliamentary party, the majority saw this as a breach of both discipline and loyalty. Voting 58 to 33, they removed the parliamentary whip from the 20 dissidents. Under the name Social Democratic Working Group, they reconstituted themselves as an independent parliamentary group. At first, the split in the parliamentary party did not, as yet, mean a split in the party itself. On 6 to 7 April 1917, in the *Volkshaus* (house of the people) in Gotha, the Independent Social Democratic Party (USPD) was launched.

There is no simple answer to the question of whether this organisational split could have been avoided. Its roots undoubtedly go back to the ideological, programmatic, and political differences within prewar social democracy. The principle which the party always adhered to has been succinctly formulated by the veteran socialist Richard Fischer: "We have always had differences of opinion and have never hidden them. [...] But from the very beginning the party has always adhered to the principle of presenting a united front to the outside world."[9] However, it was precisely the inflexible use of this dogmatic "united front" tradition of treating breaches of party discipline as mutiny which sharply aggravated those old differences. Before the war, tensions could be smoothed over by more or less theoretical compromise resolutions and tactical postponement. Now, however, in war time, the Social Democrats were being confronted with situations which could not be ducked, and which demanded instant decisions.

The very fact that, on the outbreak of war, representatives of the radical left such as Konrad Haenisch and Paul Lensch were following in the nationalist wake, while revisionists such as Eduard Bernstein and Kurt Eisner went over to the USPD, the Independent Social Democrats, was an indication that the division was not between revolutionary Marxists on the one side, and revisionists and reformists on the other. The dividing line was to be found much more on the contentious issues of war credits, the *Burgfrieden*, and in particular on attitudes towards the government and the bourgeois parties. Whereas the party majority had switched to a policy of cooperation, the USPD continued with a consistently oppositional line. They regarded themselves as the true heirs to the "old" social democracy of Marx, Engels, Lassalle and Bebel, and as a party of opposition sharply separate from all other social factions. They wished to lead the fight against the war and social evils, and for peace, democracy, and socialism, unhindered by the shackles of compromise.

Alongside representatives of the centre-left of the party, revisionists of pacifist inclination such as Bernstein and Eisner, there was also room in the USPD for radical left-wingers. While the so-called Bremen Left, as "International German Communists", chose the path of independence, the International Group, the Spartacus Group – they took their name from their "Spartacus letters" – who on 1 January 1916 had formed round Rosa

---

9 In a sitting of the parliamentary party on 20.12.1915. In Die Reichstagsfraktion der deutschen Sozialdemokratie 1898 bis 1918, edited by Erich Matthias and Eberhard Pikart (Düsseldorf 1966), vol. 2, pp. 106 ff., quotation on p. 107.

Luxemburg and Karl Liebknecht, initially allied themselves for organisational reasons with the USPD. Closely associated with the party were the Revolutionary Shop Stewards, a group of qualified metal workers in Berlin who had been pre-eminent in the organisation of strikes. The strike in spring 1917, the naval unrest in the summer of the same year, and the great strike of January 1918 demonstrated how much influence the Majority Socialists (MSPD) had lost amongst the workers. For many amongst the starving, embittered, war-weary masses, the USPD had become the party of hope. There is no simple explanation why, at first, and as demonstrated by the Reichstag by-elections, they achieved only meagre successes. It cannot be explained by sociological reasons alone. Membership and following were heterogeneous. It was undoubtedly of great significance that the Majority Socialists continued to have at their disposal the greater part of the party apparatus and the party press, that the USPD was hit harder by censorship and other repressive measures inflicted by the authorities, and that in the final resort the MSPD, despite all the aggravation, was for many workers still the traditional party, and they simply would not abandon it for something new.

3. *The Majority Social Democrats on the Path to Government Responsibility*

With the secession of the USPD, the SPD had lost its monopoly as the sole representative of the German workers' movement. If until now social democracy had encompassed the entire left-wing sector of the party landscape, the Majority Socialists now occupied only a segment of it. With the emergence of left-wing competition, the Majority Socialists shifted to the centre of the political spectrum. In spite of all the activity of the extreme right wing, which argued for a radical reorientation, the broad centre of the party, whose principal representatives were Scheidemann and Ebert, continued to dictate policy.

Philipp Scheidemann (26.7.1865 – 29.11.1939), a qualified printer, began his political career as an editor on social democratic newspapers. A member of the Reichstag since 1903, he had won a reputation as a brilliant orator. Despite his success in becoming a member of the party executive in 1911, he made his greatest impact in parliament where, after the death of August Bebel, he became the Social Democrats' most celebrated leader. In 1913 he was elected co-chairman of the parliamentary party. He took increasing *de facto* control of the party during the war, since Haase, even before resigning the party whip, had declined in importance. Typically for the party leadership, Scheidemann steered a politically middle course.

Not until the war, and as a result of disputes with a minority in the party, did he and Ebert shift to the moderate right wing of the party. Together with Ebert, he was co-chairman of the SPD from 1917 to 1919.

Friedrich Ebert (4.2.1871 – 28.2.1925) joined the social democratic workers' movement as a young saddler's apprentice. After bitter experiences as a journeyman – unemployment, lockouts – from 1891 on in Bremen he was heavily engaged in agitatory trade-union activity. At the age of twenty-three he was already carrying out a host of different functions: as editor with the Bremen Citizens Newspaper, chairman of the local Saddlers' Association and of the Bremen Trade Union Cartel, as well as of the SPD there. From 1900 on he was employed as a workers' secretary in Bremen. At the party congress in Jena in 1905 he was elected to the party executive as full-time secretary, and was also in charge of labour youth, and responsible for relations with the trade-union leadership. A member of the Reichstag since 1912, Ebert became Bebel's successor in 1913, along with Haase, as head of the party. Ebert, too, made no attempt to meddle with the party's theoretical base which was anchored in the Erfurt Programme. He staked everything on winning political power through the ballot box. His political tactics were characterised by dogged reform work, the preservation of party unity, and caution.

Both Ebert and Scheidemann attached great importance to justifying the Social Democrats' policy in the war as a logical continuation of the traditional line. Although, when the war was progressing favourably, there were various glimmerings within the party of annexationist tendencies, the basis for the "peace of reconciliation" – the "Scheidemann peace" as it became known to friend and foe alike – continued, as it had done in the pronouncement of 4 August 1914 to reject all plans for a war of conquest, and to affirm the right of self-determination for all peoples.

The Russian Revolution in February 1917 gave a powerful boost to the disappointed hopes of the war-weary masses. The longing of working men and women for peace, and their protest against hunger, those who were prolonging the war, and the failure of domestic reforms to materialise, burst forth in a massive wave of strikes in April 1917. The sheer force of these events was reflected in a resolution issued by the MSPD executive committee. It signalled its "fervent support for the victorious Russian Revolution", and expressed its solidarity with the call of the Petersburg workers' and soldiers' councils for a peace "without annexations and reparations on the basis of the free development of all peoples".[10]

10 Protokoll über die Verhandlungen des Parteitages der Sozialdemokratischen Partei Deutschlands, abgehalten zu Würzburg vom 14. bis 20. Oktober 1917 (Berlin 1917), p. 36.

In the event, the Majority Socialists were largely in agreement on this with the Independent Socialists. The founding of the USPD would certainly have had some influence on the decisions of the MSPD, fearing as they must have that their supporters might defect to their left-wing rival. The USPD, however, never managed the big breakthrough. This meant that pressure from the left remained limited, and the Majority Socialists' retained their room for manoeuvre at the centre. Instead of being the basis for unity between the various socialist groups, the formula "no annexations, no contributions!" of the so-called peace resolution of 19 July 1917 in the Reichstag brought together the MSPD, the Centre and the Progressive Party. With the decreasing likelihood of an imminent German victory, the desire grew, amongst the left Liberals and the Centre Party, who had been governed for so long by expansionist tendencies, for a "peace of reconciliation". Spurred on by the tireless agitation of the Centre Party deputy Matthias Erzberger, the three parties set up the "inter-party committee", a forum which enabled them to remain in constant contact. This meant a shift in the existing fronts in the Reichstag. A new majority sprang up which prefigured the pattern of the later Weimar Coalition. To the left of it stood the USPD, which refused from the outset to cooperate, to the right the conservative factions which, for the first time, found themselves isolated.

This new constellation of parties represented an important stage for the Social Democrats on their path from being purely an opposition party to becoming a possible party of government. On the negative side, this liaison clearly restricted their freedom to develop and implement independent policies. In the great strike of January 1918, in which the call for "peace, freedom, and bread" resounded more loudly than ever, the MSPD's bourgeois partners showed precious little loyalty, and cooperating with them brought nothing but profound alienation amongst the supporters of social democracy. Nevertheless, at the end of September 1918, the Social Democrats could no longer reject the call to participate in a new government.

At the moment when military defeat was becoming obvious, the parties which would later make up the Weimar Coalition formed a government under Prince Max von Baden, which enjoyed the confidence of the majority in the Reichstag, in an attempt to avoid the threatened collapse. There were no fundamental objections voiced within the SPD parliamentary party, merely tactical reservations. With the appointment of Philipp Scheidemann, and the spokesman of the trade unions and deputy chairman of the General Commission, Gustav Bauer, as secretaries of state, Social Democrats found themselves in a German government for the first time. Although the main concern of this cabinet was to end the slaughter and bring about a negotiated peace, it also managed to achieve one of the SPD's fundamental aims: the introduction of a parliamentary system of government in Germany. But these democratic innovations were overshadowed by the overwhelming military defeat. The fact that the government, with Erzberger well to the fore, was seemingly taking responsibility for the armistice, enabled its actual initiators to publicly disclaim all part in it. It was Hindenburg and Ludendorff, the generals at the head of Army Supreme Command, who were pressing the politicians to seek an armistice, and who, in the case of Hindenburg, had approved the acceptance of the ceasefire conditions. The military, and nationalists of every hue, exploited the concealment of the true circumstances to begin propagating the *Dolchstoßlegende*, the myth of having been "stabbed in the back", in order to discredit the forces of democracy, and disguise the fact that it was they themselves who had led the Imperial Reich to military defeat.

VI. From the Revolution to the Weimar Republic

1. The German Revolution 1918/19

When, at the end of October 1918, and behind the backs of government and parliament, the German admirals wanted to take the fleet into one last battle, the sailors extinguished the fires in the boiler rooms. With peace imminent, they saw no sense in sacrificing their lives for officers intent on death or glory. The spontaneity of their action was characteristic of the whole "November Revolution". On November 4 a revolutionary Workers' and Soldiers' Council took control of Kiel, and three days later almost the entire fleet was in their hands. The spark of revolution spread like wildfire from the ports to other parts of Germany. From Kiel to Munich, from Cologne to Breslau, and finally in Berlin, soldiers and workers rose up against authority and militarism, motivated by a desire for peace, freedom, and bread, and the hope for a new and better order.

The monarchs were not slow to vacate their thrones. It needed the merest push for the old organs of state to collapse like a crumbling wall. In the workers' and soldiers' councils, which sprang up everywhere like mushrooms, the mass movement created its organs of revolution. They were modelled on the Russian example and had already been seen in embryonic form in the naval unrest of 1917 and in the January strike of 1918. Neither the Majority nor the Independent Social Democrats, nor the Berlin Committee of Revolutionary Shop Stewards and the Spartacus Group had "made" this revolution. Its main characteristic was not careful planning and direction from the top, but the spontaneity of the war-weary masses. They chose the red flag, the symbol of socialism, as their banner because it embodied both peace towards the world at large, and opposition to the ruling forces.

Ultimately, the Majority Social Democrats as well as the leaders of the Independents yielded to the pressure of circumstances. The eagerly awaited peace, which was slow in coming, together with the revolutionary movement, determined the need to act. In the night of 7 to 8 November, Kurt Eisner of the USPD, independently of the sailor revolutionaries, proclaimed the establishment in Munich of a Socialist Soviet Republic. At the same time, the MSPD in Berlin issued an ultimatum demanding the abdication of Kaiser Wilhelm II. This was to no avail. But the wave of revolution was by now unstoppable, even in the imperial capital. On the morning of 9 November, workers in Berlin streamed out of the factories. Joined by soldiers and sections of the war-weary population, a massive procession of demonstrators marched on the parliamentary and government quarter. Under the impact of this mass demonstration, Prince Max von Baden took it upon himself to announce the abdication of the Kaiser and appointed Friedrich Ebert, the leader of the Majority Socialists, to the office of Chancellor. Thinking it would be a way of avoiding chaos and civil war, he initially considered not abolishing the monarchy. This proved to be illusory, and, under the onslaught of the masses, the monarchy collapsed. From the windows of the Reichstag building early that afternoon Philipp Scheidemann declared that Germany was now a Republic, while, shortly after, Karl Liebknecht proclaimed the free Socialist Republic of Germany from the balcony of the Berlin Imperial Palace.

It was, however, collaboration not confrontation between the various socialist factions – all under the slogan "brother shall not fight brother" – which determined the mood of the day. In this spirit, Ebert offered the Independents the possibility of forming a government with equal representation for the MSPD and USPD. Ebert was not even opposed to the participation of Karl Liebknecht, describing him as "pleasant". But Liebknecht rejected the proposal, as did Georg Ledebour from the radical wing of the USPD.

On November 10 the revolutionary government met for the first time in the Reichskanzlei, the Imperial Chancellery. This self-styled "Council of People's Commissioners" was composed of three representatives from the MSPD (Ebert, Scheidemann and Otto Landsberg) and three from the USPD (Haase, Wilhelm Dittmann and Emil Barth as spokesman for the Revolutionary Berlin Shop Stewards). The Council of People's Commissioners owed its mandate to the revolution, which was reflected in the confirmation of the revolutionary government at an assembly of workers' and soldiers' councils in the Circus Busch in Berlin. But it was no less characteristic that, in the preceding "coalition agreement"[1] between the two parties, provision was made for the existing bourgeois secretaries of state to remain in office.

With the merging of a considerable number of the functions carried out hitherto by parliament, government, the Kaiser, and the Bundesrat (Upper House), the Council of People's Commissioners now had considerable powers at its disposal. But equally great were the problems with which it was confronted: the legacy of the lost war and the oppressive

---

1 In, inter alia, Die deutsche Revolution 1918–1919. Dokumente, edited by Gerhard A. Ritter and Susanne Miller (new edition Hamburg 1975), p. 85f.

Above, photographs of deputies (Friedrich Ebert, Philipp Scheidemann, Otto Landsberg, Hugo Haase, Wilhelm Dittmann and Emil Barth) with the caption "Founding of the German Republic". Below, photograph of demonstrators carrying a banner "For Ebert, Scheidemann! Against Spartacus!"

ceasefire conditions, and the continuation of the blockade by their former enemy. Threatened by hunger and chaos, the German Reich was on the brink of total collapse. The revolutionary government coped admirably, however. The needs of the moment and the worst consequences of the war were dealt with. The threat of starvation was combated, and there was a for the most part orderly return of soldiers to civilian life. Meanwhile, a series of regulations on health insurance, job-creation and protection measures, and unemployment benefits, saw the introduction of important social and political reforms. The lifting of censorship and emergency regulations was self-evident for the Social Democrats, as were freedom of expression and individual liberty and security. The introduction of universal proportional representation for all parliaments, votes for women, and the announcement of the eight-hour working day brought about the realisation of some of their great traditional goals. In the Weimar period, the working population considered the implementation of the statutory eight-hour day as the great achievement of the revolution. Democratic to the core, the government of People's Commissioners under Ebert and Haase regarded itself as a merely provisional arrangement in a time of revolutionary upheaval. With the proclamation of the National Assembly, the cabinet immediately committed itself to an elected people's parliament as the organ of constitutional government. This was in tune not only with the will of the MSPD leadership, but was also supported by the leaders of the USPD and the greater part of the workers' and soldiers' councils. The majority of the councils, largely dominated by supporters of Ebert and Scheidemann, regarded themselves not as the advocates of a "system of workers' councils", or of the "dictatorship of the proletariat", but as an interim solution born of the revolution. The conflict between a "National Assembly" and a "system of workers' councils", of which much was made in public discussions, in no way mirrored the actual balance of political power. With its slogan "All power to the workers' councils", the Spartacist League in the first phase of the revolution had only a very narrow base, as is vividly demonstrated by the elections to the Congress of German Workers' and Soldiers' Councils. Of the 489 delegates who convened from 16 to 20 December in Berlin as a kind of revolutionary parliament, there were only ten "United Revolutionaries". With 344 votes to 98, the representatives of the workers' and soldiers' councils rejected Ernst Däumig's proposal for a socialist republic based on the construction of soviets. The great majority, consisting of Majority Socialists, the right wing of the USPD, soldiers' representatives, and the few bourgeois democratic delegates present, opted for an elected National Assembly. In accordance with the wishes of the Majority Socialist commissioners, the congress fixed 19 January 1919 as the date for the election. The MSPD emerged from these elections with 37.9 per cent of the vote, the USPD with 7.6 per cent. Neither in the National Assembly, nor one week later in the elections in Prussia, where the MSPD took 36.4 per cent of the vote, and the USPD 7.4 per cent, were the socialists able to gain a majority.

The coalition between the two parties was already in tatters at this point. In the night of 29 to 30 December, after a dispute about the deployment of the military against insurgent sailors, the USPD commissioners seceded from the cabinet and were replaced by two Majority Social Democrats, Rudolf Wissell and Gustav Noske. The euphoric mood of November had now given way to an atmosphere of confrontation within the socialist workers' movement.

One of the causes for this mounting conflict was to be found in the takeover of state responsibility. This applied as much to the attitudes towards each other of the socialist party groups, the MSPD, USPD, and the Spartacus/KPD (German Communist Party), as it did to the relationship between the leadership and the rank and file of these factions. As the opposite pole to the misery of war, 9 November seemed to herald the dawn of a new age for the revolutionary masses. The working class seemed united once more, they had seized power and the state was in the hands of their representatives. The long-cherished promises of socialism would now find their fulfilment. For decades, the talk had been of class struggle and the conquering of political power by the working classes, and it was assumed that the "socialisation" of the means of production would be the indispensable prerequisite for socialism. Now that their revolutionary governments and their organs of power were in charge at both national and federal state level, they expected that the serious business of putting promises into practice would begin.

Instead of this, they had to look on as almost everything remained the same in the bureaucracy, the military, and the economy. Apart from isolated examples of working-class delegates and "inspectors", the desks of mayors and government officials throughout the Reich, officers' posts, the control posts of industry and the economy, were still occupied by the representatives of the authoritarian state and the military caste, of the landlords and industrial bosses. As an example, half a year after the eruption of revolution there was but a single Social Democrat amongst the 470 Prussian *Landräte*, or chief district administrative officers. In the Christmas disturbances of 1918, when Berliners rushed to demonstrate their solidarity with insurgent sailors under attack from the military, clear signs of growing discontent were in the air. Unrest flared up in the Ruhr, Upper Silesia, Berlin, Bremen and Brunswick, Saxony and Thuringia. In addition to strikes for higher wages and better food, there were further mass demonstrations in favour of nationalising the factories, retaining the workers' councils, and even calls for the violent overthrow of the capitalist system.

The democratic potential at the heart of these mass demonstrations remained largely unexploited. Essentially, it manifested itself in formal legislation such as the Nationalisation Law of March 1919 and the Workers' Council Article 165 of the Weimar Constitution, but not in a genuine and lasting democratisation and a social restructuring of state and society.

Much has been written about the causes of this. In the GDR, the Central Committee of the SED, in its "Theses" on the "November Revolution of 1918 in Germany", classified it as "a bourgeois-democratic revolution which, to a certain degree, was carried out with proletarian means and methods".[2] Along with the initial lack of a "Marxist-Leninist fighting party", the "betrayal" by the SPD leaders played a decisive role in this Communist version of history. In the Federal Republic, on the other hand, the view long prevailed that in 1918–1919 the only choice was between the "social revolution in league with forces pressing for a proletarian dictatorship, or the parliamentary republic in league with conservative elements such as the officer corps"[3]. Amongst Social Democrats the pre-eminent view was that, when it had come to the crunch, the SPD had leaped into the breach and saved Germany from Bolshevism and dictatorship by workers' councils. Willy Brandt, on the other hand, argued that the claims about the dangers of Bolshevism were an "impermissible simplification", and that the alternative was embodied more by Rosa Luxemburg's "Democratic Socialist, [...] not terroristic Communist" vision.[4]

In the months of revolution, Rosa Luxemburg took a leading role in the Spartacus League, a heterogeneous group dominated by utopian and anarchistic leanings. At the founding party conference of the KPD, the

---

2 See 'Die Novemberrevolution 1918 in Deutschland. Thesen anläßlich des 40. Jahrestages'. In Zeitschrift für Geschichtswissenschaft 6 (1958), Sonderheft, pp. 1–27 (here, p. 21). See also, in the same issue, pp. 28–54: Walter Ulbricht, 'Begründung der Thesen über die Novemberrevolution 1918.' This is the basic line pursued by Georg Füllberth and Jürgen Harrer in Die deutsche Sozialdemokratie 1890–1933 (Darmstadt and Neuwied 1974), p. 127. Also by Jutta von Freyburg, Georg Füllberth and Jürgen Harrer et al., in Geschichte der deutschen Sozialdemokratie 1863–1975 (Cologne 1975).
3 This is the formulation of Karl Dietrich Erdmann. See 'Die Geschichte der Weimarer Republik als Problem der Wissenschaft', in Vierteljahrshefte für Zeitgeschichte 3 (1955), p. 6f.
4 Willy Brandt, 'Fünfzig Jahre danach. Rede auf der Feierstunde der SPD am 10.11.1968 in Godesberg.' SPD press information 10.11.1968.

German Communist Party (31 December 1918 and 1 January 1919), there was a large majority vote, in defiance of Rosa Luxemburg, Karl Liebknecht and Paul Levi, to boycott elections to the National Assembly, and instead to take the revolutionary message out onto the streets.

As with Rosa Luxemburg and Karl Liebknecht, the fear of losing touch with the radical masses largely determined the tactics of the USPD leadership under Haase and Dittmann. In the USPD, the idea of building first of all on the "achievements" of the revolution was closely linked with parliamentary democracy and the National Assembly. With disappointment growing among the workers, the left wing around Ernst Däumig and Richard Müller gained in importance and, at the workers' councils congress in December 1918, they pushed through, against the wishes of Haase, the non-participation of the USPD in the Central Council. The result was that in this institution, which served as a mechanism for keeping the Reich and the Prussian government under scrutiny, only the MSPD and soldiers' delegates were represented. The USPD commissioners had the ground taken away from under them. The left wing of the party was thrust back into opposition, and sought its salvation in a policy of confrontation with their main rivals, the Majority Social Democrats. On 28 to 29 December 1918 the USPD commissioners resigned from the government.

With Ebert, Scheidemann, Landsberg, Rudolf Wissell and Gustav Noske, the government was now made up solely of Majority Social Democrats. Their aim and guideline was a parliamentary democracy in which a responsible people made sensible decisions in free elections, and social democracy, legitimised by an electoral majority, could carry through social reforms in a climate of democratic order. Many Majority Social Democrats and seasoned trade-union leaders regarded spontaneous mass action and the high-handed activities of individual workers' councils as a betrayal of the deeply rooted principles of the labour movement, as a gross infringement of the principle of the constitutional state, and as the creation of "Russian conditions" which brought about inequality of income, rendered impossible the task of providing fairly for all of the population, and threatened the entire economic structure. The commissioners entrusted with governmental responsibility thus found themselves in mounting confrontation with the workers' councils, and increasingly sought help and support from the forces of the old system. For the entire government, from the Social Democrats to the representatives of the left-wing USPD, the civil service bureaucrats in particular were absolutely indispensable in overcoming the difficult problems of the transitional period, and as a result grew in importance.

On the question of the military, the decision was made not in favour of an army governed by a spirit of democracy, but to reconstitute the principle of a "state within a state" of the Reichswehr. The old Imperial High Command headed by Hindenburg and Groener, and responsible for the armed forces, preserved a high degree of independence. Attempts by Ebert and the executive committee of the Berlin workers' and soldiers' councils to create a democratic people's militia never got off the ground.

The so-called Spartacus uprising of January 1919, when armed insurgents threatened the almost defenceless government of People's Commissioners, sent out a signal which would determine future defence thinking. The street battles in Berlin set the seal not only on the split in the workers' movement, but this violent jeopardising from the left of the new order mobilised counter-forces from the right, and indirectly gave the military the chance they had been looking for to intervene. The Imperial government did not put its trust in the Majority Socialist volunteer units who manned the barricades, but in the old officers, and the new *Freikorps* (Free Corps) leaders of the troops deployed by Noske. His main concern was to demonstrate the power of military force, and to set a lasting example. "For Noske, the use of force was not the *ultima ratio*, but quite simply the means of establishing internal order."[5] The decisive factor for him was not the character and political beliefs of the troops: discipline was everything, and there was no call for democratic convictions. These, and similar squads of men, in whom counter-revolutionary leanings were there for all to see, formed the nucleus of the military forces deployed in the postwar years, and were the basis of the Reichswehr, the German Army. The last gasp of the revolution was stifled by machine guns, cannons, and mortars.

The deployment of the military and Noske's *Freikorps* against demonstrating, embattled workers, the complete failure to recognise the growing danger from the right, as well as the brutal murders of Rosa Luxemburg and Karl Liebknecht, mobilised not only the radicals in the labour force against the Reich government. "Noske politics" also strained the government's credibility amongst large sections of its own supporters. The January uprising marked a turning point. From here on there was a mutual build-up of tension between radicals on both left and right, while at the same time the efforts of the Social Democrats to bring about a democratic and social restructuring of society were crumbling. The workable basis for a parliamentary and democratic Republic which the Social De-

---

5 This is the conclusion of Susanne Miller in her study, Die Bürde der Macht. Die deutsche Sozialdemokratie 1918–1920 (Düsseldorf 1978), p. 270. See also pp. 225 ff.

mocratic commissioners wished and were striving for, could only have been achieved if democracy had not come to a halt outside the barracks, office buildings, and factory gates, and also if it had undertaken a thoroughgoing demolition of the existing bureaucratic and economic power structures.

2. A New State on Old Foundations

In the National Constituent Assembly elected on 19 January 1919, the Majority Socialists had gained 165 seats, while the Independents could only win 22. There were 91 deputies from the Christian People's Party (Centre), 75 from the German Democratic Party (DDP), 19 from the German People's Party (DVP), 44 from the German National People's Party (DNVP), with 7 seats going to splinter groups. The mainly new names for the parties were only in part a reflection of new party programmes. In the Centre Party, appearing very briefly as the Christian People's Party, the employees' wing gained in importance. The DDP basically continued to follow the course, enhanced by a social component, of the left-wing Liberals. In the DVP, the right wing of the old National Liberals formed around Stresemann, while the old Conservatives united with distinctly *deutschnational* (fervently nationalistic) circles to form the DNVP. The outcome of the election, in which the Social Democratic parties remained in the minority, strengthened the self-confidence of the bourgeois parties.

A citizens' bloc government would have been numerically feasible, but was out of the question for the German Democrats and the Centre Party. When the USPD rejected the offer of the MSPD to participate in a coalition government, the groups making up the inter-parliamentary party committee took on new life. In the theatre in Weimar, a venue for the National Constituent Assembly chosen for security reasons, Friedrich Ebert was elected Reichspräsident, German President, on 11 February 1919 with 277 out of the 379 votes cast. Two days later, the parliament appointed Philipp Scheidemann as Minister President (the term Reichskanzler was not reintroduced until after the Weimar Constitution came into effect on 14 August 1919). In the newly formed government, the Majority Socialists held six ministerial posts, the DDP and the Centre Party shared six, while the Minister for Foreign Affairs, the professional diplomat Count Brockdorff-Rantzau, officially held no party allegiance. The two other parties accepted three conditions from the MSPD as the basis for government policy. First, the unreserved recognition of the republican state system. Second, severe burdens in financial policy on wealth and property. Third, a radical social policy, and nationalisation of those industries deemed ready for it.

Chief among the multitude of difficulties facing government and parliament were the problem of a peace treaty, and the drafting of a constitution for the Republic. Not only the parliamentary and government representatives of the Majority Social Democrats, but also the USPD deputies worked intensively on the framing of the constitution. Cassandra-like, the USPD touched on some of the sore points which would have such fateful consequences for the way in which the Weimar Republic would develop. Their criticism was directed at a military system spiralling out of democratic control, a controversial matter given insufficient attention by their Social Democratic sister party, and neglected to the point of culpability by Noske. Equally timely was their warning about overestimating the parliamentary scope for changing the existing social structures. The ability of the USPD to make its presence felt was, however, very limited. Not only their lack of parliamentary numbers, but also increasing internal dissent over policy, proved to be a severe handicap. Alongside the proponents of parliamentary democracy who wished to see it supplemented by workers' councils, were those around Ernst Däumig, and who would soon be in a majority in the party, who advocated a system based on them alone. Their programme envisaged the workers' councils in the political, and the factory councils in the economic sphere, as *the* form in which the working population should be organised. The principle of recalling representatives at any time was held to be particularly democratic, but by excluding whole sections of the population from representation in the councils, these models were a serious infringement of the democratic principle of equality.

At the Second Congress of Workers' Councils in April 1919, the MSPD parliamentary group introduced a different concept with its motion to create a "Chamber of Labour". This would involve the councils operating not "*instead of* the parliament, but *alongside* the parliament"[6]. The idea that democracy must be firmly anchored in the economic as well as the political sphere, and that the workers' councils had to be allocated particular tasks in this, had also gained ground among the Majority Socialists.

---

6 This is the formulation of Eberhard Kolb in 'Rätewirklichkeit und Räte-Ideologie in der deutschen Revolution von 1918/19'. Reprinted in Eberhard Kolb (ed.), Vom Kaiserreich zur Weimarer Republik (Cologne 1972), p. 177. For the text of the various bills, see Zweiter Kongreß der Arbeiter-, Bauern- und Soldatenräte Deutschlands vom 8. bis 14. April 1919 im Herrenhaus zu Berlin. Stenographisches Protokoll (Berlin 1919), p. 267 and p. 269f.

In the first weeks after the revolution, the main interest of those, including figures such as Emil Barth and Kurt Eisner, who held political responsibility, had been directed towards getting productivity going again. They made no serious attempt to intervene in the sphere of private capital with which, for all their social and political experience, they did not feel entirely comfortable. With the founding of the *Zentralarbeitsgemeinschaft*, the joint industrial alliance with employers' organisations, it was the trade unions who had decided as a matter of urgency to attempt to boost the economy and combat hunger and unemployment. The agreement with the employers of 15 November 1918 secured them total freedom of association, the extension of wage agreements to all branches of trade and industry, and the legal guarantee of a maximum eight-hour day. The People's Commissioners made this regulation legally binding. Confronted with the devastation of war, both government and trade unions shrank from embarking on an immediate programme of nationalisation. Their decision was influenced both by the not unfounded fear that the victorious powers would, in their reparation demands, seize state-owned concerns first, and also, despite all the programmatic declarations, by the complete lack of any concrete plans. The reluctance to pre-empt a decision of such magnitude by the National Assembly, as well as the bitter experiences in Soviet Russia, also had an inhibiting effect on the socialists in government. In the severe crises affecting food supplies which were shaking Lenin's agricultural Russia, a man such as Karl Kautsky, now in the USPD, could see the deterrent proof of where over-hasty nationalisation measures might lead. No unreasonable experiments, increase productivity and get the economy going, and then socialisation – that was the government's argument. "No growth in productivity without socialisation" was the increasingly vocal counter-argument from the factories.[7]

Many workers, more self-confident since the revolution, and with greatly raised expectations, took exception to a bureaucracy which carried on as before, to the behaviour of the military, to material shortcomings, and to those employers, mainly in mining and heavy industry, who adopted an "I'm the master here" mentality. They felt the revolution had failed to bring adequate change to either their lives or their conditions of work. Along with socialisation, the institution of the councils seemed to be a way of restructuring the industrial concerns, and of replacing the old system of rule with a democratic economic and industrial relations code. A wave of strikes and mass action of unprecedented force in spring 1919

---

[7] See Hans Schieck, 'Die Behandlung der Sozialisierungsfrage in den Monaten nach dem Staatsumsturz', in Vom Kaiserreich zur Weimarer Republik, p. 148.

served to vent their discontent. The government and the Weimar coalition parties, the DDP and the Centre Party included, were united in the view that bans, penal measures, and the military, were not the only way of settling this crisis, and that positive regulations were also required. On 1 March 1919, with the support of the Centre Party, the DDP, and the Social Democrats, the National Assembly approved a "Socialisation Law".

In it, the Reich was empowered to introduce legislation to firstly, "transfer to collective management, in return for appropriate compensation, business enterprises suitable for socialisation, particularly those engaged in the extraction of mineral, and exploitation of other, natural resources. Secondly, in the case of emergencies, to regulate the production and distribution of goods on a collective basis".[8] The law on the regulation of the coal industry of 23 March 1919, and the laws on the potash and electricity industry, arose out of this Socialisation Law. They had barely any effect.

Almost in parallel with the passing of the Socialisation Law, the government adopted guidelines on the workers' councils. In addition to workers' councils at factory, regional, and national level, they also made provision for economic councils in which workers and employers would work together on matters affecting the economy as a whole – nationalisation in particular – and lend support to the parliament. An almost unchanged version of this draft became Article 165 of the Weimar Constitution.

Preliminary work on this constitution for the new Republic had already been undertaken at the time of the People's Commissioners. The bulk of the task had fallen to the Secretary of State for the Interior, Hugo Preuß, a member of the DDP and a convinced democrat. After lengthy consultations involving specialist commissions, People's Commissioners, representatives of the federal states, a constitutional committee, and plenary sessions of the National Assembly, the constitution was finally adopted on 31 July 1919 in Weimar. The Majority Socialists, the German Democratic Party, and the Centre Party, voted in favour. The German Nationalist People's Party, the German People's Party, the Bavarian Farmers' League, Georg Heim of the Bavarian People's Party, and the Independent Social Democrats, voted against. After being signed by the President, Friedrich Ebert, on 11 August, the constitution came into force on 14 August 1919.

The German Reich was now a parliamentary, democratic republic, with sovereignty in the hands of the people, all men and women over the age of twenty. They elected the Reichstag, the central organ of power, the

---

8 Reichs-Gesetzblatt 1919, p. 341 f.

president as head of state, and were able to exercise their will directly through popular initiative and referendum. The first part of the constitution regulated the structure and tasks of the Reich, a second part dealt with the basic rights and duties of the German people. With resort to the rights incorporated in the Paulskirche constitution of 1848, it guaranteed equality before the law, personal liberty, freedom of movement, expression, and conscience, and the right of association. This complex of rights was extended by regulations introducing equal civil rights for men and women, a minimum of eight years education – free of cost and with provision of teaching materials – and the obligation of all citizens to pay taxes.

A third group of measures was to be found in section 5 which dealt with the "economic sphere". The introductory article 151 decreed that "the organisation of economic life must conform to the principles of justice, with the goal of ensuring a dignified existence for all."[9] This general proposition could not disguise the element of compromise in this section on the economy. On the one hand, it contained a commitment to freedom of business and trade, the safeguarding of the interests of the self-employed middle classes, the guaranteeing of inheritance and property rights, while on the other it made specifically social democratic demands.

Apart from regulations on health and safety at work and the guarantee of freedom of association, the constitution committed the state to creating a comprehensive, democratically structured system of insurance to "maintain health and the ability to work, to protect working mothers, and to make provision for the economic consequences of age, infirmity, and the vicissitudes of life", and to give support to every citizen for whom no appropriate work could be found or created. In addition to this range of socio-political measures, Article 153 stated that "property imposes social obligations", thus imposing limitations on the property guarantee, and decreed that any "increase in the value of land" which came about "through neither work nor investment" should be given over to the public good. Beyond this, the state was given the right – in return, of course, for due compensation – to make expropriations, and by law "to take into public ownership business enterprises deemed suitable for socialisation".

The principle of expropriation without compensation to which the Social Democrat parliamentary groups of both tendencies subscribed, they had been unable to anchor in either the Socialisation Law, or the Reich constitution. They lacked a majority in parliament. Nevertheless, article 156 created the possibility, upon securing the necessary mandate, of in-

---

9 See Ernst Huber, Dokumente zur deutschen Verfassungsgeschichte, vol. 3 (Stuttgart, Berlin, Cologne, Mainz 1966), pp. 129 ff. Subsequent quotations are taken from this.

troducing the long-propagated socialisation of the means of production. Along with this instrument, there presented itself, in article 165, a quite different approach to restructuring the economic system. The idea of councils, which had been so prominent in the revolutionary transitional phase, emerged again here, albeit in a much weakened and restricted form. Article 165 proclaimed as its basic principle: "Workers and employees are called upon to work together with employers in the regulation of pay and working conditions, as well as in the general development of the productive forces in the economy." In order that "their social and economic interests be represented", they would be given legally guaranteed factory and regional workers' councils, as well as a central, national workers' council. At regional and national level, the employees' corporations would join with "representatives of the employers and other interested circles" in forming regional economic councils and a *Reichswirtschaftsrat* (national economic council), and would participate in "fulfilling the whole range of economic tasks", as well as in the "implementation of the socialisation laws". These guidelines constituted a framework for a democratic economic system. This task, enshrined in the constitution, was never fully carried out. The Works Councils' Act of 4 February 1920, and the setting-up of a provisional national economic council in May of the same year, represented only a very incomplete realisation of it.

The letter of the Reich constitution indicated that social democracy had achieved goals which went far beyond what it could have dared to hope for before the war. Its democratic legacy going back to the 1848 revolution, along with its socio-political programme, left their clear mark on the Weimar constitution. Even the concept of socialisation, admittedly in watered-down form, found expression there, laying down the principles of a democratically run economy.

The adoption of the constitution was celebrated with wild enthusiasm by the Majority Socialist executive committees in party and parliament. The parliamentary group in the National Assembly was even presumptuous enough to declare that: "The constitution has taken the shape demanded by our Erfurt programme."[10] No other constitution "is more democratic, or gives the people greater rights". "From now on, the German Republic is the most democratic democracy in the world"[11] was the predominant tone, with any element of criticism being drowned out at first. But behind

10 Protokoll über die Verhandlungen des Parteitages der Sozialdemokratischen Partei Deutschlands, abgehalten in Kassel vom 10. bis 16. Oktober 1920 (Berlin 1920), p. 89.
11 Ibid., pp. 89 ff., and appendices pp. 93 ff.; see also, Stenographische Berichte der Verfassunggebenden Deutschen Nationalversammlung, vol. 329, p. 2194 f.

all the euphoria could be detected a note of concern that the letter of the constitution, and the reality of it, were two quite different things. In spite of Marx and Lassalle, the men who attained political responsibility in the revolution of 1918 were overly concerned with the outward facade of democracy, and made too few fundamental changes. This was insufficient to satisfy the expectations, nourished by the old slogans about class struggle and socialisation, of the social classes, principally industrial workers, who were the mainstay of social democracy.

"In the urgent appeals to its own followers to be not only critics and onlookers, but to play a full role in furnishing and filling the new house with life, could be heard the view which would later be so bitterly confirmed: A democracy can only exist when enough democrats commit themselves to it."[12]

3. "Versailles" and the Consequences

One of the heaviest burdens on the new democracy was the Versailles peace treaty. The Social Democrats found themselves under severe pressure from two sides: from their right-wing political opponents at home, and from the Allied governments of France, England, and Italy. The armistice terms which were dictated to the German chief negotiator Matthias Erzberger, a leading figure in the Centre Party, by Frenchman Marshal Foch in the forest of Compiègne, did not punish the old ruling powers, but the forces who had stood up for peace, reconciliation, and democracy. To be precise, the real hardship was not the understandable obligation to surrender all heavy weaponry and to withdraw from occupied territory. What hit a vital nerve was the handing-over of almost a third of all locomotives, railway wagons, lorries, the releasing of the merchant fleet, the heightening of the blockade, as well as the sealing-off from the Reich of territories on the left bank of the Rhine. After tough negotiations, Erzberger had been able to wring some concessions, which had been acknowledged by German Supreme Command, from the Allies. Nevertheless, the fears which he, and also some Social Democrats, particularly Scheidemann, had been harbouring, were all too quickly borne out.

Even before the November revolution, terms such as "stab in the back" had begun to circulate. After the revolution they spread thick and fast, culminating in the assertion that a revolution planned well in advance had

---

12 See Heinrich Potthoff, 'Das Weimarer Verfassungswerk und die deutsche Linke', in Archiv für Sozialgeschichte, vol. XII (Bonn-Bad Godesberg 1972), p. 483.

assailed the German Army from the rear, and, just as Hagen had once done to Siegfried, treacherously stabbed it in the back. The legend fell upon fertile ground. Wartime propaganda had persistently conjured up an excessively optimistic picture of the military situation, thereby reinforcing the population's understandable propensity for wishful thinking. Even the Social Democrats' perspective on military realities was often clouded. Moreover, unlike in the Second World War, defeat was not experienced as an unmitigated catastrophe in which the country came under military occupation, but at the end of the Great War, the allegedly "victorious" German armies were supposed to have been still deep in "enemy territory". Unsurprisingly, there was an immediate readiness to lay the blame elsewhere, and to suspect treachery. Those who, in whatever form, had worked for an end to the slaughter, were ready-made scapegoats. The very same old ruling classes of Imperial Germany, who, like Hindenburg and Ludendorff, knew better, hid shamelessly behind this "stab-in-the-back lie", and used it as a weapon against the "lefties" and the entire "Erzberger and Scheidemann crew".

When the peace conditions of 7 May 1919 unleashed a wave of protest, the *Dolchstoßlegende*, the stab-in-the-back legend, had already gained considerable currency. Up to this point the expectation had been of lenient peace terms. Amongst Social Democrats in particular, the view prevailed that the new democracy had a claim to a just peace. They were expecting a peace treaty founded on the right of self-determination for all peoples, and hoping for a League of Nations based on equal rights and anchored in internationally binding socio-political guidelines. Instead of this, the terms of the Versailles peace treaty seemed to be an instrument of enslavement, a "Peace of Violence" (Ebert), imposed by force. "Were this treaty really to be signed", reasoned Scheidemann on 12 May 1919 before the National Assembly, arguing that the treaty was unacceptable, "then it would not be merely the corpse of Germany alone which would be left lying on the battlefield of Versailles. The equally noble corpses of the right to self-determination of all peoples, the independence of free nations, the belief in all the fine ideals under whose banner the Entente claimed to have fought, and above all, the belief in the good faith of the treaty, would lie next to it."[13] Full of outrage, he swept aside any thought of signing as, "consenting to merciless dismemberment, acquiescing in enslavement and harlotry. [...] What hand would not wither which binds itself and us in these fetters".

13 For the full text, see Stenographische Berichte der Verfassunggebenden Deutschen Nationalversammlung, vol. 327, pp. 1082ff.

Scheidemann's speech fervently expressed what many were thinking. But it was not distinguished by its realism. At this moment when the emotions of most Germans were running riot, the only party in the National Assembly to adopt the one position which was possible in view of the circumstances was the Independent Social Democrats. They too branded the terms which had been laid down as the worst kind of forcibly imposed peace, but, as they declared quite openly, there was no way to avoid signing it: "Failure to sign means the non-return of our prisoners of war, occupation of our raw materials locations, intensification of the blockade, unemployment, starvation, mass deaths, an appalling catastrophe which will put us under even more duress to sign."[14]

In the long run, and the closer it came to the Allies' ultimatum, the Majority Socialists were also forced to share this view. While Scheidemann and the German Democratic Party continued to be obstructive, the Centrist Erzberger, and David from the MSPD, supported it as the lesser of two evils. As is demonstrated by an assessment, written by Groener and approved by Hindenburg, of the hopelessness of military resistance, they no longer saw any realistic alternative. After Scheidemann resigned out of protest against Versailles, and the DDP had seceded from the government, a newly formed coalition government consisting of the MSPD and Centre Party under the social democratic trade unionist Gustav Bauer took the unavoidable step. Hermann Müller (MSPD) and Johannes Bell (Centre Party) signed the peace treaty in Versailles.

It was quickly forgotten by all sides that this step was inevitable if Germany was to be prevented from being plunged into an even greater catastrophe. Signature of the Versailles Treaty became, for the "Nationalists", a renewed "betrayal of Germany". There were constant reminders of the repercussions of the "treaty of shame". With the partition of Upper Silesia in 1921, the continued occupation of the Rhineland and the occupation of the Ruhr by French and Belgian troops in 1923, the disputed war-guilt clause in the Versailles Treaty and the constant battle about reparations, the population was repeatedly confronted with the consequences of a defeat with which it had not come to terms. Many Germans identified with the misfortune of the nation as a whole, seeing the reason for their own, entirely personal hardships in the "shame" of the "dictatorial" Versailles peace. For them, the "November criminals", the "traitors", and the whole "system" they had introduced were the guilty parties.

---

14 The decision of the USPD party conference is quoted, inter alia, by Friedrich Stampfer, in Die vierzehn Jahre der ersten deutschen Republik (Hamburg 3rd edn 1953), p. 117f.

Amongst those forces hostile to the Republic, this climate bred an atmosphere of hatred and unbridled agitation which often ended in murder. In his book *Vier Jahre politischer Mord* (Four Years of Political Murder), Professor Emil Gumbel produced a statistical balance for the years up to the end of 1922. Gustav Radbruch, the Minister of Justice, officially confirmed that in Germany since 9 November 1918, there had been at least 376 political murders, almost all of them committed by right-wing radicals, and which in the vast majority of cases had gone unpunished.[15] Victims had included, *inter alia*, Rosa Luxemburg and Karl Liebknecht, Leo Jogiches, Hugo Haase and Kurt Eisner, Gustav Landauer, Karl Gareis, Hans Paasche, Matthias Erzberger and Walther Rathenau, to name only the best known. Justice was mostly quick off the mark when it came to sentencing left-wingers, whereas crimes committed by the right were subject to the eyes of *Justitia* blindfolded in the wrong sense.

Characteristic of the anti-democratic spirit of Weimar justice and its hostility to the Republic was the treatment of President Ebert, who, in a series of legal actions, had to defend himself against a multitude of gross slanders. One court in the Republic even went so far, in one judgement, as to call the head of state a "traitor", merely because in January 1918 Ebert had participated in a meeting of a strike committee, and that with the express purpose of terminating a strike in an orderly fashion. With the methods of nationalistic incitement and the slogans "stab in the back", "treason", "November criminals", "dictate of shame", the democratic forces which had built up, and sustained, this Republic were cursed and confronted. So it was that social democracy, under simultaneous heavy attack from the left, was forced onto the defensive. This is where the roots of much uncertainty and half-heartedness in its policies during the Weimar period are to be found. The party felt pressurised to prove that it was not the party of revolutionary overthrow and betrayal, but that it represented the national interest, and was concerned to preserve peace and order.[16] This gave additional thrust to its inclination to prefer being in opposition and supporting the government indirectly, instead of itself taking charge and full governmental responsibility. This defensive strategy had the objective of persuading the bourgeois parties to share responsibility for Versailles. Nevertheless, it is valid to ask whether it might not

---

15   Emil J. Gumbel, Vier Jahre politischer Mord (Berlin-Fichtenau 1922: new edn Heidelberg 1980), esp. p. 5f., p. 78, p. 119f. and p. 145.
16   On this, see particularly the section 'Kriegsschuldfrage und Friedensvertrag: Der Nationalismus in der Sozialdemokratie', in Heinrich August Winkler, Von der Revolution zur Stabilisierung. Arbeiter und Arbeiterbewegung in der Weimarer Republik 1918 bis 1924 (Berlin/Bonn 2nd edn 1985), pp. 206–226.

have been possible to adopt a different tactic, namely by following a consistent, sober foreign policy, and one which adhered strictly to the facts, was combined with an intensive process of explanation at home, and which sought the energetic cooperation of all those forces committed to democracy.

VII. Weimar Democracy

1. Workers' Parties and Trade Unions in the Early Years of the Republic

Despite divergent tendencies, and party and trade unions being two distinct organisations, social democracy was unified in the prewar period. After the revolution of November 1918, however, the relationship between party and unions becomes one of both cooperation and confrontation.[1] At the beginning of the Weimar Republic, no less than three parties laid claim to the tradition of the socialist workers' movement. The KPD, the German Communist Party, which initially remained a splinter party, was dominated by the followers of a utopian, revolutionary course of direct action. The ideas of Rosa Luxemburg were defeated as early as the party's inaugural congress. She totally rejected Lenin's dictatorship of the proletariat as dictatorship without freedom by the party. She regarded the "abolition of the most important democratic guarantees" such as freedom of the press and the right of freedom of assembly and association, as a slap in the face for socialism, and she criticised the Bolshevists with the argument that:

"Freedom only for the supporters of the party, only for the members of one party – no matter how numerous they may be – is no freedom at all. Freedom is always freedom for the person who thinks differently. This contention does not spring from a fanatical love of abstract "justice", but from the fact that everything which is enlightening, healthy, and purifying in political freedom derives from its independent character, and from the fact that freedom loses all virtue when it becomes a privilege."[2]

After the murder of Rosa Luxemburg and Karl Liebknecht, the KPD found itself at even more of a dead end with its "all or nothing" tactics.

1 On social democracy in the Weimar Republic, see Heinrich August Winkler's Von der Revolution zur Stabilisierung, Der Schein der Normalität, Der Weg in die Katastrophe (Berlin/Bonn 1985/1990). Useful older literature: Arthur Rosenberg, A History of the German Republic, trans. I.F.D. Morrow and L.M. Sieveking (London 1936), and Richard N. Hunt, German Social Democracy 1918–1933 (New Haven/London 1964). For the early years, see Susanne Miller, Die Bürde der Macht. Die deutsche Sozialdemokratie 1918–1920 (Düsseldorf 1974). Eberhard Kolb's Die Weimarer Republik (Munich and Vienna 1984), and Karl-Heinz Dederke's Reich und Republik. Deutschland 1917–1933 (in collaboration with the Institut für Zeitgeschichte in Munich. Stuttgart 1969) both give a good overview of the development of the Republic.
2 Translated from Rosa Luxemburg, Die russische Revolution. Eine kritische Würdigung (Berlin 1922), p. 109.

Banned by the authorities and driven underground as a result of putschist excesses, they underwent a gradual reorientation. At the Second Party Congress of 20–23 October 1919 there was a split. The ultra-left and anti-parliamentary wing defected, taking with it half of the KPD membership, and, in spring 1920, formed the German Communist Workers' Party (KAPD). Although it played something of a role in the bloody struggles of the following years, it then went into decline. Under the leadership of Paul Levi, the KPD rump then decided to go down the parliamentary road. They stood for the first time in the Reichstag elections of June 1920, and polled 2.0 per cent of the vote. The KPD did not become a mass party until November 1920 when the left wing of the USPD joined with the old KPD to form the United Communist Party of Germany.

In the course of 1919, it had emerged ever more clearly that there were irreconcilable tendencies at work within the USPD. The most marked differences were over parliamentary democracy. Two opposing and equally strong bodies of opinion met at the party congress in March 1919. The one side was committed to the parliamentary system, while the other regarded it merely as an arena for "inciting the masses to revolution"[3]. Those around Ernst Däumig, Curt Geyer, and Clara Zetkin favoured the workers' councils, or Soviet system, and were prepared to fight for the dictatorship of the proletariat even without a majority in parliament. In the Munich *Räterepublik* (Soviet Republic) and a series of armed uprisings, it was the radical wing of the USPD which predominated. The party was held together mainly by the joint opposition of its two wings to the ruling MSPD. When the Majority Socialists returned to opposition, the bond collapsed. In the difficult situation in which it found itself, the USPD lost the moderating, reconciliatory influence of party chairman Hugo Haase, who was murdered on 7 November by a mentally deranged assassin. At the Leipzig party congress (30 November to 6 December, 1919), the dominant left wing finally pushed through a programme which championed dictatorship of the proletariat in the form of rule by workers' councils. Consistent with this, a majority of the congress voted to break with the Second Social Democratic International, and entrusted the party executive with the task of joining the Third Moscow International (the Comintern).

Despite internal squabbles, and, in contrast to the MSDP, its organisational weaknesses, the USPD was well on the way to becoming the protest party of the disillusioned masses. Majority Socialist supporters deserted their old party in droves, believing the government which they were

---

3 This is Däumig's formulation in a motion by the left wing. See Protokoll über die Verhandlungen des außerordentlichen Parteitages [of the USPD] vom 2. bis 6. März 1919 in Berlin (Berlin, no date [1919]), p. 250.

backing was doing neither enough to meet their material and social needs, nor to fulfil the goals of socialism, particularly since socialisation had failed to materialise, and almost everywhere the captains of industry still remained firmly at the helm. The deployment of the military against rebellious workers, the suppression of strikes, permanent supply crises, rapidly growing inflation and unemployment, did the rest in steering young workers made rootless by the war, and who had not been shaped by the organised labour movement, into the ranks of the USPD.

Representatives of the USPD, for instance, came to dominate the shoemakers' and the textile workers' associations. In the largest union, the German Metal Workers Association, the USPD took over the executive committee at the Association's national conference in October 1919, and, in the experienced and industrious Robert Dißmann, provided it with its new President. Along with these successes amongst the trade unions, the growth in membership and the Reichstag elections of June 1920 demonstrated that the USPD could successfully compete with the MSPD. Whereas their share of the vote now rose from 7.6 per cent in January 1919 to 18.0 per cent, that of the MSPD dropped in the same period from 37.9 to 21.6 per cent. If one adds the USPD and KPD vote together (18 per cent plus 2 per cent), then we are faced with two opposing camps of almost equal strength. If, however, the stance on parliamentary democracy is taken as the criterion, then the dividing lines run straight through the middle of the USPD.

At their congress in Halle in October 1920, conflict within the USPD led to a split in the party. It was precipitated by the twenty-one conditions which Moscow had stipulated for joining the Communist International. After bitter discussion, mainly between Rudolf Hilferding on the one side, and Grigori Zinoviev, chairman of the Comintern, on the other, there was a majority vote in favour of joining the Third International and merging with the KPD. The path of this United Communist Party (VKPD) was characterised in the following years by battles over direction, changes of course, and purges. In the process, the German Communists became increasingly dependent on Moscow, clearly functioning as lackeys and mere recipients of orders.

The USPD minority, who had been outvoted at the party congress in Halle, and to whom three-quarters of the parliamentary group in the Reichstag belonged, tried at first to keep the party going. In September 1922, the party rump, apart from an insignificant splinter group, joined up once again with the MSPD to form the United Social Democratic Party of Germany.

Whereas the USPD, up until their break-up, adhered strictly to an oppositional role, and bluntly rejected any participation in coalition government, the development of the MSPD after the revolution veered between governmental responsibility and opposition. The problems they were confronted with at the time of the People's Commissioners also occurred repeatedly in the period following. Until summer 1920, they were the leading party. The Scheidemann cabinet (MSPD, German Democratic Party, and Centre Party) were replaced, after his resignation in June 1919, by a government consisting of the MSPD and Centre Party (with Reich Chancellor Bauer), and which ministers from the DDP joined again in October. After the Kapp Putsch of March 1920, the Bauer cabinet resigned. They were succeeded by the government of Hermann Müller, which once again drew support from the "Weimar coalition". In addition to the office of Chancellor, which, as by far the strongest party, was its due, the MSPD held two portfolios throughout the duration of the three cabinets: the Ministry of Economic Affairs and the Ministry of Labour. The Ministry of the Interior and the Ministry of Finance, however, always remained in bourgeois hands. The remaining ministries switched between the parties. In June 1919, Hermann Müller (MSPD) replaced the previous incumbent Count von Brockdorff-Rantzau at the Foreign Office. After Hermann Müller's appointment as Chancellor, his party colleague Adolf Köster succeeded him as Foreign Minister. Gustav Noske, who had become an increasing liability for the party, had to vacate his post as Minister of Defence after the Kapp Putsch. The Social Democrats thereby gave up the important task of responsibility for the military which now fell to Otto Geßler of the DDP.

Not long after the revolution it soon became apparent that the forces on the right were recovering rapidly from their shock. The clearer the outlines of an anti-democratic faction ready to do battle became, the more trouble began to brew amongst the Social Democrats and their supporters. After the great strikes and disturbances of 1919, which the government had met with a mixture of harshness and concessions, the workers' councils movement began to ebb away. Beneath the surface, there remained a strong element of unrest amongst the workers. There was a persistent sense here that they, as the bearers of the revolution and of the new democracy, were owed much more by the state than merely formal bourgeois freedoms. Apart from the socialisation legislation, which had barely any effect, and the fine constitutional regulations about economic democracy and the eight-hour day, they could see nothing which represented any real progress towards socialism. After lengthy consultations and discussions which stretched on throughout 1919, finally, on 4 February 1920, an industrial relations law (works committee law) was passed. It gave workers in industry legally guaranteed representation, as well as the right to co-determination – fought tooth and nail by the employers' federations – in the case of hiring and firing, the fixing of working hours and regulations, holiday arrangements, and the introduction of new methods of payment. But the law incurred the displeasure not only of radical workers who, on its second reading, organised a protest demonstration under the direction of the USPD outside the Reichstag building, which ended in bloody clashes with the police. Broad sections of the moderate workforce were also disappointed. They felt cheated out of the fruits of the revolution, and could not understand why the Social Democrats in the government had not been more energetic on their behalf. Resentment at the "government of compromise", which was not "their" government, but a coalition, translated itself into disquiet about the course being adopted by the party leadership. As the MSPD party chairman Otto Wels put it at the end of 1919, there reigned "a profound uneasiness, an extraordinary discontent with the party and those leading it"[4].

The first thought of anyone consulting absolute figures for membership – which, from a million in April 1914, and down to a low point of 250,000 in April 1918, had risen to a million again in 1919, and from 1920 to 1922 were above 1.8 million – would not be of a party in crisis. If, however, one compares the development of membership with the speedy growth of the USPD, and above all with the rapid upswing in trade-union recruitment, then stagnation springs to mind. The fact that the MSPD, under the auspices of the new age, profited so little from the increasing popularity of party and trade-union organisations, is testimony to a serious decline in their attractiveness.

The Free Trade Unions underwent a very different development. At their congress in June and July 1919 they adopted a new and tighter constitution, and renamed themselves the National German Trade-Union Congress (ADGB). The General Commission was replaced by a federal executive supported by a federal committee, the organ of the executive committee chairman. The prewar membership figure of 2.5 million (labour unions and their affiliated socialist unions of white-collar employees) which, as a result of the war, had sunk by the end of 1916 to a low point of less than one million, had been overtaken once more before the end of 1918. By the end of 1919, the figure had shot up to over 7.33 million, and in June 1920 reached its high point of 8,144,981.[5]

---

4 Protokoll der Sitzung des Parteiausschusses, Berlin den 13. Dezember 1919 (Berlin no date), p. 1.
5 For more detail, see Heinrich Potthoff, Gewerkschaften und Politik zwischen Revolution und Inflation (Düsseldorf 1979), esp. pp. 40ff.

Although the tactics of the trade-union leadership continued to be marked by a sober and practical approach, this now began to be accompanied by intensive discussion of strategy and a process of politicisation throughout the movement, from the bottom up to the very top. There were a number of reasons for this: the mass influx of new and poorly educated members, the broad political spectrum of a membership which stretched from the radical, soviet wing of the USPD, through the critical Social Democrats to the trade unionists favouring the English model, the involvement of the Majority Socialists in government coalition with the bourgeois parties, insensitive military measures against striking workers, and, above all, the existence of several socialist parties. These factors led to a perceptible loosening of the trade unions' close ties with the MSPD, and to the development of an independent political importance of their own. A new note was struck by Carl Legien, chairman of the General Commission and the archetypal representative of traditional trade-union policy, with his reproach to Scheidemann that the Majority Social Democrats were becoming an "annex" of "this government of compromise", and when he stressed that the party leadership must ensure "that we remain an independent party"[6]. No less revealing were the words of his later successor, Theodor Leipart, who said he could fully understand why, in the ADGB meeting house, the Independent Socialists' paper *Freiheit* was available, and not *Vorwärts*, the official paper of the MSPD.[7]

The feeling was spreading to the top levels of the trade-union leadership that the coalition government, led by the Majority Socialists, was not in a position to radically improve the interests of working people. The trade unions would, therefore, have to intervene in economic and political matters above and beyond the traditional spheres of wages and social policy. The determination no longer to leave political decision-making solely to the parliamentary representatives of working people, but, as an independent political force, to seize the initiative in constructing a socialist democracy, underwent its first severe test in the Kapp Putsch of March 1920.

2. The Kapp Putsch and its Repercussions

Up until 1920, the hope had grown in nationalist, right-wing circles that the "republican interlude" was at an end. Around the *Freikorps* (Free

---

6 Protokoll der Parteikonferenz in Weimar am 22. und 23. März 1919 (Berlin 1919), p. 19.
7 See the Konferenz der Vertreter der Verbandsvorstände (of the Free Trade Unions). Sitzung vom 25. April 1919 (Berlin, no date [1919]), p. 6 and p. 26.

Corps) in particular, a nucleus of a new, combative, anti-democratic nationalism had gathered, for which the constitutional government was simply the "government of shame". On 13 March 1920, and supported by two of these *Freikorps* who had resisted government attempts to break them up, the Reichswehr General Lüttwitz, the former East Prussian Director General of Landscapes, Kapp, the *Freikorps* officer and naval captain Ehrhardt, and other officers, mounted a putsch against the democratic Republic. With black-white-red flags waving in the wind, and swastikas on their helmets – an omen of what was to come for Germany – the putsch troops occupied Berlin. The Reichswehr, whose duty it should have been to defend the government, refused to fight the putschists. Although General Walther Reinhardt, the head of Army High Command, remained loyal to the constitution, he was fighting a lone battle. General von Seeckt and his officers left the government in the lurch at a moment when, for the first time, it came down to offering protection against the right, and not as previously, against the left.

President Ebert, Chancellor Bauer, and other ministers of state, fled Berlin, escaping the threat of imprisonment by the skin of their teeth. In the Republic's most serious crisis to date, the Free Trade Unions under Legien's leadership sprang into the breach. The National German Trade-Union Congress (ADGB), together with the Working Group of Free Employees Association (AfA), appealed to workers, employees, and civil servants for a general strike against the putschists. The same call was issued by the SPD party chairman Otto Wels, with Ebert and the Social Democrat members of the Reich government adding their names to the appeal. The Independent Socialists, too, threw their weight behind the general strike. The mainly low-grade civil servants in the League of German Civil Servants (DBB), along with the liberal Hirsch-Duncker trade unions, added their ranks to those defying the onslaught. Despite officially rejecting strike action, the Christian German Trade-Union Congress (DGB) joined the struggle *de facto*. Even the leadership of the KPD, who initially had refused to ally themselves with a struggle to save the Republic, was constrained to join forces. Inexorably, the general strike gathered momentum, sweeping away the ground from beneath the rebels' feet. The resolute response from workers and employees – many civil servants in the various ministries also refused to cooperate with the illegal putsch government – forced Kapp and his accomplices to their knees.

Carl Legien, this sober and energetic trade unionist, revealed himself during the general strike to be not only a brilliant organiser, but he also became the key figure in coordinating the efforts of the Reich government, the coalition parties and USPD, and the mobilised labour force.

But he was not content with the capitulation of the men who had breached the constitution. Members of the Free Trade Unions now expected a radical change of political course. In a joint programme, the ADGB, AfA and DBB set nine conditions for ending the first political general strike in German history:

1. Decisive influence "on the restructuring of the governments in the Reich and the states, as well as in the revision of regulations governing economic and socio-political legislation".
2. Speedy disarmament and punishment of all involved in the Kapp Putsch.
3. Immediate resignation of Defence Minister Noske (MSPD), the Prussian Minister Wolfgang Heine (MSPD), and Rudolf Oeser (DDP).
4. The purging of all reactionary persons in the state and industrial administration.
5. The most rapid democratisation possible of the administration.
6. Immediate extension of social legislation, and real equality for workers, white-collar employees, and civil servants.
7. Immediate socialisation of mining and energy supplies.
8. Dispossession of landowners who sabotaged food supplies.
9. Dissolution of all counter-revolutionary groups and takeover of the security service by the unionised labour force.[8]

The efforts of the trade unions to give the Weimar Republic an even more stable foundation by decisive reforms was not successful. Although the leadership of the MSPD around Otto Wels demonstrated great commitment and found sporadic support from the USPD, there was never any real chance of making up for the failings of the November coup. The trade unions, in alliance with other loyal forces, had saved the Republic. But they did not make it stable. Their intervention proved to be a double-edged sword. Under battle slogans against "government by trade union" and the "trade-union state", an anti-trade union faction developed in the bourgeois camp which had longer-term repercussions than the distaste for the Kapp putschists. The trade unions only appeared to have emerged victorious from the Kapp Putsch. The real victor was the military. The cabinet assembled, after some wrangling, by Hermann Müller (SPD) was once again based on the old coalition. Although, with various ifs and buts, particularly from the DDP, it accepted the programme demanded by the unions, it implemented only a small part of it. The central domestic po-

---

8 See the Korrespondenzblatt (news letter) of the National German Trade-Union Congress, 30, 27 March 1920, p. 152f.

litical problem for the Müller cabinet was the suppression of uprisings which had flared up in the wake of the general strike in Berlin, central Germany, and especially in the Ruhr. A "Red Ruhr Army" was formed there which, after heavy, often brutal civil-war battles, controlled at times almost the entire industrial region. With undertakings from the government, State Commissar Severing managed to negotiate a ceasefire, and to prise a great part of the moderate fighters away from the Red Army. The resistance of its militant core was shattered by the Reichswehr with their bayonets, guns, and cannons. In the process, military units which, during the Kapp period had been close to the putschists, were deployed against the worker formations. Their "white terror" surpassed the "red terror" in brutality and intensity. Many workers, who, with the continuation of the strike and the formation of their own units, had wished to defend the Republic against those seeking to smash its constitution, and now had to watch these same Kapp putschists fighting, in the name of the Müller government, against themselves, or their comrades, were extremely bitter. Under the conditions of the state of emergency, strikers loyal to the Republic were often severely punished, mainly by military tribunals, merely because they had made themselves suspicious, or been denounced. Meanwhile, judgement by the Republic of its enemies on the right remained non-existent.

The lingering effect of the Kapp Putsch and the subsequent workers' uprisings exerted an influence on the Reichstag elections of June 1920. Compared to the elections for the National Assembly, there was now a landslide change in fortunes between the two socialist party groupings. The MSPD received a mere 21.6 per cent of the vote, the USPD went up to 18 per cent, with an additional 2 per cent from the KPD. But there was not only a shift to the left in the camp of the labour movement: overall they lost almost four percentage points compared to 1919. At least as serious were the shifts amongst the bourgeois parties. Of the MSPD's previous coalition parties, the Centre Party – mainly due to the splitting-off of the Bavarian People's Party – lost 6.1 per cent (13.6 per cent compared to 19.7 per cent in January 1919), while the DDP sank dramatically from 18.5 per cent to 8.2 per cent. The big winners were the national-liberal DVP (from 4.4 to 13.9 per cent) and the right-wing DNVP (from 10.3 to 15.0 per cent). Against all the expectations of Otto Wels, the chairman of the MSPD, the Kapp Putsch had not worked against the right. On the contrary, the civil-war-like conditions of spring 1920 had driven substantial numbers of voters into the arms of right-wing critics of the "system".

Hermann Müller's attempt, notwithstanding, to form a government under the leadership of the MSPD, failed. There were no Social Democrats in the new cabinet under Konstantin Fehrenbach of the Centre Party. It was the Weimar Republic's first purely bourgeois government (DVP, DDP, and Centre Party). In the eight years leading up to the formation of Müller's second cabinet, the Centre, and no longer the Social Democrats, were the party of government. In these eight years, the SPD was represented, for nine months in all, in just four, short-lived cabinets – and then only as a junior partner.

3. The Path of Social Democracy from 1920 to 1928

For the most part, the Majority Social Democrats showed no regret or concern at losing power. On the contrary, their response was one of great relief. "None of us", noted Müller, in summing up the mood of the party congress of October 1920, "has any desire to be once more part of government."[9] This was an expression of the attitude which *Vorwärts* articulated so memorably in 1925, when it said that the SPD had never pressed to be in government, and had only done so, "when the dire need of the people had demanded this sacrifice from them"[10]. Particularly after the experience of the eighteen months it had spent in power up until June 1920, and which had seen its supporters deserting in droves, only in extreme emergency would it have wished to shoulder once more the burden of government responsibility.

Notwithstanding these reservations, the Social Democrat group in the Reichstag still saw itself having to prop up governments which it frequently did not support, in order to secure a parliamentary majority and thereby avert the threat of fresh crises. The party clearly expected that this tactic of "toleration" would force the bourgeois parties to take public responsibility for unavoidable measures occasioned by crises at home and abroad, and that social democracy would thereby be removed from the firing line of its opponents on left and right. This strangely ambiguous position – half government party, half opposition – was the subject of scathing criticism in 1928 by Julius Leber, who in 1944 would pay for his resistance to Hitler with his life:

"One must either rule, or adopt a stance of absolute opposition. Not to have, in the one instance, the joy of responsibility, in the other to be lacking in courage – in other words to prefer a policy of clever fudge to

---

9 See Protokoll über die Verhandlungen des Parteitages der Sozialdemokratischen Partei Deutschlands, abgehalten in Kassel vom 10. bis 16. Oktober 1920 (Berlin 1920), p. 270. For a similar view from 1924, see Protokoll des Parteitages in Berlin 1924 (Berlin 1924), p. 83 and p. 130.
10 Vorwärts, 6.12.1925.

one of firm decision-making – this is the worst mistake which a political party can make."[11]

Unfailingly, when unpopular decisions with far-reaching repercussions became unavoidable, the SPD would leap into the breach. In contrast to many of its opponents on both left and right, it barely ever dodged matters of vital national policy. As a partner in the coalition, it supported the attempt by the government of Joseph Wirth (1921/22), through a policy of so-called "fulfilment", to bring about a revision of the Versailles Treaty. While the Social Democrats were very sympathetic towards Wirth, who came from the left of the Centre Party, they were reserved towards his successor, the right-wing businessman Wilhelm Cuno, who belonged to no party. But even his cabinet, which had no SPD representation, was extended their help in the attempt to respond with passive resistance to the occupation of the Ruhr by Franco-Belgian troops in January 1923. When this policy gave the final impulse to inflationary devaluation of the currency and the mark slumped dramatically, the Social Democrats were again at hand with help. The cabinet of Gustav Stresemann, in which they were junior partners, took over the thankless task of ending the futile battle over the Ruhr, and of subsequently stabilising the currency.

1923 was one of the years of greatest crisis for the Republic. Resistance in the Ruhr, mainly by workers, white-collar workers, and civil servants, in the course of which on 31 March thirteen Krupp workers were shot dead by French troops, could not be sustained in the long term. The colossal growth in government expenditure was being financed by printing money. The dollar was kept at roughly 20,000 marks until the middle of April when inflation then spiralled completely out of control. In August the exchange rate rose to 4.6 million marks to the dollar, in October to over 25 billion[12], and, on 15 November, the day of the currency reform, to 4.2 trillion. The unimaginable hardship this caused furthered not only the separatist movements in the Rhineland and the Palatinate. The Communists were preparing for a revolutionary offensive, the "German October". In Saxony and Thuringia they formed defence units, the "proletarian hundreds", in expectation that the worst might come to the worst. Those in the right-wing camp were contemplating a dictatorial solution to the crisis, and the handing over of power to a "strong man".[13] In Bava-

---

11 Julius Leber, Ein Mann geht seinen Weg. Schriften, Reden und Briefe, edited by his friends (Berlin 1952), p. 177.
12 According to the short scale system.
13 Views in this vein were expressed by Count Westarp, parliamentary chairman of the DNVP, and by the leading industrialist Hugo Stinnes. Seeckt, Chief of the Army Command, had similar inclinations. For the context of this, see Heinrich August

ria, the right-wing authoritarian regime under Gustav von Kahr, in league with the Reichswehr and police leaders, was in open revolt against the Republic. This was envisaged as a signal for the "march on Berlin" which would culminate in the proclamation of a "national dictatorship". On 8–9 November 1923, Adolf Hitler saw his hour approaching, and, with the support of Ludendorff, attempted a putsch in Munich. Within twenty-four hours it had collapsed.

With the effective assistance of the Social Democrats, the Republic, under Stresemann's leadership, survived this crisis. The measures adopted by the government with the help of an enabling law plunged the party into deep conflict. In view of the revolution threatened from the right, Saxony and Thuringia, where purely SPD governments with a strong left-wing component were in office, brought Communists, quite legally, into the cabinet. The SPD now had to stand by as Reichswehr troops marched into Saxony and Thuringia to forcibly dissolve the governments under Erich Zeigner and August Fröhlich, while the Reich government which it itself was supporting did virtually nothing to halt the right-wing, authoritarian, and *völkisch* (nationalistic) threat from Bavaria. The SPD no longer felt able to share responsibility for this double standard: hard towards the left, but prepared to make concessions to the right. Their withdrawal from the government was a prelude to them bringing down Stresemann. This was understandable from the party's standpoint at the time, but made no sense in terms of national policy. It met with a furious response from Ebert: "The reasons why you have brought down the Chancellor will be forgotten in six weeks, but you will feel the effects of your stupidity for the next ten years."[14]

The Social Democrats were undoubtedly "forced out of the government"[15], but this was also a victory for party common sense after its previous half-hearted fudging. The withdrawal from power was also influenced by pressure from their left-wing rivals, the mood of the rank and file, and consideration for the left wing of the party's dislike of coalitions. In September 1922, the USPD rump had returned to the bosom of the old mother party. Although the reunion brought a growth in membership,

---

Winkler, Von der Revolution zur Stabilisierung. Arbeiter und Arbeiterbewegung in der Weimarer Republik 1918 bis 1924 (Berlin and Bonn 2nd edn 1985), pp. 612–624.

14   See Gustav Stresemann, Vermächtnis (Berlin 1932), vol. 1, p. 245. Also, Waldemar Besson, Friedrich Ebert, Verdienst und Grenze (Göttingen 1963), p. 89.

15   This from Erich Koch-Weser, a leading DDP politician. In Karl-Dietrich Erdmann and Martin Vogt (eds), Die Kabinette Stresemanns I and II. 13. August bis 6. Oktober 1923, 6. Oktober 1923 bis 30. November 1923 (Boppard am Rhein 1972), vol. 2, p. 945.

and reached a figure of 1,261,072 which would never be surpassed, it exerted barely any pulling power outside the party. The KPD had firmly established itself to the left of the SPD. Its share of the vote went from 2.0 per cent (1920) to 12.6 (May 1924), 9.0 (December 1924), 10.6 (1928), and to 13.1 per cent (1930). The aggressive policy of the KPD towards the Republic and social democracy contributed to the SPD leadership equating socio-revolutionary tendencies in the labour force with "Communist" ones. This made the prospect of winning back the support of radicalised workers a sheer impossibility.

Their role in opposition could not make good the severe setback which the ruling SPD had suffered in the 1920 elections. In May 1924, the re-unified party's share of the vote fell to 20.5 per cent. In the December elections of the same year they achieved a respectable result with 26 per cent. Following the stabilisation of the Republic, they fell just short of the 30 per cent margin in 1928 with 29.8.[16] It emerged quite clearly from the election results that the SPD could not make up the ground lost to the KPD, and that only a third of the electorate were potential left-wing voters. The SPD were never able to gain more than a part – albeit by far and away the largest part – of the vote of workers who, according to the employment census of 1925, made up 45.1 per cent of those in full-time employment. Catholic workers remained, by and large, loyal to the Centre Party. Protestant workers, insofar as they were members of Christian trade unions, preferred the "national" parties. The SPD also found it difficult to secure a foothold amongst agricultural workers, who were still under the strong political and economic influence of the big landowners.

Even in the Weimar Republic, the SPD was only able to make minor inroads amongst other social classes: office workers and minor civil servants, for instance, pensioners and small farmers, some craftsmen and small shopkeepers, all of whom found themselves in a similar financial situation to workers. Admittedly, the proportion of workers in the party declined from 90 per cent before the war, to 73 per cent in 1926, and to 60 per cent in 1930, while the proportion from other groups rose. In 1930, 10 per cent were white-collar employees, 3 per cent were civil servants, and 17 per cent were housewives. Of consideration here is that the workers' sector of the population was beginning to stagnate, while the proportion of civil servants and white-collar employees was growing, and by 1926 comprised 16.5 per cent of those in employment. Sections of the middle class also now belonged to the lower part of the social pyramid, having

---

16 For more detail, see Heinrich August Winkler, Der Schein der Normalität. Arbeiter und Arbeiterbewegung in der Weimarer Republik 1924 bis 1990 (Berlin and Bonn 2nd edn 1988).

been plunged into economic hardship, and proletarianised, by inflation. According to socio-statistical calculations, over 50 per cent of the population belonged to the economic underclass.[17] A further 12 per cent from the lower middle class were not much better off. In view of these figures, the question arises why the SPD did not succeed in better exploiting this voter potential and become *the* party of the underprivileged.

The burdensome legacy for the party of defeat, revolution, and "Versailles" was one reason. A further debit for democratic socialism was that, in the division of power in the Republic, the social scales had quickly tipped back in favour of the employers. It was entirely in character that they should soon question the eight-hour day. They argued that it would prevent Germany from fully bearing the brunt of the lost war and reparations. Employees were very aware that they had to make their contribution to overcoming the burdensome consequences of war, but could detect no such readiness on the part of those who employed them. In the period of hyperinflation they saw their real incomes continually sinking as prices outstripped wages, while industrialists and businessmen on the other hand received their payment in hard gold marks.

The loss of trade-union power (dwindling membership and empty coffers) was paralleled by an enormous growth in power for those with material assets. Big industrialists in particular, with their low production costs and speculative ventures, capitalised taxes, and debts which evaporated to nothing overnight, could make huge profits. Although Hugo Stinnes' famous industrial empire outstripped everything else in size, it was by no means the only one of its kind. This first process of industrial concentration after the stabilisation of the mark was followed by a second. After the question of reparations had been regulated by the Dawes Plan, foreign capital, attracted by high interest rates, poured into Germany and triggered a strong upturn in the economy. These loans formed the basis for the stormy process of rationalisation which was getting underway. The main beneficiaries were the modern, export-oriented electrical, mechanical engineering, and chemical industries. The best-known examples of this concentration of economic power were the amalgamation in 1926 of the chemical industries to form IG Farben (roughly nine-tenths of the chemical sector), and Vereinigte Stahlwerke, a merger in the same year which resulted in ownership of two-fifths of coal, iron, and steel production.

Workers, too, profited from this economic boom, their real wages rising by 37 per cent in the years 1924 to 1927. Nevertheless, given that

---

17 See Theodor Geiger, Die soziale Schichtung des deutschen Volkes. Soziographischer Versuch auf statistischer Grundlage. Reprint of the 1932 edition (Darmstadt 1967), esp. p. 73.

Cartoon from **Der wahre Jacob** *entitled "The Distribution of the Load"*

actual wages had fallen far behind their prewar level in the period of high inflation, this growth did not seem quite so rosy. In only one year, 1929, did the net real weekly income surpass that of 1913, and then only by a miserly 2 per cent. An additional negative factor was that almost every year of the Weimar period was dominated by chronic unemployment. It is true that in the brief postwar boom, the number out of work dropped from roughly one million officially registered principal recipients of unemployment benefit in the middle of 1919, to between roughly 120,000 and 400,000. But in the winter of 1923–24, the number climbed rapidly to 1.25 million. In total, at this time, there were four million wholly, or for the most part, without work. After a rapid drop, there were still two million relying on unemployment benefit in 1922. In 1927 and 1928, unemployment remained high – despite considerable seasonal variations – at an average figure for the year of 1.4 million, before shooting up to hitherto unprecedented levels in the great economic crisis.

The difficulty of switching to a peacetime economy was responsible for the high unemployment figures immediately after the war. After 1923, they were the result of demographic changes and economic slump, as well as the consequence of socially ruthless rationalisation. Along with the increasing monotony and lack of variation which resulted from new production methods (the conveyor belt, for instance), workers also saw their jobs in jeopardy. Wage earners were under constant threat of economic insecurity. Persistent undermining, despite unemployment, of the eight-hour day – in October 1926, 53 per cent were working more than 48 hours a week – and painful setbacks in social policy, demonstrated how vulnerable the crisis-afflicted employees' organisations were *vis-à-vis* "business". The so-called "Golden Twenties" brought no economic miracle either, merely a brief, unsteady upswing. Economic growth was insufficient to bring prosperity to all sections of the population, and to eliminate the conflicts about distribution of wealth. Thus it was that the new welfare state found itself on a weak footing.

On the political front, the right-of-centre parties, in alliance with the Centre, which had become the party of government, were calling the shots. After the bitter election defeat of 1920, the Social Democrats' room for manoeuvre had been considerably restricted. The great national and economic crisis of 1923 reduced it even further. There were several reasons for this. But the most pressing question is the extent to which the SPD's own theory and practice were responsible for their political importance and ability to impose themselves remaining so limited.

It was noticeable that theoretical discussions, apart from in fringe groups inside and outside the party, were extremely rare. There were lively internal discussions in 1921 in Görlitz when the MSPD gave itself a new programme, but they revolved mainly around practical, concrete conference issues. With the Görlitz Programme, the party presented itself as "the party of working people in town and country", and as a "fighting group for democracy and socialism". Despite this definition as a people's party, the concept of class struggle remained an integral part of the programme. It was interpreted here as an "historical necessity", a "moral imperative", brought about by the capitalist economic order. In the "transference of the great, concentrated industrial concerns into public ownership", and the "continuing transformation of the whole of the capitalist, into a socialist economy", the programme saw a "necessary means" of "elevating mankind to higher forms of economic and moral community". With an unreserved affirmation of the democratic Republic, the Social Democrats simultaneously proclaimed their determination to "defend to the last the freedom they had attained" and to repel any attack on democracy "as an attack on the life and rights of the people"[18].

In 1922, after reunification with the USPD, a commission was set up to draft a new party programme. Approved by the party congress in 1925, the programme, in which, amongst others, Karl Kautsky had a big hand, contained loud overtones of Marxist class struggle. This was not only a concession to members of the old USPD, but a reflection of the social conflicts aggravated by the years of crisis. The main section of this Heidelberg Programme drew in large measure on the Erfurt programme of 1891, and included passages, in the main from Rudolf Hilferding, on the growing influence of finance capital on state power, and the striving for imperial power which emanated from it. Long before other parties had pinned their European colours to the mast, German social democracy committed itself in this official party programme to "the creation, on urgent economic grounds, of European economic unity, and to the formation of the United States of Europe"[19].

Even before the war, at the party congresses of 1894 and 1895, a vain attempt had been made to draw up a special agrarian programme. This was tried again at the Kiel party congress of 1927, with a programme committed to land reform and helping small farmers being approved unanimously. This initiative to tap into fresh strata of voters by creating a programme to meet the needs of a particular social group foundered to a great extent on the reservations about social democracy which had become entrenched in the farming community over the decades.

Of even more serious consequence for the party was the fact that their political programme was, apart from isolated instances, met with a wall

18 Protokoll über die Verhandlungen des Parteitages der Sozialdemokratischen Partei Deutschlands, abgehalten in Görlitz 18. bis 24. September 1921 (Berlin 1921), pp. III ff.
19 Sozialdemokratischer Parteitag 1925 in Heidelberg; Protokoll mit dem Bericht der Frauenkonferenz (Berlin 1925), pp. 5 ff.

of suspicion in lower middle-class and white-collar workers' circles. In battling to win them over, the SPD accused them of "false consciousness", and addressed them as proletarians, or proletarians in the making. But the majority of them did not want to be the workers' comrades. Some, even if of proletarian origin, were all too eager to cast off anything which reminded them of their earlier status. The other, larger group was composed mainly of members of the old middle class. As a result of inflation and changes in the economic structure they were downwardly socially mobile. In spite, or precisely because of, their depressed economic situation, they continued to believe that they were something better. They were inclined to attribute the loss of their own security to the misfortune of the nation as a whole. They were quick to blame the Social Democrats for this humiliation. Their ideal was not a classless society, but, for them, the way out of their sad situation was to find an acknowledged place in the *Volksgemeinschaft* (national community), and the rise of the Reich to new greatness and recognition in the world.

The right-wing, *völkisch* groups, and ultimately National Socialism, could offer them emotionally fuelled visions of this sort, but not the SPD. The Social Democrats also regarded the recovery of Germany as a priority to which they were wholeheartedly dedicated, in both word and deed. But their policies remained sober, devoid of inspirational spark and zest. Women owed their right to vote to the Peoples' Commissioners, but the main beneficiaries of their voice at the polls were the Catholic Centre Party and the National German People's Party. Their contribution to the SPD vote was below the average. The attraction of social democracy for young people was comparatively low. In 1930, for instance, only eight per cent of members were under twenty-five years old. By the end of the Republic, the Social Democratic parliamentary group in the Reichstag had the highest average age of all the parties in the parliament. Anyone once elected to the party executive committee remained a member virtually for the rest of their life. The character of the party was determined by men who were reliable and industrious, but lacking in any great personal charisma. Toiling in painstaking and tenacious fashion, they led the struggle for social improvements and modest reforms. In the referendum on the *Fürstenenteignung* (expropriation of the princely families) initiated by the KPD and SPD in 1926, they admittedly managed to mobilise uncommitted voters far beyond the ranks of their own supporters, but this was an isolated case which brought them no long-term benefit or concrete success.

In thousands of towns and communities Social Democrats played an active and exemplary role in the development of local politics, although there were far fewer "red town halls" than is generally supposed. In addition, they wielded influence in several federal states, with one-third of all Landtag deputies in 1929 belonging to the SPD. While in Bavaria, the "custodian of law and order", where reactionary conservative forces had ruled the roost since the Soviet Republic, the party had, by 1932, become almost a splinter group with a mere 10 per cent of the vote, they played a major role in the state governments of Hamburg, Baden, Hesse, and Prussia. With brief interruptions, the Social Democrats had been at the helm in Prussia since 1919. After 1920, Otto Braun, one of the most impressive political personalities of the Weimar Republic, took over the office of Minister President from Paul Hirsch. With coalition governments comprising the SPD, Centre Party, and DDP (and occasionally the DVP) he attempted to make Prussia the model of a "republican people's state". Well-functioning and properly administered democratic institutions, along with the energetic response of SPD Minister of the Interior Carl Severing and Chief of Police Albert Grzesinski to any activity from left or right hostile to the state and democracy, made "red Prussia" the prime target for the hatred of all those who were enemies of the Republic.

However, even the "Prussian bulwark" of the Republic manifested a weakness characteristic of the SPD in the Weimar period. As the experienced veteran Wilhelm Keil, at the party conference of 1925, put it, the Social Democrats felt themselves to be "the real force behind the democratic Republic", to be the "advocates of the poor, of working people, and of the dispossessed". Social Democrats were, indeed, the custodians of the constitution and democracy. But their concept of democracy remained too restricted to the formal functioning of the democratic institutions, and to merely defending them. The reasons repeatedly given for their belief in the democratic Republic was that it was a "base" they had secured on the path "to the socialist people's state". At the Kiel party conference in 1927, Karl Ulrich, the Minister President of Hesse, formulated this argument as follows: "We must inform the masses that we are determined to fight tooth and nail for the democratic Republic because it offers us a much more promising arena than the monarchy in which to fight for our social and political demands and socialist goals."[20] But the alternative to the Weimar Republic was not a restoration of the Wilhelmine monarchy. The real danger was the threat of the modern "Führer state" of militant, nationalistic, and fascist forces to which a merely defensive posture was a completely inadequate response. Hilferding's argument

---

20 Protokoll über die Verhandlungen des Parteitages der Sozialdemokratischen Partei Deutschlands, abgehalten in Kiel vom 22. bis 27. Mai 1927 (Berlin 1927), p. 196 (Paul Löbe) and p. 210 (Karl Ulrich).

that, historically, democracy had been the business of the proletariat, and still remained so, had little appeal. Voices on the right and left wings of the party were calling for democracy not merely to be safeguarded, but to be actively promoted, and to be implemented in all areas of state and society.

A policy of this kind demanded consistency and an ordering of priorities: a subordination of all other aims and considerations to the one overriding goal. His early death robbed the Social Democrats of the one man who had adopted this stance most tenaciously, and who had the requisite authority. On 28 February 1925, Friedrich Ebert died as the result of a burst appendix. In his six years in office as head of state he had proved to be an effective custodian of the Republic, a champion of the nation, and a conscientious democrat. He had subordinated everything to safeguarding the democratic system and the unity of the Reich, and had sacrificed his health and energy in the process. However, with his implacable opposition to the left, his over-reliance on specialist advice, and his failure to replace relics of the old order with convinced democrats, he has to share responsibility for the limited impact made by social democracy. Hindenburg, a legendary national hero, would now step into Ebert's shoes.

In the first round of the presidential election on 29 March 1925, the DNVP and DVP candidate, the Mayor of Duisburg, Karl Jarres, achieved the largest proportion of the vote with 10.7 million, over Otto Braun (SPD) with 7.8 million, and Wilhelm Marx (Centre Party) with 3.9 million. Since none of the contenders achieved the requisite absolute majority, a second electoral round took place on 26 April. The Centre Party, the DDP, and the SPD had jointly nominated Marx as their candidate, while Hindenburg was the choice of the right-wing parties. It was a close result: Hindenburg was the victor with 14,655,000 votes, followed by Marx with 13,751,000, while Ernst Thälmann, once again the KPD candidate, polled 1,931,000, taking the vote of those who, had he not run, would have been inclined to vote for Marx. Much more responsible for this outcome, however, was the Bavarian People's Party, a kind of precursor of the CSU (Christlich Soziale Union). They appealed to their supporters not to vote for Rhineland Centre Party man, Marx, the candidate of their sister party, but for the venerable Field Marshal. The highest office in the land was thereby delivered into the hands of a man who exercised his military values in matters of state, and who, deep down, was opposed to parliamentary democracy.

4. The Second Hermann Müller Cabinet

In 1928, the Social Democrats once again had the chance to determine the politics of the Reich from the government benches. A new Reichstag was elected on 20 May 1928. The SPD increased its vote of 26.0 per cent in the 1924 elections to 29.8, and won 153 seats (as opposed to 131 earlier) in the Reichstag. At the same time, the KPD share of the vote rose from 9 to 10.6 per cent. The gains for the SPD resulted mainly from greater success in mobilising their core voters. The bourgeois centre parties, DPP and Centre, worn out by the strains of coalition government, were left weaker.[21] After long and difficult negotiations, Hermann Müller formed a cabinet from the SPD, Centre Party, DDP, and DVP. The participation of the German People's Party was rather half-hearted. It had taken energetic efforts on the part of Gustav Stresemann, who had been ill for some time, to persuade them to join the government of the "Grand Coalition".

In spite of domestic tensions, a successful joint course was pursued in foreign policy. Whereas it had met with stubborn resistance within his own party, the policy of reconciliation of the long-standing Foreign Minister Stresemann had found firm support from the SPD in the years when it was in opposition. After the signing on 27 August 1928 of the Kellogg Pact renouncing war, the government applied itself to the problem of reparations. After difficult negotiations and meetings of experts, the so-called Young Plan was finally accepted at a conference in The Hague in August 1929. It not only brought Germany a reduction in the burden of reparations and a liberation from existing Allied controls, but an agreement was also signed about the evacuation of the occupied Rhineland. Under it, Allied troops would vacate German soil in 1930, five years earlier than had been agreed at Versailles.

This great foreign policy success nevertheless found little favour with the nationalists, as little, indeed, as had Hermann Müller's plea before the League of Nations – of which Germany had been a member since 1926 – for disarmament on the part of other nations, too. So-called nationalist circles were not so much interested in general disarmament, as they were in German rearmament. This sentiment had inspired the previous bourgeois government to decide to build the *Panzerkreuzer A*, the armed cruiser "type A". The SPD, which had campaigned against this in the election on the slogan "Food for children, not armed cruisers", now saw itself confronted with the fact that its own government was seeking to make finance available for the ship's construction. This evoked a wave of out-

---

21 For a detailed analysis of the elections and their outcome, see Winkler, Der Schein der Normalität, pp. 521–527.

rage at both grassroots and parliamentary level, with the party finding itself up in arms against its own comrades in the cabinet. The SPD ministers bowed to the prevailing mood and party discipline and voted against *Panzerkreuzer A* in the Reichstag. Barely had this rock, on which the ship had threatened to run aground, been negotiated with great difficulty, than economic catastrophe shook the Republic to its very foundations.

Even before the outbreak of the great world economic crisis with the New York stock market crash on 24 and 29 October 1929, the fragile German economy was already flagging, and the country was in the grip of rising unemployment and mounting social tensions. The ugly Ruhr iron producers' dispute of late autumn 1928 in the Rhenish-Westphalian coalfield spotlighted the ruthless conflict strategy adopted by the entrepreneurial classes in their efforts to take advantage of the situation. With their complete disregard for the government arbitration decision which Minister of Labour Rudolf Wissell had declared binding, the Ruhr industrialists drove a coach and horses through the Weimar system of wage bargaining. Their battle against compulsory arbitration was simultaneously a declaration of war on the democratic state. Under the impact of the on-going dispute, which began in 1929, about unemployment insurance, the entire foundation of the Weimar social order began to totter. Although the seasonal high of 2.85 million unemployed in January 1929 dropped in summer, it climbed again the following winter to 3.2 million. After a cabinet compromise deal, the growing levels of relief expenditure were to be maintained by increasing the contributions of both employers and workers from 3 per cent to 3.5 per cent. The growing deficit in unemployment insurance brought the issue back onto the political agenda in spring 1930. The DVP, who inclined to favour industry and the employers, were arguing – as were the employers' organisations – for a settlement which offered lower relief payments to the unemployed. The main criterion for the SPD, however, was the security of employees who, through no fault of their own, were suffering great hardship. They therefore called for increased contributions of 3.75, then 4 per cent. There was no majority in the SPD parliamentary group for the compromise suggested by the Centre Party and accepted by the DVP. Minister of Labour Wissell and the trade unions regarded unemployment insurance as the safety net for the whole wage-rate system and as the cornerstone of social policy. It was the point "at which the patience and tolerance demonstrated by the labour force and its organisations towards SPD considerations of national policy runs out."[22] This unyielding stance was supported by the left wing

---

22 Gewerkschaftszeitung (Trade Union Newspaper), no. 14, 4 April 1930, p. 209.

of the party who, at the last party conference, had already called for withdrawal from the coalition. But for the party leadership too, enough was enough in the matter of concessions for a Social Democratic-led government. Thus it was that, on 27 March 1930, a majority of the parliamentary party rejected the possibility of compromise. The Centre Party, and particularly the German People's Party, who had deliberately engineered the break with the Social Democrats in order to fulfil their own financial and socio-political agenda[23], took this decision by the SPD as a pretext for wrecking the coalition. On the same day, the Müller cabinet, Weimar's last constitutional government, resigned. The death throes of the Republic had begun.

---

23 See the declarations of the DVP chairman Ernst Scholz. On this and the decisions of the party, see also Werner Conze and Hans Raupach (eds), Die Staats- und Wirtschaftskrise des Deutschen Reiches 1922/33 (Stuttgart 1967), p. 198. For a comprehensive account of the collapse of the coalition, see Winkler, Der Schein der Normalität, pp. 736–823, and on the DVP, particularly p. 783f., and pp. 798–801, and p. 816.

VIII. The Destruction of Democracy

1. Factors in the Crisis in State and Society

There are many causes – domestic and foreign, economic and social, national and emotional, objective and subjective – for the destruction of democracy and the seizing of power by the National Socialists.[1] Barely any of those exercising political responsibility at the time, Social Democrats included, are entirely free of guilt. But the extent and nature of that guilt, as well as of the degree of dereliction, are so great that it is impossible to reduce them to a single common denominator. It stretched from those fighting for the National Socialist regime, to nationalistic politicians such as Hugenberg who deliberately exploited Hitler as their drummer-boy, accomplices from industry, judges, academics, teachers, all of whom supported Hitler directly or indirectly, to the Communist Party who directed their main attack at the Social Democrats, and believed they could be the heirs to National Socialism. Anti-democratic tendencies amongst the middle classes, authoritarian and nationalistic trends, along with divisive social fault lines, provided the fertile soil in which National Socialism could flourish.

The results of the Reichstag elections in the period from 1919 to 1933 reveal that, apart from the special case of the National Assembly, those parties committed to, and bearing responsibility for, power in the Weimar Republic never, in fact, succeeded in securing the votes of more than half of the electorate. In the elections of 14 September 1930, 31 July 1932, 6 November 1932, and the last ones on 5 March 1933, held after the Nazi seizure of power, and subject to great interference, this last vestige of democracy shrank even further. The SPD vote fell from 29.8 in 1928, to 24.5 in 1930, and 21.6 and 20.4 in July and November 1932. In 1933, and with Hitler in power, they were still able to gain the support of 18.3 per cent of the electorate. The DDP, which since 1930 had called itself the German State Party, had almost completely disappeared apart from a tiny residue (1.0 percent in November 1932). By contrast, the Centre Party was

---

1 On what follows, see: Erich Matthias and Rudolf Morsey (eds), Das Ende der Parteien (Düsseldorf 1960); Karl Dietrich Bracher, Die Auflösung der Weimarer Republik. Eine Studie zum Problem des Machtverfalls (Villingen/Schwarzwald 4th edn 1964); Heinrich August Winkler, Der Weg in die Katastrophe. Arbeiter und Arbeiterbewegung in der Weimarer Republik (Berlin/Bonn 2nd edn 1990).

able to maintain its Catholic vote virtually intact in the elections between 1930 and 1933 (11.8; 12.5; 11.9; 11.2. In comparison: 13.6 in 1924, and 12.1 in 1928). It had, however, changed course politically. The new leadership elected at the party congress of 1928 in Cologne steered the party into emphatically conservative and national waters, thereby completing a development begun much earlier by its Bavarian sister party. The German People's Party, which had joined the Hermann Müller government only after much wrangling and, until his death in 1929, had prospered mainly from Stresemann's reflected glory, were relegated to the status of an insignificant splinter party in the elections after 1930 (1.2 per cent in July 1932, 1.9 per cent in November 1932).

To the right of the DVP were the German National People's Party (DNVP). After the election of Alfred Hugenberg as party chairman in 1928, its initially strong representation of conservative and monarchist forces was weakened. After the departure of the moderate wing under Count Westarp in 1930, the party was reconstituted as the "Hugenberg Movement". Organisation on the lines of the "Führer" principle, the creation of combat units, and the deliberate undermining of the democratic political system now determined the party's political direction. After 1924, its election results followed a downward trend. From 14.2 per cent in 1928, it fell to 7 per cent in 1930, 5.9 per cent in July 1932, 8.5 per cent in November 1932, and 8 per cent in 1933.

In the National Socialist movement the DNVP had found a rival who far outstripped them in unscrupulousness and skilful propaganda. In the Reichstag elections of May 1924, *völkisch* groups, with National Socialism soon playing first fiddle, had entered parliament for the first time with 6.5 per cent of the vote. In the years of economic and political stabilisation, their proportion of the vote sank from 3 per cent in December 1924, to 2.6 in the 1928 elections. In September 1930 votes for the NSDAP rocketed to 18.3 per cent, rose to 37.4 in July 1932, and, after dropping to 33.1 per cent in November 1932, reached 43.9 per cent in the elections of 5 March 1933 which had been overshadowed by intimidation and terror.

The fortunes of the KPD were also governed by economic and social developments. After declining in the period of stabilisation, their share of the vote rose in 1930 to 13.1 per cent, in July 1932 to 14.3, and in November 1932 to 16.9 per cent. In the last elections of March 1933, when the KPD was the party most exposed to Nazi terror, their percentage of the vote fell to 12.3.

Both the political factions, on left and right, who radically questioned the existing state and used every means at their disposal to fight it, profited from the economic catastrophe which plunged the Republic into unimaginable misery. By January 1930, the number of registered unemployed had already risen to over 3.2 million. Above 2.7 million in July 1930, the figures rose to 4.887 million in January 1931, 6.042 million in January 1933, and 6.014 million in January 1932. The highest figures of 6.128 million were recorded in February 1932. The actual figures must have been some 600,000 higher. Only roughly 12.7 million blue and white-collar workers were still in some form of employment, with several million of these being on short-time work. On average in 1932, 43.8 per cent of trade-union members were without work, and a further 22.6 per cent were working short time.

After hours of queueing, and in exchange for a stamp on their unemployment card, those in distress through no fault of their own would finally receive their benefit allowance. Up until June 1932 it was calculated on the basis of providing half of the basic minimum needed to exist. Then, the cabinet of Franz von Papen, which was governing without parliament and was backed only by the Field Marshal in his presidential chair, slashed the sum to an amount which was no longer sufficient to live on. A family of two adults and one child, for instance, received 51 marks a month, of which 32.50 marks alone went on rent, heat, and light. That left just 18.50 marks for food. At contemporary prices, that could buy each family member a daily ration of half a loaf, a pound of potatoes, 100 grams of cabbage, and 50 grams of margarine. Three times a month one could buy a cheap herring, and for a child even one extra, along with half a litre of milk a day.

This family would have been relatively much better off than many others, since unemployment benefit, including so-called "emergency relief", was granted for up to a year at most. In February 1932, 12.6 per cent of the unemployed received no support at all. The 29.9 per cent, or 1.833 million, who were no longer paid any unemployment money or, like many of the poor and old, young people and the self-employed, had never belonged to the social security scheme, remained dependent on charity. In many places this was not even sufficient to buy something warm to eat, let alone enough to pay the rent. People vegetated aimlessly out in the open, in waiting rooms and hostels for the homeless, waiting for a miracle that would put an end to their misery. They had long abandoned any hope of help from the government.

After the break-up of the Grand Coalition under Hermann Müller, various forces from the political and economic sphere, as well as the Reichswehr, felt the hour had come for a "cabinet of the right" with special powers. Bypassing parliament, it would take tight control, either by means of an enabling law, or by using the President as a front. Whereas some entrepreneurs, mainly in manufacturing, had settled for a system of partnership between capital and labour, others saw the "trade-union state" as an obstacle to a full exercise of their economic power. This is why heavy industry in particular supported predominantly those associations and parties who promised to rein in the work force by means of an authoritarian form of government.

By the middle of January 1930, and with the Hermann Müller government still in power, Hindenburg too was set on a cabinet subject to his good graces alone. It was to be, firstly, anti-parliamentary and free of the usual coalition negotiations, and secondly, "anti-Marxist", to preclude any Social Democratic influence. And moreover, the Braun government in Prussia was to be replaced by a cabinet in the same Hindenburg mould.

On 30 March Hindenburg appointed the conservative Centre Party deputy Heinrich Brüning as Chancellor. This led to the first, if somewhat disguised, presidential cabinet. The Reich President gave the new Chancellor the mandate, based on the ominous article 48 of the constitution, to rule by emergency decrees. When, with the very first trial of strength, a recalcitrant parliament rejected these emergency decrees by a narrow majority, Brüning simply made use of his power of authority and dissolved the Reichstag. With this step, which went against the spirit of the constitution, the transition to an open presidential system with the dictatorial power of the Reich President as the basis for the power of the state, was complete.[2]

The winners of the elections of 14 September 1930 – much influenced by the economic crisis, Brüning's rigorous economy measures, and the wave of nationalistic agitation – were the radical opponents of the democratic Republic. The National Socialists profited far more than the Communists: their mandates rocketed from 12 to 107. Brüning's government, "above party alignments" and backed by the President, fell the moment on 29 May 1932 when – after whispers in his ear from Reichswehr General Kurt von Schleicher, and pressure from East Elbian landowners – the Field Marshal withdrew his confidence in him.

The new cabinet under the ultra-conservative former Centre Party man Papen found itself in open confrontation with parliament: "It was no longer government supposedly 'above party alignments', but government against the parties".[3] With the lifting of the Brüning cabinet's ban on the

---

2 On these events, and what is dealt with in the following pages, see Winkler, Der Weg in die Katastrophe, chapters 2 to 4.
3 See Karl Dietrich Bracher, Deutschland zwischen Demokratie und Diktatur. Beiträge zur neueren Politik und Geschichte (Berne and Munich 1964), p. 45.

SA, Papen opened the streets once again to the terror of the "Brown Army". They wrought havoc as never before. Plans for a dictatorship, and the *coup d'état* of 20 July 1932 which removed from office the Prussian government of Otto Braun, were characteristic of the course adopted by the "Cabinet of the Barons". On 1 December, Papen was ousted, mainly due to pressure from the Reichswehr. For two months Hindenburg now allowed, to use his own words, "the [Reichswehr General] Herr von Schleicher to try his luck in the name of God".[4] The general had no luck. On 30 January 1930, the ex-Field Marshal once again launched a government on its way, this time under Adolf Hitler, with a rousing phrase: "And now, gentleman, onward with God!".[5] And onward things went: into the Nazi dictatorship.

In the period of the presidential cabinets, the National Socialists not only became the strongest party, they also became, for large sections of the bourgeois party camp, socially acceptable and fit for government. The first to offer the Hitler movement his hand was Alfred Hugenberg, chairman of the DNVP. In the "Reich Committee against the Young Plan", Hugenberg and Franz Seldte, the leader of the Stahlhelm, a nationalistic para-military organisation of former front-line soldiers, joined forces with Hitler and unleashed an unprecedented hate campaign against the Republic and its representatives. In December 1929, a plebiscite, initiated by the committee, which threatened with imprisonment those responsible for the signing of the Young Plan, fell well short of its objective with only 13.8 per cent of the votes.

Beneficiaries of this cooperation were Hitler and his movement who now, deploying the whole gamut of demagoguery, began to embed themselves in the consciousness of broad swathes of the population. In the wake of the catastrophic economic crisis, the masses began to flock to them. In contrast to their party name, the "National Socialist Workers' Party" was more of a populist people's, than a workers' party. Those who voted for, or were members of, the NSDAP, came from a broad social spectrum: the upper class, the new and old middle class, the petit bourgeoisie, and the proletariat. They were often people who had been knocked sideways by the war and the economic crises, and who felt equally threatened by both capitalism and socialism. There was a particularly high proportion of senior civil servants and white-collar workers, the self-employed, downwardly mobile middle-class tradespeople, Protes-

---

[4] This according to Franz von Papen in Der Wahrheit eine Gasse (Munich 1952), p. 240.

[5] Quoted from Theodor Duesterberg, Der Stahlhelm und Hitler (Wolfenbüttel-Hanover 1949), p. 41.

tant farmers, and high-school and university students. In the labour force, the NSDAP had its successes amongst the socially deracinated or those close to the land, as well as workers of nationalistic and anti-Marxist disposition. The Social Democratic and Christian and Catholic labour force, on the other hand, proved to be largely immune. High unemployment was also a factor in drawing industrial workers and, above all, the so-called "unpolitical" and particularly many young people, into the National Socialist net. After leaving school or finishing their education they looked in vain for work, and, in their desperation, turned to those who promised them employment and bread, power and greatness. Particularly those who were inwardly insecure, who had no firm social or religious ties, felt at home in the NSDAP. The "movement" offered compensation for their own feelings of inferiority and a safety-valve for their aggressions. Envy of competition and prejudice, anger and hatred, violence and destructiveness, could find a ready outlet when directed at the enemy: the Jews and Bolshevism, social democracy and the whole "system".

Instead of erecting a common front against National Socialism, more and more parts of this "system" began to embrace fascism. It is not surprising that National Socialism could gain a foothold in the Reichswehr, this "state within a state", and that younger officers should sympathise with its bellicose, pugnacious ideas. Even the Reichswehr leadership was beginning to show certain signs of turning towards the NSDAP. With the knowledge of Chancellor Brüning, General von Schleicher sounded out Hitler and Röhm about the possibilities of a "strong national government of the right".[6] The government did virtually nothing to counter the outbreak of vicious political terrorism, since Brüning wanted to gain National Socialist support for Hindenburg in the presidential elections due in 1932.

Things turned out differently. Hitler, along with Ernst Thälmann for the KPD, and Theodor Duesterberg of the Stahlhelm, stood against Hindenburg on 13 March 1932. In the second electoral round on 10 April 1932, the Field Marshal won with 53 per cent of the votes (19.3 million), with Hitler gaining 36.8 per cent (13.4 million), and Thälmann 10.2 per cent (3.7 million). Alongside the German People's Party and the Bavarian People's Party who had already supported him in 1925, the Centre Party, the German Democratic Party, and the SPD – in a reversal of the fronts – now also backed Hindenburg. While the Centre Party now feted him as the "rock of national security", the "saviour", and the

---

6 See the note of Major General Curt Liebmann of 25.10.1930, in Vierteljahrshefte für Zeitgeschichte 2 (1954), pp. 406 ff.

"leader of the German nation"[7], the decision of the SPD was based on the slogan "against Hitler". Seen in this light, even the victory of Hindenburg was a victory for the Republic.

Once again, the assault of the National Socialists on the state had been halted. In April 1932, it even seemed as if the government was about to steel itself to take energetic counter-measures. After pressure from the state governments who did not want to stand idly by as the columns of Nazi thugs rampaged murderously through the streets, the SA and SS were banned. After the resignation of Brüning, the newly fledged Chancellor Franz von Papen found nothing more pressing to do than promptly dissolve the Reichstag and rescind the ban on the SA and SS. This was the price Papen had to pay for the toleration of him, negotiated by General Schleicher, by the Nazis.

In the subsequent Reichstag elections on 31 July, the NSDAP became far and away the biggest party with 37.4 per cent of the vote. Despite the brutal murder by Nazis of a Communist miner in the Silesian village of Potempa (10 August 1932) to which Hitler ostentatiously gave his backing, the Centre Party conducted lengthy coalition negotiations with him and Göring, albeit ultimately to no effect. Although parliament passed a no-confidence vote against him by 512 votes to 42, Papen remained in office. Instead of resigning, he used the *carte blanche* powers of the President to dissolve the Reichstag.

In the subsequent fresh elections the National Socialists dropped by 4.3 points, while at the same time the KPD went from 14.3 to 16.9 per cent. This confirmed the expectations of the Communist Party leadership that NSDAP voters would ultimately defect to them. In the political struggle, the KPD tarred every political tendency but their own with the brush of "monopoly capitalism". Although their attacks were also directed at "national fascism" (NSDAP), their main target was "social fascism" (SPD). The "Bloody May" of 1929, when the Social Democrat Berlin Chief of Police Zörgiebel suppressed the Communist May Day demonstrations, had certainly left deep scars. But even after the Reichstag elections of 1932, when the Social Democrats had only secured 24 per cent of the vote, the KPD continued to attack the SPD as the "main social support of the bourgeoisie". Their analysis of the elections concluded that "the importance of the SPD for the fascist policies of finance capital" had grown much stronger.[8] Cautious moves to initiate a change of

---

7   See, inter alia, Schultheß' Europäischer Geschichtskalender 1932, p. 59; Das Zentrum. Mitteilungsblatt der Deutschen Zentrumspartei (Berlin) 3 (1932), p. 89f.
8   See Siegfried Bahne, 'Die Kommunistische Partei Deutschlands', in Das Ende der Parteien, pp. 674ff.

course on this in April 1932 were retracted and condemned as right-wing opportunism. Moreover, at the moment when they were mounting a frontal attack on the SPD, the KPD was even warning against overestimating the dangers of fascism. Their leaders round Ernst Thälmann adhered unwaveringly to tactics dictated by Moscow. In August 1931 the KPD colluded with the NSDAP and DNV in initiating a plebiscite in Prussia to dissolve the Social Democrat government under Otto Braun. Once again, in the Berlin transport workers strike at the beginning of November 1932, they did not shrink from working with the National Socialists. In tangible demonstration of their hostility to the Republic, and to the SPD in particular, fascists and Communists were patrolling side by side.

To left and right, troops were ready and waiting to deliver the death blow to a Republic undermined from within. Naked fascism, Communism of Stalinist complexion, authoritarian striving to be in government, and nationalistic dreams of power were all threatening the Republic. Where hostility did not manifest itself openly, there reigned passive acceptance of the circumstances, or resignation. After the end of the Müller government and the transition to the presidential cabinets of Brüning, Papen, and Schleicher, "social democracy was alone in its single-minded defence of the democratic constitution and the parliamentary system"[9].

2. *The Social Democrats' Defensive Battle*

After Brüning's appointment as Chancellor, the Social Democrats in the Reichstag adopted an initially ambivalent stance. They criticised the use of Article 48 as a threat, but simultaneously offered their willingness to cooperate. Confrontation arose in July 1930 when Brüning promulgated his budget by emergency decree, despite the SPD being ready, given certain conditions, to approve it. The SPD parliamentary group regarded this bypassing of the Reichstag as a breach of the constitution. They then voted with the parliamentary majority to abrogate the decrees, whereupon the Chancellor promptly dissolved the Reichstag.

After the substantial gains made by anti-democratic party factions in the elections of September 1930, the Reichstag had reached a point of total impasse. Those parties openly hostile to the state (NSDAP, DNVP, KPD) held 225 (39.1 per cent) of the 577 seats in the Reichstag. The SPD finally came to the point where, in Wilhelm Keil's words at the end

9 This, from Hans Mommsen, is just one of many academic verdicts. See 'Sozialdemokratie in der Defensive. Immobilismus der SPD und der Aufstieg des Nationalsozialismus', in Hans Mommsen (ed.), Sozialdemokratie zwischen Klassenbewegung und Volkspartei (Frankfurt/Main 1974), p. 107.

of September 1930: "In the present political situation our only option, if we wish to prevent the National Socialists from seizing power, is to support Brüning"[10]. Preservation of the democratic system, safeguarding the constitution, and protecting the already severely battered parliamentary process were the overriding priorities for the Social Democrats in the Reichstag. Toleration of the Brüning cabinet and its emergency decrees was, for them, the lesser evil. The fear that Brüning would otherwise seek alliance with the NSDAP, or that he would be replaced by an openly rightwing cabinet, or dictatorship, made up of all the reactionary and fascist forces, thrust the Social Democrats increasingly on the defensive. They had to defend unpopular emergency and economy measures to which their own supporters were passionately opposed, while swallowing the fact that laws were being passed which favoured solely the interests of the large estate-owners.

What other possible course of action lay open to them? Certainly not the one being propagated by some of their own rank and file that "one should let the right-wingers, including the National Socialists, get into office so that they finish themselves off, once and for all".[11] Otto Braun's plea for a "Grand Coalition of the reasonable", and for a close interlinking of the national with the Prussian government, failed because of the very fact of Brüning's inability to overcome his prejudices towards the Social Democrats. However, in view of competition from the Communists and pressure from its own left wing, there was barely any readiness in the SPD either for a solution of this kind. It became very clear at the party conference in Leipzig in 1931 that the majority still backed the tactics of toleration. Even the young Wilhelm Hoegner, who warned his comrades against underestimating fascism, once again argued in favour of this course:

"Fascism is certainly not an enemy with whom we can cross swords in cosy fashion. It is an enemy who wants to grab us by the throat, who wants to slaughter everything we hold sacred: peace amongst nations, democratic equality, the liberation struggle of the working class. That is why we must subordinate everything to what is required in this fight against our strongest enemy, even the tactics, especially the tactics, of the parliamentary party in the Reichstag."[12]

10 Quoted from Erich Matthias, 'Die Sozialdemokratische Partei Deutschlands', in Das Ende der Parteien, p. 106.
11 See Otto Braun, Von Weimar zu Hitler (New York 1940), p. 308.
12 Sozialdemokratischer Parteitag in Leipzig 1931 vom 31. Mai bis 5. Juni 1931 im Volkshaus, Protokoll (Berlin 1931), p. 134. For a comprehensive account see especially, Wolfram Pytha, Gegen Hitler und für die Republik. Die Auseinandersetzung der deutschen Sozialdemokratie mit der NSDAP in der Weimarer Republik (Düsseldorf 1989).

In spite of reluctance from within the party, the SPD brought itself to support Hindenburg in the presidential elections because:
"Hitler instead of Hindenburg means chaos and panic in Germany and the whole of Europe, worsening of the economic crisis and the misery of unemployment, the greatest danger of bloody confrontations at home and abroad. Hitler instead of Hindenburg means: victory of the reactionary sections of the bourgeoisie over the progressive sections, and over the working class, the annihilation of all civil liberties, of the press, and trade-union and cultural organisations, a worsening of exploitation and wage-slavery. Against Hitler! That is the slogan for 13 March." (SPD election appeal of 27 February 1932.)[13]

Given the gist of this appeal, even the re-election of Hindenburg was a victory. The considerable gains made by the NSDAP in the Land elections (*inter alia* in Prussia), and the replacement of Brüning by Papen, destroyed all hope of overcoming the crisis. The onslaught by anti-democratic forces could no longer be warded off by parliamentary and purely formal democratic methods alone. For some time, in circles within, and close to the SPD, there had been calls for the use of extra-parliamentary methods against the "reactionaries" and fascism.

As in the debates at the beginning of the century about mass strike action, the calls for more action now came mainly from the fringes, of the left, as well as of the right. The International Socialist Combat League (ISK) arose out of the International Youth Organisation (IJB), founded in 1917 by the Göttingen philosopher and mathematician Leonard Nelson, after the IJB had been excluded in 1925 from the Socialist Workers' Youth (SAJ) and the SPD. Influenced by the ideas of Kant, the ISK followed a non-Marxist, idealist socialist philosophy, rejecting the SPD leadership's policy of accommodation, and arguing for a joint alliance of SPD and KPD in the struggle against right-wing radicalism.[14]

The German Socialist Workers' Party (SAPD)[15], founded in October 1931 under the aegis of Reichstag deputies Max Seydewitz, Kurt Rosenfeld and Heinrich Ströbel, developed a more militant activism in their efforts to preserve the democratic Republic. The lack of electoral success of this new party (which Willy Brandt joined as a schoolboy in Lübeck) was mainly because traditional loyalties were more a determinant of how people voted than dissatisfaction with the party leadership.

13 Quoted from Walter Tormin (ed.), Die Weimarer Republik (Hanover 1962), p. 214.
14 On the ISK, see Werner Link, Die Geschichte des Internationalen Jugend-Bundes (IJB) und des Internationalen Sozialistischen Kampfbundes (ISK) (Meisenheim 1964).
15 On this, see Hanno Drechsler, Die Sozialistische Arbeiterpartei Deutschlands (SAPD) (Meisenheim 1965).

SPD election poster from 1932. The text reads: "The Worker in the Reich of the Swastika. That's why you should vote List 1 – the Social Democrats!"

On the right, the Hofgeismar Young Socialists' Study Group were working towards a theoretical and practical reorientation of SPD policy.

Under the motto of *Volksgemeinschaft* (national community) their ideas were consciously national in direction. In addition, younger reformers were battling with the immobility of the party leadership. They were calling for much more single-minded and militant efforts on behalf of democracy. Under the Nazi dictatorship, their leading figures – men such as Carlo Mierendorff, Julius Leber, Theodor Haubach, and Kurt Schumacher – put their lives and freedom on the line in the struggle for a better Germany.

The rise of new organisations such as the ISK, or splinter groups such as the SAP, as well as the call for action – particularly by young people in the party – were an expression of disquiet about the inflexibility and obsolescence of the party apparatus. The criticism in publications such as *Jungsozialistische Blätter*, or *Neue Blätter für den Sozialismus*, was countered, as Theodor Haubach has remarked, fairly ruthlessly.[16] The anathema of disciplinary measures afflicted opposition from the right, as well as from the left, which was all too readily accused of being close to Communism. The alliance in which the two critical wings of the party sometimes found themselves in relation to the centre, demonstrated that these disagreements over direction were not so much between pragmatic reformers and revolutionary Marxists. It was more the case that the warring front ran between those, be it on the left or right, who demanded action, and those who insisted on retaining the traditional strategies and tactics. The political ideas of the latter had been shaped by the experiences of Imperial Germany, and by thinking in terms of organisational power. Discipline and the unity of the movement were values which they would not gamble away lightly. Cautious jockeying for position, tolerance of the lesser evil, and waiting for the next elections were the defining measure of their politics.

As Julius Leber put it so bitterly[17], even the meteoric rise in the Nazi vote on 14 September 1930 was unable to prompt any decisive change of tack. Amongst the SPD rank and file, on the other hand, this alarm signal triggered a wave of militant impulses. Younger supporters in particular were not content to stick with the old and trusted methods: they were urging that the Nazi civil war troops be confronted with a democracy prepared to defend itself by force.

The "Alliance of Republican Front-Line Soldiers", founded by the SPD, Centre Party, and the German Democratic Party in 1924, became the backbone of these efforts as the *Reichsbanner Schwarz – Rot – Gold*.[18] Just six

16 See the essay by Hans Mommsen quoted in footnote 9.
17 Julius Leber, Ein Mann geht seinen Weg, p. 238.
18 On the Reichsbanner, see Karl Rohe, Das Reichsbanner Schwarz – Rot – Gold. Ein Beitrag zur Geschichte und Struktur der politischen Kampfverbände zur Zeit der Weimarer Republik (Düsseldorf 1966).

days after the Reichstag elections, the Reichsbanner, which in practice had become an outstanding peace-keeping force for the Republic, decided to set up a powerful protection unit. The trade unions, too, began to create similar units, the *Hammerschaften*. At the end of 1931 these democratic combat units merged with workers' sports organisations to form the Iron Front. According to Julius Leber, this initiative had the same effect on the "nameless masses of the old Bebel party" as would an "old, half-forgotten signal to attack on battle-hardened soldiers used to winning"[19]. The Iron Front underlined its desire to stand up to the fascists with mass demonstrations. Along with preparations for self-defence and to protect party and trade-union premises, precautionary measures were taken in various places, particularly Magdeburg, against the eventuality of civil war. The SPD in the Reichstag called upon workers' organisations to be prepared to support the parliamentary struggle for democracy and the securing of the interests of society "by every appropriate means"[20].

For a time, the exhilarating effect of this mood of awakening disguised real weaknesses. The Iron Front made barely any impact beyond the Social Democratic camp, and even within the SPD there were reservations about an extra-parliamentary, para-military organisation of this kind, as well as about the use of violence in general. Neither the Reichsbanner nor the Iron Front was a genuinely effective fighting force. At bottom, they were no more than useful auxiliaries who would stand by the Republic in an emergency. Most Social Democrats clung to the belief that the state had a monopoly on force. They trusted it to use the powers at its disposal to overturn any putsch by the National Socialists.

Their hopes rested mainly on the republican "bulwark" Prussia where, with Carl Severing as Interior Minister and Albert Grzesinski as Chief of Police, Social Democrats were operating the police's levers of power. But on a single day, control of this "fortress" was ripped from their hands. After the Prussian elections of 24 April 1932, which left the coalition parties in a minority, the cabinet, as in other states in the Reich, only remained in government in a caretaker capacity. Otto Braun, whose energy and decisiveness distinguished him from many other Weimar politicians, went on sick leave on 6 June, overcome with resignation, and with the "firm intention of never returning to office"[21]. He felt totally unsure of himself after the election defeat, and was left a broken man.

19 Julius Leber, Ein Mann geht seinen Weg, p. 240.
20 Quoted from the "Kochel-Brief" of May/June 1955, p. 43. See also Matthias, 'The Social Democratic Party', in Das Ende der Parteien, p. 121.
21 Otto Braun, Von Weimar zu Hitler, p. 396.

On 20 July 1932, Papen delivered the *coup de grace*. He lured the representatives of the Prussian cabinet to the Reich Chancellery and used Hindenburg's *carte blanche* decree to depose Braun and Severing. The burden of responsibility at this moment was borne principally by Minister of the Interior Carl Severing. This illegal suspension from office and the takeover of power by Reich Commissar Papen, who had barely any backing in parliament, was met by Severing with the proud statement that it was force alone which had made him yield.[22] The declaration of a state of emergency in Berlin and the surrounding area, and placing the Prussian police under the regional commanders of the Reichswehr, passed off without a hitch. Following the arrest of the Berlin Chief of Police Grzesinski and the Commander of Police, Severing cleared his office that same evening. The tactics of the politically utterly ruthless Papen had proved to be somewhat different from those of the SPD.

Already days before, the party executive had discussed the feared attack on Prussia and consoled itself with the information from the Reich Chancellery that nothing was planned "for the time being". There had been enough advance warnings. Nevertheless, the news of the "Prussian *coup*" had a paralysing shock effect on the session convened on 20 July, and attended by Otto Wels, Franz Künstler from the party organisation in Berlin, Theodor Leipart, chairman of the ADGB, and the head of the Reichsbanner, Karl Höltermann. "The news", in Wels's description, "left us all depressed. There was not a word of outrage, no visible sign of disquiet. I had the impression that no one had the remotest idea what to do".[23] The chances of a political general strike were deemed to be nonexistent. National Socialists and Communists opposed them, as did the government and the Reichswehr. It was thought that a general strike would only provoke an immediate military dictatorship. The reaction of the SPD and the leaders of the trade unions to the *coup d'état* was encapsulated in Wels's slogan, "Safeguard the Reichstag Election on 31 July".

This response was often pilloried, particularly in retrospect, as failure and spineless capitulation. But it was not just Otto Wels and the SPD party executive, Theodor Leipart and the ADGB, but also Karl Höltermann of the Reichsbanner who rejected active resistance. In view of the desolate situation and the armies of unemployed, the prerequisites for a political general strike were decidedly poor, not to say potentially disas-

---

22 On this and the following, see especially: Winkler, Der Weg in die Katastrophe, pp. 646–680; Hans J.L. Adolph, Otto Wels und die Politik der deutschen Sozialdemokratie 1894–1939 (Berlin 1971), pp. 240ff.
23 In a handwritten note by Otto Wels 'Um den 20. Juli 1932. Einige Erinnerungen', quoted from Adolph, Otto Wels, p. 243.

trous. It seemed more than doubtful whether any show of force by the Iron Front might achieve anything. Challenging the state machine, as well as the bulk of the population, seemed hopeless: it was a battle lost even before it had begun. Admittedly, here and there, units of the Iron Front were awaiting their marching orders, and workers in the factories the signal for a general strike. But the clarion call to defend the Republic never came. No one at the top wanted, as Severing put it, "to be courageous at the cost of the comrades".[24] The seeming futility of active resistance, the possibility of a disastrous bloodbath, paralysed both the trade-union and party leadership. Moulded by a long, humanitarian and democratic tradition, schooled in the practice of realpolitik and the avoidance of experiments, anchored firmly in the conviction that the main priority was to keep the organisation as intact as possible, they went to the state Court of Justice, invoking in time-honoured fashion the power of the ballot box in the forthcoming Reichstag elections of 31 July 1933.

Apart from the elections of March 1933, which were no longer free, these elections brought the National Socialists their greatest success. Encouraged by the smoothness of Papen's *coup d'état*, the right-wing antidemocratic forces gambled more than ever on achieving their ends by surprise and sheer cold-blooded force. Typical of this is Joseph Goebbels's diary entry for 20 July 1932: "Everything goes off according to plan. [...] You only have to bare your teeth at the 'Reds', and they come to heel". A day later he notes: "The 'Reds' have let slip their opportunity. They will never have another."[25] The moment had arrived for National Socialism to mount its decisive onslaught on the Republic.

The lack of any concerted defensive action on 20 July proved a death blow to the will of democracy to assert itself. Nothing, not even failure, could have had a more paralysing effect than the SPD and trade-union leaders giving up without a fight. But to be fair to them, one has to bear in mind that by 1932, the Social Democrats, the most reliable and consistent supporters of parliamentary democracy, were virtually alone in still upholding the principles laid down in the Weimar constitution. The strength of the SPD, however, was merely relative to the other representatives of democracy who were barely able to keep their heads above water. With a share of just over 20 per cent of the vote in 1932, the Social Democrats were more than ever thrown back on their own resources. Despair and lethargy, however, were rife both amongst the rank and file and the leader-

24 See Carl Severing, Mein Lebensweg, vol. 2 (Cologne 1950), pp. 347 ff.
25 See Joseph Goebbels, Vom Kaiserhof zur Reichskanzlei (Munich 1934), pp. 131 ff. For an English version of this, see Dr. Joseph Goebbels, My Part in Germany's Fight (London 1935). Translation by Dr. Kurt Fiedler.

ship. The authority of the democratic constitutional state, which the Social Democrats had built on up until the Prussian coup, lay shattered. They could no longer expect any effective help from the state in their struggle against the superior National Socialists, and the majority of people were against them. There was no way out of the dilemma for the weakened band of Social Democrats prepared to defend Germany's fundamental constitutional and democratic order. They consoled themselves with the thought that the SPD "had gone through worse times", and in the course of its development had "successfully overcome many a danger [...], and many an adversary"[26]. Under attack from all sides, the Social Democrats fought on two fronts: with socialist slogans against the social injustices of the capitalist system, and with democratic and rational maxims against the irrational agitation of the fascists. It was precisely their deeply rooted belief in the principles of reason and humanity, of justice and the rule of law, which made it difficult for them to grasp the essential nature of the Nazi movement. They braced themselves against the danger, and sought to prevent Hitler taking power. But despite their passionate condemnation of National Socialism, the Social Democrats failed to recognise the totalitarian nature of German fascism, which never for a moment considered respecting the principles of law and liberty, but trampled on them, having no scruples whatsoever about the murderous use of violence and terror against their opponents.[27] The few months still remaining to the Social Democrats after the Prussian *coup* offered no real chance of fending off, at the last moment, the Hitler movement's attempt to seize power. With the *Machtübernahme*, the taking over of power, on 30 January 1933 the dark night of dictatorship descended over Germany.

---

26 This from Rudolf Breitscheid, inter alia, in his address to the Leipzig party conference in 1931: 'Die Überwindung des Faschismus', Sozialdemokratischer Parteitag in Leipzig 1931 vom 31. Mai bis 5. Juni 1931 im Volkshaus, Protokoll (Berlin 1931), pp. 119 ff.
27 In the light of this, the verdict of Franz Walter – in Die SPD. Vom Proletariat zur Neuen Mitte (Berlin 2002), p. 81 f. – that the SPD majority had been "under no illusion about the character of National Socialism", does not hold true. This even applies to the "acute analyses of modern right-wing dictatorships" which he lists.

IX. The Struggle for a Better Germany

1. Resisting Totalitarian "Gleichschaltung" (Co-ordination)

On the afternoon and evening of 30 January 1933, as the columns of SA marched baying and intoxicated with victory through the streets, there were spontaneous mass demonstrations against Hitler by socialist supporters in several larger cities. The next day meetings took place in Berlin of the highest SPD and trade-union (ADGB) bodies, as well as representatives of the Iron Front. Scepticism and resignation prevailed: no provision was made for one last, desperate act of defiance. Nevertheless, and despite checks by the SA auxiliary police, individual groups continued to make preparations for acts of resistance. Night after night, many slept in their clothes, awaiting the signal to strike back. But the terror which the National Socialists inflicted, with the backing of the state, had a visibly intimidating effect on people's will to resist. After the Reichstag fire, Hindenburg's decree of 28 February for the Protection of People and State abolished important basic rights and engineered sweeping special powers for the Hitler government. The Nazi tyranny became increasingly uninhibited. Violence was used in the suppression and persecution of the Communist Party and the mass arrests of its functionaries, bans were imposed on the Social Democratic press in the election campaign, meetings were prohibited or disrupted, many SPD officials were beaten up and arrested. Prisons were full to overflowing, and the first of the concentration camps (Dachau) appeared in March. Despite all the aggravations, Social Democrat voters in the elections of 5 March 1933 demonstrated almost to a man their loyalty to the party. Some 7.181 million voters, just 66,400 less than in November 1932, had the courage even now to stand by their party. Some 4.8 million still showed their allegiance to the KPD, but the government simply excluded their 81 elected deputies and had them arrested. Their Reichstag mandates were not formally revoked until 31 March 1933.

On 23 March 1933, in the Kroll Opera House where the Reichstag rump was sitting, Hitler secured himself the phoney legal basis for the construction of his totalitarian system of government. Along with the NSDAP and DNVP, the German People's Party, the State Party (the former DDP), the Centre Party, the Bavarian People's Party, and the splinter parties all voted for the *Ermächtigungsgesetz* (Enabling Law). Not a single

136

one of their members voted against, none abstained. The Centre, BVP, DVP, and State Party would not even support an SPD motion to release the imprisoned deputies. The Social Democrats were beseeched by the parliamentary parties of the so-called "bourgeois centre", either not to attend the sitting, or to abstain in the vote on the Enabling Law. The SPD stood firm, even though the first of their 120 deputies were already behind bars, and others were only able to avoid the threat of being arrested by fleeing. Wilhelm Sollmann, a former Minister of State, lay badly beaten in hospital. Julius Leber and Carl Severing[1] were arrested on their way to the building. To reach the chamber, the Social Democrat deputies had to run the gauntlet of gangs of Nazis, and on arriving were immediately surrounded by armed SS and SA. Ninety-four SPD deputies were able to take part in the Reichstag sitting, and when the roll was called, ninety-four gave their courageous and unforgettable "No" to the vote on the Enabling Law.

The party chairman Otto Wels rose to speak on their behalf. Urgent warnings had been unable to dissuade him from taking on this dangerous task. As he stepped up to the rostrum, the baying of the Nazi mobs outside could be clearly heard. He defied the Nazi philosophy of terror and violence with the SPD credo: "They can rob us of our lives and freedom, but not of our honour". In full view of the SS with their murderous threats, Wels concluded his speech with the following declaration:

"The Weimar Constitution is not a socialist constitution. But we stand by the principles of the rule of law, equal rights, and social justice which are enshrined in it. At this historical hour, we German Social Democrats solemnly pledge ourselves to the principles of humanity and justice, of freedom and socialism. No Enabling Law can give you the power to destroy ideas which are eternal and indestructible. You yourselves have professed belief in socialism. The Anti-Socialist Law did not destroy social democracy. And German social democracy can also draw fresh strength from this most recent persecution. We greet the persecuted and oppressed. We greet our friends in the Reich. Their steadfastness and loyalty deserve our admiration. The courage of their beliefs, their undaunted optimism, give promise for a brighter future."[2]

Otto Wels's speech is one of the great historical testimonies to freedom and humanity, courage in one's beliefs, and the will to resist. Nevertheless, it cannot be ignored that the brutality and single-mindedness of Hitlerite

---

1   Severing managed to get free before the end of the Reichstag sitting, and was able to take part in the vote.
2   Stenographische Berichte über die Verhandlungen des Deutschen Reichstages, vol. 457, p. 33f.

fascism was still being underestimated. The frequent comparison, used again here by Wels, of the Nazi regime with the Anti-Socialist Law, revealed that the Social Democrats were still barely capable of imagining the true horror of totalitarian rule. Many of them were still hoping that the lawlessness was only temporary, and that National Socialism would remain a short-lived episode. This resulted – particularly in the trade unions, but even in the party – in an attempt to do everything possible to keep the organisations intact. Under Leipart's leadership, the ADGB sought to maintain its independence by distancing itself from the SPD and adopting a neutral stance towards the state and its regime. This policy of accommodation, whose most vociferous opponent was Siegfried Aufhäuser of the white-collar workers' union (AfA), was rejected by the SPD leadership. It was also a tactic which had not helped the unions one jot. After several trade-union offices had been attacked in the weeks leading up to 1 May 1933, the SA and SS occupied all trade-union premises in one fell swoop on 2 May 1933. Dozens of officials were arrested, beaten up, or, as in Duisburg, murdered.

This blow led the SPD party executive to expect a similar, sudden onslaught on them. On 10 May, party assets were confiscated. After Otto Braun and Albert Grzesinski, Philipp Scheidemann and Wilhelm Dittmann, Artur Crispein, Rudolf Breitscheid, and Rudolf Hilferding had already been forced to emigrate, the party executive now sent three of its members, Otto Wels, Siegmund Crummenerl and Friedrich Stampfer to Saarbrücken which was still under French administration. Hans Vogel, Erich Ollenhauer, and Paul Hertz had to follow them a few days later. When, on 17 May 1933, the parliamentary party in the Reichstag voted in favour of a "peace resolution", this provoked conflict with the executive majority in exile. The remnants of the parliamentary party consisting of only 65 of the 120 deputies found themselves in a dilemma, after a majority, in the face of resistance from a minority to which Kurt Schumacher belonged, had voted to take part in the sitting. Hitler's government statement had been dripping with waffle about peace and willingness to come to an understanding. The SPD parliamentary group were denied their own resolution which welcomed the calls for equal rights, but simultaneously censured the outrages and repression being perpetrated by the regime. This had the effect of provoking open death threats from Frick, the Nazi Interior Minister. Paul Gerlach put it in a nutshell: "Either we set the world an example by standing under the *Siegessäule* (the victory column in Berlin) and shooting ourselves collectively in the head, or we have to vote for the government statement in the Reichstag. There's no third way."[3] Voting in favour on 17 May reflected badly on the SPD, casting a shadow over the moral credit gained by rejecting the Enabling Law. It was illusory to think that clinging to the facade of parliamentary democracy would lessen the terror and rein in the Hitler regime.

The exiled party executive now moved to Prague to intensify its underground resistance work. The conflict with the rump executive in the Reichstag under Paul Löbe, who still subscribed to the fiction of the regime's legality, was rapidly overtaken by events. On 21 June, Interior Minister Frick proscribed all SPD activity on the grounds that they had insufficiently distanced themselves from the "treasonable" activities of the party executive in exile. On 14 July 1933, the party was officially banned. With any form of legal party work now at an end, the roots of the dispute between Prague and Berlin also disappeared. In the struggle against Hitlerite fascism, all that remained was to go underground, or emigrate.

2. Resistance in the Labour Movement

With the exception of some specialised academic studies, the resistance of German workers to Hitler was for a long period of barely any public interest in the Federal Republic. This was due not only to lack of knowledge and a one-sided focus on 20 July 1944. Rather did it mirror a specific self-image of the Federal Republic in which, in so far as there was any interest at all in resistance, it was examined only as it had manifested itself in Church, conservative, and military circles. The resistance amongst SPD and Communist workers, to which the other, SED-led German state laid claim, was largely excluded from traditional research in the Federal Republic.

Under the totalitarian regime, not only active resistance was a threat to the system, but every manifestation of oppositional behaviour – from political jokes and listening to foreign radio, to refusal to work and helping the persecuted. When three to four thousand old party colleagues attended the funeral in May 1936 of the former SPD Reichstag deputy Clara Bohm-Schuch, this was not only an expression of personal courage, but also a demonstration of unbroken solidarity.[4]

---

3 For more detail, see Winkler, Der Weg in die Katastrophe, pp. 932ff. On p. 127 of his Geschichte eines Deutschen (Stuttgart/Munich 2001), Sebastian Haffner makes false accusations. See Heinrich Potthoff, in Die Neue Gesellschaft/Frankfurter Hefte, no. 1/2 (2002), pp. 79ff.

4 See Frank Moraw, Die Parole der "Einheit" und die Sozialdemokratie (Bonn-Bad Godesberg 1973), p. 44.

Despite the oppression and temptations, the Social Democratic community proved at first to be remarkably stable. In the works committee elections of April 1933, the first results for the National Socialist Factory-Cell Organisation (NSBO) were so unsatisfactory that the elections were halted. A count of the incomplete results showed that the Free Trade Unions had won 73.4 per cent of the votes cast. And again, the shop stewards' elections of 1934 and 1935 produced such negative figures for the Nazis that they had to resort to manipulating and falsifying the results. There was no question of these being free and secret elections. The workers were going to be forced to vote for the single list of the German Labour Front (DAF), the National Socialist monopoly organisation. Nevertheless, many still had the courage to vote against the DAF. After this, the National Socialists decided to abandon altogether the use of the ballot box in factory elections.[5]

There is a clear reflection in Gestapo reports of unrest amongst the work force, and criticism of political and social conditions under the Nazi regime. They reveal the myth of a single "national community", united in combat, to be mendacious propaganda. Even though it is not possible to equate symptoms of disgruntlement such as this with resistance, its basis was nonetheless "considerably broader than can be assumed and observed by outsiders. Committed Social Democrats were able to maintain contact with one another even without the organisation."[6] That alone, under the swastika, was a moral victory. But even the labour force proved not to be immune. With the disappearance of unemployment and successes in foreign policy, not least with the *Anschluß* (annexation) of Austria, Hitler had clearly become popular, even with German workers, and it was only a minority who rejected the Nazi regime completely.[7]

Even before Hitler's seizure of power, a number of Social Democratic groups had begun to make provision for going underground should they be banned. The idea for this had come, amongst others, from Otto Wels. The main impetus, however, for the formation of Social Democratic resistance groups came from local initiatives. Since May 1933, activity by

---

5 On works committee elections, see Theodor Eschenburg, 'Streiflichter zur Geschichte der Wahlen im Dritten Reich, Dokumentation', in Vierteljahrshefte für Zeitgeschichte 3 (1955), pp. 311 ff. There are various other studies which give information about individual results.
6 See Ludwig Bergsträsser, Geschichte der politischen Parteien in Deutschland (Munich 10th edn 1960), p. 297.
7 For a comprehensive account, see Michael Schneider, Unter dem Hakenkreuz. Arbeiter und Arbeiterbewegung 1933 bis 1939 (Bonn 1999).

groups working covertly had been on the increase.[8] Without the approval of the remnants of the SPD executive which had remained in Berlin, and was still clinging desperately to the notion of working within the law, individual sections of the party began to adapt to the underground struggle. First and foremost, sections of the Socialist Labour Youth (SAJ), the Reichsbanner, or Iron Front, and the Social Democratic student movement attempted – notwithstanding the conditions of Nazi rule – to stick together as closely as possible. Although under often only very flimsy disguise, they initially had a somewhat better chance of oppositional activity than older and more prominent Social Democrats who were well known to the authorities and the Nazis. They were held to be suspicious from the beginning, as is demonstrated by the case of Franz Klühs, the editor in chief of *Vorwärts*, who quickly fell victim to the Nazi state.

It has proved hard to measure precisely the full extent of Social Democratic resistance to the Hitlerite dictatorship. The "White Paper on German Opposition to the Hitler Dictatorship", published by the SPD in exile (Sopade) in 1946, offers some informative insights.[9] In addition to the Reich capital Berlin and the traditional SPD regions of Thuringia and Saxony with their numerous cells, the main, known centres of resistance were in the Rhine-Main-Neckar region, Stuttgart, Nuremberg, Munich, Cologne, and the Ruhr. A well-organised group, the Socialist Front, which had undergone thorough preparations well before the Nazi seizure of power to work underground, operated in Hanover under the leadership of Werner Blumenberg. It had roughly 3,000 reliable, active members. Despite taking every precaution, a great number of them fell into the hands of the Gestapo in 1936. Over 200 men and women were convicted in a show trial and given long prison sentences.[10] At the end of 1937, the

8   For the overall picture see, principally: Richard Löwenthal and Patrik von zur Mühlen (eds), Widerstand und Verweigerung in Deutschland 1933 bis 1945 (Berlin/Bonn 1982); Günter Weisenborn (ed.), Der lautlose Aufstand, Bericht über die Widerstandsbewegung des deutschen Volkes 1933–1945 (Hamburg 2nd edn 1954); Peter Grasmann, Sozialdemokraten gegen Hitler 1933–1945 (Munich/Vienna 1976); Hans-Joachim Reichardt, 'Möglichkeiten und Grenzen des Widerstandes der Arbeiterbewegung', in Walter Schmitthenner and Hans Buchheim (eds), Der deutsche Widerstand gegen Hitler (Cologne and Berlin 1966), pp. 169–213. This latter volume is available in English translation as The German Resistance to Hitler (London 1970). For studies of local resistance see: Hans-Josef Steinberg, Widerstand und Verfolgung in Essen 1933–1945 (Hanover 1969); Kurt Klotzbach, Gegen den Nationalsozialismus. Widerstand und Verfolgung in Dortmund 1930–1945. Eine historisch-politische Studie (Hanover 1969).
9   Weißbuch der deutschen Opposition gegen die Hitlerdiktatur, published by the executive committee of the SPD (London 1946).
10 See Moraw, Die Parole der Einheit, p. 37; Günter Weisenborn, Der lautlose Aufstand, pp. 141 and 179.

Red Shock Troop (RS), which was structured along similar lines with roughly the same numbers and operated mainly in the Berlin area, was smashed.

In the overall spectrum of democratic, socialist resistance, the splinter groups, which in 1933 kept a critical distance from the party executive, and were even outside the party itself, have a particular importance. Their greater militancy, a much more realistic assessment of fascism, as well as their organisational structure which was often based on the cell principle, made them much better equipped for the underground struggle than the SPD organisations. The International Socialist Combat League (ISK), for instance, despite great sacrifices of lives and freedom, was initially able to make some impact. The Gestapo situation report for 1937 records "some considerable activity. [...] Typical of the ISK pamphlets is the symbol at the end of them which depicts a swastika hanging from a gallows."[11]

In addition to the SAP[12], which had its main roots in Saxony, of particular prominence was a group which became known under the name *Neu Beginnen* (New Beginning). Initially a clandestine organisation of oppositional Communists and critical young socialists, their influence grew in spring 1933 when the Socialist Labour Youth (SAJ) in Berlin prepared to go underground, at first against the wishes of the SPD executive rump. The cooperation between the numerically small *Neu Beginnen* and the majority of the Berlin SAJ formed the basis for an independently operating unit. The group was led, firstly, by Walter Löwenheim (pseudonym Miles), and later by Richard Löwenthal (pseudonym Paul Sering), and worked intensively, and with success, to create effective methods of underground activity and a close collaboration with the SPD in exile.[13] The young Fritz Erler, an SAJ official, also worked with this group. He was arrested in 1938, and sentenced to ten years imprisonment the following year. The apparatus of resistance, organised decentrally by *Neu Beginnen*, lasted until 1944, when it fell victim to the regime. A great number of the leaders of the individual groups were executed. Amongst trade-union ranks, the efforts of the opponents of Nazism after 2 May 1933 were initially directed at maintaining solidarity, creating a clandestine information network, and

---

11 Quoted from Weisenborn, Der lautlose Aufstand, p. 152.
12 On this, see Jörg Bremer, Der Sozialistische Arbeiterpartei Deutschlands (SAP). Untergrund und Exil 1933–1945 (Frankfurt/M.-New York 1978).
13 On Neu Beginnen, see Kurt Kliem, Der sozialistische Widerstand gegen das Dritte Reich, dargestellt an der Gruppe "Neu-Beginnen", typewritten PhD thesis (Marburg 1957). Also Hans-Joachim Reichardt, 'Neu Beginnen. Ein Beitrag zur Geschichte des Widerstandes der Arbeiterbewegung gegen den Nationalsozialismus', in Jahrbuch für die Geschichte Mittel- und Ostdeutschlands (Sonderdruck), vol. 12, 1963.

establishing contact between different resistance groups. With increasing pressure and persecution, it became ever more important to demonstrate at home and abroad that there was another, different Germany. Railwaymen and transport workers round Hans Jahn and Adolph Kummernuss, as well as the International Federation of Transport Workers, supported and encouraged by the Secretary General Edo Fimmen, became especially active in the struggle against the Nazi regime. After its proscription, the Communist Party attempted initially to mount its resistance on the basis of the old organisational structure. The campaign against Hitler, conducted with extraordinary energy and readiness to take risks, paid a high price in human lives. The courage and loyal conviction of many Communists did not prevent their resistance cells being infiltrated by spies and the Gestapo. With the mass arrests, the accommodation of the KPD to Moscow's Popular Front strategy, and the sudden shift to the Hitler-Stalin pact, the basis for a large-scale offensive collapsed. Resistance intensified once more after the attack on the Soviet Union, but it now lacked the broad impact of earlier.

If only for security reasons, it was vital for all resistance groups to draw on support from former political and trade-union alliances. Alongside the SPD's underground organisations, there were those such as the socialist trade unions, the Working Men's Sports Association, the *Reichsbanner*, the SAP, ISK, *Neu Beginnen*, Christian trade unions and employees, and KPD and Communist trade-union opposition groups. The common goal of the fight against Hitler and the mortal danger that threatened all opponents of Nazism created a feeling of closeness. This contributed to the dismantling of old prejudices and the relativisation of political differences in the battle being fought. Although there were strong reservations amongst the supporters of social democracy about the methods and goals of the KPD, independently operating resistance organisations began to cooperate in ways which transcended all party boundaries. In the "Saefkow" Group, for instance, one of the most widely spread groups, Social Democrat and Communist workers cooperated with opponents of Hitler from bourgeois circles.

Most resistance groups from the Social Democratic camp were primarily concerned, through dissemination of information, to keep democratic awareness alive and to unmask the Nazi terror regime. This was done by means of leaflets and pamphlets, which were either distributed clandestinely, or found their way into streets and factories at a given moment. These publications were partly self-produced. The groups used what connections they had with the exiles as a source of material. Until the war brought an end to all contact, enormous quantities of brochures were smuggled into Germany and distributed there – mostly disguised under various, different imprints and titles. One of the most impressive and shattering examples is the report on Oranienburg concentration camp by the SPD party executive in Prague. In it, the former SPD Reichstag deputy Gerhart Seger[14], who was one of the few who managed to escape, revealed early on the horror of the concentration camps.

Helping the persecuted and those threatened with prison, concentration camp, and the hangman, was another crucial task for the resistance fighters. An example of this emerges in 1944 from the verdict delivered in the People's Court by the notorious Nazi judge Roland Freisler, against the group "European Union" who had taken up the cause of foreign forced labour:

"What a shameless attitude has been displayed by the accused. It seems that they have been systematically supporting Jews living under cover, and have even been fattening them up. But not only that, they even provided them with false passports to disguise their identity from the police, as if they were Germans, not Jews. […] Another pamphlet proclaims with wordy phrases that the "European Union" is fighting together with the SPD, the SAP, and KPD, but also that they do not spurn help from representatives of the bourgeois political tendency. Even more clearly than the manifesto, the leaflets churn out all the old mendacious principles of human rights in the Weimar Constitution, and even go as far as saying that they are counting on the masses of foreign workers [sic!] in Germany."[15]

The resistance fighters' lack of conspiratorial experience and organisational techniques often allowed Hitler's police to quickly track them down. By the middle of the 1930s, the Gestapo had succeeded in smashing most of the early Social Democratic resistance groups. Thousands of people were arrested, others managed to escape in the nick of time by fleeing abroad or going into hiding with friends and colleagues. In the first year of the Nazi state the "Statistical Yearbook of the German Reich" recorded 20,565 political convictions. Designed to intimidate, they resulted mainly from the emergency decrees for the "Protection of People and State", to "combat political extremism", for the "Defence against attacks on the Government of National Revival", and also on the grounds of

14 Gerhart Seger, Oranienburg. Erster authentischer Bericht eines aus dem Konzentrationslagers Geflüchteten. Mit einem Geleitwort von Heinrich Mann (Karlsbad 1934); see also the documentation produced by the SPD executive in exile: Konzentrationslager. Ein Appell an das Gewissen der Welt. Ein Buch der Greuel. Die Opfer klagen an (Karlsbad 1934).
15 Quoted from Weisenborn, Der lautlose Aufstand, p. 169.

"high treason", and the "Law on weapons and ammunition". The main victims of this Nazi justice in the early years were followers of the socialist workers' movement. They included KPD functionaries, members of socialist splinter groups, leading Social Democrats such as Paul Löbe and resolute anti-fascist fighters such as the young Kurt Schumacher, members of active resistance groups, and those who openly expressed at work their opinion of the Hitlerite dictatorship. In its original form, resistance from the labour movement was almost crushed by the heavy onslaught by the Gestapo. In 1936 alone, 11,687 people were arrested for illegal socialist activity. Then around 1937, having benefited from its earlier experiences, the anti-fascist resistance launched new initiatives. These were based for the most part on a cell system of groups of three, four, or five, so that even if individual groups were arrested the resistance work of the others could continue.

"A new generation of resistance fighters who were young, experienced, and with no illusions, joined the groups. "Hard" groups were formed which covered their tracks so carefully that over many long years they escaped being caught – an enormous achievement, bearing in mind how all-powerful the Gestapo was."[16]

All in all, this resistance "from below" came at a high price. Thousands paid for their courageous commitment to freedom, justice, and their fellow human beings, with prison, torture and their lives. Sober statistics convey virtually nothing of the enormous suffering and willingness to make sacrifices, of the struggle against oppression and tyranny, of the help for the persecuted and endangered, of the man and woman who rescued a Jew from the clutches of the Nazi thugs, saving him or her from certain death. Who can still recall a Gestapo statistic of 10 April 1939 recording 302,562 political prisoners? By far the largest contingent of political prisoners held by the Nazi regime came from the labour movement. Among the tens of thousands who were executed was an especially large number of Communists. According to a report from the Reich Ministry of Justice, 11,881 death sentences were carried out in accordance with supposedly "legitimate" court decisions between 1933 and 1944. Military justice and special courts, particularly in the last months of the war, sent countless people to their deaths. This list of victims as yet includes none of those who would perish in concentration camps and prisons, or who were executed in connection with the attempted assassination of Hitler on 20 July 1944.[17] This latter "rebellion of conscience" has been

16 Ibid., p. 146.
17 See, inter alia, Bruno Gebhardt, Handbuch der deutschen Geschichte (Stuttgart 9th edn, vol. 4, part 2 1976), pp. 570, 572 and 579; see the article by Manfred Funke in

given due acknowledgement. The "silent rebellion" of the army of the nameless, the burden of which rested mainly on the shoulders of men and women in the labour movement, has, on the other hand, received scant attention. The "book of commemoration" for those who were persecuted for being Social Democrats, and often lost their lives, sends out a clear signal here.[18]

In the midst of a brutal war, the International Trades Union Association was already remembering these victims. At a rally of the "Union of German Socialist Organisations in Great Britain" on 29 January 1943, Secretary General Walter Schevenels expressed his thanks for the courageous efforts of the socialist labour movement in Germany. His words my be read as recognition of all those who actively resisted National Socialism and fought for a Germany of freedom and democracy, social justice and humanity:

"Today, it is too easily forgotten that hundreds of German workers lost their lives in these battles, that tens of thousands risked their lives. It is true that the German labour movement made mistakes and showed weaknesses, but it is not true to claim that our German comrades did not fight. [...] I would like to say one more word for our anti-Nazi fighters in Germany. Before I left Germany, I had a conference with our German colleagues. One week later most of those who attended this conference were arrested. I shall never forget the conference. In the crowded room, the chairman shook my hand and said: 'You are now returning to the free world. Say to our friends that whatever mistakes we made in the past, we were always honest and upright in our endeavours. Tell them that we will remain true to our beliefs, and that they should never forget us.' I can say today that the majority of German workers have kept their word."[19]

Men such as Kurt Schumacher, Julius Leber, Wilhelm Leuschner, Carlo Mierendorff, Theodor Haubach, Gustav Dahrendorf, Adolf Reichwein, and very many others exemplified the Social Democrats' unbroken spirit of resistance. Imprisonment and concentration camp could not deter them from continuing and renewing their struggle against the injustices of the regime. Even under these appalling conditions they managed to mount new initiatives. In Buchenwald concentration camp near Weimar, a Communist-led prisoners' organisation operated over many years. In February 1944, Hermann Brill and Ernst Thape (both SPD) formed a popular front

---

    Widerstand und Exil 1933–1945 (Bonn 1985), pp. 60–75, esp. p. 66; Weisenborn, p. 149, and Grasmann, Sozialdemokraten gegen Hitler, p. 109f.
18 Der Freiheit verpflichtet. Gedenkbuch der deutschen Sozialdemokratie im 20. Jahrhundert, edited and produced by the SPD Executive Committee (Marburg 2000).
19 Quoted in Weisenborn, Der lautlose Aufstand, p. 181f.

committee with Werner Hilpert (Centre Party, later CDU) and Walter Wolf (KPD) and worked out a programme for the "Buchenwald Manifesto" which was published after the liberation.[20]

His militant activity against National Socialism made Kurt Schumacher a particular object of Nazi hatred. When he was arrested in July 1933, the *Stuttgarter Zeitung* announced triumphantly that "one of the Social Democrats' leading and most shameless rabble-rousers has been put out of action"[21]. Seriously wounded in the war, there began for Schumacher ten years of suffering in prison cells, concentration camps, and finally in the infamous Neuengamme camp. Despite being tortured by the guards, Schumacher remained unbowed, and, through his courage and solidarity, won respect and authority amongst his fellow prisoners. With the Americans advancing, he was ordered to be shot, but managed to escape the Nazi henchmen in the nick of time.

Wilhelm Leuschner, deputy chairman of the disbanded ADGB, was prominent in the building up of a trade-union resistance organisation. Together with Jakob Kaiser from the Christian trade unions and Max Habermann of the Association of German Business Employees (DHV) he created the concept for the future of unified trade unions. They wanted to embark in unison on "the right path for the German people of a healthy synthesis of socialism and freedom"[22]. Leuschner's importance in the resistance movement is demonstrated by the fact that he was earmarked by the 20 July 1944 movement for the post of deputy Chancellor. He, like his friend Julius Leber, who was earmarked for the post of Minister of the Interior, had taken up early contact with the circle round Goerdeler, the former Mayor of Leipzig.

"The decision by trade unionists and Social Democrats who participated in the 20 July conspiracy that it was the generals who should precipitate the downfall of the system was correct. Previous historical experience of totalitarian or authoritarian regimes proves that a successful coup is impossible without the help of the military."[23]

20 Buchenwald. Mahnung und Verpflichtung (Frankfurt/M. 1960), pp. 394 ff.
21 Stuttgarter Zeitung, 12.7.1933. On Kurt Schumacher, see inter alia the biographies of Lewis J. Edinger, Kurt Schumacher, Persönlichkeit und politisches Verhalten (Cologne and Opladen 1967), pp. 80 ff. and esp. Peter Merseburger, Der schwierige Deutsche. Kurt Schumacher. Eine Biographie (Stuttgart 1995).
22 Quoted from Peter Hoffmann, Widerstand – Staatsstreich – Attentat (Munich 1969), p. 229.
23 Hans Mommsen, 'Gewerkschaften zwischen Anpassung und Widerstand', in Heinz Oskar Vetter (ed.), Vom Sozialistengesetz zur Mitbestimmung. Zum 100. Geburtstag von Hans Böckler (Cologne 1975), p. 297 f.

Leber was a personal friend of Colonel Claus Schenk von Stauffenberg, the leading military figure in the 20 July plot. An approach to Communist groups, which was observed by the Gestapo, led to the arrest of Leber and Reichwein. Concern that the plot would be blown led to Stauffenberg taking speedy action on 20 July 1944. This revolt by the "other Germany" failed. The vicious response of the Nazi police state afflicted those directly, and indirectly involved, as well as those who were neither. Before they fell victim to the hangman, these men were subjected to cruel and brutal interrogation. The words of Julius Leber, shortly before his execution on 3 January 1945 in Plötzensee, may serve as a fitting epitaph for Leuschner, Leber, Haubach, Reichwein (Mierendorff had been killed in an air raid), and many others: "The sacrifice of one's life is the appropriate price for such a good and just cause."[24] They gave their lives for those Social Democratic principles which had found such impressive formulation in 1933, "humanity and justice, freedom and socialism".[25]

3. The Path and Goals of Democratic Socialism in Exile

The words "emigration" and "émigré" had long carried undertones of reproach, seeming to imply that one should not simply abandon community and people to their fate when threatened by personal danger. Such reservations held sway for many years, and influenced the political climate. Those who adopted, blithely or maliciously, this argument, were either playing down the Nazi dictatorship, or were themselves prisoners of its philosophy of national community. None of those who fled Germany after 1933 left the country whose language they spoke, and where their roots were, with a light heart:

"Common to almost all émigrés who left the country, be it because of their political leanings or their Jewish origins – often both factors applied – did so because they felt their existences, their freedom, and their lives threatened by the dictatorship; and more than a few of them decided to flee only after they had made the acquaintance of terror and the regime's concentration camps and prisons."[26]

---

24 Julius Leber, Ein Mann geht seinen Weg, p. 295.
25 See the declaration of Otto Wels in the Reichstag on 23 March 1933 (note 1).
26 This from Erich Matthias in Mit dem Gesicht nach Deutschland. Eine Dokumentation über die sozialdemokratische Emigration. Aus dem Nachlass von Friedrich Stampfer ergänzt durch andere Überlieferungen, published by Erich Matthias, edited by Werner Link (Düsseldorf 1968), p. 8. Further important literature on exile as a whole and SPD emigration: Werner Röder, Die deutschen sozialistischen Exilgruppen in Großbritannien 1940–1945. Ein Beitrag zur Geschichte des Widerstandes gegen

For the Jewish refugees who, up until the onset of the "Final Solution" in October 1941, had been able to leave the Hitler Reich in time, there was no going back. As a result of Hitler's lightning conquests, tens of thousands who thought themselves safe fell into the clutches of the murderers.

The bulk of those emigrating had been persecuted because of their race, were Jewish citizens of a once free country who were now threatened with concentration and extermination camps. Roughly one in ten of all émigrés – Social Democrats and bourgeois democrats, Communists and pacifists, Christians and others – had had to leave Nazi Germany for mainly political reasons. The hard core of active opponents of Hitler was recruited mainly from this group. Exile for them was a political task: it was the basis for their struggle against the Nazi dictatorship and for a different, better Germany. Apart from those who emigrated to the Soviet Union, their numbers were dominated by democratic socialists.

After the banning of the SPD in June/July 1933 and the abrogation of their mandate in the Reichstag, the one remaining mouthpiece for the party was the executive committee in exile. It saw itself as representing the whole party and chose Prague as its base. It consisted of Otto Wels as chairman, Hans Vogel as vice-chairman, Siegmund Crummenerl as party treasurer, along with Friedrich Stampfer, Paul Hertz, Erich Ollenhauer, and, from autumn 1933, Siegfried Aufhäuser, the former chairman of the white-collar workers' union (AfA). The exile party executive saw its main task as "telling the world the truth" and putting itself at the service of clandestine activity back home.[27] This involved securing and providing finance, the provision of information material (often disguised as advertising brochures or editions of the *Reclam* classics), help for the victims of Nazism, as well as the attempt to open the eyes of the world to the nature of Hitler's dictatorship.

A network of sixteen "frontier secretariats" all round the borders of Germany maintained communication with representatives in the Reich, helping those carrying on the fight there. With Gerhart Seger's book on his experiences in Oranienburg and the documentation put together in 1934 on the other Nazi concentration camps, the exiled SPD endeavoured to arouse the conscience of the world. From 1934 on, the "Grüne Berich-

---

den Nationalsozialismus (Hanover 1968); Erich Matthias, Sozialdemokratie und Nation. Ein Beitrag zur Ideengeschichte der sozialdemokratischen Emigration in der Prager Zeit des Parteivorstandes 1933–1938 (Stuttgart 1952). Strangely, emigration is not dealt with at all in Arno Klönne's book, Die deutsche Arbeiterbewegung. Geschichte – Ziele – Wirkungen (Düsseldorf-Cologne 1980, new edn Munich 1989).

27 Neuer Vorwärts, 18.6.1933.

te" ("Green Reports")[28] edited by Erich Rinner appeared, in which information collected by contacts in the Reich were assembled and then passed on. They presented, notwithstanding understandable errors, an unvarnished picture of the harsh reality of the Nazi regime. The Social Democrats were set on countering Nazi violence and lies with the power of truth and enlightenment. "Hitler means war" was the main slogan in their battle against Hitlerite fascism before and after 1933. Stampfer, in *Neuer Vorwärts*, published in Prague, put it as follows: "If the whole of Europe is not to be reduced to rubble, with the mangled corpse of Germany buried beneath it, then we cannot simply sit back and watch as catastrophe approaches."[29]

The appeal to the "civilised world" to take a decisive stance against Hitler while there was still time, fell on deaf ears. Not only this, the great European powers regarded the warnings of the German Social Democrats as a disruption to their appeasement policy towards the Third Reich. As the British government admitted, reports were kept under lock and key so as not to cloud relations with Nazi Germany. Just as the hopes of action from abroad remained unfulfilled, so did the prospect under the circumstances of the Nazi dictatorship for a successful uprising in Germany. All the courage and dedication of the active opponents of the Nazi regime, who before the outbreak of war came predominantly from the socialist camp, could not alter the fact that an overthrow of Hitler rule by an isolated uprising from below was not possible.

The "Prague Manifesto" of the SPD, or Sopade (Social Democratic Party of Germany) as it now called itself, of 28 January 1934 evoked the revolutionary component of the struggle against Hitler. This programmatic statement by the executive committee in exile was a mixture of Marxist theories about the nature of the Nazi counter-revolution and up-to-the-minute political appeals to fight for peace and the "overthrow of despotism". "The unity and freedom of the German nation can only be saved by the conquering of German fascism." The appeal concluded with a commitment to the "great and unchanging ideas of mankind": "We do not wish to live without freedom, and we shall seize it. Freedom without class rule, freedom to the point where every last shred of exploitation and domination of one human being by another is abolished. [...] Through freedom to socialism, through socialism to freedom! Long live revolutionary German social democracy, long live the International!"[30]

28 So called because they were duplicated on green paper, the official title being "Reports from Germany". They have been published under the title: Die geheimen Deutschlandberichte der SPD 1934–1940, 7 vols (Frankfurt/Main 1980).
29 Neuer Vorwärts, 8.4.1934.
30 Reprinted in Stampfer, Mit dem Gesicht nach Deutschland, pp. 215 ff.

Konzentrationslager

Ein Appell an das Gewissen der Welt

Ein Buch der Greuel
Die Opfer klagen an

DACHAU — BRANDENBURG — PAPENBURG
KÖNIGSTEIN — LICHTENBURG — COLDITZ
SACHSENBURG — MORINGEN — HOHNSTEIN
REICHENBACH — SONNENBURG

Documentation by the Party Executive in Exile. The text reads: "Concentration Camps. An Appeal to the World's Conscience. A Book of Horrors. The Victims accuse: DACHAU – BRANDENBURG – PAPENBURG – KÖNIGSTEIN – LICHTENBURG – COLDITZ – SACHSENBURG – MORINGEN – HOHNSTEIN – REICHENBACH – SONNENBURG"

This avowal of faith in the revolutionary character of socialism was a reflection of circumstances. It was a product of the only conditions – i.e. revolutionary and subversive – under which the struggle against the Nazi dictatorship could be conducted. The rejection of compromises, reformism, and legality was, however, also a reflection of a new radicalism. It grew out of efforts to bring the splinter groups back into the fold of the old mother party. In the struggle against dictatorship, the uncompromising dedication of the Social Democrats to both cause and idea raised their profile.

In the exceptional situation in which socialists found themselves in exile, it was inevitable at first that differences old and new should erupt.

There were debates about the causes of the victory of fascism, about the failures and mistakes of democratic socialism in the past, as well as about the most effective ways of fighting National Socialism. Potentially explosive was the question of the extent to which Communists should be included in the united socialist front against Hitlerite fascism. The KPD's offer of a united front in November 1935 led, in part, to fierce controversy. Reaction varied from unconditional rejection, to partial cooperation, to hopes of healing the split in the socialist labour movement.

The working group "Revolutionary Socialists" with Karl Böchel formerly of the USPD, and Siegfried Aufhäuser of the AfA, demanded a radical break with all reformist traditions and the "class struggle of the united German proletariat".[31] In contrast to these ideas of the so-called "old left", which had disbanded again in 1937, the champions round Wilhelm Sollmann and Wenzel Jaksch of a "people's socialism" were propagating the repudiation of theories of class struggle and advocating the "patriotic socialism of Lassalle"[32].

In the case of the International Socialist Combat League (ISK), there were, initially, several obstacles in the way of a rapprochement: mainly old, as yet unhealed wounds, as well as ideological differences and the ISK's part in attempts to bring about a concentration of left-wing socialist exile groups. As late as 1939, the party executive pointed out the incompatibility of belonging to both organisations. There were lively, sometimes stormy debates with the "new left" focused on *Neu Beginnen*, to which, amongst others, Karl Frank, Richard Löwenthal (pseudonym Paul Sering), Waldemar von Knoeringen and Erwin Schoettle belonged. The Sopade executive were particularly bitter about the fact that one of its members, Paul Hertz, and other colleagues, had secretly worked for *Neu Beginnen* and that *Neu Beginnen* claimed to be a branch of German social democracy of equal status within the International.

The groups of socialist émigrés were scattered across many countries. Initially, their main centre was Czechoslovakia which offered them something approaching a second home. Ultimately, however, the Czechoslovakian government had to bow to pressure from Hitler, which became even stronger after the interventions of the British Prime Minister Neville Chamberlain who was seeking a settlement with the Third Reich. Sopade, along with their Austrian sister party, decided in 1938 to move to Paris.

---

31 See "Der Weg zum sozialistischen Deutschland/Plattform für die Einheitsfront", Zeitschrift für Sozialismus, Monatsschrift für die Probleme des Sozialismus, 12/13 (Karlsbad 1934), pp. 375 ff.
32 Wilhelm Sollmann's formulation, Zeitschrift für Sozialismus, 24/25 (Karlsbad 1935), p. 736.

In the Czechoslovakian Republic they had, as Friedrich Stampfer wrote, "breathed the air of freedom and found understanding friends. Things were now going to change. The word was passed from mouth to mouth: 'Our emigration is only just beginning'".[33]

What awaited the Social Democrats in Paris was described in a letter to the party executive from Rudolf Breitscheid, who had fled to France earlier: "Never have émigrés had to cope with so many difficulties as we have. We are, at least in France, nothing more than troublesome foreigners whom one would like to be rid of as quickly as possible."[34] With the German attack on France, things turned from bad to worse for émigrés who had dedicated themselves to the fight against Hitler and fascism. Influenced by widespread xenophobia towards "hostile foreigners", the Daladier government, who themselves had failed miserably in face of the Nazis' expansionist drive, now rounded up German nationals indiscriminately. While German troops surged ever deeper into France in a lightning campaign, tens of thousands of Germans who had had to fear for their lives at the hands of the Nazi henchmen now sat in internment camps. Active politicians of every persuasion, unpolitical opponents of Nazism, and above all, great numbers of Jews who had escaped to France, underwent weeks of anxiety and appalling hardship.

The gates of the camps were opened only at the last minute. People fled in desperate haste to escape the clutches of the SS and Gestapo. The armistice agreement of 22 June 1940 obliged the French government to hand over the German refugees. The only way out for most of them was to cross the border illegally into Spain where, following a bloody civil war, General Franco's dictatorship, supported by Mussolini and Hitler, had just begun. The route then went via Portugal to the United States – the goal of the main flood of refugees – or to Great Britain. Only a fraction of them managed to overcome the obstacles and dangers they encountered en route.

The main source of help were the United States, socialist mayors in France, nameless unknown individuals who risked their lives for others, and the so-called "German Labor Delegation" in the USA. This had been founded on 10 March 1939 in New York by the Social Democrat émigrés Albert Grzesinski, Rudolf Katz, Gerhart Seger, Max Brauer, Hedwig Wachenheim, and others. With the support of the Jewish Labour Committee and the American Federation of Labour they organised exemplary help and rescue operations. Hundreds owed their lives to them.

---

33 See Stampfer, Mit dem Gesicht nach Deutschland, p. 101.
34 Ibid., p. 109.

Not everyone reached safety. Many others shared the fate of Rudolf Breitscheid and Rudolf Hilferding, who were captured by the French authorities and handed over to the Nazis. Hilferding met his death in a Paris prison, Breitscheid died in Buchenwald concentration camp. The case of the Frankfurt Social Democrat Johanna Kirchner is particularly tragic. After French resistance workers had freed her from the infamous internment camp of Gurs, she fell into the clutches of the Vichy authorities and was extradited to Nazi Germany. Sentenced by the notorious "hanging judge" Roland Freisler, she went to the guillotine.

Those who had managed to escape to Great Britain were out of acute danger, but difficulties and hardship lay in wait for them even here. The situation of these refugees as well as that of the émigrés who had fled to England earlier, mostly because of their Jewish origins, was unfavourable to say the least. Although a number of aid committees worked unsparingly on their behalf, strict immigration regulations and the lack of opportunities to work drove many refugees to leave and emigrate overseas. After the fall of France, thousands underwent the bitter experience of compulsory internment as "hostile aliens". In July 1940, almost 8,000 were deported to Australia and Canada, with almost twice as many being placed under strict police supervision.

Only when the shock of the first few months of war had abated, and the hysteria about espionage given way to more sober consideration, was there, under pressure of public opinion and the efforts of individual members of parliament, a proper scrutiny of the internments instigated. The British government admitted, self-critically, that serious mistakes had been made. This resulted in the Sopade representatives who had fled to England being freed. The various socialist émigré groups received support from the Fabian Society, figures such as Victor Gollancz, James Middleton, and others, as well as in some measure from the Labour Party with whom the *Neu Beginnen* exiles in particular enjoyed good relations. At the same time, attempts were made by the Labour Party to bring together the various rival exile factions.

With war raging across Europe, many of the intensely controversial issues which had hitherto beset the exiled democratic socialists now seemed much less important. The idea of a popular uprising in Germany, as well as the hopes of unconditional cooperation from the Social Democratic parties in those countries fighting against Hitler, proved to be illusory. There could be no counting on assistance from the Allies for German opposition from within. Expectations of a peaceful settlement after the overthrow of Hitler had been pinned on Roosevelt and Churchill's "Atlantic Charta" of 14 August 1941 and earlier statements by the Labour

Party. They were bitterly dashed. As the war went on, a strongly national element coloured the thinking of a majority within the Labour Party about solidarity with the German democrats. The conservative British Prime Minister Churchill declared that the principles of the Atlantic Charta would not apply to Germany. In parliament, he dismissed the attempted coup of 20 July 1944 as a mere power struggle between "people in high places in the Third Reich" who were trying to murder each other. From virtually no quarter could the German exile groups expect support for preserving the unity of the Reich after the defeat of Hitlerite fascism.

With the Hitler-Stalin Pact, the left wing of the exiled Social Democrats, who seemed prepared to cooperate with the Communists in the struggle against National Socialism, lost a good deal of their credibility and authority. In the London group of the Socialist Workers' Party, their emphasis on "socialism without bureaucratic dictatorship" and "with democratic freedoms" represented a rapid process of rapprochement with Sopade.[35] Equally worthy of note in the group *Neu Beginnen*, after parting from their founder Walter Löwenheim, and under the influence of their leading theoretician Richard Löwenthal, was a move towards the social democratic movement as a whole. After settling disputes about organisational matters, there were no longer any fundamental obstacles to close collaboration with the exile party executive. During the war, and under Willi Eichler – its leader abroad who had had to flee Germany in 1933 – the ISK had already begun to move towards social democracy, and now showed its willingness to cooperate.

In the exile organisation founded in 1935, German Trade Unions Abroad (ADG), led by Heinrich Schliestedt, and from 1938 by Fritz Tarnow, attempts to bring émigrés in different countries together did not get beyond the first stages. It is true that basic agreement existed about the concept of a future unified trade union. Controversial, however, was Tarnow's view that it should take as its starting point the DAF, the Nazi German Labour Front which would be broken up once Hitler had been overthrown. In the regional group of "German Trade Unionists in Great Britain", and under the leadership of Hans Gottfurcht and influence of Walter Auerbach, the policy of complete reconstruction prevailed. Under the aegis of this émigré trade-union organisation, various socialist groups sat down together for the first time at the same committee table, and laid

---

35 On this and what follows, see Werner Röder, Die deutschen sozialistischen Exilgruppen in Großbritannien (Bonn-Bad Godesberg 2nd edn 1973), pp. 43 ff., quotation on p. 44, as well as Jörg Bremer, Die Sozialistische Arbeiterpartei Deutschlands (SAP), p. 252 f. and pp. 259 ff.

the basis for the "Union of German Socialist Organisations in Great Britain".

The force of circumstance, personal friendships, and exposure to the same hardships of emigration contributed in no small measure to the overcoming of reservations and differences. Vogel and Ollenhauer from Sopade, Knoering and Schoettle from *Neu Beginnen*, and Eichler from the ISK were men who knew how to put what they had in common before what divided them, and they grew to trust one another. On 25 February 1941, official negotiations were opened to set up a merger of the SPD (Sopade), *Neu Beginnen*, the International Socialist Combat League (ISK), Socialist Workers' Party, and the regional group of "German Trade Unionists in Great Britain". Agreement was soon reached on the basic issues. On 19 March 1941, the "Union" came into being. It was headed by Hans Vogel (SPD) as its chairman. Alongside him, Ollenhauer, Fritz Heine (SPD), Schoettle (*Neu Beginnen*), Eichler (ISK), and Hans Gottfurcht (for the trade unions) bore main responsibility for the policy of the "Union" over the coming years. With an unanimously approved statement, the socialists who had joined forces in the "Union" expressed their determination to work "with all the powers at their disposal" for the subjugation of the "totalitarian forces" and a democratic peace "which would give a new Germany the possibility, as a free member of the European community of peoples, to make its contribution to the reconstruction of Europe". "German socialists in Great Britain are united in the conviction that the military defeat and overthrow of the Hitler regime, the final vanquishing of German militarism, and the elimination of the social basis of Hitler's dictatorship are the indispensable prerequisites for lasting peace and a democratic and socialist future for Germany."[36]

Fruitful cooperation in the "Union" pushed the old organisational demarcations into the background. Also, in the discussions about the path democratic socialism should take in the future, clarification of different standpoints began to emerge. Although, as before, there was varying emphasis here and there, an increasingly stronger common line was fashioned on a whole series of crucial points. Long-cherished hopes of deposing Hitler through an alliance of all free and democratic forces from within Germany and outside had to be abandoned. It seemed the only likelihood of overthrowing the Nazi dictatorship was by force of arms. This presented the SPD exiles with a dilemma. On the one hand, they were at one with the Allies in the common struggle against Hitlerite fascism, but

---

36 In Zur Politik deutscher Sozialisten. Politische Kundgebungen und programmatische Richtlinien der Union deutscher sozialistischer Organisationen in Großbritannien (London 1945), p. 26.

on the other there was a widening gulf between their ideas on a peace settlement and the war aims of the anti-Hitler coalition. It was clear after the Tehran conference between Stalin, Roosevelt, and Churchill in December 1943 that the war would end with the dismemberment of Germany.

With protests and memoranda, the "Union" expressed its opposition to any plans for partition and foreign rule. It also rejected the thesis of collective guilt and anti-German "Vansittartism"[37], which attributed National Socialism to something in the German character. In this struggle, the unifying bond of the émigrés' national feelings became much more evident. The politically active SPD exiles regarded themselves as part of the German people and felt that they had to share their fate after the overthrow of Hitler. As Germans among Germans, they wanted to help carry the burden of the consequences of war and, supported by their moral claim to be the earliest fighters against fascism, wished to represent the interests of the nation *vis-à-vis* the victors.

This national dimension widened the rift with the Soviet Union whose expansionism the exiled SPD was in fear of. Following the attack on Russia, when the Soviet Union became the bulwark of the defence against Hitler, making enormous sacrifices in the process, their crucial role in overcoming the Nazi dictatorship was in little doubt. The attitude of the Social Democrats to the Communist system had little of the friendliness towards the Soviet Union which existed in parts of the western Allied camp. Notwithstanding the strong sympathies which *Neu Beginnen* and SAP had traditionally shown for the "great socialist experiment" of the Leninist Soviet Republic, these groups could not turn a blind eye to the excesses of the Stalinist system. The Hitler-Stalin Pact was living proof of the unscrupulousness of Russian power politics. Stalin's dictatorship with its purges and show trials, to which thousands of German émigrés had fallen victim, revealed the totalitarian nature of a system which claimed to be socialist. The well-nigh unconditional loyalty of the exile KPD to Stalin, its defence of annexations and expulsions by advancing Soviet troops, and the abusing of Social Democrats as the "agents of Hitlerism abroad"[38] destroyed any thought of a unified front with the Communists, even for those on the left wing of the SPD.

"They were not part of the unified socialist movement"[39], the clear future shape of which was emerging in "Union" discussions. Their aim was

37 So called because of the chief diplomatic advisor to the British government and former Under Secretary for State at the Foreign Office, Sir Robert Vansittart.
38 Röder's summing-up in his Sozialistische Exilgruppen, p. 214.
39 See Willi Eichler, Hundert Jahre Sozialdemokratie (Bielefeld 1963), p. 69.

to overcome splits in the labour movement and to absorb all organisations, factions, and tendencies based on a free and democratic socialism into a new and unified Social Democratic Party. As early as 1943, the "Union" presented a joint programme on foreign policy in which it proposed, among other things, a "federation of European nations", disarmament, reparation and compensation, and an international security system. The durability, however, of any future peaceful co-existence between nations "depended largely on the German people being given the possibility of following their own initiative in the shaping of their domestic political, social, and economic life".[40]

In 1945, in their "Programmatic Guidelines", the democratic socialists in the "Union of German Socialist Organisations" demonstrated how they thought a German state based on freedom, justice, and peace should be forged. In their statements on cultural policy, education, the judicial and administrative systems, and especially the guidelines on economic policy and a "constitution for the German state", they sketched the framework for a radically democratic republic whose economic and political structure would avoid the mistakes of Weimar:

"The goals of socialists for the economy are: freedom from economic exploitation, equality of opportunities for economic development, the guaranteeing of a dignified existence for all, full-time employment for all those able to work, raising of the general level of prosperity, and free development of the abilities of all."[41]

In the preamble to the guidelines for a German constitution, the "Union"[42] sent social democracy on its way with the benefit of all its experiences. A new state and social order had to be constructed on the following principles:

"Respect for, and protection of the freedom and dignity of the individual are the inalienable basis for the national and social life of the German Republic.

In this spirit, it strives for a social order based on justice, humanity, and peace;

a political and social democracy in which all citizens participate and have responsibility;

the liberation of the economy from the fetters of private monopoly capital and the introduction of a planned economy;

---

40 Decision of the "Union" of 23.10.1943, reproduced in Zur Politik deutscher Sozialisten, p. 16f.
41 Ibid., 'Richtlinien für die Wirtschaftspolitik', p. 3f.
42 On 2.12.1945 in London the "Union" was replaced and amalgamated into an "integrated party organisation".

protection from all economic exploitation;

the securing of a dignified human existence for all;

equality of opportunity in economic and cultural development;

fostering of the intellectual and cultural life of the nation and the education of youth in the spirit of moral responsibility, democracy, and international understanding;

elimination of war as a political weapon;

international institutions to which, for the securing of peace and prosperity for all nations, individual national sovereignty would be subordinated."[43]

---

43 Ibid., 'Richtlinien für eine deutsche Staatsverfassung', pp. 5 ff. This quotation, p. 5.

X. The Legacy and the Task Ahead

It retrospect, it may seem self-evident that the Social Democratic Party should become the great left-wing people's party it did. This was not what it was in 1945 after the collapse of Nazi Germany. To the left of the Social Democrats, and unlike in the Weimar period when it had grown to become the third largest party, the KPD remained limited to those following the Leninist path. Even for the millions suffering hunger and misery in western Germany, they were never a serious alternative. In the eastern part of Germany, however, with the help of the Soviet occupying power and (after the forced amalgamation with the SPD) as the SED, the government party, they were able to establish a new state, and one destined to be Communist.

Supporters of a liberal socialism had found *their* political home in the SPD. Freed from the irksome restrictiveness of Weimar, it became the party of all those who, regardless of their theoretical grounding, were striving for a democratic and free socialist society. Social Democrats who had survived twelve years of Nazi dictatorship under Hitler joined with Social Democrats who had suffered the bitter fate of foreign exile. Transcending the old organisational and theoretical conflicts, the banner of democratic socialism united men and women of diverse backgrounds and who came from differing starting points. Social Democrats who, as a matter of course, had remained loyal to the party through thick and thin, came up against socialists who had engaged in long conflicts with the old mother party, as well as committed democrats who saw the SPD as the guarantee of a better future. The experience of Nazi dictatorship and communism of the Stalinist variety, recognition of the weaknesses of the Weimar Republic, and the need to stand together in the struggle for a social democracy enabled them to surmount what might have divided them.

1945 constituted not a break, but a fresh beginning for social democracy. Socialism arose in Europe as a protest against the excesses of early capitalism, as a movement which campaigned against exploitation, economic hardship, and repression, and worked for a solution to the social question through a change in the structure of state and society. Unlike the West European states where the liberal bourgeoisie became the pioneers of parliamentary democracy, the main burden in Germany in the struggle for democratic freedoms fell on the shoulders of the socialist labour movement. In the dual task of battling for both justice and democratic freedom, social democracy had little but its own resources to fall back on. In the struggle to eliminate social ills, there was some support from the employees' wing of the Christian Centre Party, while the most likely source of help in the battle for democracy came from the left-wing Liberals. The weight of opposition came from two quarters: the state and business. Both of these summoned up all their energies to consolidate, or renew, their positions of power. Social democracy it was which offered the strongest, most persistent, and yet ultimately ineffectual resistance to National Socialism.

It was precisely this experience of fascism, as well as the perversion of Communism to Stalinism, which enlivened and deepened the urge amongst freedom-loving socialists to reflect on the driving force and principles behind this great emancipatory movement. A common thread throughout the entire history of democratic socialism had been the struggle against exploitation and oppression, whether it was directed against classes, races, or individual human beings.[1] Its goal was the liberation from need and fear and from economic and social insecurity, a just distribution of income and wealth, and the elimination of inequality and injustice by an economic system which operated in accord with the interests of the community as a whole. For Social Democrats, democracy was not only the structuring principle for the state, but also the model on which the whole of social life should be organised.

In this sense, democratisation was not simply about granting rights. It also charged people with exercising their freedoms. Upbringing and education, along with the creation and extension of the organisational and material prerequisites for them, had a vital role in this. State and society need the critical scrutiny of the responsible citizen who, in respecting the views of others, can take an active and independent part in shaping the life of the community. From its very first beginnings, the preservation and safeguarding of peace with the outside world and the solution of conflict by non-violent means have been social democracy's most basic requirements for a better future. Throughout the course of its history, the great goal with which the labour movement set out has imposed, time and time again, tasks and obligations: a world at peace in freedom and equality, a social order in which the personality of the individual can develop freely in solidarity with that of others.

1 This is the wording, or similar, in the Erfurt, Görlitz, and Heidelberg Programmes.

Part Two

Susanne Miller:

The SPD –
the People's Party of the Left

Revised Version by Heinrich Potthoff

I. Social Democracy in Postwar Germany

1. Organisational Refoundation

On 8 May 1945, the war unleashed by Nazi Germany was at an end. At great sacrifice, the Third Reich with its murderous crimes had been brought to its knees. Europe had been divided into two spheres of influence – one Eastern, one Western – with German territory east of the Oder-Neisse line being placed under Polish or Russian administration, and the rest of Germany being divided up into zones of occupation between the four victorious powers. The cities lay in ruins, with millions who had been bombed out, evacuated, or driven from their homes in search of a roof over their heads. Hunger and homelessness were daily realities, dire hardship, chaos, and the struggle for survival were to be found almost everywhere. The victorious Allies were in command, the Germans left in the dark about their future. This, they felt, was their "hour zero", and only slowly and gradually did it dawn on them that the collapse was in truth a liberation.

On 6 May 1945, even before the unconditional surrender sealed the defeat of Nazi Germany, Kurt Schumacher took to the postwar political stage with a programmatic speech[1] in which he marked out the future course of social democracy. The strong-willed, charismatic Kurt Schumacher was to become the dominant leading German Social Democrat of the postwar period. His influence lasted long beyond his death on 20 August 1952. The fixation on this one single SPD hero-figure, as well as the long-standing concentration on events from a predominantly Federal Republican, West German viewpoint, has also led, however, to a narrowing of perspective. As a result, even the complex dimensions of the party in the three Western occupied zones have been somewhat neglected, with the development of social democracy in the Soviet zone of occupation and influence being almost completely lost sight of.

As in Hanover, where, nine days before the capture of the city by Allied troops on 19 April, a meeting of Social Democrats had already taken place at which it was decided to revive the party, groups assembled in many other places to take similar initiatives. The SPD was the party with the longest unbroken historical tradition. The process of reorganising it

[1] Published in Kurt Schumacher, Erich Ollenhauer, Willy Brandt, Der Auftrag des demokratischen Sozialismus (Bonn-Bad Godesberg 1972), pp. 3ff.

began, in most cases, immediately after the collapse of the Nazi regime. It happened spontaneously at local and regional level, and initially without the permission of the Allied military governments, which did not allow the registration of democratic political parties until the Potsdam Conference at the beginning of August 1945. The organisational structure had been restored within a few months, mainly in the large cities and industrial centres. In summer 1945, Social Democrats in Leipzig reported to their regional committee that "the greater part of the old local associations are functioning again"[2]. Although party-political activity was generally more slow to get going in villages and small towns, nevertheless, many new local organisations were founded, particularly in rural areas, by Social Democrat refugees from the East who were well versed in party work.

Membership and party cadres were recruited overwhelmingly from among Social Democrats who had been schooled in the Social Democratic labour movement of the Weimar Republic, and had kept faith with the movement throughout the twelve years of dictatorship.[3] But just to reform along the old traditional lines was simply not enough. Many activists from former socialist splinter groups such as the ISK, SAP and *Neu Beginnen* – people like Willy Brandt, Fritz Erler, and Willi Eichler who saw the SPD as the party for them, along with newcomers to social democracy from a bourgeois background such as Carlo Schmid and Adolf Arndt, a seasoned former Communist labour leader such as Herbert Wehner, and young ex-soldiers or naval men of the ilk of Helmut Schmidt, Peter von Oertzen and Hans Matthöfer – were now drawn to the party. This was a broad spectrum, and despite the links with Weimar and a return to the tried and tested, there were tentative attempts to construct the house from new. Amongst the Social Democratic rank and file, the variants on a fresh start stretched from leaving the old party as it was, to a new-style democratic and socialist workers' party, from a socialist unity party to something on the model of the British Labour Party, and a left-wing peoples' party. After the collapse of Nazi rule and the liberation from fear and horror, more than a few Social Democrats and many left-wing socialists longed to see an end to the split in the labour movement which had made things so much easier for their enemies. But despite such

---

2 Quoted from Helga Grebing, '"Neubau" statt "Wiederaufbau" der SPD – Die Lehren aus der Weimarer Republik', in Dieter Dowe (ed.), Kurt Schumacher und der "Neubau" der deutschen Sozialdemokratie nach 1945 (Bonn 1996), p. 85.
3 See Albrecht Kaden, Einheit oder Freiheit. Die Wiedergründung der SPD 1945/46 (Berlin/Bonn 2nd edn 1980), p. 125f. and p. 321f.; Klaus Schütz, 'Die Sozialdemokratie im Nachkriegsdeutschland', in Parteien in der Bundesrepublik (Stuttgart and Düsseldorf 1955), p. 158.

longings, there was only "the semblance of working-class unity", as Klaus-Dietmar Henke put it.[4]

Less than eighteen months after the unconditional surrender of the Reich, the SPD, on 30 September 1945, had a membership of 633,244 in Berlin and the three Western occupation zones, and by the end of the year had increased this by over seventy thousand more. This meant that the figure for the same region in 1931 had risen by 18 per cent. The newly founded SPD had managed – primarily because of changes to the structure of the population brought about by the war, by people fleeing or being driven out, and various other factors – to extend its organisational network to a point far beyond that of the Weimar period. At the end of 1946, there were more than 8,000 Social Democrat associations in the Western zone, almost 3,000 more than there had been in 1931.[5] The strength of the organisation in the Soviet occupied zone (SBZ), where the traditional bastions of the SPD were located, was even higher. At the end of March 1946, there were 92,000 members in Thuringia alone, in the province of Saxony over 170,000, and in the state of Saxony over 200,000. By the end of 1945, in the SBZ, the SPD had succeeded in achieving membership figures which roughly equalled the prewar level. Despite the intimidation and obstacles put in their way by the Soviets and Communists, they gained 300,000 further members in 1946, so that by the end of March 1946 their 685,000 members exceeded the number of Social Democrats in the three Western zones overall.[6]

In this first year after the war, crucial decisions determining the future existence and course of social democracy in the divided Germany were made. Under Schumacher in the West the party moulded itself into a free and independent force, in the East it was forced to merge with the KPD. The members of the exile SPD executive living in London, Hans Vogel and Erich Ollenhauer, had declared themselves prepared to put their mandate at the disposal of a party once more operating legally in Germany.[7] In the middle of June 1945, the "Central Committee of the SPD", which had been formed in Berlin under the chairmanship of Otto Grotewohl, announced its leadership claims. Its first appeal ended with a declaration of its intention "to lead the struggle for reorganisation on the basis

---

4 Klaus-Dietmar Henke, Die amerikanische Besatzung Deutschlands (Munich 1995), pp. 646–656.
5 Jahrbuch der SPD 1946 (The SPD Yearbook for 1946), pp. 18ff.
6 Beatrix Bouvier, Ausgeschaltet! Sozialdemokraten in der Sowjetischen Besatzungszone und in der DDR 1945–1953 (Bonn 1996), pp. 42ff., esp. p. 61.
7 See Schütz, Die Sozialdemokratie im Nachkriegsdeutschland, p. 160.

of the organisational unity of the German working class".[8] On behalf of the KPD, however, which had initially presented a reformist image, and even professed its commitment to a parliamentary democratic Republic, Walter Ulbricht rejected an immediate merger.

In his speech of 6 May 1945, Kurt Schumacher had already delivered an unambiguous, uncompromising rejection of any attempt to form a "party of unity" with Communists. The decisive factor in this was the German Communists' firm ties to Russia, and their function as lackeys of the Soviet system and its policies. Social Democrats, he maintained, must refuse to be "the autocratically manipulated instrument of some foreign, imperial interest or other". What divided Social Democrats and Communists was not "the degree to which they were radical, but the perspective from which they viewed the political world, a different way of evaluating circumstances and ideas"[9].

The rigorousness with which Schumacher rebuffed the Communists was not something to be readily expected at that time, even in the West. The Allies regarded them as one of the "democratic parties", and they were initially considered in the Western zones as partners in a kind of antifascist consensus. Moreover, it was more common then to encounter a diffused urge for unity in the labour movement. Joint initiatives with the Communists which had been started in many towns in the West after the war[10] were, however, soon halted, and for the most part without any great internal party conflict. The treatment of Social Democrats in the Soviet occupied zone destroyed any hopes which still existed of being able to work together with Communists. But not until the advent of the Cold War would Communists finally disappear altogether from West German state governments.

In the immediate postwar period, Kurt Schumacher and the Social Democrats were mainly occupied with the struggle against the Communist system. In this, they put freedom above unity, and set the course for an, at that time, by no means self-evident anti-Communist democrat consensus. When, at the conference in Wennigsen in October 1945, Schumacher secured the support of Social Democrats in the West for his course, the "Central Committee" under Otto Grotewohl had already distanced itself from a fusion with the KPD. After their experiences with the

8 See loc. cit. Kaden, Einheit oder Freiheit, p. 26 f.
9 Kurt Schumacher et al., Der Auftrag des demokratischen Sozialismus, p. 30.
10 On Bremen, see Peter Brandt, Antifaschismus und Arbeiterbewegung (Hamburg 1976); on Hamburg, see Holger Christier, Sozialdemokratie und Kommunismus. Die Politik der SPD und KPD in Hamburg 1945–1949 (Hamburg 1975); for a general account, Lutz Niethammer et al. (eds), Arbeiterinitiative 1945 (Wuppertal 1976).

Kurt Schumacher at an SPD Rally in 1946

Communists and the occupying Soviet powers, the desire grew amongst Social Democrats in the SBZ for autonomy and independence, while the inclination towards a merger waned. A linking up of the SPD at national level was now the priority. With this all-German strategy and the demand for a "Reich party conference" the "Central Committee" was playing for time. But the pressure from the Soviet occupying powers and their German Communist accomplices became increasingly insistent. The denunciation, intimidation, and arrest of Social Democrat functionaries were designed to break their resistance. Under this physical and psychological pressure to fall in line, the "Central Committee" collapsed, and a number of regional chairmen and functionaries began to conform by going along with the seemingly inevitable merger with the KPD. Following the so-called "Conference of Sixty" on 21 and 22 December 1945, which was organised by tricks and force, manipulated reporting gave the impression that the East-SPD had agreed to the KPD line on uniting. On 11 February 1946, in a kind of self-sacrifice, the "Central Committee" finally voted in favour of merging with the KPD.[11]

There was hardly any alternative for the Social Democratic party organisation in the SBZ since a ballot was just as unfeasible as was open protest. The real battle was about the party in Berlin. The district association in Berlin organised opposition to the merger under the leadership of Franz Neumann. It made contact with Kurt Schumacher, who had finally made a clean break with the "Central Committee". At a dramatic functionaries' conference in the *Admiralspalast*, the Berlin Social Democrats decided to hold a ballot. It took place on 31 March 1946 in the three Western sectors of the city; in the Eastern sector the ballot had been prohibited by the Soviet military authorities. Despite a majority of 62 per cent affirming their loyal willingness to cooperate, over 82 per cent answered in the negative the question: "Are you in favour of the immediate merger of the two workers' parties?". On 7 April 1946, the Social Democratic party of Greater Berlin was constituted anew.

The result of a ballot by Social Democrats in the Soviet occupied zone would probably have been scarcely any different. But it was not possible to hold a vote there, and the merger went through in accord with the fixed timetable of the Soviets and the KPD. On 22 and 23 April 1946, a party conference celebrating the merger took place in the *Admiralspalast* in the Eastern sector of Berlin, at which the Socialist Unity Party of Germany (SED) was constituted with due pomp and pathos. The founding of the

---

11 Bouvier, Ausgeschaltet, pp. 54ff. Contains pointers to other literature on the topic, inter alia Andreas Malycha, Auf dem Weg zur SED. Die Sozialdemokratie und die Bildung einer Einheitspartei in den Ländern der SBZ. Eine Quellenedition (Bonn 1995), as well as a series of publications by Harold Hurwitz. In Walter, Die SPD, pp. 112–117, there is strong insistence on Social Democrats in the SBZ having sought "the unity" of the two parties "off their own bat".

SED was the result of a "unity" brought about by massive intimidation, repression, and deception, and was as such – for all the self-delusion and opportunistic conforming – ultimately a *Zwangsvereinigung*, a merger brought about by sheer force.

In the Soviet occupied zone, the SPD had now ceased to exist as an independent force. Only in East Berlin, where it enjoyed the protection of the Four Power status, was the SPD able to continue to exist and establish itself. In the local council elections of 20 October 1946, it secured 43.6 per cent of the vote in the Eastern sector of Berlin, well ahead of the SED with 29.9 per cent, and the CDU with 18.7 per cent. With the blockade of West Berlin in 1948, the SPD in the Eastern sector was put under conspicuous pressure, and membership figures in the following years sank by two-thirds: 15,437 in 1948, 7,621 in 1952, 6,627 in 1956, 5,327 in 1961. But not until after the building of the Berlin Wall in 1961 was the party organisation in the Eastern sector wound up for good.[12]

Until 1989, when courageous men and women called a new Social Democratic party into life in the GDR, a free and independent SPD existed only in the West. The organisational framework was created on 9 May 1946, when delegates from the three Western zones and Berlin met for the party conference in Hanover. Kurt Schumacher was elected unanimously as the party chairman, with Erich Ollenhauer as his deputy. The salaried members of the executive committee, in addition to Schumacher and Ollenhauer, Fritz Heine, Herbert Kreidemann and Alfred Nau, formed the so-called "bureau", the inner leadership circle. The twenty-five members of the party executive committee elected in Hanover consisted largely of men and women who had survived the years of Nazi rule in prisons and concentration camps, or in exile. They had all been members of the SPD prior to 1933, albeit that some of them had left or been expelled from the "mother party" during the Weimar period and the time of underground activity, and had been active in independent socialist groups. From the moment of its re-foundation, the SPD became the "unity party" of non-Communist socialists, while the SED, the "Socialist Unity Party" in the East, mutated into a Communist-Stalinist cadre party.

2. *Programmatic Political Perspectives*

The rebirth of the party, which for half a century had laid claim to being based on the secure foundations of "scientific socialism", occurred in what

---

12 For more on this, see Manfred Rexin, Die SPD in Ost-Berlin 1946–1961. Mit Beiträgen von Siegfried Heimann und Horst Hoffke (Berlin 1989), pp. 1–30, esp. p. 8 and p. 29.

was virtually a theoretical vacuum. Despite, or perhaps thanks to, the relative lack of interest of many party managers, functionaries, and members, in ideological questions, a "party line" embracing basic SPD policies was developed at a very early stage, and one which would determine the policy and character of the party over many years. Overwhelmingly responsible for this process was Kurt Schumacher.

Schumacher was born on 12 October 1895 in Kulm in West Prussia, where he attended the grammar school. On the outbreak of the First World War he volunteered immediately and was seriously wounded two weeks after first going into battle. He lost his right arm, was discharged from the army, and then dedicated himself to his studies, graduating with a doctorate in politics. A member of the SPD since 1918, he was elected to the Württemberg Landtag in 1924, and to the Reichstag in 1930. Imprisoned for ten years by the Nazis, and held in various concentration camps where he was tortured almost to the point of death, he was eventually released in summer 1943, but arrested again for several weeks after the bomb plot on 20 July 1944. Thereafter, he lived near Hanover until the end of the war. In this old stronghold of social democracy he resumed contact with former SPD colleagues and led the rebuilding of his party at first from the "Schumacher Bureau" in Hanover which, after he had been joined by Ollenhauer and Heine in February 1946 (Hans Vogel had died in October 1945 in London), was expanded into the "Bureau of the Western zone".

Idle though the attempt may be to construct a rounded political philosophy from Schumacher's ideas, the elements of socialist theory which were of lasting influence on him are unmistakable. First and foremost among them was Lassalle's affirmation of the state, and the emphasis so characteristic of this thinker on the indissoluble connection between the democratic freedom of a people within the state, and its independence outside it. Schumacher's declaration that there was more to thank Marxism for as a method "than any other scientific and sociological method in the world"[13] was undoubtedly more than just an attestation of respect for a doctrine which, for twelve years, it was only possible to profess at danger to one's life. Schumacher's interpretation of social phenomena, his criticism of society, and particularly his conception of where his party was located in the political process were frequently dominated by terminology from the sphere of Marxist thought. Much more crucial, however, for the formation of Schumacher's intellectual stance than any scholarly system,

13 From his speech to the SPD party congress in May 1946, in Protokoll SPD-Parteitag 1946, pp. 23–56. Also in Willy Albrecht (ed.), Kurt Schumacher, Reden – Schriften – Korrespondenzen 1945–1952 (Berlin/Bonn 1985), pp. 385–422.

was direct, personal *experience*: the First World War, the crisis-ridden Weimar Republic, his suffering at the hands of National Socialism, the Second World War, and the reduction of the Reich to rubble.

Schumacher's affirmation of state and nation and his militant commitment to the Republic of Weimar drew him to Social Democrats such as Carlo Mierendorff, Julius Leber, and Theodor Haubach. Even though he was sharply critical of the *immobilisme* and ineffectiveness of his party in the final phase of Weimar, the SPD still remained for him the representative of the "other Germany", the very antithesis – its substance still intact – of Hitler's state and those who had prepared the ground for, and supported, it. There was, it seemed to him, a compelling moral and historical claim for his party to lead the new Germany, as there was for this new Germany to be given equal rights and to be able to determine its own destiny.

Schumacher, with his anti-Communism, his free and democratic socialism, and his efforts on behalf of a free Germany, was diametrically opposed to everything the KPD/SPD leadership stood for. His charisma radiated deep into the Eastern zone. For the Communist regime, he was the epitome of the enemy. Social Democrats who had resisted the merger, had reservations about the party line, or were suspected of "Social Democratism" were persecuted as "Schumacher agents" and "put out of action". This process was deliberately stepped up in the course of remoulding the SED into a "new-type party" – i.e. the Stalinisation of it. With the claim that the SPD "Eastern bureaux" in Hanover and Berlin (West) were collaborating with Western secret services, Social Democrats were persecuted, arrested, and condemned as "spies" and "agents". The mere suspicion or insinuation that the person in question had contacts with the SPD in the West or its Eastern bureau was sufficient for them to be accused of espionage or sabotage and be thrown into prison or a Soviet "special camp". After the closing of these camps at the beginning of 1950, over 10,513 individuals who had been sentenced by the Soviet Military Administration (SMAD) received further prison terms, while 3,482 other prisoners were handed over to the GDR authorities for sentencing.[14] Both the Soviets and their German vassals proceeded with the utmost harshness. Sentences of 25 years hard labour or prison were almost the rule, 15 years was mild, the death penalty not infrequent, and the same applied to the "Waldheim trials". Bautzen and Hoheneck are representative of the suffering and intolerable prison conditions to which many fell victim.

---

14 See Wolfgang Eisert, Die Waldheimer Prozesse. Der stalinistische Terror 1950. Ein dunkles Kapitel der DDR-Justiz (Esslingen/Munich 1993), pp. 15 ff.

At the beginning of the 1960s, the West-SPD listed 20,000 members of the SPD in the Soviet occupied zone who had been subject to repressive measures in the period from December 1945 to April 1946 alone. According to statistics from the Kurt-Schumacher-Circle, roughly 5,000 Social Democrats were sentenced to prison by Soviet or East German courts, 400 of whom died there. According to recent Russian figures and West German surveys, "a realistic figure for the number of Social Democrats convicted could be around 5,000 to 6,000"[15].

For Social Democrats committed to freedom, resistance began with the forced merger. After the founding of the SED, opposition – which was already fraught with danger – switched to "illegal" forms of political struggle. The borderline between self-assertion, resistance, protest, political opposition, and subversive activity was often hard to define. Those Social Democrats who had more or less voluntarily gone down the SED path were then sidelined or, like Otto Grotewohl, conformed to such an extent that they became little more than minions of the Communist-Stalinist dictatorship. Many others simply withdrew out of protest or/and fled to the West. Others fell victim to purges and now themselves met the sorry fate of being outlawed and persecuted. The spirit of Social Democratic values was preserved, however, mainly by like-minded Social Democrats who stuck together in loose-knit conspiratorial circles and groups. It was a difficult and dangerous line to walk. The unrelenting battle of the persecutors against "saboteurs", "espionage groups", and "oppositional elements" was indicative of a wider potential for opposition and resistance. The activity and resistance of these Social Democrats were motivated by the hope of a reunified Germany. Kurt Schumacher was for them the rock in a stormy sea, which sustained their will to resist and hold out, and to which they clung.

Schumacher identified his own role totally with that of social democracy. Almost nobody seriously disputed his unique position in the organisation. If there was any open criticism of him, it was mainly directed at his personal style of leadership. But beneath the surface there was a degree of conflict about the structures and goals of the party. Faced with Schumacher's determinedly centralist course, criticised by some as militantly Prussian in character, men like Hoegner in Bavaria and Kaisen in Bremen were pressing for a federalist model more in tune with peoples' needs.[16] By sheer force of personality, and due to the great esteem he en-

---

15 Bouvier, Ausgeschaltet, p. 258.
16 See Emil Werner, Im Dienst der Demokratie. Die bayerische Sozialdemokratie nach der Wiedergründung 1945 (Munich 1982), esp. p. 40f. and p. 56.

joyed, however, Schumacher was able to keep the opposition at bay and leave his indelible mark on the party.

To the outside world, complete harmony reigned at central party level. In retrospect, this does not seem as self-evident as it might, since there were people who had joined the SPD, and risen to leading positions in it, whose political past and outlook differed from that so characteristic of Weimar social democracy, and in many cases were even in conflict with it – Carlo Schmid, Adolf Arndt, Herbert Wehner, and Karl Schiller for instance. Moreover, men such as Willy Brandt, Waldemar von Knoeringen, Erwin Schoettle, and Willi Eichler, who had left the SPD in the Weimar period, now also held important functions in the organisation. Undoubtedly, this ability to integrate such individuals into the re-founded party was in great measure due to Schumacher's charismatic personality. He it was who also emphasised from the outset the openness of the reborn party in ideological and spiritual matters, addressing in particular people who were socialist out of religious conviction and inviting them to become politically active in the SPD.

"Socialism as a task for the present" was the slogan used by the Social Democrats in the early days to publicise their social and political goals. It embodied the conviction that the reconstruction of a devastated country could and should not be governed by capitalist economic principles. These were neither effective, nor just. Victor Agartz defined this position precisely at the first SPD party congress after the war in May 1946. The party rejected "as unjust and inappropriate, especially in the present situation of the German people": 1. "Liberalism in its original form", 2. "monopoly capitalism with imperialist tendencies", 3. "the corporate state", 4. "centralist state capital in the form of the marketless economy", and 5. "emerging neo-Liberalism".[17] The election of the executive committee was a vote of confidence in Agartz: with only two less than Schumacher, he received the second-highest number of votes.[18]

"A controlled economy and socialisation", according to Erik Nölting, rapporteur for the executive's economic policy committee the following year, meant the "realisation of the socialist idea in the economic sphere", but this did not mean that socialisation was identical with nationalisation.[19] "A new framework based on socialist principles" had to be created for the economy, which would encompass the "basic industries, which would be socialised, and the state-controlled financial institutions".[20] As late as 1950,

17 Protokoll des SPD-Parteitags 1946, p. 65f.
18 Ibid., p. 180.
19 Protokoll des SPD-Parteitags 1947, p. 158 and p. 161.
20 Party congress resolution, ibid., p. 228.

Hermann Veit, in a paper to the party conference, presented a comprehensive programme of socialisation: mining, iron and steel, energy, large chemical concerns, large suppliers of building materials, the big banks and insurance companies – ultimately all those monopoly concerns which it was deemed preferable to transfer to public ownership and control.[21]

But the day was long gone when there was even half a chance of bringing this about. In the Soviet occupied zone the big landowners had been dispossessed under the slogan "Junker land in peasant hand", banks and savings banks had been nationalised, larger businesses transferred to state ownership without compensation, and Soviet-style joint-stock companies set up for heavy industry. Under the heading of "denazification" and "anti-fascism", capitalism was to be smashed and replaced by a socialist system. In the West, social intervention was kept within strict limits. It operated mainly in the breaking up of IG Farben and the largest coal and steel companies. The desire for a thoroughgoing structural change to the social system was nevertheless in the air during the initial phase of political reconstruction after the collapse of Nazism. The idea of socialisation left its mark on the CDU's Ahlen Programme of 1947, as well as on several state constitutions and, albeit somewhat diluted, on the *Grundgesetz* (Basic Law). In a plebiscite in Hesse in December 1946, 71.9 per cent voted for the transference of big industrial concerns to public ownership. In summer 1948 in the North Rhine-Westphalian Landtag, an SPD bill seeking the authorisation of the British military government to transfer the mining industry into public ownership received the approval of roughly a third of the CDU parliamentary party. Plans for socialisation, which foundered on the objections of the occupying power, were not only determined by economic and socio-political considerations. Their initiators wanted to prevent the rise of any future "big-business dominance hostile to democracy", to "set aside fears that reconstruction in the Ruhr" could become "a threat to the security of Europe", and to fend off "calls for the dismantling of German industry".[22] If "the transference of the means of production to common ownership" was *the* classical demand of Social Democratic programmes from Gotha (1875) to Heidelberg (1925), there was now a new dimension to it. Its aim now was to smash the power of big business and heavy industry which had made Hitler possible. At the very moment when the economy was in total ruins, they saw the chance of creating a radically new system which would be egalitarian and a safeguard of both peace and democracy. This presup-

21 Protokoll des SPD-Parteitags 1950, p. 192.
22 This from the chairman of the SPD caucus in the North Rhine-Westphalian Landtag, Fritz Henßler, Protokoll des SPD-Parteitags 1948, p. 54.

SPD election poster 1946.
The text reads: "Vote SPD. No more War! No more Dictatorship!"

posed two things: that any attempt to solve the problems of reconstruction with capitalist methods would be doomed to rapid failure, and that the mass of people who had been severely tested and proletarianised by National Socialism, war, collapse, and being forced to flee their homeland, would be seized by anti-capitalist longings which social democracy could and must satisfy by concrete action. Both premises were to prove erroneous.

In matters of foreign policy which, under Schumacher's influence, for the first time in the history of German social democracy had become of primary importance, the reunification of Germany in freedom was the goal against which everything else was to be measured. Central to the desire for reunification was of course the relationship of the Soviet occupied zone to the Western zones, but in general, the policy of the SPD was directed towards the restoration of Germany within the borders of 1937, which entailed the reincorporation of the Saar, the maintenance of Berlin as the capital city, and the non-recognition of the Oder-Neisse line. The emphatic fashion in which these demands were promoted, particularly by Schumacher, is frequently seen as the expression of a new nationalism designed to wipe out the odium of being unpatriotic to which the SPD was subjected in the Wilhelmine and Weimar periods. Accusations of this kind overlook how emphatically the SPD had been committed to preserving the "intactness of the Reich", and how unequivocally it had rejected any separatist tendencies during the revolution and the Weimar period. Throughout its entire history, and going back to its founding, the SPD can be seen to have striven for the "unity of the Reich": its policies after 1945 in no way constitute a break with this tradition. They were given a contemporary emphasis by the consideration, which also had its roots in traditional SPD values, that it must be the task of every free German politician to make unification their goal on the basis of the right to national and democratic self-determination. In addition, there was the consideration that a divided Germany represented a constant latent or immediate danger to peace in Europe and the world. Although, for fifteen years, the fixation on reunification lent an inner logic to SPD foreign policy and its stance on defence, there was at the same time an inflexibility to it which considerably diminished the party's chances of electoral success.

The Social Democrats' unification policy has, of course, always to be seen in connection with the fact that Schumacher – as Peter Merseburger demonstrates in his biography of Schumacher, and Hans-Peter Schwarz puts it in his analysis of SPD foreign policy in the postwar years – "had, from the beginning, taken the SPD in a direction for which they could only count on support in the West. And since in 1945 and 1946 he had firmly reckoned on the Social Democrats coming to power, this could only mean Germany opting prematurely, and, at least under his leadership, irreversibly for the West".[23] The implication of this was far greater than the matter of a helpless object caught up in the interplay of international forces prefering to opt for one of the power blocs rather than the other. It was more a profession of faith in a political system, with all its values and forms, which had emerged from the Western tradition, than it was in any way an affirmation of particular policies of the Western powers. Not only then did Schumacher find himself – with this basic decision – in complete agreement with the entire party[24], it was also never called into question at any later phase.

3. *Opting for Opposition*

In answer to a question in an opinion poll by the British military government in 1947 about who was the most admired postwar politician, the only person named was Kurt Schumacher. A survey at roughly the same time by the American military government in their zone showed that 40 per cent of the respondents had heard something about Schumacher; Adenauer was not mentioned at all.[25] There was, however, a crass disparity between the degree of familiarity with the party chairman and the esteem in which he was held, and the trust which voters had in his party, even though the SPD was held to be "the Schumacher party" in the public consciousness. In the first elections to be held in the Western zones they for the most part lagged behind their greatest rivals, the CDU, as can clearly be seen from the votes:[26]

---

23 Hans-Peter Schwarz, Vom Reich zur Bundesrepublik. Deutschland im Widerstreit der außenpolitischen Konzeptionen in den Jahren der Besatzungsherrschaft 1945–1949 (Neuwied and Berlin 1966), p. 500; Peter Merseburger, Der schwierige Deutsche. Kurt Schumacher. Eine Biographie (Stuttgart 1995).
24 "What we need most urgently", wrote Erich Ollenhauer on 6.4.1946 to the chairman of the Dutch Socialists, "is the moral and political support of the West European labour movement and of all truly democratic forces in the West. […] We will not be bowed, and we will tread our own path as far as our strength allows, for this is not a matter of tactics and manoeuvering, this is the be or not to be of a free, democratic German labour movement, and with it the possibility of a new and viable German democracy." Quoted from Schwarz, Vom Reich zur Bundesrepublik, p. 499.
25 See Lewis J. Edinger, Kurt Schumacher. Persönlichkeit und politisches Verhalten (Cologne and Opladen 1967), p. 271.
26 These election results are taken from Richard Schachtner, Die deutschen Nachkriegswahlen (1956), as well as statistical yearbooks and monthly reports from the individual federal states. For the elections in the French zone, the results from the Saar were also taken into consideration; Union parties trading under different names in various states were subsumed under CDU. The material was put together by Rüdiger Wenzel.

American zone
Municipal elections (1946)   SPD 17.3%   CDU 35.2%
District elections (1946)   SPD 27.2%   CDU 62.6%
Landtag/City Parliament elections (1946/47)   SPD 36.2%   CDU 41.5%

British zone
Municipal elections (1946)   SPD 24.4%   CDU 28.2%
District elections (1946)   SPD 35.1%   CDU 46.4%
Landtag/City Parliament elections (1946/47)   SPD 49.0%   CDU 27.4%

French zone
Municipal elections (1946)   SPD 11.9%   CDU 45.9%
District elections (1946/47)   SPD 23.9%   CDU 61.0%
Landtag elections (1947)   SPD 28.0%   CDU 52.4%

Greater Berlin
Town council elections (1946)   SPD 48.7%   CDU 22.2%
Borough council elections (1946)   SPD 48.9%   CDU 22.9%

The SPD succeeded in only very few elections in defeating the CDU: in the Hanseatic cities (City Parliament elections of 13.10.1946, and in Bremen the supplementaries on 12.10.1947), in all the municipal, district, and Landtag elections in Hesse, Lower Saxony, Schleswig Holstein, as well as the municipal elections in the district of Württemberg in the state of Württemberg-Baden. Its most impressive result was in Berlin.[27]

The election results in the three Western zones resulted in disappointment for the Social Democrats, but not, however, in a general discussion. Most active functionaries were completely taken up with tackling everyday public and personal needs, and were scarcely in a position to embark on more thoroughgoing deliberations about the future of the party. But the party leadership, too, had obviously not taken into consideration that, in view of the way the electorate had voted, many of the premises on which the basic programmatic positions of the party were founded were possibly the result of miscalculations, and needed to be examined.

The Landtag election results were indirectly of considerable importance for setting the course which would determine the SPD's political stance for years ahead. At the beginning of 1947, the British and the Americans decided to economically unify their two zones, and, by the creation of an economic council for this Bizone, grant the Germans political and parliamentary representation above federal state level. Delegated

---

27 See Willy Brandt and Richard Löwenthal, Ernst Reuter. Ein Leben für die Freiheit. Eine politische Biographie (Munich 1957), p. 357.

by the state parliaments, the members of the economic council, which had Frankfurt am Main as its designated seat, were then to elect the directors of five central economic administrative bodies. Of the originally 52 members of the economic council (the number was later doubled, with party proportions being maintained), which began its work in May 1947, 20 were SPD, 21 CDU, 4 FDP, 3 KPD, with the rest distributed among smaller parties. The SPD demanded the right to fill the post of director of economic administration with a Social Democrat. When they failed, because the CDU, backed by the FDP, insisted on appointing one of their own men, they declined – urged to do so by Schumacher – to take any part in the administration and decided on a policy of opposition. It would, of course, as the SPD emphasised, be "constructive opposition". In fact, Social Democrat deputies worked intensively with the economic council and, as their chairman stated with satisfaction, exerted a considerable "influence on the business detail which never received any wider public recognition".[28] When, however, living conditions gradually improved after the currency reform of June 1948, it was Ludwig Erhard and the parties supporting him who got the credit for the developing economic upturn, while the SPD were branded as "the opposition".

And yet it was precisely from their role in opposition, decided on in the economic council, that the party had hoped for a decisive increase in public acceptance and popular approval. In the federal states created after 1945, coalition governments had been formed in which the SPD had, along with other posts, most often been allocated the Ministry for Economic Affairs. External circumstances, particularly dependence on the military governments and the limited possibilities of getting a grip on the problems of reconstruction within the federal state framework, were regarded by Schumacher's SPD as an obstacle to success. They were now building on the hope, in opposition, of being able to open the eyes of the people to the fact that, as Schumacher described it in his speech to the 1948 party congress, "the ruthlessness of this class struggle from the top" was so great, "that in the last year it would not have been possible to come to an understanding on a single important issue without abandoning the interests of the working masses and disowning the task we have set ourselves to win the battle for socialism"[29].

---

28 Herbert Kriedemann's account at the party congress in September 1948, Protokoll, p. 120. Deserving of special mention in this context is the work of Anni Krahnstöver and Wilhelm Mellies (deputy SPD chairman 1952–1958) on the Equalisation of Burdens legislation.
29 Protokoll des SPD-Parteitags 1948, p. 32.

But the SPD was not only mistaken with respect to the effects of Erhard's economic policy. Even more crucial was their calculation that the social injustices it inflicted would drive the "working masses" into the socialist camp, whereas it turned out that the majority of them were, in fact, prepared to put up with them if their own standard of living, by comparison with the impoverishment of the immediate postwar years, was rising. Furthermore, experience of the wartime and postwar economy had led to widespread rejection of state *dirigisme* and to an identification of socialist planning with the command economy and shortages.

It is clear with the benefit of hindsight that, had the SPD ever found itself in a comparable situation to that of spring 1947, it would not have taken the decision to go into opposition. Also worthy of our attention is Ulrich Dübber's point about the national political implications of the decision which, he maintains, resulted in the "young democracy" being made a present of "a reliable opposition party, free of the suspicion of radical intentions".[30] The political constellation in the Frankfurt economic council anticipated that of the Bundestag and its governments during the first seventeen years of the Federal Republic. The decision which made this constellation possible represented a caesura in the history of postwar German social democracy. For a long time, from then on, the roles would be divided. A coalition of "bourgeois" parties would make up the federal government, while the Social Democrats formed the "constructive opposition".

4. The Creation of the Grundgesetz (Basic Law)

The attitude of the SPD to the formation of the Federal Republic was a logical consequence of its decision to gear itself towards the West. This was related to what Schumacher described as the "magnet theory". Its starting point was the attractiveness of Western living conditions for the population in the Soviet sphere of influence, and this "magnetic effect" was expected to yield political results. Attempts to enter into negotiations with politicians in the Soviet occupied zone, or even to strike compromises with them, he held to be senseless and damaging.[31] Schumacher was hostile to initiatives aimed at reaching economic, and then also political agreements by holding conferences of the Minister Presidents of the

---

30 See Ulrich Dübber, 'Die deutsche Sozialdemokratie nach 1945'. In Aus Politik und Zeitgeschichte. Beilage zur Wochenzeitung Das Parlament, vol. 21/62, 22.5.1963, p. 56.
31 See Albrecht (ed.), Kurt Schumacher. Reden – Schriften – Korrespondenzen, p. 124f.

four zones, and did not shrink from conflict over this with leading Social Democrats whose party loyalty was above all suspicion.[32]

When the Soviet Union was visibly "pushing forward", as Schumacher put it in a speech of December 1947, "with the transformation of its zone of occupation into a totalitarian one-party state along the lines of its own"[33], the path to the founding of a West German state lay clear ahead. It went hand in hand with the Marshall Plan, which was announced in June 1947 and implemented in April 1948, the introduction of currency reform on 20 June 1948 in the Western zones, and the lifting of government controls by Ludwig Erhard at virtually the same time. In the consciousness of most West Germans, the economic and currency reforms were significant signposts pointing towards the Federal Republican state, and they also represented a watershed separating them from the East. In 1947/48, the dark clouds of the Cold War loomed evermore threateningly on the horizon. The *Gleichschaltung* of the central European states on the Soviet model was in full operation. The Defenestration of Prague in February 1948, i.e. the takeover of sole control by the Communists, sealed the final hope of any semblance of partial democracy in those states located in the Soviet sphere of influence. From April 1948 traffic to and from Berlin was impeded, and in summer 1948 the Soviet Union responded to currency reform and the Deutschmark with a blockade of the Western sector of Berlin. The entire traffic, by road, rail, and water, was brought to a standstill. For nine months, the Western Allies ferried supplies into West Berlin by air. In Berlin, adversaries and occupiers became helpers and protectors, and ultimately friends. Ernst Reuter, the already elected, but not yet confirmed Lord Mayor of Berlin, became a symbol of the courageous self-assertiveness of this island of freedom in a sea of red. As a party of freedom defying the Communists, the SPD emerged victorious in the West Berlin elections of 5 December 1948 with 64.5 per cent of the vote, and Reuter was elected as Governing Mayor.

The word and arguments of the charismatic Ernst Reuter carried weight. Alongside the party leader Kurt Schumacher he was social democracy's great political figure, and in Minister-Presidential circles his vote counted. With the "London Recommendations" of June 1948, the Western Allies had issued the guidelines for a West German federal state. In principle, the Minister Presidents and the parties, including the SPD, in the Western zones were positive about the creation of a provisional

---

32 See, in particular, Wilhelm Kaisen, Meine Arbeit, mein Leben (Munich 1967), pp. 236 ff., p. 267 f.
33 Willy Albrecht, Kurt Schumacher. Ein Leben für den demokratischen Sozialismus (Bonn 1985), p. 59.

Western state, and they took upon themselves the most important task in the recommendations, the working-out of a constitution. At a meeting of the West German Minister Presidents with the Military Governors on 20/21 July 1948, Ernst Reuter set aside any remaining doubts about whether this would not ultimately seal the division of Germany, with the convincing argument that "the political and economic consolidation of the West is also a fundamental prerequisite for our recovery, and for a return of the East to the common motherland".[34]

On 1 September 1948, the Parliamentary Council held its constituent assembly in Bonn. The SPD participated on the understanding that the constitution to be devised could only be provisional, since the "rest of Germany" had no sovereignty, and the Russian zone of occupation, as well as the former German territory east of the Oder-Neisse line, were excluded from the process.[35] The SPD laid great stress on these points at the preceding conferences of the Minister Presidents and the preparatory constitutional convention in Herrenchiemsee. Nonetheless, the honing of the Basic Law is unmistakably attributable not least to the intensity of Social Democratic involvement. But even in retrospect, Social Democrat members of the Parliamentary Council described the main characteristic of their activity there as endeavouring to "avoid arrangements which would be permanent".[36]

Given the numerical strength and expertise of the Social Democrat representation on the Parliamentary Council – of the 65 members, 27 belonged to the SPD, the same number as belonged to the CDU/CSU – and their outstanding leading constitutional lawyer Carlo Schmid (chairman of the central committee), it is somewhat surprising that the Basic Law, particularly in the social area, is largely lacking in concrete detail. There are different levels of explanation for this. After 1945, the SPD concerned itself with constitutional questions much sooner than the other parties, and adopted "guidelines for the construction of the German Republic" as early as its second postwar conference.[37] In these "guidelines", however, as well as in a paper given by the chairman of the constitution committee Walter Menzel, there was no real discussion of basic social

---

34 See Brandt/Löwenthal, Ernst Reuter, pp. 468 ff., quotation on p. 474.
35 See the report on the Parliamentary Council in the Jahrbuch der SPD 1948/49, pp. 12 ff., esp. p. 13.
36 The formulation of Fritz Eberhard in a letter of 16.11.1972 to Susanne Miller.
37 Protokoll des Parteitags 1947, pp. 225 ff. For a detailed account, see Werner Sörgel, Konsensus und Interessen. Eine Studie zur Entstehung des Grundgesetzes für die Bundesrepublik Deutschland (Stuttgart 1969), pp. 59 ff.

rights and obligations[38], something which betrayed programmatic uncertainty, as well as a conception of goals "in which democracy was understood solely as a state and social system run along socialist lines".[39] The reason given by Carlo Schmid was that "they had restricted themselves to the classical basic rights, and had deliberately not dealt with the basic rules of life", since otherwise "they would have exceeded their brief, which was to create no more than a provisional arrangement (pending future unification)".[40] Twenty years later, one SPD member of the Parliamentary Council summed up the Social Democrats' particular motivation with the formulation: social articles should not be devised "without our comrades in Saxony".[41]

While, on the one hand, the Social Democrats emphasised the transitional nature of the future Federal Republic, they expended a great deal of energy on the other to ensure that this provisional arrangement functioned at optimum efficiency. This required the formation of a common front with the FDP against the federalism of both the CDU/CSU and the German Party, as well as that of the Americans and French. This collaboration with the Liberals was a further, immediately urgent reason for the SPD not to be more precise on the subject of basic social rights. Under Schumacher's leadership, the battle against federalistic solutions took a dramatic turn which reached its climax at a meeting in Hanover on 20 April 1949 to which – barely recovered from the amputation of his leg – he summoned top party officials, SPD members of the Parliamentary Council, and the Social Democrat Minister Presidents. The resolution passed at the meeting was directed against the intervention of the Western occupying powers who were demanding a greater measure of federalism in the construction of the Federal Republic, and particularly in its system of public finances. The six points of this resolution demanded "the necessary freedom for Germans to make their own decisions" *vis-à-vis* the occupying powers, "the preservation of German judicial and economic unity", and a regulation of finances which "grants the Federal Government the means and resources required to meet its responsibilities". It announced, furthermore, that the SPD would reject a Basic Law which

---

38　Ibid., pp. 121–142.
39　See Volker Otto, Das Staatsverständnis des Parlamentarischen Rates. Ein Beitrag zur Entstehungsgeschichte des Grundgesetzes für die Bundesrepublik Deutschland (Düsseldorf 1971), p. 205.
40　See the introduction to Werner Matz, Grundgesetz für die Bundesrepublik Deutschland und Besatzungsstatut (Stuttgart and Cologne 1949), p. 7.
41　Volker Otto, Das Staatsverständnis des Parlamentarischen Rates, p. 86.

did not satisfy all of the six demands.[42] Shortly afterwards, the Parliamentary Council reached an agreement with the Allies which, although not meeting the Social Democrats' conditions entirely, nevertheless yielded significant concessions regarding judicial and economic unity and the powers of the Federal Government in matters of public finance. It represented a clear victory for Kurt Schumacher.[43]

The experience of Weimar had motivated the SPD to make stability a basic priority of the constitution being created. It is also very understandable, therefore, that the Social Democrats should have been very much in favour of the Federal Chancellor having a strong position, and one firmly anchored in the constitution. Their support for this was, furthermore, linked to the optimistic expectation that the first, and possibly also succeeding Chancellors of the Federal Republic, would come from the SPD. The Social Democrat men and women who drafted the Basic Law could not have foreseen Adenauer's "Chancellor democracy".

42 Jahrbuch der SPD 1948/49, p. 139. The proposal by Ernst Reuter, Wilhelm Kaisen, and Hermann Lüdemann (Minister President of Schleswig Holstein) to remove the ultimatum in the final sentence, was defeated by eight votes. See Brandt/Löwenthal, Ernst Reuter, p. 487.
43 The interpretation of Theo Pirker (Die SPD nach Hitler (Munich 1965), p. 100) that this was a "Pyrric victory" rests on his assumption that Schumacher wanted to wreck the constitution in order to prevent the widening of the division between the two Germanies which the creation of a West German state would have caused. Susanne Miller considers this to be a faulty assumption. The thesis that Schumacher was informed about the decision of the Allies – arrived at on 8.4.1949, but kept secret – to make concessions, is the one unanimously held by scholars, but is disputed by Schumacher's closest colleagues.

II. "Constructive Opposition"

The Basic Law was approved by the Parliamentary Council on 8 May 1949, the anniversary of the capitulation. After ratification by all the state parliaments except Bavaria, it was promulgated with due ceremony on 23 May 1949. Constituted specifically for a "transitional period", the Basic Law gave the German people a new system of national government pending reunification. In the words of the Preamble: "The entire German people are called upon to achieve in free self-determination the unity and freedom of Germany."

Voters in the election campaign for the first Bundestag were presented with two alternatives: the SPD's "planned economy" or Ludwig Erhard's "social market economy". In the elections on 14 August 1949, the SPD received 29.2, the CDU/CSU 31.0, the FDP 11.9, and the KPD 5.6 per cent of the vote. The rest of the vote was distributed amongst tiny parties which, without exception, disappeared over the following years. This result gave the SPD practically no chance of forming a government. The initiative for forming a coalition was in the hands of the strongest party, the CDU/CSU, whose chairman, Konrad Adenauer, had neither cause nor inclination to enter into talks with the marginally weaker party of his rivals. There was no question of the FDP and the other bourgeois parties doing anything but opt for Adenauer's party and Erhard's economic policies. Thirteen years would go by before the electorate, and the shift in political location by individual parties, would loosen the SPD's fixation with its role as opposition. Moreover, it would take a further four years for it to succeed in changing this role. This, when German social democracy had never before had someone who had pressed its case to be the party of government so urgently and self-confidently as Kurt Schumacher had done. And yet his policies were unmistakably a factor in it being denied power for so long.

Two weeks after the general election, the executive committee of the SPD passed a resolution on the sixteen so-called "Dürkheim points" which were approved soon after by the parliamentary party and the SPD Minister Presidents. They mapped out the SPD's understanding of its function and responsibility as a "constructive opposition". Erich Ollenhauer, now Schumacher's deputy not only as the party, but also the parliamentary party chairman, emphasised this with the slogan: "Our opposition programme of today will be our government programme of tomorrow."[1] In Dürkheim, the SPD had, for the first time after 1945, worked out a comprehensive programme of their most immediate tasks and goals. The bulk of the Dürkheim resolutions was concerned with economic and sociopolitical demands. They were directed towards planning and direct controls, the *Lastenausgleich* (equalisation of burdens, i. e., compensation for damage and loss caused by the war), co-determination, and the "disempowering of big business" while "safeguarding the free development of medium-size businesses and farms".[2]

In the first year of the Federal Republic, the principal target of the SPD's criticism of the government was the passivity of its labour-market policy: in the winter of 1950 there were almost two million out of work. In the wake of economic upturn and falling unemployment, however, the substance of Social Democrat accusations changed: the effectiveness of Erhard's policies were subject less and less to question, while the social injustices and hardship they produced came increasingly under fire. In a memorable phrase, they made the rich richer, and the poor poorer. Nonetheless, the differences of *principle* with the government were diminishing. Instead of stressing nationalisation and planning, the parliamentary party, and gradually the party too, laid increasing stress on more co-determination and on stimulating the economy. The programme for action adopted at the party congress in Dortmund in September 1952 demonstrated an important change of emphasis. The SPD, it was declared, would, along with planning, encourage "genuine competition in all branches of the economy, where appropriate", as well as "private ownership on a small and medium scale". In the changes and extensions made to the action programme two years later at the party congress in Berlin, the relationship between planning and competition was defined by the motto devised by the Hamburg Senator for Economic Affairs, Karl Schiller: "Competition as far as possible. Planning as far as necessary."[3]

In the sphere of domestic politics in its widest sense, the parliamentary practice of the SPD was entirely in keeping with its early resolution to be a "constructive opposition". This expressed itself not only in the important part it played in framing the considerable body of new legislation introduced in the first parliamentary terms of the Bundestag, but also in the fact that by far the largest proportion of all laws were passed with the

1 Protokoll des SPD-Parteitags 1950, p. 91.
2 Jahrbuch der Sozialdemokratischen Partei Deutschlands 1948/49 (Bonn 1950), pp. 18 ff.
3 See Dowe and Klotzbach (eds), Programmatische Dokumente (2004), pp. 276–323, quotations p. 295 and p. 298.

votes of the Social Democrats. Especially worthy of mention was their part in the legislation on the construction of public-sector housing, the integration of refugees, and reform of the national pension scheme. They also enjoyed a high profile in judicial policy with the Public Prosecutor Adolf Arndt, in the parliamentary decision on the Federal Constitutional Court, and reparations for the victims of National Socialism. The SPD deviated from the pragmatic policy of partial cooperation only on some pieces of important social legislation, on which the CDU/CSU adopted a confrontational stance, and which the SPD were insufficiently able to reconcile with their principles. They withheld their agreement, for instance, on the Equalisation of Burdens Law, as well as that on child benefit. While, in spring 1951, the law on the right of "co-determination" for employees in the mining and the iron and steel producing industries was adopted with the combined vote of the CDU and SPD, and against that of the FDP, the SPD found itself isolated on the question of the industrial relations law, and rejected the government draft. The Social Democrat parliamentary group regularly delivered a no to the federal budget. This was not a contravention of their policy on political cooperation on the domestic front, but a time-honoured, symbolic act of opposition.

The real rough-and-tumble took place not on domestic issues, but in the field of foreign, European, and defence policy. This is where the image of the SPD as the party of permanent negation was formed, and which forced it onto the defensive.[4]

1. *The Struggle for a "New National Self-Awareness"*

The most spectacular clash between the two dominant figures of the early years of the Federal Republic took place at the end of 1949 when Schumacher, in the debate on the Petersberg Agreement, denounced Adenauer as a "Chancellor of the Allies". As a punishment he was suspended for twenty sessions of the Bundestag. Shortly before his death on 20 August 1952, Schumacher summarised, in the foreword to the Dortmund action programme, the basic ideas which had governed his policies since 1945. It read like an angry and painful day of reckoning with Adenauer in stating that the Germans must "under no circumstances sink into a position

---

[4] Klaus Schütz demonstrates the repercussions which disputes over foreign policy issues had on the possibilities of the CDU and SPD reaching an understanding over social and economic policy – exemplified by the legislation on works committees and the Equalisation of Burdens Law. See Klaus Schütz, Die Sozialdemokratie im Nachkriegsdeutschland, pp. 251 ff.

of subservience; [...] the politics of German democracy must never become a function of the Western Allied powers"; the German people must be given "a new national self-awareness which is as far removed from the criminal arrogance of the past, as it is from the widespread inclination of today to regard every wish of the Allies as a revelation of European thinking". And even the leitmotiv-like sentence that, for the SPD, "German unification is not a distant, but an immediate goal", had a polemical undertone.

The decisions of the SPD – brought about by Schumacher and pursued by his successor Erich Ollenhauer – have to be seen against the background of this concept of the SPD chairman, one which he advocated all the more passionately, the more it clashed with the goals and tactical adaptability of his victorious opponent in the battle for state power. It revolved round three closely interconnected issues: the political and economic integration of the Federal Republic into Western Europe; its position within the Western bloc; its military rearmament.

At the instigation of the French Foreign Minister Robert Schumann in spring 1950, the Council of Europe invited the Federal Republic, along with the Saar – which due to France became independent – to join. This was followed by the Schumann Plan, drafted by Jean Monnet, for a European Coal and Steel Community. Adenauer, the European from the Rhineland, welcomed both plans, the "national" German Kurt Schumacher rejected them out of hand. His counter-argument was based primarily on the fact that the acceptance of the Saar would lead to its independence being abrogated in Strasbourg, but more generally on the character of the "Europe of the Six", now fast approaching, which he described as "conservative, clerical, capitalist, and cartelistic"[5]. He was undoubtedly motivated at a deeper level by the concern that integration would create even greater obstacles to the reunification of Germany. Moreover, his objections to the limitation of German sovereignty were lent an additional nationalistic twist by the weightiest argument against German participation in the European Coal and Steel Community, namely that the French would profit at the cost of their German partners.

At the party congress in Hamburg in May 1950, Schumacher, effectively supported, particularly on the question of the Council of Europe, by Carlo Schmid, received an overwhelming vote of confidence for his

5 Schumacher repeatedly invoked these "four c's" as typifying the "Europe of the Six", or "mini-Europe". The most concise summary of his overall criticism of these plans is to be found in one of Schumacher's speeches which was published as a pamphlet under the title 'Deutschlands Forderung: gleiches Risiko, gleiches Opfer, gleiche Chancen!' (Hanover, no date).

position: the resolution of the party executive was accepted, with only eleven votes against. However, the dissenters were men of some political weight: Ernst Reuter, Willy Brandt, Max Brauer, Paul Löbe. The Mayor of Bremen, Wilhelm Kaisen, who did not attend the congress, was on the side of the opposition and lost his seat on the executive.

Despite rejecting German entry to the Council of Europe, the SPD did of course send their representatives to Strasbourg, and soon they counted among its most respected members. Social Democrats also played an important, sometimes a leading role in every other European political and economic institution during the following period. In the economic organisations this was due not least to the fact that the German Trade Union Federation (DGB) had a positive, if not uncritical attitude to the ECSC. Notwithstanding their initial resistance to the "Europe of the Six", the SPD played a significant part in the development, shaping, and extending of it.[6]

Government and opposition were furthest apart over the dispute about rearmament. After the attack by Communist North Korea on the south of the divided country in June 1950, Konrad Adenauer offered to make a German contribution to the Western security system by militarily rearming the Federal Republic. Although, with the Korean War, the fear of Communism was growing, and in the GDR, even before it was founded, para-military organisations were being set up under the guise of the *Kasernierte Volkspolizei* (the People's Police in Barracks), rearmament was very unpopular. The attitude of the SPD membership was basically pacifist and anti-militaristic, as was that of many trade unionists and left-wing Protestants. The opposition of the SPD leadership to the creation of the Bundeswehr (Federal armed forces) and integration into a European Defence Community was able to draw support from this position without, however, identifying with it.

Schumacher was not in principle against German rearmament. His concept of defence – summed up in the formula, Germany must be defended at the Oder, not at the Elbe – called for the Federal Republic to be a completely equal partner of the victorious powers, and to play a central role. Just as when the Social Democrats rejected joining the first European institutions, their objection now to a German defence contribution was largely determined by the priority they gave to the reunification of Germany. The Stalin Note of 10 March 1952 is one of the most contentious events in the history of divided Germany. Adenauer regarded it as

---

6 Impressive testimony to this from the viewpoint of a leading French "European" was a letter from Jean Monnet to Herbert Wehner, published in Die Zeit on 13.10.1972.

nothing more than a disruptive manoeuvre by the Soviets, others saw it as a possible chance of Germany being united. The SPD urged that its seriousness be put to the test. They wanted to exhaust every possibility of the four occupying powers reaching an understanding on German reunification, in order to avoid West German forces, as part of a Western defence system, being responsible for hardening even further the two opposing fronts which ran through the middle of Germany. The federal government, however, was irrevocably committed to its "Western course" and a "policy of strength", and was not prepared to negotiate with Stalin who had called for this line to be reversed.

The death of the Soviet dictator Stalin on 5 March 1953 aroused hopes, in the East as well as the West, of a less restrictive and aggressive course. After the founding of the German Democratic Republic (GDR) in October 1949, the authorities pushed ahead with the sovietisation of state and society on the Moscow model of Communist dictatorship. The consequences of the "construction of socialism" were a rising tide of people fleeing the country, and chronic shortages and economic crisis which the politburo attempted to stem, after the change of leadership in Moscow, by introducing the "New Course". Discontent spread throughout almost the entire population, and from 11 June 1953 there were protest rallies and occasional strikes. The strike and demonstrations by building workers in East Berlin on 17 June 1953 escalated, in Berlin and many other towns and cities in the GDR, into a mass movement, a general workers' revolt which was tantamount to a national uprising. Social Democratic thinking and traditions were clearly still alive, and manifested themselves in calls for the SPD to be reinstated, and in the singing of the old Social Democrat song "Brothers, into the sunshine and freedom". The uprising was far more than a social protest: it was also a broad political movement pressing for both free elections and German unification.

With the forces at the disposal of the GDR regime not up to the task, the Soviets deployed their tanks and the army to quell the uprising. At least 50 demonstrators were killed, 3,000 were arrested by the Soviets, and 13,000 later taken into custody by the GDR authorities. But 40 Red Army soldiers also lost their lives: most of them shot for refusing to carry out orders. The Ulbricht regime responded to this mass revolt by extending the network of spies and surveillance. For the great majority of people in the GDR, 17 June was traumatic: first the bloodbath, then increased repression – all with the West standing by in silence.[7]

---

7 See Heinrich August Winkler, Der lange Weg nach Westen. Deutsche Geschichte vom "Dritten Reich" bis zur Wiedervereinigung (Munich 2001), vol. II, p. 157f.

In summer 1953, the Bundestag declared 17 June the "Day of German Unity", which was thereafter celebrated annually with commitments to unity and freedom. For Willy Brandt, the insurgent workers were "combatants in the forefront of the fight for unity in freedom"[8], for Konrad Adenauer the events in the GDR were an affirmation of his policy of integrating with the West and rearmament as a safeguard against the threat posed by the Soviet Union.

In the Bundestag elections on 6 September 1953, the big winner was the CDU/CSU with 45.2 per cent (1949 only 31.0), while the SPD, with its poorest result of 28.8 per cent, losing even its blocking minority, and Adenauer, with his coalition, having a two-thirds majority which allowed him to amend the constitution. With the SPD voting against, the Bundestag decided in February 1954 on an amendment to the Basic Law which made possible the introduction of armed forces and military service. Every effort by the Social Democrats to prevent the creation of the Bundeswehr was in vain. When the French parliament scuppered the European Defence Community in 1954, the West German defence contribution was made within the framework of the newly founded NATO. With the Paris Treaties of October 1954, the Federal Republic, by means of a revision of the *Deutschlandvertrag* (German Treaty) of 1952, received almost all the powers of a sovereign state – with the exception, however, of so-called ABC and strategic weapons. The Western powers, however, retained all their rights "with respect to Berlin and Germany as a whole". When on 5 May 1955 the amended *Deutschlandvertrag* and the Paris Treaties came into force, the Soviet Union responded on 14 May by setting up the Warsaw Pact with its satellites. The provisional solution to the Saar question agreed in Paris, in which Adenauer relinquished Germany's claim on it, was bitterly opposed by the Social Democrats and, in the plebiscite of 23 October, rejected by the Saarlanders by a large majority (67 per cent). On 1 January 1957, the Saar was returned to Germany, a first step (secured in the face of French resistance) on the path to freedom in unity.

The SPD rejected the Paris Treaties and all the laws serving the setting up of armed forces as "laws resulting from treaties". Their opposition to political, economic, and military Western integration attracted them the odium of being the party of permanent negation, and left them out in the cold as regards the Atlantic Alliance. Only gradually, when confronted by *faits accomplis* and the realities of world politics, did the party begin to modify its approach, even to questions of defence and security policy.

---

8 Speech of 1.7.1953 in the Bundestag. Verhandlungen des Deutschen Bundestages, Stenographische Berichte, vol. 17, p. 13883. See also, Willy Brandt, My Road to Berlin (London 1960), pp. 233–4.

The efforts of Fritz Erler played a large part in this. The Stuttgart party conference of 1958 argued for "a limited number of mobile and well-trained troops made up of volunteers"[9]. There was intensive collaboration from the SPD on the drafting of laws dealing with soldiers' basic rights, and, with their help, these were approved by the Bundestag.[10] They were instrumental in creating the office of Defence Commissioner. In contrast to their opposition in principle to Adenauer's policy of Western integration, in the day-to-day running of parliament they showed themselves to be a "constructive opposition".

The SPD's opposition to rearmament was lent an extra dimension by the fact that the party's battle was also being fought outside parliament.[11] By collecting signatures for a "German Manifesto", which was drawn up in the Paulskirche in Frankfurt on 29 January 1955, it attempted to initiate a mass movement against rearmament and Western treaties. The result did not, however, come up to their expectations. True, the SPD managed to win over several well-known writers, academics, and theologians for their ban-the-bomb campaign launched four years later with the aim of securing a nuclear-free zone. They also managed to organise some impressive mass rallies. But it helped the SPD to bring about neither the plebiscite on atomic weapons they were seeking, nor to influence the general mood in their favour – as is demonstrated by the North Rhine-Westphalian elections of July 1958, where the CDU achieved an overall majority. It was understandable, therefore, that the ban-the-bomb campaign should have been broken off so abruptly, but it was nevertheless a disappointment, particularly for those people who, attracted by it, had only just begun to warm to the SPD.

After Nikita Khrushchev's Berlin Ultimatum at the end of 1958 and the offensive from the East to change the status quo in Germany, the SPD embarked on a desperate, but problematical attempt to propagate – in order to make the reunification of Germany an "immediate goal" – a "Third Way" in the form of a "confederation". The "SPD Plan for Germany", largely inspired and formulated by Herbert Wehner, was presented in March 1959. It provided for a militarily "diluted" zone in central Europe, from which both NATO and the Warsaw Pact countries would

---

9 Protokoll des SPD-Parteitags 1958, p. 488.
10 See Udo F. Löwke, Für den Fall, dass ... Die Haltung der SPD zur Wehrfrage 1949–1955 (Hanover 1969), pp. 119–121.
11 See Hans Karl Rupp, Außerparlamentarische Opposition in der Ära Adenauer: Der Kampf gegen die Atombewaffnung in den fünfziger Jahren. Eine Studie zur innerpolitischen Entwicklung der BRD (Cologne 1970), esp. pp. 47 ff., pp. 98 ff., pp. 127 ff., pp. 149 ff., pp. 173 ff., pp. 213 ff., pp. 250 ff. and pp. 263 ff.

withdraw, as well as a step-by-step political and economic drawing together of both halves of Germany as preparation for all-German elections. The plan was fiercely attacked from all sides. It was illusory from a power-political point of view, was incompatible with the interests of the West which, at that point, was putting its faith in *détente* and solving the Berlin question, a step which involved relegating German unification to a back seat. And finally, even the Soviet Union regarded it merely as an indication that the West was going soft. The plan was quickly shelved. The fact that its publication coincided with the return of Fritz Erler and Carlo Schmidt from a trip to Moscow, bringing with them the impression of Soviet intransigency, may also have contributed to its being quietly buried.

And so, the first decade of the Federal Republic ended with the recognition by the SPD that the achievement of their "most crucial national goal, the restoration of the unity of Germany in freedom [...] was more remote than at any time since the end of the war". And "domestically too, nothing has basically changed in the conflicting positions of the Adenauer one-party government and the Social Democratic opposition". In July 1960, when Erich Ollenhauer presented this balance sheet of stagnation[12], a new direction was already being set in the party which would send the stalled party machine off down quite a different track.

2. *Party Reform and the Godesberg Programme*

The development of the Social Democrats' share of the vote in the Bundestag elections from 1949 to 1972 shows an upward curve, with an almost constant increase of three to four per cent in each election. The only downward blip is at the beginning. In 1953 the SPD lost 0.4 per cent of its share of the vote compared to 1949, and the CDU/CSU gained 14.2 points, with Adenauer and Erhard being the big winners. This result unleashed a discussion in the party of a breadth and liveliness unprecedented in the postwar era.[13] Criticism was directed at the organisation of the party, as well as at its image and propaganda. The actual policy of the SPD since 1945 was excluded from the discussion. The calls were not to change it, but to find better ways of "selling" it.

12 In the foreword to the Jahrbuch der SPD 1958/59, p. 7.
13 Heinz-Joachim Mann gives a concise account of this internal party debate in 'Das Godesberger Programm als Ergebnis innerparteilicher Willensbildung', in Geist und Tat, 24, no. 4 (1969). A more comprehensive account is to be found in Kurt Klotzbach's Der Weg zur Staatspartei. Programmatik, praktische Politik und Organisation der deutschen Sozialdemokratie 1945 bis 1965 (Berlin/Bonn 1982), pp. 308–325. (New edition, Bonn 1996).

One way of characterising the unrest which gripped the SPD from 1953 might be to see it as an attempt to come to terms with the party's past. It was Carlo Schmid who talked of the necessity of "jettisoning ideological ballast", something immediately seized on, and which provoked intense discussion. All part of this "ballast" were the party symbols and conventions: the red flag, the address form "comrade", the use of "Du", the familiar "you". But beyond these minor matters, there was the whole question of the role played by Marxism in shaping party thinking.

The executive set up two commissions to evaluate the discussion: one to deal with organisational points, the other to handle all the other issues. While the recommendations accepted by the executive[14] had no visible effect, other decisions were of significance for the further development of the party. The 1954 preamble to the 1952 Dortmund action programme contained some of the important principles of the Godesberg Programme of 1959, as for instance, ideological openness in arguing the merits of socialism and the SPD's conception of itself as a workers' party which had become a *Volkspartei*, a party of the whole people. In addition, there were moves to step up the work of education within the party and to found a theoretical journal. At the party conference in Berlin (1954), which brought the discussion of 1953 to a kind of close, it was decided to establish a commission to work out a basic political programme.

The debate about personalities had already played something of a role after 1953. It became even livelier after the disappointing Bundestag elections of 1957 when, although the SPD gained three percentage points, the CDU/CSU still won an absolute majority. At the centre of the discussion was the party chairman Erich Ollenhauer, whose lack of appeal as Chancellor candidate was held partially responsible for the election defeat. The *Apparat*, or the "bureau" of salaried members of the executive committee at party headquarters, were accused of blocking the selection of attractive Chancellorship contenders and a prospective government team who would appeal to the electorate. The reforms which influential figures and the party organisations behind them were seeking, were aimed at disempowering the *Apparat*, and at restructuring the leadership of both party and the parliamentary party and replacing them with fresh personnel. The parliamentary party went ahead with this in 1957. They elected three new deputy chairmen in Fritz Erler, Carlo Schmid, and Herbert Wehner who threw their political weight behind a modernisation of the party and its policies. The party followed suit at the Stuttgart party conference in May 1958. Although Erich Ollenhauer was re-elected party chairman, he was

---

14 Published in the Jahrbuch der SPD 1954/55, pp. 320 ff.

allotted two deputy chairmen in Waldemar von Knoeringen and Herbert Wehner who were chosen to represent the full spectrum of Social Democratic opinion. Wehner, at that time, was held to be the most prominent exponent of the left, Knoeringen was – particularly in Bavaria – a very popular politician in the tradition of his important fellow-Bavarian Georg von Vollmar. The institution of the "bureau" was abolished, and two of its members, Herta Gotthelf and Fritz Heine, were not re-elected to the executive. After the changes made in Stuttgart to the organisational statute, a committee the 'party presidium' elected from the party executive committee was now responsible to the management.

Also in Stuttgart, there was the first reading of a political programme drafted by a commission chaired by Willi Eichler. Although instigated at the Berlin party conference of 1954, the commission's work on the programme did not begin until March 1955 and made slow progress. After the shock of a third electoral defeat, Erich Ollenhauer pressed for it to be brought to a speedy conclusion, and approved. His belief in the possibility, at this stage, of creating a political programme, and his expectation that it would be an important lever with which to boost the appeal and impact of the party, were by no means shared by the entire party leadership. Particularly those who were considered to be "reformers", such as Willy Brandt, Fritz Erler, Helmut Schmidt, and Herbert Wehner, had misgivings about laying down a new programme of principles for democratic socialism and committing the party to them for the long term. They would have much preferred the party to limit itself to an action programme.

Up until Stuttgart, the party as a whole had demonstrated virtually no interest in the preparation of the programme, and even after the publication of the draft, only a mild one. But then, an intensive discussion got underway at all levels of the party. At hundreds of meetings, Eichler in particular, as chairman of the programme commission, and Heinrich Deist as author of the economic section, debated the very numerous objections and suggestions for changes. On the instructions of the party presidium a second, substantially tightened up and amended draft was drawn up and the section "The Order of the State" reformulated by Adolf Arndt. After the executive committee of the party had adopted the second reworked draft, an extraordinary party conference was called to reach a decision on it. Some 340 delegates gathered in Bad Godesberg from 13 to 15 November 1959, and had to deal with 200 motions on the second draft. In the final vote on the draft, some parts of which had been amended in Godesberg, it was passed almost unanimously. There were only 16 votes against.

The most remarkable thing about the Godesberg Programme was its refusal to identify with any particular ideological or theoretical line. It

Corrected draft of a page from the Godesberg Programme (Willi Eichler)

committed itself to "basic values" and "basic demands" which were open to various religious or philosophical interpretation. This openness removed barriers which had hitherto prevented the SPD from gaining followers from especially amongst those who held religious beliefs.[15] The programme also made explicit its respect for the "particular task" of the Church and its "independence".

In Godesberg, the most controversial parts of the programme were still the statements on economic policy. The stress on competition which was already to be found in the Dortmund action programme was emphasised even more strongly in the Basic Programme. The term "socialisation" no longer crops up, but one paragraph, however, is dedicated to "public ownership" which is "useful and necessary" as "a legitimate form of public control" where "a healthy organisation of economic power cannot be guaranteed". In connection with the statements on "the trade unions and the economy", reference was made to the fact that the co-determination which already existed in some industries would have to be "extended to all branches of the economy".

The section on national defence stated unreservedly that the SPD was "in favour of national defence". What followed marked out its policy goals for security and peace: international *détente*, disarmament and the outlawing of weapons of mass destruction, prohibition of the production and use of atomic and other weapons of mass destruction in the Federal Republic, the inclusion of the whole of Germany in a European zone of *détente*.

For the rest, the Godesberg Programme was basically a *résumé* of the principles which had guided the SPD since 1945: a commitment to parliamentary democracy, sharp demarcation between itself and Communism, protection of the right to freedom of the individual, striving for social justice, solidarity with the weak, promotion of science and education. There was very little on the controversial term "socialism". The Programme made reference to the historical roots of democratic socialism in Europe: Christian ethics, humanism, and classical philosophy. Then in "Our Path" we find: "The purpose of socialism was, and is, to eliminate the privileges of the ruling classes and to bring freedom, justice, and prosperity to all people". Earlier conceptions of a socialist "final goal", which had their origins in Marxism, were implicitly rejected in the observation that socialism was "a task in perpetuity – to battle for and preserve freedom and justice, and to prove oneself in them".

The adoption of the Godesberg Programme undoubtedly contributed much to the calm and clarity of the party internally, but its main value lay in changing the image of the SPD in the public eye. This was the prereq-

---

15 Although, after 1945, there had already been a loosening in this respect, the SPD had in North Rhine-Westphalia, for instance, never succeeded in the fifties in securing a direct mandate in districts where there were more than 40 per cent Catholics.

uisite for achieving their goal of becoming a *Volkspartei* which people of all classes would vote for.

Of course, even more important decisions affecting personnel and policies needed to be made after Godesberg in order to finally escape the "30 per cent ghetto". The SPD in the Weimar and Wilhelminian eras had offered its members a "parental home and a purpose in life" (to use Otto Bauer's apt description) in the shape of a comprehensive club life – workers' gymnastics, sports, and ramblers organisations, the free-thinkers' association, the workers' choral union and orchestra, book clubs, people's theatre, chess clubs, etc. – but at the same time this had also isolated it from the rest of society. After the Second World War, the social democratic milieu in the GDR was, despite considerable resistance, broken up and destroyed. In the West, a social democratic sub-culture in the old sense had either collapsed or been absorbed into society at large. In a region such as the Ruhr, for instance, where the party had been rather weak before 1933, a broad culture of work and leisure developed amongst ordinary people which was very much SPD-influenced. Based on close links between workplace and the community, it was best exemplified by the local "multi-functionary" who was always on hand to offer moral and practical support where needed. This gave the Social Democrats a firm anchor point in everyday social life which, over time, helped to widen their influence. This was demonstrated most clearly by the popularity enjoyed by many prominent local and regional SPD *Landesväter*, widely trusted patriarchal figures such as Hinrich Wilhelm Kopf in Lower Saxony and Georg August Zinn in Hesse, Max Brauer and Wilhelm Kaisen in the city states of Hamburg and Bremen, and the well-known mayors who, in most cities from Kiel to Regensburg, and from Cologne to Kassel, were members of the SPD. Beginning with Louise Schroeder, the mayors of Berlin all seemed to embody the city's vitality and love of freedom. The importance of Ernst Reuter, of course, went far beyond that of a city head. In his relatively short time in office – he died in 1953 – he became a statesman of European significance. The same applied to Willy Brandt.

The esteem enjoyed by SPD state and local politicians rested primarily on their concrete achievements. In addition, many of them gained their particular celebrity by taking part in traditional events and festivals which enabled them to reach a far wider public than through conventional political channels. These popular SPD politicians of the fifties and sixties were mostly seasoned Social Democrats from the Weimar period; many of them, such as Kaisen, Brauer, and Reuter, had held responsible posts at that time. Labelling them, therefore, as "new-style" Social Democrats,

Willy Brandt and Erich Ollenhauer in conversation (1954)

in contrast to Ollenhauer and other *Apparat*-"functionaries"[16], did not quite meet the case. These were people who were the product of various different jobs and functions. This was vital: for the image of the SPD as a *Volkspartei* it was important to come up with personalities who were independent of the *Apparat*, and whose work and public activity had made them known and popular with large sections of the population. By comparison with the other parties, the SPD at state and local level had the greatest reservoir of politicians of this sort. At national level, too, with Brandt, Erler, Möller, Helmut Schmidt and Schiller, men were coming

---

16 See H.K. Schellenger, The SPD in the Bonn Republic. A Socialist Party modernizes (Den Haag 1968), pp. 131 ff.

forward who would not be shackled by the restraints of the *Apparat*, and whose charisma, competence, and energy gave them a high public profile. It was to the credit of Erich Ollenhauer, and the men and women who had helped him to lay the foundations for the SPD after 1945, that they were able to change its image without becoming either a party of notabilities, or an election machine. The SPD remained a members' party, and one which was able to extend its base considerably over the coming years.

3. A Party in Waiting

"We have to acknowledge that, given the present state of society, we are not swimming with the tide, but against it". When Fritz Erler made this statement in 1950 at the highest level of the party[17], the insight it expressed was still far from being generally accepted within the SPD. Erler's image of swimming against the tide is nevertheless a perfect description of the politics of German social democracy from the end of the Second World War until the late 1950s. The Godesberg Programme considerably increased the party's room for manoeuvre, but its real shift in policy was not determined directly by the principles enshrined in it, but rested on a constellation of changed circumstances and the conclusions drawn from them.

The integration of the Federal Republic into the West and the Atlantic Alliance was complete. Moscow had consolidated its empire with the bloody and violent suppression of the Hungarian uprising and of Polish workers in 1956. The Soviets' possession of intercontinental ballistic missiles, and the "Sputnik" shock of 1957, demonstrated the gradual establishment of an atomic balance of power, and it was becoming clear that there were now only two players on the world stage. The international climate was showing the first tentative signs of détente and partial cooperation between the two leading powers, while the issue of Germany was in a state of stagnation. Nikita Khrushchev's Berlin ultimatum had been on the table since 1958, and the negotiations on the German question at the Four Powers Foreign Ministers' Conference in Geneva in 1959 had reached deadlock.

Clear signals now emerged from the SPD inviting a common approach, where possible, between government and opposition on crucial issues affecting the German people, particularly in foreign affairs and *Deutschlandpolitik*. The main driving force behind this "common approach strategy" was Herbert Wehner – which is why the "Germany Plan" of 1959 seemed as if they were endeavouring to shoot themselves in the foot.

17 Protokoll des SPD-Parteitags 1950, p. 247.

After Khrushchev's dramatic scuppering of the Paris summit conference in May 1960, Wehner gave a speech on 30 June 1960 in the Bundestag foreign affairs debate which caused a sensation. It had not come out of the blue, however: the product of intensive party discussion, it was a tactical *tour de force*. It proposed a joint foreign policy, invoked the community of interest of all democrats, and committed the SPD unambivalently to Western integration and NATO. Wehner saw it as a "sign of the times that, while we may continue to maintain a healthy difference on domestic policies, a divided Germany cannot tolerate Christian Democrats and Social Democrats being endlessly at each other's throats. Instead, therefore, of tearing each other apart, we should work together within the overall democratic framework."[18]

With Wehner's speech, the SPD were acknowledging the realities created in the Adenauer era of being tied firmly to the West. By voting unequivocally for joint action in the interests of the nation and democracy they built the first bridges to the FDP and demolished the barriers separating them from the CDU. The static relationship between government and opposition now showed signs of change. Even though it was criticised by the intelligentsia, the policy of cooperation which the SPD continued to pursue was overwhelmingly popular with ordinary citizens. Even the Springer press, with the *"BILD"-Zeitung* to the fore, lent the SPD its support.

The Bundestag election campaign of 1961 was marked by a sense of fresh style. Its most noticeable characteristic was the decisive change in personnel. At the party conference in Hanover at the end of November 1960, Willy Brandt was introduced as the new Chancellor candidate, along with his "team": Max Brauer, Heinrich Deist, Fritz Erler, Wenzel Jaksch, Alex Möller, Willi Richter, Carlo Schmid, Fritz Steinhoff, Käte Strobel and Georg August Zinn. These had been selected by a commission of seven members of the party executive for their suitability for government office, but also because of their popularity and the influence they had with particular electoral groups: Jaksch, for instance, was a leading figure in the Union of Expellees, Richter was chairman of the Federation of German Trade Unions.

When measured by traditional party-hierarchical standards, the boldest decision was to make Willy Brandt the SPD's candidate for the Chancel-

---

[18] Verhandlungen des Deutschen Bundestages (stenographic report), vol. 46, pp. 7058–61. For the context and preparation of this speech, see Heinrich Potthoff, 'Herbert Wehner '60. Anerkennung der außenpolitischen Realitäten', in Die Neue Gesellschaft/Frankfurter Hefte, 1/2 2001, pp. 39 ff. Walter, in his Die SPD. Vom Proletariat zur Neuen Mitte (Berlin 2002), p. 164, perpetuates the myth that Wehner "had not breathed a single word of it to anyone beforehand".

lorship. Brandt had only been elected to the executive in 1958, and was not even a member of the party presidium. His party power base was in Berlin where, after a long, tough power struggle with Franz Neumann and his supporters, he became regional chairman of the SPD in 1958. He achieved great public esteem as Governing Mayor of Berlin and was respected far beyond the confines of the Federal Republic. He had taken over this post after the death of Otto Suhr in 1957. Particularly in situations of crisis, he revealed himself to be a prudent, convincing politician who also enjoyed a high measure of trust with the USA, the city's "guardian angel". Brandt was a man of the West who, like Ernst Reuter, came to embody the self-assertive courage demonstrated by Berlin in facing the Communist threat. His belief in being firmly anchored in the Atlantic Alliance, while at the same time cautiously seeking a rapprochement with the East, was largely at one with the new course which the party leadership had adopted since summer 1960.[19] Brandt also appealed to the non-core vote. He was popular. As a kind of German Kennedy he would soon eclipse the eighty-four-year old Konrad Adenauer.

At the party conference in Hanover, Brandt described "community of interest and decency" as the "two pillars of a new-style politics".[20] The conference resolutions focused on a range of domestic political demands up to and including environmental protection ("Blue skies over the Ruhr once more" was the slogan), while in foreign policy the emphasis was on achieving "a broad basis" for the representation of the right to self-determination and reunification, as well as on preventing Berlin being separated from the West.[21] The government programme of April 1961 contained more concrete proposals: namely, rejection of the two-states theory and calls for the extension of the EEC, more objective handling of relations with the peoples of eastern Europe, and the improvement of development aid.

Circumstances changed dramatically with the building of the Berlin Wall on 13 August 1961. The "hour of great disillusionment"[22] had come.

19 The significance of Brandt's foreign policy orientation for his nomination as Chancellor candidate is recognised, but over-emphasised by Abraham Ashkenasi in his Reformpartei und Außenpolitik. Die Außenpolitik der SPD (Berlin-Bonn, Cologne, and Opladen 1968), p. 196. This is neglected by Gregor Schöllgen in Willy Brandt. Die Biographie (Berlin/Munich 2001). His account, which sees Brandt's political life as a series of defeats, is superficial and does not do Brandt justice.
20 Protokoll des SPD-Parteitags 1960, p. 674.
21 Jahrbuch der SPD 1960/61, p. 420.
22 The CDU politician Heinrich Krone's description in his notes on Deutschland- and Ostpolitik in Rudolf Morsey/Konrad Repgen (eds), Adenauer-Studien (Mainz 1974), vol. 3, p. 162f.

But it was inevitable that Berlin would eventually be cut off. The flood of refugees had risen rapidly since 1960, due mainly to the forcible collectivisation of agriculture. Already in March 1961, at a meeting of the Warsaw Pact, Walter Ulbricht had called for the border in Berlin to be closed. Fearing that this last escape hole would be blocked, the flood of refugees became even greater. In the early hours of the morning of 13 August, the border with West Berlin was sealed off with barbed wire and barricades, and then subsequently made impassable with a wall, and behind that, with a restricted zone. From now on, anyone attempting to escape risked life and limb.

The reaction of the federal government was one of helplessness, dismaying even Adenauer's close party allies. The *"BILD"-Zeitung* reflected the general public mood with its front page of 16 August: "The West is doing NOTHING! President Kennedy remains silent [...] MacMillan is off shooting and Adenauer is abusing Brandt". The initial reaction of the population, particularly Berliners, was one of absolute outrage. Chancellor Adenauer kept resolutely out of it, continuing his tirade against "Mr Brandt, alias Frahm". Willy Brandt immediately interrupted his election campaign: his place was now in Berlin. Energetically, and yet responsibly, he faced up to the Moscovites and urged the hesitant Americans to take a more active role. But the three Western Allies merely accepted the building of the Wall. Their function as a protecting power extended only to West Berlin. The request of the USA, that German policy should simply acknowledge the reality of the divided city, came as a disillusioning shock.

It gradually began to dawn, however, that 13 August 1961 marked the end of one phase in postwar history, and the beginning of another. The building of the Wall represented a deep caesura. For people in the GDR, it meant being almost completely cut off, the apparently final banishment to a camp from which there was virtually no escape. It seemed as if the GDR had firmly established itself as an independent Communist German state, and for many people under this dictatorship their only hope was to somehow come to terms with the system. On the other side, the citizens of the Federal Republic increasingly resigned themselves over the coming years to the fact of a divided Germany. They sought the right to an independent existence for their provisional Federal Republic and to find their political and social identity within Europe and the Western world.

In the federal elections of 17 September 1961, the SPD won 36.2 per cent of the votes, their best result so far at national level, and an increase of 4.4 points. After the building of the Wall, Brandt and the SPD at first outstripped Chancellor Adenauer and the CDU/CSU, but the mood changed in the shadow cast by the fear of war. The SPD remained the opposition party in Bonn. Although their proposal to form an all-party government for these troubled times met with some resonance among the general public, Adenauer soldiered on in coalition with the FDP.

But it was becoming clear that the government could not continue for ever in face of the SPD challenge, and the political fronts began to crumble. Adenauer's authority had suffered, and his days as Chancellor were numbered. In foreign policy, the CDU/CSU was split by the rift between "Gaullists" and "Atlanticists"[23], and there were repeated tensions and conflicts within the coalition over domestic policy, ignited by issues such as social, budgetary, and taxation policy and the statute of limitations on Nazi war crimes, as well as by Franz Josef Strauß and the many dubious deals associated with his name: the FIBAG, HS 30, and Starfighter affairs, for instance. This opened up possibilities for the SPD to flex its muscle by cooperating variously with the FDP or sections of the CDU/CSU, thus putting some of its own ideas into play and continuing to loosen the bonds of the coalition.

With the world gripped by anxiety over the Cuban missile crisis, and the break-up of the CDU/CSU-FDP coalition in November 1962 over the *Spiegel*-affair, it was clear that the SPD already had its foot in the door of government. On the one hand, in the cooperation of left-wing Liberals and Social Democrats, there was the hint of a possible SPD-FDP coalition, on the other, the talks between Wehner and the CDU/CSU deputies Karl Theodor Freiherr von Guttenberg and Paul Lücke led to the first negotiations on a Grand Coalition. It was true that neither produced any tangible result, and that the old coalition was renewed, but after December 1962 all three parties in the Bundestag were *koalitionsfähig*, or capable of forming a coalition with one another. The possibility of both options was open to the SPD. The debate about the necessity and expediency of a Grand Coalition continued to smoulder away, while the prospect of an SPD-FDP coalition was visible on the horizon. The SPD had a bargaining chip in the Emergency Laws, since their vote was needed to introduce an amendment to the Basic Law. With tenacity, circumspection and vision, they used this situation to draw the authoritarian teeth of the government's draft bill and to facilitate a solution which was compatible with the spirit of parliamentary democracy. To be sure, the course adopted by the parliamentary party and the leadership met with often severe criticism from sections of the SPD, the trade unions, young people, and left-wing

---

23 The Gaullists advocated close cooperation with France, the Atlanticists favoured stronger ties with the USA.

liberal professors, but it also raised the profile of the SPD as a mature party ready to take on the responsibilities of state.[24]

The public increasingly came to regard the SPD during this time as a political force which combined a sense of responsibility with both expertise and modernity. They were seen as the champions of forward-looking policies on education, science, and transport, and in charge of budgetary, finance, and economic policy were figures such as Alex Möller and Karl Schiller who were the very essence of authority and solidity. In *Deutschlandpolitik* and foreign policy they found a way out of the political dead end which the 13 August 1961 had thrown so dramatically into focus. In tandem with global efforts to bring about *détente* between East and West, Brandt and his Berlin team introduced the "policy of small steps". This led to the first of several subsequent permit agreements (up to 1966) which allowed West Berliners to cross into East Berlin at Christmas 1963, making the Wall less impenetrable and giving people fresh hope.

After the death of Erich Ollenhauer on 14 December 1963, Willy Brandt was elected party chairman. At the head of the parliamentary party was Fritz Erler, who impressed both as a brilliant and competent parliamentarian and as an acute analyst who combined liberal views with leadership ability. Herbert Wehner had a firm grip on the reins of the party organisation. Together with such outstanding intellects as Alex Möller and Karl Schiller, this "triumvirate" was clearly superior to their opposites in government who were showing palpable signs of wear and tear. In Helmut Schmidt, who as Minister for Internal Affairs had demonstrated his leadership qualities in the catastrophic Hamburg floods of 1962, and had gained wide respect, there was another hopeful waiting in the wings.

The result of the 1965 elections did not, however, come up to expectations. With a 39.3 per cent share of the vote, the SPD lagged far behind the CDU/CSU with 47.6 per cent. Ludwig Erhard, who was elected Adenauer's successor in 1963, fulfilled his role as an "electoral locomotive". In 1965, the aura he enjoyed as the father of the economic miracle brought the Union yet another electoral victory. But on his very own territory, and as a symbol of affluence, Erhard and his reputation went into rapid decline. Budget deficits and the withdrawal of pre-election bonuses, a worsening economy, and the coal crisis all affected the political climate. In the Landtag elections in North Rhine-Westphalia, which Erhard had made a test of national policies, the CDU suffered a severe setback. The SPD, which, since spring 1966 with its planned exchange of speakers with

---

24 For a comprehensive account, see Michael Schneider, Demokratie in Gefahr? Der Konflikt um die Notstandsgesetze. Sozialdemokratie, Gewerkschaften und intellektueller Protest (1958–1968) (Bonn 1986).

the SED, had mounted an offensive in the sphere of *Deutschlandpolitik*, now seized the initiative in financial and economic policy through Karl Schiller. They received support from business, parts of the Union, and above all from the federal states, a majority of which opposed the course being steered by Erhard, and then unanimously rejected the government's budget.

III. The Social Democrats in Government

1. *The SPD in the Grand Coalition*

The SPD's chance of coming to power came when the existing government coalition found itself in what was widely regarded as a serious crisis. By autumn 1966, it was abundantly clear that Erhard was no longer up to the task of dealing with the domestic political difficulties which were manifesting themselves in economic recession, rising unemployment, the "affair of the Generals" in the Bundeswehr, and NPD gains in Landtag and local elections. Moreover, in its foreign policy, and against the background of *détente*, the Federal Republic was in danger of becoming isolated. When the four FDP ministers resigned from the government, Erhard was abruptly dropped by his party. A proposal by Willy Brandt that fresh elections should be held immediately, stood no chance of being accepted.[1] Negotiations on a new government coalition had begun with Erhard still in office. Various possibilities had been considered – a fresh version of the old coalition, a Grand Coalition, and a social-liberal coalition – and coalition talks held on all of them. Things were clearly running in favour of a Grand Coalition, however, as was shown by the nomination of Kurt Georg Kiesinger, who had defeated the advocate of a CDU-FDP coalition, Gerhard Schröder, as the CDU/CSU's Chancellor candidate. The concern over the stability of the Bonn democracy aroused by the entry of the NPD into the Hesse Landtag, and the pressure to consolidate the budget by means of economy measures and tax rises, spoke in favour of a broadly based government. On 26 to 27 November, negotiations between the CDU/CSU and the SPD reached a positive conclusion. The SPD parliamentary group and the responsible party committees finally decided by a large majority in favour of forming a government composed of the CDU/CSU and the SPD. In the history of German social democracy, the formation of the Grand Coalition in 1966 belongs to the chapter on hotly debated, internal party-political decisions.[2] An alternative might

---

1 Brandt had already made this suggestion on 22.10.1966 at a meeting of the SPD in Berlin. See the Stuttgarter Zeitung of 24.10.1966. Also the SPD-Jahrbuch 1966/67, p. 21.
2 The documentation published by the SPD executive gives a good overall account. See Bestandsaufnahme 1966 (Bonn 1966). Even at the Nuremberg party conference of 17 to 21.3.1968 the coalition was still the subject of vigorous debate.

have been to form a government with the FDP, which, with the Chancellor coming from the SPD, would have given them much greater leverage. The SPD, however, could not afford the risk of going into government with such a narrow parliamentary majority, particularly with that risk being increased by differences within the FDP. As the negotiations revealed, the pressing financial, budgetary, and economic problems could hardly have been solved, given that the FDP was plagued with anxieties about its continuing existence. With the CDU/CSU on the other hand there was a broad consensus on these issues, and in *Ost-* and *Deutschlandpolitik*, the CDU/CSU had moved closer to the SPD agenda. Brandt answered those critics of the Grand Coalition who were of the opinion that "those who had driven the cart into the mud should pull it out" by retorting: "We have become too big for that". The effort "must be made to make a limited but attainable success of this for the sake of both Germany and the SPD, who will, if they can demonstrate their competence in the crucial areas, gain themselves further trust"[3].

Subsequent developments proved him right. The Grand Coalition government under Kurt Georg Kiesinger, in which there were nine ministers and eight secretaries of state from the SPD, was successful in several important areas, and the "bonus of office" which the SPD gained in the process would help them to reach their ultimate goal. The most decisive, immediately discernible results were achieved in the economic and financial spheres. Minister of Economics, Karl Schiller, together with Minister of Finance, Franz Josef Strauß – whose presence in the coalition cabinet was hard to swallow for many Social Democrats – managed to lower the number of unemployed remarkably quickly: by autumn 1968 it stood at under one per cent. Industrial output rose by almost 12 per cent in 1968. An important factor in the successful economic and financial policy of the new Bonn government was persuading both trade unions and entrepreneurs to accept a programme of "concerted action". In general, the cooperation between the trade unions and the employers enabled the government to implement their plans for a revitalisation of the economy relatively smoothly.

Of particular importance were the various measures undertaken jointly by the state and national governments to solve the crisis in the Ruhr mining industry. In the North Rhine-Westphalian Landtag elections of July 1966, the SPD had been the strongest party, and had only narrowly missed

---

[3] Brandt to the SPD Party Council on 28.11.1966. Ibid., Bestandsaufnahme. A shorter version in Wolther von Kieseritzky (ed.), Willy Brandt. Berliner Ausgabe, vol. 7: Mehr Demokratie wagen. Innen- und Gesellschaftspolitik 1966–1974 (Bonn 2001), pp. 114–124, quotation on p. 124.

winning an overall majority. Their breakthrough in small towns and rural areas, as well as their gains amongst the Catholic population, were unmistakable signs of change in the political climate: the SPD was now electable in what had been CDU strongholds. After five months in office, the increasing difficulties forced the resignation of the CDU Minister President, and the Social Democrat Heinz Kühn formed a cabinet with the FDP.[4] The positive outcome of the "Small Coalition" in the biggest of the federal states and the personal influence of Minister President Kühn had no little effect on later FDP decisions at national level.

Just as the initial disquiet that many members and supporters of the SPD felt at the association with the CDU began to wane, it sprang to life again in spring 1968 with the passing of the Emergency Laws. Since the arguments about the military rearming of the Federal Republic, no piece of legislation had, over so many years, caused such strong public reaction and unleashed such protest amongst SPD voters. Even within the SPD parliamentary group there was a minority who had basic misgivings about an emergency constitution, exerted a not-to-be-underestimated influence while it was being debated, and ultimately voted against the legislation. However, after these laws were passed, and by a large majority which included the SPD vote, the furore rapidly evaporated, or, at least, had no further political part to play.

The work of Willy Brandt as Foreign Minister on the other hand met, from the outset, with an unreservedly positive response within the party. His efforts were directed towards consolidating and extending the European Community, continuing to cultivate the relationship of the Federal Republic with its Western neighbours – with Brandt doing his utmost to return relations with France, which had cooled under Gerhard Schröder as Foreign Minister, to a more amical basis – and complementing the policy towards the West with a systematically developed *Ostpolitik*. Steps along the way were the signing of a non-aggression treaty with the Soviet Union, the restoration of diplomatic relations with Yugoslavia which had been broken off in 1957, and finally the initiation of negotiations with the GDR.

Aside from the incalculable gains which the Grand Coalition brought the SPD by giving it the opportunity, for the first time at national level, to persuade the populace that the "party of eternal opposition" was fit to govern, it also created internal party problems. At that time, unrest was

---

4 It was characteristic of the mood within the SPD that Kühn's original intention to follow Bonn and go into coalition with the CDU foundered on the objections of the Social Democrats in the Landtag. See Heinz Kühn, Aufbau und Bewährung (Hamburg 1981), p. 163f., p. 167, p. 169, pp. 196–200, p. 203f.

brewing as never before amongst the *Jusos*, younger party members who belonged to the Young Socialists Association. Admittedly, at the end of the 1950s, the party leadership had already had such great differences with the SPD-financed and sponsored League of Socialist Students (SDS) that they finally decreed that membership of the SDS was incompatible with being a member of the SPD, and set up instead the Social Democratic Association of University Students (SHB). The youth organisation "The Falcons" had also been the cause of frequent aggravation and trouble, but for two decades the Young Socialists had never given the party serious cause for concern, particularly since they wielded no political power. Now, with the student revolts and the protest movement, things would change fundamentally.

Originating in the universities, a process of radicalisation began amongst the ranks of the *Jusos*. There was widespread protest by critical youth against the US war in Vietnam, against the suppression of the Nazi past, against actual and supposed fascist tendencies, and against unbridled capitalism. It was combined with an anti-authoritarian rebellion against the "Establishment" and the lifestyle of the older generation. After the highpoint of the "'68 movement" with the campaign against the emergency legislation, a gradual process of decline – but at the same time one of differentiation – began. The more realistic and moderate young academics and their pupils embarked on their "march through the institutions", starting with the Social Democrats, the trade unions, and the small FDP.

In the SPD at that time, taking their cue from successful political models so outweighed all other considerations that ironic observers of this process described it as the attempt by the party to become the best CDU there had ever been. There was barely any discussion of fundamental issues, Godesberg was at best referred to, but never interpreted. Young party members reacted to this pragmatic approach to power with scepticism, criticism, and opposition, an attitude which met with no understanding from the party "Establishment", and often, as they saw it, with authoritarian rejection. But the young socialists, who frequently came from the academic milieu, learned to develop strategies and to deploy tactics – successfully, but not always fairly – which in many places brought them key organisational positions and secured them important offices at local and state level. This was one aspect of *Juso* activity: it often speeded up the necessary generational changes in responsible positions, increased the reservoir of party activists, and sharpened the competition for electoral seats. This led to many a bruising conflict and, particularly in university towns, to an excessively academic and theoretical approach. It is true that the pragmatism which Godesberg had brought to the SPD worked as an antidote to this, stimulating a discussion which, despite the half-baked nature of many of the *Jusos* demands and their excessive emphasis on theories and "models", nevertheless stimulated reflection on questions of fundamental Social Democratic policy. But this onward march of the "'68ers" also burdened the party with long-term internecine political skirmishing which proved extremely wearing, driving party officials almost to the point of desperation.

2. *Off to Pastures New*

Even the architects of the Grand Coalition, whatever their individual motives may have been, knew very well that this coalition represented a "short-term marriage". Towards the end of the legislative period, the election of the Federal President in March 1969 opened up the prospect of a constellation more favourable to the SPD, and one which held out the promise of a more permanent arrangement. Both parties put forward a candidate: the CDU/CSU the then Minister of Defence, Gerhard Schröder, the SPD Gustav Heinemann, the Minister of Justice in the Grand Coalition cabinet. The outcome of the election depended on the two opposition parties, the FDP, and the right-wing radical NPD, on whose votes the Union parties were counting in order for their candidate to win. The FDP leadership had opted for Heinemann, but it remained uncertain right up until the election whether all their deputies would abide by the decision. The eventual unanimous vote of the Free Democrats for Heinemann was not only crucial in securing his election, but it also set aside any remaining doubts the Social Democrats may have had, on the basis of past experience, about the reliability of the FDP.

At the end of the 1960s, a shift had occurred in the social climate of the Federal Republic. The movement known as the "student revolt", which had begun in the USA, and reached its climax in May 1968 in Paris, spread rapidly to universities in the Federal Republic. The protest against existing conditions to which this generation of students gave such powerful expression was the spearhead of a much wider mood of upheaval and fundamental change which had been coming for some time. Critical questions began to be asked about "conservative democracy" and the Nazi period, and demands were being made for a more liberal approach and a reassessment of the past. A change of mood could also be detected in circles which had hitherto been socially and politically passive. Women began to express dissatisfaction with their situation in both the private and public spheres, and, with a new-found self-confidence and awareness,

*Helmut Schmidt and Gustav Heinemann
after the election of the Federal President in 1969*

formed groups to represent their interests. At various levels of society people began to call into question established authority, traditional allocation of roles, outmoded ways of thinking and behaving. Topics became the subject of public discussion which had hitherto been the preserve of experts or outsiders. An increasing number of citizens were convinced that much had to change and that old encrusted habits had to be swept away. Politically, this critical, anti-conservative trend favoured the SPD. The project of a more open civil society which had been in the offing since the beginning of the 1960s, as well as reaching a settlement with neighbouring countries in the East, and the call for more democracy in state and society, were now firmly on the agenda. In the final phase of the Grand Coalition, the SPD, with its "strategy of limited conflict", made a name for itself as a reform party on the move.

After a campaign in which the SPD received the unprecedented backing of well-known personalities outside the party – actors, directors, writers, academics, journalists, sportsmen – they won 42.7 per cent of the vote in the election on 28 September 1969. Their most striking gains were among the middle classes, white-collar workers, and civil servants, but fewer from among the self-employed. By comparison with 1966, the SPD had gained 3.4 points, while the CDU/CSU suffered slight losses but still remained the strongest party. After their shift to the left, the FDP dropped from 9.5 to 5.8 per cent. A change of government was numerically possible but, in view of the narrowness of the majority and unreliable elements within the FDP, had hidden dangers.

Before the election night was out, Willy Brandt had energetically grasped the opportunity of forming a coalition with Walter Scheel's FDP. Foreign policy and *Deutschlandpolitik* were the main driving force which brought the Social and Free Democrats together. Coalition negotiations went ahead speedily. The new government alliance was in place by the beginning of October, and Willy Brandt was elected Federal Chancellor on 21 October 1969. The FDP received two key posts. Walter Scheel became Foreign Minister and also Deputy Chancellor, while Hans-Dietrich Genscher was made Minister of the Interior, with Josef Ertl becoming Minister of Agriculture, thereby bringing on board the right wing of the FDP. The SPD received eleven ministries. Karl Schiller, the SPD's "election locomotive", remained Minister for Economic Affairs, and the well-respected Georg Leber, Minister of Transport. New to the cabinet were, amongst others, Alex Möller as Finance Minister, and as Minister of Defence, Helmut Schmidt, who was succeeded as leader of the parliamentary party by Herbert Wehner. The appointment to the post of Minister of Education and Science of Professor Leussink, who belonged to no party, raised eyebrows amongst some sections of the SPD, since educational reform was considered to be a specifically Social Democrat concern. After Leussink's subsequent resignation, his post was taken over by the Social Democrat Klaus von Dohnanyi.

The policy of the social-liberal coalition would be one of "continuity and renewal", declared Willy Brandt in his statement on government policy on 28 October 1969. On foreign policy, he emphasised continuity with the previous government and, in domestic policy, he signalled the breaking of new ground under the motto "we want to venture more democracy". He concluded with the words: "We are not at the end of our democracy, we are only just beginning. We want to be and become a nation of good neighbours at both home and abroad."[5]

If one measures the achievements of the Brandt government against the two criteria of "continuity" and "renewal", then continuity looms larger in domestic policy. Economic and financial policy were subject less to reform than to attempts to adapt to the particular state of the economy or the budget. There was considerable legislation on domestic issues, particularly in the socio-political sphere, even though there was not a single instance of it being pioneering, but rather a continuation along the path taken by the Grand Coalition, and even by earlier governments. Many reforms were not carried through because the Brandt/Scheel government's period in office came to an end after just three years. Others, such as land reform and taxation, presented such great inherent difficulties that they were never brought to a conclusion. With *Bafög*, the Federal Educational Grants Act, the coalition government opened up better chances of higher education for children from low-income families, but their efforts to democratise the universities met with limited success. They showed signs of being more liberal and meeting the expectations of the young generation with the right to demonstrate and lowering the voting age to eighteen. But the agreement, reached in January 1972 between Chancellor Brandt and the heads of the state governments, on the so-called *Radikalenerlass* (Decree Concerning Radicals), had critics at home and abroad up in arms. It was designed to bring a halt to left-wing extremists entering the civil service and, as with the decision in winter 1970/71[6] to draw a clear line between Communists and the SPD, demonstrated the will of the government and of Social Democrats as a whole to bolt the door on left-wing infiltration. This was done not only with a view to voters in the political

---

5 Verhandlungen des Deutschen Bundestages (stenographic report), vol. 71, pp. 20–34. See also Willy Brandt. Berliner Ausgabe, vol. 7, pp. 218–224.
6 Jahrbuch der SPD 1970–1972 (Bonn, undated), pp. 557 ff. (Party Council of 14.11.1970 and executive committee of 26.2.1971).

middle ground, but was also a result of the new *Ost-* and *Deutschlandpolitik*. The Social Democrat leadership was thereby making it absolutely clear that peaceful coexistence and *rapprochement* with eastern Europe must not be permitted to blur the fundamental differences between free democracies and Communist dictatorships.

The social-liberal government under Willy Brandt immediately took bold new steps in foreign policy. Already by the middle of November 1969 it agreed negotiations with Moscow on a mutual non-aggression treaty, and a week later Bonn and Warsaw reached an understanding about future talks. At the end of November, the Non-Proliferation Treaty was signed. At the beginning of December, Willy Brandt proposed an extension of the European Community and closer cooperation with the aim of achieving economic and currency union. Immediately afterwards, NATO suggested holding negotiations with the Warsaw Pact on troop reductions in Europe and gave the Federal Republic backing for its political initiatives with the East.

Being firmly anchored in the Atlantic Alliance was the basis for the new *Ost-* and *Deutschlandpolitik*. It was Willy Brandt who had often emphasised that his *Ostpolitik* was only the logical completion of Adenauer's *Westpolitik*. It is indisputable, however, that it carved out new paths, loosened rigid fronts, and opened up the prospect of an international *modus vivendi* which had hitherto been considered unthinkable. In the realisation that the key to *détente* lay with the Soviet Union, Bonn directed its easternpolitical antennae primarily towards Moscow. In January 1970, Egon Bahr embarked on discussions with Andrei Gromyko and other Kremlin delegates. Parallel with this, representatives of the Four Powers were conducting negotiations on Berlin, and the first two German summit conferences took place in Erfurt (March 1970) and Kassel (May 1970) between Chancellor Brandt and the East German Prime Minister, Willi Stoph. In addition, there were talks with Poland. This whole series of negotiations was all interlinked and connected. The breakthrough finally came at the end of May 1970, when Foreign Minister Gromyko, and with him the Soviet leadership, declared themselves prepared to accept the famous "letter on German unity".

On 12 August 1970, the Moscow Treaty was signed. It was followed on 7 December by the Warsaw Treaty. In kneeling at the memorial to victims of the Warsaw ghetto Willy Brandt made a powerful symbolic gesture. With the Four Power Agreement on Berlin of September 1971, the city was finally given a guarantee which secured its viability and future. It was supplemented by the transit agreement between the Federal Republic and the GDR. With the *Grundlagenvertrag* (Basic Treaty) of December

1972 between the Federal Republic and the GDR, the final piece of this pioneering policy of treaties with the East was now in place.

The Brandt government's *Ost-* and *Deutschlandpolitik* was an initiative of historical proportions. It enabled the social-liberal coalition to make an invaluable contribution to *détente* and the breaking down of mutual hostility between East and West, and to create a climate of trust, and of understanding and reconciliation between Germany and its neighbours in the East. The legal status of beleaguered West Berlin was now on a much firmer footing, travel on the transit routes was faster, safer and simpler, many citizens were once more able to make journeys from West to East Germany, and it was now possible, for older GDR citizens at least, to travel to the West. The Wall and barbed wire had finally become less impenetrable, and the consequences of the division of Germany less intolerable. This was politics for people in a divided land, and was felt particularly keenly by those Germans who had spent years without freedom under the SED regime. The veil was briefly torn aside when, at the meeting in Erfurt in 1970, the crowd assembled in front of the "Erfurter Hof" could be heard chanting loud and clear: "Willy, Willy (Brandt)". These were unmistakable signals. The feeling that Germans belonged together was alive and well in the GDR. Hopes for a turn for the better were being firmly pinned on the Social Democrat Federal Chancellor Willy Brandt. Erfurt became a symbol of people's longing for change, which was all inextricably linked with Brandt's policy of dialogue and increased contact.

The new *Ost-* and *Deutschlandpolitik* liberated the Federal Republic from its old shackles of political paralysis *vis-à-vis* the East. The settlement with its Eastern neighbours, in consensus with the Western powers, strengthened Bonn's hand internationally and enhanced its political reputation. The awarding of the Nobel Peace Prize to Willy Brandt in October 1971 was testimony to the deep respect for, and recognition of, the policies, embodied and symbolised by Brandt, of peace and reconciliation of a democratic Germany which wished to become a nation of good neighbours. The aura of this spread throughout the GDR. For many of its citizens, the charismatic Willy Brandt became the bearer of hopes of liberalisation and change, a figure who had shown Germany the way to peace and freedom at the heart of Europe.

With the Moscow and Warsaw treaties and the *Grundlagenvertrag*, the Federal Republic acknowledged the existing borders as being "inviolable", but not as "unchangeable", and recognised the DDR "constitutionally", but not "under international law". Nothing was given away which had not already been lost as a result of the war unleashed by Nazi Germany. The new *Ost-* and *Deutschlandpolitik* required a break with taboos and met with fierce resistance in the Federal Republic. It came under heavy attack from sections of the CDU/CSU. In January 1972, the CDU federal committee voted unanimously to reject the Eastern Treaties. After three FDP deputies had gone over to the CDU/CSU, with three from the SPD following in their steps[7], and others being viewed as potential defectors, the coalition no longer had a secure majority in the Bundestag. The CDU/CSU attempted to topple Willy Brandt and to elect Rainer Barzel as the new Chancellor by means of a vote of no-confidence. On 27 April it failed by two votes, one of which was certainly bought, and the other in all probability.[8] Amidst unprecedented excitement, the SPD and FDP, as well as countless Brandt supporters amongst the public, were jubilant. But this was followed by stalemate in the Bundestag, and the treaties with the Eastern bloc were on a knife edge.

Government and opposition found a way out of the crisis by working out a compromise: the Bundestag reached a joint decision on the treaties with Moscow and Warsaw, and most CDU deputies abstained in the vote on them. In the battle over the Eastern Treaties, which had put everything else in the shade, the Brandt government had survived by a whisker. But further tribulations lay ahead. The RAF, the Red Army Faction, had begun challenging the authority of the state in May 1972 with a series of bomb attacks. The cheerful mood of the Olympic Games in summer 1972 was completely overshadowed by a terrorist attack on the Israeli team by a radical Palestinian group. The attempt to free the hostages ended in disaster. At the beginning of July, the at times very popular "Superminister" Karl Schiller who, in addition to his economics portfolio, had taken over Alex Möller's post as Finance Minister, resigned. The former Defence Minister Helmut Schmidt took charge of the "Super Ministry". After the previous stalemate, and with Schiller's resignation and the defection of the SPD deputy Günther Müller to the CSU, the situation had now become untenable. Since neither the government nor the opposition had a "Chancellor majority", all parties agreed to bring forward new elections. After a complicated parliamentary procedure required by the *Grundgesetz*, the Federal President Heinemann dissolved the Bundestag.

It was a rough-and-tumble election campaign, conducted in an emotionally overheated atmosphere. *Ostpolitik* played a leading role. On 8 November, a few days before the election, the *Grundlagenvertrag* (Basic Treaty)

---

7 Klaus-Peter Schulz in 1971, and Franz Seume and Herbert Hupka in 1972.
8 In addition to Julius Steiner (CDU), the CSU deputy Leo Wagner had "with a probability bordering on certainty" been "rewarded" by the MfS, the GDR security services, for "his vote against Barzel". See Willy Brandt. Berliner Ausgabe vol. 7, p. 60 and p. 552, note 91.

was initialled. The coalition acclaimed it as a contribution to peace, with those sections of the media well-disposed towards it celebrating it as the dawn of a new age. The elections inevitably became a kind of plebiscite on the whole of Willy Brandt's peace policies, as well as on the charismatic Nobel Peace prize winner himself.

The political interest and commitment of those sympathetic to him were enormous. The whole focus was on the policy of reconciliation with the East, the arguments revolving as never before round individual politicians. On the one hand, Barzel and Strauß whom the public regarded with little affection, and on the other, the well-loved and celebrated Willy Brandt. In this unprecedented personalisation of the campaign, there was a danger of opponents being defamed not only politically, but also morally. This had the positive effect, however, of mobilising the electorate. Along with many intellectuals, writers, academics, and artists, sections of the population who had been more or less politically indifferent now began to get involved. With voters' action groups, street and house discussions, by sporting badges and other symbols, they expressed their support publicly and openly for their party of preference. The SPD and Willy Brandt profited more from this politicisation of the electorate than did the CDU/CSU. These federal elections, with people voting in record numbers, disproved the then current theory that a high turnout favoured the SPD's opponents.

In the new elections brought forward to 19 November 1972, the SPD with 45.8 per cent outstripped the CDU/CSU (44.9) for the first time, and achieved the greatest election victory in their history. Compared to earlier elections, they achieved their biggest gains amongst women, younger voters, and workers in the lower income bracket. The vote of their FDP coalition partner went up to 8.4 per cent, and the government now had a solid parliamentary majority. Annemarie Renger of the SPD became President of the Bundestag, the first time a woman had held this high office. With 269 of the 493 votes cast, Willy Brandt, on 14 December 1972, was once again elected Federal Chancellor. As Finance Minister with increased responsibilities, Helmut Schmidt was now the strong man in the cabinet. Newcomers to the cabinet were the former Mayor of Munich, Hans-Jochen Vogel, as Minister for Regional Development, Katharina Focke in the Ministry for Family Affairs, and, with the Ministry for Economic Affairs now in the hands of the FDP, Hans Friderichs. Horst Ehmke, who had previously been Brandt's right-hand man in the Chancellor's office, moved to the Ministry for Research. Herbert Wehner remained chairman of the parliamentary party. The coalition negotiations and forming of the government had not been particularly auspicious for Willy

Brandt. Handicapped by a stay in hospital and a this time protracted depression, Brandt made heavy weather of it. After the euphoria of the "Willy" elections and getting his Ostpolitik through, he came down to earth with a bump. Brandt's statement on government policy of January 1973 stressed continuity, balance, and "staying power". The ratification of the Basic Treaty by the Bundestag in May went smoothly. The CDU had been weakened by a leadership crisis. After the resignation of Rainer Barzel, the CDU/CSU parliamentary group elected Karl Carstens in May as its new chairman, and in June Helmut Kohl replaced Barzel as CDU party chairman. The Basic Treaty came into force on 21 June 1973, and on 31 July the Federal Constitutional Court adjudged that it was compatible with the Basic Law, but at the same time stressed the obligation to restore the unity of the two German states. On 18 September, the Federal Republic of Germany, and simultaneously the GDR, were admitted as full members of the United Nations.

The circle had now been closed as regards the new *Ost-* and *Deutschlandpolitik*. A breakthrough had been achieved, but there were disappointments. For the SED Communists who damned "Social Democratism", Bonn remained, despite the social-liberal government and *détente*, the "class enemy" who employed "ideological diversion in order to infiltrate us with bourgeois ideology"[9]. The Soviet Union continued to treat West Berlin as a special political entity, and the SED regime in the GDR had, hedgehog-like, turned in on itself. The border areas were made even more deadly by mines and SM 70 automatic firing devices, the circle of people forbidden contact with the West was widened, the *Stasi* (state security) apparatus extended and refined, and ideological *Abgrenzung* or "delimitation" stepped up.

Since the signing of the *Grundlagenvertrag*, there had been no movement on the humanitarian front: the reuniting of families and the buying free of prisoners which had formerly been carried out at "lawyer level" ground to a halt. Round two thousand GDR citizens who had originally been given permission to leave now found themselves literally waiting with their bags packed. Herbert Wehner, who, since his time as Minister for all-German Affairs, was well acquainted with, and committed to this buying prisoners free, made himself their advocate, and, at the end of May 1973, travelled to a meeting in the GDR – a cause of great excitement – with Erich Honecker, his younger comrade-in-arms from their earlier

---

[9] This from politburo member Werner Lambertz. See Die Aufgaben von Agitation und Propaganda bei der Verwirklichung der Beschlüsse des VIII. Parteitags der SED (Berlin [East] 1972), p. 52.

Communist days together.[10] Wehner was successful on the humanitarian front: families were reunited, and the buying free of prisoners resumed once more. This system of human trafficking, in which the SED regime was profiting from people's misery, remained in place to the end, with the price rising all the time. In addition to countless families who were reunited in this way, over 33,000 prisoners were ransomed between 1964 and 1990. The SED state made almost 3.5 billion Deutschmarks from this grim trade in human lives.

Brandt and others were kept informed about Wehner's journey, and Wolfgang Mischnick from the FDP was also present for parts of the meeting with Honecker. But after German-German relations began to stagnate, there was palpable disagreement in Bonn about how to proceed *vis-à-vis* East Berlin. In addition, there were animosities between the close circle round Brandt and the powerful chairman of the SPD parliamentary group who began to operate a kind of parallel foreign policy towards the East. While on a visit to Moscow at the end of September 1973, Wehner openly criticised the policy on Berlin of his own government, even stooping to critically malicious remarks about Brandt, calling him "spineless", "distant", and "worn out".[11] Brandt was outraged and deeply hurt, but he shied away from an open conflict and split. Wehner's behaviour was disloyal and unforgivable. But there were, nonetheless, widespread doubts in the upper echelons of the party about Brandt's leadership and his ability to master the office of Chancellor. His decision to cover up the split indirectly confirmed this view of him. The Chancellor's prestige had taken a knock, and a series of other factors would damage it further: the Steiner-Wienand affair, or the well-founded suspicion that votes had been bought in the vote of no confidence; the first oil-price shock following the Yom Kippur war in autumn 1973 and the ban on driving; bitter setbacks in *Deutschland-* and *Ostpolitik* with the doubling in November 1973 of the amount of hard currency visitors to the GDR had to change, along with the impeding of traffic to Berlin; the air traffic controllers' strike in 1973 which led to six months of chaos; and finally the strike at the beginning of 1974 by the ÖTV, the union of transport and public-service workers led by Heinz Kluncker, which extorted wage and salary increases of just under 11 per cent from the public purse. The government was

---

10 Heinrich Potthoff, Bonn und Ost-Berlin 1969–1982. Dialog auf höchster Ebene und vertrauliche Kanäle. Darstellung und Dokumente (Bonn 1997), p. 38f., pp. 102ff. and pp. 208ff.
11 Süddeutsche Zeitung of 6.10.1973 and Der Spiegel of 8.10.1973. On Wehner's Moscow trip, see Arnulf Baring, Machtwechsel. Die Ära Brandt/Scheel (Stuttgart 1982), pp. 616–620.

*Willy Brandt and Helmut Schmidt on his election
as Federal Chancellor on 16 May 1974*

widely felt to be helpless and feeble, with its reputation and authority in tatters.

In spring 1974, with some of the faithful thinking that Brandt was beginning to regain a measure of control, the news broke of the arrest of Günter Guillaume, one of the Chancellor's senior aides. Many people in the Federal Republic were open to reproach over failures and mistakes in the Guillaume affair, and it must not be forgotten that no less than Markus Wolf, the head of espionage in the GDR, and *Stasi* boss Erich Mielke had been directly responsible for the planting of the spy. A more resolute Chancellor would have survived this crisis. But Brandt had been weakened by successive crises since 1972, as well as by the intrusions into his private life, and no longer had the necessary staying power. The die was cast on the famous weekend of 4–5 May in Bad Münstereifel.[12] Brandt submitted his resignation in a letter to Heinemann, the Federal President, on 6 May 1974.[13] There was enormous disappointment amongst Willy Brandt's supporters and sympathisers. But the smoothness with which the baton was handed on to Helmut Schmidt forestalled any deeper crisis of trust which might easily have arisen. Willy Brandt remained chairman of the SPD, and continued to enjoy respect as its great father figure and as the Chancellor who had taken the Social Democrats to pastures new.

3. *A Party in Flux*

Even though the federal elections of November 1972 had been principally about Willy Brandt and *Ostpolitik*, the results confirmed that the claim made in the Godesberg Programme that the SPD was "a party of the working class which had become a party of all the people" was increasingly a reality. This was also mirrored in the sociological make-up of the party. Whereas new membership in 1960 comprised 55.7 per cent workers, this fell in 1969 to 39.6, and to only 27.6 by 1972. At the same time, the proportion of white-collar workers and civil servants amongst new members rose from 21.2 to 33.6, and finally to 34 per cent. The figure for the self-employed remained steady at 5 per cent, amongst the intellectual and free-lance professions it rose from only 2.7 in 1960 to 7.8 per cent in 1969. It was 9 per cent for housewives and 5 per cent for retired people and pensioners. In 1972 there were, for the first time, separate

---

12 For Brandt's view of events see his notes on the "Guillaume case". In Willy Brandt. Berliner Ausgabe, vol. 7, pp. 508–537, and also the footnotes on pp. 606–609.
13 Ibid., p. 538 and p. 609. The letter was written on the evening of 5.5.1974.

statistics for students and pupils, who made up 15.9 per cent.[14] It is true that amongst the party membership workers were still the largest group, but there was still an unmistakable decline in their numbers[15], and a shift in favour of the middle classes. A further development was the drop in the age of new members. Whereas 55.3 per cent of those who had joined in 1960 were under 40, this had risen to 67.2 in 1969, and to as high as 75.2 per cent in 1972 (with 19.7 of these under 21). These tendencies would be even more pronounced in any comprehensive evaluation of the changes, at various levels, of the age and profession of the executive committees and parliamentary representation. The membership of the party, which was almost a million in spring 1973, consisted at that point of people, two-thirds of whom had joined the party in the previous ten years. In the second half of the 1970s, the German Social Democrats were, therefore, a rejuvenated and sociologically much changed party.

The SPD had been in government since 1966, and since 1969 their candidate, Willy Brandt, had been Chancellor. This had, of course, a decisive effect on the relationship between party and government. The fate of the government led by the Social Democrat Chancellor Hermann Müller (1928–1930) reveals what problems this relationship was exposed to in the Weimar period. In Bonn during the Grand Coalition, as well as during Brandt's Chancellorship, it was never severely tested. The reason for this remained, on the one hand, a change of thinking in the party as a whole: having grown tired of their role in opposition, they had gone all out to be in power, and now wanted to retain that power. But it was also due to personalities. Herbert Wehner, the most influential figure in the party organisation, was also the main driving force behind the Grand Coalition, and, as chairman of the parliamentary party during the social-liberal coalition, was regarded as the one cracking the whip. The in general relatively smooth running of the Grand Coalition was due, in large measure, to the work of Helmut Schmidt, who had become chairman of the parliamentary party after the death of Fritz Erler.[16] But the most important factor in building trust between the party and government was the fact that Willy Brandt, in addition to being Foreign Minister and Chancellor, was also chairman of the party. He admittedly allowed the party its head

---

14 Source of information, Jahrbücher der SPD, as well as information supplied to Susanne Miller by the office of the SPD executive committee.
15 As is shown by job statistics for the population as a whole, the proportion of workers was dropping (from 1961 to 1970 by 1.2 per cent), but by nowhere near as much as in SPD membership.
16 Erler died on 22.2.1967.

at times, but his great popularity usually allowed him successfully to impose his authority.

Although the SPD's fundamental loyalty to the Brandt government was never in question, it was no accident that, after the election victory of 1972, Brandt should strongly emphasise that the electorate had opted for a coalition of Social and Free Democrats, and that – along with Wehner – he should give a firm warning to the SPD's governing committees about forming right or left-wing factions within the party. Behind these admonitions lay fears that, by means of systematic efforts within the parliamentary party and the organisation as a whole, attempts might be made to restrict the freedom of the government to act and make decisions, and to undermine trust in it. In view of the demand of many local party organisations to proceed according to the principle of the "imperative mandate", these concerns could not be rejected out of hand. The growth of the party, the shift in social background and average age of party membership, the increasing influence of young academics in the SPD parliamentary groups and executive committees at all levels, excessive expectations after the great election victory of 1972, and the strong position of the SPD in the Bundestag which made earlier considerations no longer necessary – all this made it more difficult to avoid tensions between party and government. It could no longer be ignored that programmatic aspirations and perspectives within the party at large were at odds with the realities of a coalition government and what it could reasonably achieve.

This was clearly evident at the SPD party conference of April 1973 in Hanover. Admittedly, the governing committees of the party got their way on almost all important matters of substance, remaining loyal to Godesberg and the coalition's course on foreign policy, and Willy Brandt seemed to emerge from the conference stronger than he went in. But while concessions to the young socialists were kept within strict limits, the "left wing" scored a great personnel success. Roughly a quarter of the newly elected executive committee belonged to it, more or less reflecting the composition of the party as a whole. Internal polarisation was avoided at Hanover. But it was there for all to see that there were various tendencies being voiced in the left-wing people's party, the SPD, and that those on the left of the party were now moving into positions of power. This testified, of course, to the democratic vitality of the party, preventing it from stagnating, and reducing the chances of conflict. Nevertheless, the ability and efforts of Willy Brandt to unify his party and to integrate its young rebels clearly had their limits.

In view of the *Jusos*' continued pressing for "system-changing" reforms, the party chairman warned in September 1973 against "tearing ourselves apart" and "self-destructive tendencies".[17] Unimpressed by this, the young socialists decided at their Munich conference of January 1974 on a "two-track strategy" with which they would seek to challenge the SPD's socialist goals both inside and outside the party. Even for Brandt, this now went beyond what was reasonable. The executive committee responded with a sharp reprimand: "A two-track strategy against one's own party" was impermissible, and majority opinion had to prevail. "Without the centre", ran the main part of the argument, there could be "no majority in a democracy". Those who "abandon it, sacrifice their ability to govern".[18]

If they wished to remain in government, the Social Democrats had to make an impact with the centre. With Schmidt replacing Brandt as Chancellor a few weeks later, the course was set to achieve this. This was the path he would follow as Chancellor, governing the social-liberal coalition soberly and with realism, and winning over those voters in the middle ground. Seemingly as a matter of course, Willy Brandt continued as party chairman. Even though he first had to recover from the shock of resignation, his identification with the SPD was never in doubt. He knew very well what he had in the party, and the party drew its strength from him, his charisma, his ability to integrate and motivate.

Intensive efforts were underway to define precisely what the SPD stood for. Fundamentally, it was not about catchphrases such as "stabilisation of the system" or "overcoming the system", which caused more confusion and unrest then they were worth, but about how far, and in what form, the party should be guided by longer-term perspectives. Since Schmidt was concentrating all his attention on the office of Chancellor, and Brandt had the party on a fairly loose rein, a whole series of Social Democrat practitioners and theoreticians felt they could offer their views for public consumption.[19] They were at one on at least three basic points: 1. The measure and guideline of Social Democratic policy were the basic values of freedom, equality, and solidarity laid down in the Godesberg Programme. 2. The fresh challenges demanded not the abandoning, but the continuation of reforms, albeit with different emphases. 3. Social Democratic policies could only be carried out with the assent and cooperation of the people.

---

17 Brandt at the party executive meeting of 9.9.1973. In Karl Dietrich Bracher, Wolfgang Jäger, Werner Link, Republik im Wandel 1969–1974. Die Ära Brandt (Stuttgart 1986), p. 100. This is vol. 5 of Bracher et al., Geschichte der Bundesrepublik Deutschland.
18 See Baring, Machtwechsel, p. 715 and p. 717 (the "Aprilbeschlüsse").
19 See the writings of Willy Brandt, Helmut Schmidt, Horst Ehmke, Erhard Eppler, Horst Heimann, Peter Glotz, Thomas Meyer, Joachim Steffen, Johano Strasser, Hans-Jochen Vogel, and others, listed in the bibliography.

But the emphasis given to these points varied. In a publication written under the direction of Hans-Jochen Vogel, Heinz Ruhnau, and Hermann Buschfort – a contribution of sorts to the party programme by reflective pragmaticians – a call was made to undertake the immediate task of "preserving what has been achieved", and of keeping threats to it at bay.[20] Erhard Eppler, on the other hand, thought that a "structural policy" to change the existing power structures in the economy, bureaucracy, and international relations was absolutely essential if basic human values were to be preserved.[21] Peter von Oertzen, as a respected representative of convinced but moderate left-wing views, advocated a thoroughgoing democratisation of society.

Typically, in an effort to coordinate these various and very different approaches and players, the party set up a commission. Its task was to continue and give direction to the work which had already begun, and to bring it to a conclusion. In accordance with the conference resolution in Hanover in spring 1973, the commission set up by the executive had thirty members. It was led by Peter von Oertzen, Horst Ehmke, and (after the death of Klaus Dieter Arndt) Herbert Ehrenberg. It had the support of specialists and experts from within the party. In addition, there were contributions and proposals from countless party organisations and working groups. The draft, therefore, which was presented for approval at the SPD party conference in November 1985 was "the result of a lengthy, comprehensive, and profound discussion" in which not only party members, but also the Christian Churches, trade unions, and even critics of the party had participated.[22]

At the party conference in Mannheim (11.–15.11.1975), "Orientation Framework '85" was, after a few amendments, adopted almost unanimously. Horst Ehmke gave a positive summing-up: "We have worked out an orientation framework which, if not a patent remedy, gives us what we were looking for: political direction for the work of the party, and for the politics of this country, over the next ten, undoubtedly difficult years." It seemed to him equally important that they had "succeeded after long years of sometimes difficult discussion, particularly with the young generation and what is called the 'young left', in reaching wide-

---

20 Godesberg und die Gegenwart (Bonn-Bad Godesberg 1975), pp. 29 ff.
21 Ende oder Wende (Stuttgart, Berlin, Cologne, Mainz 1975), esp. pp. 28–37, pp. 72–79.
22 See Peter von Oertzen's introductory talk on "Orientation Framework '85" at the Mannheim party conference. In Peter von Oertzen, Horst Ehmke, Herbert Ehrenberg (eds), Orientierungsrahmen '85, Text und Diskussion. Bearbeitet von Heiner Lindner (Bonn-Bad Godesberg 1976), p. 79 f.

spread agreement in the party on matters of policy. The party can", he maintained, "draw fresh self-confidence and new strength from this."[23]

Willy Brandt characterised "Orientation Framework '85" as being "a halfway house between day-to-day politics and a Basic Programme".[24] Peter Glotz, in detecting an "unresolved residue of helplessness" in this document which "absorbed the fresh ideas of the late 1960s, but rejected the errors and illusions"[25], put his finger on both the strength and the limitations of such a "halfway house". More differentiated, and yet more modest than any other programmatic statement of the Social Democrats had ever been, the orientational framework indicated where the party was going, and what its aims were. It outlined, in its four main chapters: 1. The goals of democratic socialism. 2. Conditions and frame of reference. 3. The implementation of the principles of democratic socialism as the task of the Social Democratic Party. 4. Main areas of emphasis – the crucial problems for a modern, democratic party of reform. In other important areas, however, this document had been overtaken by developments. Unemployment, which had become an enormous problem during the recession, was not mentioned at all. The orientational framework had barely any effect, and sank without trace.

In view of the problems which had occurred, and even before the approval of the orientational framework, the executive committee had set up a commission in October 1974 to define more precisely and concretely the basic values of the Godesberg Programme: freedom, equality, and solidarity.[26] Under the chairmanship of Erhard Eppler, with Richard Löwenthal and Heinz Rapp as his vice-chairmen, it produced discussion papers on topics such as: "Basic values in an endangered world" (1977), "Basic values and basic rights" (1979), "On political culture in a democracy" (1980), "The labour movement and the change in social consciousness and behaviour" (1982).[27] These contributions illuminated the chances and dangers for a changing world, and their significance for policies determined by the values of democratic socialism. They offered stimulus and

---

23 Ibid., p. 297.
24 Ibid. See his preface, p. 3.
25 'The Mannheim SPD party conference 1975' In, Aus Politik und Zeitgeschichte. Beilage zur Wochenzeitung Das Parlament, 11/1976, 13 March 1976, p. 3.
26 The setting up of the Commission on Basic Values was at the suggestion of Willi Eichler in 1971. See Willi Eichler, Zur Einführung in den demokratischen Sozialismus (Bonn-Bad Godesberg 1972), pp. 117–124. Also Klaus Lompe and Lothar Neumann (eds), Willi Eichlers Beiträge zum demokratischen Sozialismus (Berlin and Bonn 1979), p. 187.
27 All published in Erhard Eppler (ed.), Grundwerte für ein neues Godesberger Programm (Reinbek bei Hamburg 1984).

guidelines for serious discussion amongst those in positions of influence who were intellectually aware and interested in the party's political programme. However, the hopes of the commission that they would have widespread effect were disappointed. In truth, the government had more concrete challenges on its plate, and a quite different agenda was making the headlines: oil crises and unemployment, terrorism, and finally the approach of "the second Cold War".

The orientational framework and the work of the Commission on Basic Values were the SPD's contribution to the clarification of its own political programme: they reopened the discussion about basic principles which had been broken off after the adoption of the Godesberg Programme. The orientational framework was not a rejection of Godesberg, but a continuation of its policy of a socialism based on freedom and basic values. But "Orientation Framework '85" could not offer a political direction for the future because social democracy in the wake of worldwide economic crisis since the second half of the 1970s was faced with problems which challenged previous assumptions, and which the framework had barely taken into consideration. The Commission on Basic Values was an attempt to plug this gap. But many in the party found their identity in Willy Brandt rather than in theoretical papers. Despite the occasional critical voice, this was undoubtedly advantageous for internal party solidarity, and the image of the German Social Democrats abroad was helped enormously by the esteem in which Brandt was held. This two-pronged leadership, however, with Willy representing the soul and vision of the party, and the soberly rational Chancellor Helmut Schmidt with his reputation for getting things done, was not without its problems. Amongst Social Democrats, this had long been swept under the carpet. Structurally, at least, having one person in charge of both offices seemed a better way of holding government and party together. The splitting up, on the other hand – even between two such well-respected politicians as Willy Brandt and Helmut Schmidt – of the office of Chancellor and the chairmanship of the party was liable to lead to alienation in certain quarters.

IV. The Social-Liberal Coalition in the Shadow of Worldwide Economic Recession

The fresh direction so characteristic of the Brandt era manifested itself most strikingly in a new *Ost-* and *Deutschlandpolitik*. This is where Brandt made his greatest impact. His period in government was identified with both a process of internal reform of the democratic system and society in the spirit of "venturing more democracy", and greater social justice. The initial great élan of the social-liberal coalition began to fizzle out in 1973, to be replaced by widespread disillusionment. It was clear that there would be setbacks, and that not every dream could be fulfilled. But global changes were now taking place which would have profound repercussions for the Federal Republic. With its negotiated withdrawal from Vietnam in 1973, the USA acknowledged defeat. The People's Republic of China and the Soviet Union were the main beneficiaries of the American disaster, with the USA suffering a loss in prestige and standing. The coordinates of world politics were shifting. Their effects were being felt in the Middle East, where the Arab-Islamic world began to flex its muscle. The regional conflict with Israel escalated into a global dispute, with far-reaching consequences for the world economy.

It was triggered by the attack on Israel by Egypt and the Arab states in October 1973 (the Yom Kippur War). This led to a boycott on supplies to the Western industrial nations by the oil-producing states of the Middle East, and, after it was lifted, by drastic increases in the price of crude oil. The Federal Republic, too, could not escape the effects of the worsening worldwide economic recession produced by the energy crisis. Its gross national product which, compared with the corresponding period in the previous year, rose in real terms in 1973 by 4.7 per cent, grew by a mere 0.2 per cent in 1974, and in 1975, at the height of the crisis, fell by 1.4 per cent. It did not rise again until 1976, and then by 5.6 per cent. The growth rate in the following years was 2.7 per cent in 1977, 3.3 in 1978, 4.0 in 1979, and 1.5 in 1980. Worldwide recession resulted in rising prices and an increase in unemployment, which rose from less than 250,000 in 1972 to over a million in the period 1975 to 1977.[1]

---

[1] See below the tables and diagrams 12 (Economic and Social Data) and 14 (Developments in the Labour Market).

The bitter experience of inflation in 1923, unemployment in the 1930s, and the depreciation of the currency after the Second World War all contributed to a feeling of crisis which was heightened by the dependency, as a mobile, affluent society, on heating oil and petrol. Admittedly, by international standards, the Federal Republic was relatively well off: it had one of the lowest rates of increase in consumer prices of any industrial nation, and one of the lowest levels of unemployment. Even more than its symptoms in Germany, the development of the world economy as a whole demanded a radical examination of the changed circumstances, and the consequences to be drawn from them. The Godesberg Programme, along with the various SPD election platforms and the plans for reform which the social-liberal coalition governments had envisaged since coming to power, were based on the presupposition of unhindered growth in material prosperity. This premise was now in question. The much discussed study by the "Club of Rome" published in 1972 had already pointed to the "limits of growth".[2] The experiences of autumn and winter 1973/74 with the ban on driving on Sundays and unprecedented energy-saving measures were an even stronger call for a radical policy rethink. In the shadow of the "oil shock", diminished resources, and with the OPEC cartel holding the whip hand, it was clear that the global economy was in the grip of structural crisis. This changed the social climate, and optimism now gave way to growing concern.

1. Setbacks and Testing Times

The oil-price shock hit the Brandt government and the Social Democrats at a time when the party was no longer in best fettle. After the splendid victory in the federal elections of November 1972, they experienced a series of defeats in the Landtag elections, the heaviest in Hamburg and Bremen, where their vote fell by around ten per cent compared to the previous elections. The SPD did not do well in the local elections either. In Frankfurt and Munich, where they had had a majority since the end of the Second World War, the office of mayor went, for the first time, to the CDU and CSU respectively. The downward trend at these elections could be explained not only by the fact that the symptoms of economic and social crisis were blamed on the governing party, despite the fact that they were due to global factors, and were much less severe in the Federal Republic than elsewhere. There were other causes. After decades in power

---

2 Dennis Meadows, Donella Meadows, Erich Zahn, Peter Milling, Die Grenzen des Wachstums. Bericht des Club of Rome zur Lage der Menschheit (Stuttgart 1972).

in traditional SPD strongholds such as Hesse, Lower Saxony, Hamburg, and Berlin, the party began to show signs of wear and tear. Some of the successors of popular and universally respected Social Democrat worthies at state and city level did not enjoy the same degree of authority, and were unable to prevent irregularities in administration and the public institutions. Internal party strife, which assumed ugly proportions in the Munich SPD, hampered fruitful political activity in many other places and frightened people off. A further cause of unrest in the SPD, and amongst many of those concerned about liberal values in the Federal Republic, was the handling of the so-called *Radikalenerlass* (Decree Concerning Radicals).[3]

The euphoria following the electoral victory of November 1972 could not last. It tipped over, not always for rational reasons, into disappointment with the government. Many reform plans did indeed become bogged down: in the sphere of schools, education, and science, for instance, due to financial cuts; in judicial matters because of the verdict of the constitutional court on the reworking of paragraph 218 of the criminal code (abortion); on co-determination because of the stance taken by the FDP coalition partners. Despite significant improvements – easier travel, re-uniting of families, access to Berlin – the limitations on what the federal government could achieve with its *Deutschlandpolitik* were also becoming apparent. While the increasingly polemical and aggressive CDU/CSU opposition was accusing the social-liberal coalition of getting irresponsibly carried away by its reform programme, members and supporters of the SPD were criticising the government for its indecisiveness in combating the unmistakable trend towards conservatism in the Federal Republic.

Following Willy Brandt's resignation, Helmut Schmidt was elected Chancellor on 16 May 1974. The previous day, the Federal Convention had chosen the former Foreign Minister Walter Scheel as Gustav Heinemann's successor as Federal President. The change from "Citizens' President", as Heinemann regarded himself, to Scheel, who was succeeded as Foreign Minister and FDP chairman by Hans-Dietrich Genscher, was a significant shift of emphasis. This was even more true of the transfer of the Chancellorship to Helmut Schmidt. The political visionary, spirited exponent of foreign policy, and symbol of Social Democrat integration was succeeded by Schmidt, an energetic and "morally responsible pragmati-

---

3 This had its origins in the principles agreed by the Chancellor and the Minister Presidents on "the membership of civil servants of extreme organisations". There is a very informative account in Peter Frisch, Extremistenbeschluß (Leverkusen 2nd edn 1976). See also, Hans Koschnick (ed.), Der Abschied vom Extremistenbeschluß (Bonn 1979).

cian"[4] with a highly developed sense of duty, and someone who had profound expertise in almost every area of politics. The new faces in his cabinet were tried and tested practical politicians such as Hans Apel, Hans Matthöfer, Helmut Rohde, and Kurt Gscheidle. But there was no place for the intellectual trio in Brandt's cabinet of Egon Bahr, Klaus von Dohnanyi, and Horst Ehmke.

Chancellor Schmidt stressed the continuity of, and necessity for, social-liberal policy. But the pathos of 1972, with its talk of bold new directions and reforms, had vanished. The alliance of SPD and FDP saw itself as a convenient arrangement for solving urgent problems. It concentrated with sobriety and realism on what had to, and could be, done. In the shadow of a world economy in crisis, this meant steering a difficult course through tricky waters. The coalition government attempted to counteract and overcome the effects of recession by means of a mixture of fiscal consolidation and the stimulation of economic activity.

The energy and expertise of Chancellor Helmut Schmidt, particularly in the economic sphere, met with speedy recognition at home and abroad. He proved himself to be a master at crisis management and in the international arena. The close personal ties between Schmidt and Valery Giscard d'Estaing brought a whole new quality to Franco-German friendship. At the world economic summit meetings which they initiated, the Chancellor's competence and political judgement gained him great respect. He played an outstanding part in East-West relations with carefully considered and balanced policies aimed at maintaining military equilibrium, while at the same time furthering *détente* and seeking to alleviate the plight of Germans living in the East. An agreement on financial credits with Poland gave over 100,000 citizens of German origin the possibility of resettling in the Federal Republic. A high point for Schmidt was the Helsinki Conference on Security and Cooperation in Europe in 1975, attended by statesmen from Europe, North America, and the Soviet Union, and its Final Act with the famous Basket III on basic rights and humanitarian issues.

Chancellor Helmut Schmidt was a man of international authority. At the beginning of 1976, he was able to give the following summary of the comments of leading newspapers in the USA, France, and England:

"They confirm that we have coped with the problems of a dramatically changing world economy far better than comparable industrial nations; that we are constructing a balanced and just society, and that we are in-

---

[4] This is the description of Heinrich August Winkler. In Der lange Weg nach Westen (Munich 2nd edn 2001), vol. 2, p. 329.

creasing and recognising the freedom and participation in the democratic process of all our citizens; and finally, that we have played an active part in securing peace in Europe."[5]

The federal elections of 3 October 1976 were the acid test. They demonstrated that, despite the SPD's internal problems and some loss of favour with the electors, there was a majority, albeit a narrow one, which was prepared to reward the Chancellor for his achievements.

2. *Renewal of the Mandate*

The governments led by Social Democrat Chancellors had successfully steered the country through difficult times. The Union parties had no constructive alternative to offer. Their opposition to *Ostpolitik*, which in 1975 had gone as far as rejecting the Helsinki Agreement, had left them isolated. They were alone on this, even amongst other European Christian Democratic parties. The fact that the opposition often mounted exaggerated attacks on SPD weaknesses, criticised, or blocked government measures – in the Bundesrat (upper house) or by appealing to the Federal Constitutional Court – was not of itself an infringement of the rules of a functioning democracy. In indulging, however, in confrontation, polarisation, and polemics for their own sake, they were abandoning the principles of objective political debate. Franz Josef Strauß initiated this with a speech in Sonthofen published in *Der Spiegel* on 10 March 1975. Hans Filbinger then fought the Landtag election in Baden-Württemberg in spring 1976 under the slogan "Freedom or Socialism". This, along with terms such as "red menace" and "socialist bondage", was part of the catalogue of tired old clichés with which conservatives and the Union were attempting to smear the SPD. Even though doubts about this strategy of defamation – particularly when directed at someone like Chancellor Schmidt – were raised within the Union parties, two variations on this slogan were adopted in the federal election campaign: "Freedom instead of/or Socialism". The opposition either blurred or demagogically twisted any real matters of substance, with the result that the electorate was given barely any information at all on the controversial issues. The Konrad-Adenauer-Foundation, which was close to the Union, commented that the election was "characterised by the fact that, as far as the population was concerned, it was a

---

5 Schmidt's speech of 29.1.1976 in the Bundestag on the state of the nation. Verhandlungen des Bundestages (typed report), vol. 96, pp. 15081–15093, quotation on p. 15091.

campaign devoid of issues".[6] This was to some extent due to the CDU and CSU slogans, but even more so to the campaign being reduced to the question of who should be Chancellor. The choice was between Helmut Schmidt and Helmut Kohl, and the majority of voters trusted the well-respected incumbent.

The SPD called for "Further work on Model Germany" in its election manifesto for 1976–1980. Bearing the clear imprint of Chancellor Schmidt, its central core was a balance sheet of the social-liberal coalition's achievements in power. It looked impressive: a successful policy of peace and understanding; relatively high economic stability; a tight social safety-net with significant improvements, such as flexible retirement age, guaranteed works' pensions, pension schemes for the self-employed, health insurance for farmers, a new youth employment protection law, revision of child benefit, adjustments and increases in war victims' pensions, rehabilitation and special employment rights for the severely handicapped; extension of co-determination; new married couples' and families' legislation; the initiation of reforms to paragraph 218 of the penal code on abortion; a considered, but of necessity hard response to the challenge of terrorism. "We know", ran the manifesto, "that millions of people would be happy if they were able to live under the material conditions of our Republic, and with the measure of personal freedom and social security which we take for granted. But we also know that there remains a lot to do to secure and consolidate our position."

In the federal elections of 3 October 1976, the SPD received 42.6 per cent, the FDP 7.9 per cent, and the CDU/CSU 48.6 per cent of the vote, which gave the SPD and FDP combined ten more seats in the Bundestag than the Union parties. Helmut Schmidt was elected Chancellor once again; the FDP chairman Hans-Dietrich Genscher remained Foreign Minister and Deputy Chancellor. The social-liberal coalition set up in 1969 was still in power. Nevertheless, the SPD had every reason to be worried since, even with the pulling power of Helmut Schmidt, they had lost votes. There were various reasons for this. The possibility of influencing many of them – the development of the global economic crisis, for instance, the international power constellations, the age distribution of the population – was strictly limited. Other weak points were of the SPD's own making. The party reacted to the outcome of the elections, however, by showing that it was prepared to scrutinise its own defects and weaknesses, and to draw the consequences.

6 Werner Kaltefleiter, 'Der Gewinner hat nicht gesiegt. Eine Analyse der Bundestagswahl 1976', Aus Politik und Zeitgeschichte. Beilage zur Wochenzeitung "Das Parlament", 50/76, 11.12.1976, p. 31.

Holger Börner, from 1972 to October 1976 the SPD party manager, and Hans Koschnick, from 1975 to 1979 deputy party chairman, concluded the following about the 1976 election campaign:[7] The Social Democrat image had been damaged by party infighting, shortcomings in the exercise of public office, and an inability to accommodate to the new life style of the average citizen. The balance sheet of its achievements which the SPD presented had made insufficiently clear what the values guiding its policies were[8], and yielded insufficient perspectives for the future. By contrast with 1972, the SPD had not succeeded in going on the offensive with topics which would stimulate widespread discussion and mobilise the voters. The challenge of a CDU/CSU which was driven by its right wing had not been countered early and aggressively enough. In addition to these deficits in the substance of the campaign, there had also been organisational weaknesses and problems with communication. Egon Bahr, Börner's successor as party manager, indicated the way ahead: "The organisation must establish relations between people, between citizen and party, and within the party itself. In today's German, the word is 'communication'."[9] It seemed the SPD had lost its old verve and profile as a party, and was sustained largely by the respect still enjoyed in the Federal Republic by Chancellor Helmut Schmidt.

The social-liberal coalition government between 1976 and 1980 enjoyed a high measure of stability. This was remarkable given that its period in office coincided with years of great upheaval and crises: global economic problems persisted, with most of the industrial nations unable to prevent inflation and unemployment. Terrorism in the Federal Republic at times reached threatening proportions. In the "German autumn" of 1977, with the kidnapping and murder of Hanns Martin Schleyer, President of the Confederation of German Industry (BDI) and the German Employers' Confederation (BDA), the skyjacking of Lufthansa jet Landshut and the

---

7 Their paper, entitled 'Bundestagswahlkampf 1976: Analyse und Folgerungen für die Arbeit der SPD', is published in the appendix to the Protokoll der Tagung des SPD-Parteirats am 27./28.1.1977 in Bad Godesberg, edited by the executive committee (Bonn 1977). See there also Willy Brandt's 'Anregungen zur sozialdemokratischen Vertrauensarbeit'.
8 These themes were dealt with splendidly by Marie Schlei and Joachim Wagner in Freiheit – Gerechtigkeit – Solidarität. Grundwerte und praktische Politik. Mit einem Vorwort von Helmut Schmidt (Bonn, Bad Godesberg 1976). An account of the thinking behind the government's socio-political reforms is also to be found in Marie Schlei and Dorothea Brück, Wege zur Selbstbestimmung. Sozialpolitik als Mittel der Emanzipation. Mit einem Geleitwort von Herbert Wehner (Cologne and Frankfurt/Main 1976).
9 Protokoll der Tagung des SPD-Parteirats am 27/28.1.1977, p. 57.

freeing of the hostages in Mogadishu by the GSG 9 anti-terrorist squad, and the suicide of terrorists in Stammheim prison, the democratic constitutional state faced its severest test. It passed it, setting an example of how to deal with terrorism and its destructive contempt for human life. Rising oil prices increased the difficulties of the developing countries; conflicts in the Middle East and the dictatorship of Islamic fanatics in Iran presented a challenge to the USA, Germany's most important partner in the Atlantic Alliance; the armaments policy of the USSR with its SS-20 missiles and the Russian invasion of Afghanistan altered the equilibrium between the military and political blocs. Difficulties in the European Union were an additional burden for the Federal Republic, which had given it vigorous support and energetic backing for direct elections to the European parliament.

The social-liberal coalition had succeeded in maintaining the country's standard of living, in avoiding grave, domestic social conflicts, and on the international front had pursued well-considered policies with great conviction. This had brought the government, and particularly Chancellor Helmut Schmidt, great respect at both home and abroad. The course followed by the governments led by Helmut Schmidt was characterised by tenacious pursuit of what had been embarked on, by the successful safeguarding of what had been achieved, but not, however, by bold new initiatives in search of fresh horizons.

3. New Tasks for the SPD

The trust which Helmut Schmidt had won during his time in office went far beyond the so-called "Chancellor bonus". And his party of course profited from this, as is demonstrated by the Landtag elections at the end of the 1970s: by comparison with earlier ones, they showed an upward trend for the SPD. The attractiveness of the SPD as an organisation, however, had not increased under Schmidt's Chancellorship. There were factors other than the stagnating, sometimes falling, membership figures which demonstrated this. Far fewer non-SPD members offered their active support in the 1976 and 1980 election campaigns than had done in 1969, and particularly in 1972. Even party members were frequently less committed than they had been previously. Those who were prepared to become politically and socially active, especially young people, found refuge in citizens' initiatives or small pressure groups. Although the proportion of new women SPD members had risen considerably, discontent was particularly rife in female circles. Egon Bahr's appeal for more "communication"[10] was, it seems, only partially successful. Compared to the previous decade, any upturn for the SPD in the second half of the 1970s failed to materialise.

The fact that the SPD had become the party which for years had led a successful coalition government, was the cause of many internal party problems. More than a few party members were afraid the SPD was becoming nothing more than a "Chancellor party", or was even degenerating into an apparatus for distributing posts at various levels. Many cast a critical eye on the "Establishment", as they called it, or sometimes even regarded it with mistrust. Their commitment to the party began to wane.

And yet, there was no shortage of fresh initiatives, originating and being developed at grassroots level. There were, for instance, the Social Democrat newspapers produced in factories and local districts and wards, and the many information stalls and offices set up to offer citizens personal help and advice. Activities such as this showed that the organisational life of the SPD, more than that of any other party, was a product of the members themselves. Nevertheless, the party had reason enough to repeatedly scrutinise its organisational defects, and to remain open to fresh impulses, in order to be able to intensify the "trust building" which had been sketched out in "Orientation Framework '85".

The internal conflicts with which the *Jusos* were riven led to a lessening of tensions between them and the party. In 1977, when Klaus Uwe Benneter, a representative of the "Stamokap" wing[11], was elected *Juso* chairman, and set his sights on working together with communists, the party executive committee reacted harshly. He was removed from office and thrown out of the party. The dust soon settled over the whole affair.[12] After the "Benneter case" there were no further confrontations between the *Jusos* and the party executive, even though the young socialists remained sharply critical of various aspects of the then current Social Democrat policy. They were, it must be said, not the only ones in the party with their criticisms.

Particularly controversial with the SPD rank and file and beyond, were the tightening of the laws to combat terrorism, the attitude towards com-

10 See note 9.
11 On this, see Hans Koschnick, Richard Löwenthal, Johano Strasser, Zur Klärung des Verhältnisses zwischen Sozialdemokratie und Stamokap-Richtung, edited by the SPD executive committee (Bonn, no date), p. 7: "The essence of the Stamokap theory lies [...] in the dogmatic assertion that even the planned intervention of a democratic state in the economy must of necessity and one-sidedly serve the interests of monopoly capital".
12 See Dieter Stephan, Jungsozialisten: Stabilisierung nach langer Krise? (Bonn 1979), esp. pp. 83–87.

munists in the civil service (the Extremists' Decree), security and defence policy, and the use of nuclear energy. After the "German autumn" of 1977, the danger of terrorism in the Federal Republic gradually died away. The extremist opposition had been weakened, and confidence in the democratic rule of law boosted. With this, the measures to combat the terrorist threat no longer seemed relevant. Accordingly, and following the principles adopted by the party conference of December 1978 in Cologne, the states governed by the SPD made substantial modifications to the practice of the Extremists' Decree.

Security policy and questions about the use of atomic energy remained problems of central importance. At the SPD party conference in Berlin in December 1979, they were the most significant and controversial points of discussion. The policy of *détente* was put to the test by the Soviets' installation of SS-20 nuclear missiles in Eastern Europe. The talk was of a second Cold War. Helmut Schmidt pushed emphatically for a strategy of nuclear balance designed to lead ideally to a "zero option" for medium-range missiles, and, should this fail, made provision for an upgrading of the Western nuclear response. There were, however, some Social Democrats, and not only those close to the peace movement, who had misgivings. Egon Bahr expressed massive reservations, Herbert Wehner kept his distance, and even the party chairman Willy Brandt declined to lend Schmidt his full support. The dissent in the party on security policy could no longer be ignored. In the run-up to the NATO dual-track policy (on 12 December 1979), the SPD party conference in Berlin had to reach a decision on a party executive committee motion on the issue. While still emphasising arms control and negotiations, it proposed the installation of medium-range ballistic missiles should these prove to be unsuccessful.[13] A clear majority of the delegates was in favour, but a considerable minority remained stubbornly opposed. Schmidt had staked his whole authority on a successful outcome, and had been helped by the fact that Franz Josef Strauß was his opponent in the next federal elections.

Resistance was even stronger, and the number of opposers even greater, to the assertion in the motion on energy that the peaceful use of atomic energy was indispensable. The most telling argument of the opponents of atomic energy was the unforeseeable dangers for today's and future generations which its use would bring. The ecological movement in the Federal Republic had formed powerful organisations hostile to atomic

13 The motion on atomic energy is in Energiepolitik. Dokumente, edited by the SPD party executive committee (Bonn 1980), p. 3 f. The one on security policy is in Sicherheitspolitik. Dokumente, edited by the SPD party executive committee (Bonn 1980), pp. 8 ff.

energy. Particularly successful amongst them were the Greens, who had made some electoral impact. At first in Bremen (1979), and then in Baden-Württemberg (1980), they overcame the five per cent hurdle and entered parliament. The Greens took votes mainly, if not entirely, from the SPD which, as for instance in Schleswig-Holstein in 1979, was crucial in giving the CDU the narrowest of victories. The obvious consideration, therefore, was for the SPD to adopt "green" themes, thereby eliminating the feather which tipped the electoral scales. On the other hand, the SPD's rejection of the use of atomic energy would have been the cause of disagreement with an important section of its supporters and voters, as well as provoking conflict with the trade unions. Moving closer to the Greens would, therefore, have hardly been worthwhile, even for tactical, electoral reasons.

The rise of the Greens, along with the numerous citizens' initiatives and protest campaigns by opponents of atomic energy and environmentalists, changed the domestic political climate. The SPD was inevitably affected by this. But at the party congress in Berlin it was the determination of the SPD to develop political concepts in close conjunction with their representatives in both federal and state governments, and to take joint responsibility for their implementation, which predominated. This had been an unmistakable feature of SPD policy since coming to power. But equally clear was the determination to influence SPD-led governments in such a way that their policies could be supported by the party as a whole. It was therefore inevitable that tensions would occasionally arise between groups both within the party and the Social Democrat parliamentary group on the one hand, and SPD members of the government on the other. Differences of opinion of this kind, which in some cases revealed themselves in voting in the Bundestag, were certainly aggravating, and damaged the party's public image, but they never put the social-liberal government in jeopardy.

The SPD played a leading role in the Socialist International in the 1970s. Unlike most other Social Democratic parties in Europe at this time, it enjoyed an uninterrupted spell in power. In November 1976, Willy Brandt, the internationally highly respected chairman of the SPD, became President of the Socialist International, an honour both for him personally, and for his party. After being elected, he called on the International to mount a three-pronged offensive: for a secure peace, for new relations between North and South, for human rights. Recognition of Brandt's efforts on behalf of these goals, and an encouragement to pursue them further came, when, at the end of 1977, he was appointed chairman of the Independent Commission on International Development Issues (North-

South Commission). The commission's report[14] published in 1980 set out a programme of urgent action: conquering world hunger; comprehensive political agreements on energy; increased transfer of resources; reform of international agencies.[15]

The growing importance of the Federal Republic as one of the world's richest and most stable industrial countries increased the SPD's sphere of responsibility. Separating the national from the international tasks of a Social Democrat party, particularly when it was in power, was becoming less feasible than ever.

4. The Federal Elections of 5 October 1980

Faced by a Chancellor who was more popular than his party, and a Deputy Chancellor Hans-Dietrich Genscher who, with his FDP, was demonstrably close to Schmidt, it was virtually impossible for the Union parties to win the federal elections of 1980. Their Chancellor candidate was Franz Josef Strauß, chairman of the CSU and Minister President of Bavaria. Following the success of the social-liberal coalition in the federal elections of 1976, Strauß had uninhibitedly criticised the then candidate of the Union parties, the CDU chairman Helmut Kohl, as "completely incapable", and threatened to break away from the CDU.[16] Strauß then abandoned his intention to extend the CSU to the whole of the Federal Republic in favour of a new plan: he wanted to be the "strong man" of the Union parties. When, after great resistance from the CDU, he finally managed to secure the Chancellor candidacy, he seemed to have achieved his goal. This would set the tenor for the 1980 federal election campaign. With the slogan "Against the SPD-State – Stop Socialism", Strauß sought to win by adopting a course of demagogic confrontation. Given that a man such as Helmut Schmidt was Chancellor, this could hardly cut any ice with centre-ground voters. "Schmidt or Strauß" was the alternative suggested by the SPD, largely with the agreement of the FDP. The federal elections of 5 October 1980 became a plebiscite against Franz Josef Strauß.

The SPD made narrow gains (0.3 points), achieving 42.0 per cent; the FDP went up to 10.6 percent (an increase of 2.7); the Union parties lost

---

14 North-South: A Programme for Survival (MIT Press Boston 1980).
15 See Willy Brandt's speech in Santo Domingo on 26.3.1980, published in an SPD press briefing of 27.3.1980.
16 See 'Strauß' Wienerwaldrede: Kohl ist total unfähig zum Kanzler', Der Spiegel, 29.11.1976.

4.1 percentage points, but remained the numerically strongest party. This gave the social-liberal coalition a comfortable margin of 45 seats in the Bundestag, compared to one of only ten in the previous parliamentary term.

Despite the coalition's broadened parliamentary basis, the outcome of the 1980 federal elections was unsatisfactory for the SPD. After its great success in the North Rhine-Westphalian Landtag elections of May 1980, when, under their new, but already popular Minister President Johannes Rau, they achieved an overall majority in this state for the first time ever, and were able to form a government on their own, a greater increase in SPD votes might have been expected. It also had to be disappointing for the SPD that the much greater sympathy and trust – shown by all the polls – which Schmidt enjoyed amongst the general public as compared with Strauß did not translate into greater numbers of votes for the Chancellor's party in the federal elections. It was also clear that in these elections both SPD and FDP received support from people who were only voting for them to prevent Strauß from becoming Chancellor. The fact that under these circumstances the Greens received only 1.4 per cent of the vote, was principally to the good of the SPD, while the FDP profited from the distaste of potential Union voters for their own candidate, and also received the vote of those who were inclined to favour the SPD, but did not want the FDP to fall at the five per cent hurdle.

The elections of 5 October 1980 were a vote of confidence in the eleven years of the social-liberal coalition. The election results demonstrated that the electorate, particularly north of the Main, did not want the change in the politics of the Federal Republic promised by the Union, but which it never concretely defined. But neither did it give the SPD the clear victory it had expected. Basically, the party had retained its core vote, but had been unable to extend it to new regions and sections of the population.

V. Crisis and the End of the Social-Liberal Coalition

1. Discontent and Conflicts in the SPD

The statements of both the SPD and FDP in the 1980 election campaign left no doubt that both coalition partners intended to continue to work together in government. On 9 November the Bundestag again elected Helmut Schmidt as Chancellor. On the same day he appointed his third cabinet, which contained thirteen SPD, and four FDP ministers, who, with few exceptions, retained the same portfolios as before. Continuity seemed guaranteed.

But negotiations about the future policy of the social-liberal coalition did not run smoothly. The consequences of the second "oil shock" of 1978/79 were only now making themselves felt. Production slumped, and consumer prices rose, the economy was sliding into recession, and there was a clear rise in unemployment after autumn 1980. Overcoming this crisis proved to be a severe test of endurance. The coalition was faced with having to impose cuts in order to halt state borrowing, and to take measures to balance the budget without stifling economic growth. A compromise had to be sought and found between the FDP's call for cuts in welfare benefits, and the plan favoured by the SPD to introduce an employment programme. On the essentials, the junior partner got its way over the senior partner. A widely read news magazine commented that it was the SPD's traditional voters who would have to carry the main burden of the economy measures.[1] No measures were agreed on unemployment, a decision on safeguarding co-determination in the iron and steel industries was postponed, and the FDP Minister of Agriculture was able to fend off the cutting of aid to farmers. The FDP insisted on the SPD not attempting to get legislation through with changing majorities, which would have mobilised the employees' wing of the CDU against the Liberals.

The course of future government policy which had been set in the coalition negotiations was received with disappointment, and also, in part, with bitterness by large sections of the SPD and the trade unions. But Social Democrats were also completely realistic about the dilemma in which they found themselves. Even those – and there were a lot of them – who reproached Helmut Schmidt for being too accommodating towards the

---

1 Der Spiegel, 10.11.1980, p. 20.

Liberals, did not want to break up the coalition and thereby bring about the demise of a Social Democratic government. They knew, moreover, that their relatively good performance in the 1976 and 1980 elections was due to the appeal of Helmut Schmidt, and that for this reason alone his position within the party must not be jeopardised. For those determining SPD policy, another possibly lengthy spell on the opposition benches was a frightening prospect. On the other hand, the party had no wish to abandon its criticisms of coalition policy, and its objections to concessions which their comrades found intolerable. A great part of the SPD membership did not regard opposing coalition measures with demands which had been formulated after an opinion-forming process within the party as being disloyal towards their representatives in government. They saw their criticism and counter-suggestions as a legitimate and necessary way of showing them the way forward, and of giving them support *vis-à-vis* their coalition partners. "We trade unionists do not want a different government, we want different policies", wrote Leonhard Mahlein, chairman of the printers' and papermakers' union, in April 1982.[2] A left-wing trade unionist, Mahlein was not only representing the wishes of his close political allies, but also those which many other trade unionists and Social Democrats had also been expressing since the advent of Schmidt's third cabinet. However, the group under Egon Franke within the parliamentary party, who saw themselves as the backroom boys and the vigorous mainstay of Helmut Schmidt's policies, regarded this as an attempt to square the circle. With their public campaigns against the government's economy measures, and harsh protests under the slogan "enough is enough", the trade unions distanced themselves from the government. The ruling Social Democrats, and those in the unions with the greatest say, began to drift apart at this point.

In the social-liberal coalition's third period in office, there was much more divergence of opinion within the SPD over the policies and performance of the Chancellor and the SPD ministers than in the first two. Nonetheless, the party was still determined to keep the social-liberal government in power. Even those members of the parliamentary party who were at odds with the "backroom boys" refrained from any activity in the Bundestag which might have seriously jeopardised the coalition. When, after years of friction, two left-wing SPD deputies, Manfred Coppik and Karl-Heinz Hansen, abandoned the party whip, they found themselves

---

2 Quoted by Klaus Bohnsack, 'Die Koalitionskrise 1981/82 und der Regierungswechsel 1982', Zeitschrift für Parlamentsfragen, 1 (1983), p. 11.

completely isolated, and their attempt to set up a new party was a miserable failure.

While the government could rely on the absolute discipline of the parliamentary party under Herbert Wehner, conflicts outside parliament were unavoidable. Resistance to NATO's installation of Pershing missiles began to grow. The peace movement sprang into action. There was criticism from the Protestant Church, and sections of the SPD were moving inexorably closer to the peace movement. Erhard Eppler, as well as Oskar Lafontaine, the *Jusos*, and 150 SPD deputies openly criticised NATO's dual-track policy as a "disastrously wrong decision".[3] Although the party chairman Willy Brandt outwardly supported the Chancellor, he showed some sympathy for the peace movement and its concerns about an arms race. The dissent was dramatically exposed by a peace demonstration in Bonn on 10 October 1981, in which 250,000 people, including many Social Democrats, took part. Members of the SPD and FDP parliamentary parties also showed their solidarity with the demonstrators. Helmut Schmidt regarded this as a mass protest against his own policies, and was opposed to Social Democrats taking part. He failed, however, to impress this on the SPD presidium. Supported and encouraged by Willy Brandt, Erhard Eppler – member of the presidium and chairman of the SPD Commission on Basic Values – was one of the prominent speakers at the demonstration.

Increasing numbers of Social Democrats abandoned their loyalty to their own Chancellor over security policy, and adopted a path which, with its somewhat one-sided criticism of NATO rockets and anti-American reservations directed mainly, but not exclusively, at Ronald Reagan, led to a rather distorted situation. The moves to unseat Schmidt were not limited to just the younger left-wingers in the party; Egon Bahr made a start with his "parallel foreign policy", and Willy Brandt, after his trip to Moscow, praised Brezhnev's desire for peace. No few Social Democrats distanced themselves from the struggle for freedom of the Solidarity movement in Poland. Solidarity was perceived as disruptive, as a threat to stability and *détente*, and, unlike Pinochet's military dictatorship in Chile, the establishment of the Jaruzelski regime and the introduction of martial law in December 1981 did not provoke mass protests. Helmut Schmidt was, at this point in time, on an official visit to the GDR. The meeting with head of the SED and Chairman of the State Council Erich Honecker at Werbellin and Döllnsee was overshadowed not only by the events in Poland, but

---

3 Winkler, Weg nach Westen, vol. 2, p. 373f. Erhard Eppler was a member of the SPD presidium, Oskar Lafontaine was Mayor of Saarbrücken.

Peace demonstration in Bonn on 10 October 1981

also by the ghostly scenes in Güstrow.[4] Uniformed and plain-clothes *Stasi* (secret police) and peoples' police lined the streets. GDR citizens were harassed and banned from public places out of the well-justified fear that the Social Democrat West German Chancellor would be greeted sympathetically. In spite of the hardened fronts in the East-West conflict, Schmidt, with his considered policies of dialogue, and by fighting tenaciously for the alleviation of human problems, had achieved far more than mere damage limitation in the difficult terrain of all-German relations. He had sown the seed which would then bear fruit under his successor Helmut Kohl.

Not only the peace movement, but also the environmental and alternative movements, along with various citizens' initiatives and protest campaigns – principally those against the building of atomic power stations and the extension of Frankfurt airport ("runway West") – were attractive to some members of the SPD and, above all, to young people who hitherto had been potential SPD voters. Opinion within the party was divided over these movements and protests, and whether it was permissible for Social Democrats to participate in them. Equally controversial was the question of whether sections of this movement could be won over to the SPD. It was important to find an answer to it, given the various successes the Greens were having in Landtag and local elections.

On the question of "Social Democrat identity", Willy Brandt pleaded for openness towards these new tendencies which "were striving for nothing which was foreign to the goals of democratic socialism"[5]. "They were", he argued, "resisting the uncontrolled and exultant progress of a technology which is destroying nature and ways of living which should be preserved. Many are resisting the anonymity of modern life, the inhumanity of vast organisational structures and their attendant bureaucracies. Many are endeavouring to re-establish old patterns of life and experience. They are searching for new ways to live together, new ways of linking work and leisure, and reuniting work and culture". Brandt concluded his description of what "restless youth", "awkward probers" were pressing for with questions to which he himself had already given positive answers:

---

4 On this visit, see Helmut Schmidt, Die Deutschen und ihre Nachbarn (Berlin 1990), pp. 57–73; Heinrich Potthoff, Bonn und Ost-Berlin 1969–1982 (Bonn 1997), pp. 79–81 and pp. 652–697, and Im Schatten der Mauer. Deutschlandpolitik 1961 bis 1990 (Berlin 1999), pp. 188–194.

5 In a speech at a symposium held in Bonn on 21.10.1982, which the SPD executive had organised in commemoration of the tenth anniversary of the death of Willi Eichler. The symposium is documented in Die Neue Gesellschaft, 28, 12.12.1981, pp. 1062–85.

"Are not these also our own goals? [...] Is there not something being expressed here of the principle of 'venturing more democracy' which I myself took as our motto when, in 1969, we embarked on breaking the encrusted mould of the CDU state?"[6]

Willy Brandt met with resistance. Professor Richard Löwenthal, his old companion and well-respected advisor to Social Democrat politicians, reproached Brandt for not having taken his answer "seriously enough".[7] Löwenthal's point of reference was that, on the one hand, the SPD was losing potential new young voters to the Greens, on the other, that either their core vote was defecting to the Union parties, or that they were not voting at all. He warned the SPD against seeking, by being accommodating towards them, to integrate groups who wanted nothing to do with the legal norms of parliamentary democracy, and who rejected the division of labour in industrial societies. In the conflict between the "drop-outs" and the mass of "employees of all kinds", the SPD had to take an unambiguous stand against the "drop-outs": otherwise the party itself would merely "disintegrate".[8] This clash – widely regarded as one between Helmut Schmidt (whose position Löwenthal wished to bolster) and Willy Brandt – received particular publicity when Löwenthal's argument, drawn up in six theses, was presented for signing by Annemarie Renger, Vice President of the Bundestag, and prominent Social Democrats and trade-union chairmen. This attempt to strengthen the position of the Chancellor within his own party had little long-term effect. The party executive brushed it aside, and it had no influence whatsoever on the coalition.

2. *Genscher's Call for a Wende (turnabout)*

It was less the controversies in the SPD, which had mainly to do with peace and security policy, which weighed heavily on relations between the coalition partners in summer and autumn 1981, than the problems arising from the worsening situation in the economy. It became increasingly difficult in the government camp to find common, agreed solutions to them. The number of unemployed had passed the million mark and was continuing to rise. Unemployment was altering the balance of power between employers and employees, putting the trade unions on the back foot, and producing amongst traditional SPD supporters feelings of resig-

---

6 Ibid., p. 1066.
7 Ibid. Löwenthal's essay 'Identität und Zukunft der SPD' is published on pp. 1085–89 (here, 1086). It also appeared in the weekly newspaper Die Zeit.
8 Ibid., p. 1087.

nation and disappointment towards both party and government. At the same time, unemployment made the problem of state financing and the funding of the welfare safety net even more acute. The government was faced, on the one hand, with sinking revenues because of the drop in national insurance contributions and taxes, and on the other by rapidly rising welfare expenditure. The financial problem was not helped by the high interest rates which all Western industrial countries had introduced to counter creeping inflation. The prerequisites for a classical Keynesian counter-strategy were poor: no reserves had been accumulated because, for years, politicians and experts had been in the grip of an uncritical belief in growth. In view of high interest rates and the burden of public debt, there were misgivings about the financing of job-creation schemes by the extension of net borrowing.

The social-liberal coalition was no longer in a position to defuse conflicts about wealth distribution by everyone being able to improve their standard of living through a growth in gross national product. Any policy to tackle the financial and economic crisis had, of necessity, to impose burdens on the population. The source of conflict was how, precisely, these should be distributed. The FDP blocked proposals by the SPD to finance an employment programme by means of a surtax on high earners. They believed in the power of the market to heal itself. The economic liberals in the FDP wanted to make up the deficits in the public purse by cutting national expenditure in the social sector.

On 20 August 1981, the FDP chairman and Deputy Chancellor Hans-Dietrich Genscher, addressing his party in the so-called *Wendebrief* (turnabout letter), wrote: "Our country is at a crossroads". He compared the current controversy about basic principles with the decisions about political direction "during the period of reconstruction after the Second World War." It was a matter, he said, of "breaking the mentality that everything should be provided", which had arisen "because much legislation directly encourages, even induces people, to make claims on the state". Genscher's subsequent, often quoted conclusion was that: "A *Wende* (turnabout) is necessary."[9]

Against the background of coalition policy since October 1980, Genscher's considerations were not very plausible. After all, the FDP with Count Otto Lambsdorff as Economics Minister had been able to assert itself on crucial issues in cabinet without a "debate on basic issues". A critical observer without any particular sympathy for Social Democrat

---

9 Wolfram Bickerich (ed.), Die 13 Jahre. Bilanz der sozialliberalen Koalition. Spiegelbuch (Reinbek bei Hamburg Nov. 1982), p. 241.

complaints noted in retrospect: "The economic wing of the FDP ruled, the employees' wing of the SPD was given a hearing."[10] The Liberals had taken a battering at this time from the party donations scandal. It had damaged the credibility of all the parties, but had hit the FDP and its Economics Minister Count Otto Lambsdorff particularly hard. When the amnesty initially proposed foundered on the veto of the new Justice Minister, and resistance from the SPD parliamentary party, the coalition atmosphere was soured.

But probably the most credible motive for Genscher's call for change was the coalition parties' fall from grace with the electors. In the local elections in Hesse in March 1981, and the elections to the Berlin Chamber of Deputies in May 1981, the CDU became the strongest party, the SPD suffered heavy losses, and the FDP only just managed to surmount the five per cent hurdle. Opinion polls in those months revealed a steady decline in support for the SPD throughout the Federal Republic. Given this situation, the FDP wanted to raise its profile, and to be able to choose its coalition partner. Its loyalty to the SPD ceased at the point where its own chances of being in power were on the line. In the Rhineland-Palatinate, for instance, the FDP declared itself prepared to form a coalition with the CDU, should they not win an overall majority. In March 1977 it had joined the CDU government in the Saar. In May 1979 they had demonstrated that they were symbolically keeping their options open to a certain extent when, in the election for the Federal President, they voted neither for the CDU candidate, Karl Carstens, nor for the SPD candidate, Annemarie Renger. At local level, FDP support for the Union parties was not an exception. For the time being, however, this did not call the Bonn coalition in question.

Developments in Hesse had a significant effect on the relationship of the SPD to its partner in the federal government. The FDP had been a member of the SPD-led state government there for twelve years. In the Landtag elections set for the end of September 1982, they opted in favour of forming a coalition with the CDU. There were no local political factors in this decision: the Minister President of Hesse, Holger Börner (SPD), had, in the face of stiff resistance from the left wing of his party, and above all from the Greens, steered a course to which the FDP could hardly object. It was uncertain, however, whether the SPD would once again form the government after the Landtag elections in Wiesbaden. After all, the Social Democrats had lost their overall majority in their traditional stronghold of Hamburg, with the CDU becoming the strongest group in the

---

10 Ibid., Wolfram Bickerich, p. 47.

"Hitch-hiking in both directions".
Cartoon of Hans-Dietrich Genscher by Klaus Pielert

parliament, and the FDP – as they had done in 1978 – falling at the five per cent hurdle. The idea immediately suggested itself to the FDP that they might profit from the trend towards the CDU. Hesse, however, proved to be a miscalculation, since the September elections brought the Liberals not a single seat. Nonetheless, the FDP's coalition choice in Hesse sent out a signal for the Federal Republic as a whole.

3. The SPD Munich Party Congress

After the conflicts in the coalition over balancing the budget and the party donations amnesty, Chancellor Schmidt wanted to persuade the FDP to show its colours, and his own party to be more united. The SPD and FDP deputies unanimously stuck by him in the vote of confidence on 5 February 1982, but the fact that Helmut Schmidt had put it at all was a sign of how brittle the coalition had become. A cabinet reshuffle at the end of April, in which Schmidt surrounded himself again with his trusted allies Hans-Jürgen Wischnewski and Klaus Bölling, brought no lasting relief. It affected only SPD ministers; the FDP was left untouched.

The FDP, along with commentators favourably disposed to it, cited the resolutions of the SPD party conference of April 1982 as the reasons for the subsequent collapse of the social-liberal coalition. The delegates meeting in Munich were indeed determined to raise the profile of their own Social Democratic Party. As the SPD information service put it: "This was not a coalition party congress, but a party congress at which the Social Democrats redefined their position."[11] Chancellor Schmidt also recognised this in principle when he noted: "The SPD must provide the intellectual force behind forward-looking, concrete solutions. It must not get caught up between techniques of government and alternative movements. The party must not merely be allowed to be ahead of the government, the coalition government, it has to be ahead of it."[12] At the end of the social-liberal coalition, he called upon the SPD to draw up a short catalogue of its policies "in keeping with our previous decisions, including, of course, those made in Munich".[13]

Unemployment and how to tackle it were of central importance in the Munich discussions; it was also the topic on which the differences between the two coalition partners were at their most obvious. The party conference finally approved, by a large majority, a document of some considerable length. It was headed: "Social Democratic perspectives on regaining full employment – work for all". It did not escape public notice, and was strongly criticised by both Union parties and the FDP, that it contained demands which had been rejected in the cabinet, mainly due to pressure from the FDP Minister of Economics, Count Otto Lambsdorff. Among them were: increased borrowing to combat unemployment; a fixed-term surtax on higher incomes and a labour-market tax to finance job-creation schemes; abolition of unjustified tax breaks; raising of the higher rate of income tax; introduction of a tax on land-value increases. Clearly in tune with the trade unions was the demand that co-determination and industrial codes should "maintain parity between capital and labour in all important decision-making processes". The demand for shorter working hours was also a sop to the trade unions.[14]

With these resolutions on economic and financial policy, the party conference upped its left-wing profile, while Helmut Schmidt succeeded, by a large majority, in pushing through his line on security and energy

11 Informationsdienst der SPD intern, 7/82, 28.4.1982, p. 1.
12 Ibid., p. 2.
13 Schmidt to the SPD party council on 19.9.1982; SPD-Service 416/82, p. 5.
14 Dokumente. SPD-Parteitag München 19.–23. April 82, Beschlüsse zur Wirtschafts- und Beschäftigungspolitik, part 1, pp. 1–14, edited by the SPD executive committee (Bonn 1982).

policy in the face of opposition to NATO's dual-track policy from critics such as Erhard Eppler and Oskar Lafontaine. The Chancellor had passed this trial of strength, albeit after making certain concessions. The "Munich Declaration" affirmed the party's commitment to the Western Alliance, as well as to a "security partnership with the eastern states", and also expressed its sympathy for the peace movement. A decision on what conclusions the SPD would draw from current negotiations between the USA and the Soviet Union on the question of stationing new missile systems on German soil was postponed pending a special party conference in autumn 1983.[15]

The SPD, battered by defeats in local and Landtag elections, internal party strife, and compromising revelations about goings-on in the trade-union-owned housing construction company *Neue Heimat*, drew fresh courage from the Munich party congress. The party had succeeded there in pulling itself together, in engaging in controversy but simultaneously demonstrating a common purpose. The plethora and variety of activities at local level, demonstrated for the first time at the party congress, were testimony to the vitality and inventiveness of the party. Helmut Schmidt, who once again was elected deputy SPD chairman, along with Johannes Rau, the North Rhine-Westphalian Minister President – with Schmidt getting 365 out of 436, and Rau 367 out of 432 votes – could assume from this that his party was in favour of a continuation of the social-liberal coalition under his leadership.[16] This was vital since tensions within the coalition were rising. That they were substantially increased by the SPD's Munich party congress is part of the legend fashioned by the FDP to justify changing its coalition partner.

4. *The Collapse of the Social-Liberal Coalition*

In early summer 1982, the coalition partners engaged in laborious negotiations on the basic points of the 1983 budget. The result satisfied no one, and the indications that the government would collapse were increasing. Since the turnabout by the FDP in Hesse, it was generally assumed that the social-liberal coalition would come to a premature end; the only question was how and when. Some prominent Social Democrats openly spoke out against remaining in the government. The most drastic of them was

---

15 SPD-Parteitag, München, 19.–23. April 82, Beschlüsse zur Außen-, Friedens- und Sicherheitspolitik, pp. 3–7, edited by the SPD executive committee (Bonn 1982).
16 See the "Munich Declaration" of 19.4.1982. In Informationsdienst der SPD intern, no. 7/82, 28.4.1982.

the Mayor of Saarbrücken and member of the SPD executive Oskar Lafontaine. "The SPD must get out of the government in Bonn", he loudly demanded. It could only regenerate itself, he maintained, in opposition. This approach was accompanied by harsh criticism of Chancellor Schmidt.[17]

But those who advocated leaving the government as soon as possible did not represent the views of members of the government and the parliamentary party. They were intent on avoiding the accusation that the SPD had capitulated to the difficulties of government responsibility by seeking refuge in opposition. Admittedly, Helmut Schmidt, when amongst close party colleagues, occasionally made no secret of how hurt he felt by criticism from within the party – and particularly when it was as defamatory as that of Lafontaine – and of how much he missed having some reaction from the party leadership.[18] But Schmidt was far from drawing the consequences of internal SPD wrangling, and abandoning his post as head of government. He did not want either himself or the SPD to bear the responsibility for failure.

The final blow then to the social-liberal coalition was delivered by the FDP. The declarations of war from the Free Democrats were mounting. On the evening of 9 September, Schmidt received from the Economics Minister Count Lambsdorff a memorandum which read like the economic Liberals' credo against the Social Democrats, and which was clearly aimed at bringing the coalition with the SPD to an end.[19] At the cabinet meeting of 15 September 1982, five days after publication of the note, Schmidt declared that Lambsdorff's concept was not in accord with government policy, and he asked him to clarify where he stood on it. Schmidt, along with the parliamentary party, found Lambsdorff's explanation in the Bundestag unsatisfactory.[20] The "divorce note" remained on the table.

---

17 In a telephone conversation with the reporter Jürgen Serke, Lafontaine said: "Helmut Schmidt continues to speak about a sense of duty, predictability, feasibility, steadfastness [...] These are secondary virtues. To be absolutely precise: they are what you need to run a concentration camp." In Stern, 15.7.1982, p. 55 f. This statement was also published in Bild-Zeitung on 15.7.1982.
18 See, for instance, the excerpts from Schmidt's remarks to the SPD parliamentary party on 26.10.1982. In Helmut Herles, Machtverlust oder das Ende der Ära Brandt (Stuttgart 1983), p. 11 f.
19 See Klaus Bölling, Die letzten 30 Tage des Kanzlers Helmut Schmidt. Ein Tagebuch (Reinbek bei Hamburg 1982), p. 47 f. On the dissemination of the Lambsdorff note and its discussion in SPD and FDP committees, see Klaus Bohnsack, Die Koalitionskrise 1981/82 (see note 2), pp. 19 ff.
20 Ibid., Bohnsack, pp. 29 ff.

There was also opposition to the intention to split with the SPD from within the FDP. But the majority of the FDP parliamentary party were not prepared to drop their Economics Minister Lambsdorff in order to rescue the coalition with the SPD, at least in the short term. Genscher had intended to postpone any decision on a *Wende* until after the Hesse elections on 26 September. Schmidt drew a line through this plan. The Lambsdorff memorandum, with its "list of reactionary requests", which "were a flagrant contradiction of the jointly formulated economic and financial policies of the coalition"[21], and the FDP departure signals not only undermined the authority of the government, but were also a threat to parliamentary democracy. Since neither Helmut Kohl with his CDU/CSU nor the FDP round Genscher and Lambsdorff dared to bring the *Wende* into the open, Schmidt was now determined to fix the separation date himself.

In an impressive speech in the Bundestag on 17 September 1982, Helmut Schmidt announced the end of the social-liberal coalition. He had given a written copy of it to Genscher beforehand, who then shortly afterwards submitted the resignation of the four FDP ministers. Schmidt praised the social-liberal era as "an historical epoch in the development of our democratic community", and emphasised that, through the behaviour of its leading politicians, the FDP had abandoned the basis for honest cooperation. He proposed that the Bundestag be dissolved, and called for fresh elections to be held as soon as possible. After a discussion with Willy Brandt and Herbert Wehner, he had concluded that this was the best way "of leading us out of the present domestic political crisis".[22]

Schmidt's suggestion was disregarded. Helmut Kohl, as well as Hans-Dietrich Genscher, fought shy of risking an election against the popular Helmut Schmidt with his "bonus" as the Chancellor in office. Although the FDP were punished for their "treachery" in the Hesse elections on 26 September, Genscher brought the Wende he had planned and arranged with Kohl to a conclusion. On 1 October 1982, the Union parties brought a constructive vote of no confidence against Chancellor Schmidt, which resulted in a majority for Helmut Kohl (CDU). Four days later, the new cabinet, formed from the Union parties and the FDP, was appointed under Chancellor Kohl.

A strong minority in the FDP parliamentary party was opposed to Genscher's tactics, which had led to their party switching coalition partners. Very few FDP deputies, however, drew the obvious conclusion of

21 Schmidt at the SPD party council on 19.9.82, SPD-Service 416/82, p. 1 and p. 3.
22 Text of Schmidt's speech in Verhandlungen des Deutschen Bundestages, stenographic reports, vol. 122, pp. 7072–7077.

their opposition: Ingrid Matthäus-Maier, an acknowledged financial expert, Günter Verheugen, former Secretary General of the FDP, and Andreas von Schoeler, former parliamentary Secretary of State in the Ministry of the Interior, joined the SPD: Mrs Matthäus-Maier and Verheugen received SPD mandates on 6 March 1983, Helga Schuchardt left the FDP, and soon after became Senator for Culture, with no party allegiance, in the SPD Senate in Hamburg.

Helmut Schmidt had presided over a dignified exit for himself and his party. His great prestige, based on expertise, judgement, and sense of duty, outlasted his fall. The sovereign way in which he cut through the Gordian knot of an intolerable crisis gained the grudging respect of even his opponents, and his own party was grateful to him for it. He had liberated them from a situation which had plunged them into uncertainty and shaken their self-confidence. This came as a relief to many. But there was scarcely a single Social Democrat, whether amongst the rank or file or the party leadership, who did not feel deep down that the loss of governmental power had ushered in a period – possibly of long duration – on the unforgiving opposition benches, and one in which the domestic political reforms and the foreign policy successes which the social-liberal coalition had achieved might be put in jeopardy.

VI. A Balance Sheet for the Social-Liberal Era

As the party in government, the Social Democrats achieved the best result in their history in the 1972 federal elections. In the following years, however, the party suffered setbacks which could only be made good – as in May 1980, for instance, in the North Rhine-Westphalian Landtag elections – in exceptional cases. In nine Landtag elections in 1974/75, while the Union parties made gains (except in Schleswig-Holstein), the SPD vote, as compared to the four previous years, went down everywhere except in the Saarland, with Hamburg and Berlin seeing the biggest drop.[1] There was a similar development in municipal elections in many large cities where the SPD had, for decades, enjoyed an overall majority.

In a process of self-scrutiny, it did not escape the party's notice that Social Democrats at state and local level had not managed to retain the hard-won respect they had once enjoyed. This was not only due to adverse external circumstances, but had causes within the party itself. Internal wrangling, for instance, which had ruined the standing of the SPD in Munich; the filling of posts with party cronies who were intellectually and personally not up to the job, whose actions were not subject to control, and whose mistakes were subsequently hushed up (in short, nepotism and corruption); wrong decisions and weak leadership from Social Democrats in charge of state governments and town halls, as demonstrated by the affair of the Hesse regional bank, or the toxic-waste scandal in Hamburg. When Alfred Kubel, Minister President in a social-liberal coalition in Lower Saxony and a seasoned Social Democrat who had been in government office since 1945, resigned, by agreement, in the middle of the legislative period, this was a gamble which proved to have serious consequences for the SPD. Kubel's designated successor (initially Helmut Kasimier, Minister of Finance in Kubel's cabinet, then Karl Ravens, Minister of Housing in Bonn) did not get a majority in the parliament, whereupon the CDU candidate Ernst Albrecht formed a new state government and won the next Landtag elections.

In addition to the inadequacies of SPD personnel at state and local level, there were political measures which were not supported by large sections of the population. A prime example was educational policy, and in particular the guidelines for schools in Hesse, which put more value

---

[1] See the Jahrbuch der SPD 1973–1975, p. 241.

on critical thinking than on transmission of knowledge. The conception of comprehensive education came under attack from all sides, not just from conservative parents who had grown tired of the constant experimentation and yearned for a degree of calm, order, and consistency. So-called "regional reform" also met with fierce criticism, particularly in states governed by social-liberal coalitions such as Lower Saxony and Hesse. The creation of large administrative units, partly under new names, was seen as showing no understanding of established traditions, and as demonstrating a complete disregard for local interests. The most vociferous protest was reserved for the amalgamation (subsequently revoked) of Giessen and Wetzlar under the name "Lahnstadt", after the river Lahn which flows through both towns. "Regional reform" was not something specific to Social Democrat state and local policy. It was carried out by the CSU in Bavaria[2], and the main impetus for it in Hesse came from the FDP coalition partner. But the objections to educational and regional reform were directed principally at the SPD, because, as the governing party in Bonn, they were identified in the mind of the average citizen with every government measure at national and state level, and also because they were *the* party of reform. A negative influence on the public's judgement of the SPD were the protest activities of, for the most part, young people – demonstrations, often of a violent nature, as well as the occupation of universities and empty houses – which, in the opinion of many, the Social Democrat state and local governments were not dealing with in a sufficiently energetic fashion. The "ungovernability" of Frankfurt, where Social Democrat mayors had endeavoured to quell the ongoing disturbances which had begun with the rebellion of the 1968 APO-generation[3] – two of these mayors, Willi Brundert and Walter Möller, had found the whole business so gruelling that they had died in office – was regarded almost as a matter of fate. But after the SPD had lost its majority in Frankfurt, and the CDU candidate Walter Wallmann had become Mayor in 1977, the riots died away. It was the same in Berlin and various other university towns and cities. The impression arose that this was not because the CDU/CSU office-holders were politically superior to their SPD predecessors, but probably because there was an awareness that the conservatives would have fewer scruples than the liberal-minded Social Democrats in using the full force of the state to deal with the excesses, and that this

---

2 The Bavarian SPD reported that "the [SPD] parliamentary party made countless submissions in an attempt to implement the justified demands of many communities for the rectification of senseless regional reforms". See the Jahrbuch der SPD 1977–1979, p. 163.
3 Außerparlamentarische Opposition (extra-parliamentary opposition).

had an inhibiting effect on the protestors. Perhaps they also thought that there was no point in mounting protests against conservative authority, whereas the Social Democrats would always feel obliged to give them some consideration.

One of the fundamental aspects of the SPD's involvement in government has been the high expectations it has aroused. This is understandable given that the party has always set itself the goal of changing society in the direction of more freedom, more justice, and more humanity. It never lost sight of this in all the sixteen years it was in power in Bonn. In 1976, when it drew up a balance sheet for the social-liberal coalition – which had been preceded by three years of crucial SPD participation in the federal government – the party could look with justifiable pride on what it had achieved.[4] But even then, it was clear that there were problems for which the social-liberal government would have no solutions.

It was true that the social safety net prevented the worst extremes of poverty (a fate which befell millions in the USA, the richest industrial country in the world) and that, by comparison with other nations, a large proportion of the population lived in affluence. But the crass differences in income and standard of living amongst various groups in the Federal Republic still left social justice as a distant ideal. This was acceptable to those disadvantaged groups as long as they could count on the hope of steady economic growth, and on themselves being able to benefit from it in due course. But with a sinking rate of growth and rising unemployment, the yawning gap in the distribution of material goods grew even wider.

People whose jobs and incomes were destroyed or jeopardised by economic developments – and counted amongst them were not only ordinary workers, but also self-employed tradesmen, middle-class shopkeepers and entrepreneurs, members of the freelance professions, small farmers – found their situation particularly oppressive in view of the fact that there was an ever larger group who were not affected by the same risks as them: workers in the public sector, and civil servants in particular. Their privileges were even increased by the social-liberal coalition. This caused a lot of bad blood amongst the population at large, and fed mistrust of "them up there" who were wangling favours for one another. Increasing resentment inevitably came to influence the way the state was regarded.

The problem of *Gastarbeiter*, foreign workers, was a further burden on the social-liberal coalition. Since the beginning of the 1960s, workers from all over the world had been recruited for jobs which Germans did not want to do, without employers and the state bothering about their needs

---

4 See p. 236 above.

and interests. In 1980 there were two million foreign workers, and 4.5 million foreigners in all, living in the Federal Republic. At a time of growing unemployment, this led to increasing difficulties. Tension arose between different cultural groups, mainly Germans and Turks, in residential districts, pubs, and on the street. It bred widespread xenophobia, which was most marked amongst workers since it was their lives which were most closely affected by foreigners and, in addition, they saw them as competitors in the labour market. Politicians were worried, but they had no clear policy on foreigners, and, apart from halting the recruitment of foreign workers, had no solutions to offer. The attempt to integrate foreigners into German society met with rejection from Germans, as well as from in particular the Turks. On legal and humanitarian grounds, sending foreigners back to their country of origin was not an option for the social-liberal government. This did nothing for the government's popularity.

The Social Democrats had taken up the subject of environmental protection earlier than other parties and movements. The SPD's call, in the 1960s, for "Blue skies over the Ruhr once more" was the cause of some amusement. But since the 1970s there had suddenly been a growing awareness of the importance of ecology for the quality of life, even the survival, of mankind. As in no other Western industrial society, it was linked in the Federal Republic to disquiet at an excessively organised state, and the development of a readiness to protest into a real political force. After decades of a stable three-party system, which at times seemed to be moving towards one made up of two parties, a fourth, ecologically oriented party, the Greens, came on the scene. They had soon won seats in local and state parliaments, and in March 1983 they entered the Bundestag.

The SPD was in something of a dilemma on the question of ecology. It was not only of a current, political nature, but was connected with its whole tradition. Social democracy had always been positive towards technology; Ludditism was foreign to the German labour movement. The SPD had long considered the peaceful use of atomic energy as a splendid opportunity for the development of affluence and greater opportunities for everyone. Were there sufficient irrefutable arguments for rejecting the construction of atomic power stations as citizens' initiatives, which Social Democrats were joining, were claiming? Even scientists were divided as to whether it was advisable or expedient to accelerate the development of atomic power. This made the decision particularly difficult for politicians. That the Social Democrats in government were hesitant and disunited in making it, seemed to many to be yielding to the Greens, or even showing sympathy for those "dropping out" of industrial society.[5] In reality there was an understandable and responsible reluctance to take a step in possibly the wrong direction, and one which could have unforeseen consequences for generations to come.

In the final years of the social-liberal coalition, however, none of the publicly criticised SPD shortcomings already mentioned weighed as heavily as the obvious inability of the government to actively master the severe economic difficulties. Almost without exception, all the industrial countries in the Western world – most of them under conservative governments – were suffering the same difficulties, but to a much greater degree than the Federal Republic. It was senseless, therefore, to make the SPD-led government responsible for these difficulties. Nevertheless, the question arises whether government policy could have combated the effects of economic recession more efficiently if the causes and extent of it had been diagnosed more accurately.[6] It was shortsighted of the SPD to trivialise the problem of financing pensions in the election campaign of 1976, and that of the national debt in the 1980 campaign: both problems would soon come home to roost. Immediately after the elections, the government had to own up and admit it had deceived the electorate.

For a long period under the social-liberal coalition, the Federal Republic had got to grips much better than most comparable states with its social and economic problems. This had probably led Helmut Schmidt to believe that things would remain so. It is surprising, therefore, that he above all – a man whose economic competence enjoyed international recognition – should not have seen earlier that the world was going through an extended period of structural economic crisis at the end of the 1970s, and that it was therefore impossible to offer voters the prospect of an improvement in their economic situation. By the 1980 election campaign at the latest, the population should have been informed that economy measures in various areas and cuts in welfare benefits would be unavoidable. Had the electorate been better prepared for this, the government would have found it easier to take the decisions it thought necessary. There would certainly have been disagreements over this between the coalition partners, but a less sharp reaction from the groups affected by the financial cuts would have left the SPD in a more favourable position.

Closer contact with the trade unions would have been important preparation for the coming hardships, and for settling the disagreements they caused. What was required, particularly at this time of increasing difficul-

---

5 See p. 248f. above.
6 See below, p. 274, the formulation in the SPD manifesto for 1983–1987.

ties, was close cooperation. The relationship between the SPD and the trade unions, however, was now much looser, and the unions themselves had been hit hard. They had been weakened by unemployment, and compromised by the *Neue Heimat* scandal. Publication of how the directors of this trade-union construction company had lined their pockets through shady deals, the publicising of the high additional income of leading trade unionists, and the admittedly legal, but for men in their positions, nonetheless unacceptable exploitation of ways of avoiding tax, along with reports of the unfair treatment of *Neue Heimat* tenants – all of this was greatly detrimental to the reputation of the unions, and also indirectly to that of the SPD.

The Social Democrats' room for manoeuvre had shrunk, partly due to factors which could have been corrected or avoided, but in much greater measure due to developments which they were hardly in a position to influence. On the world stage, the most threatening was the increased conflict between the USA and the Soviet Union, and the resulting intensification of the arms race between the two military blocs. Since the election of the Republican Ronald Reagan to the presidency in November 1980, there was deep mistrust of the American government in the Federal Republic, particularly in circles close to the SPD. The Reagan government put the increasing of American military potential at the heart of its policies, supported reactionary regimes in Central and South America and other parts of the world, slashed welfare benefits at home, allowed unemployment to grow, and pursued a high interest policy which had an unfavourable influence on economic development in Europe. Conservatives in the Federal Republic warmed to these policies, and accused critics of them of "anti-Americanism", an argument which worked against the SPD. During President Jimmy Carter's period in office, Helmut Schmidt had pushed for the NATO dual-track policy, because he wanted to help bring the USA and the Soviet Union together in order to negotiate on the new ballistic missiles in Europe, with a view to renouncing them. For the Soviet Union, this meant doing away with those which had been already installed. Negotiations in Geneva, however, left little hope that this goal would be achieved. In the SPD, opposition to the NATO dual-track policy was growing, but the party did not renege on the decision it had made at its 1979 party conference in Berlin, wishing to postpone until 1983 accepting the consequences of it. The SPD could not therefore be accused of disloyalty towards Chancellor Schmidt, even though they were increasingly critical of him and his policies, and sections of the party had renounced their allegiance to him.

This relationship, not only with Helmut Schmidt, but also with other Social Democrats in government office, highlighted a problem which had existed at least since the formation of the Grand Coalition in Bonn, and which had worsened over the years: the mistrust, by both SPD members and supporters, of "those at the top", the "Establishment". Willy Brandt, who was the very image of the thoughtful politician, was better at counteracting this mistrust than Helmut Schmidt, who made no attempt to hide his intellectual and political superiority. Everything which both Schmidt and Brandt did was ethically motivated. But Schmidt was less able than his predecessor in office to convey to people in and outside the party the motivation, considerations, and goals which guided his policies. The long-standing image of him in the media as "Schmidt the Doer" was a hindrance to this. For many it gave a distorted view of his true personality: that of a reflective, cultured, and – in the real sense of the word – conscientious man.

*

One can say without reservation that *Ostpolitik* and *détente* were the Social Democrats' great historical achievements in government. Singlemindedly pursued by Foreign Minister Brandt and effectively supported by Egon Bahr, they reached their decisive phase with the Moscow and Warsaw Treaties (1970), the Four Power Agreement on Berlin (1971), and the Basic Treaty with the GDR (1972), and were an integral component of social-liberal coalition policy under Chancellor Schmidt. The position of the Federal Republic was strengthened by the normalisation of its relations with the Soviet Union and its allies, while at the same time it remained firmly anchored in the Western Alliance and totally committed to the European Union. Its international reputation as an important economic and political force grew enormously in the 1970s. Richard Löwenthal summed it up when he said: "The once so accurate description of West Germany as an economic giant, but a political dwarf, has disappeared from the international lexicon"[7]. With the conclusion of the Eastern Treaties, all the world could see that the Federal Republic had accepted the consequences of a Second World War unleashed at German instigation, and had thereby enhanced its ability to play an international role. Its tireless efforts to ease tensions between East and West were a significant contribution to the preservation of peace and equilibrium between nations and states. With the heightening of these tensions at the end of 1979 when the Soviets invaded Afghanistan, Helmut Schmidt ensured

---

7 Richard Löwenthal, 'Bilanz der deutschen Ostpolitik', Das Parlament, no. 49, 11.12.1982, p. 12.

that the Federal Republic showed solidarity with America – by boycotting the Olympic Games in Moscow, for instance – without damaging relations with the Eastern bloc countries. Schmidt sought to do everything in his power to avoid a return to the Cold War, and he used the great international esteem he enjoyed to bring the two great powers back to the negotiating table.

The Federal Republic succeeded in maintaining the progress it had achieved with its *Ostpolitik*. The treaties and subsequent agreements with the GDR made the Wall and barbed wire a little less impenetrable, and facilitated a lively exchange of visitors between the two German states, even though the severe restrictions imposed by the SED regime made travelling from West to East, albeit with conditions, much easier than visiting the Federal Republic from the GDR. The human contacts which had been severed by sealing off the GDR were now extended and made easier. Alongside contacts at the political and economic level, cultural, academic, and personal connections were also important for the relationship with the Soviet Union and the states within its sphere of influence. Although *Ostpolitik* was very controversial in its initial phase, and individual details of the treaties were subject to harsh criticism, most people in the Federal Republic came to recognise the results they had brought, and many made use of them.

The principle of the social welfare state is enshrined in the constitution of the Federal Republic. From the outset, and with the cooperation of various forces in society, laws have been created and measures taken, often jointly by the Union parties and the SPD, in order to fulfil this commitment. But it was only when the Social Democrats came to power in Bonn that the provisions of the welfare safety net reached a level which few other countries could equal. Whether every individual measure was the right one, and whether the great centralised public institutions with their sprawling bureaucracy – to which the SPD had contributed – had proved their worth, or whether a different line of social policy might have been followed, has been the subject of much controversy, even amongst Social Democrats themselves. Their discussions stressed on the one hand the importance of getting rid of cronyism and malpractice, and on the other putting more emphasis on the idea of self-help. The principle of a legal right to state welfare, which was the product of, and designed to benefit, a caring society, as well as the view that these benefits were also designed to cancel out as far as possible the injustices of an unequal distribution of material goods and opportunities in life, were not at issue. Even under changed economic conditions, the SPD held fast to the principles which determined Social Democrat social policy, and the standards which this set. It attempted to defend it from cuts which had already been made, and which could be expected to be made, and to preserve the basic principle of a caring social policy.

The formation of the social-liberal government was preceded in the Federal Republic, as it was in other Western countries, by a movement comprising many different groups which was pressing for the breaking down of ossified structures, the abandoning of traditional conventions, and for more humane ways for people to live together. At the universities, students were up in arms against the old hierarchical order, women were banding together and developing a new self-confidence, in kindergartens, schools, and families anti-authoritarian education was being experimented with. This wave – characterised by a striving for more freedom, emancipation, and participation in the shaping of society – swept the SPD along at elections and was a boost to its policies of reform.

Willy Brandt's call "to venture more democracy" had particular appeal to those new to supporting and voting for the party. There was an interaction between the widely predominant mood of the time and the intention of the SPD to push ahead with the democratisation of public life, the workplace, of relations between men and women and the generations, and of the cultural and educational establishments. Without the political climate produced by this mood, the SPD would probably not have reached the pinnacles of power, and without the SPD in government, the positive impulses in the 1968 movement would probably have withered away. The policies of reform were welcomed by large sections of this insurgent movement, which meant that some of them could be integrated into the SPD.

The reformist zeal of the first years of social-liberal government did not last. It was stifled by increasingly depleted finances, judgements by the Federal Constitutional Court, the recalcitrance of the CDU/CSU-dominated Bundesrat (upper house), resistance from the FDP, global economic problems, and a change in the climate of opinion. Under Chancellor Schmidt the euphoria of reform was replaced by sober realism, resolute crisis management, and damage limitation. What was important to Schmidt, and in which he was supported first and foremost by Hans-Jochen Vogel, the Minister of Justice, and the FDP Ministers of the Interior, Werner Maihofer and Gerhart Baum, was to emphasise the liberality of the state in legislation and the implementation of the law. Doubts about whether this liberality existed had been raised under Willy Brandt's Chancellorship when the *Radikalenerlass* was deployed so comprehensively as to provoke sharp criticism, both in the Federal Republic and abroad. This was one of the examples, during the Social Democrats' period in office, where the results of a political measure were in conflict with the purposes for which it had originally been devised.

The liberality of the Federal Republic was put to its severest test in the mid-1970s by terrorist acts of violence: hostage taking, kidnappings, murders, arson. Legislation was tightened up, leading to misgivings not only in left-wing circles. The fact that security measures such as barbed wire, tanks, heavily armed police, became a permanent feature of the government district in Bonn, was a source of further disquiet. Many people reacted with alarm when it became known that the authorities had secretly installed bugs in the flat of the atomic scientist Klaus Traube, who had been wrongly suspected of having contacts with terrorists. The concern that this bugging operation aroused – Maihofer, the Minister of the Interior, was forced to resign – was a sign of how sensitive the public had become in the Federal Republic to intervention by the authorities. This too was ultimately a product of social-liberal policy, since they had contributed to this sensitivisation. Chancellor Schmidt reacted firmly, and without panicking, to the actions of the terrorists. No state of emergency was called, life went on as usual in the Federal Republic just at the time when the terrorists were seeking to bring about the very opposite. Civil rights were preserved, and it transpired that this was entirely reconcilable with the obligation to protect the population against terrorists.

Sixteen years of Social Democratic government in Bonn gave the lie to Adenauer's remark in the 1950s that a victory for the SPD would mean the end of Germany. With Willy Brandt and Helmut Schmidt, there were SPD Chancellors from 1969 until 1982. Compared to the task Brandt and the Social Democrats set themselves, a lot remained undone. But the record of the social-liberal coalition was a respectable one. They set in train urgent domestic reforms, and, in the shadow of worldwide recession, the Social Democrats ensured that cuts did not one-sidedly affect those less well off. With its *Ostpolitik* and furthering of *détente*, the social-liberal government freed itself from the burden of the Cold War and created the basis on which the Federal Republic could become a much more significant player on the international political stage. The stature of the two Social Democrat Chancellors contributed to this in no small measure. During the SPD's period in government, and encouraged by it, society developed a greater openness and tolerance, as well as the desire for more democratic self-determination and participation. *Ostpolitik* and *détente*, the extension of the welfare safety net, and a greater degree of social liberality were the fruits of Social Democratic government during this period which served as a pointer to the future and increased the respect in which the Federal Republic was held, both in Europe and throughout the world.

Part Three

Heinrich Potthoff:

A Party in Transition
Stagnation – Search for Direction –
The Responsibility of Government

I. The Predicament in Opposition

After the Social Democrats had lost power, perspicacious observers and politicians realised that the party would have to settle for a lengthy and difficult period in opposition. A figure subsequently bandied about by journalists and commentators was the fifteen years prophesied by Herbert Wehner.[1] It would, in fact, be sixteen years. Initially something of a figure of fun, and underestimated, Helmut Kohl put every effort during this period into consolidating his power base. The new Chancellor, who had already been CDU chairman for nine years, had a keen nose for power, and the means of retaining it. His for the most part infallible instincts, and a network of loyal followers and individuals personally indebted to him, helped him maintain a firm grip on his party. One by one he got rid of unwelcome rivals, and he made his seat in office so secure that he even surpassed Adenauer's record term as Chancellor.[2] The Kohl system, the darker side of which had already been glimpsed during his Chancellorship, but only really became public after he had been voted out of office, left a permanent imprint on the German political and social landscape. The network of power under his regime left lasting traces, and the damage he inflicted on democratic culture still lingers on. Even though the long years of conservative-liberal dominance under the Kohl system were certainly not the product of some law of nature, and Kohl, after 1989/90, clearly profited from the myth of being the "unification Chancellor", the Social Democrats in 1982 nevertheless had grounds for concern.

But in fact, the overwhelming response of many in the party was to give a collective sigh of relief. As if the onerousness of government and the constraints of compromise had been a sacrifice of their identity, many Social Democrats regarded the replacement of their Chancellor Helmut Schmidt almost as a liberation. In the pointed judgment of the political analysts Peter Lösche and Franz Walter, by the last years of his Chancellorship, "the bulk of Social Democratic activists supported the Chancellor and ministers of their own party at best out of a sense of duty and discipline, often with a feeling of distaste, but hardly ever with a feeling of

---

[1] In an interview on Saarland radio on 18.9.1982: "...it can take fifteen years."
[2] Konrad Adenauer was Chancellor for fourteen years, from 1949 to 1963.

sympathy and enthusiasm"[3]. In the wake of the arms-race debate and the peace and ecology movement, the gulf widened between large sections of the party and its own Chancellor and SPD ministers. When, in October 1981, the party chairman Willy Brandt defended his policy of integrating those disposed towards the Greens and the peace movement, and turned emphatically against those more inclined towards the SPD "core vote", open conflict broke out.[4] The opposite position formulated by his old comrade Richard Löwenthal got short shrift, and the party executive lined up almost to a man behind their revered and much-loved Willy Brandt. Based on personalities, it came down to an argument between Willy Brandt, who was pressing for a move in the direction of the ecology movement and those of alternative disposition, and Helmut Schmidt, who was seeking to secure the support of the trade unions and the political centre, and to reject the "drop-outs" and supporters of the peace movement. As every opinion poll confirmed, Helmut Schmidt was by far the most popular politician in Bonn. But nonetheless, the SPD party lost voters not only to the Greens, but even more – twice as many in fact – to the CDU. Their popularity was at an all-time low.[5] If something of an overstatement, the often quoted dictum: Helmut Schmidt is a very good Chancellor, it's just that he is in the wrong party, was indicative of an increasingly apparent dilemma. The party could not identify with the Chancellor. But it also demonstrated that the Chancellor, for his part, was insufficiently in touch with the feelings of his party.[6]

1. Adjusting to Opposition

After the social-liberal coalition had finally collapsed, but before Helmut Kohl had been appointed as the new Chancellor on 1 October 1982, Willy Brandt, in the party council, called for continuity of Social Democrat policy: "Our party cannot rediscover the world while in opposition. It has to build on what was achieved while in government."[7] Helmut Schmidt reiterated this statement[8], but he also recognised, and expressed it openly

---

[3] Peter Lösche/Franz Walter, Die SPD: Klassenpartei – Volkspartei – Quotenpartei. Zur Entwicklung der Sozialdemokratie von Weimar bis zur deutschen Wiedervereinigung (Darmstadt 1992), p. 120.
[4] See pp. 249 above.
[5] See Wolfgang Jäger and Werner Link, Republik im Wandel 1974–1982. Die Ära Schmidt (Stuttgart and Mannheim 1987), p. 216.
[6] See Lösche and Walter, Die SPD, p. 120.
[7] Unpublished minutes of the meeting of the party council in Bonn on 19.9.1982, p. 2.
[8] At the party council on 19.9.1982, SPD-Service 416/82, p. 5.

to the parliamentary party on 26 October, that the party was moving away from issues of central importance – and for which he stood – such as security policy and atomic energy.[9] It was therefore not only health and personal reasons which deterred Helmut Schmidt, despite the urgings of his political friends, from putting himself forward once more as Chancellor candidate. Just a few months after his fall, the SPD seemed almost to have forgotten that they had spent many years in power, and that their man had been Chancellor. Hans-Jochen Vogel was worried that, after having lost power, the SPD was now also "under threat of losing – and for a long time – the ability to function as an opposition"[10].

The voting out of the respected Chancellor Helmut Schmidt by the switch of allegiance of an FDP plagued by fears of survival aroused the ire not only of the SPD, but also of large sections of the electorate. For the FDP to have pocketed votes intended to bolster Schmidt seemed now, two years later, to have made a travesty of the 1980 elections. Before being voted out, Helmut Schmidt had favoured fresh elections as the basis for a democratically legitimate change of Chancellor and government. Following the FDP U-turn which had enabled Helmut Kohl to become Chancellor, he now needed a mandate from the electors in order to legitimise the change of government in the eyes of the public. For transparently tactical reasons, Kohl and Genscher decided to postpone fresh elections – which the new Chancellor announced in his government declaration on 13 October 1982 – until March 1983. The way was smoothed for this by the engineering (which aroused serious constitutional reservations) of a vote of confidence with a deliberately negative outcome. Even the CDU Federal President Karl Carstens expressed serious misgivings.[11] Fresh elections were fixed for the 6 March 1983.

Helmut Schmidt was no longer a candidate for the Chancellorship, and this already lessened the SPD's electoral chances. Johannes Rau, the popular Minister President of North Rhine-Westphalia, was also not available. The SPD selected Hans-Jochen Vogel as its Chancellor candidate: he in no way felt himself to be a "stopgap or even one of the party infantry", but was certain he was fit enough for the "office of Chancellor". This was undoubtedly true, but even he had no illusions about the "chances of success".[12] Hans-Jochen Vogel, born in 1926 and a brilliant lawyer, had

---

9   Archiv der Gegenwart, 52, 1982, p. 26161.
10 Hans-Jochen Vogel, Nachsichten. Meine Bonner und Berliner Jahre (Munich and Zurich 1996), p. 165.
11 A complaint by four Bundestag deputies was rejected by the Federal Constitutional Court on 16.12.1983. Its verdict, however, was the subject of much controversy.
12 Vogel, Nachsichten, p. 170f.

*Chancellor candidate Hans-Jochen Vogel at the
SPD electoral party congress on 21 January 1983 in Dortmund*

made a considerable name for himself as Mayor of Munich from 1967–1972. The move to the left of the SPD in Munich blighted his work in Bavaria. Minister of Housing and Construction under Brandt, he became Minister of Justice under Helmut Schmidt in 1974. He gained particular respect in the SPD when he gave up his ministerial post in Bonn to help the party in Berlin, who were in severe crisis. In January 1981, he became Governing Mayor of Berlin. Following the elections to the House of Deputies in June, he lost this post to Richard von Weizsäcker (CDU). Vogel remained chairman of the parliamentary party in Berlin and, as a member of the SPD presidium, a leading figure in the party. For the first time in his career he got to know at first hand the rigours and frustrations of being in opposition. His experiences in Berlin – turmoil, squatting, the alternative scene, and an SPD riven by dissent and politically at rock bottom – had a lasting effect on Vogel. He was transformed into a politician who pursued an integrational course in the SPD.

"The SPD manifesto for 1983–1987", agreed at the party election conference on 21 January 1983 in Dortmund, was largely Vogel's conception.[13]

---

13 Published 1983 by the SPD in Bonn. The basic elements of this can already be found in Vogel's speech to the SPD party conference in November 1982. Full text, Politik. Aktuelle Informationen der Sozialdemokratischen Partei Deutschlands, no. 8, December 1982, pp. 18–26.

It contained a commitment to the "continuation of 16 years of Social Democrat work in government", as well as an admission of mistakes and failings. Its ambivalence and critical reflectiveness, however, made it hard to get across. The SPD manifesto and the election campaign covered a wide spectrum of issues: economic and social policy, the future shape of society, the law, ecology ("seeking peace with nature and saving the environment"), peacekeeping. The party was unable to offer a plausible, attractive concept for restoring economic prosperity and combating unemployment. The majority of voters, including former SPD supporters, believed that the Union parties were in a better position to stimulate investment, boost the economy, and overcome the financial problems.[14] In the run-up to the elections, there was a brief swing to the SPD, but its campaign, with its employment programme and environmental plans, opposition to the arms race and the stationing of ballistic missiles, was able to make little headway with the voters.

The SPD found itself falling between two stools. It was easy for the Union parties with their electoral message about the "inherited financial burden", unemployment, and "spiritual and moral change", all of which evoked the glory days of the economic miracle and full state coffers when they had been in power in Bonn. They attributed the blame for the miserable situation and the collapse of middle-class culture to the SPD. They also held the better cards in foreign affairs. They knew that with their commitment to NATO, being firmly anchored in the Western Alliance, and favouring the installation of ballistic missiles, they not only had Reagan and the USA behind them in the election, but François Mitterrand as well. The socialist French President openly and unambiguously supported the policy of counter-arming, and with it, Helmut Kohl. What Hans-Jochen Vogel described as an affront to the SPD[15], was in fact of their own making. By turning away from Schmidt and his security policy, the party was virtually sidelined in the West on matters of foreign policy, and throughout the entire history of the Federal Republic this had always had a knock-on effect domestically. Using the old trick of denigrating the Social Democrats as being patriotically unsound and "socialistically" dangerous, the Union once again operated, and not without success, with insinuations that the SPD was in Moscow's pocket. On the other hand, however, the SPD was unable to win over young voters who belonged to the peace and ecology movements. For them, the Greens were a more

---

14 See Ursula Feist, Hubert Krieger, Pavel Uttitz, 'Das Wahlverhalten der Arbeiter bei der Bundestagswahl 1983', Gewerkschaftliche Monatshefte, 7 (1983), pp. 414–427.
15 Vogel, Nachsichten, p. 174.

attractive alternative, and they duly entered the Bundestag for the first time with 5.6 per cent of the vote.

The SPD suffered a severe defeat in the fresh elections on 6 March 1983. They won just 38.2 per cent of the vote, while the CDU and the new Chancellor Helmut Kohl went up from 44.5 to 48.8 per cent. The FDP had paid the price for their earlier stunt, when, at the Landtag elections in Hesse (26 September) and Hamburg (19 December), they gained a mere 3.1 and 2.6 per cent respectively and were thrown out of office. They also lost 3.6 points at the federal elections, winning a mere 7 per cent overall. On the whole, however, the voters gave their seal of approval to the *Wende* of autumn 1983, thus legitimising the conservative-liberal coalition in government. Kohl was now firmly in the saddle, supported by an FDP obsessed with remaining in power and their permanent fixture as Foreign Minister, Hans-Dietrich Genscher. Kohl could now set about bringing on board and taming his awkward party rival Franz Josef Strauß. With the thousands of millions of credit for the GDR, which the conspiratorial Strauß negotiated with the East German hard-currency trader Alexander Schalck-Golodkowski, and the visit which the Bavarian paid to the SED party boss Erich Honecker in July 1983, Kohl succeeded in neutralising his adversary.

With Helmut Schmidt, the Social Democrat with the highest popularity rating amongst the voters, having departed the political scene, it was now the turn of Herbert Wehner, that dyed-in-the-wool politician, to retire. He had toiled away at maintaining party discipline during the social-liberal era, but became less effective as illness began to take its toll. Hans-Jochen Vogel became his successor as chairman of the parliamentary party on 8 March 1983. He had been the SPD's Chancellor candidate in the federal elections. This had been a thankless task, but his new post was no picnic either, far from it. The parliamentary party was left weakened by the bitter electoral defeat, many experienced parliamentarians were no longer in office, and being in opposition was an unaccustomed role. That voters had not turned their backs on the FDP for switching loyalties, and that the Liberals were once again in government, this time at Kohl's cabinet table, was a deep disappointment. But first and foremost the SPD had to swallow the fact that with the Greens, there was now another, young opposition party who, with their unconventional and unusual ways, brought new life to the Bundestag. They made for a strange presence amidst the long-established parliamentary routines, but with their irreverent approach and "events" were popular with the media, and stole the SPD's thunder.

"As chairman of the parliamentary party", said Hans-Jochen Vogel looking back, "my primary objective, particularly at that time, was to hold the parliamentary party together, and, after the loss of power, to make it the focus for uniting and renewing the party as a whole, and once more a political force to be reckoned with".[16] This began with a process of organisational and structural reform. The plethora of committees and working groups, deputy chairmen, and business managers, with their overlapping confusion of responsibilities and tasks, was – to some murmurings of discontent – given a radical overhaul. The functions of the chairmen of the work groups were fused with those of the deputy chairmen of the parliamentary party. To a certain degree, this helped to see the wood for the trees, but at the cost of eight deputy chairmen, new frictions, and "bureaucratisation".[17]

The parliamentary party "rapidly became a viable parliamentary team"[18] and set about the task in hand. Hans Apel, the former Defence Minister and close ally of Helmut Schmidt, who was somewhat reserved with Vogel, nevertheless acknowledged the commitment he had shown in "bringing the wretched parliamentary party and the 'Barracks' (SPD headquarters in Bonn) up to scratch".[19] But his leadership style and his plastic folders with their resubmitted motions, which earned him the nickname "the schoolmaster", also aroused antipathy in some quarters. It was not only Hans Apel and Horst Ehmke who found him authoritarian and bureaucratic, and lacking in political message. The SPD parliamentary party drew up a five-point programme: on peace and security, tackling unemployment, the environment, social justice, and a more liberal approach domestically. As was only to be expected with Hans-Jochen Vogel, the parliamentary party was very diligent, and, in the first two years of the legislative period alone (up to summer 1985), submitted almost two hundred parliamentary motions. But industriousness and quantity were no guarantee of political effectiveness. In the 1960s, when the SPD was girding its loins for government, it had consciously abandoned the endless production of parliamentary motions as a largely futile activity.

With a stream of published surveys on the government's so-called negative record, the SPD sought to demonstrate to the public at large that, under Kohl, unemployment and the tax burden had risen, and that poverty and the number of those on welfare benefits were on the increase, while at the same time income from property and business was growing. While the rate of growth for net income from these sources in the years 1983

---

16 Ibid., p. 182.
17 See Horst Ehmke, Mittendrin. Von der Großen Koalition zur Deutschen Einheit (Berlin 1994), pp. 323–325.
18 Vogel, Nachsichten, p. 180f.
19 Hans Apel, Der Abstieg. Politisches Tagebuch 1979–1988 (Stuttgart 1990), p. 233.

and 1984 was 17.7 and 11.4 per cent respectively, wages and salaries had grown by barely 2.0 and 1.7 per cent.[20] With its programme "Work and the Environment" of April 1984, the SPD was presenting a forward-looking project which attempted to reconcile environmental protection with the creation of new jobs by means of an increase in the price of energy. As was to be expected, the SPD, with its call for a speed limit of 100 km an hour on the motorways, did itself no favours with the car-loving West Germans who were attracted much more by the slogan "A free run for free people". Resistance to changes to paragraph 116 of the Employment Promotion Act[21], with which the government coalition sought to weaken the ability to strike, earned the plaudits of the trade unions, but virtually no bonus points from the population as a whole. The scandal-ridden crisis and collapse of *Neue Heimat* not only permanently discredited the idea of joint ownership, but also did severe damage to the already not particularly favourable reputation of the trade unions. For some time, one only needed to mention the words *Neue Heimat* to stop the trade unions, as well as the Social Democrats, in their tracks. Playing up this affair was for the Union and the FDP a way of distracting attention from the scandal over political donations, which had hit them the hardest.

2. Stirring Topics of the Day

On 13 May 1983, the Bundestag investigative committee began its work on the "Flick affair". Work for a political party costs money, and parties need public funding for their activities. In addition to direct contributions, they also profited from tax relief on membership subscriptions and smaller donations. With large donations the state even offered further incentives by making them tax-deductible up to 60,000 and 100,000 Deutschmarks respectively. The contribution of the state towards financing the parties continued to rise, to the point finally where it amounted to half of party revenue.[22] The time was over when the SPD depended almost exclusively on the "worker's penny", and its members bore the main burden of campaigning by sticking up posters and knocking on doors. But compared with other parties, and depending on the strength of the membership and progressive subscriptions, the SPD was still very much reliant on its

---

20 See table 12 in the appendix.
21 The revision of paragraph 116 made the payment by the Federal Employment Office of benefits to employees outside the contested wage agreement more difficult.
22 This from von Arnim, the main critic of the system in his many publications. See, inter alia, Hans Herbert von Arnim, Die Parteien, der Abgeordnete und das Geld (Mainz 1991).

members' contributions. Between 1984 and 1987 this made up some 42 per cent of its income[23], and as much as 58.2 per cent in 1988, which amounted to some 114 million Deutschmarks.

Much of what had formerly been done by SPD members was now carried out by professional organisations, who were paid accordingly. The sums of money which had to be found grew with the increasing obsession with image and the media. Election campaigns were becoming ever more costly, and the expenditure of the parties was constantly rising. This affected first and foremost the party central offices who were responsible for managing the main election campaigns. They were always chronically short of cash, and often had to take out loans. But it had also long been an open secret in Bonn that the parties did not always stick to the financial letter of the law, and sought extra funding by various roundabout routes. The famous/infamous "civic associations", which channelled money into mainly Union coffers, played an important role here. But also in disrepute, particularly as regards political education, were the foundations with party affiliations: the Konrad-Adenauer linked with the CDU, the Friedrich-Ebert with the SPD, the Friedrich-Naumann with the FDP, and the Hanns-Seidel-Foundation with the CSU.

Investigations by the public prosecutors had already brought something of the Flick affair out into the open in 1981. A series of meticulously researched exposés, mainly by the *Spiegel* – although other organs of the press and media, the public prosecutor's office, tax officials, court proceedings, and a Bundestag investigative committee also played their part – revealed the practices whereby a large business concern might exert influence on politics. The money from Flick came mostly from a slush fund laundered through the Steyl missionary society in St. Augustin, which was then handed over to the recipient in cash in sealed envelopes. All of the parties in the Bundestag profited from this "landscape conservation", as it was called, but especially the Union. Between 1969 and 1980 the CDU and CSU alone received 15 Million Deutschmarks from Flick, the small FDP party 6.5, and the SPD some 4.5 million. "The venal Republic" was the appropriate sub-title of a well-regarded book of the time.[24] There was a widespread impression in Bonn that political decisions were up for sale. In 1985/86 the Federal Chancellor, Helmut Kohl, found himself for the first time in difficulties over donation practices. At the end of the 1970s, the Flick concern had furthered his political career with a cash payment totalling 55,000 Deutschmarks in all. This, however, now seemed to have

---

23 See, inter alia, Karl-Heinz Nassmacher, 'Parteifinanzierung im Wandel', in Die Parteien in der Bundesrepublik (Stuttgart, Berlin, Cologne 1990), p. 146.
24 Hans Werner Kilz and Joachim Preuss, Flick. Die gekaufte Republik (Reinbek 1983).

slipped his mind completely. To get him off a possible charge of lying under oath, the wily General Secretary of the CDU, Heiner Geißler, maintained that he must have been suffering from a blackout. Kohl was saved on that occasion by his closest financial henchmen Walther Leisler Kiep, Horst Weyrauch, and Uwe Lütje, who gave false testimony to get him off the hook and ensure that he remained Chancellor.[25]

The impetus for the investigation by the public prosecutor came from the Bundestag deputy Otto Schily of the Greens. This was typical of the climate in Bonn during the party donations affair. Newly arrived on the scene, the Greens were the only party whose credibility was left unscathed by the scandal. The SPD were unable to benefit from the misdemeanours of the Union and the FDP in the Flick affair because they themselves were involved in this system of illicit financial payments, even though they did not profit from "landscape conservation" to the same extent as the two other parties. When, in December 1983, the Bundestag decided on new regulations for party financing, the SPD concurred. As a consequence of the scandals, the rules on illegal donations were tightened up, and accepting gifts from foundations and charitable organisations prohibited. But the new regulations also increased to 100,000 Deutschmarks the upper limit at which large donations were tax-deductible, gave those parties who were less well-disposed towards "capital" a fairer chance by granting them state subsidies, and raised the overall level of election expenses. Only the Greens voted against, and in 1984 they even lodged a complaint with the Federal Constitutional Court. In its judgement of 1986 it reduced the level at which party donations were tax-deductible. In the new regulations, this necessitated the Bundestag in 1988 increasing the amount which could be reimbursed for election expenses, and, once again, the Greens voted against.

On this issue of central importance for the public reputation and credibility of the political parties, only the Greens had pinned their colours to the mast, while the SPD, by and large, had been lumped together with the other parties and politicians, all of whom were suspected indiscriminately of having their snouts in the trough. The popular view was that the financial greed of the established political parties was insatiable. With expenditure rocketing, even the greatly increased revenue could not keep pace. It was once again the Greens, with their fresh complaint of 23 May 1989 in Karlsruhe (the seat of the Constitutional Court), who took a stand against the system of party financing. It was not until after German re-

---

25 See Winkler, Weg nach Westen, vol. 2, p. 411, as well as p. 704, note 16 which gives details of additional material on the subject.

unification that, with its verdict of 9 April 1992, the Constitutional Court declared that the rules calculating the *Sockelbetrag* (basic payment) were faulty, as was the handling of the *Chancenausgleich* (equalisation of opportunities). Furthermore, however, while declaring a whole series of other regulations to be unconstitutional, it held that state funding of the parties which went beyond the reimbursement of election expenses was in accordance with the constitution.[26] With the change to the Party Law and other legal regulations, the Bundestag finally approved in January 1994 a system of party funding which conformed to the Karlsruhe guidelines.

Helmut Kohl and his Union parties learned nothing whatsoever from all the scandals over party donations and their own misdemeanours. After what came to light at the end of the Kohl era about the complicated network of illegal accounts, envelopes stuffed with cash, and contributions from big business, we know that he and other of his Union cronies persistently broke the law and the rules of common decency. When power was at stake, this selfsame Chancellor of "intellectual and moral change" abandoned every shred of political morality, and placed himself above both justice and the law. The devastating impression that politics was up for sale left a permanent stain and completely undermined its credibility with the public. In the sixteen years of the Kohl system, however, the Social Democrats never managed to derive any party advantage from the morass into which he and his Union had sunk over political donations. The skill and unscrupulousness with which everything had been covered up, as well as the fact that the SPD itself was tied into the system of party funding, prevented them from mounting a full-frontal assault. For as long as they were not yet firmly established, the Greens, in alliance with the media and the constitutional lawyer Hans Herbert von Arnim, a very effective public operator, took on this role. It seemed as if the young and still highly principled party was the real opposition here.

The Greens, for whom feminism also played an important role, had first come to prominence as an ecological and pacifist peace movement.[27] The imminent stationing of Pershing II rockets and Cruise missiles following the NATO dual-track decision made for a turbulent autumn in 1983. This was the subject that most concerned public opinion at the time. The peace movement in the Federal Republic was at its height. Many Social Democrats took part in the huge rallies, and most regional party conferences expressed their opposition by voting overwhelmingly no. In Bonn

---

26 Peter Ebbighausen and others, Die Kosten der Parteienfinanzierung. Studien und Materialien zu einer Bilanz staatlicher Parteienfinanzierung (Opladen 1996), pp. 141 ff.
27 See, particularly, Joachim Raschke, Die Grünen. Wie sie wurden, was sie sind (Cologne 1993).

on 22 October 1983, the SPD party chairman Willy Brandt addressed a mass rally of 300,000 people. At the extraordinary SPD party conference on 18/19 November 1983 in Cologne, Willy Brandt and the new chairman of the parliamentary group Hans-Jochen Vogel gave their joint reasons for the SPD rejecting the stationing of missiles, and the delegates voted by an overwhelming majority for the party executive committee to table a motion to this effect. Only fourteen delegates voted against. It was a bitter moment for Helmut Schmidt, and not an honourable chapter in the history of the German Social Democrats. In truth, all the arguments that not every avenue of negotiation had been fully explored, and that this was the only way of combating the arms race, could not disguise the fact that the Social Democrats were pursuing a policy which would alienate them from the Western mainstream, and even from their great European sister parties. In the vote in the Bundestag on 22 November on the stationing of missiles, the SPD deputies who were present, along with the Greens, voted against. The stationing began at the beginning of January 1984, accompanied by sit-down protests. In the eyes of the West, Helmut Kohl was able to present himself as the reliable Alliance partner, while the SPD were viewed with political suspicion.

This was a reality which for many years made the American administration, as well as West European governments, no longer regard them as a really reliable partner, even though the SPD as a whole never questioned Germany's membership of the Atlantic Alliance. But by turning their backs on the course adopted by Helmut Schmidt, they were rejecting the concrete requirements of political alliances. It was not just Oskar Lafontaine's book of 1983, *Angst vor den Freunden* (Fear of one's Friends),[28] which seemed to suggest that non-alignment was the logical consequence of being a democratic socialist, but also other criticisms aimed at the USA and its attitude to the East, which raised eyebrows in friendly Western countries, and also amongst dissidents in Eastern Europe. Following the change in government to Helmut Kohl, the SPD in opposition set about cranking up its own "parallel foreign policy". It was directed mainly towards the GDR and the Soviet Union, and, concretely, that meant cooperation with the ruling parties there. Some saw this "second phase of *détente*" in a positive light[29], while others among the SPD's political opponents attacked it vigorously.

28 Oskar Lafontaine, Angst vor den Freunden. Die Atomwaffen-Strategie der Supermächte zerstört die Bündnisse (Reinbek bei Hamburg 1983).
29 The account by Klaus Moseleit, Die "Zweite" Phase der Entspannungspolitik der SPD 1983–1989. Eine Analyse ihrer Entstehungsgeschichte, Entwicklung und der konzeptionellen Ansätze (Frankfurt/Main 1991), was prompted by Egon Bahr.

Ost- and *Deutschlandpolitik*, which became the trademark of the Social Democrats in the Brandt era, was implemented under the regimes of Chancellors Willy Brandt and Helmut Schmidt at government level. Below this, there were individual contacts such as Wehner's visit to Honecker in 1973 and Egon Bahr's talks in East Berlin in September 1981. They supplemented the system of political dialogue between the two states, but were not entirely uncontroversial. Now that they were no longer in power in Bonn, the SPD were faced with the basic decision of how, in opposition, they might continue to influence policy towards Europe and the USA, as well as *Ost-* and *Deutschlandpolitik*. Their many rhetorical, distancing statements aside, the new Kohl government's foreign policy was a continuation of that pursued by Helmut Schmidt. By renewing the ex-Chancellor's invitation to Honecker to visit the Federal Republic, telephoning the SED party chief, and granting two credits in the order of a billion (1983 and 1984), Chancellor Kohl put his energies into continued dialogue and a "coalition of reason".[30] This was something to which the SPD could hardly raise any fundamental objections.

The real bone of contention was over security policy. In the wake of the arms debate and the peace movement, the SPD had moved away from the line adopted by Schmidt. Step by step, the concept that security was only possible on a joint basis began to clearly establish itself. Egon Bahr had been the first to formulate this in 1981.[31] The concept of "common security" dominated the (Olof) Palme Commission's report of May 1982[32] in which, with Egon Bahr playing a leading role, politicians from East and West worked on disarmament proposals, as well as the attempts by Social Democrat defence experts to reach agreements with the Soviet Union and the SED on collective security measures. The focus on the "preservation of peace", "security in partnership", and a "community of responsibility" between the two German states "developed a momentum

---

30 On this, see Heinrich Potthoff, Die "Koalition der Vernunft". Deutschlandpolitik in den 80er Jahren (Munich 1995), pp. 21 ff., and the same in Im Schatten der Mauer (Berlin 1999), pp. 223 ff. Also Timothy Garton Ash, Im Namen Europas. Deutschland und der geteilte Kontinent (Munich/Vienna 1993), p. 231 f. and p. 248 f.; Karl-Rudolf Korte, Deutschlandpolitik in Helmut Kohls Kanzlerschaft. Regierungsstil und Entscheidungen 1982–1989 (Stuttgart 1998), p. 129 f., pp. 136–140, pp. 161–180, pp. 185–194.

31 See Egon Bahr, Zum europäischen Frieden. Eine Antwort auf Gorbatschow (Berlin 1988), p. 23; Andreas Vogtmeier, Egon Bahr und die deutsche Frage. Zur Entwicklung der Ost- und Deutschlandpolitik vom Kriegsende bis zur Vereinigung (Bonn 1996), pp. 243 ff.; Garton Ash, Im Namen Europas, p. 460 ff.

32 The Palme-Report, the Report of the Independent Commission on Disarmament and Security Issues, was published as Common Security: A Blueprint for Survival (New York 1982).

and laws of its own which brought a problematic 'anti-ideologisation' of East-West relations, tended to neglect questions of freedom and human rights, and gave highest priority to the maintenance of international peace".[33]

The talks and agreements on security were part of the formal contacts in which the SPD and SED had been engaging since 1983. In May 1983 the new chairman of the parliamentary party Hans-Jochen Vogel paid his first formal visit to Erich Honecker. It was the first of the meetings which then regularly took place in May.[34] Honestly and unambiguously, Vogel made it absolutely clear that the Social Democrats continued to be committed to NATO and the values of Western democracy. This was, and remained, the SPD's official party line. Nevertheless, there was no hiding the fact that amongst sections of the party there was a shift of emphasis. The postulate of German unification was no longer sacred, the party was visibly distancing itself from the USA, and an illusory over-estimation of what it might achieve was rampant. Doubts were being raised in the West as well as the East about whether the SPD was still the party of freedom. Critical observers had the impression that some Social Democrats had quietly pushed to one side the fundamental differences between a free democracy and a Communist dictatorship. The preoccupation with the ruling Communist power elites on the other side of the Wall and barbed wire had seriously discredited the Social Democrats in the eyes of the upsurgent opposition movements in Eastern Europe. This was particularly true of Solidarity in Poland, but also of dissidents in other countries. There were few – far too few – Social Democrats who maintained contact with them, and lent them their support. Driven by a kind of anti-anti-Communism, which was as widespread amongst the ranks of the West German left as were notions of a post-national identity, many of the '68 generation, who were increasingly setting the tone in the SPD, were insensitive to what the situation required.

3. *The Internal Development of the SPD*

For a *Volkspartei* seeking to secure as wide a social base as possible, and also to make itself attractive to the coming generation, the development which the SPD underwent while in opposition was problematical. It is true that its overall membership figures changed very little, and that after falling from 926,000 in 1982 to 910,063 at the end of 1987, they had risen

33 Potthoff, Im Schatten der Mauer, p. 230.
34 Vogel, Nachsichten, p. 192f.; Potthoff, Koalition der Vernunft, pp. 119–144.

to 921,430 by the end of 1989.[35] The change in the social make-up of the party membership resulting from the decision to aim at all sections of the population led to an increasing domination by the new middle classes and civil servants. As a proportion of those in employment, workers were under-represented in the SPD by comparison with white-collar workers and civil servants. This trend was even more marked amongst party officials and those elected to government. Academics played a dominant role in the crucial decision-making committees at the middle and top levels. It was shown that 61 per cent of the delegates to the 1986 party conference had an academic degree.[36] The '68 generation of students were now making careers for themselves. Those who followed them, and who were committed to peace and ecology issues, looked for and found their home with the Greens. Characteristic of the internal development of the SPD, and also a cause for alarm, was the increasing age of the membership. The proportion of *Jusos*, i.e. of those under thirty-five, which had been over thirty per cent in the 1970s (30.9 per cent in 1974), dropped below the twenty per cent mark, and was some 18.62 per cent in 1989.[37] While young people tended to give the SPD the cold shoulder, the proportion of women members continued to rise: after being 18.7 per cent in 1972, it went up to 27.1 per cent in the mid-1980s, and almost 37 per cent of new members in 1989 were women. More women were also being elected to parliament and becoming party officials. Whereas at the party conference in 1976 only 10 per cent of the delegates were women, ten years later the number had risen to almost 33 per cent. In 1986 women made up a quarter of the party executive committee, and although in 1987 only 16.1 per cent of the parliamentary party were women, 29 per cent of its executive committee were female.[38] The move towards a greater involvement of women was already well underway in the SPD when the Münster party conference of 1988 decided on fixed quotas.

In May 1984 the SPD held its first full party conference since the change of government. It was uneventful, the change in security policy having already been decided in 1983. The party also reversed its previous policy on nuclear energy. Its use was accepted merely for a transitional

35 Statistics of the SPD party executive provided by the political archive of the Willy-Brandt-Haus in Berlin. See too, Lösche and Walter, Die SPD, p. 162.
36 Hermann Schmittgen, Von den Siebzigern in die Achtziger Jahre: Die mittlere Parteielite der SPD im Wandel (Mannheim, no date), p. 6. (Quoted in Lösche and Walter, Die SPD, p. 166 and p. 407).
37 Lösche and Walter, Die SPD, p. 166f.; Schöllgen, Brandt, p. 258.
38 Lösche and Walter, Die SPD, p. 167; for the Bundestag see Peter Schindler, Datenhandbuch zur Geschichte des Deutschen Bundestages 1949 bis 1999 (Berlin 1999), vol. 1, p. 636.

period. Barely any of the delegates would have expected it to take until Gerhard Schröder's red-green coalition government in 2001, and the regulation of the decommissioning of nuclear power stations, for this to be implemented. A few days after this conference, on 23 May 1984, Richard von Weizsäcker (CDU) was elected as the new Federal President by the Federal Convention. The Greens had nominated their own candidate in Luise Rinser. The SPD supported Weizsäcker in his candidacy and in the election. President Richard von Weizsäcker was a great asset to the political culture of the Federal Republic. With his fine speech of 8 May 1985 on the anniversary of the unconditional surrender he achieved a breakthrough in the perception of the 8 May as a day of liberation from the Nazi dictatorship and the savage war it had unleashed.

While in part a gesture of respect towards Weizsäcker, the decision by the SPD not to put forward a candidate of their own was also symptomatic of their diminished political power. Their position had been weakened, not only in Bonn but also in the federal states, after losing control of Lower Saxony (1976) and Berlin (1981). The CDU/CSU were in power in most of the states, and in five of them – Baden-Württemberg, Bavaria, Lower Saxony, Rhineland-Palatinate, and Schleswig-Holstein – with an overall majority, and held 41 seats in the Bundesrat, as opposed to the 15 held by the SPD. Since 1982 Hesse had been governed by Holger Börner in a caretaker capacity, and since 1984 with a minority cabinet. The Greens, with whose votes he had been re-elected in June 1984, did not become part of his government until December 1985. This was the first red-green governing coalition, and the public had to get used to the spectacle of a minister in jeans and running shoes, Joschka Fischer, who had won his first political spurs in the alternative Sponti scene in Frankfurt. Only in the city states of Bremen and Hamburg, as well as in North Rhine-Westphalia, did the SPD have an overall majority. The result of the three Landtag elections in 1985 was important for the continuing development of the SPD. On 10 May 1985, the once proud Berlin party suffered a further setback with the loss of almost 6 percentage points of the vote. On the same day, however, the Mayor of Saarbrücken, Oskar Lafontaine, won a magnificent victory in the Saarland. He and his party gained 49.2 per cent of the vote, won an overall majority, and, in April, he was elected Minister President of the Saarland. Lafontaine, who was not one to fight shy of a measure of populism and anti-Americanism, became a symbolic figure for a brand of Social Democratic strategy which, with its determinedly ecological and peace-movement vocabulary, was able to win over younger voters who inclined towards the critical, alternative movement. He went down well in the transformed SPD, and became the favourite "grandson" of his idol in the party, Willy Brandt.

At the opposite pole was the North Rhine-Westphalian Minister President, Johannes Rau, who, with his warm, charismatic personality and his consensus politics, enjoyed widespread popular support. At the Landtag elections on 12 May 1985, the SPD increased its overall majority in North Rhine-Westphalia, winning 52.1 per cent of the vote. Sober assessment urged that the Minister President of the most populous federal state should be assigned a leading role in the SPD at national level. In fact, this made the already problematical leadership question in the party even more complicated. There were various, different centres of power: the diligent parliamentary group under the respectable, conscientious "leader of the opposition", Hans-Jochen Vogel; the party patriarch, Willy Brandt, who towered over everyday events and who roamed around the world in the role of elder statesman; then the party apparatus around the guiding intellectual presence of party business manager Peter Glotz; the ever busy, reddish-green "little Napoleon" from the Saarland, a master of self-orchestration; and the patriarchal Johannes Rau with his North Rhine-Westphalian SPD, who represented an SPD of the little people averse to all green experiments and was anchored firmly in traditional values. It was impossible to ignore the differences of style, personality, and politics. Whereas earlier the "troika", for all its peculiarities, had toed the same line, the image now was of a quadriga which was having problems with the fine tuning of its direction and steering. The party was split from top to bottom by unbridgeable rifts. There were irreconcilable differences which could only grow worse.

In September 1985, Hans-Jürgen Wischnewski, one of the faithful stalwarts of the Schmidt government, threw in the towel as SPD party treasurer, ostensibly because of suggested economy measures occasioned by mounting deficits arising from the ailing *Vorwärts* magazine. He was replaced by Hans Matthöfer, a former Minister of Finance (1978–1982). Also in September, the party executive made a preliminary decision to nominate Johannes Rau as its Chancellor candidate. After his outstanding election victories in heavily populated North Rhine-Westphalia, the most recent in May 1985, Johannes Rau was considered to be the only Social Democratic political personality who had any chance of bringing the SPD success in the 1987 federal elections. Rau left no doubt that he excluded any possibility of coalition with the Greens and would be aiming for an overall majority. With a programmatic speech in Ahlen, the location in 1947 for the CDU's launching of their soon-to-be-abandoned Ahlen programme with its social and anti-capitalist overtones, the SPD on 15 September

Chancellor candidate Johannes Rau at the electoral party congress in Offenburg on 25 October 1986

1985 launched the election campaign. This was extremely early, and, as it turned out, much too early.

After the iciness of the "second Cold War"[39], the election of Mikhail Gorbachev as the new General Secretary of the CPSU in March 1985 brought a fresh momentum to international politics. At almost the same time, the USA and the Soviet Union renewed their talks on arms control. Following his re-election, President Ronald Reagan began to pursue a more flexible policy. At a meeting in Moscow, Chancellor Kohl and the GDR Head of State Honecker expressed, in the "Moscow Declaration", their common purpose that "Germany must never again be responsible for war, it must make peace its responsibility."[40] In July 1985, a joint SPD

---

39 See above, p. 240.
40 Bulletin of the government "Presse- und Informationsamt" of 14.3.1985, p. 230; Potthoff, Koalition der Vernunft, pp. 305–310.

and SED working group led by Egon Bahr and Hermann Axen respectively presented their "framework" for a chemical weapons-free zone in Europe.[41] There were many indications therefore of a return to a period of *détente*. With Gorbachev's *glasnost* and *perestroika*, hopes were raised that the rigidities of "real-existing socialism" were relaxing, that reforms and change, as well as the gradual ending of confrontation between the two power blocs, were in the offing. For many Social Democrats this was a chink of light which lent fresh impetus to their battered party.

The Chernobyl nuclear reactor accident in April 1986 aroused deep anxiety in the Federal Republic and strengthened the already existent concerns about the peaceful use of nuclear power. There were immediate calls in the SPD for a speedy abandonment of nuclear energy programmes. Gerhard Schröder, who was the SPD's leading candidate in the Landtag elections in Lower Saxony, put himself in charge of these moves. Although the SPD made considerable gains in these elections on 15 July, going from 36.5 to 42.1 per cent, they were insufficient to bring about a change of government. Ernst Albrecht (CDU), together with the FDP, was able to continue in power with a one-vote majority. This caused some disappointment in the SPD. Instead of concentrating more intensively on the electoral middle ground, which is what their Chancellor candidate Johannes Rau envisaged, the party, under the impact of Chernobyl, was driven ever deeper into "alternative" waters. At the party congress in Nuremberg from 25–29 August 1986, the opponents of nuclear energy finally got their way.[42] But the majorities for the requisite legislation were a long way off – the coalition government in Bonn was not in favour of it – and the only chance of acquiring them was through an electoral victory for the SPD in alliance with the Greens. There was, furthermore, no broad consensus in favour of abandoning nuclear energy. Even within the SPD there were still those who supported the peaceful use of nuclear energy, not least in the SPD in North Rhine-Westphalia. For Johannes Rau the party's decision came at an inopportune moment. Nonetheless, in an impressive speech, the Chancellor candidate demonstrated, outwardly at least, his solidarity with his party.

The SPD felt they were on an up. They thought that their main policy issues – cautioning against missiles and the lunacy of the arms race, opposition to nuclear energy, and an emphatic commitment to peace and *détente* – were in tune with the popular mood. The CDU/CSU on the other hand,

---

41 For a summary of this, see Moseleit, Die "Zweite Phase" der Entspannungspolitik, pp. 58 ff.
42 Protokoll vom Parteitag der SPD in Nürnberg, 25.–29.8.1986, esp. pp. 279–337 and pp. 827–837.

with some improvements in the economy, were pursuing an optimistic campaign while playing up the subject of asylum. Overt and covert suspicion of foreigners was rife. It was aroused primarily by the so-called flood of asylum seekers. Many of them arrived by *Interflug* via East Berlin. Wolfgang Schäuble, a minister in the Chancellery, sought to seal off this door to the West by striking deals with the East German leadership. At the same time the CDU/CSU used the asylum issue to put the SPD under pressure. At the behest of the SPD leadership, Egon Bahr attempted in summer 1986 to reach an agreement, via his SED contacts Hermann Axen and Erich Honecker, which would plug this hole in the Wall, and then allow the SPD and its Chancellor candidate Rau to take the credit. This electoral "helping hand" from the SED was ambivalent, and, in more than one respect, problematical.[43] But it did not of course decide the outcome of the elections.

There were sources of irritation within the SPD. In an interview with *Die Zeit* in July 1986 Willy Brandt cast doubt on Johannes Rau's electoral objective of securing an overall majority. The two election teams in the Erich-Ollenhauer-Haus in Bonn and the Bodo Hombach team in Düsseldorf were at odds with one another, with the result that no single, clear political course emerged. In the Bavarian Landtag elections on 12 October the SPD lost four points and dropped to 27.5 per cent. They suffered an even worse blow in the city parliament elections on 9 November in Hamburg. They dropped almost ten points, plummeting to 42 per cent. Wolfgang Clement, the SPD press spokesperson and Rau's confidant at the "barracks", resigned the same night. And as if this were not enough, Gerhard Schröder announced in Hanover at the beginning of December that Oskar Lafontaine ought to be the SPD's next Chancellor candidate. The so-called and self-styled "grandsons" of Willy Brandt were not above promoting each other when it was a matter of going against leading figures in the SPD who were blocking their own further upward progress. This was enough to sour the atmosphere within the SPD. But it was to become a real burden when, as they were about to make the final push for the top, they got in each other's way. This conflict left its long-standing mark on the party, seriously impaired its effectiveness, and, together with smouldering differences on policy matters, left it paralysed.

---

43 For a more comprehensive account, see Vogel, Nachsichten, p. 215 f., and Potthoff, Im Schatten der Mauer, pp. 249–257.

4. Falling in Step and Hopeful Prospects

In the federal elections on January 27, 1987, the SPD, despite its popular Chancellor candidate Johannes Rau, achieved only 37 per cent of the vote. This was 1.2 percentage points less than four years previously, and barely more than in 1961. Discussions and differences amongst the SPD in the run-up to the election had certainly not helped, but even if the party had shown greater unity it would hardly have been able to dislodge the Kohl government. The real winners in the election were the two small parties. The Greens went up to 8.3 per cent and established themselves as the fourth new force in parliament. The FDP, who sold themselves as the corrective element in the coalition and exploited the esteem enjoyed by the well-respected Foreign Minister Hans-Dietrich Genscher, went up to 9.1 per cent and had clearly consolidated their position after the confusions of the coalition change. The Union parties on the other hand had to swallow considerable losses, losing 4.5 percentage points, and going down to 44.3 per cent. Overall, the government camp had suffered a slight loss (53.4 as opposed to 55.8 per cent), the opposition had gained somewhat (from 43.8 to 45.3 per cent). But it was clearly split into Greens and SPD, with the Social Democrats still at odds, furthermore, over their attitude to the Greens. The Kohl government, however, was also far from being the united front it liked to present to the outside world. In the secret election of the Chancellor on 11 March, sixteen of the coalition deputies failed to vote for Helmut Kohl. These symptoms of crisis, however, were disguised by the fact that the Social Democrats were still attracting hostile reports in the press.

For some time speculations about Willy Brandt retiring as party chairman had been doing the rounds, fed in part by a remark he himself had made at the last party congress in August 1986. Doubts were being voiced about his leadership qualities.[44] In the middle of February 1987, a small group – Brandt, Vogel, Rau, and Lafontaine – met to quietly discuss the succession. After the negative outcome to the election, Johannes Rau had already declared he would not stand. A possibility was Hans-Jochen Vogel, who had just been re-elected as chairman of the parliamentary party, but Willy Brandt favoured Oskar Lafontaine as his successor in the change-over set for 1988. Lafontaine, however, hesitated, and a little later (the end of February 1987) sent out a clear political signal. Instead of the candidate chosen by Brandt and the presidium as successor to Matthöfer, Lafontaine, in a surprise coup, succeeded in pushing through Hans-Ulrich Klose for

---

44 Vogel, Nachsichten, p. 220; Schöllgen, Brandt, p. 259; Willy Brandt, Erinnerungen (Berlin and Frankfurt/Main 1989), p. 367 f.

the post of party treasurer, thereby undermining even further Willy Brandt's already severely dented authority.

Ultimately, however, it was Brandt himself who, through a personal miscalculation, provided the impetus which finally led to his resignation on 23 March 1987. He proposed Margarita Mathiopoulos as successor to Wolfgang Clement in the post of party spokesperson. She was the daughter of a well-known opponent of the Greek colonels' regime; she was young, good looking, but with no journalistic experience, and was not a member of the SPD. Despite the tactfully expressed misgivings of the party presidium, Brandt stuck with his decision. A discreet withdrawal could have cleared the matter up internally. But matters escalated out of control. Leading Social Democrats lined up publicly against Mathiopoulos and indicated that it was time for a change of party leadership. A meeting of the "grandsons" on 20 March signalled "generational change". After a short period of reflection, however, Oskar Lafontaine bowed out. The ambitious Margarita had no thought of giving up in order to defuse the conflict, but was already lobbying the two potential candidates for successor – Hans-Jochen Vogel and Oskar Lafontaine.[45] On 23 March Willy Brandt gave in and announced to the party executive that he was considering taking his leave. It was a hasty, undignified exit, adding insult to injury and hardly the "jolly leave-taking" with which Willy Brandt entitled the relevant passage in his memoirs.[46]

This step marked "the end of an epoch in which Willy Brandt in great measure shaped and was the embodiment of German social democracy for almost a quarter of a century"[47]. He was admired and revered amongst Social Democrats and beyond, and was regarded with real affection by many. As Chancellor and the symbol of a new Germany, as the hero of social-liberal *Ostpolitik* and Nobel Peace Prize winner, as a statesmanlike thinker and politician with vision and charisma, he lodged himself firmly in the collective memory. For very many, he continued to be remembered as "our Willy". But even this great Social Democrat, a kind of August Bebel of the postwar epoch, had to accept that his authority had been dented, and that his time as party chairman had run its course.

At the suggestion of Willy Brandt, the party executive nominated Hans-Jochen Vogel on 23 March as its designated party chairman. His election was made official at a special party congress on 14 June in Bonn, and Willy Brandt was elevated to honorary party chairman. Oskar Lafontaine

---

45 For more on this, see especially Ehmke, Mittendrin, p. 336; also Vogel, Nachsichten, p. 223.
46 Brandt, Erinnerungen, pp. 367–373.
47 Vogel, Nachsichten, p. 225.

The election of Hans-Jochen Vogel at the party congress in Bonn 14 June 1987

was promoted to deputy party chairman, with Anke Fuchs becoming the successor to Peter Glotz as party business manager. This change in the leadership and management of the party brought with it a change in style. At the weekly presidium meetings, the monthly sessions of the executive committee, and the regular discussions in the Erich-Ollenhauer-Haus, as well as the committee of the parliamentary party, the agenda was painstakingly worked through point by point and down to the very last detail. Membership strength was a particular hobby horse of the new chairman, who also committed himself wholeheartedly to anchoring a female quota for party posts and parliamentary seats in the SPD party statutes.

At federal level, the SPD was much preoccupied with itself. In spite of five years of Chancellor Helmut Kohl, at the first Landtag elections after the federal elections they found the wind in their faces. The red-green coalition in Hesse under Holger Börner and with Joschka Fischer had collapsed in February 1987. At the early fresh elections, the SPD suffered a severe setback (just 35.5 per cent), with the Greens also being left badly bruised. The electorate showed no appreciation of the red-green coalition. The CDU became the strongest party and formed the new government. The presidium's verdict was as follows: "Losing power in the most markedly Social Democratic territory in the Federal Republic has inflicted severe damage on the ability to implement Social Democratic policies."[48]

48 Statement of the SPD presidium of 6.4.1987, in Service der SPD für Presse, Funk, TV, no. 292/87, 6.4.1987.

And so it had. Having been on a losing streak since 1982 at national level, the party had now lost one of its traditional regional strongholds. But any process of regeneration had to come from the federal states since the rules of electoral behaviour dictated that the particular party in power in Bonn was invariably punished in Landtag elections, and, that by raising its profile at state level, a party gained plus points nationally. The Barschel scandal in Schleswig-Holstein was helpful in this respect.

But before this, it was the SPD-SED discussion paper and the Honecker visit which hit the headlines. Following their first joint document on a chemical weapons-free zone in Europe, the bilateral SPD and SED political working group on security had presented in October 1986 their "Principles for a nuclear weapons-free corridor in Central Europe".[49] Since 1985, members of the SPD's Commission on Basic Values under Erhard Eppler had, prompted by *glasnost* and *perestroika*, been engaged in talks with the Academy for Social Sciences of the SED Central Committee. At the end of August 1987, the joint document "The Conflict of Ideologies and Common Security" was produced. It aroused great interest, mainly due to its being published in the SED party newspaper *Neues Deutschland*. It dealt with peaceful competition between the systems, peace-keeping, and a culture of dialogue, as well as of "political conflict". Talks and cooperation should become the norm, as well as "open and clear criticism" when "human rights and democracy" were infringed. Controversial, also amongst the ranks of the SPD, were, above all, the statements: "No side" should deny the other "the right to exist", and that "both systems are capable of reform", and that each acknowledged the other's "capacity for development and reform". This was open to interpretation as a watering-down of the fundamental rejection of the Communist SED system. In spite of these problematical passages, the document was received positively in some quarters in Bonn, even in government circles (amongst others, by Deputy Chancellor Genscher), but was heavily criticised, however, in others.[50] With the "culture of conflict", the Commission on Basic Values was aiming for openness, a plurality of views, and reform. There was a considerable hidden risk for the SED in the document, since, fol-

---

49 For more detail see, inter alia, Moseleit, Die "Zweite" Phase der Entspannungspolitik, pp. 60 ff.; Bahr, Zu meiner Zeit, pp. 530 ff.; Vogtmeier, Egon Bahr, pp. 279 ff.
50 Document published in Neues Deutschland on 28 August 1987. For Genscher's positive evaluation, see Detlef Nakath and Gerd-Rüdiger Stephan, Von Hubertusstock nach Bonn. Eine dokumentierte Geschichte der deutsch-deutschen Beziehungen auf höchster Ebene 1980–1987 (Berlin 1995), pp. 329 ff.; for a summary, see Garton Ash, Im Namen Europas, pp. 475–480; Potthoff, Im Schatten der Mauer, p. 267, and Winkler, Weg nach Westen, vol. 2, p. 453.

lowing the Helsinki Final Act and the so-called Basket III, there was now a further document signed by the SED to which dissidents and critical citizens could appeal, and they promptly did so. From the viewpoint of the SED regime, the SPD-SED document fitted into a context of measures designed to have a positive influence on the climate for the Honecker visit. The abolition of the death penalty, a general amnesty, even for those convicted of political offences, as well as the institution of a court of appeal, were all part of this, and were devised to create an appearance of liberality. On 7 September 1987, the red carpet was rolled out for comrade Chairman of the Council of State. Honecker's visit to the Federal Republic lasted until 11 September. The horde of some 2,400 journalists, 1,700 of whom were foreign, was testament to the enormous interest and the great political importance of this all-German summit. Its tangible results, however, were somewhat modest, its real significance being in the symbolism – red carpet, guard of honour, national anthems, receptions – all of which, apart from small nuances, were the same as for any other prominent visiting head of state. Of central importance were the negotiations and events with Chancellor Kohl. Federal President Richard von Weizsäcker held a reception for Honecker in the Villa Hammerschmidt. Anyone of rank and reputation in the political life of the Federal Republic was on hand to exchange a word or two. The array of Union politicians stretched from Franz Josef Strauß, who received Honecker in Munich with full honours, to Bernhard Vogel, and as far as Alfred Dregger. From the SPD, there were meetings with the chairman of the party and the parliamentary group, Hans-Jochen Vogel, the elder statesmen Willy Brandt and Helmut Schmidt, North Rhine-Westphalian Minister President Johannes Rau, as well as two of the "grandsons" Oskar Lafontaine and Gerhard Schröder. A further one, Björn Engholm, who was the SPD's leading candidate in the Schleswig-Holstein Landtag elections, also had the honour, alongside Hans-Jochen Vogel, of a meeting.[51] This was arranged at the wish of the SPD, who wanted to give their candidate some media exposure.

It was not this favour by the SED General Secretary, supposedly intended as a big helping hand, but the revelations about the machinations of the CDU head of government Uwe Barschel which in fact secured Engholm his breakthrough in the Schleswig-Holstein Landtag elections on 13 September. The *Spiegel* had already on 7 September published the first reports about disreputable infringements of Engholm's private life

---

51 Notes on the conversations held by Honecker on his visit to the Federal Republic are to be found in Potthoff, Koalition der Vernunft, pp. 564–661; see also the same in Im Schatten der Mauer, pp. 267 ff.; Winkler, Weg nach Westen vol. 2, pp. 454–459.

such as being spied on by a detective agency, insinuations about Aids, and false accusations of tax fraud. In announcements about the next edition, Uwe Barschel, the ruling CDU Minister President, and Anton Pfeiffer, a member of his office, were named as the authors of these machinations.[52] The *Spiegel*-affair included, this was a highpoint in the rich history of CDU government scandals, at least as regards the methods employed. When the retention of power was at stake, any means to outmanoeuvre the sympathetic and popular rival Björn Engholm was seemingly justified. But the despicable game could be laid not solely at Barschel's door. At bottom, it had always been common practice in Germany to discredit and denigrate the "Socialists". There was a common thread leading from Adenauer's "All paths of Marxism lead to Moscow", through the campaigns against the emigrant Willy Brandt, the slogan "Freedom instead of Socialism", and up to Barschel and then the party-contributions scandals under the Kohl system. It had always been the way of the so-called Christian Democrats to secure their predominance in postwar Germany by demagogic and underhand methods, even if the revelation of the scandals to which they gave rise discredited them in the eyes of responsible citizens.

In the Landtag elections on 13 September 1987, the CDU suffered heavy losses and received just 42.6 per cent of the vote. The SPD became the strongest party with 45.2 per cent. After a Landtag investigating committee had confirmed the essential accusations made against Barschel, the political parties, the CDU included, agreed to hold fresh elections on 8 May 1988, which the SPD then won with an overall majority and 54.8 per cent of the vote. On 31 May, Björn Engholm was elected as the new Minister President. After thirty-eight continuous years in power, the CDU lost their stronghold in Kiel. This was a bitter blow for the Union parties, and a tremendous fillip for the Social Democrats. The handsome and likeable Engholm, who belonged more to the generation of sons rather than grandsons, became a new figure on whom the Social Democrats could pin their hopes and laid the basis for his short spell as party chairman from May 1991 to May 1993. This has been largely forgotten, unjustifiably, since under him the SPD embarked on a discreet change of course and attempted to make itself more open to a broader section of society.

The Barschel affair inflicted grave damage on political culture in Germany and was a severe blow to the credibility of its politicians. It was not surprising that disreputable machinations of this kind should add consid-

---

52 Der Spiegel, 7.9.1987, pp. 17–21, and 14.9.1987, pp. 17–27. See also, Archiv der Gegenwart, 57 (1987), pp. 31418ff. and pp. 31666ff.

erably to the sum of so-called *Politikverdrossenheit*, a general disillusionment with politics, or rather with politicians and political parties. Compared to the wretched Barschel, Björn Engholm at that time was like a shining beacon of light for social democracy. But in 1993 he too was accused of misdemeanours and had to resign as party chairman. And once again, politics lost something of its credibility. Scandals were always followed by pledges of improvement and/or the attitude that this was the last of them. But it was not long before all the good intentions had been forgotten, and even for the electorate these affairs were soon a thing of the past. But, beneath the surface, deep-rooted misgivings were growing about those "obsessed with power"[53] and politicians intent on feathering their own nests. The clear drop in voter turnout resulting from the conscious decision not to vote is one, but not the only, important indicator of this.

The campaign backed by the keen amateur pilot Franz Josef Strauß to remove the tax on aircraft fuel for private use added further to the disillusionment with politicians and political parties. In June 1988 a narrow coalition majority approved this tax break for apparently impecunious leisure-time fliers, while at the same time other taxes were raised. Two serious plane crashes involving military aircraft, one at an air show in August 1988 in Ramstein, and another in December in Remscheid, which resulted in many deaths, alerted the public and produced a backlash against the Kohl government, which was stubbornly refusing to abandon low-level flights in heavily populated areas. In the Rhineland-Palatinate, ambitious CDU politicians deposed their party chairman Bernhard Vogel, who then resigned as Minister President. The President of the Bundestag, Philipp Jenninger (CDU), caused a great stir and widespread outrage in November 1988 with his speech to mark the fiftieth anniversary of the night of the pogroms. His use of terms and images from the Nazi period – which could not be explained away as quotations – and the attempts to explain Nazi ideology and its successes struck entirely the wrong note and occasioned enormous offence. Hans-Jochen Vogel saw it as revealing an "appalling lack of sensitivity", and told Jenninger on the same day that he was unacceptable to the SDP as Bundestag President. He resigned the following day.[54]

Helmut Kohl and his government suffered a series of embarrassing setbacks. They were showing unmistakable signs of wear and tear, and Kohl's clinging on to power – he would not tolerate any potential rivals

---

53 This is the acerbic verdict of Federal President Richard von Weizsäcker. See Richard von Weizsäcker im Gespräch mit Gunter Hofmann und Werner A. Perger (Frankfurt/Main 1992).
54 Vogel, Nachsichten, p. 275f.

– contributed to the loss of respect for Union politicians. After the Chancellor had seriously put his foot in it with a singularly inappropriate comparison of Gorbachev with Goebbels, it was left to Federal President Richard von Weizsäcker and Foreign Minister Genscher to smooth things over prior to Kohl's meeting with Gorbachev in Moscow in October 1988.[55] With the SED regime it remained business as usual, with the Kohl government declining to intervene in internal developments and the growing repression of dissidents in the GDR. The Chancellor had few foreign policy successes in this period, which was characterised primarily by the interplay between the two super powers, the USA and the Soviet Union under Gorbachev. In domestic politics, along with the Barschel affair, it was the massive protests against the closing of the Krupp steel works in Rheinhausen around the end of 1987 and the beginning of 1988 which caused the greatest stir. The CDU, it seemed, had no social conscience at this time of crisis, and it was left to the North Rhine-Westphalian state government under Johannes Rau to take up the cause of employees and their jobs.

On the women question which was preoccupying public opinion at this time, the Union parties were obstructive, while the SPD took a step forward with the *Quotenregelung*, the regulation regarding the adequate representation of women. After lengthy discussions in which, quite naturally, the *ASF*, the Working Group of Social Democratic Women under Inge Wettig-Danielmeier played a leading role, with Hans-Jochen Vogel arguing energetically for a quota system, the party congress in Münster from 30 August to 2 September 1988 decided by the necessary two-thirds majority that in future there should be a representation of women of at least 40 per cent in party posts (as from 1994) and in parliamentary seats (as from 1998).[56] Herta Däubler-Gmelin was the first woman to be promoted to deputy party chairman, and in Ingrid Matthäus-Maier, a politician with financial qualifications and charisma succeeded Hans Apel as deputy chairman of the parliamentary group. The proportion of women in the SPD parliamentary group in the Bundestag rose to 27.2 in 1990 and then to 33.7 per cent in 1994.[57] With increased self-confidence, more women party members became involved in party work and community politics. Not every expectation made of the quota system was fulfilled. But the SPD were now on a better footing with women, and the Greens with their

---

55 Archiv der Gegenwart, 57 (1987), p. 30831 f.; Potthoff, Im Schatten der Mauer, p. 290; Korte, Deutschlandpolitik in Helmut Kohls Kanzlerschaft, p. 439; Garton Ash, Im Namen Europas, pp. 160 ff.
56 Protokoll vom Parteitag in Münster, 30.8 – 2.9.1988, pp. 84–128.
57 Schindler, Datenhandbuch Deutscher Bundestag 1949 bis 1999, vol. 1, p. 636.

*The "Women Quota" approved in Münster in 1988
is displayed at the party congress in Bremen in 1991*

female lineup were no longer so dominant in the sphere of equality between the sexes.

Initially, the negative trend for the Union continued uninterrupted in 1989. The CDU lost heavily in the elections to the Berlin parliament, thereby losing control of yet another state. Walter Momper formed a new red-green senate from the SPD, who had climbed to 37.3 per cent, and the so-called "Alternatives". With his trademark red scarf, Momper signalled a fresh wind in symbol-laden Berlin (West) which, as a result of its isolated position, had become a strange mixture of the old and crusty and the young and alternative. On sober reflection, however, the situation of the SPD was not all that favourable. Its 37.3 per cent of the vote was less than the 38.3 per cent of eight years before which had sent them into opposition, and the internal party situation was, and remained, desolate. But in Berlin with the Greens/Alternatives, who had had their biggest successes in cities dominated by universities and the service industries, they had a potential coalition partner with whom they would have a majority once more.

At state level in the local elections in Hesse, the CDU dropped eight percentage points and lost control of Frankfurt/Main. Martin Wentz, the local chairman, and Volker Hauff, the mayoral candidate, were aiming for a successful, modern red-green model which would appeal to the upwardly socially mobile. A total of 40.1 per cent in their old stronghold was enough to give the SPD a narrow victory. After years of seeing their vote collapse in the big cities, the SPD now seemed to be regaining ground. Once again, Munich had an SPD mayor in Georg Kronawitter. It was significant that they had had success there with Hans-Jochen Vogel's successor, whose life had been made difficult by the left, and also in Frankfurt with Helmut Schmidt's former Minister for Research and Technology. With attractive politicians who combined approachability with competence and modernity there was the possibility of regeneration in the large cities and the service industry centres. But this was often irresponsibly squandered amidst the old, internal party quarrels. As early as March 1991, Volker Hauff threw in the towel. In Berlin, Walter Momper resigned in summer 1992.

In 1989 all the CDU/CSU's hopes seemed to have been dashed. The opinion polls showed them to be permanently lagging several points behind the SPD. Helmut Kohl in particular came under critical fire. The Mayor of Stuttgart Manfred Rommel, something of a liberal, along with other representatives of the Union, suggested the very shrewd Minister President of Baden-Würtemberg, Lothar Späth, as a successor to Helmut Kohl as Federal Chancellor. In a startling article in *Die Zeit*, the right-wing conservative publicist Rüdiger Altmann described Kohl's "wretched style of leadership" as at the "roots of the malaise" and demanded that he give way to Lothar Späth.[58] At this time, respect for Kohl in the popularity ratings reached rock bottom. When polled by the Allensbach Institute in 1988 and 1989, a mere 29 and then 27 per cent respectively declared themselves satisfied with the Chancellor's policies.[59] In April 1989 Kohl attempted to stabilise his precarious position with a cabinet reshuffle. Taking the wind out of the sails of his critics and putting a firm stop to the rumours of a putsch, he sent the awkward Gerhard Stoltenberg off to the Hardthöhe (Defence Ministry) and brought the CSU more firmly on board by giving the Finance Ministry to Theodor Waigel. How tense the situation had become for him is demonstrated by the slip of the tongue he made when saying that the coalition partners wanted to "sink [he meant 'work'] together" considerately. In discussion of Kohl's government state-

---

58 See Vogel, Nachsichten, p. 277 (quoted from Die Zeit end of March 1989). For the context, see Kai Dieckmann and Ralf Georg Reuth, Helmut Kohl. Ich wollte Deutschlands Einheit (Berlin 1996), pp. 75–80.
59 Allensbacher Jahrbuch der Demoskopie, vol. 2 (1984–1992), p. 684; see also Korte, Deutschlandpolitik in Helmut Kohls Kanzlerschaft, p. 464.

ment, Hans-Jochen Vogel quoted this Freudian slip "not without a certain *Schadenfreude*"[60].

The Kohl government was ailing, and Helmut Kohl's days as both Chancellor and party chairman seemed numbered. The SPD saw themselves as on the up, and it was widely felt that they would once again provide the next Chancellor. But in the European elections of June 1989 they received a setback. Admittedly, with 37.3 per cent, they received almost the same percentage of the vote as the Union, who suffered heavy losses and stood at 37.9 per cent. As far as the public was concerned, however, the SPD had simply not managed to pull it off. Despite all their weaknesses, the CDU/CSU still had their noses out in front. This had a not-to-be-underestimated psychological importance. The main beneficiaries of the discontent felt by many voters were the right-wing radical Republicans under Franz Schönhuber, whose demagogic campaign focused on unemployment, housing shortages, and the "flood of asylum-seekers". But European elections also serve as warning lessons in which protest parties do better in terms of percentages. On more sober analysis, the race for the next federal elections seemed to be wide open. The Union had a reasonably reliable coalition partner in the FDP. Its occasional barbed asides served more to raise its profile with the electorate than to signal actual moves to cut itself loose.

The SPD had the problem that, in the task of gaining governing power in Bonn, it had no dependable and viable partners. The Greens were not yet ready for the responsibility of government in Bonn. At state level, the first red-green coalition in Hesse had collapsed after barely eighteen months, the second red-green/alternative project in Berlin was running into difficulties, at federal level the Greens were beset with internal squabbles, and any overtures to them met with considerable resistance within the SPD as a whole. Decisive for their electoral chances, however, was whether the Kohl government would discredit itself even further. In summer 1989 Kohl was at absolute rock bottom, and a showdown seemed likely at the forthcoming party congress in Bremen (11 to 13 September 1989). But rapid developments in the East with the wave of refugees, peaceful revolution, and finally German reunification, brought a complete reversal of mood. Kohl's seat in power was not only secured, but he was also set to rule for a further nine years, thereby surpassing Adenauer's record and basking in the aura of being the Chancellor of unification.

---

60 Vogel, Nachsichten, p. 278.

5. A New Basic Programme

The Godesberg Programme had signalled the transition of the SPD to an open, left-wing *Volkspartei* and paved the way to government power in Bonn. After being banished to the opposition benches, the need had grown, in the wake of new social movements and the changing orientation of values within the party, for a new programme of basic principles. This was intended to take account of social and technical changes and give the party fresh political direction. The programmatic concept was prepared by the Commission on Basic Values, which endeavoured to produce a synthesis of Social Democratic principles and new social tendencies.

At the party congress in Essen in May 1984, a programme commission was set up. It was chaired by Willy Brandt. With a high degree of personal commitment he mapped out the course towards a revised programme and indicated the path the commission should take. Assisted by some political practitioners with an interest in the programme, the Social Democrat theoreticians convened at the isolated monastery of Irsee in the Allgäu for a long-term meeting. In a process of discussion lasting two years, the differing positions of the ecological pragmatists, who were sceptical about growth, and the open-minded economic and employment pragmatists grew closer. The intended process of integration, which is at the heart of all debates about political programmes, was therefore, from an internal perspective, successful.

In June 1986, the commission presented its draft, the basic tenor of which had been set by Willy Brandt. The so-called Irsee draft programme was a collection of ideas, some 107 pages in length. It read like a response to complex realities and the burgeoning tasks of integration. The Irsee pointers to the future were ecologisation of production and consumption instead of growth, controls on technology and production capacity, supplementing the established welfare state by means of non-state self-help, a repudiation of "masculine patterns of thought", and a turning towards feminist-influenced "female" virtues. With its deep-seated doubts about existing concepts of politics, the Irsee score was in a distinctly minor key, and the basic message got lost amidst its fat programmatic package. With its process of self-reflection, Irsee fulfilled a limited function in addressing members with programmatic interests and integrating various divergent tendencies in the party. Beyond this, however, it had very little influence. Carl-Friedrich von Weizsäcker disguised his criticism thus: "Alongside much that was misguided in the pastoral letters of old, there was also a lot of truth."[61] Even within the party, it failed to strike any real spark.

61 As reported in Ehmke, Mittendrin, p. 330.

The Nuremberg party congress in 1986 discussed the draft rather as if it were – to use the barbed comment of the Social Democrat political analysts Peter Lösche and Franz Walter – "a tiresome obligation"[62]. Its resonance with the general public was not encouraging. Amongst the media there was widespread mockery of its grumpy pessimism about the future and of Erhard Eppler's pietistic hostility to progress. Peter Glotz criticised the Social Democrats' image as one of "crabby anti-modernism"[63]. Others, such as the two Baden-Württemberg Social Democrats Dieter Spöri and Ulrich Maurer, saw the SPD's reputation as the "party who always says no" as being responsible for their decline. This made no impact with those who were upwardly mobile and working in communications and the computer and information technology industries. It was a fact that the SPD had suffered its greatest losses in the federal elections amongst those working in these modern boom areas.

Based in Baden-Württemberg, a group of Social Democrats emerged who were dedicated to modernisation, technical progress, and a culture of achievement. Oskar Lafontaine was thinking along similar lines, and under his direction work was begun on the programmatic concept for "Progress 90". After Willy Brandt had retired as party chairman, and no longer wanted to be in charge of the programme commission, Lafontaine "indicated" that he was interested in taking over.[64] Potential conflict was smoothed over by giving the post to party chairman Hans-Jochen Vogel, and making Lafontaine executive chairman. For a time, formulaic compromises such as this became a trademark of the SPD, which was having difficulties in finding its way. Possible obstruction of work on the programme was avoided, however. Lafontaine, head of the SPD in the Saar, found it very difficult to get on with members of the commission as independently minded as Erhard Eppler and Peter von Oertzen. As chairman, he was "generally badly prepared and had no enthusiasm for the job in hand", and made the others feel that all their efforts "were not worth the candle"[65]. Teamwork and programmatic nitty-gritty were not the Saarlander's forte. He was out for the big effect, the media orchestration of eye-catching messages with which he could appeal to the voters and put himself firmly in the spotlight.

62 Lösche and Walter, Die SPD, p. 127. See also the Protokoll vom Parteitag der SPD in Nürnberg, 25.–29.8.1986, pp. 522–529, pp. 532–556, and pp. 558–566.
63 Peter Glotz, 'Plädoyer für kollektive Lernprozesse der SPD im Spannungsfeld zwischen "konservativer" Entsolidarisierung und "grünem" Subjektivismus'. In Perspektiven ds (1984), p. 50. On this and what follows, see Lösche and Walter, Die SPD, p. 127f.
64 Vogel, Nachsichten, p. 234.
65 Lösche and Walter, Die SPD, p. 129.

The debate initiated on this "new progress" by Spöri and Maurer found favour with other leading representatives of the "grandson generation" such as Björn Engholm, Rudolf Scharping, and Gerhard Schröder, and received a further boost when Oskar Lafontaine "put himself at the head of the SPD's modernisation movement in 1988"[66]. With instinct, skill, eloquence, and media professionalism, he initiated controversial public debates. He produced the biggest headlines and greatest television impact with his attacks on the trade unions. These were linked to a plea for a forward-looking, modern market policy, and for more flexibility in working hours and the labour market.[67]

While Lafontaine, with his modernisation and profile-raising course, was becoming a sought-after political star, he was also meeting resistance from within the party. Many of the very same people who thought of themselves as being on the left, and to whom he had once been a hero, now energetically resisted his presumptions, and even the party's programme makers took exception to him. The programme commission which had been set up by the Nuremberg party congress found itself in something of a quandary. At first its course was affected primarily by proponents of Marxist visions as well as by less dogmatic left-wingers in league with reflective analysts and political theorists. Active political and parliamentary practitioners showed less interest, and, with their full diaries, could only seldom find the time and patience for the debates on the programme. The demand of a majority of the commission for economic and political controls and planning was completely out of tune with the times, and threatened to take the party back to the pre-Godesberg era. Following the appalling echo this had in the media, the party leadership and economic experts got together and brought the programme commission back on course. "Nothing", according to Lösche and Walter, "could have demonstrated more clearly what a fiasco the programme debate had been than the sigh of relief that at least things had not got as bad" as had been feared: "The debate about the SPD's programme in the second half of the 1980s was, as regards the effect it had outside the party, an enormous, historically unprecedented flop."[68]

Oskar Lafontaine was hitting the headlines with an orchestrated media campaign on his conflict and modernisation strategy. He knew how to take firm grip of a topic, and to captivate groups of sympathisers and vot-

66 Ibid., p. 128.
67 Oskar Lafontaine, Die Gesellschaft der Zukunft. Reformpolitik in einer veränderten Gesellschaft (Hamburg 1988); Vogel, Nachsichten, p. 237f. For an evaluation of the role of Lafontaine in this period, see too, Walter, Die SPD, pp. 222–224.
68 Lösche and Walter, Die SPD, p. 130.

ers who at first sight had little in common. With his vigorous stand on the arms race and his voting in favour of ecology and eco-taxes, he spoke to a whole generation of peace and environmental campaigners, and with his pleas for modernity and flexibility addressed the concerns of those seeking the break-up of the old fossilised structures and looking for new ways forward. The discussions about the new party programme, on the other hand, threatened to become bogged down. It was not until the beginning of 1989 that this stagnation had been overcome to the extent that the draft could be made public. The provisional end product which, according to Horst Ehmke, "still, in parts," resembled "more a political educational programme than a political one"[69], was, despite its great size and complexity, greeted initially with some degree of interest by the party and the media. From summer 1989, however, the debate was increasingly obscured by the dramatic events in the GDR, and was ultimately lost sight of. The extraordinary party congress, originally scheduled for Bremen, was shifted to Berlin, but still timetabled for the middle of December. Accordingly, the new basic programme – approved in the middle of the period of rapid upheaval between the peaceful revolution and approaching unification – was entitled the "Berlin Programme".

The SPD party congress on the programme was held from 18 to 20 December 1989 in the conference centre at the *Funkturm* (radio tower). In the main, the draft programme was a reflection of the ecological peace-movement and the post-national tendencies of the SPD in the 1980s. It was designed to lift the party's profile, and had to bring together various, different currents. Hans-Jochen Vogel did an excellent job on the necessary task of integration. The ecological renewal of industrial society, social equality for women, fewer working hours and a society "with humane conditions of work for all", the "equal distribution between the sexes" of employment and housework, improved quality of life, "a democratic community of peoples", and a liberation of mankind from the "madness of war and the arms race" were the programme's highly ambitious goals. They were discussed and explained at length, and presented in measured, academic fashion. In particular, the term "progress" was defined much more critically than had traditionally been the case with the SPD and its long-standing attachment to social and technical progress. "Progress", as it was understood in the Berlin Programme, meant a rejection of "quantity" in favour of "fresh thinking and direction, being selective, and shaping things" with the aim of "enhancing the quality of human life".

---

69 Ehmke, Mittendrin, p. 330.

Congress on the Party Programme in Berlin, 18–20 December 1989

Beyond its narrower historical task – the fashioning of state and society in the direction of a democratic and social community – the Social Democrats, with their Basic Programme, were committing themselves to the struggle for a humane world in which future generations could lead dignified lives in peace. Taking their cue from the United Nations statement of human rights, the Social Democrats saw the "point of departure and objective of our activity" as being the "dignity of the individual". In "Our Image of Man" it states that "the human being is destined to be neither good nor bad, but is capable of learning and reason. This makes democracy possible. He is fallible, can err, and is susceptible to inhumanity. This makes democracy necessary." Compared to Godesberg, this justification of democracy, based on a realistic view of humanity, represented a step forward. But quotable passages such as this were a rarity in the Berlin Programme. For a supposedly symbolic and eye-catching programme, it was much too long, overly reflective, and too far removed from the practical requirements of day-to-day politics. This draft for the future, intended as the "offer of a reformist alliance of the old and new social movements", was already being overtaken by the present. While the party was in conference in Berlin, it was not it which was determining events, but the hundreds of thousands out on the street celebrating the unexpected coming-together. The party congress was then eclipsed entirely by Helmut Kohl's show-stealing appearance in Dresden amidst a sea of black-red-gold flags.

II. Peaceful Revolution and the Process of Unification

The years 1989/90 represented a caesura for Germany, Europe, and the world which brought enormously dramatic and far-reaching changes. The epoch of East/West conflict, in which the blocs led by the two superpowers, the USA and the Soviet Union, confronted each other, was coming to an end. The opposing arsenals of weapons were being dismantled, and the old hostilities transformed into partnership. The deep gulf between free and democratic constitutional states and totalitarian dictatorships which had characterised the "short twentieth century" so crucially, leading to brutal wars, appalling crimes, and enormous expenditure of resources to compete in the power struggle between the systems, seemed to have been bridged. American political scientists such as Francis Fukuyama were already celebrating the victory of democracy as the end of history.[1] The dream of genuinely peaceful cooperation seemed to have been realised, and the age of lasting peace to have arrived.

The revolution in Eastern Europe and the breakthrough to freedom and democracy came at a breathtaking pace, with one turbulent event following another. With the exception of Romania, where the regime used armed force in its attempt to crush the uprising, the change in Central and Eastern Europe took place without bloodshed and the use of violence. The citizens in these states liberated themselves from Communist dictatorships in peaceful revolutions. This seemed like a miracle, given that there had, from time to time in the past, been violent mass insurrections against these regimes: in the GDR in 1953, in Hungary in 1956, in Czechoslovakia in 1968, in Poland in the mid-1950s, and then once again with the rise of the popular trade-union movement, Solidarity. But these manifestations of protest were all crushed by Soviet tanks, or, as in Poland in 1981, suppressed by a military regime fearful of Soviet intervention.

With the introduction of *glasnost* and *perestroika* under Mikhail Gorbachev, the fear vanished. The people felt encouraged to throw off the yoke of Communist rule. Without the changes in the Soviet Union and the outstanding role played by Mikhail Gorbachev, the peaceful revolution could not have happened as it did. We should, and must not, forget this. But countries such as Hungary and Poland also played their part. They paved the way for reforms and an opening up of the system, embarking in spring

---

1 Francis Fukuyama, The End of History and the Last Man (New York 1992).

1989 on a process of democratisation. When Hungary grew tired of being misused as a lackey of the inflexible SED system, and opened its borders to GDR citizens, they were sending out an unmistakable signal. After Czechoslovakia and Poland also allowed refugees from the GDR to leave, and Gorbachev critically distanced himself from Honecker, the GDR "gerontocracy" found itself increasingly isolated. The East German Communist regime was inwardly and outwardly a sham, its governing elite increasingly insecure, and its very foundations were beginning to crumble. Finally, it imploded.

With its *Ost-* and *Deutschlandpolitik*, as well as its policies of reconciliation, peace, and understanding, the SPD had contributed to the demolition of conventional concepts of the enemy, and built up a climate of trust which had made possible the peaceful change in Eastern Europe. Without this, *glasnost* and *perestroika* could not have flourished, nor could the peaceful revolution have succeeded. But the possibilities of the SPD – initially up to 1982 as the party of government, and thereafter in opposition – having a direct impact on conditions in the GDR were limited. *Deutschlandpolitik* under Willy Brandt and Helmut Schmidt, as well as under Helmut Kohl, meant the painstaking task, through dialogue, cooperation and treaties, of making division more tolerable, facilitating human contacts, and easing communication between Germans from the two states. But it was limited to this. There was no attempt, or even intention, on the part of the Federal Republic's ruling powers, to actively destabilise the GDR. The decisive impetus came from the people of the GDR themselves who insisted on being allowed to leave, who raised their voices for freedom and democracy, and who brought about the peaceful revolution with their mass demonstrations. The people of the GDR were the most important players; they it was who seized the initiative, and who swept politicians, parties, and policies along with them as on an onrushing tide.

1. *From the Citizens' Movement to the SDP/SPD*

Under the decades of SED rule, not only were Social Democratic organisations and endeavours suppressed, combated, and eradicated, but Social Democratic traditions were also outlawed and banished from historical consciousness. After the dissolution of the Social Democratic organisation in East Berlin following the building of the Wall in 1961, there was ultimately nothing left in the second German state of the old party and its rich traditions. The early Social Democratic opposition groups had been smashed, many Social Democrats incarcerated and brutally persecuted.

After being released, many went to the West, others lived under dismal circumstances in the GDR, condemned to remain silent about their sufferings, and without the support of a Social Democratic "party family". There were repeated instances of opposition and resistance to Communist rule in the 1940s, 1950s, and also in the 1960s, but, as Markus Meckel put it at an event commemorating the founding of the SDP, "there was no real tradition of opposition [...] no continuity or tradition of resistance", and they "had to develop each time from scratch".[2] Nevertheless, this was how Marianne Birthler, at the same conference, described her own experiences: "The GDR was a kind of fertile ground for Social Democratic ideas. Very many people there identified closely with the SPD in the West, followed its discussions and debates very closely, and took a lively interest in the fortunes of the SPD and its representatives in the public eye".[3] Willy Brandt in particular was a figure with whom people could identify.

Oppositional and resistance thinking and activity received important support from the Helsinki process, since dissidents now had an official document to which they could appeal: the Final Act of the CSCE conference in Helsinki (1975) with its Basket III, to which the GDR state and party leadership had been co-signatories. Impulses were also coming from Poland which, compared to the GDR, permitted a greater degree of intellectual freedom. The Solidarity movement there was a powerful mass movement opposed to the regime and, despite the serious setbacks inflicted by the Jaruzelski regime, managed to squeeze change and some degree of personal freedom from it. Even though the Chancellor of the time, Helmut Schmidt, after a first rather problematical comment, announced in the Bundestag that he "was wholeheartedly on the side of Polish workers"[4], and the DGB (Federation of German Trade Unions), with its secretary for international affairs, Chris Christoffersen, did a lot for Solidarity, as did individual Social Democrats, the West German left as a whole frequently struck the wrong note in dealing with the Polish freedom movement. Harsh words, for instance, about rampaging strikers, whom, they maintained, they were not going to allow to destroy the policy of *détente*, Willy Brandt's hesitant approach *vis-à-vis* Lech Walesa, Wehner's problematical trip immediately after the Jaruzelski *coup*, all this amounted to a considerable list, with the result that "the already damaged reputation

---

2 Bernd Faulenbach and Heinrich Potthoff (eds), Die deutsche Sozialdemokratie und die Umwälzung 1989/90 (Essen 2001), p. 19.
3 Ibid., p. 20.
4 Verhandlungen des Deutschen Bundestages (stenographic report), vol. 120, pp. 4289 ff. (statement by Federal Chancellor Helmut Schmidt in the session on 18.12.1981).

of the SPD amongst many Poles sank to rock bottom"[5]. For many Poles who supported the changes, these experiences aroused deep-seated reservations about the German Social Democrats, and these continued to reverberate long after 1989/90.

With the nuclear arms race and the "second Cold War" at the end of the 1970s and beginning of the 1980s, a peace movement developed not just in West Germany. In the GDR too there arose an independent, separate peace movement at grassroots level, which met for the most part under the aegis of the Church, and attempted – insofar as the conditions of an authoritarian and dictatorial system permitted – to develop into a wider network. Whereas the West German peace movement protested for the most part solely against Western missiles, in the GDR they set their sights on those in both East and West. With the distinctive symbol "swords into ploughshares", of which 100,000 screen prints alone were made, it was chiefly young people who committed themselves publicly from 1980/81 on to the cause of peace, submitting themselves in the process to humiliation by the state. The spectacular reforging of a sword into a ploughshare on the Lutherhof in Wittenberg gave this grassroots peace initiative a fresh boost.[6] Via the networking and the annual meetings of the groups "Frieden konkret" (Concretely Peace), a platform was set up which provided a basis in 1989 for the demonstrations, warning vigils, and the monitoring of elections.

Along with peace issues, it was often ecological problems, and increasingly the call for human rights, which prompted critical GDR citizens to band together. After the security services had come down heavily on the young audience at a rock concert at the Brandenburg Gate in June 1987, the environmentalist library in the *Zionskirche* in East Berlin was searched, and several people arrested. Before and during Honecker's visit to the Federal Republic, which also opened the door to other Western capitals for the party chairman and head of state, the regime adopted a moderate approach. But then after the visit was over, it tightened the reins of repression and took rigorous measures against nonconformists and dissidents. The activities of the security apparatus were, however, un-

5 The comment of Klaus Reiff, Polen. Als deutscher Diplomat an der Weichsel (Bonn 1990), p. 303.
6 For an account of the development of these movements see, especially, Ehrhart Neubert, Geschichte der Opposition in der DDR 1949–1989 (Berlin 1995), and the volumes VI/1–2 "Möglichkeiten und Formen abweichenden und widerständigen Verhaltens und oppositionellen Handelns, die friedliche Revolution im Herbst 1989, die Wiedervereinigung Deutschlands und Fortwirken von Strukturen und Mechanismen der Diktatur" of the enquiry commission "Aufarbeitung von Geschichte und Folgen der SED-Diktatur in Deutschland".

able to extinguish the flame of protest, and indeed gave rise to a wave of solidarity with those arrested. Members of civil-rights and peace groups used the traditional parade on 17 January 1988 commemorating the murder of Karl Liebknecht and Rosa Luxemburg to display unofficial banners carrying Luxemburg's memorable phrase "Freedom is always the freedom for the person who thinks differently". The state and security apparatus responded by detaining, convicting, and sometimes deporting to the West, numerous dissidents and opponents of the regime – the biggest wave of arrests since 17 June 1953.

There were many services of intercession held in churches throughout the GDR. The tough treatment of dissidents met with a vigorous response from the West German media. Leading Social Democrats such as the party and parliamentary party chairman Hans-Jochen Vogel, Erhard Eppler of the Commission on Basic Values, and the chairmen of the SPD parliamentary parties at state and federal level were scathing in their condemnation of these repressive measures. Helmut Kohl and his government, on the other hand, held back. They quite deliberately refused to be critical, to avoid, as they put it, "adding fuel to the fire". Their cooperation with the SED regime continued almost undisturbed, the Chancellor even giving the GDR a kind of "survival guarantee".[7] The SED General Secretary Erich Honecker noted with satisfaction "that the FRG government, in contrast to the SPD, has been restrained in its comments about the most recent provocations against the GDR"[8]. His irritation was now directed not only at the Greens, who for some time had been using their influence to help dissidents in the GDR, but now increasingly at the Social Democrats. Gert Weisskirchen, who was heavily engaged in working on behalf of peace and civil-rights activists, was repeatedly refused entry to the GDR. Weisskirchen, Horst Sielaff, and Jürgen Schmude had forged contacts with circles round Friedrich Schorlemmer and Rainer Eppelmann. Schmude, along with Johannes Rau and Erhard Eppler, used their function in the Protestant Church to meet with members of civil-rights and peace groups at Church congresses in the GDR.

---

7 See, inter alia, Korte, Deutschlandpolitik in Helmut Kohls Kanzlerschaft, p. 384f., and p. 392f.; Potthoff, Koalition der Vernunft, pp. 698–720 and pp. 730–752; Werner Filmer and Heribert Schwan, Schäuble. Politik als Lebensaufgabe (Munich 1994), p. 219; Detlef Nakath and Gerd-Rüdiger Stephan, Countdown zur deutschen Einheit. Eine dokumentierte Geschichte der deutsch-deutschen Beziehungen auf höchster Ebene 1980–1987 (Berlin 1996), pp. 82ff.; Potthoff, Im Schatten der Mauer, pp. 278–281.
8 Quoted from Honecker's conversation with Milos Jakes of the Czechoslovakian Communist Party. In Bundesarchiv SAPMO, DY 30, IV 2/1/679.

When, on the night of New Year's Eve, fireworks heralded the beginning of 1989, barely anyone expected that this would be the year in which the Wall would come down. In his report on the state of the nation on 1 December 1988, Chancellor Kohl was still saying that his government viewed the "internal difficulties of the political system of the GDR" with concern, and that he had no interest in seeing them "continue to increase".[9] A month later, in January 1989, a young, unknown GDR theologian, Martin Gutzeit, suggested to a priest friend of his, Markus Meckel, that he should set up a Social Democratic Party in the GDR, to which he agreed. Pure fantasy perhaps, and yet this was the moment which gave birth to the idea of the SDP. There were no doubt also others who were quietly cherishing the vision of a revival of social democracy. But in contrast to the cautious sceptics, Meckel and Gutzeit set about achieving it. On 24 July 1989 they put the final touches to the "Call for the Establishment of an Initiative Group" to found a Social Democratic Party.[10]

A lot had happened in the GDR in these months. Since the beginning of the year, the number of applications to leave the country had risen rapidly. In the local elections on 7 May 1989, independent observers from the civil-rights movement had kept a sharp eye on officialdom, and succeeded in revealing the regime's well-tried methods of fiddling elections. The process of rebellion was encouraged and driven forward by events in Poland and Hungary, countries which had gone down the road of democratic reforms ("round tables" in Poland, transition to a multi-party system in Hungary), and where a pluralistic democracy had begun to take shape. In May and June 1989, after the Hungarians had begun to remove the barbed wire along their border with Austria, more and more GDR citizens were using this route to escape to the West.[11] Many others forced their way into the West German embassies in Budapest, Prague, Warsaw, and East Berlin; they numbered 6,000 in Budapest alone. This "voting with their feet" was the first act in a mass exodus which, after 11 September with the public announcement of the opening of the Hungarian border with the West, would become increasingly dramatic.

9 Printed, inter alia, in Texte zur Deutschlandpolitik, third series, vol. 6, p. 472f.; Verhandlungen des Deutschen Bundestages, stenographic report, vol. 147, pp. 8094–8099, here p. 8097.
10 Report of the historical commission of the SPD party executive, Von der SDP zur SPD (Bonn 1994), pp. 44–48. Gero Neugebauer and Bernd Niedbalski, Die SPD in der DDR 1989–1990. Aus der Bürgerbewegung in die gesamtdeutsche Sozialdemokratie (Berlin 1992).
11 The best account of this is Axel Schützsack, Exodus in die Einheit. Die Massenflucht aus der DDR 1989 (Melle 1990); See also Fischer Weltalmanach, Sonderband DDR (Frankfurt/Main 1990), pp. 138–142.

The destabilisation of the GDR was now well underway, but no one could yet anticipate how the regime would react. The revolt of 17 June 1953 had been suppressed in bloody fashion, as had the popular uprising in Hungary in 1956, and the Prague Spring of 1968. On 4 June 1989, the Chinese hardliners round Li Peng put an end to the democracy movement with the bloody massacre on Tiananmen Square, the "Square of Heavenly Peace", and the SED, in alliance with the bloc parties (CDU, LDPD, etc.) gave the Chinese leadership their backing. A "Chinese solution" hung like a Damocles sword over the peaceful revolution. The founders of the SDP knew that they might be arrested at any moment. They represented a far stronger direct challenge to the SED than those who regarded themselves as a civil-rights movement. On 26 August 1989, in the congregation of the Golgotha Church in East Berlin, they went public with their "Appeal" for the founding of a Social Democratic Party. It bore the signatures of Martin Gutzeit, Markus Meckel, student chaplain Arndt Noack, and Ibrahim Böhme. It was rapidly distributed throughout the GDR via the Protestant Church and the network of dissidents and civil-rights groups, with the press publicising it in the Federal Republic.[12] A so-called initiative group of some ten persons met several times to make preparations for the founding of the party. They took various precautions against the possibility of being raided by the state security by, for instance, having a "secret preliminary founding". The date of the formal foundation ceremony, the 7 October, was deliberately chosen to coincide with the fortieth anniversary of the founding of the GDR. It took place at the vicarage in Schwante, to the north of Berlin. After signing the four foundation documents and the decisions on the statutes, as well as the request to join the Socialist International, an executive committee was appointed, and the party posts allocated. Stephan Hilsberg was elected as spokesperson, with Angelika Barbe and Markus Meckel as his deputies, Ibrahim Böhme was made business manager and Gerd Döhling treasurer.[13]

In founding this Social Democratic Party, the small Schwante gathering was directly challenging the SED's monopoly on power. They were thereby defining the SED "not as a party of unity, but as a Communist

12 Markus Meckel and Martin Gutzeit, Opposition in der DDR. Zehn Jahre kirchliche Friedensarbeit – kommentierte Quellentexte (Cologne 1994), p. 350f.; Petra Schuh and Bianca von Wieden, Die deutsche Sozialdemokratie 1989/90. SDP and SPD im Einigungsprozess (Munich 1997), pp. 9–180 for the beginnings of the SDP.
13 Of the wide range of literature on Schwante see, in addition to what has been named already, Dieter Dowe (ed.), Von der Bürgerbewegung zur Partei. Die Gründung der Sozialdemokratie in der DDR (Bonn 1993); Wolfgang Herzberg and Patrik von zur Mühlen, Auf den Anfang kommt es an: Sozialdemokratischer Neubeginn in der DDR, Interviews und Analysen (Bonn 1993).

**Gründungsurkunde
der
Sozialdemokratischen Partei
in der DDR (SDP)**

Schwante (Kr. Oranienburg), den 7. Oktober 1989

Copy of the "Foundation Document of the Social Democratic Party in the GDR (SDP)", dated Schwante (Oranienburg district) 7 October 1989

party, which it was. This was an attack on its very roots."[14] The SDP was very deliberately linking itself to the tradition of the oldest German party, and reclaiming for itself the democratic and social heritage of the workers' movement. They were taking their cue directly from the great Social Democratic personalities such as Willy Brandt. Their policies were to be democratic and social, as well as ecological. They committed themselves to parliamentary democracy. This distinguished them from various other civil-rights groups who were establishing themselves at the same time, such as "New Forum", "Democracy Now", and "Democratic Awakening", since these regarded themselves as adherents of grassroots democracy. The SDP, however, was a political party, and the only independent one to boot. This is why, in autumn 1989, they attracted people from various backgrounds who were no longer satisfied with the alternative scene of the citizens' movements groups, and who were eager to become politically active. By reviving a Social Democratic alternative they succeeded in

---

14 Markus Meckel, in Faulenbach and Potthoff (eds), Die deutsche Sozialdemokratie, p. 25. Konrad Jarausch gives a good summarising analysis in '"Die notwendige Demokratisierung unseres Landes" – Die Rolle der SDP im Herbst 1989'. Ibid., pp. 52–67.

reaching a wider section of the population. The SDP made a decisive contribution to the destabilisation of the SED system, as well as to the politicisation of the opposition. Amidst the upheaval, they single-mindedly drove the process forward along the road to parliamentary democracy, and were in the front line of this peaceful, democratic, and successful revolution.

The West German public first heard about the intention to set up a Social Democratic Party in the GDR with the publication of the SDP appeal in the *Frankfurter Rundschau* and the *taz* of 31 August. It met with enormous response throughout almost the entire West German press. The West German media played a decisive role not only in this, but during the whole process of peaceful revolution. They ensured that it received a lot of public attention, which was then transmitted via them back to the GDR, giving people fresh strength, encouragement, and inspiration. The initial reactions of the great SPD sister party in the West, however, to all of this were more than reserved. In the presidium session of 30 August there was no mention of the new party, on the 11 September it was discussed merely peripherally, with the conclusion being reached that "the requisite degree of maturity for the founding of a party of this kind has not yet been achieved", that the SPD in the West was not going to become involved, and that a decision about the establishment of a new party would have to be made in the GDR.[15] Public statements by Karsten D. Voigt, Walter Momper, and Egon Bahr were similarly somewhat cool.[16] Others were deliberately restrained out of understandable concern not to put the intrepid founder members of the SDP in even greater danger than they already were. Social Democrats in the West were, at this phase of the upheaval in the East, preoccupied mainly with themselves and the prospect of election year 1990. The relationship between East and West, including developments in Eastern Europe and the GDR, was of secondary concern. Their main interest was in how to handle the attacks by the Union on their contacts with the East. The party was struggling to find a change of direction, but amidst the chorus of different opinions it was difficult to find a single clear line, and instead they arrived at a compromise: suspension of the discussions of the Commission on Basic Values, the carrying-out of already arranged visits, the encouragement of *glasnost*, reforms, properly conducted elections, and pluralism. In a resolution of

---

15 From the minutes of the presidium sessions on 30.8 and 11.9.1989, in the SPD-Vorstandsarchiv, now the Archiv der sozialen Demokratie in the Friedrich-Ebert-Stiftung.
16 See Wolfgang Jäger, Die Überwindung der Teilung. Der innerdeutsche Prozess der Vereinigung 1989/90 (Stuttgart 1998), p. 258, with documentation in notes 506, 507, and 510 on p. 596.

18 September, a week after the opening of the Hungarian border, the party executive committee pressed for freedom of travel, information, and expression, as well as the "responsible participation of all citizens of the GDR in the shaping of social conditions". The GDR, it maintained, would "be stabilised, not destabilised, by reforms".[17]

At bottom, the great SPD declined to undertake any initiatives of its own to revive social democracy in the East, leaving it to the young and courageous initiators to attempt the feat of setting up the SDP. "For a party such as the SPD, with its tradition of freedom, this was too half-hearted."[18] Social Democrats in the West such as Gert Weisskirchen and Norbert Gansel who had already had contact with dissidents, and who showed some concern for their new "little sister", were few and far between. It was not until the visit of Steffen Reiche to Bonn at the end of October that the party began to show some real interest. Two weeks after its foundation, the SDP used Reiche to seize the initiative. Of great help here was the committed radio journalist Manfred Rexin, and Tilman Fichter from the SPD party school. Reiche's appearance on the television programme "Brennpunkt", which was discussing the fall of Honecker and his replacement by Egon Krenz, secured the necessary publicity. There he was, a young East German Social Democrat, alongside such illustrious guests as Helmut Schmidt, Oskar Lafontaine, and Rudolf Seiters, a CDU minister in the Chancellor's office, and then being given an official reception in the Ollenhauer-Haus. Hans-Jochen Vogel was immediately prepared to engage in talks, took him to a meeting of the executive committee on 23 October, and then thereafter to a sitting of the parliamentary party's executive committee. These meetings left a deep impression. The leadership of the SPD suddenly realised what had been set in motion in Schwante, and was now clearly ready to embrace its sister party. Willy Brandt and Hans-Jochen Vogel then took it upon themselves to fulfil the SDP's ambition to join the Socialist International. At the beginning of November 1989, they received their formal status as a member, and, with this, a measure of protection against those still in power in the GDR.

The founding of the SDP by a group of individuals with backbone represents a milestone in the long and chequered history of social democracy as the champion of freedom and civil rights. At the point at which they dared to take this step, the future of the GDR was still uncertain. Two days later, on 9 October, the assembled ranks of security forces in Leipzig pulled back in the face of the demonstrators. The peaceful pro-

17 See Vogel, Nachsichten, p. 288 f.
18 Potthoff, Im Schatten der Mauer, p. 300.

test of a few thousand had by this point grown into a mass movement, and the peaceful revolution had achieved a breakthrough. Week by week in the "heroic city" of Leipzig and many other towns, the number of demonstrators was growing, finally reaching over a million at the end of October and beginning of November. On 4 November, more than half a million, and according to some sources, a million people gathered on the Alexanderplatz in East Berlin alone.[19] On 7 November the government of Willi Stoph resigned, followed the next day by changes in the SED Politburo, and on 9 November Helmut Kohl travelled to Poland with a large delegation. In East Berlin the Central Committee of the SED and the Council of Ministers were working on a new law on foreign travel. Just before seven o'clock in the evening, Günter Schabowski pulled out his famous note, and, in answer to a journalist's questions, announced that new legislation allowing the right to travel freely would be implemented, "immediately, and without delay". Late that evening, under the onslaught of massed crowds of GDR citizens, the Wall was breached. At first, the border guards at Bornholmer Straße allowed just a few people to cross, invalidating their identification papers as they did so. Finally, at 11.30 they were forced to give way. In the course of the night, people began to flood unchecked over the border there and at other crossing points into West Berlin and the Federal Republic. The human tide which swept across the border in the next hours and days was so enormous, and the pressure so irresistible, that the fall of the Wall, that symbol of separation and division, became inevitable. The jubilation was indescribable, with people embracing each other, delirious with joy. Berlin was one enormous party. As far as their Trabis could take them, East Germans set out to explore the West. In the first two weeks alone, most of the population made a trip to West Berlin or the Federal Republic.

The SED had no desire to see the Wall come down: shaken and undermined by the mounting pressure, however, the regime imploded and collapsed. But politicians and governments in Bonn, Moscow, and the Western world were also caught unawares by the Wall coming down. The Bundestag in Bonn interrupted its sitting at 8.20 in the evening and, after a short pause, the spokespersons for the parliamentary parties, with Hans-Jochen Vogel on behalf of the SPD, gave their response to the more liberal travel regulations. Finally, a few of the Union deputies began singing the national anthem, and, apart from some of the Greens, were joined by the members of the other parties, the FDP and the Social Demo-

---

19 Statistical table in Konrad Jarausch, Die unverhoffte Einheit 1989–1990 (Frankfurt/Main 1995), p. 77.

crats.[20] This unusual scene was characteristic of the political stance of the West German parties in the coming process of unification. Chancellor Kohl and the Union set the tone and direction, while the Social Democrats (in the West) were always struggling to keep up with the rapid development of events.

Chancellor Kohl interrupted his visit to Poland to attend, first, the great demonstration in front of the Schöneberg town hall, and then a separate one organised by the CDU. Kohl was greeted with catcalls, and his speech constantly disrupted, by a crowd in front of the town hall consisting mainly of SPD and Green/Alternative supporters. Foreign Minister Hans-Dietrich Genscher and the Governing Mayor Walter Momper also spoke. But the man of the hour was Willy Brandt. He received the loudest applause, and hit exactly the right note at this moment with his speech about Germans coming together in freedom, and the growing together of Europe. His phrase "What belongs together, now grows together" would become legendary.[21] It was used for an SPD poster, together with a picture of a benign, happy Willy Brandt against a bright, blue sky.

In these days and weeks, Willy Brandt, the patriot, opened up his heart to events, demonstrating an unerring instinct for the right words. For a man who had been Governing Mayor of Berlin at the time of the building of the Wall, and Chancellor responsible for the new *Ostpolitik*, the fall of the Wall and the coming together of the Germans meant the realisation of a dream, and he was now dreaming, somewhat less realistically, of the dawn of a new Social Democratic age. Others in the SPD leadership also felt that a move in the direction of unification was called for. Johannes Rau, who already in September in the presidium had ventured the prognosis that "the issue of reunification [was] ripe for fresh evaluation"[22], summarised the impressions he was getting from the GDR to the effect that: "Amongst people in the street, reunification euphoria is rampant."[23] The chairman of the party and the parliamentary group, Hans-Jochen Vogel, saw quite clearly that German unification was firmly on the agenda, and was counting on a closer, step-by-step interlocking and confederation of the two states. But other leading colleagues in the party, such as the

---

20 See Winkler, Weg nach Westen, vol. II, p. 511 f.; Verhandlungen des Deutschen Bundestages (stenographic report), vol. 151, pp. 13221–13223.
21 This version did not occur in Brandt's speech in Schöneberg, but he used it several times on the same day at other rallies, at the Brandenburg Gate for instance, and in interviews with journalists.
22 In the minutes of the session of the SPD presidium on 11.9.1989. In the SPD-Vorstandsarchiv, now the Archiv der sozialen Demokratie.
23 The session of the SPD presidium on 13.11.1989. Source as in previous note.

SPD poster 1989. The text reads:
"What belongs together, now grows together" (Willy Brandt, 10.11.1989)

new rising star Björn Engholm and Gerhard Schröder, reacted somewhat hesitantly, and Egon Bahr could not be distracted from the primacy of security structures, stability, and European peace. Despite Willy Brandt, the change of heart about the SDP, and agreeing to Kohl's plan for a confederation, the West German SPD as a whole was not really up with the times.

The SDP consisted of no more than a small handful of Social Democrats when the Wall came down. Contacts had to be made, new members signed up, and organisational structures put in place. Despite the virtual non-existence of their own infrastructure, membership rose rapidly, and is said to have reached between ten and fifteen thousand by the end of 1989.[24] Compared, however, to the 1.4 of the formerly 2.3 million party members who belonged to the re-christened "SED/PDS"[25], and the several hundred thousand in the old bloc parties now in the process of change, the membership base was, and remained, weak. Alongside this building of the party, in which they were being helped by the SPD in the

---

24 See Jäger, Die Überwindung der Teilung, p. 260.
25 This extension of the name took place at the party congress on 16./17.12.1989. From 1990 on it was known simply as the PDS (Party of Democratic Socialism).

West, the work at the so-called "Round Tables" played a very important role. Of main concern was how to control the old forces still in place, the implementation of counter-structures, and preparing the way for the democratic reorganisation of future elections. In contrast to most other civil-rights groups, who were based on grassroots democracy, the SDP were aiming unambiguously for parliamentary democracy, but there was overwhelming agreement amongst them on the concept of a "Third Way", and of a civil society in the GDR living in peace and democracy. It was above all the mass demonstrations which brought about a change in the revolution. Instead of "We are the people!", there was the increasingly vociferous call of "Germany, united fatherland", taken from Johannes R. Becher's GDR national anthem, and then thereafter the chanting of "We are one people!". The SDP could not, and would not, resist being drawn along by this, and at the beginning of December its executive committee expressed its commitment to the "unity of the German nation", declaring itself in favour of a confederative "treaty community".[26]

2. Social Democracy and German Unification

It was Hans-Jochen Vogel, the first speaker in the Bundestag debate of 28 November 1989, who raised the question of creating a "German confederation". This was lost, virtually without trace, when Chancellor Helmut Kohl afterwards announced his "ten-point programme" in which he spoke in favour of free elections, breaking the SED's monopoly on power, and of "confederative structures with the eventual goal of a federation of the two Germanies".[27] The majority of the SPD parliamentary group gave their assent, the West German media welcomed overwhelmingly the suggestion that this could bring unification closer. It was only when loud criticism was voiced from abroad that many began to find fault with Kohl's policy of going it alone.

"Only the left are rocking the boat" was the verdict of the American historian Konrad Jarausch.[28] It was certainly not Willy Brandt or the SPD chairman Vogel whom he had in mind, more left-wing intellectuals such as Günter Grass, the Greens, and certain sections of the West German SPD. A particularly inflammatory contribution came from Oskar Lafontaine, who inveighed against Germanic jingoism and, at the end of November,

26 Jäger, Die Überwindung der Teilung, p. 261; Potthoff, Im Schatten der Mauer, p. 313.
27 Complete text in, inter alia, Verhandlungen des deutschen Bundestages (stenographic report), vol. 151, pp. 13502ff.
28 Jarausch, Die unverhoffte Einheit, p. 110.

demanded that GDR citizens resettling in the Federal Republic should be halted by no longer treating them simply as German citizens as laid down in the Basic Law.[29] Lafontaine was the protagonist of the so-called grandsons' generation who were Western, post-national, and internationalist in orientation, who inwardly found it hard to relate to the idea of a German nation state, and who were looking to drive Kohl into a corner at the next federal elections on ecological and social issues. And these were the Social Democrats who were principally responsible at that time for the SPD's public image.

At their programme congress in Berlin from 18 to 20 December, and in a context in which Germany was being radically changed by the peaceful revolution and the inexorable push towards unification, the party resembled dancers doing the splits on a slippery floor. Markus Meckel, who brought greetings from the SDP along with their backing for "German and European unification", was given a warm welcome. Willy Brandt's speech, which focused entirely on German nationhood and imminent unification, was met with wild applause. Oskar Lafontaine's great hour came the following day, on 19 December. The purpose of his speech was supposedly to explain the Berlin Programme. He used it, however, to distance himself from the patriotic attestations of honorary chairman Brandt and the nation state, and to give his backing to the internationalism of "liberal social democracy".[30]

The applause was so long and loud that it seemed to signal his selection as the party's next Chancellor candidate. Even though the party congress, in the Berlin Declaration, which had been formulated beforehand by the executive, professed its belief in a united Germany as the goal of the unification process, it contained no message which demonstrated that the Social Democrats were adopting a positive stance on unification. The cornerstones for it were provided the same day by Helmut Kohl on his visit to Dresden. Amidst a sea of black, red, and gold flags virtually every utterance of the Chancellor on peaceful revolution and solidarity, freedom and "the unity of our nation", was greeted with jubilation and frenetic applause. There were chants of "Helmut, Helmut", "Germany, Germany", and "We are one people". With these images of unification euphoria, transmitted by television throughout Germany and beyond, the dif-

---

29 Interview in the Süddeutsche Zeitung of 25.11.1989; see also Vogel, Nachsichten, pp. 306 ff.; Winkler, Weg nach Westen II, p. 527 f.
30 Protokoll vom Programm-Parteitag Berlin. 18.–20.12.1989 (Bonn 1990), p. 93 f. (Meckel), pp. 127–130 (Brandt), pp. 151–153 (Grass), pp. 246–254 (Lafontaine), and pp. 539–545 (Berlin Declaration "Die Deutschen in Europa" ("The Germans in Europe")). See too Vogel, Nachsichten, pp. 316–318.

fuse and growing hopes of unification became inextricably linked with the person of Helmut Kohl.

As became abundantly clear at the Berlin party congress, the SPD was in a quandary. The various irreconcilable positions prevented the development of any coherent, forward-looking strategy. The main contentious issues were glossed over by formulaic compromises of the "not only, but also" variety, and various different brands of social democracy emerged into the open, spreading confusion, and ultimately paralysing the party. Johannes Rau's urgent warning that "If the SPD misses the unification boat, it will also for many a long year be missing the chance of winning elections and of once again exercising governmental power"[31], proved to be an accurate prognosis.

In January 1990, the people of the GDR were presented with the *de facto* bankruptcy of their state and the threat of a complete collapse in public order. In this difficult situation, the SDP and the other opposition groups went along with the gamble on a "government of national responsibility" under the continuing office of Hans Modrow. This proved, however, unable to get to grips with either the economic or the political crisis. The population at large now had virtually no ear for the calls of the civil-rights movement for real democracy, civil society, and the "Third Way". Instead of this, there were increasingly vocal calls for free elections, the social market economy, and German unification as a haven of hope. The mood of Germans in both East and West pointed increasingly towards German unification. According to polls conducted in February 1990, the demonstrators in Leipzig were almost unanimous in their support for it. Two-thirds of people in the GDR as a whole were in favour.[32] At the same time in the Federal Republic, three-quarters of those questioned supported German unification, even though many of them were worried about the speed of it. Even abroad there was great sympathy for German unity, most noticeably in Italy (78 per cent), 70 per cent were for it in Spain, France, and Hungary, 60 per cent in Great Britain and the USA, and even in the Soviet Union there was a small majority of 51 per cent in favour. Only in Poland was there a clear majority (64 per cent) against unification. The people in most of these countries were invariably ahead of the politicians there, let alone of the intellectuals, whose reaction ranged from scepticism to downright rejection.

At the beginning of 1990, the view was emerging in Moscow that German unification was now virtually unstoppable, and that Soviet policy

31 From the minutes of the sitting of the SPD presidium on 27.11.1989. In the SPD-Vorstandsarchiv, now the Archiv der sozialen Demokratie.
32 See Jarausch, Unverhoffte Einheit, p. 366, note 48.

must adapt accordingly. The beginnings of a breakthrough occurred with the visit at the end of January of GDR Minister President Hans Modrow, of the U.S. Secretary of State for Foreign Affairs James Baker on 8/9 February, and finally of Helmut Kohl on 10/11 February. Two days later in Ottowa, the Two Plus Four discussions (Federal Republic and GDR, USA, Soviet Union, Great Britain, and France) ended in agreement. Chancellor Kohl was determined to speed up the process of unification. With the surprising offer on 6 February of a currency union, and the "Alliance for Germany" formed the previous day, Kohl, the power politician, rapidly moved things on, having now created a platform for the implementation of his political strategies. Offering the Deutschmark as an incentive, and with the promise of "blossoming landscapes" in the East at zero cost to the West, he was determined to push ahead with unification, and thereby win over voters in East and West for both himself and his party.

On 18 March 1990, at the first free elections to the *Volkskammer*, the new People's Chamber, the citizens of the GDR gave a decisive pointer as to the future. The outcome seemed uncertain, but most prognoses seemed to indicate a probable victory for the young Social Democrats. Since their delegates' conference in the middle of January 1990, they had adopted the official title of SPD, had finally dismissed the idea of an independent GDR, and now gave their full backing to German unification. At their first full party congress in Leipzig (22–25 February 1990) the 524 delegates approved a Basic Programme. The Leipzig Programme was notable for the clarity of its language, its sensitivity towards the past, succinct formulations, stringent organisation, and its lucid, comprehensible message. It proclaimed a self-confident commitment to the independence of the new party whose roots were in the "human-rights, peace, and ecology movement", while at the same time locating itself "quite consciously in the time-honoured tradition of German and international social democracy". It saw the SPD "as a broad, democratic party of the people" and formulated its immediate goal as the desire "to live together in the GDR, and soon in a unified Germany, in freedom, security, and equality".[33] Along with the Basic Programme, the congress approved a party statute, as well as an election manifesto. Ibrahim Böhme, whose rhetorical talents, and especially his media appearances, had brought him great popularity, was elected party chairman and leading candidate for the People's Chamber elections. The delegates appointed as his deputies, Markus Meckel – who had earlier also expressed interest in the chairmanship – along with Angelika Barbe

---

33 Full text, inter alia, in Dowe and Klotzbach (eds) Programmatische Dokumente der deutschen Sozialdemokratie (Bonn 2004), pp. 422–464.

and Karl-August Kamilli. Stephan Hilsberg became business manager, and Willy Brandt honorary chairman.

Up until shortly before the People's Chamber elections, Ibrahim Böhme was thought to be a certain winner and the future Minister President. He was officially received as such in Moscow. But on the evening of 18 March 1990 the Social Democrats in the GDR, and their big sister in the West, suffered a bitter disappointment. The SPD received a mere 21.8 per cent of the vote, while the "Alliance for Germany", supported by Kohl, along with the re-formed East CDU, was the big winner with 48.1 per cent. The reasons for the SPD's poor showing were not only organisational weaknesses and problems of communication, inadequate electoral experience and resources, but also the growing strength of the Kohl camp, and the stance of the Social Democrats in the West on the approaching process of unification. The Chancellor and his allies in the GDR had immeasurably greater power and organisational resources at their disposal. Moreover, Kohl knew how to focus people's hopes for a change for the better on himself, and to imply that there would be rapid agreement on article 23 of the Basic Law, in other words on joining the Federal Republic. The power politician Kohl had no scruples about taking on board the old, tainted CDU bloc party, and insinuating that the undoubtedly democratic and untainted young SPD was close to Communism and the SED. The height of this campaign of defamation was a poster bearing the letters "PDSPD".[34] This unsettled not only potential voters, but even the young SPD itself, and to the extent that they called to a complete halt the already very restricted admission of former SED members to the party.

The fact that their strategy on the overriding issue of unification was neither clear nor purposeful had further negative consequences for the SPD. The SPD in the East voted to join the Federal Republic by way of article 23, the speedier way, while the SPD executive in the West was divided, although a majority were in favour of proceeding via article 146, after more thorough dialogue and a more gradual process of merging together. To the outside world, the chorus of Social Democrats in the West was singing a tune which went from multi-voiced to dissonant. In January, the financial expert Ingrid Matthäus-Maier, assisted by the parliamentary group's spokesman on economics Wolfgang Roth, was the first to venture the suggestion of a currency union. Objections came from Oskar Lafontaine who, after his great electoral victory in the Saarland when, on 28 January, he registered a record 54.4 per cent, was now proclaimed officially as the SPD's designated Chancellor candidate. His plea against an early

---

34 See, inter alia, Vogel, Nachsichten, p. 321 f.

currency union, and in favour of taking unification at a "more conservative pace" was, in view of the prevailing mood and the high level of expectation, a "catastrophe for the SPD in the East as well as in the West".[35] After lengthy negotiations, the new, democratically legitimated GDR government under Lothar de Maizière came into being. Along with the parties of the "Alliance for Germany" and the Liberals, it also contained representatives of the SPD. Markus Meckel, who, along with Richard Schröder, was one of the strongest advocates of participating in the government, became Foreign Minister. In the process of unification, and particularly in the Two Plus Four negotiations, he represented the interests of the GDR, now truly democratic, in a tough and emphatic manner. Ibrahim Böhme, for a few months the star of the SPD in the East, had resigned at the beginning of April as chairman of the party and the parliamentary group. It was revealed at the end of March that he had been working for many years for the *Stasi*. The charges proved well-founded. His task had been to subvert the opposition and the young SDP/SPD. This was a bitter blow for all concerned, but it was testament to the inner strength of this young party that they were able to take even this in their stride. He was replaced by Markus Meckel as acting chairman, and Richard Schröder was made chairman of the parliamentary group.

The mere fact that the Social Democrats in the GDR were now in government, while those in the West were in opposition to the Kohl government, gave the appearance of an awkward split. Matters were made worse by diverging views on the manner in which unification should be achieved and by the tragic attempt on the life of Oskar Lafontaine. On 25 April he was stabbed by a mentally disturbed woman at a rally in Cologne, and left seriously wounded. His life was only saved by a swift emergency operation. The shock lingered on, and, during Lafontaine's enforced period of convalescence, relations between the Chancellor candidate and sections of the parliamentary group and the party grew increasingly fraught. Neither telephone calls nor pilgrimages to Saarbrücken were of any avail. With the SPD becoming the strongest party, and Gerhard Schröder the new Minister President, following the Landtag elections in Lower Saxony, the Social Democrats had a majority in the Bundesrat for the first time since 1949. Since the economic and currency union needed the approval of the Upper House, Kohl could no longer carry out his declared aim of

---

35 See Dieter Grosser, Das Wagnis der Währungs-, Wirtschafts- und Sozialunion. Politische Konflikte im Kampf mit ökonomischen Regeln (Stuttgart 1998), p. 190f.; by the same author, 'Zeit der Führung, Konsens und Konflikt 1989/90', in Peter März (ed.), 40 Jahre Zweistaatlichkeit in Deutschland. Eine Bilanz (Munich 1999), p. 309.

implementing it without the SPD. This meant that the SPD now had to show where they really stood.

Lafontaine's slippery tactics, whereby the SPD was to vote no in the Bundestag, with the SPD-governed states following suit in the Bundesrat – with the exception of Hamburg which, by voting yes, would secure approval of the bill – descended into complete farce. The reaction amongst the general public, as well as in the SPD, was one of almost universal incomprehension and understandable irritation. After a series of crisis talks a difficult compromise was finally reached, which, although keeping the worst at bay, certainly did nothing to enhance the image of the SPD: Oskar Lafontaine would remain the party's Chancellor candidate, the SPD would, after certain amendments, approve the treaty on currency union, and Lafontaine, providing he was willing, become the new SPD party chairman at the forthcoming unification party congress. But when Horst Ehmke, with the backing of Gerhard Schröder, publicly set the ball rolling to replace Hans-Jochen Vogel as party chairman, Lafontaine backed out.[36] This was not the only time that the so self-confident Saarlander had put himself forward, only to get cold feet when push came to shove. The dismal bickering over the SPD chairman posts was the first of the various disputes over the leadership role. It was followed later by infighting amongst the "grandsons", in which none of them exactly covered themselves with glory.

Riven by internal squabbles and differing positions, the West German Social Democrats found themselves out in the cold in shaping the process of unification. Basically, all that remained for them was to attempt to make minor corrections, in which North Rhine-Westphalia with Johannes Rau and Wolfgang Clement played the most important part, and to simply accept the *faits accomplis* of the Kohl government. Apart from the Saarland and Lower Saxony, all the other SPD states voted on 22 June for the currency union, as did the vast majority of the parliamentary party in the Bundestag on 21 June. And when the unification treaty was ratified on 20 September, all the SPD deputies voted in favour. The effect of this, however, was quickly forgotten in the face of the impression of wavering, scepticism, and misgivings which had been created by Lafontaine. Instead of the joy expressed by Brandt and many others at German unification, and the welcoming of it as an imposing task which, with a huge effort, could be overcome, there remained in the public mind, and thereby clouding its opinion of the Social Democrats, virtually only those aspects of it to which objection, quite justifiably, had been taken.

---

36 See Vogel, Nachsichten, p. 336; Ehmke, Mittendrin, p. 429.

The SPD also drew hardly any benefit at all from the merger on 27 September, even before the two states were unified, of the two Social Democratic sister parties. The previous day, after the West and East SPD had formally approved this step at two separate party conferences, the delegates assembled in the symbolic setting of Berlin for their first joint party conference. Instead of electing a new executive committee, the old West committee was simply expanded to include ten members from the East.[37] In this case, as well as in the distribution of delegates, the large West SPD with almost 900,000 members was being accommodating towards its little sister party in the East with its not quite 30,000 members. Wolfgang Thierse, who at a special party conference on 9 June in Halle had been elected as the new party chairman of the East SPD, now became deputy chairman of the whole party. An impressive speaker with a capacity for reflection, and an ability to communicate in a balanced, considered, and yet lucid fashion, Thierse won great respect not only in the East, but also established himself as a leading presence in the SPD as a whole, as well as with the German public.

Both joy and pride were the dominant emotions at this party conference, with notable speeches from Willy Brandt, Hans-Jochen Vogel, Wolfgang Thierse, and Oskar Lafontaine. In an impressive "Manifesto on the Restoration of the Unity of the Social Democratic Party of Germany", the SPD evoked its history as the party of democratic freedom. "From today, the SPD is once again what it had sought to be since its foundation over much more than a century ago. The party of social democracy for the whole of Germany."[38] But the euphoria at being united again led to the goals being set far too high. "Oskar Lafontaine will be Federal Chancellor" was the motion passed by 470 votes to 12 after the Chancellor candidate's speech, and the manifesto contained the even more ambitious statement: "The German Social Democratic Party lays claim, as the determining democratic force, to the leadership of Germany in the 1990s." Neither of these ambitions would be fulfilled. Lafontaine did not become Chancellor, and it would take until 1998 for the electors to become so tired of Kohl that they got rid of him, thereby opening the door of the Chancellor's office to Gerhard Schröder.

The SPD, who before the peaceful revolution had thought they were on an upsurge, fell increasingly behind in the course of the unification process. Helmut Kohl, whose position as Chancellor and party chairman had seemed exceedingly shaky in 1989, rose, by taking advantage of the

---

37 See the minutes of the SPD party conference (East), SPD (West) in Berlin 26.9.1990; minutes of the party conference in Berlin 27.–28.9.1990.
38 Jahrbuch 1988–1990 SPD (Bonn, no date), p. 181 f.

Hans-Jochen Vogel, Willy Brandt, Wolfgang Thierse, Oskar Lafontaine with the "Manifesto on the Restoration of the Unity" of the SPD on 27 September 1990

moment, and through instinctive touch and great political skill, to become the Chancellor of unification, and seemed to be unassailable. On 2 October at 00.00 reunification became a reality. It was welcomed ceremonially with the ringing of the freedom bell, the hoisting of an enormous black, red, and gold flag in front of the Reichstag building, and a colourful firework display. Half a million people thronged the streets in Berlin. Millions watched the historical events on television. A certain pathos was unavoidable in the official ceremonies. All in all, however, these ceremonies were conducted in a dignified and democratic fashion. The hundreds of thousands on the streets celebrating the day they had been reunited did so with an exuberance free of nationalistic overtones. By making 3

Ceremony at the Reichstag marking German Unification, 3 October 1990

October 1990 a new national holiday, Kohl, the Chancellor of unification, was deliberately marking it out as a day to be celebrated, aiming to build the unification of Germany into a myth with which he would be forever linked. It has been solemnly celebrated every year since. But as an historical and epoch-making event, it is the fall of the Wall on 9 November 1989 which has most impressed itself on people's consciousnesses. These were the emotional hours in which citizens from the GDR paved the way for freedom, when the bell tolled unexpectedly for German unity, and on which states and statesmen then formally set their seal on 3 October 1990.

III. The Search for Direction in Unified Germany

1. Elections, Fluctuating Events, and Change

In the first all-German elections on 2 December 1990, the SPD suffered a heavy defeat. Although the CDU/CSU dropped 0.5 percentage points as compared to the previous Bundestag elections, they remained by far the strongest grouping with 43.8 per cent. Helmut Kohl was able to continue in government with the FDP, who had climbed from 9.1 to 11.0 per cent, and, since the Greens had failed to surmount the 5 per cent threshold in West Germany, had a comfortable majority at his disposal. The election result represented a severe setback for the prospect of a red-green reform project, since not only were the Greens stopped in their tracks, the SPD suffered too, even though in the new Eastern states the Social Democrat vote had risen by almost three per cent compared to the *Volkskammer* elections. This was also a result of the disappointment which had set in in the East following the initial flush of unification euphoria. In the West, the SPD had lost by a decisive margin. Admittedly, the party had made clear gains in the Saarland, where Chancellor candidate Oskar Lafontaine was on home territory. But in all the other federal states, as well as in Berlin, the SPD had come off even worse than in the previous Bundestag elections. With a mere 35.7 per cent in the old Federal Republic, and 33.5 in unified Germany as a whole, they had slumped in popularity to the level of the 1950s. Lafontaine's strategy of courting the voters with ecological and social issues, of presenting himself as a Western internationalist, and expressing misgivings about the way in which unification had come about, had been unsuccessful. Helmut Schmidt was certainly a little over the top, and not entirely free of old animosities, when he had been driven to comment in an interview: "Lafontaine will lose the election, and deserves to do so."[1] He was not the only Social Democrat who thought like this. In these first all-German elections, it was no wonder that many potential SPD supporters declined to give their vote to someone who was clearly not in favour of unification.

The SPD had every reason to rethink their previous strategy. The process of unification made it very clear that their policy at the time had

---

1 See Vogel, Nachsichten, p. 361. For Lafontaine's harsh criticism of Schmidt see p. 255 above, note 17 in particular.

331

left them as mere spectators. As in the 1950s, when, with their resistance to Western integration, they had found themselves swimming against the political tide, they were once again failing to read the signs of the times, something which Kohl, the instinctive power politician, could do all too well. On the day following the election defeat, the honorary chairman Willy Brandt observed that the impression had arisen "that unity and freedom were being regarded as more of a burden than an opportunity". This was aimed at Lafontaine. Brandt was supported in his criticism by, amongst others, Erhard Eppler, Klaus von Dohnanyi, Hans Koschnick, and Wolfgang Thierse.[2] In the other camp were the post-national Social Democrats of the "grandsons'" generation who had difficulty in coming to terms with the idea of the German nation. This conflict had split and paralysed the party during the period of upheaval and unification. On the absolutely crucial point of reunification they resembled a party with two faces. For their future as a *Volkspartei* in a united Germany, it was vital that they position themselves in relation to the free and democratic nation state of the new Germany and its role in Europe and the world in such a way as to be capable of, and prepared for, the responsibility of office.

A generational shift in the leadership was in the offing. But this was bedevilled by the fact that the 1968ers coming to the fore were dominated by the post-nationals who felt at ease with the limited sovereignty of the old Federal Republic, and harboured misgivings about the taking on of international responsibility by the new German nation state. It was predictable, therefore, that a long and arduous learning process would have to be gone through before the SPD could once again present itself to the people as a party capable of governing, and which could be entrusted with steering unified Germany through the choppy waters of the challenges of globalisation and international conflict. The difficulty was that Lafontaine was the only heir apparent envisaged for the party chairmanship. The stubborn and cocky Saarlander had not an iota of insight into his own shortcomings, was constantly lamenting the lack of solidarity, and was sensitive to any suggestion of criticism. The presidium, consistently supported by the executive, was unanimous in offering him the party chairmanship and, if he had so wished, that of the parliamentary party too. He turned down both of them. And so, on 5 December 1990, Hans-Jochen Vogel was once again elected chairman of the parliamentary party. The search began for a new party chairman. Johannes Rau was not willing

---

[2] From the minutes of the meeting of the executive on 3.12.1990, in Archiv der sozialen Demokratie; cf. also Winkler, Weg nach Westen II, p. 603f. For a view on the estrangement from Brandt from Lafontaine's own perspective, see Oskar Lafontaine, Das Herz schlägt links (Munich 1999), p. 31f.

to stand. Expectations were therefore directed towards the Schleswig-Holstein Minister President Björn Engholm. He was sympathetic and engaging, was held in high esteem by the public, and, at 51, was representative, at least by German standards, of the younger generation of politicians. On 10 and 17 December respectively, the presidium and the party executive were unanimous in nominating him for the party chairmanship. Engholm was then finally elected to the post at the party congress in Bremen in May 1991. One crisis had been overcome, but the deep political differences in the SPD were by no means at an end.

After the depressing election results in the *Volkskammer* elections of March 1990, and the Bundestag elections in December of the same year, the party was urgently in need of a success. In the East they were, and remained, weak. In the first local elections on 6 May 1990, they even performed slightly worse than in the *Volkskammer* elections, winning a mere 21.3 per cent overall. The first Landtag elections in the new states on 14 October were also not very satisfactory. The CDU were victorious in Mecklenburg-Western Pomerania, Saxony-Anhalt, Thuringia, and Saxony (there with an overall majority), which meant that the SPD lost its majority in the Bundesrat. The situation was even more dismal in the Landtag elections in Bavaria, where the party slumped to 26 per cent. Only in Brandenburg with 38.2 per cent were the SPD the strongest party. This was principally due to Manfred Stolpe. The Consistory-President of the Protestant Church – held, along with Johannes Rau, in high regard by Helmut Schmidt – had, with his sovereign, personable manner, great electoral appeal. Together with the popular Regine Hildebrandt, he succeeded in establishing a feeling of identity between his fellow Brandenburgers and the SPD. The campaigns against him later did not succeed in damaging the great respect in which he was held as one of Brandenburg's patriarchal *Landesväter*. In the Landtag elections in 1994, he achieved a great personal success, with 54.1 per cent of the vote going to the SPD. Manfred Stolpe was now one of the team of Minister Presidents whose word would carry weight over the coming years.

Following the Landtag elections in Hessen on 20 January 1991, Hans Eichel also joined this group. The SPD finally saw a clear increase in their vote once again, outstripping the CDU with 43.6 per cent. With the new red-green government under Hans Eichel, and in partnership with Joschka Fischer, the balance of power in the Bundesrat had now changed. The SPD had another success on 21 April 1991 in the Rhineland-Palatinate, and replaced the CDU as the ruling party in the state from which Kohl originated, and where he had governed for so long. Rudolf Scharping, who for many years had wooed the people of this winegrowing region so patiently

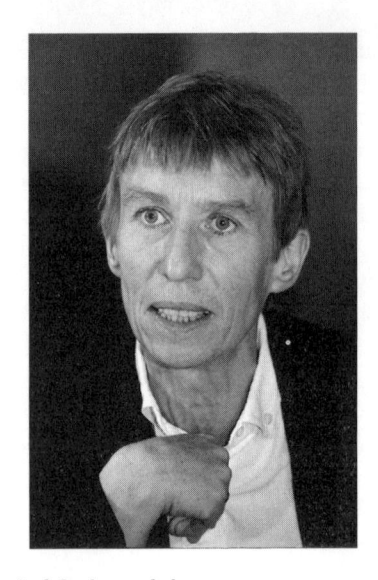

*"Elder statesman" Manfred Stolpe and the
"Mother Courage" of the East Regine Hildebrandt*

and purposefully, now became its new Minister President. He was soon to become one of the party's new hopefuls. In Hamburg, too, the SPD improved its vote on 6 June 1991, and achieved an overall majority. The successes in these states were, of course, in great measure due to the candidates and the effort put in by the local parties. They also mirrored, however, the loss of respect for the CDU at federal and state level, as well as a change in the political climate.

The USA and its allies launched a counter-attack against Saddam Hussein following his invasion of Kuwait in summer 1990. "Operation Desert Storm" began on 17 January 1991, at first with air strikes, and then on 24 February with ground operations. The Gulf War was not only a cause of great anxiety in the Federal Republic of Germany, it also mobilised pacifist voices. This undoubtedly influenced the elections in favour of red and green. Not only most of the Greens, but also prominent Social Democrats such as Oskar Lafontaine and Gerhard Schröder were resolutely opposed to the Gulf War. In making their case they made allusion, *inter alia*, to Nazi war crimes.[3] Given that Saddam Hussein had fired rockets at Israel this was somewhat embarrassing, and, in the context of the lessons to be learned from Germany's past, grossly wide of the mark. However, this

---

3 See, for instance, the article 'Oskar Lafontaine Verzweifelte Aussichten', in the taz of 9.2.1991.

brand of pacifism, and using Auschwitz to justify German isolationism and taking a separate path, met with clear opposition in the Social Democratic and left-wing camp.[4] Jürgen Habermas argued for a more differentiated approach: resistance to power-political arrogance "which endangers the civil coexistence of nations", but caution in the face of any manifestation of the old forcefulness and "belligerency".[5] With his cautioning against "warmongers", the intellectual guru of the West German left was availing himself of a fashionable label. The charge of allegedly supporting wars was wielded like a moral cudgel against politicians and publicists who did not pay homage to pacifist dogma. The contrasting, of which even the *Spiegel* was so fond, of "warmongers" and "pacifists", with its implicit moral and ethical dimension, was more of a hindrance than a help in the need for urgent political debate on these matters.

With the Gulf War, unified Germany was confronted for the first time with the possibility of participating in military measures for which it was prepared neither politically nor militarily. The Federal Republic and its government manoeuvred their way through with the offer of some assistance with US supplies, Bundeswehr troops in Turkey, and minesweepers in the Mediterranean, as well as some costly "chequebook diplomacy". There was also some sign of cautious movement from the SPD. In the run-up to the party conference in Bremen from 28 to 31 May 1991, the executive had, after tough discussions, approved a motion in which participation "in military engagements", even under UNO mandate, was rejected, but which for the first time allowed for so-called blue-helmet intervention for peace-keeping purposes. At the Bremen conference a majority of delegates voted in favour.[6] Gunter Hofmann entitled his article on the conference for *Die Zeit* "Out with the Old, but Nothing New"[7]. Although almost the whole of the Social Democrats' established foreign-policy elite, from Willy Brandt and Helmut Schmidt to Egon Bahr and Erhard Eppler, gave their backing to military intervention under UNO command, the majority of party activists were not prepared to do so.

The SPD continued to lag behind on foreign policy, something in which the party had led public opinion in the Federal Republic in the late 1960s and the 1970s. Foreign policy remained an unloved stepchild. It took the dramatic developments in the Balkans and the massacres at

---

4 On this, amongst others, Hans-Ulrich Klose, 'Die Deutschen und der Krieg am Golf – eine schwierige Debatte', Frankfurter Allgemeine Zeitung, 25.1.1991; Cora Stephan, 'Der anständige Deutsche – zum Fürchten', Süddeutsche Zeitung, 9./10.2.1991.
5 Winkler, Weg nach Westen II, p. 625f.
6 Protokoll vom Parteitag Bremen 28.–31. Mai 1991, pp. 558 and pp. 649–651.
7 Die Zeit, 7.6.1991.

Srebrenica in July 1995, in which some 7,000 people were murdered, to make them revise their thinking. Anyone who was opposed to dictatorships, and who took seriously their belief in human rights and international law, could hardly stand aside and watch as these were trampled under foot, and brutal atrocities were being committed. Even the Greens could no longer wash their hands in innocence. Joschka Fischer pointed the way forward with his demand that, in the case of genocide, the "obligation to intervene" must be at the "inalienable core of anti-fascism".[8] In 1995 the SPD, and even the Greens, voted in favour of sending medical orderlies to Bosnia, and the moving of Tornado fighter jets to Italy. German participation in the two UNO missions, IFOR and SFOR, to Bosnia-Herzegovina in 1995/96 was no longer a matter of debate for most SPD deputies. This policy continued with the Bundestag resolution in October 1998 approving participation in a possible air war against the rump of Yugoslavia. But only when the party was in government once again, and with an SPD Chancellor, did they pin their colours unambiguously to the mast. They accepted that increased sovereignty brought with it increased obligations, and these also included a commitment to military action.

Under Björn Engholm, who was elected as the new party chairman by the Bremen conference, there also emerged a change of course in other areas. In summer 1992, Engholm, who had always been considered a liberal, took many by surprise by introducing a change in asylum policy. At first sight it seemed like an authoritarian move from above, pushed through in the face of vociferous opposition from many officials, delegates, and other party activists.[9] In fact, however, the party leadership was reacting to Social Democrat politicians at local level, and to a widespread mood in the SPD heartland. The grassroots often evoked by many activists, and which these activists saw themselves as constituting, were not actually the real grassroots: these were in fact the party members themselves. In a poll in the *Unterbezirk* (sub-region) of Rhein-Sieg which caused a great stir, over three-quarters of those questioned opted in favour of a change to the law on asylum and of Bundeswehr involvement under the aegis of the UN. In contrast to many party officials, the membership backed what they saw as a politically necessary change of course.[10] This was because, after al-

8 See Der Spiegel, 12.11.2001, p. 38.
9 See Franz Walter, 'Die SPD nach der deutschen Vereinigung – Partei in der Krise oder bereit zur Regierungsübernahme'. In Zeitschrift für Parlamentsfragen, 1 (1995), p. 87, and the newspaper articles mentioned there in note 4.
10 In the last week of October 1992, the SPD in the sub-region of Rhein-Sieg held a poll of its members after the party conference in the region of Mittelrhein on 10.10.1992 had rejected the resolutions on asylum and Bundeswehr involvement. It resulted in

Björn Engholm at the Party Congress in Bremen, 28–31 May 1991

ready losing voters to the Greens, the SPD was now being threatened at the beginning of the 1990s with a slump in its traditional support. These voters were, out of protest, defecting in droves to the right-wing Republicans. Every fourth Republican voter came from the Social Democrat camp, roughly 40 per cent of them were workers, and, which was particularly alarming, members of trade unions were more susceptible to the Republicans than those who were not.[11]

In the Landtag elections in 1994, the SPD were only able to gain ground in the new states, with the exception of Saxony under "King Kurt"[12],

---

77.1 per cent of party members who were questioned voting for Engholm's suggestion on asylum, refugee, and immigration policy, and 75.3 per cent voting in favour of the executive's blue helmet (UNO) concept. Documentation with the results of the votes and newspaper reports in the sub-regional archive. The author thanks the sub-regional manager Achim Tüttenberg for the material.

11 For information on the relevant material and analyses of Matthias Jung and Dieter Roth of the research group "Wahlen", and the results of the Allensbach Research Institute, see, inter alia, Süddeutsche Zeitung, 1.10.1991, Frankfurter Allgemeine Zeitung, 18.3.1993, and Die Zeit, 24.9.1993.
12 A widespread term for the respected Minister President Kurt Biedenkopf and his style of government.

where they fell even further behind. In Thuringia and Mecklenburg-Western Pomerania their vote went up to almost 30 per cent, in Saxony-Anhalt they almost drew level with the CDU with 34 per cent, and in Brandenburg Manfred Stolpe won an outstanding victory with 54.1 per cent.[13] In the West, however, the SPD's future electoral chances did not look rosy. What they had to offer new social groups emerging yielded barely any fruit at all. Particularly in university towns and service industry centres, the party continued to lose ground, and the Greens to make gains. As a rule, the attempt to govern in coalition with the Greens, and to thereby bring them on board, did not pay off. Red-green municipal governments had their wings clipped as painfully by the voters as had the red-green experiment at state level in Hesse.[14] Only in Lower Saxony, where Minister President Gerhard Schröder allowed the Greens little room for manoeuvre, were the SPD able to make their presence felt.[15] On the other hand, a determined strategy of modernisation such as the SPD was pursuing in the south-west under Dieter Spöri also failed to bring the hoped-for success with the voters. Despite getting good marks from the public for their performance as junior partner in coalition with the CDU in Baden-Württemberg, the SPD share of the vote in this region nevertheless continued to decline throughout the 1990s. It seemed that the overtures being made towards the upwardly mobile were not having the desired effect, not least because the transition from the pietistic Erhard Eppler to the trendy yuppie Dieter Spöri had been far too abrupt, and, in the short term, lacked conviction. The dilemma grew even worse when, in the 1990s, workers began to turn their backs on the SPD and either defected to the Republicans, or stayed at home out of protest or lack of interest. The situation was at its most bleak amongst the young, who had made a decisive contribution to the SPD's electoral successes of the late 1960s and early 1970s. Young voters up to, and including, those in their mid-thirties tended overwhelmingly to vote Green. The SPD came a very poor second, with this trend on the increase.[16] It has been generally overlooked that dynamic, success-oriented young people were at the same time turning towards the Union or the FDP. Amongst the internet generation – gripped

13 The exact percentages for the SPD in these elections between June and October 1994 were: Brandenburg 54.1, Mecklenburg-Western Pomerania 29.5, Saxony 16.6, Saxony-Anhalt 34.0 per cent.
14 After achieving 43.6 per cent in 1991, they fell to 38.0 in the Landtag elections of 19.2.1995.
15 See Walter, Die SPD nach der deutschen Vereinigung, p. 93. In the Landtag elections on 13.4.1994, the SPD went up slightly to 44.3 per cent (44.2 in 1990). The Greens, too, increased their vote from 5.5 to 7.4 per cent.
16 Ibid., p. 92f.

in the second half of the 1990s by stock-market and enterprise fever – the FDP, under their energetic party manager Guido Westerwelle, became an increasingly attractive proposition. For the FDP, who had been virtually written off, a climate was developing which was opening up new political opportunities.

2. The Internal Problems of a Fragmented Party

The SPD's problems with the electorate were also mirrored, in a different way, in party membership. In the 1990s its numbers continued to shrink at an accelerating rate. From 919,129 in the year of German unification, they had slumped to 734,657 by 2000. The number of women members also sank in this period from 250,906 to 215,633, although the proportion of women overall rose slightly from 27.30 to 29.35 per cent, due to the fact that the drop in the number of male members, from 668,223 to 519,034, with their lower life expectancy, was considerably greater. The SPD in the new states was, and remained, organisationally extremely weak: on 31 December 2000 they numbered just 3,462 members in Mecklenburg-Western Pomerania, 5,870 in Saxony-Anhalt, 7,518 in Brandenburg, 5,694 in Thuringia, and 5,198 in Saxony – a mere 27,742 in all. In other words, roughly the same as at the beginning of the 1990s. This made it difficult, at all political levels, to find candidates willing to stand for office. In view of this paucity of personnel it is astonishing, and a matter of great credit, how much the Social Democrats managed to achieve, politically, in the new states.

In comparison to the growing academicisation of the SPD in earlier years, far fewer academics were now attracted to a party which had spent so long festering on the opposition benches, others turned their backs on it, or withdrew from party activity altogether. A consequence of this was a lessening of the emphasis on theory and a move towards more practical politics. The SPD was now a little closer to its traditional roots, even though the party continued to be dominated by people in the public services. Of the SPD membership on 31 December 2000, white-collar workers were the largest group with 27.64 per cent, with civil servants making up 10.32 per cent – 37.96 overall. Workers made up 21.05, pensioners 11.71, housewives 10.76, and the unemployed 2.08 per cent. Pupils and students who had figured for the first time in 1972 with 15.9 per cent, now accounted for only 7.22 per cent. This was an illustration of how unattractive the party had become for young people. The rapid drop in younger members which had begun in the 1980s now continued unchecked in the 1990s. After 30.9 per cent of members being of *Juso* age in 1974, and 18.62 in the year of the peaceful revolution, the quota had slumped by the end of 2000 to just 8.99 per cent. A mere 2.41 per cent were under twenty-five.[17] If this trend cannot be halted and younger members not be persuaded to do political work for the party, the SPD threatens to become a gerontocratic organisation, doomed to virtually die out as a vibrant membership party. Whether, however, projects such as the "network party", or tightening up the organisation as in North Rhine-Westphalia can have a mobilising effect remains doubtful. Stronger control and centralisation may perhaps produce more efficiency, but it also inhibits people's willingness to engage at grassroots level. Even in the age of media democracy and the internet, a party's strength lies with those people who are prepared to show some commitment.

A party which wishes to govern, of course, needs leadership and has to set a clear and comprehensible course with an expert hand on the tiller. The problems of finding the right destination, and steering single-mindedly towards it, however, resulted from the fact that the position of the Social Democratic flotilla was difficult to determine. The SPD of the 1990s was a decidedly federalist party, in which self-confident state governors embodied the real centres of power.[18] There was, furthermore, the plethora of working groups operating fairly independently at all levels of the party, from the local association, to the sub-region and region, and right up to the federal level. This made it difficult to pinpoint where a sense of the party as a whole was located at any one time. The political analysts, Peter Lösche and Franz Walter, used the term "loosely linked anarchy" to describe this, which was certainly a little exaggerated, but nevertheless contained a grain of truth.[19]

The *ASF* (Working Group of Social Democratic Women) had firmly established themselves alongside the numerically dwindling *Jusos*, and, in the haggling in the party over posts, they had enjoyed, and for the most part successfully, working together. The former long-term *ASF* chairperson, Inge Wettig-Danielmeier, who was succeeded in this office in 1992 by Karin Junker, became Federal Treasurer. This function enabled her to achieve an important political and personal position of power within the

---

17 The author was provided with these figures by the political archive of the SPD executive. On 31.12.2001 the quota of members of Juso age was 9 per cent. The total party membership had declined further to 717, 513.
18 See Gerhard Schröder's comment: "The SPD's centre of power is not in Bonn, but in the states." Presidium session of 28.8.1995, minutes in Archiv der sozialen Demokratie. See also, Walter, Die SPD, p. 227.
19 Lösche and Walter, Die SPD, p. 77 in the chapter heading, and again as section heading on p. 192.

Heide Simonis, Minister President of Schleswig-Holstein

SPD leadership apparatus. The internal success story of the *ASF*, however, was of barely any help, even among women, in making the party more attractive to the outside world. Self-assured, younger, dynamic women tended to make their careers elsewhere – in the media, for instance, with the Greens, or, as in the case of Angela Merkel, even in the CDU – while rejecting the self-focused *ASF* with its paradigms from the 1960s. Female politicians with specialist expertise were also able to make their mark without the ASF: women such as Heide Simonis, who in 1993 became Minister President in Schleswig-Holstein, the only woman in Germany to occupy this office, Jutta Limbach, who in 1994 became the first President of the Federal Constitutional Court, or Ingrid Matthäus-Maier. In opposing her candidacy in the constituency of Rhein-Sieg II in favour of their own somewhat colourless candidate, the *ASF* rather shot itself in the foot. It did the party no credit that Ingrid Matthäus-Maier was later consigned to the political wilderness.

The Working Group for Employees' Issues (*AfA*), set up in 1973 as a counterbalance to the *Jusos*, was, under its new chairman Rudolf Dreßler, who had taken over from Helmut Rohde in 1984, certainly able at times to make its presence felt. Its social and political traditionalism met with some resonance following German unification, and Rudolf Dreßler gained in stature as a recognised spokesman on social policy. It was unable, however, to relate successfully to the modern branches of today's economy. Rooted in a brand of honourable tradition, it was insufficiently forward-looking. With an increasingly aging German population, the elderly became an ever more important political target group, and, in 1994, the SPD set up *AG 60plus* (Working Group 60 plus), aimed at bringing pensioners more on board and utilising their experience and possibilities of communication. Apart from an increase in special events, however, and separate activities for active older party members, the effect was limited. Despite staunch commitment here and there the overall impact of *AG 60plus* on the community at large was virtually nil.

The fragmentation of the SPD into many parallel, occasionally mutually hostile, and in the main self-contained sub-organisations, had to be counteracted if the SPD were ever again to be viewed as an integrated unit. What was required was organisational reform, and this was got to grips with under Björn Engholm. It began with the surprise choice of Karl-Heinz Blessing as federal business manager. He came from the *IG Metall* trade union, was young, and had scarcely figured in the SPD up until then. He did not find things easy in the Erich-Ollenhauer-Haus. No progress was made in transforming party headquarters into a modern, efficient communication and control centre. The dismantling of certain posts and responsibilities, for instance in the departments of economics, the Bundeswehr, and the environment, together with poor inter-communication, deficiencies in personnel, and dwindling motivation, resulted in the "Barracks" (as party headquarters was called) diminishing in importance. This was aggravated by Rudolf Scharping rapidly succeeding Björn Engholm as party chairman, and the heavy reliance of both on their own party teams in Kiel and Mainz – a further cause of friction. Despite the resolutions of the 1993 party conference in Wiesbaden and various projects "to make the *Volkspartei* more open", the campaign of modernisation and motivation with which Engholm wanted to bring fresh impetus to party life, open it up to new forms of commitment, and encourage outside talent never got beyond a series of half measures.[20] Although the party experimented with elements of direct democracy with the ballot on the new party chairman in 1995, no real mobilisation of party energies was discernible.

20 Protokoll Parteitag in Wiesbaden 16.–19. November 1993, esp. pp. 781–786 and pp. 1158–1163; see also Thomas Meyer, Klaus-Jürgen Scherer, Christoph Zöpel, Parteien in der Defensive? Plädoyer für die Öffnung der Volkspartei (Cologne 1994), and Karl-Heinz Blessing (ed.), SPD 2000. Die Modernisierung der SPD (Marburg/Berlin 1993).

For SPD members and supporters it was not easy to find fixed points of orientation which might give the party a firm, symbolic profile. When Willy Brandt died on 8 October 1992, many people felt this was the end of an era. Over the years and decades Brandt had shaped, guided, and been the epitome of social democracy. He was a democratic socialist, a German patriot, a convinced European and internationalist with a sense of tradition, and had great charisma. For the Union, and particularly after unification, Helmut Kohl had become the supreme father figure on whom almost everything seemed to be focused: from his personal leadership of the party and the conduct of elections, through to the instrumentalisation of the apparatus of the state to boost his own importance and consolidate his power. In the SPD, in which Willy Brandt had once been the personification of the party while Helmut Schmidt had been making policy in Bonn, there was no even remotely comparable power figure with whom to identify. Hans-Jochen Vogel resigned the chairmanship of the parliamentary party in autumn 1991. Three candidates put themselves forward for election: the legal expert and deputy party chairman Herta Däubler-Gmelin, the expert on social policy and *AfA* chairman Rudolf Dreßler, and the former Mayor of Hamburg and current SPD treasurer Hans-Ulrich Klose. With no result forthcoming in the first ballot, Klose won the runoff by a margin of fifteen votes over Däubler-Gmelin.[21] This led to a loosening of the previously bureaucratically tight organisational structure of the parliamentary party. It was none the more effective for this. Under the cultured, reflective Hans-Ulrich Klose the parliamentary party lost even more of its clout. Ultimately, the real reason for this was that since 1991 the centre of power in the SPD had shifted from Bonn to the state capitals.

Following German unification, North Rhine-Westphalia with Minister President Johannes Rau, and his head of office Wolfgang Clement, played the leading part in representing the concerns, as well as the social interests, of the federal states as German unity began to take effect. From May 1991 there were Social Democrat Minister Presidents in nine states in all, including eight out of the ten in the West. While the parliamentary party in the Bundestag could do little more than exhort and warn, the A-states were able to wield real political power with their majority in the Bundesrat.[22] Their majority was insufficient, however, to mount a tough strategy of opposition such as that envisaged by Oskar Lafontaine. In 1991, in the battle over the raising of value-added tax, when Brandenburg under

21 See Vogel, Nachsichten, p. 389 f.; Jahrbuch der SPD 1991/92, p. 62.
22 The A-states were those with SPD-led governments, the B-states were those governed by the CDU and CSU.

Manfred Stolpe withdrew from the group of those rejecting it, it became abundantly clear that fundamental opposition had become impossible. The fact was, that on many issues, the states had widely diverging interests. Those in the East were financially so dependent on the federal government that the help they received was contingent on reaching a consensus with the Kohl regime. At bottom, therefore, the A-states, and particularly when it was a matter of finance, favoured the path of compromise and cooperation with the Kohl government, which, since 1990, had found itself in a much stronger position.[23]

For many years, Johannes Rau had stood out head and shoulders above other SPD state governors in terms of popularity, and yet within the party his role was basically more that of a moderator. As Minister President of Brandenburg, Manfred Stolpe had gained in stature beyond the borders of his own state as a spokesman for the concerns of people in the East as a whole. This, however, was the limit of his reputation. As regards the real leadership question in the SPD, in other words the chairmanship and Chancellor candidacy, the ball was in the court of the "grandsons". For the time being Lafontaine had blown his chances, and Björn Engholm was now the favourite. But there was no end to their continuing rivalry. Under Engholm's chairmanship some changes in political strategy, such as organisational innovation, were set in motion. Part of this was a new, modern image relating to economic policy, with the party declaring itself in favour of innovations and the "key technologies for the future". In the Hesse local elections of 7 March 1993, however, the modernisation course suffered a severe setback. The SPD lost over eight percentage points. It was mainly traditional supporters who turned their backs on the party. This marked the beginning of a change in which a move back to grassroots seemed called for. It was initiated with Engholm still in power. In spring 1993, however, when it became known, and the media made a meal of the fact, that he too had been guilty of misconduct during the Barschel Affair, he threw in the towel on 3 May 1993 both as party chairman and Chancellor candidate. He withdrew from politics almost entirely.

3. A Short Interregnum

One hope for the future was out of the race. Johannes Rau took over for a short time as caretaker party chairman, until a new one could be chosen. It was only partly the newly discovered love of direct democracy, but just as much an expression of weakness in the decision-making process, or

---

23 Walter, Die SPD nach der deutschen Vereinigung, p. 97f.

rather perplexity and helplessness amongst the higher echelons of the party, that a decision was to be made by balloting party members. Gerhard Schröder from Hanover threw down the gauntlet by asking simultaneously for the chairmanship and the Chancellor candidacy. Rudolf Scharping, who had pursued successful policies as Minister President of an SPD-FDP government in the Rhineland-Palatinate, was more modest and came across as moderate and solid, albeit without demonstrating any great charisma. The third candidate was the former *Juso* chairwoman Heidi Wieczorek-Zeul, who argued that a woman should stand for the chairmanship. As an out-and-out left-winger she attracted votes which would otherwise have gone to Schröder. At the count, Scharping had his nose in front with 40.3 per cent, followed by Schröder with 33.2, and Wieczorek-Zeul with 26.5 per cent. The party conference in Essen on 25 June 1993 confirmed the decision of the party membership.[24] Scharping chose as his party manager Günter Verheugen, who, after Genscher's switch of loyalties in September 1982, had resigned his office as FDP General Secretary and joined the SPD. Scharping's decision was, of course, meant as a signal to Free Democrats past and present.

With the "man from the Palatinate", a "grandson" was now party chairman whom many had not even considered up to then. He led the party somewhat soberly, and with discipline and circumspection. There was some consternation, however, when, after the asylum law, a further alteration of course was made urging a "tougher line from the state" in combating crime. This was introduced by Engholm, and then completed under Scharping. In the face of resistance from mainly the middle ranks of party functionaries, the party conference in Wiesbaden in November 1993 voted by the narrow majority of 196 to 181 of the delegates in favour of the "great bugging operation".[25] At the same time, Social Democrats under the aegis of Oskar Lafontaine were seeking a more modern approach to economic policy, one oriented towards the market economy, and which at the same time set its sights on structural ecological reforms. It sank without trace in a mire of misgivings and special interests within the party. Ultimately, all that remained was the call for "work, and more work". After the brief boom brought by unification in the early 1990s, mass unemployment had risen rapidly. In 1994 unemployment levels were at 9.2 per cent, or 2.55 million, in the West. But the hardest hit were those in the new states. At over 14.8 per cent in 1992, the figure then rose to

---

24 See the Archiv der Gegenwart, (63) 1993, p. 38031 f.
25 On this, see Walter, Die SPD nach der deutschen Vereinigung, p. 88.

Rudolf Scharping with Oskar Lafontaine and Gerhard Schröder as the "triumvirate" in the election campaign of 1994

16 per cent, meaning that more than 1.14 million people were without a job at this point.[26]

The Social Democrats found some common ground in their criticism of the "social coldness" of the Kohl government and its "abhorrent social policies". They made it the focal point of their political agitation and promised the people more social safeguards in the event of them winning the next election. In the winter of 1993/94, with many Germans afraid of losing their jobs and taking a pessimistic view of the future, the Social Democrats' electoral chances seemed rosy, particularly since for the first time in years they were being seen by voters in some polls as more competent than the CDU/CSU. But early in 1994 the wind began to change. People looked to the future with greater confidence. In the elections for Federal President on 23 May 1994, Johannes Rau was defeated by the Union candidate Roman Herzog in the third ballot, a result of symbolic significance. In the poll on Chancellor preferences, the old warhorse Kohl, despite his obvious inadequacies, had just nosed in front of the

26 Statistisches Jahrbuch 1995 für die Bundesrepublik Deutschland. Published by the Statistisches Bundesamt (Wiesbaden 1995), p. 122f.

challenger Scharping, albeit narrowly in the West, but by a much clearer margin in the new states.[27] In the eyes of the public, the SPD were above all found wanting on financial and economic policy, even by comparison with the Union who were playing this selfsame economic card. When Scharping mixed up gross and net when discussing income tax limits, the media had a field day and were merciless in denigrating his competence.[28] Only on the question of social responsibility did the SPD and its candidate have a clear advantage with the electorate, while Kohl was clearly ahead as someone seen as having the "winning touch", and who would stand up for "German interests". Scharping showed great stamina in the election campaign, and the opposition, of course, also profited from the disappointment and disquiet which were widely felt amongst the population about the Kohl government and the inadequacies of its policies.

In the Bundestag elections on 16 October 1994, the CDU suffered heavy losses in the East, but by and large managed to maintain its position in the West. Overall, the CDU/CSU dropped to 41.4, and the FDP to 7.3 per cent. The Greens increased their vote to 7.3 per cent, and for the first time since 1972 the SPD showed a clear growth of almost three percentage points. It achieved 36.4 per cent, with its main improvement in the East. The conservative-liberal coalition was only able to survive by the skin of its teeth. The narrow margin of two seats became ten as a result of the *Überhangmandate* (overhang seats). The optimistic prognosis of Rudolf Scharping immediately after the election that Kohl's days in power were numbered, and that the SPD's hour was imminent, was not of course borne out.

With Scharping taking over the chairmanship of the parliamentary party, the SPD's two leadership posts were now in one hand. Structurally this meant that there was now a better basis for the party to be able once more to speak with a single voice, and to present a much more unified political image at federal level. But instead of the hoped-for tailwind there began, from within their own ranks, and actively promoted by the media, the demolition of the somewhat unfortunate endeavours of the "man from the Palatinate". At the end of 1994, for instance, he announced a change of course for the SPD in economic policy, only to then rapidly disavow it. The mood grew even more awkward as the SPD in North Rhine-Westphalia, who were spoiled for success, lost their overall majority in the Landtag elections in May 1995, and Johannes Rau was forced to form an

---

27 In the West, the percentages were 50.9 to 49.1, whereas in the East, they were 53.9 to 46.1. See Oscar W. Gabriel and Angelika Vetter, 'Die Chancen der CDU/CSU in den neunziger Jahren', in Aus Politik und Zeitgeschichte 6 (1996), p. 14.
28 See, for instance, Bild-Zeitung 26.5.1994, and Stuttgarter Zeitung 18.5.1994.

unwelcome coalition with the strengthened Greens.[29] The Annual Tax Law became a bone of contention in the SPD, with the interests of the states in conflict with the financial demands of the SPD parliamentary group and their economic policy. The disputes were conducted in public and via the media. There was an increasing lack of support for Rudolf Scharping, who was labelled as wooden and stiff. The appeals to close ranks fell on deaf ears. His show of strength, after serious conflict, in "suspending"[30] Gerhard Schröder as economics spokesman (August 1995) brought no relief.

Behind the scenes, what was really at stake was the question of the Chancellor candidacy. Scharping and Schröder were sharply at odds. Schröder, with one eye on his chances for the federal elections in 1998, objected to an early decision being made. Scharping, on the other hand, stubbornly insisted that with his re-election as party chairman in Mannheim he was simultaneously "the natural contender for the Chancellor candidacy", and that he "intended to lay claim to it".[31] The "triumvirate" of Scharping, Lafontaine, and Schröder was now "to all intents and purposes dead"[32]. Both Scharping and Schröder, on opposite sides of the conflict, had been damaged. The winner was Oskar Lafontaine, who lambasted the lack of loyalty amongst the SPD leadership, as well as urging solidarity and clarity. Thus it was that *Der Spiegel* put it to Scharping that Lafontaine might be the "beneficiary of this dispute?".[33]

The SPD leadership conflict, which lasted for several months, was reflected negatively in the opinion polls and growing irritation at SPD grassroots level. At a private meeting on 8 and 9 September, the party manager Verheugen reported that the mood in the party was veering "between frustration, anger, and aggression".[34] Shortly after, utterly dispirited, he threw in the towel and resigned. In the middle of October he was replaced by the chairman of the powerful SPD region of West Westphalia, Franz Müntefering, a decision which was to point the way ahead to an SPD revival. He radiated trust and solidity and had the ability to speak directly

29 In the Landtag elections on 14.5.1995 the SPD received 46.0 per cent (in 1990 it was 50.0), and the Greens climbed to 10.0 per cent.
30 See the presidium sitting on 4.9.1995, minutes in the Archiv der sozialen Demokratie.
31 Presidium sitting on 28.8.1995 with the corresponding resolution, Archiv der sozialen Demokratie. See too, Scharping's interview with Der Spiegel of 7.8.1995. Also, Lafontaine, Das Herz schlägt links, p. 35 f., and p. 41 f.
32 According to Hans Eichel in the presidium sitting of 28.8.1995.
33 Der Spiegel, 7.5.1995, interview with Rudolf Scharping.
34 Private meeting of the presidium in Berlin 8–9 September, minutes in the Archiv der sozialen Demokratie. See, too, the presidium sitting on 28.8.1995 with data from FORSA and EMNID.

to the hearts of the *Genossen* (comrades). Nevertheless, on the evening before the Mannheim party conference, he had to admit that "the grass-roots were consumed with a mixture of anger and rage".[35] The disastrous rebuff to the Berlin SPD who, in the elections to the Chamber of Deputies, had slumped to 23.6 per cent, was a stern warning about the querulous image which the party leadership was projecting at federal level.

Discord and strife were clearly looming for the party congress in Mannheim in November 1995. Scharping's performance, an attempt to put the ship back on course, was feeble. He failed and was made to feel the delegates' displeasure. The next day, Oskar Lafontaine had an enthusiastic plenary session on its feet with his skilful rhetoric, and brought about the so-called *putsch*. Scharping was deposed, with Lafontaine subsequently being enthroned on 16 November.[36]

4. Shadows from the Past

Over the years, the party had always profited, particularly amongst young people, from the fact that Social Democrats had actively resisted the Nazi regime. With the revival of the *AvS*, the Working Group of Persecuted Social Democrats (1979), this liberal, anti-fascist heritage found a special niche under its enterprising chairman Heinz Putzrath. At his instigation, the all-party association "Against Forgetting, for Democracy" was founded in 1993. Under the chairmanship of Hans-Jochen Vogel, this project became very active in encouraging debate about the legacy of the Nazi past, and in the struggle against right-wing radicalism and racism. The re-activation of the *AvS*, as well as the founding of the Historical Commission of the SPD Executive in 1981, had been championed by Willy Brandt in 1981. Under its first chairman Susanne Miller, and her successor Bernd Faulenbach, it organised regular and well-respected forums on historically and politically relevant topics.[37] These represented an intellectual counterweight to the lavishly funded and staffed history projects of the Kohl government, such as the House of the History of the Federal Republic in Bonn, and many other institutions and organisations of similar ideological inclination.

---

35 Siegfried Heimann, 'Die SPD in den neunziger Jahren'. In Werner Süß (ed.), Die Bundesrepublik in den 90er Jahren (Leverkusen 2002), p. 89.
36 In the election for the chairman, Lafontaine received 321 votes, Scharping only 190. For Lafontaine's view, see Das Herz schlägt links, pp. 42–44.
37 On the activities of the AvS, see in particular the periodical information service of the AvS; most of the Historical Commission's forums have been published by rowohlt or Klartext-Verlag.

In the 1990s, the SPD felt the cold wind of the more recent past. The prelude to this was an article by the journalist Christian von Ditfurth in *Der Spiegel*, in which he gave a critical and tendentious account of contacts between the SPD and the SED.[38] At the beginning of 1994, Brigitte Seebacher-Brandt mounted an attack on the dead Herbert Wehner, accusing him of having promoted the "cause of the other side" (by which she meant Communists in the GDR and Moscow) and of using his contacts in the East to engineer the downfall of Willy Brandt.[39] In doing this, Brandt's widow made herself indirectly an accomplice to a campaign by the CDU, whose Secretary General Peter Hintze had not only the PDS, but also the SPD in his sights with his so-called "Rote Socken" (red socks) polemic.

In March 1992, the Bundestag had, at the suggestion of Markus Meckel amongst others, set up a commission of enquiry to "review the history and consequences of the SED dictatorship in Germany". The CDU deputy and former civil-rights campaigner Rainer Eppelmann was made chairman. The impressive work of the commission is reflected in the substantial eighteen-volume publication which appeared in 1995.[40] Even though the members of the commission and the co-opted academics were generally intent on honest elucidation and fair evaluation, it was clear that many in the Union camp, in alliance with those research assistants favourably disposed towards them, were attempting to instrumentalise the enquiry against the Social Democrats. An important role in this was played by the "Research Association SED-Dictatorship" at the Free University in Berlin which included "converted" former *Spontis* and Maoists. In conjunction with sensation-seeking sections of the media, this developed into a campaign against prominent Social Democrats, who were accused of having been excessively chummy towards the SED. In the face of the massive campaign against them, those being pilloried in this way went onto the defensive. Only very few in SPD circles retaliated with some basic spade-work of their own to demonstrate that the Union too, including Chancellor Kohl, had fallen over themselves to make contact with the upper echelons of the SED.[41] This no longer seemed opportune after German unification, and was kept quiet. For its part, the SPD showed

---

38 Der Spiegel, no. 35, 24.8.1995, pp. 44–63.
39 On this, see Vogel, Nachsichten, p. 430 f.
40 Enquete-Kommission Aufarbeitung von Geschichte und Folgen der SED-Diktatur in Deutschland, published by the German Bundestag (Baden-Baden and Frankfurt/Main 1995).
41 A basic work here, Potthoff, Koalition der Vernunft (1995); also, Potthoff, Bonn und Ost-Berlin (1997), and Im Schatten der Mauer (1999).

too little interest in bringing these facts more insistently to public attention.

In spring 1995, in time for the Landtag elections in North Rhine-Westphalia, Brandt's widow went into action once more. Her criticisms were now also directed against Egon Bahr, Hans-Jochen Vogel, and Johannes Rau. She then left the party. Egon Bahr, Karsten Voigt, and the "grandsons" were, because of their contacts with the SED, the main targets of the Union hardliners in the commission of enquiry, their helpmates in the SED Research Association, and a willing press, mainly the *Welt am Sonntag* and the *Frankfurter Allgemeine*. Johannes Rau was also on the receiving end. This was particularly unfair, since German unification had always been close to his heart, and he had worked energetically on behalf of the citizens of the GDR. It was transparently clear that this was not about getting at the truth, but an attempt to discredit the popular Johannes Rau in the run-up to the elections.[42]

Egon Bahr caused a great stir in 1996. He, who had himself come under suspicion from the Union because of his diplomacy in the East, openly accused Herbert Wehner of "betraying" Willy Brandt, and of engaging in underhand dealings with Erich Honecker.[43] In spite of the accusations being refuted, the attacks on Wehner continued. The perpetual bombardment of Social Democrats with accusations of having been in cahoots with Communists had its effect, even though there was nothing new in either them, or the supposed evidence for them: they were merely rehashes, but nevertheless sparked uncertainty in people's minds.

There was in fact good reason for the SPD to get to grips with the nature and intensity of their contacts with Communist parties in the East. The party had always maintained a clear and hostile stance towards right-wing dictatorships, whereas the CSU, and sections of the CDU, were far less scrupulous in their dealings with, for instance, Franco's Spain or the Pinochet regime in Chile. This is as much a subject for examination as is the attitude of the SPD towards Communist dictatorships and their relationship with citizens' movements in eastern Europe, including the GDR. In the light of the conflict between the different power systems and their potential for mutual nuclear destruction, stability was felt to be the key. The SPD hoped that the creation of a civilised network of relations would

---

42 This was the case in the NRW Landtag elections on 14.5.1995, as well as on the earlier occasion of the federal presidential elections on 23.5.1994.

43 Egon Bahr, Zu meiner Zeit (Munich 1996), pp. 438–447. The relevant section on Wehner had already appeared in Die Zeit of 20.9.1996. For a refutation of Bahr's accusations, see, inter alia, Heinrich Potthoff in Der Spiegel, 14.10.1996; also in Im Schatten der Mauer, p. 125 f.

further the potential for reform in the East. In this process, the correct balance between cooperation in the service of *détente*, building trust, and offering people concrete help on the one hand, and maintaining the appropriate distance between free democracy and an authoritarian and dictatorial system on the other, was not always preserved. Critical consideration should be given to the fact that some politicians – and not solely from the ranks of the Social Democrats, but from other parties too – became too close, and problematically so. Many political commentators and representatives of social organisations were also guilty of this. Conversely, many people in West Germany who lived in affluence and freedom, and were fond of basking in their western, post-national identity, should ask themselves why they had lost all interest in those Germans whose fate it was to live in the other Germany of the GDR.

Initially, the collapse of the Communist regimes in eastern Europe and the Soviet empire certainly did not improve the framework conditions for the Social Democratic project. Willy Brandt's vision of a new Social Democratic dawn was slow in coming. Amongst the opposition groups such as *Solidarnosc* in Poland who were now coming to power, the West German Social Democrats were often viewed with suspicion because of their overly close contacts with the old Communist regimes. Generally speaking, they preferred to have the long-standing Chancellor Helmut Kohl and his CDU/CSU as partners, and regarded a liberal economic course such as that being pursued by the USA, and by Kohl in the Federal Republic, as offering the most promising hope of success for them. The western capitalist system in conjunction with a somewhat conservatively oriented parliamentary democracy had carried the day. With the fall of communism, anything to do with socialism seemed to be discredited.

It was not only the SED state which had presumed to present itself as "real-existing socialism", but in everyday usage in the Federal Republic the talk was mostly of the "socialist states". Others spoke of "real socialism", or of "socialism in eastern Europe", thereby indirectly conceding to the Communists the claim they persisted in maintaining to represent a version of, or rather *the* socialism. The damage done to the term socialism by the Communist systems caused the SPD to soft-pedal its traditional trademark "democratic socialism". Opponents of the SPD repeatedly exploited the discredit brought about by "state socialism" to associate the party closely with collectivism and lack of liberty. After the collapse of the Communist dictatorships they were, under the banner of the "End of Socialism", not only intent on condemning out of hand "democratic socialism", but along with it social democracy itself. The American political scientist Samuel Huntington, who would later predict the "clash of civilisations", proclaimed, as did his colleague Francis Fukuyama, the final victory of democracy. What he had in mind was the model embodied by the USA with its neo-liberal, private capitalist social system, in other words a "liberal", not a "social" democracy.

The sense of deep caesura was widespread. The world was indeed at an epoch-making turning point. The system of a largely bipolar world, dominated by the two great power blocs, had been the cause of anxiety because of the weapons arsenals involved, but it also gave a certain, controlled stability. The collapse of the Soviet empire and the upheavals in the eastern central European states, including the GDR, and the dissolution of the Council for Mutual Economic Aid (Comecon), along with the Warsaw Pact (both in 1991), was followed by the disintegration of the old Soviet Union. In the same year, 1991, the declaration of independence by Slovenia and Croatia brought about the collapse of Yugoslavia. It led in Croatia, Bosnia-Herzegovina, and finally in Kosovo, to the lengthy and brutal conflicts with the Serbs and Slobodan Milosevic's rump Yugoslavia. With its wars and ethnic cleansing, the Balkans was once again becoming a dangerous European trouble spot.

After the demise of the Soviet Union, the USA were left as the sole world power. Economically they were number one, they could dictate the rules of the game, they acted as a kind of global policeman, intervening wherever American interests were threatened. Admittedly, the Europe of the EU was internally stronger following German unification. This was a result of Franco-German cooperation between Helmut Kohl and François Mitterrand, who were in agreement that Europe was most likely to tolerate an enlarged Germany if it were firmly embedded in a tighter European alliance. Chancellor Kohl held a much better hand than the SPD, not only with regard to German unification. He also behaved like, and throughout Europe was seen as, the better European. The SPD, which, in its Heidelberg Programme of 1925, had been the first German party to advocate a "European economic union" and the "building of the United States of Europe", but after 1945 had initially kept aloof from integration with the West, now once again found itself lagging behind. And this despite having, in Klaus Hänsch, who amongst other things had been the President of the European Parliament, an established, capable, and thoughtful politician with European credentials. But apart from the elections to the European parliament, Europe, as far as Social Democrats in the 1990s were concerned, was of secondary importance. The party's policy as regards both the smaller EU, as well as the larger European project with the opening up towards the East, was neither internally consistent, nor did it have any purposeful continuity. It was almost as if the Social Democrats had no overall concept, but were making pro-European pronouncements one minute, and reiterating populist, nationalistic reservations the next. Scharping and Schröder, for instance, in the run-up to the Mannheim party conference, presented themselves "as the guardians of the Deutschmark and currency stability", and were warning against the European currency union, while shortly before, at a meeting with representatives of the banks, the presidium had committed itself to the rapid implementation of a currency union.[44] The Mannheim party conference kept faith with this, but its credibility had taken a knock. There was a lasting impression of querulousness, incompetence, and lack of leadership. This was regrettable since the Social Democrats had good historical and political grounds for giving the new and enlarged Germany a more precise location in Europe and the world, and determining the crucial basic values by which a European Germany and the European alliance should be guided.

Already at the beginning of the 1980s, the celebrated sociologist Ralf Dahrendorf, once one of the pioneers and theoreticians behind the FDP switching to a social-liberal coalition, had caused a stir with his thesis on the "end of the Social Democrat century". His argument, summarised in the book *Die Chancen der Krise* (The Chances of Crisis)[45], was in effect a testimonial for social democracy. As a party, the SPD had been responsible for "promoting and defending the connection between the constitutional state and the institutions of an open society", for democracy in other words. This was its achievement. He justified the "end" of social democracy with the thesis that its particular concerns – "growth, equality, rationality, state, and internationalism" – had been taken up and implemented by various social groups, so that in effect "(almost) all of us had become Social Democrats". It was true that the conclusion following from this analysis, that social democracy had fulfilled its historical task, and could now abdicate, fitted well with an age in which neo-liberalism and a pronounced individualism determined the social climate. But it misrepresented and distorted the problem, since it was this selfsame neo-liberal renaissance which was beginning to call the socially responsible welfare state into question. In view of mass unemployment, turbo capitalism, and the power of international finance capital, even Lord Dahrendorf had had to modify his position.

As an idea and a movement, social democracy had for decades influenced and shaped both politics and society. One of its central concerns,

---

44 Peter Lösche, 'Die SPD nach Mannheim: Strukturprobleme und aktuelle Entwicklungen', in Aus Politik und Zeitgeschichte, B 6 (1996), p. 25f.
45 Ralf Dahrendorf, Die Chancen der Krise. Über die Zukunft des Liberalismus (Stuttgart 1983), esp. pp. 16–18.

emancipation and equality for the labour force in industry and trade, had, in the developed societies, been largely achieved. Following the change from an industrial to a modern service and microelectronic society, the original social basis of social democracy had shrunk. The proportion of workers dwindled, and the old Social Democratic milieu lost its broad ability to bind people together. The growing class of white-collar workers, public service employees, and those in the high-tech and communications sector, were a heterogeneous group, and – unlike workers once had been – were not rooted in a political and social culture which had the power to shape and influence. The urge to better oneself, preoccupation with possessions and affluence, and individual freedoms, became increasingly important. This was at odds with the traditional Social Democratic and trade-union orientation towards collective organisation and comprehensive social state intervention. The desire for individual development on the basis of material prosperity was in direct conflict with the at times very lively ecological awareness and scepticism about progress and growth, which, for years, had been fostered particularly amongst the ranks of the left.

The problems which this caused the SPD manifested themselves especially in the large conurbations. It is true that in 1995 there were SPD mayors in more than two-thirds of cities with populations of over 100,000. And yet, especially in the large cities, the party was very much on the slide. In comparison, for instance, with the 1969 federal elections, in Frankfurt/Main they were down by 19.3, in Munich by 16.9, in Stuttgart by 15.9, and in Hamburg by 14.9 per cent. The decline was most dramatic in Berlin, where, in the former West Berlin in 1963, they had 61.9 per cent of the vote, but in the 1995 elections in Greater Berlin they plummeted to 23.6 per cent.[46] The diminishing attractiveness of the SPD manifested itself particularly in those regions where the high-tech and communications service industries were concentrated, where there was a high standard of education and housing, and at the same time a large proportion of foreigners. Here many people favoured the Greens, whilst others were turning towards right-wing populist parties. The SPD lost even more to non-voters. Overall, both popular parties, the CDU/CSU included, lost some of their traditional support[47], but the fact that the SPD were unable to capitalise on the Union losses had a much more negative impact on them since they were in opposition. The Social Democrats needed a strategy

---

46 On this, see particularly the report of an internal SPD working group, SPD und Großstädte. Der Bericht. Arbeitsgruppe unter Günter Verheugen (Bonn 1995); see too, Lösche, Die SPD nach Mannheim, p. 23f.
47 See below, chapter IV, section 3.

with which to activate the latent mood of hostility towards the government. It was a matter of gaining the economic credibility which was usually the crucial factor in winning elections, and of finding political personalities with charisma and media skills who could serve as a convincing alternative to Kohl, the "Chancellor in perpetuity".

But the SPD had been suffering for years from the rivalry between the various pretenders to the throne, men who had neither the word loyalty, nor solidarity, in their vocabulary. Above all, there was no real centre giving leadership and direction. This had begun to be a problem in the latter years of Willy Brandt, who operated very much off his own bat and sometimes kept even the presidium very inadequately informed. His bad example was emulated by the "grandsons", even though they were not remotely of the same stature as Brandt. Each went their own way, advancing their careers and making their mark with spectacular campaigns which were often in conflict with the party line. In the process, and the attempt to get one over on their potential rivals, they often clashed.

The media, of course, gleefully lapped up these rivalries. Politicians and journalists were all too frequently hand in glove in this. In the transformed media landscape, with competition from the private channels, the craving for sensation and eye-catching, short-lived headlines had a field day. "Politics as theatre", with carefully staged appearances and trenchant offerings characterised this "new power, the art of presentation".[48] But there were also other reasons for much of the malice directed at the SPD, not least the effect of the Kohl system on the media landscape. The many years of dominance of the "black giant" (Kohl) and his regime of personal allegiances led to a penetration of the media by government supporters and spin doctors who did not hesitate to interfere in publicly administered institutions, bringing to heel and paralysing even those current affairs programmes viewers thought were of a critical nature. Even a news magazine such as *Der Spiegel*, which saw itself as a guardian of democratic culture, seemed a little too reverent towards the government. Other newspapers and journals were immeasurably worse. Moreover, with *Focus*, a new magazine sympathetic to the government had become firmly established. Whereas in the 1960s the SPD had profited from the fact that influential newspapers and political commentators promoted and backed their political direction, they had had to survive in the 1990s largely without this encouragement. The media were, for the most part, hostile to them. Only

48 Thomas Meyer and Martina Kampmann, Politik als Theater. Die neue Macht der Darstellungskunst (Berlin 1998); see also Thomas Meyer, Die Inszenierung des Scheins. Voraussetzungen und Folgen symbolischer Politik (Frankfurt/Main 1992).

when the end of the Kohl era was in sight was there any perceptible change.

5. Fresh Impetus under Lafontaine's Regency

After the Mannheim party congress of November 1995, and with Lafontaine now as party leader, the SPD bottomed out in the opinion polls, gained six percentage points, and at least ended up with 34 per cent once more on the "Sunday question" (German elections are held on Sundays). This left them still far behind the CDU/CSU, despite the Union parties falling from 47 to 43 per cent.[49] After the appalling picture at Mannheim of the leadership team totally at loggerheads, the first priority was to demonstrate solidarity, and for the party to close ranks. Even though the *putsch* left a sour taste in the mouths of some Social Democrats, Oskar Lafontaine was for the time being the man of the moment. Despite his bitter defeat, Rudolf Scharping received a lot of credit for continuing to put himself at the service of the party. He became deputy party chairman and remained chairman of the parliamentary party.

Gerhard Schröder was basically the last remaining rival from the "grandsons'" generation. But his position in the SPD seemed weakened. With his plea in 1995 for a "modern economic policy", he had not only provoked the party chairman of the time, Scharping, who had relieved him of his function as SPD economics spokesman, but a propensity for doing things off his own bat had also turned many of the party rank and file against him. He was heavily criticised in Mannheim as being responsible for the decline of the party. The delegates' punishment was to almost not elect him to the executive committee.[50] Heide Simonis, Minister President of Schleswig-Holstein, who had ventured a judgement in favour of more realism in financial policy, also received an angry reception. Mannheim seemed to represent a real setback for long overdue economic and financial reforms. Instead of setting their sights more firmly on potential electors, delegates sought salvation from a man who knew how to exploit their mood. This brand of conference democracy was historically one of the strengths of this great members' party, but it also clearly hampered the attempt to extend its appeal to a broader segment of society and its citizens. The attitude of activists who attended party meetings and congresses did not, of course, correspond to that of ordi-

---

49 See Lösche, Die SPD nach Mannheim, p. 20.
50 In the first ballot Schröder did not secure the necessary 263 votes, and was only elected to the executive in the second round when he received 303 votes.

nary party members[51], and it was markedly different from that of traditional SPD voters, let alone that of voters from the middle ground whom they were attempting to woo. This is where the SPD had to pick up points if it was going to win the Bundestag elections, and for that they had to have an effective Chancellorship candidate who would appeal to these voters and be able to stand up to the tried-and-tested electioneer, Helmut Kohl.

The first priority, however, was to strengthen and bring up to scratch a party riven by internal rivalries and frustrated by long years in opposition. Franz Müntefering remained party manager. With his solid base in West Westphalia, he was in a strong position. Somehow, he made the *Genossen*, the comrades, feel that they belonged. His big plus point was the great respect he enjoyed within the party, along with his talent for organisation, openness to fresh ideas, and ability to get across his point of view. He ensured that friction was avoided wherever possible, that the rank and file remained on board, and that a firm campaign basis was established. The new party chairman, Oskar Lafontaine, who himself had not always been known for these qualities, now called for discipline, loyalty, and solidarity, and indeed imposed them with skill and a firm hand. Potential troublemakers and deviators from the party line were either brought on message or neutralised. Whereas under Scharping the parliamentary party had been in the foreground, and the SPD state governors often felt their concerns were being insufficiently met, Lafontaine now made the presidium into an effective mechanism for coordinating and steering policy. The heads of the SPD-led states were always consulted, and their needs addressed, above all when it came to financial matters.[52] Guidelines laid down by the presidium were binding on the parliamentary party. After the off-putting chorus of dissonant voices in 1995, the SPD leadership were once again operating as a team, and were, as a result, a much more effective opposition. The SPD, recently such a ragbag of different factions and plagued by internal rivalries, now had the feeling that it once again had a proper chairman, and one who knew how to lead, was in tune with the mood of the party, and could motivate the rank and file.

51 See p. 337 above.
52 SPD Minister Presidents, or their deputies, were brought in as a matter of course when topics relevant to the federal states were under discussion in the presidium sessions. Under Scharping, this happened only occasionally. See the minutes of the presidium sessions in the Archiv der sozialen Demokratie. See also Lafontaine's comment (session of 22.4.1996) that the presidium "must be able to control and coordinate the SPD position". Where required, specialists within the parliamentary party were also brought in for presidium sessions.

Oskar Lafontaine seemed to be the man of the moment, someone who could visibly lift the party with his rhetorical skills, feeling for the grassroots, and ability to exploit the media effectively. The year 1996 was a period of "consolidation" in which the SPD succeeded in regaining the support of its core voters.[53]

There was a feeling that the party was finally on the move, and had a good chance of leaving the opposition benches in Bonn behind, and taking up the reins of power once again. The SPD were making gains in polls on the famous "Sunday question" which asked people how they would vote, and were also catching up in the more realistic electoral projections. According to raw data from the Allensbach Institute, in the period January to September 1996 alone, the SPD reduced the gap between them and the Union from 9 to just 2 per cent.[54] By winter 1995, popular satisfaction with the Kohl government had begun to fall off dramatically, dropping in 1997 to an all-time low which lasted until early summer 1998. In the same period, following the Mannheim congress, the SPD experienced a steady upward trend – both as regards the general political mood and the verdict on their work in opposition – which left them well ahead of the government.[55]

Lafontaine's high period lasted until 1997. Until then, most in the SPD, along with many other observers, had assumed that the party chairman would be the Chancellorship candidate who in 1998 would step into the ring with Helmut Kohl, the Chancellor who had presided over the *Wende* and unification. But the wind began to change during the course of the year. The very same media who had previously treated him with kid gloves, now set about demolishing him. In the usual opinion polls, his standing as Kohl's challenger was not good. His lead over the "Chancellor in perpetuity", who had become very unpopular, was extremely slim. He met with less approval amongst the public than did his party, the SPD. Gerhard Schröder, on the other hand, in the evaluation of the parties' top politicians, had, since 1997, always received a positive assessment. He was clearly more popular than Chancellor Kohl, and, according to the voters, the SPD would have a better chance with him than with Lafontaine. Since

---

53 It was Lafontaine who talked of a period of "consolidation". Other leading Social Democrats spoke in similar terms.
54 In January 1996 the difference between the parties was SPD 31.7, CDU/CSU 40.7 per cent; in September, SPD 35.1, CDU/CSU 37.1 per cent. See Malte Ristau, Der Wahlkampf der SPD – Eine chronologisch-systematische Darstellung (unpublished). These statistics are also to be found in the press.
55 See Matthias Jung and Dieter Roth, 'Wer zu spät geht, den bestraft der Wähler. Eine Analyse der Bundestagswahl 1998'. In Aus Politik und Zeitgeschichte, B 52 (1998), p. 5f.

November 1997 he had been well ahead of Helmut Kohl in the Chancellorship stakes.[56] But the dice had not yet been cast in the SPD. Lafontaine certainly held the better cards within the party, but Schröder was more highly regarded amongst the population at large. This led to lively public speculation about who would actually be the SPD's Chancellorship candidate.

Early in 1997, Helmut Kohl had announced that he would stand once more in the 1998 elections. It was characteristic of his arrogant sense of power, along with his insufferable smugness and feeling of indispensability, that he should do this via television, and from his holiday location. Wolfgang Schäuble, the eternal crown prince who enjoyed widespread trust in the Union and was greatly respected by the population at large, had to take a back seat. He would have been a far more dangerous opponent for the SPD, particularly since his popularity rating experienced a continuous rise throughout 1997 and 1998.[57] Kohl, on the other hand, had squandered most of his credit. He was becoming a burden to his own party. The "old" Chancellor could barely be trusted any longer with a problem, and many voters had grown thoroughly tired of him. Instead of a "Chancellor bonus" – the bonus accruing to the incumbent Chancellor – there was now a "Chancellor deficit", but, increasingly out of touch with reality, the power-mad Kohl simply could not accept that he was no longer up to the job. There was an unmistakable desire for change. The CDU/CSU/FDP government had also lost a vast amount of credit on important election issues such as economic competence, financial policy, and unemployment. Kohl had boasted that he would halve unemployment. But the statistics told a different story: in reality, the numbers of unemployed were soaring, and it was obvious that the government was unable to do anything about it.

In the new states, unemployment had been the chief talking point ever since unification. After a minimal improvement in 1995, the percentage of registered unemployed in the East rose rapidly, and had reached 19.5 per cent by 1997/98, so that by the middle of the year there were over 1.37 million without a job. But there had also been a continuous rise in unemployment since 1991 in the West, and in the years 1996–1998 it consistently went above the 10 per cent mark. This meant that in Germany as a whole there were around 4.3 million people without work.[58] The nadir was reached with 4.9 million in January 1998. In addition to the registered

56 See Oscar W. Gabriel and Frank Brettschneider, 'Die Bundestagswahl 1998: Ein Plebiszit gegen Kanzler Kohl?'. In ibid., p. 23 f.
57 See Jung and Roth, 'Wer zu spät geht, den bestraft der Wähler', p. 11 f.
58 See the Statistisches Jahrbuch 1999 for the Federal Republic, p. 120 f.; see too, Facts about Germany (Frankfurt/Main), p. 301 f.

unemployed, there were also several hundred thousand who were not registered. Many were in part-time work, or engaged in so-called "employment measures" offering no long-term prospects. Mass unemployment was the main topic of conversation amongst the population. Since the beginning of 1997, on average 80 per cent of those questioned regarded it as the most pressing problem. There was virtually no longer any faith whatsoever in the Union and the Kohl government which had failed people so dismally on this issue. Even though the majority of citizens were generally sceptical about the ability of politicians to solve the problem of unemployment, there were more on the whole who believed that the SPD was the party more likely to create jobs.[59]

The Kohl government seemed hapless, too, as regards its budgetary policy. The failure of the tax reform bill in autumn 1997 seemed almost predictable. Technically, it collapsed because of the SPD majority in the Bundesrat, in other words because of Lafontaine's blocking tactics, to which the Union was so often fond of drawing attention. But it was also socially unbalanced and, above all, unpopular. For all their scepticism, it was true that on the question of economic competence the voters had more faith in the Union than the SPD, but in comparing Kohl and Schröder they considered the latter to be the much more competent politician.

In weighing up their electoral chances, therefore, the SPD had in fact since autumn 1997 been contemplating making Gerhard Schröder their Chancellorship candidate. For this to happen, Lafontaine would have to set aside his own ambitions and give way to a more promising rival. Which of the two would carry the day occupied the media for months, ensuring that the SPD remained in the public eye. The decision was made in the Landtag elections in Lower Saxony on 1 March 1998[60], in which the candidacy issue helped to bring out the voters in favour of the SPD. With 47.9 per cent of the vote and an overall majority in parliament, Gerhard Schröder won a magnificent victory for the SPD. The day after the election, the presidium and party executive unanimously nominated him for election as the Chancellorship candidate by the party congress on the 17 April in Leipzig.[61] This was an occasion for the SPD to get solidly, and

---

59 See Jung and Roth, 'Wer zu spät geht', p. 8; see also, Forschungsgruppe Wahlen, Bundestagswahl 1998. Eine Analyse der Wahl vom 27. September 1998 (Mannheim 1998).
60 See Lafontaine's account of his promise to Schröder in Das Herz schlägt links, pp. 81–90: "If you achieve, or improve upon, the result of the last elections in Lower Saxony, then you can be the candidate. If not, the party must decide." See too details of the minutes listed in the following footnote (n.61).
61 See the minutes of the presidium and the executive committee meetings on 1.3.1998. In the SPD-Vorstandssekretariat, as well as the Presseservice der SPD 78/98 of the 2.3.1998.

impressively, behind their candidate Gerhard Schröder and their party chairman Oskar Lafontaine. "Work, innovation, and justice" were the slogans on which the campaign would be fought. The call for social justice was aimed primarily at the SPD core vote and those voters, particularly in the East, who had become disillusioned with the CDU. Innovation and political leadership were intended to appeal to those citizens who clearly found them missing in the lethargic federal government. And finally, the general slogan of political change summed up the desire, particularly evident in potential non-voters, for the replacement of a Kohl regime which had become so stuck in its ways.

In the Landtag elections in Saxony-Anhalt on 26 April 1998, the SPD vote went up to 35.9 per cent[62], with the ruling CDU suffering a severe setback. Magdeburg, however, put a damper on the feeling that the party was on the move. Horror at the 12.9 per cent for the right-wing extremist Republicans and conflict over the role of the PDS were a cause for concern. Reinhard Höppner formed a minority government of SPD and Alliance 90/Greens which had some support from the PDS. The CDU, under their General Secretary Pastor Hintze, dragged up the old, moth-eaten spectre of the Popular Front. The image of the "red hands" of the PDS/SPD – an allusion to the foundation motif of the SED – was scurrilous, particularly given the conspicuously large number of *Blockflöten* (the pejorative term for parties aligned to the old SED) who had found their way into the Saxony-Anhalt CDU. Nevertheless, the so-called Magdeburg model put a strain on the inner harmony of the SPD, as well as on the party's election campaign strategy. An own goal, however, by the Greens at their Magdeburg party congress in March 1998 gave the SPD an indirect advantage in the battle for the voters' favour. Their decision to gradually raise the price of petrol to 5 Deutschmarks a litre[63] alarmed many voters who wanted a change of government in Bonn. This drove them into the arms of the SPD, where party chairman Oskar Lafontaine was catering more for the post-industrially inclined clientele, while Gerhard Schröder was attempting to appeal to voters from the modern, high-tech industries with the slogan the "New Centre".

The Schröder/Lafontaine duo worked to virtual perfection in the campaign phase of the election. This was chiefly due to the two main players. The SPD's main themes were combating unemployment, and a measured combination of social responsibility and modernity. The slogan "We will do a lot differently, but above all, a lot of things better" aimed at avoiding

---

62 In the Landtag elections on 26.6.1994 they won 34.0 per cent.
63 See the Archiv der Gegenwart, 68 (1998), p. 42669.

SPD election poster 1998. The text reads: "The whole of Germany eagerly awaits For Whom the Bell Tolls. Must finish on 27 September. SPD We are ready"

negative expectations of change, whilst also encouraging positive associations in the minds of the voters. It was coined to fit Gerhard Schröder with his image as a Chancellor candidate of the centre ground. "Kampa", the campaign centre managed by Franz Müntefering, performed sterling work. The SPD presented itself as a fresh, vibrant party which was managing to combine its basic, traditional values of freedom, justice, and solidarity with the demands of a modern industrial service industry and communications' society.

"What matters is the Chancellor" was an old recipe for electoral success by a CDU/CSU which had grown used to being in power. In the 1998 election, the SPD turned the slogan successfully on its head, with the media going along with this personalisation of the campaign. Longtime Chancellor Kohl was cleverly satirised as last year's model. With the hand over in Düsseldorf, where, on 27 May 1998, the respected and longserving Minister President Johannes Rau passed on the baton to the dynamic moderniser Wolfgang Clement, the SPD introduced a change of leadership which was well received by the media and the public at large[64],

---

64 See Ristau, Der Wahlkampf der SPD, p. 8.

and increased the pressure on the Union. Gerhard Schröder was "without doubt the more popular politician, with the aura of a winner and of a man who gets things done, extremely personable, but who in addition is seen quite clearly as the person most likely to solve Germany's future problems."[65] The election result on 27 September 1998 was therefore also a success for him personally, just as it represented a clear personal defeat for Helmut Kohl.

Changes of government in the Federal Republic had hitherto only taken place in the context of changed coalitions: in 1966, for instance, with the SPD entering government, 1969 with the previous FDP opposition joining the SPD in government, and in 1982 when the FDP had switched allegiances to Helmut Kohl. For the first time in German postwar history, the change of government and power had been directly brought about by the electorate. The CDU/CSU had been severely rebuffed, and fallen to 35.2 per cent. The FDP suffered slight losses (6.2), as did the Greens (6.7). The single, great victor, and by a clear margin, were the SPD who increased their vote from 36.4 to 40.9 per cent. They were the strongest party with all age groups apart from the over-sixties, made above average gains amongst white-collar workers, and, in the new states, were streets ahead of the Union: the CDU had been six points ahead of them in 1994, whereas the SPD now led there by 15 per cent. In comparison with 1994, the Social Democrats had gained some three million second ballots more, mainly from former CDU/CSU voters and previous non-voters.[66] Whereas, prior to the election, a grand coalition of CDU/CSU and SPD had seemed the most likely outcome, and for many citizens the most desirable one, the way the electorate had voted had produced a decision in favour of a red-green coalition, which was arguably what many people had not wanted. Nonetheless, it was clear by the night of the SPD's magnificent election victory that the name of the next Federal Chancellor would be Gerhard Schröder.

---

65 Ibid., p. 12.
66 See Forschungsgruppe Wahlen, Bundestagswahl 1998. Eine Analyse der Wahl vom 27. September 1998 (Mannheim 1998), esp. pp. 21 ff. and pp. 71 ff.; Jung and Roth, 'Wer zu spät geht', pp. 13–16.

IV. The Schröder Government and the SPD as the Party of Government

1. Shaky Beginnings and Consolidation

After the election victory on 27 September which had paved the way for a coalition of the SPD and the Greens, it was a matter not only of mapping out the direction Gerhard Schröder's government would take, but also of settling the balance of influence between the two parties and their leading figures. In the coalition discussions with the Greens the tone was set primarily by the party chairman Lafontaine. This led to the red-green coalition agreements taking on a social and ecological character. The themes of "innovation", the "New Centre", and the modernisation of state and society on which Gerhard Schröder had stood in the election campaign took something of a back seat. In view of the huge mountain of debt which had accumulated under the Kohl government, there was precious little scope for closing the gap between rich and poor. It was precisely in the social sphere, however, where improvements were expected. The practical difficulties faced by the new red-green government under Gerhard Schröder were enormous. It was all too understandable, given the time they had spent in opposition, that there would be teething troubles. Moreover, the administration had been heavily influenced by sixteen years of Kohl government. Even in the handing over of government affairs there were unfair practices. The removal of files and the wiping of computer data in the Chancellor's office immediately following the CDU/CSU's losing the election are glaring examples of this. Also, right from the start, the complicated nature of relationships amongst the SPD leadership proved to be a strain.

With Wolfgang Thierse, the German Bundestag had its first East German President. On 27 October 1998, Gerhard Schröder was elected Federal Chancellor by the unanimous vote of the 345 coalition deputies, with a further six votes coming from the opposition benches. There were few surprises in the allocation of ministerial posts, with eight going to the SPD, and three to the Greens.[1] The prominent lawyer Herta Däubler-Gmelin was given the Ministry of Justice, and Otto Schily, the spokes-

---

1 On the selection of the ministerial team, see Lafontaine, Das Herz schlägt links, pp. 112–118.

man on domestic affairs and former Green, the Ministry of the Interior. Giving the Ministry of Labour and Social Affairs to Walter Riester, who came from the trade union IG Metall and was known to be receptive to political reform, also symbolised the readiness to tread new paths in social policy. The recruitment by Schröder of the independent Werner Müller as Minister for Economic Affairs[2] signalled his keenness to bring in expertise from the business world. The successful election campaign manager Franz Müntefering was given the transport portfolio, and Heidi Wieczorek-Zeul the Ministry for Development. Edelgard Bulmahn and Karl-Heinz Funke from Lower Saxony took over the Ministry for Research and the Ministry of Agriculture respectively, Christine Bergmann from the ranks of the East German Social Democrats was made head of the Ministry for Families, Youth, and Pensioners. Somewhat surprisingly, Bodo Hombach was put in charge of the Chancellery. From the Greens, Foreign Minister Joschka Fischer convinced the initially sceptical with his political skill, and rapidly gained in stature and respect. Jürgen Trittin, who for some time had been to many like a red rag to a bull, gradually began to toe the line. For Rudolf Scharping, who would have liked to remain leader of the parliamentary party with his own power base, the path to the Hardthöhe and the Ministry of Defence was not easy. He had not emerged unscathed from the earlier political and personal skirmishes, but loyalty and common sense finally convinced him to step into line.[3] Peter Struck, who had been the party's parliamentary business manager, was elected leader of the party in the Bundestag.

These, however, were just the preliminaries of the real power struggle to come. It began "when, on the day of the change of government, the marriage of convenience between Lafontaine and Schröder collapsed"[4]. Lafontaine took the leading role in the coalition negotiations, extended the authority of the Ministry of Finance which he had taken over, and made it his control centre. With the chairmanship of the party in his hands, the media regarded him as a kind of "counter-Chancellor". Erhard Eppler described this existence of two power centres as a basic design fault in the red-green coalition.[5] In the initial phase of government, it seemed as if it was mainly Lafontaine who was determining policy. This

---

2 Jost Stollmann had originally been in line for this post, but he withdrew at the last minute.
3 Lafontaine gives an account of this which is very critical of Scharping in Das Herz schlägt links, pp. 121–126.
4 Der Spiegel, 4.10.1999, p. 24. See also the article in the same issue, 'Der lange Weg zum kurzen Abschied', pp. 116–130.
5 Ibid., p. 125.

was very much dictated by the promise of greater social justice which had been made. The changes introduced by the previous government on the law on wrongful dismissal, the continued payment of wages in the case of sickness, and to pensions, were all revoked. Child benefit was increased, a programme on combating youth unemployment introduced. In addition there were new regulations on 630-DM jobs, which now became subject to national insurance contributions, and measures designed to put a stop to those designating themselves as "self-employed" for tax purposes.

The revision of the law on nationality was intended, amongst other things, to ease the naturalisation and integration of foreigners living in Germany and, under certain conditions, permitted the holding of dual nationality. This was actually long overdue, since the old law ("jus sanguinis") still bore the imprint of *völkisch* (nationalistic) thinking from the time of Imperial Germany and National Socialism. The population at large, however, had its reservations. Roland Koch (CDU) inflamed and exploited these in populist fashion during the Landtag election campaign in Hesse, with money from dubious sources also playing its part. On 7 February, in spite of small gains by the SPD and Hans Eichel, the CDU carried the day. Lafontaine now wanted to "bring the CDU in on the responsibility for the nationality question", and, after the Kurdish riots, spoke in favour of looking at "easier methods of deportation". His main opponent on this was Herta Däubler-Gmelin. Behind Lafontaine's complaints about lack of coordination and the government's failure to present a "united front" lay unmistakable frustration.[6]

Lafontaine's initiatives on financial policy – attempting to control international financial capital, for instance – met with resistance in Germany, and from its Western partners. They were scarcely compatible with the free market principles favoured by Atlanticists and the Chancellor, nor with the need to boost the economy, consolidate the budget, and simplify the tax system.

Lafontaine had overestimated himself and the extent of his powers. Clear moves to counteract him emanated from Bodo Hombach and the Chancellery, with a campaign being mounted to embark on a market-oriented "modernisation course" such as the one Tony Blair had successfully implemented in Great Britain under "New Labour". Faced by a

6 See especially the minutes of the presidium meeting on 22.2.1999 in the secretariat of the SPD executive. On the reservations about the revision of the nationality laws, see Lafontaine, Das Herz schlägt links, pp. 172–177, as well as the presidium meeting of 9.2.1999. On the revision, which was finally passed on 7.5.1999, see the account in Archiv der Gegenwart, vol. 69 (1999), p. 43533.

Chancellor whose right to determine policy guidelines gave him the upper hand, and who had a well-developed instinct for power, the party chairman found himself sidelined. There could only be one hand on the tiller. It came as a bombshell when, on 11 March 1999, Lafontaine announced his resignation both as Finance Minister and party chairman.[7] On 14 March he gave "poor teamwork", as well as his "private life" as the reasons for this step, concluding with the comment, "the heart is still not traded on the stock exchange, but it has a firm location: it beats on the left"[8].

Many Social Democrats, particularly on the left of the party, but also members of the Greens, were taken aback by the resignation, and felt offended that he had dumped the party chairmanship as he would a damp towel. Looking back in *Das Herz schlägt links* (The Heart beats on the Left), Lafontaine accused the ruling Social Democrats, as well as the Greens, of having sacrificed principles and making errors.[9] Chancellor Schröder described his surprising step as a "logical and honourable decision".[10] Fundamentally, it was in fact a decision of principle between the old opposition profile of the SPD, and what was required of a party now in government who were committed to their international obligations, and were tackling urgent domestic reforms (budget, taxes, labour market, and the economy). The well-known Polish political commentator Adam Krzeminski put it as follows: "It is clear that a 'social duel' has taken place", in which Schröder, "representing the Blair line", has "won the day" with the "so-called New Centre". He suspected that Lafontaine's resignation "would basically strengthen the SPD".[11] At the party congress in Bonn on 12 April 1999, Gerhard Schröder was elected Lafontaine's successor with an "honest" majority.[12] The offices of Chancellor and party chairman were now in one hand. This prepared the ground for a closer relationship between government and the party, and for the avoidance of friction.

7   Already in an article in 1990, Peter Glotz characterised him as "unpredictable", saying that he "was capable at any moment of chucking everything in, and getting on with his life." See, 'Versuch über Lafontaine', in Neue Gesellschaft/Frankfurter Hefte, no. 7 (1990), pp. 583 ff. Lafontaine has given his own view and explanation of the run-up to, and circumstances of, his resignation in Das Herz schlägt links. See esp. p. 143, p. 153, p. 223, pp. 225–233, p. 243 f., and p. 276.
8   Quoted from Archiv der Gegenwart, vol. 69 (1999), p. 43387 f.; wording also in Lafontaine, Das Herz schlägt links, pp. 230–232.
9   Lafontaine, Das Herz schlägt links, passim; on the Greens, esp. p. 150 f., and pp. 153 ff.
10 "Special session" of the presidium "on the resignation of Oskar Lafontaine", minutes in the SPD-Vorstandsarchiv.
11 Quoted from the Archiv der Gegenwart, vol. 69 (1999), p. 43388.
12 He received 75.98 per cent of the votes cast.

*Gerhard Schröder at the party congress in Bonn, 12 April 1999.
Caption reads: "Responsibility"*

The unresolved leadership conflict had contributed considerably to the problems of coordination which surfaced initially in the work of the government. Although the head of the Chancellery, Frank-Walter Steinmeier, rapidly gained respect internally, he could only fully develop his abilities as an efficient coordinator in the style of a Manfred Schüler[13] after Bodo Hombach had vacated his post as Chancellery Minister. The verdict of the political analysts Richard Stöss and Oskar Niedermayer on this first phase was that "given the current extremely differentiated process of formulating political demands and objectives and decision-making, there was a lack of a vital central control mechanism, and of a reliable early-warning system with which political mistakes could have been spotted and corrected at an early stage"[14]. There were problems of coordination and communication within the government, as well as in the relations between the government and the party, the parliamentary party, and the SPD-led

---

13 Manfred Schüler was head of the Chancellery under Helmut Schmidt from 1974 to 1980.
14 Richard Stöss and Oskar Niedermayer, 'Zwischen Anpassung und Profilierung. Die SPD an der Schwelle zum neuen Jahrhundert'. In Aus Politik und Zeitgeschichte, B5/2000, p. 7.

federal states. On sober reflection, this was no wonder. After so many years in opposition, how to operate in government has to be learned. The Kohl government after 1982 had also had its share of teething troubles and mishaps. Moreover, after the years of stagnation, the red-green coalition wanted too much, too quickly. This led to basic errors and inadequately prepared legislation which often had to be amended and revised.[15] This frequently led to irritation and confusion. Difficulties over the 630-DM jobs, the law against those designating themselves as "self-employed" for tax purposes, as well as the to-ing and fro-ing on health reform, are all examples of this.

On 23 May 1999, Johannes Rau was elected as the new Federal President. His talent for reconciliation, his reflective manner, his Christian beliefs, and his sensitivity in dealing with the Nazi past seemed to make him absolutely predestined for this office. Only once in the entire history of the Federal Republic had it been occupied by a Social Democrat – from 1966 to 1971, by Gustav Heinemann, Johannes Rau's patron. He took up office on 1 July. In his own, particular way, his main energies were directed against xenophobic excesses and attacks on Jewish institutions which were reaching frightening proportions, and he made the integration of foreigners living in Germany one of the central concerns of his presidency.

The image of the red-green government was not the best. The coalition rapidly lost popular support. In the European elections on 13 June the CDU made considerable gains, and, by comparison with the 1994 election, the SPD dropped 1.5 percentage points, and 10.2 points compared to the Bundestag elections. Then after the summer "silly season", they received a severe battering in Landtag elections in autumn. On 5 September 1999, the party slipped by 5 percentage points in the Saar, losing their overall majority. Reinhard Klimmt (SPD) was succeeded as Minister President by Peter Müller of the CDU. In Brandenburg the SPD slumped by 14.8 percentage points, and Manfred Stolpe was reduced to forming a coalition government with the CDU. A week later the next disaster struck: In Thuringia a loss of 11.1 points, and a similarly grim result in the local elections in North Rhine-Westphalia, where the SPD lost some of its traditional strongholds in the Ruhr to the CDU. Across the country as a whole they achieved only 33.9 per cent, whereas the CDU were up to 50.3. In Saxony on 19 September they suffered a loss of 5.9 percentage points, and in Berlin, after the all-time low of 23.6 per cent in 1995, there was a fur-

---

15 Lafontaine lays the blame for this exclusively on other people, mainly on Chancellor Schröder. See Das Herz schlägt links, esp. pp. 161–168.

ther decline to 22.4 per cent.[16] Along with factors specific to individual states, policy at federal level played an important part in these electoral setbacks. There was an evident and almost universal loss of approval, most marked, however, among the unemployed, who were disappointed that a drop in unemployment was slow in coming, and the low and middle-income self-employed who were upset by the regulations on 630-DM jobs, as well as on those describing themselves as "self-employed" for tax purposes. Those in the East who abandoned the SPD voted, in roughly equal measure, either for the CDU or the PDS, or did not vote at all. According to data from the Forsa Institute, countrywide in autumn 1999, less than 20 per cent expressed a preference for the SPD; the CDU/CSU were in the lead, and many of those polled were undecided.[17] The result of the celebrated "Sunday question" was that by October 1999 the SPD had steadily declined from the 40.9 per cent in the Bundestag elections to 32 per cent, while in the same period the CDU/CSU had made strong gains.[18] Popular acceptance of the Schröder government was dramatically low, and they found themselves in a serious crisis.

Gerhard Schröder, whom sections of the press, not without their own particular agenda, had subjected to malicious comment, dubbing him the "Brioni-", "Cashmere-", and "Cohiba-cigar-Chancellor", also found himself in the firing line. Sections of the media were already proclaiming Rudolf Scharping as the "Chancellor in reserve", who was just waiting for his hour to come.[19] With the Schröder/Blair paper of June 1999, the Chancellor had made a surprise intervention in the discussion about policy. It bore the hallmark of the "modernisers", taking its direction from the market-oriented policies of "New Labour" under Tony Blair, and from the "Third Way" propagated by his influential advisor Anthony Giddens. This was, according to Schröder, Germany's "New Centre".[20] The aim of the paper was to reduce state expenditure, also in the social sphere, to make the economy more dynamic, to introduce tax reforms, and it also advocated that the Social Democrats should adopt some aspects of liberalism. The "traditionalists" in the party on the other hand, taking their cue from Lionel Jospin in France, were emphatically in favour of state control

16 For a good overview of these elections, see Archiv der Gegenwart, vol. 69 (1999), pp. 43767–43770.
17 See Stöss and Niedermayer, pp. 6 ff., and the chart, 'Political mood after the Bundestag elections'.
18 See the chart giving the corresponding data in Der Spiegel, 6.12.1999.
19 See Der Spiegel, 15.11.1999, and Stern, 25.11.1999.
20 See Anthony Giddens, The Third Way. The Renewal of Social Democracy (Cambridge 1998); Anthony Giddens, Beyond Left and Right. The Future of Radical Politics (Cambridge 1994).

as a way of turning things round.[21] Many comrades had difficulties with the concept of the "comrade of the bosses". Instead of globalisation and modernisation, they favoured greater social justice, redistribution of wealth, and even more state intervention. In a party somewhat unsure of itself, the Chancellor and party chairman found himself swimming against the tide. The state of the party apparatus was such that it was unable to offer strong support. A further aggravating factor was the moving of party headquarters from Bonn to the Willy-Brandt-Haus in Berlin in late summer 1999, along with the transferring of the seat of government and parliament. This created not only logistical problems which had to be dealt with, but it also required adjustment to a different media landscape in the federal capital, and a much rougher political climate.

Late autumn of 1999 saw a change in fortunes, with both government and party returning to an even keel. Ottmar Schreiner, the party's business manager appointed under Lafontaine and who belonged to the left-wing "traditionalists", vacated his position, and was replaced by the successful 1998 election campaign duo, Franz Müntefering and Matthias Machnig. Initially as business manager, and then from December on, as General Secretary directly elected by the party congress, Müntefering successfully managed to remotivate the battered party and to restore its effectiveness. Schröder sought support for his policies at four regional conferences in the run-up to the Berlin party congress (7 to 9 December), emphasising the importance he attached to the basic principle of social justice.[22] With a decisive rescue operation for the Holzmann building concern and its 30,000 workforce[23], the Chancellor Schröder showed both resolve and a social conscience. "The people want leadership", he declared. He was confirmed in this by EMNID polls, according to which 78 per cent of SPD supporters blamed the poor image of the coalition for the election failures, but only 24 per cent the Chancellor.[24]

To many observers, the appointment of Hans Eichel as Finance Minister seemed no more than a stopgap solution. After an initial package of economy measures, and with the programme aimed at reducing the deficit in public expenditure, the discontent only seemed to intensify. It was directed at the economy measures as well as the plans for the reform of pensions, which, in the first instance, were to be pegged for two years to

21 See S. Heimann, Die SPD der neunziger Jahre, p. 96 f.; by same author, 'Von den Franzosen lernen? Lionel Jospins Reformprojekt: links und sozialistisch – trotzdem erfolgreich, in spw, no. 118 (2001).
22 See Gerhard Schröder, 'Starke Partei', Vorwärts, December 1999, p. 6.
23 See Archiv der Gegenwart 69 (1999), p. 43913 f.
24 See Der Spiegel, 6.12.1999, p. 33.

the rate of inflation. The "ecology tax", out of which the burden on pension funds was to be relieved, thereby lowering additional wage costs, was criticised as socially unbalanced. But, in fact, Eichel's economy measures represented a move to more convincing government policies. However, his argument that a state paying 82 billion Deutschmarks in annual interest was barely able to function, and that the financing of that interest through taxes was "a major redistribution of wealth from the bottom to the top", and therefore unjust, only gradually began to sink in.[25] A well-known political commentator praised him for this "different social philosophy for the twenty-first century", and, for the first time having taken the future into consideration on a social issue.[26] The ground was being prepared on which the Schröder government could sow the seed for the harvest to come. Hans Eichel played a decisive part in this. As Finance Minister he became one of the pillars of the cabinet, and soon won wide popular respect. Following the enormous mountain of debt left by the Kohl government, which amounted to 1.5 trillion, or 1,500 billion Deutschmarks, and was only in part a result of the financing of German unification[27], the immediate political priority was to put state finances on a solid footing, something the conservative-liberal coalition had singularly failed to do. The Social Democrats, so often discredited as the party of redistribution of wealth, now set about tackling this thorny problem under their Finance Minister and Chancellor. As a prelude to "winning back viability for the future", savings in the region of 27 billion Deutschmarks were made in the 2000 budget. This took courage and tenacity, particularly with regard to party comrades and large sections of their supporters.

The SPD party congress in Berlin in December 1999 was a harmonious affair, although things had looked rather different in the run-up to it. In many of the motions from local party organisations there could still be heard an outdated insistence on wealth redistribution, whereas the message from the executive was one of "independence", "taking responsibility for oneself", and "personal initiative". "Responsibility for Germany" and "the future needs courage" were the slogans with which the party leadership and the Chancellor were advocating the need for measured policies. Exuding energy, Schröder emerged from this test of strength with flying colours.

25 See Eichel's speech of 15.9.1999 on the budget. In Verhandlungen des Deutschen Bundestages (stenographic report), vol. 197, pp. 4649–4660.
26 This was Warnfried Dettling, former head of the planning department in the Konrad-Adenauer-Haus. See Der Spiegel, 6.12.1999, p. 35.
27 Of the 1.5 trillion, or 1,500 billion DM, some 900 billion went towards the cost of German unification. The figure of "900 Million DM" given in the text of the Eichel speech in the Archiv der Gegenwart 69 (1999), p. 43771, is incorrect.

In Wolfgang Clement, the Minister President of North Rhine-Westphalia, a proven moderniser was promoted to deputy party chairman. At this party congress, the SPD closed ranks and took fresh courage. The Schröder government had fallen in step, and the party had recovered itself. The mood in the country changed. Between November and December the SPD went up by ten points in the polls, while the CDU/CSU simultaneously plummeted from 55 to 43 per cent.[28]

The CDU party-finances scandal excited a good deal of attention. It was a setback for the CDU/CSU Union, who had thought themselves to be on the road to victory. Since November, the headlines had been dominated by reports about a whole range of dubious CDU financial practices. The investigation of what amounted to infringements of common law had been instigated by the district court in Augsburg which, on 4 November, had issued a warrant for the arrest of the former CDU treasurer Walther Leisler Kiep. It emerged that Helmut Kohl, once the herald of a spiritual and moral *Wende*, and who liked to be regarded as a politician of integrity, had been the recipient of large, undeclared donations which had been squirreled away in illegal special accounts. On 30 November, the ex-Chancellor publicly admitted this. He was reluctant to reveal the names of the alleged donors, and has not done so to this day. Around the turn of the year 1999/2000, it was revealed that the CDU in Hesse had transferred millions of Deutschmarks abroad, thereby breaching the Law on Political Parties, and had used this money to finance their election campaigns. These illicit practices had been covered up by claiming that the money had come from bequests made by Jewish citizens. The favoured instrument for concealing these schemes by the Hessian CDU, as well as by the CDU at federal level, was a network of fictitious "foundations" in Liechtenstein, and a whole variety of special accounts.[29] Barely a week went by without fresh news of the scandal surrounding CDU donations hitting the headlines. Bundestag and Hessian Landtag committees of investigation attempted to pick their way through the morass. Investigations were set in train by the public prosecutor's office.

These unbelievable infringements of the law and common decency brought the Union down to earth with a bump, leaving them at rock bottom in the polls. In the first months of 2000, they plummeted to 31 per cent on the "Sunday question" asking people how they intended to vote,

---

[28] See the findings of the Forschungsgruppe Wahlen (electoral research group), in Politbarometer no. 12 (1999), p. 1.

[29] See the accounts in the Archiv der Gegenwart 69 (1999), pp. 44000–44003, and 70 (2000), pp. 44039–44043. Also Der Spiegel in its issues from November 1999 on, and many articles in the Süddeutsche Zeitung, particularly those of 5./6.2. and 1./2.7.2000.

with the SPD enjoying an upward curve at 43 per cent. But opinions were not the same as votes. In the Landtag elections on 27 February in Schleswig-Holstein, the CDU suffered losses, but, in view of the scandals, these were not as heavy as might have been expected. With gains for the SPD, Heide Simonis was able to remain in power with the red-green coalition. In North Rhine-Westphalia as well, Wolfgang Clement was able to carry on in government with the Greens, even though both the SPD and the Greens had suffered losses in the elections on 14 May. Winners were the FDP, who, under their ever busy leader Jürgen Möllemann, went up to 9.8 per cent.[30] They benefited from the loss of respect for the CDU and were now calculating their chances of once again being able to tip the scales as a party of government at both federal and state level.

The SPD was also affected by scandals in this period, but they were peanuts compared to those of the CDU. The Minister President of Lower Saxony, Gerhard Glogowski, resigned on 26 November 1999 because of a travelling expenses affair. He was succeeded by Sigmar Gabriel. In North Rhine-Westphalia, Finance Minister Heinz Schleußer resigned in January 2000 as a result of the "flight affair" – stirred up mainly by *Focus* – admitting he had made mistakes, but declaring his innocence.[31] The CDU in North Rhine-Westphalia also attempted to pin something on Federal President Johannes Rau. Although the CDU at federal level was not directly involved, on the quiet the campaigns against leading Social Democrats in North Rhine-Westphalia continued. The new Minister of Transport, Reinhard Klimmt, who in November 2000 was in the headlines because of bogus contracts for his football club 1. FC Saarbrücken, resigned on 16 November. His successor was the former parliamentary Secretary of State, Kurt Bodewig.[32] Social Democrats were certainly open to temptation and liable to make mistakes. But there was a huge gulf between affairs such as these, and the criminal energy with which the CDU set about its illegal machinations. The SPD miscreants were always taken to task, and, despite the solidarity so often evoked by the party, were invariably thrown out of office. The appalling scandals surrounding the patronage exercised by small party cliques in Cologne, which came to light early in 2002, desperately needed clearing up, and for firm action to be taken against the guilty parties.[33] These and other misdemeanours inflict untold damage.

30 Archiv der Gegenwart 70 (2000), p. 44103 and p. 44242. In Schleswig-Holstein, the SPD won 43.1 and the CDU 35.2, in North Rhine-Westphalia the SPD 42,8 and the CDU 37.0 per cent of the vote.
31 Archiv der Gegenwart 69 (1999), p. 43999f., and 70 (2000), p. 44045.
32 See Archiv der Gegenwart 70 (2000), p. 44584.
33 See press reports at the beginning of March 2002.

Throughout almost the entire first half of 2000, the CDU continued to excite attention and create a bad impression. Wolfgang Schäuble, who had succeeded Helmut Kohl as party chairman on 7 November 1998, was forced to resign on 16 February 2000 following a dubious financial transaction and severe internal party pressure. His successor as chairman of the parliamentary party was the former financial spokesman, Friedrich Merz, with General Secretary Angela Merkel being elected as the new party chairman at the party congress in Essen in April 2000.[34] Their General Secretary Ruprecht Polenz threw in the towel after only six months, and was replaced by Laurenz Meyer, who had made a name for himself with his vigorous attacks on the SPD-led state government in North Rhine-Westphalia. To get off the back foot – a situation largely of their own making – the Union found themselves almost desperately clutching at every straw in an effort to attack the government. After Merz, the chairman of the parliamentary group, had scored an own goal with the debate he had fomented about German *Leitkultur* (core cultural values), they seized upon the BSE crisis[35] to attack the Minister of Agriculture, Karl-Heinz Funke, and then unleashed a campaign against the steep rise in the price of petrol which had resulted from the high cost of crude oil and a strong dollar, and was annoying many drivers. The federal government introduced social measures to compensate for the increased energy costs, and the Chancellor took the personal and political consequences of the BSE crisis. Renate Künast of the Greens proved to be a good choice as Minister for Consumer Protection. She rapidly gained recognition and respect and became one of the cabinet's great assets. The thorny task of health reform was now in the hands of the new minister, Ulla Schmidt (SPD).

The crisis in the Union was certainly helpful to the red-green coalition. But after a shaky start, Gerhard Schröder's government had steadied itself. After difficult negotiations with the big energy providers, it had begun the phasing-out of atomic power. It had inherited not only a huge mountain of debt from the previous government, but also mass unemployment. In January 1998, still under Kohl, the number of unemployed had risen to almost 4.9 million. Gerhard Schröder had optimistically declared that he and his government would be "measured" by their ability to reduce unemployment. He had set a target of 3.5 million for the end of his first term in office. Under the new government there was indeed a reduction in unemployment, which had fallen to 3.724 million by June

---

34 Ibid., p. 44099 and p. 44125 f.
35 The first cases of mad cow disease in Germany occurred at the end of November 2000.

2000, the lowest figure since 1995.[36] Helped by a reviving economy, the number of people in work rose by 500,000 in both 1999 and 2000, an annual increase of 1.5 per cent.[37] Thanks to the ecology tax, pension insurance contributions were reduced and comprehensive tax reforms set in train. With an energy of which barely anyone beforehand had thought it capable, the government had set about the reorganisation of public finances, and had also proved itself in the difficult challenge for German foreign policy presented by the war in Kosovo.

On 25 July 2000, Chancellor Gerhard Schröder drew up a mid-term balance sheet. On the credit side he stated that the log jam of reforms had been overcome and that there was no longer any talk, as there had been for years, of the "German disease". With the biggest tax reform "in the history of our country", the citizens and the economy would be relieved by 2005 of a burden of some 93 billion Deutschmarks. The consolidation of the budget was underway, measures against youth unemployment had been successful, and in the course of the current and coming year more than half a million further jobs would be created. Difficult negotiations over compensation for forced labourers under the Nazis had been successfully concluded, the decision to phase out nuclear energy had been taken, reform of the Bundeswehr had been set in motion, and with the "green-card initiative" the way ahead had been smoothed for the recruitment of urgently needed specialists from abroad.[38] The record so far of the red-green government was indeed respectable. And especially on foreign policy it had been tested, and had achieved, far more than emerges from Schröder's understatement: "In our foreign and European policy we have finally demonstrated our value as an alliance partner and our sense of international responsibility."

2. *Growing Maturity in the Face of Difficult Challenges*

The main and ambitious goal of the Schröder government on coming to power was to bring about social and political reforms, an improvement in the labour market, innovations, and a modern economic policy. In foreign policy the red-green coalition persisted with a calm and self-confident continuation of the tried and tested European and Atlantic course.

---

36 Statistisches Jahrbuch 2001 für die Bundesrepublik Deutschland, p. 118 and pp. 124–127; see too, Archiv der Gegenwart 70 (2000), p. 44368.
37 Statistisches Jahrbuch 2001, p. 112; see, also, the comments of Finance Minister Eichel in the budget debate on 1.12.2000, text in Archiv der Gegenwart, pp. 44634–44637.
38 For the text of his statement at a press conference on 25.7.2000 in Berlin, see Archiv der Gegenwart 70 (2000), p. 44371 f.

And yet, when the conflicts which had been simmering for years in the Balkans escalated in spring 1999 in Kosovo, it was faced with difficult decisions. Following the outbreak of civil war in Bosnia-Herzegovina, the SPD had finally managed to bring itself to vote in the Bundestag in favour of participating in peace-keeping missions under UN control. Military intervention in Kosovo, however, was a whole new dimension. After the failure of the conference at Rambouillet near Paris, the fighting and ethnic cleansing continued. On 24 March 1999, Nato began air strikes against rump Yugoslavia, with German fighter jets playing their part. NATO was waging war in Kosovo even without a UN mandate. The red-green coalition gave its assent to this. Foreign Minister Joschka Fischer and Chancellor Schröder had played an important part in seeking a peaceful solution. They continued their efforts during the negotiations on the war, attempting to bring Russia on board.

Within the SPD, NATO intervention and the bombings were controversial. The debate revolved round the basic issue of the use of military force by NATO, without UN approval. Criticism was also voiced about the point of these air strikes, which were killing innocent people and not preventing the expulsion of Kosovan Albanians. At the SPD special congress in April 1999 in Bonn, not only the Chancellor but also Defence Minister Rudolf Scharping justified the course being pursued by the government, with the great majority of the delegates giving them its backing. Erhard Eppler played an important role in winning the support of left-wingers of pacifist inclination. Regarded as the party's moral authority, Eppler expressed in his speech his commitment to NATO intervention.[39]

The war in Kosovo put the architecture of unified Germany's foreign policy to the test. For decades, the Federal Republic had played its role in the era of East/West conflict under the protective shield of the superpower USA and NATO. Being closely integrated into the Western system of treaties and security was an integral part of its *raison d'État*. Only as a reliable partner was it able to exert effective influence in a NATO dominated by the USA. Any stepping out of line could arouse nothing but discord in the European-Atlantic common chorus. This was one of the lessons which the Schröder and Fischer government would learn from the Kosovo conflict after only a few months in office. Hand in hand with the increased sovereignty of unified Germany went a greater degree of international responsibility. This included, when other peaceful methods failed,

---

39 See the Protokoll of the party congress in Bonn 12 April 1999, pp. 34–54, pp. 58–67, pp. 110–113, pp. 141–144.

participating in operations requiring military force. It was not until 11 September 2001, however, that this was voiced openly.[40]

The lessons of the Nazi past were often adduced, mainly by Defence Minister Rudolf Scharping and Foreign Minister Joschka Fischer, to justify German participation in military intervention. This was a major turnabout, since many Social Democrats, as well as the Greens, had for years been urging that German soldiers should never again set foot in countries which had been conquered and laid waste by German troops during the Nazi period. There was a widespread view, held far beyond the ranks of the left, that, as a consequence of the experience of Nazism, war should never again spring from German soil, only peace.

The Basic Law states that the dignity of man is inviolable. In a short speech of thanks following his election as Federal President on 23 May 1999, Johannes Rau emphasised that human rights and human dignity were inseparable, and applied to all people.[41] This was the essential lesson of the experience of the murderous Nazi dictatorship and its contempt for human life. Only by powerful military action could this expansionist, criminal system be defeated. The Germans in particular had a special obligation to do what they could for the persecuted and the oppressed, and to oppose dictators and every manifestation of genocide. Throughout its history, the SPD has always regarded itself as the party of peace and international understanding. Its aim, wherever possible, has been to find appropriate ways of nipping threatening conflicts and troubles in the bud, and to endeavour to resolve them peacefully. But this has never excluded the use of coercive measures as a last resort, which in borderline cases can also entail military force.

The war in Kosovo came to an end in June 1999. The Yugoslavian army and the Serbian defence forces withdrew from Kosovo, NATO troops together with Russian units moved in, and the Albanian refugees and expellees began to return. This did not yet, however, bring with it real peace. But with military intervention against the Milosevic regime, even though at the cost of human lives and serious destruction, conditions were created under which, even in Serbia, democracy was given a chance. For the states of the former Yugoslavia there was the prospect of a better future free of violence. In the clashes in Macedonia in 2001, the timely intervention of NATO put a stop to the further escalation of violence. Here too, as in Kosovo and Bosnia-Herzegovina, German soldiers were deployed to ensure order and peaceful coexistence amongst former ad-

---

40 See, in particular, Schröder's government statement of 11.10.2001 in the Bundestag, Bulletin der Bundesregierung no. 69/1 of 12.10.2001.
41 Full text in Archiv der Gegenwart 69 (1999), p. 43537f.

versaries. They also proved their worth as emergency workers. The German government had committed itself to reconstruction and the implementation of cooperative structures in this region. By patiently seeking to bring these countries gradually closer to Europe, they were pointing the way forward.

Under the red-green coalition, the Federal Republic was playing an important part on the foreign-policy front. Foreign Minister Joschka Fischer won great international recognition and respect for his sensitivity and skill in a crisis, and for the firmness he demonstrated whenever necessary. Chancellor Gerhard Schröder was a confident performer on the international stage. He represented German as well as European interests with dignity and the appropriate clarity. The international significance of unified Germany was increasing under the red-green government. In Europe it built bridges to the candidates for entry to the European Union, and nurtured its contacts with Russia as a way of keeping it more firmly in touch with the sphere of the Atlantic Alliance. In their dealings with the one remaining superpower, the USA, Schröder and Fischer found a viable path between the respect demanded by the marked difference in economic, political, and military power, and their own political concerns which were governed more by avoidance of conflict, mediation, and preservation of peace. This became clearer than ever after 11 September 2001.

Chancellor Gerhard Schröder found just the right words in branding the terrorist attack as an assault on the entire civilised world.[42] There were admittedly some reservations about his promise of "unlimited solidarity" with the USA. This was, however, the only way of creating a climate in which the Federal Republic, in alliance with other European states, could at least exert a certain influence on US-American policy. In *Der Spiegel*, Erhard Eppler impressively described the real significance of 11 September: namely as a new dimension in the undermining of the state by private, non-state, and barely controllable violence.[43] There was a broad consensus amongst political parties in the Federal Republic about the principle that the democratic state had to defend itself against this terrorist threat. Only the PDS (Party of Democratic Socialism), which certainly had no pacifist past whatsoever, played the peacemaker, probably in the hope of winning over former green voters. A minority of Greens and a few Social Democrats had certain reservations, mainly about the sending of Bundeswehr soldiers to Afghanistan. For the government's ability to act it was vital that it should secure a majority of its own, by means of a vote of con-

---

42 See the Bundespresseamt, text of Chancellor Schröder's press statement of 12.9.2001.
43 Der Spiegel, 8.10.2001, pp. 56–59.

fidence, for the deployment of troops to Afghanistan.[44] Both the SPD party congress in November in Nuremberg, as well as that of the Greens in Rostock which followed, gave their backing to government policy. On foreign affairs the red-green coalition demonstrated considerable strength and skill, and showed that it was able to cope with the increased responsibility. It steered the country through extremely troubled waters with a very steady hand.

The adoption of military tasks and responsibility in the theatres of crisis in Europe and the world cost money. Considerable additional resources had to be found for the Bundeswehr, which was stretched to the limit, and for internal security. At the same time the economy began to stagnate, and unemployment to rise. After foreign-policy challenges having been for so long to the forefront, by the winter of 2001/2002 economic problems were once more firmly on the agenda.

3. Profile and Practice of a Transformed SPD

"The Transformation of Social Democracy" was the title which, in 1998, the political scientist and Social Democratic theoretician Thomas Meyer gave his book on the change undergone by Social Democratic parties in Europe.[45] As in earlier publications, Meyer set his critical sights primarily on the trend towards politics as theatre. While clearly understanding the rules of modern media society, he made a plea for the preservation of programmatic principles and a lively and open internal party democracy. When Meyer published his studies, the SPD was still in opposition, but in the meantime Germany had a Social Democrat Chancellor, and the party was in government with the Greens. The responsibility of government brought with it actual as well as tactical restraints, with the main task of the party being to support the government and ensure that it always had a majority. This had asked a lot of the SPD, particularly on foreign affairs, ranging from the war in Kosovo to the military actions in the wake of 11 September 2001. But on the domestic front, too, directions had been taken for which an SPD which had been languishing in op-

---

44 See, inter alia, the Süddeutsche Zeitung of 17.11.2001 ("Dokumentation der wichtigsten Redebeiträge") and the Frankfurter Rundschau of 17.11.2001 (inter alia, speeches). The negative evaluation by Der Spiegel that the "agreement reached by brute force" possibly marked "the beginning of the end for the red-green coalition", and that the Chancellor had been left "battered", was a spectacular misreading of the true situation. See Der Spiegel, 19.11.2001, pp. 22–27.
45 Thomas Meyer, Die Transformation der Sozialdemokratie. Eine Partei auf dem Weg ins 21. Jahrhundert (Bonn 1998).

position for so long was ill-prepared. After the initial teething troubles, however, the party faced up to – smoothly for the most part – the changed tasks with which it was being confronted.

This was particularly visible in two areas: that of economic and financial policy, and in the sphere of internal security. The "alliance for work", on which initially many hopes had been pinned, brought only limited results. Given the empty coffers, the government could scarcely be a distributor of social munificence. It was counting on boosting the economy, and the creation of an investment-friendly climate. The party went along with this, as it did with the consolidation in fiscal policy. The billions resulting from the auctioning of UMTS licences went exclusively towards paying off the national debt, and the interest this saved was used for investment.[46] With the so-called "Riester pension", the coalition built a second pillar into the pension system which depended on subsidised self-provision for old age. With this, the SPD was taking into account not only the strains imposed by the serious shift in the age pyramid, but also the need for people to take more responsibility for themselves. Just as their sister parties in other West and North European countries, the German Social Democrats were initiating new policies in the social and state sector. While sticking to their basic principles, they were attempting to find solutions to current problems which would also benefit future generations. The tax reforms brought relief to those on lower incomes and benefited families. Social Democrat traditionalists found it harder to swallow the lowering of the highest rate of tax and improving the tax situation for business, from which the large joint-stock companies in particular profited. Schröder's government was determined to strengthen Germany as a base for economic investment. Globalisation, competition, and the free movement of capital had put business under increasing pressure. The boom in exports showed that the large concerns could withstand it, and the very large ones had long since become global players. The problems were with the small and medium-sized entrepreneurs and their complaints about non-wage costs and the complicated regulations on tax and labour law. There was increased pressure to free up job-protection laws and liberalise the labour market. This proved difficult for the trade unions, but despite these strains they maintained a working relationship with the government. The European social democracies once set standards with the welfare state. Throughout Europe, this has now been subject to reorganisation. Along with having to adapt to external and internal constraints, the SPD was faced with the task of anchoring the principles of social democracy much

---

46 See, for instance, Archiv der Gegenwart 70 (2000), p. 44438.

more effectively beyond the country's national borders, and of committing itself, in Germany's own self-interest, to the worldwide implementation of minimum social standards.

German social democracy has always attached great value to freedom and justice. Even before coming to power, the SPD put great emphasis on "internal security" and the need to combat organised crime. The attacks of 11 September made protection from terrorist threats a high priority. Otto Schily set the tone on this. Comments in the media that he was pursuing a law-and-order policy close to that of the CSU were not far off the mark. They were unfair, however. An adequate measure of internal and external security is indispensable for the preservation of freedom. The call for "security and order" was by no means as foreign to Social Democratic circles as it might seem. The state has an obligation to protect citizens and society from terrorist threats. For a society accustomed to freedom this also entails unaccustomed constraints. It is of the essence in a liberal democracy that as little harm as possible is inflicted on the freedoms of an open society. The SPD as the party of freedom knows the value of individual human rights. It holds the individual and his dignity to be the measure of all things. As an anti-totalitarian party, it has learned from history that tolerance has its limits. Confronted with those who use murderous methods and who trample human rights underfoot, a free society has to defend itself. Freedom and security are not antithetical, the one is a condition of the other.[47]

With a Social Democrat as Chancellor, the decisive power to shape affairs now lay with the comrades in government. The party inevitably declined in importance as an independent factor. The parliamentary party also lost some of its significance. Gerhard Schröder's style of government was largely focused on himself as Chancellor. He was at the centre of political power, supported by his cabinet. The SPD now seemed primarily a Chancellor party. There were, moreover, other factors emerging which were connected to changes to the political landscape as a whole. Historically, the SPD had always regarded itself as a party which drew its identity from its political programme and its members: this was the image it cultivated. Many historical accounts of the party had also taken their orientation largely from its programmatic statements. Real-existing social democracy, however, also had another face that was determined by the concrete, day-to-day demands and constraints of having to prove itself to

---

[47] These are the words of Chancellor Schröder in his speech "The Centre in Germany" on 22.02.2002 (text from the party executive, office of the SPD chairman); "According to our understanding of culture and openness, freedom and security are not opposites. We understand security as a civil right."

the voter and in government. Throughout the long years under Helmut Kohl, with the SPD occupying the opposition benches in Bonn, this was demonstrated mainly in the work of the local authorities and the states where the SPD was in government. The signature of the Social Democrats was often only marginally different, however, from that of the CDU-led local authorities and states. This led to frequent complaints about loss of profile, and the indistinguishableness of the big parties, with the spectre being raised of the "Americanisation" of the political landscape. The consequence of this has been that in political debate, and especially during election campaigns, opponents are attacked come what may, and differences of no real substance get blown out of all proportion. These skirmishes are frequently nothing more than show, put on to score points with the public. But they have become visibly bored and alienated, and even a party's particular clientele has seemed increasingly reluctant to get politically involved.

Years ago, the catchwords *Politik- und Parteienverdrossenheit* (disenchantment with politics and parties) did the rounds. There is barely any talk of them today, with electoral turnout having stabilised once again, albeit at a lower level. Yet in 1998 the electoral sociologist Stefan Immerfall asserted that the situation of the parties had in no way improved: "Instead of people's irritation with the parties – which at least shows that there is something on their minds – something worse is creeping in: indifference."[48] Membership figures for the large parties are an example of this. Since 1992, they have, without exception, been in decline. This has been much more marked in the case of the CDU than the SPD, due to exorbitant losses in the new states.[49] The prestige of the parties, and respect for them, have been decreasing, their loss of trust and credibility are as equally obvious as the decline in their appeal. The young in particular seem to be unattracted by the idea of becoming actively involved in a political party. This has been dramatically reflected in the SPD in the rapid drop in the number of younger party members.[50]

The days of the old members' party seemed numbered. Earlier attempts to make it more attractive by introducing directly democratic elements and opening it up to non-members did not bring the desired success. It was almost as if the party leadership had resigned itself to the fact that a living grassroots social democracy was finally a thing of the past.

---

48 Stefan Immerfall, 'Strukturwandel und Strukturschwächen der deutschen Mitgliederparteien', in Aus Politik und Zeitgeschichte B, 1–2 (1998), pp. 3 ff.
49 See Elmar Wiesendahl, 'Wie geht es weiter mit den Großparteien in Deutschland?', in Aus Politik und Zeitgeschichte B, 1–2 (1998), table 2 on p. 19.
50 See above, p. 339.

The new catchphrases were "professionalisation", "efficiency", and "network party". Matthias Machnig, the party manager, was a main proponent of this course. Criticism that factors such as the individual, and motivation, were getting short shrift in all of this, were largely overlooked. It is, of course, beyond dispute that in regions where membership is low it is often difficult to find enough candidates to fill posts and seats. In many other places, too, the grassroots were hardly falling over themselves to help and to take on functions. Most noticeable, in a negative sense, was the small number of younger members. Most young people were turning their backs on the parties, including the Greens. And this, despite the fact that, particularly in the SPD, there were great opportunities for talented young politicians.

The crisis year of 1999, with bitter election defeats in the states and at local level, led to a generational shift in the SPD. It marked the introduction of new personnel. Younger, pragmatic politicians were making their mark in the party. After the resignation of Reinhard Klimmt following the election defeat in the Saar, the 33-year-old Heiko Maas replaced him as head of the SPD. Christoph Matschie, 38 years old, became chairman of the SPD in Thuringia, and the 35-year-old Ute Vogt became SPD leader in Baden-Württemberg. In Lower Saxony Sigmar Gabriel succeeded Gerhard Glogowski, becoming at 40 the youngest Minister President in the history of the Federal Republic. The so-called '68ers, who had set the tone for so long, were beginning to lose ground. Young, fresh, and industrious politicians who were not ideologically hidebound and were able to assert themselves now began to emerge. In many sub-regions 20-year-olds were making a name for themselves.[51] Amongst the political staff there were many lively, young go-getters who were obsessed with technology, and saw their main task as being "public relations". Barely any of them had what the Irish call "the smell of the nest", that genuinely Social Democrat feel to them. Even the SPD party congresses, which were once a forum for the discussion of issues of basic principle, had radically changed in character. By the end of the 1990s, they were being professionally orchestrated, and at the party congress in November 2001 in Nuremberg the SPD presented an image of itself as a faithful Chancellor party. With the loud and previously critical voices falling virtually silent, it gave its full blessing to Gerhard Schröder's action on Afghanistan.[52] From a party all too fixated on its programmes and principles, the SPD was transformed into a pragmatic party of government which closed ranks behind its leader Gerhard Schröder.

51 The then 26-year-old Jochen Ott, for instance, in 2001 in the sub-region Cologne.
52 See, for instance, Christoph Schwennicke, 'Nachbetrachtung zum Nürnberger Parteitag', in Die Neue Gesellschaft/Frankfurter Hefte, 1/2 (2002), p. 6.

The Social Democrats occupied a position in the party spectrum which gave them various options. Gerhard Schröder had been in national government with the Greens since 1998, when, in the course of 2001, the FDP made no secret of its wish to become a possible coalition partner. In the states, Kurt Beck in the Rhineland-Palatinate was still set on maintaining the SPD-FDP coalition which had existed since 1991, whereas in Brandenburg the SPD under Manfred Stolpe formed a coalition with the CDU. In North Rhine-Westphalia under Wolfgang Clement, and Schleswig-Holstein under Heide Simonis, the constellation was red-green. Following the controversial "Magdeburg model" of Reinhard Höppner, Harald Ringstorff's alliance in Mecklenburg-Western Pomerania with the PDS hit the headlines, as did the new red-red government coalition in Berlin under Klaus Wowereit. Even over a decade after the peaceful revolution and German unification there still existed well-founded qualms about the successor party to the SED. They were a result not only of the long-term legacy of Communist dictatorship in the GDR, but also of the political and ideological direction of the PDS. The Social Democrats still regarded them as their political opponents. But just as the CDU at local level was entirely capable of cooperation, even with the PDS, so in the East with the many PDS voters the SPD could not refuse to collaborate if responsible policies at state and local level were to be implemented. "Left-wing" competition from the Greens and PDS caused the SPD to move further to the centre. Under the motto "The Centre in Germany", Gerhard Schröder evoked a "political culture of the centre", characterising it as a "policy which preserves balance" and "combines innovation and justice", "self-responsibility and solidarity" as well as "renewal and cohesion".[53] Where, unlike in Lower Saxony, it did not have an overall majority, this position gave the SPD various coalition possibilities. In the democratic party spectrum, the Social Democrats had now occupied ground on which government power could flourish.

The era of the old three-party system in the Federal Republic was over. After the Greens came the establishment of a regional party, the PDS, and on the right a whole spectrum, ranging from right-wing populists such as Roland Schill to the right-wing extremists of the NPD, were jostling for favour. Tribal loyalties were in decline, and the readiness to teach parties a lesson by changing how one voted was on the rise. Deciding on the spur of the moment whom to vote for was playing an ever greater role, as was the image projected by the media of leading political personalities.

53 Speech by Gerhard Schröder on 20.2.2002, text from the party executive, office of the SPD chairman.

How politicians looked and performed was increasingly more important than what they actually had to say. Embarrassing situations and gaffes, eagerly pounced on by sensation-seeking journalists, could prove very damaging. Presenting a convincing image in the media was just as vital to the Schröder government as were its actual achievements: sorting out state finances, the Riester pension, foreign policy. Chancellor Gerhard Schröder was the SPD's strongest card. The Bundestag election on 22 September 2002 came down to a race between the Bavarian challenger, Edmund Stoiber, and Gerhard Schröder, who had demonstrated that he was capable of leading unified Germany through difficult terrain. With his charisma, and skill at using the media to get his message across, he and the Social Democrats held a very decent hand.

The orientation of political parties towards power, and the rejection of ideologically loaded, programmatic ballast, is the sign of a normal, well-grounded democracy. For the citizen, the significance of the parties has been reduced to a functional level. The lack of interest in them, as with almost all firmly established large organisations, must not be confused however with a general lack of interest in politics as such. Large numbers of citizens participate in society in a voluntary capacity. Citizens' action groups continue to thrive. Groups such as Greenpeace who mount spectacular "events" are very popular. Political parties can certainly not compete with them, since they are geared to a more permanent, broader spectrum of commitment. This is indispensable for the viability of our parliamentary democracy. Despite the difficulties, it would be in the parties' own interest to create more inducement to become involved. This cannot be achieved by the usual local constituency meetings, conferences of executive committees, study groups, and district organisations. Many of these are somewhat exclusive and tend to scare people away. An age in which society is dominated by the modern media demands new and open forms of communication, and these are in part being successfully pursued. Even more crucial is the need to let people feel that their commitment is welcome and worth the effort. The main burden here falls on the lower echelons of the party and the local and regional political representatives. But it applies equally at the top level too. The campaign to increase efficiency by being more professional also has its down side. According to one commentator, the "emotional bond with the party" has suffered, and "there have been endless complaints about the impersonal 'management system' in the Willy-Brandt-Haus in Berlin".[54] Many of those who had committed themselves to, and worked for, the party, mostly on a volun-

---

54 Heimann, Die SPD in den neunziger Jahren, p. 98.

tary basis, felt rejected. There was the impression that party managers were concentrating so much on their projects (the lavish Kampa 02[55], for instance) that, as a result, other areas which were of equal significance for the profile and standing of the SPD were suffering. There was a danger of losing touch, and critical feedback from the early danger signs was not always forthcoming.

There was a clear need to tighten up the SPD's decision-making structures. The system in the regions, which had developed historically, did not in many cases overlap with that of the states. In North Rhine-Westphalia, for instance, internal party power lay with the four regions. In addition, the decline in membership resulted in financial problems. When General Secretary Franz Müntefering attempted to bring about a unified state association, he met with particularly stiff resistance from his own old region West Westphalia. Not until the beginning of 2001 was it decided to abolish the regions. Since January 2002 a state association with sweeping powers and solid decision-making structures has been in existence. The Rhineland-Palatinate also made the change to a state association, albeit with vested rights for the old regions. Those responsible for getting things done hoped that this firming up of the organisational structures would strengthen their effectiveness.

In the modern media democracies it is political personalities in the main who determine the party image. Only those who understand the art of self-presentation on the TV screen have a chance of being successful with the public. The development is towards "presidential parties", and away from parties based on members and political programmes. But a democracy lives from the commitment of democrats. That is why it is not merely an isolated problem for the SPD, but one which affects the profile of our parliamentary democracy as a whole. The parties have played a large part in shaping it, and parties remain indispensable. But they cannot ignore the laws of the modern media world. It seems, therefore, that if we wish to strengthen people's involvement, even more urgent consideration must be given to increasing the ways in which citizens can participate in the political process. It is hard to conceive a genuinely civil society without a lively democracy. Social democracy still has enormous tasks ahead of it. The circumstances under which the SPD, as the party of freedom, has to prove itself have changed entirely.

---

55 The SPD's election campaign centre in the Oranienburger Straße in Berlin, set up in September 2002 on the lines of the 1998 Kampa.

The Willy-Brandt-Haus in Berlin, seat of the SPD executive committee

4. A Provisional Balance Sheet

In the party system of the old Federal Republic the "bourgeois camp" almost always had the upper hand over the Social Democrats. This had social as well as economic causes. The Union profited above all from the fact that, in the founding and construction phase of the Federal Republic, the Chancellor was always from the CDU, and that in the eyes of the population they represented a positive counterpart to the years of misery and war. The Social Democrats, restricted for many years to their role as the main opposition party, had to wait until the social changes of the 1960s for their chance to take on the responsibility of government in Bonn. They passed the test. Domestic reforms were set in train, and the great task of creating understanding with Germany's eastern neighbours was accomplished. After losing power, the party lapsed into oppositional patterns of behaviour which were not helpful for their public reputation. In the process of German unification the Social Democrats were left lagging well behind by the government coalition in Bonn. This was a burden they would have to bear for many years to come. Only when the majority of the electorate had grown tired of the "eternal" Chancellor Kohl, and the SPD was once more on an even keel, did the the red-green coalition under Gerhard Schröder have its opportunity.

For many years, the conflict between the "grandsons" paralysed and weighed heavily on the party. With the spectacular resignation of Oskar Lafontaine as Finance Minister and party chairman in spring 1999, the Gordian knot was cut, and the way left open for a Chancellor Gerhard Schröder who grew and became more convincing with the job, and for the transformation of the SPD into a mature party of government. There was occasional talk of a "presidential party" and a *Kanzlerwahlverein* (Chancellor-election association). But it was imperative in demonstrating what it could do in power that the party should get behind the Chancellor and support the policies for which he and his ministers bore responsibility. The SPD was therefore not a party which had been "shut down", and was "somewhat despondent, unsure of itself, and faint-hearted", as Franz Walter has described it.[56] It had become more realistic and mature and was facing up to urgent tasks in a rapidly changing world. The Social Democratic project of a humane society founded on freedom, justice, and tolerance was, and has remained, of urgent concern. It is a task in which modern social democracy has had repeatedly to prove itself.

In a modern society dominated by the leisure and entertainment industries, the process of formulating political demands and objectives has also undergone change. The written word and factual information count for less than personal image and the messages this conveys. In a media world dominated by television, one of the ground rules of the political landscape is to concentrate attention on a handful of outstanding politi-

---

56 Walter, Die SPD, p. 262 and pp. 264–266.

cians. Even the Greens, who once saw themselves as a kind of anti-party, have grasped this. Joschka Fischer, a one-time *Sponti* and the Minister in trainers[57], who since 1998 had developed into a widely respected and esteemed politician, was their trump card in the election. In confronting the opposition, the Social Democrats were counting first and foremost on their Chancellor. After getting to grips with important reforms, withstanding the challenges in foreign policy, and getting the economy going again, he was looking, with a "calm hand", to bring his first period in office to a successful conclusion.

But in 2001 the coalition ran into choppy waters. After years of boom, there was a downturn in the US economy which hit export-oriented Germany particularly hard. The 11 September 2001 and its consequences affected almost the entire world economy. In 2000 the gross domestic product had grown by 3 per cent[58], and according to prognoses from the economic institutes the economy was due to rise in 2001 and 2002 by 2.8 per cent. But the economy stagnated, and instead of falling as had been anticipated, unemployment rose.[59] At the end of January 2002 it stood at 4.29 million. This was still half a million less than in January 1998[60], but the envisaged goal of 3.5 million now seemed barely achievable. The CDU/CSU opposition under their Chancellor candidate Edmund Stoiber seized on this with great delight. The government camp lost popular support, the SPD's approval ratings declined, and the Union as well as the FDP began to realise they were in with a chance. A victory for Gerhard Schröder in the Bundestag election on 22 September, which many had viewed as a dead certainty, no longer seemed such a safe bet. It was down to the Chancellor to pull his party up by their bootstraps, and make one last push to win over the floating voters.

Almost as they had at the outset of the Schröder period in office, sections of the media began scoffing at the mistakes and weaknesses of the government over the labour market, sniping at them over setbacks and failures such as the bill to ban the NPD, and the new military transport plane, Airbus A 400 M. Defence Minister Rudolf Scharping had been under almost constant fire since his Mallorca escapade.[61] The inexcusable events

---

57 When being sworn in as a minister in Hesse, he turned up in trainers and jeans: see above, p. 286.
58 See the Statistisches Jahrbuch 2001 für die Bundesrepublik Deutschland, p. 656.
59 See Archiv der Gegenwart 70 (2000), p. 44208.
60 Because of a change in the way statistics were recorded, the figures often vary.
61 After being flown with his female companion to Mallorca by the Bundeswehr, Scharping, – to the delight of the popular press – made a spectacle of himself with his holiday antics.

at the Federal Employment Office[62] led to negative headlines. There were also the embarrassing examples of cronyism in Cologne, which, along with other damaging scandals, led to a loss of confidence amongst sections of the party and put a damper on the mood of *élan*. The Union were using delaying tactics to block the immigration law, even though it had been welcomed unanimously by the Churches, business, and the trade unions. With the votes of Manfred Stolpe on behalf of Brandenburg it only just managed to get through the Bundesrat. Although the complicated balance between the parties in the Bundesrat – made even more difficult by the different party-political constellations in the states – was, on the one hand, an inducement to consensus, it nevertheless limited the federal government's room for manoeuvre on the other. The opposition, as well as the public, were exercised almost more by political tactics than they were by matters of policy. It is true that the red-green coalition was open to attack on various fronts. But the Schröder government could really not be held responsible for the collapse in the world economy and its consequences for the labour market. In view of the difficult conditions, the balance sheet could bear scrutiny. Unemployment began to fall in spring 2002, and the first silver linings for the economy began to appear on the horizon.

The problem of mass unemployment cannot be solved by economic growth alone. The German labour market was ailing because of structural problems and weaknesses in the service sector. The fall of the Iron Curtain left "low-wage countries", with their competitive cheap labour and inexpensive goods, directly on the doorstep of the "high-wage countries". New technology, along with social and ecological dumping, mean that production can be relocated comparatively easily. It will take enormous effort, through modernisation and flexibility, to make *Standort Deutschland* (Location – Germany) so attractive and efficient that more people might again find paid employment. This is a task for society as a whole, and one in which entrepreneurs as well as the trade unions are under particular pressure. In principle, government policy can only establish the framework conditions with which to encourage the necessary innovations and reforms. Despite the shortage of funds, investment in education and specialist qualifications, particularly in a society where knowledge is all, must be an urgent priority.[63] Not only the state, but business too, must meet this challenge. For the next SPD government and the difficult tasks it had

---

62 The figures on finding people work had been massaged. Under the new head, Florian Gerster (SPD), the Federal Employment Office underwent reforms.
63 The results of the first OECD PISA Report of 2000, 'Literary Skills for the World of Tomorrow', which revealed the educational shortcomings of German schoolchildren, are convincing testimony to this.

to face in late 2002, a reform of public finances at federal, state, and local level which would give greater incentive for self-responsibility was on the agenda.

The world today is different from what it was in the twentieth century. The only remaining superpower is the USA. The globalisation of capital and markets have reached gigantic proportions. Businesses operating worldwide are the embodiment of independent economic power, and the flow of capital knows no borders. Globalisation has severely strained the capacity of nation states for individual action. This is what makes Europe and the extension of the European Union so vital. The dream of a "supranational Europe"[64] held out great promise. But this concept of replacing the nation states with a single, unified Europe was unrealistic. With the Maastricht Treaty of 1992, the further development of the European Community into the European Union was set in motion. Tangible consequence for the citizen of the coming together of the European states was the abolition of border controls under the Schengen Agreement. With the euro, people now carry daily concrete evidence of Europe around in their pockets. The continuing expansion of the European Union eastwards also raised the question of its reorganisation, mainly with regard to the separation of authority between Brussels and individual states, as well as the role of the regions. Historical factors meant that the EU had hitherto functioned principally as a European free-market economy. The social dimension barely got a look-in. This was left to individual member states, which resulted in distortions. Neither the European Social Democratic parties, nor the trade unions, have so far demonstrated sufficient energy in tackling the European project. In practice, they seem far too ensconced in their particular national setting. Setbacks notwithstanding, they have great tasks ahead of them in the future. The SPD, too, should regard itself as part of a European-wide social democracy, and one which seeks to champion a European Germany[65] as well as a social Europe.

It was not only the foreign-political parameters which shifted after the collapse of the Communist bloc. The power struggle between different systems which absorbed so many resources also resulted in pressure in the Western world to ensure a certain equilibrium in the social sphere. This compulsion no longer exists. It is hard to ignore a certain inbalance between the interests of capital and social obligations. It is therefore the

---

64 This idea was already evoked by Peter Glotz on 20.6.1991 in the dispute about the capital, when he reproached Helmut Kohl for shifting to a Europe des patries (de Gaulle). See Winkler, Weg nach Westen, vol. 2, p. 609.
65 The term "European Germany" is Thomas Mann's: it is often quoted or used without acknowledging Mann.

bounden duty of social democracy, along with the necessary modernisation of structures in the economy and labour market, to interpret the imperative of social justice in a manner appropriate to the age. This is also a Pan-European task. If the basic value of freedom has always been central to the European heritage, so too have been the goals of justice and fraternity. It is on precisely this point that Europe differs from the USA, where the flag of freedom is held high, but the term social justice does not figure in the vocabulary. Democracy as it is understood in the USA is somewhat different from social democracy as it has developed in Europe.[66] Despite the common ground in the emphasis on freedom and civil rights, they differ on one crucial point: "liberal" democracy is built on a largely unbridled "competitive capitalism", social democracy on a market economy committed to the social imperative. Justice and solidarity are an indispensable part of the Social Democratic and European understanding of freedom.

It is vital that the German Social Democrats develop the European dimension more strongly. Chancellor Gerhard Schröder stressed emphatically in 2002 that "the strategy of the SPD must on principle be pro-European", and that it must "adopt a clear pro-European position".[67] Europe, he maintained, was "much more than a geographical term": it was an economic force, and had become a "genuine community of values".[68] Achieving an economically strong and politically united Europe, living in freedom and democracy, is a supremely worthwhile challenge. In Germany, despite its many shortcomings, the SPD had, in the period 1998 to 2002, passed the test of being in power. The priority now in the long run was for Social Democratic voices to be heard more clearly amidst the European chorus. Europe, with its various nations and states, is united not only by a tradition of freedom and enlightenment, but also by a rich common heritage of civilisation and culture. Today it stands for reconciliation, understanding, and tolerance, for its own, singular way of defending freedoms, ensuring peace, and opposing inequality and discrimination.[69] The European Union, according to Gerhard Schröder in 2002, was "our answer to globalisation and the challenge of terrorism". It was

---

66 On this, see Thomas Meyer, Soziale Demokratie und Globalisierung. Eine europäische Perspektive (Bonn, 2002).
67 Session of the SPD presidium of 28.2.2002, minutes in the secretariat of the SPD executive.
68 Speech of Gerhard Schröder on 18.3.2002 in Amsterdam. Issued to the press by the SPD executive on 18.3.2002.
69 See the remarks of Lionel Jospin on the speech of the American President George W. Bush of 29.1.2002. In Der Spiegel, 18.2.2002, p. 163f.

"the successful international model for the twenty-first century".[70] A European civil society with political weight and power, cultural attractiveness and civilising appeal, is a project which is as exacting as it is worthwhile. It represents a challenging task ahead for both the SPD and its European sister parties.

---

70 Gerhard Schröder's speech in Amsterdam on 18.3.2002, published by SPD-Parteivorstand, Mitteilung an die Presse, 18.3.2002.

Addendum
The SPD at the Crossroads

1. A Laborious Start after Re-election

When the original German version of this history of the SPD was published in early summer 2002, very few politicians, opinion pollsters, and political observers expected Gerhard Schröder's red-green coalition to come out on top in the federal elections on 22 September 2002. The CDU/CSU, and their Chancellor candidate Edmund Stoiber, who had thought themselves well on the road to victory, were overtaken on the finishing straight. They gained 38.5 per cent, their partners, the FDP under Guido Westerwelle, who had boasted of winning 18 per cent, a mere 7.4. It was the governing coalition, however, who emerged victorious from these elections – albeit narrowly. The SPD gained 38.5 per cent, some 2.4 percentage points fewer than in 1998, but nonetheless winning 9,000 more votes overall than the Union, and the Greens under their well-respected Foreign Minister, Joschka Fischer, managed 8.6 per cent, a gain of 2.1 percentage points. With 306 Bundestag seats in all, 251 of them going to the SPD and 55 to the Greens, the red-green coalition had a working parliamentary majority.[1] Once again, they had managed to pull it off.

Two factors were adduced in explaining this, to many, surprising shift in electoral favour: the widespread floods in August, which mainly affected eastern Germany[2], and the threat of war in Iraq. It is certainly true that catastrophes offer politicians in government the opportunity to get themselves into the public eye. But this does not happen automatically: it requires a certain amount of political and media savvy. Gerhard Schröder demonstrated that he had more of this than his rival Edmund Stoiber. His call "to pull together", and his plea that the election should take second place to helping the victims, resonated with the public at large. Over 120,000 helpers were at work in the flooded areas, by the end of August 137 million euros had been collected in private donations, and postponing tax cuts in favour of repairing the flood damage sat well with the popular mood. In the two big pre-election TV duels, Schröder came across more sympathetically than the Bavarian Minister President.

1 Archiv der Gegenwart 2002, p. 45852f.
2 See Archiv der Gegenwart 2002, p. 45782.

By the final stages of the election campaign in late summer 2002, the Iraq war was firmly on the political agenda. In the conflict over the action against Saddam Hussein's Iraq, the government – with Gerhard Schröder to the fore – made it quite clear that it would not go along with the military intervention envisaged by the USA under George W. Bush, and his ally Tony Blair. Although the categorical rejection of any military action, even with the backing of the UNO, was not uncontroversial even in coalition circles, it was nevertheless overwhelmingly in tune with the sentiments of the German people. From this point of view, the slogan "War or Peace for Germany", which reduced matters to a simple emotional choice, undoubtedly brought about a shift in voting intentions. But with the Iraq war and the deliberate distancing from Bush and the USA, there was more at stake than a tactical game played out with an eye to the electorate. There were signs at this point of a new direction in German foreign policy.

The decision by the Bush administration to go to war in Iraq also met with widespread rejection in many other European countries. On foreign affairs, the Schröder government was not only operating in tandem with Jacques Chirac, but there was also talk of a Paris-Berlin-Moscow axis. The polemics of Donald Rumsfeld, the US Secretary of State for Defence and one of the hardliners in the Bush administration, against the "old Europe" in fact brought the citizens and governments of these countries closer together. Given the determination of the USA's leaders to go to war, the arguments of the Union leadership, Angela Merkel and Edmund Stoiber, that the USA had to be supported, fell on deaf ears, leaving them politically out in the cold. It was clear that the mood in Germany had begun to change since the summer.

On the government side, the election campaign was dominated by the two great individual battlers, Gerhard Schröder and Joschka Fischer. The SPD as a party tended to take a back seat. It was the Chancellor and party chairman who set the pace, fought to the point of exhaustion, and succeeded in turning things around. In eastern Germany in particular, the Social Democrats were able to make an impact on voters on the topics of flood aid and Iraq, and made clear gains there (39.7 per cent of second votes, as opposed to 35.1 in 1998). This was at the cost of the PDS who, in Germany as a whole, fell at the 5 per cent hurdle. Moreover, the SPD succeeded in mobilising its traditional vote in the West, particularly in North Rhine-Westphalia. After the difficult times in spring, it had once again tasted the fruits of victory, and, for the second time in succession, it was the strongest parliamentary group.

The coalition negotiations which began on 25 September were overshadowed by the crisis in public finances and the social security systems.

Despite differences flaring up, in particular over increases in social security contributions and the phasing out of atomic energy, on 16 October the SPD and Green negotiators agreed to a comprehensive coalition package which had three goals: justice, growth, and sustainability. It was approved on 20 October by an SPD party congress in Berlin which, at the same time, elected Olaf Scholz General Secretary as successor to Franz Müntefering, who was now free to concentrate on his role as leader of the parliamentary party.

On 22 October, Gerhard Schröder was once again elected Federal Chancellor. He received three votes more than required, albeit not all of them coming from the government camp. On the SPD side, the formation of the government brought a surprise. Walter Riester had to go, and Wolfgang Clement became "Superminister" for Economic Affairs and Labour. He was appointed to pep up the cabinet and demonstrate that the government was eager to tackle the modernisation of the labour market, and that its main goal was a more dynamic economy. Initially, this new star in the cabinet made a good impression, but he left a real gap in the Social Democratic stronghold of North Rhine-Westphalia. The then Minister of Finance, Peer Steinbrück, succeeded him as Minister President. There were very few fresh faces in the new cabinet. Ulla Schmidt was given the re-jigged Department of Health and Social Security, Renate Schmidt from Bavaria took over the joint department in charge of families, senior citizens, women and young people. The then Secretary of State in the Ministry of the Interior, Brigitte Zypries, was the successor to Herta Däubler-Gmelin, who had had to resign as Justice Minister following her harsh attack on Bush, whom she had compared to Hitler. As the representative of the new states, Manfred Stolpe was given the Ministry of Transport and Construction, with special responsibility for reconstruction in the East. Manfred Struck, who, after the resignation of Rudolf Scharping over the Mallorca affair (19 July), had become Minister of Defence, remained in office, as did Hans Eichel, Otto Schily, Heidemarie Wieczorek-Zeul, and Edelgard Bulmahn, along with the team of Green ministers, Joschka Fischer, Renate Künast, and Jürgen Trittin. Apart from Clement, and, in his own way, Otto Schily, and the Green superstar Joschka Fischer, the cabinet was a little lacklustre. This made it even more important that the coalition should gain respect and profile by demonstrating its competence.

In fact, however, the first months of the second red-green coalition verged on the chaotic. The coalition agreements contained more than a few totally unrealisable, even nonsensical policy guidelines.[3] It seemed as if, after having won the election against all expectations, everyone of greater or lesser competence amongst the leadership now wanted to present the whole world with their particular wish-list. It was as if no one was singing in tune, and a vexed Gerhard Schröder was soon using the word "cacophony". But this was just the tip of the iceberg. Fundamentally, these were the voices of Social Democratic and Green "idealists" who were indulging their visions of a better world. For decades – and this is what they failed to recognise – not only in the Federal Republic, but also in other West European democracies, more had been delivered in the way of social benefits than was either economically or financially responsible.

Following the initial difficulties of the first Schröder government, it appeared that the Social Democrats had grasped this fact, at least as far as government policy was concerned. Consolidation of the budget and the "Riester pension" were proof of this. In view of the exploding costs of the health system, it must have been more than obvious that reform was an urgent priority. Yet even the sensible attempt of one health insurance scheme[4], to offer as an alternative a voluntary excess scheme with financial inducements, was initially blocked by the traditionalists in the Ministry of Health under the new minister Ulla Schmidt.

After a long delay, the reform of statutory health insurance finally got onto the political agenda. After lengthy and tough negotiations, government representatives under Ulla Schmidt came to an agreement with delegates from the CDU/CSU led by Horst Seehofer on a framework for limiting costs in the health service.[5] It met with frequent harsh criticism from the public and those affected, because of its complicated, bureaucratic regulations, and patients having to make contributions themselves, something widely regarded as an imposition. This health reform demonstrated, positively as well as negatively, the pros and cons of consensus democracy, something which had a long tradition in the Federal Republic. On the one hand, it was testimony to the ability of the two people's parties, the Union and the Social Democrats, to cooperate on matters of basic social concern, on the other it documented the paralysing constraints of a rigid federal system.

---

3 One example would be the taxing, for an indefinite period, of speculative financial ventures. It would have been completely unworkable, and, since losses could also have been offset against tax, with the inevitable fall in the stock market, would have reduced even more drastically public tax revenues.
4 It was the technicians' health insurance scheme.
5 Agreement was reached between the government and the CDU/CSU on 21.7.2003.

Unlike states organised on a centralist principle, where the regions are restricted for the most part to administrative tasks, and are dependent on the centre, the German federal states enjoy far-reaching independent powers. They have autonomy in cultural and educational matters, which means they control, *inter alia*, the education system, and also have responsibility for the police. Through the Bundesrat, the upper house which represents the governments of the states, they have a large say in federal legislation. As a consequence of the growing entwinement of federal and state responsibilities, the Bundesrat has had an increasingly important role to play.

The fact that the electorate has tended to punish the federal government at Landtag elections has frequently led to the opposition having a majority in the Bundesrat. This was the situation at the end of the Kohl era when the SPD dominated the Bundesrat, and this was repeated in reverse during Gerhard Schröder's period in office. While it was occasionally possible in the early years to persuade individual Union-led states to break ranks, since the beginning of 2003, the CDU/CSU, in alliance with the FDP, had enjoyed a solid majority in the Bundesrat. This meant, in consequence, that the government was forced to bring the Union on board for certain important pieces of legislation, rather than risk them being thrown out.

The problems resulting from this were demonstrated in 2002 with the planned Immigration Law. After painfully lengthy negotiations, the Bundestag finally produced a draft bill. It was clear to anyone with any understanding of the situation that Germany was in urgent need of a law on immigration, and it was welcomed almost unanimously by business and the Churches. But hardliners in the Union, banking on the widespread prejudice against foreigners, asylum seekers, economic migrants and immigrants, were seeking a trial of strength with the red-green coalition. After an undignified spectacle and wrangling about procedure in the Bundesrat, the third round of voting produced a disputed majority in favour of the Law. In December 2002, however, the Federal Constitutional Court overturned the vote on the grounds of procedural shortcomings.

It was, in effect, virtually impossible to get important legislation through the Bundesrat in the face of opposition from the CDU/CSU majority. It was either blocked totally by the Union, or the red-green coalition was forced to make substantial concessions. Barely any progress was made, for instance, with the proposal to abolish senseless tax subsidies in the region of billions.[6] The only solution to this dilemma for the SPD was to

6 Subsidising, for instance, the building of private homes to the tune of 11 billion euros (contributing in the process to the detriment of the countryside), and even reducing value added tax on goods such as dog and cat food, and cut flowers.

take the difficult step in advance, as they had done on health reform, of coming to an understanding with the Union, very laboriously, on an overall package. This was the only way open to them of pushing through necessary and urgent measures. A complicated monster emerged which produced savings, but offered no real solutions to basic structural problems.

Following the many problematic experiences with the blocking structures operating in the upper chamber, there was growing recognition that a thoroughgoing reform of Germany's federalist system was needed. (Over 60 per cent of legislation now required the approval of the Bundesrat). The so-called federalism commission under the dual chairmanship of Franz Müntefering for the Bundestag, and Edmund Stoiber for the states, seemed at the end of 2004 to be on the verge of a solution. It collapsed at the last minute, mainly because of the dispute over where the responsibility for education should lie. The jealousy between federal and state governments, between politicians and parties, along with the endless entanglement of responsibilities, finances, and personal vanity, once again revealed themselves as an insuperable obstacle to much-needed structural reforms. Once the Federal Republic's respected trade mark, federalism had, over time, spiralled completely out of control, and was now a hindrance to political action.

In the era of the Grand Coalition of 1966–1969, the finance reform of 1969 and the shared financing of the tasks of the federal government and those of the states had undermined the autonomy of the states, but at the same time considerably extended the say which they had in federal government. The consequence, according to Klaus Schönhoven in his thorough study of the Grand Coalition, "was a fusing and combining of the federal state with the party state", in which the "contours of government and opposition [...] became ever more blurred". With this "institutional change of course", which belonged to "the lasting legacy of the Grand Coalition", the "definitive establishment of a democracy of negotiation" had been achieved.[7] Despite a much stronger public sense of parties in dispute, this was what characterised, over years and decades, the style of the Bonn, and subsequently the Berlin Republic.

Under the new and great challenges of globalisation, competition, and the necessity for economic and social modernisation, however, a darker side began to emerge. The decision-making processes in the implementation of urgent reforms were often long and painfully drawn-out. In the conflict between diverging interests, objectives were not infrequently

---

7 Klaus Schönhoven, Wendejahre. Die Sozialdemokratie in der Zeit der Großen Koalition 1966–1969 (Bonn 2004), p. 694 f.

watered down, or even blocked almost entirely. Where the real responsibility for this lay was often virtually impossible to say.

In his government statement of 29 October 2002, Gerhard Schröder promised to push ahead with the social and ecological renewal of Germany. "Superminister" Wolfgang Clement was the main impetus behind the implementation of the proposals of the Hartz Commission[8] on the reform of job provision, and the re-regulation of the labour market. The first measures were designed to tighten the rules on what job-seekers might or might not turn down, to bring about structural changes in job provision procedures, as well to ease the regulations on subcontract labour. A second reform package aimed to encourage very small businesses, the so-called *Mini-Jobs* and *Ich-AGs* (one-man enterprises). Measures such as these, which had been diluted even further by the Union in the Bundesrat, were merely a drop in the ocean. The economy was stagnating, unemployment was rising, tax revenues were collapsing, and public expenditure was growing due to the burden of benefit payments. It was seen as a shot across the bows when the EU Commission instituted proceedings against Germany, once a watchword for stability and financial solidity, because of its balance of payments deficit.[9] The unsuccessful top-level talks in the "alliance for labour"[10] demonstrated that it was impossible to reach a consensus between employers and employees in the implementation of any fundamental structural reforms.

In the face of this, Gerhard Schröder went up a gear, and spiritedly seized the initiative. In a government statement of 14 March 2003, he pressed on with his Agenda 2010, with which he sought to cut social spending in order to boost the economy and bring some movement to the labour market.[11] The main points of the Agenda were: limiting the period for which unemployment benefit could be drawn; the merging of unemployment and social security benefit into "unemployment benefit II"; relaxing the law on wrongful dismissal for small firms; adding a "sustainability factor"[12] to the formula for calculating pensions; a gradual raising

---

8   This commission of experts under the chairmanship of Peter Hartz, the head of personnel management at Volkswagen, had submitted its proposals on 16.8.2002 to the Chancellor. See Chronik 2003. Der vollständige Jahresrückblick in Wort und Bild, Übersichten und Vergleiche (Gütersloh/Munich 2004), p. 23.
9   According to the EU stability pact, the upper limit for the overall deficit was set at 3 per cent of gross domestic product. After being at 3.6 per cent in 2002, the deficit rose to 3.8 per cent in 2003.
10 On 3.3.2003. See Chronik 2003, p. 23.
11 See Chronik 2003, p. 23 and p. 59.
12 The "sustainability factor" was designed primarily to take demographic changes into account.

of the retirement age; employees taking on the cost of sickness benefit; and the lifting, in the case of most trades, of the requirement to train under a master craftsman – this, in order to promote the setting up of new businesses.[13]

Agenda 2010 saw a determined Gerhard Schröder with the "Courage to Change"[14], who was seeking to set the country on course for the future, and was not deterred by criticism from within his own party. Egged on by the media, numerous comrades and trade unionists began to give vent to their disgruntlement. At a special party congress on 1 June 2003, however, the Chancellor secured prior approval for his hard line by making it a prerequisite for his continuing in office. Schröder was demanding painful concessions from many of those in his party who felt strongly committed to social issues. He was now acting as a Chancellor whose main duty was to the country, and who saw his task as using his office to make Germany fit for the challenges of globalisation. He left the party with no choice but to follow him along this road of reform, whether out of conviction and loyalty, or reluctantly and under protest.

2. The Party and its Development

The SPD as a party found itself barely at all in the political spotlight. The focus of public interest was on the ubiquitous media presence of the Chancellor, and the activity of the government, or rather its frequent political and personal squabbles. Initially, any friction arising from the cuts in social spending was allayed and obscured by the very high-profile US war in Iraq. Schröder's blunt repudiation of US military action and his distancing himself from the Bush administration were in tune with the prevailing mood in his party. Even if scepticism about military intervention of this kind was thoroughly justified, criticism of Germany's great ally occasionally went too far, bordering at times on anti-Americanism. After American troops had carried the day and occupied Baghdad in April 2003, the German government had to come to terms with the power-political realities, and to attempt to repair the damaged relationship with the USA. For those at the grassroots and on the left who were sceptical about the USA there still remained plenty to criticise, not least the abuse of prisoners in camps and military prisons. But basically, the US victory had broken the political and psychological link which had bound government and the party closely together.

13 The only person allowed to be in charge of a workshop was a qualified master craftsman who had undergone many years of training and a final exam.
14 This was the motto of the special SPD party congress of 1.6.2003 in Berlin.

After Peter Struck, the leader of the parliamentary party, had moved to defence in July 2002 as the successor to Rudolf Scharping, Ludwig Stiegler took over his post, initially until the end of the legislative period. Then, on 24 September 2002, Franz Müntefering was elected leader of the parliamentary party. General Secretary for many years, and a man of great organisational and political experience, he seemed particularly suited to leading the parliamentary party, and to ensuring the necessary close cooperation with both the government and the Chancellor. Olaf Scholz, leader of the SPD in Hamburg, was appointed by the SPD party congress of 20 October 2002 as the new SPD General Secretary. He was thought to be a good choice, but, unlike Franz Müntefering, was unable to bring about the internal integration of the party. This was, however, not only due to him, but was also a result of the severe setbacks and loss of trust which the SPD had suffered.

It was somehow symptomatic that the party continued to be plagued by dwindling membership. After declining to 717,513 and 693,894 at the end of 2001 and 2002 respectively[15], on 31 December 2003 the SPD numbered just 650,798 members. This corresponded to the figure for 1963 in what was then just West Germany. The decline was roughly the same in both East and West, with the proportion of women members remaining constant at 29.5 per cent. Alarm bells began to ring, however, when membership fell below that of the CDU in North Rhine-Westphalia, long a bastion of SPD support.

The mood among the SPD grassroots had imperceptibly changed over recent years. Admittedly, there had been some notable initiatives and signs of admirable commitment here and there. But party activity had a tired and jaded feel to it, and in many places seemed to be confined to an established and exclusive circle. Outsiders were often frightened away, even invited guests were put off by a tone which was not infrequently discourteous. One had the impression of inward-looking individuals who were shutting themselves off from the outside world. The execution of day-to-day practical tasks was still functioning smoothly, but there was a lack of any real buzz or conviction. Moreover, tighter control by higher party authority over grassroots finances and responsibilities was having a demotivating effect.

The middle and upper levels of the party were preoccupied with routine business administration. A sober pragmatism began to make its pres-

---

15 Jahrbuch der Sozialdemokratischen Partei Deutschlands 2001/2002, published by the SPD executive (Berlin 2003), p. 190. An overview of the figures for this year, as for others, can be found in the political archive run by Peter Munkelt in the Willy-Brandt-Haus.

ence felt. Party congresses, which had once been a forum for productive debate, now resembled theatrical media events designed to extol the Chancellor's policies. This gave rise, it has to be said, of occasional signs of discontent from the grassroots. There was never any real debate about the framework for the reforms and their goals. The SPD yearbooks became a mirror of the party's lack of genuine substance. Spiced up for the media, produced by an outside publisher, their actual content became ever thinner.

In 2004, there was once again a marked drop in membership, down by 45,000 to 605,807.[16] In addition to natural losses through age, and too few young people joining, members were increasingly leaving the party in 2003/04 out of disaffection with the direction of the Schröder government and the way the party leadership was operating. After the unexpected election victory in 2002 had revived hopes of a left-wing, red-green project, there was now much irritation over the envisaged reforms and the course which the government was taking. Following the Chancellor's announcement of Agenda 2010 on 14 March 2003, there were audible rumblings from within the party. Many members who equated social democracy with the striving for social justice and equality could simply not accept that cuts to the social safety net had become unavoidable. They also objected to the way in which this course was to be ruthlessly imposed from above, and without consultation. As a concession to the mutinous comrades, a special party congress took place on 1 June 2003, at which 90 per cent of the delegates then gave the reform plans their blessing.

In the implementation of the complicated health reforms, the greatest bone of contention was the "surgery fee"[17]. Sections of the tabloid press made great play of the discontent. The government's completely "wrong path" was not to the liking of many in and close to the SPD, and those who were basically in favour had a hard time defending it. The trade unions, apprehensive and shaken by unemployment, economic downturn, cuts in social expenditure, the growth of individualism, and a negative public image, announced protest action against the dismantling of the welfare state and government policy. The Hartz IV package approved at the beginning of July 2004, which merged unemployment and social security benefit, provoked particularly angry reaction. In summer 2004, tens of thousands, especially in the new states, went onto the streets and squares in protest against Hartz IV, with many clearly now no longer giving two hoots for the SPD.

16 Figures apply to the end of the particular year in question.
17 Those insured with the statutory health insurance scheme had to pay 10 euros per quarter out of their own pockets to visit the doctor. The regulations passed at the end of 2003 came into force at the beginning of 2004.

After the federal elections, the SPD slipped inexorably in the polls, going from around 30 per cent at the end of 2002 to around 25 per cent at the end of 2003.[18] In the first half of 2004 they polled on average between 23 and 27 per cent. After recovering somewhat at the end of the year to 33 per cent, they experienced a clear drop again in the first half of 2005, and by May 2005 were at 29 per cent.

The performance of the SPD in the Landtag and local elections in 2003 was disastrous. Their only success was in Bremen, which was mainly due to their popular mayor, Henning Scherf.[19] At the Landtag elections in Hesse and Lower Saxony on 2 February, and in Bavaria on 21 September 2003, they in each case made two-figure losses. In what was once "red Hesse", they slumped to 29.1 per cent. In Lower Saxony they plunged from 47.9 per cent in 1998, to 33.4 per cent. Not only did Sigmar Gabriel lose the office of Minister President to Christian Wulff of the CDU, but the Union parties increased their majority in the Bundesrat to 41 (35 previously) out of 69 seats in all.[20] In Bavaria under Edmund Stoiber, the CSU even won a two-thirds majority, and the SPD dropped from their already modest 28.7 per cent (1998) to below the twenty per cent threshold with 19.6 per cent.[21] They also suffered similarly drastic losses in the local elections in 2003 in Schleswig-Holstein (2 March) and Brandenburg (26 October).[22]

It was no wonder, in view of these shattering results and the annoyance over reform policy, that the mood in the party was absolutely dreadful. The party congress in Bochum from 17 to 19 November 2003 was unable to bring about the change of mood that many had hoped for. It is true that the delegates applauded Schröder's speech on the party programme, supported him on foreign policy, and confirmed him as party chairman with 80.8 per cent of the vote. But this was nonetheless 7.8 percentage points fewer than last time in 2001.[23] The men who bore the full brunt of the delegates' displeasure were Wolfgang Clement, labelled as too business-friendly and made the scapegoat for the cuts in social

18 For a survey of the SPD's standing in the polls, from the federal elections in September 1998 up until May 2005, see Der Spiegel, 30.5.2005, p. 24f.
19 In the city parliament elections on 25.5.2003 they won 42.3 per cent (almost the same as in 1999), while their coalition partner, the CDU, suffered severe losses. See Chronik 2003, p. 52.
20 Ibid., p. 14.
21 Ibid., p. 94.
22 Ibid., p. 32 and p. 102.
23 Protokoll. Bundesparteitag Bochum 2003. 17.–19. November 2003. Published by the SPD executive (Berlin, no date). The results of the election for the chairman, his deputies, and the party business manager are on p. 159, p. 174, and p. 180.

benefits, and General Secretary Olaf Scholz. In the election for deputy chairmen, Clement got in with by far the worst result at 56.7 per cent, and Scholz, who in 2002 had received the backing of 91.3 per cent of the delegates, just squeezed in again with 52.6 per cent.

When Schröder then announced on 6 February 2004 that he would hand over the chairmanship of the party to Franz Müntefering, many interpreted this as admitting the beginning of the end. The polls found the SPD at rock bottom, the reforms which had been set in motion were heavily criticised, even within the party. People were leaving the party in droves, and the disaffected discussed the founding of a new, left-wing party. In the early elections to the city parliament in Hamburg, the CDU under the popular Ole von Beust won an overall majority, and the SPD slumped in this former stronghold to a mere 30.5 per cent.[24]

At a special party congress in Berlin on 21 March 2004, the handover from Gerhard Schröder to Franz Müntefering was completed. Müntefering registered the best result for a party chairman since the election of Björn Engholm in 1991. With his solid base at grassroots level, his talent for expressing himself briefly and succinctly, and an ability to get his message across, Franz Müntefering was above all a man who could appeal to the heart and soul of the party. The hope cherished by many that the SPD would benefit from this change with the public, and in the opinion polls, was not fulfilled however.

Surprisingly, Klaus Uwe Benneter succeeded the somewhat hapless Olaf Scholz as General Secretary. As leader of the *Jusos*, he had been expelled from the party in 1977[25] because of his communist associations, but had been re-admitted in 1983. But since then he had distinguished himself neither in the Berlin SPD, nor (since 2002) as a Bundestag deputy. He was not exactly the best choice for the post of General Secretary: his sole qualification was that he was a friend of Gerhard Schröder from the old *Juso* days. Benneter was, and remained, colourless; he had no charisma, and was blessed with no great luck. There were, however, no convincing alternatives for this post, one which demanded loyalty, conviction, and the ability to keep people on board. This was not the only example of how few outstanding politicians the SPD could draw on.

Peer Steinbrück, Wolfgang Clement's successor as Minister President in North Rhine-Westphalia, was solid, but he lacked the popular touch displayed, for instance, by Kurt Beck in the Rhineland-Palatinate. Sigmar Gabriel, who (in 1999)[26] had been promoted to Minister President in

24 See Chronik 2004, p. 15 and p. 32.
25 See p. 239 above.
26 See p. 375 above.

Lower Saxony, and whom many were soon regarding as the new political heavyweight, lost the Landtag election in 2003, thus bringing his career to a sudden halt. In Brandenburg, in coalition as Minister President with the CDU, Matthias Platzeck was demonstrating his talent for crisis management, but he was barely known nationally. Heide Simonis enjoyed a certain reputation outside Schleswig-Holstein, but after losing the office of Minister President in spring 2005 she resigned herself to withdrawing from political life. Klaus Wowereit as Governing Mayor of Berlin, and Harald Ringsdorff as head of impoverished Mecklenburg-Western Pomerania, had enough problems of their own.

The most likely SPD local politician was Wolfgang Tiefensee in Leipzig. In 2002 he turned down a post in the federal government, and in 2004 managed to win in Leipzig, despite the otherwise catastrophic election results for the SPD in Saxony. Bärbel Dieckmann, the Mayoress of Bonn, was widely respected and had great personal charisma. Among the younger generation of politicians, whose early successes had often seen them crowned too prematurely, there were barely any deserving of higher office. A few such as Andrea Nahles, for instance, attempted to make a name for themselves as critical left-wingers, banking on a reconstitution of the party's personnel and policies.

In view of the distribution of party seats in the Federal Assembly, Johannes Rau decided against standing again as Federal President. In spring 2004, with the election imminent, there were two candidates, neither of whom belonged to the political establishment. In March 2004, Angela Merkel had pushed through Horst Köhler, head of the International Monetary Fund, as the candidate of the CDU/CSU and the FDP. Together with the Greens, the SPD put forward the political scientist Gesine Schwan. Up until then, neither was at all well known to the wider public. In the campaign, however, both came across as of independent mind, winning respect and esteem, particularly since there was nothing of the party footsoldier about them. For Gesine Schwan, the narrow defeat on 23 May 2004 was at least a partial success, since she even received several votes from the conservative-liberal camp. But given the clear Union/FDP majority, victory for Horst Köhler was inevitable, and from the very first he pressed for energetic reforms and exuded optimism.[27]

Gesine Schwan's *succès d'estime* faded as the SPD had to swallow heavy defeats in the upcoming Landtag elections in Thuringia (13 June), the Saar (5 September), as well as in Brandenburg and Saxony (19 September), and

---

[27] Köhler received 604 of the 1204 votes cast, Gesine Schwan 589. There were nine abstentions and two spoiled ballots. See, Chronik 2004, p. 52.

in the European elections in July. In Thuringia and Saxony they even fell behind the PDS, not even managing to get into two figures in Saxony. This not only weakened the position of the comrades in the two states in question, but it also had a negative effect on the mood of the party as a whole. The protests against the Hartz IV measures had been so vigorous that many Social Democrats were extremely reluctant to discuss them. The trade unions, having taken a severe battering as a result of the cuts in benefits and their own shortcomings, kept their critical distance, and interminable smart alecs such as the ex-party chairman Oskar Lafontaine, and a handful of left-wing SPD Bundestag deputies, continued to whinge and cavil in public.

In its annual review, *Der Spiegel* characterised 2004, somewhat maliciously, as a "year of wear and tear". The red-green government had, it said, "exhausted itself in the implementation of reforms, as had the opposition in fashioning a reform programme, and the population, in part, in opposing the reforms. Germany looks tired, but different"[28]. Nonetheless, it maintained, 2004 had not been an entirely futile year.

At the beginning of the year, it had looked as if Gerhard Schröder's days as Chancellor and SPD chairman were numbered. In March 2004, Franz Müntefering had taken over as party chairman. This had brought little relief. Although he had managed to hold the party together, and to keep the Chancellor's back covered, he had been only marginally effective in reaching beyond the boundaries of the party.

In summer 2004, the protests against Hartz IV were at their height, and the SPD touched rock bottom in the polls, both in terms of public opinion and also the respect in which the government was held. Then, at the end of the year, there seemed to be a gradual change of mood. The CDU, who thought that 2006 would see them on the road to victory, were not having things all their own way. Their good showing in the polls was less a result of their positive image than of the negative one of the governing coalition. Internally, the Union was by no means as united as Angela Merkel liked to pretend. On 12 October 2004, the deputy leader of the parliamentary party Friedrich Merz, who had been known as an energetic moderniser, announced that he was resigning from all his leadership posts. Two weeks later, Erwin Teufel, the Minister President of Baden-Württemberg, threw in the towel following criticism from within the party, and finally on 22 November 2004, Horst Seehofer, the Union's conscience on social matters, resigned in protest over the compromise on health policy. Now that both parties had to pin their colours to the mast

---

28 Der Spiegel, 27.12.2004, p. 18.

on the question of reforms, tensions began to surface publicly in the CDU/CSU.

There were the first signs that a growing number of people were beginning to accept the Schröder government's tough policy on reform. The protests against Hartz IV were gradually fading away. The SPD were very slowly getting a better response on the "Sunday question" on people's voting intentions, and the public was also rewarding some of their politicians with somewhat better marks. Franz Müntefering as party chairman was pulling out all the stops to be cheerful and optimistic. The SPD appeared to have bottomed out, and expectations for the next federal elections (it was assumed in autumn 2006) seemed somewhat more positive. The mood looked much brighter at the turn of the year 2004/2005.

The years in government since 1998 had seen a change in the Social Democrats. They had become recognisably more pragmatic. They had even lent their backing to military operations abroad which they had earlier rejected, and to economic and social measures which impinged in the main on ordinary people, and benefited business and commerce. The party had been neither programmed nor really politically and psychologically prepared for this when it came to power in September 1998. Under the pressure of the decisions being demanded of the Schröder government in both domestic and foreign affairs, it was difficult to conduct a comprehensive debate on matters of principle.

Almost unnoticed by the public, a commission was preparing a new party programme which was intended to revise and update the Berlin basic programme of 1989. A kind of orientation framework which could have given direction to government policy and the line pursued by the party, would certainly have been useful. A programmatic concept of this sort was as legitimate as it was necessary. The final work on this proposed new basic programme was overshadowed, however, by the approaching end of the red-green project. It was due to be approved at the party congress in November 2005. The early elections called for September 2005, however, changed all this. It may be surmised that a new party programme, if and whenever it comes, will ultimately be somewhat different from the one as originally conceived and planned.

3. In Troubled Waters

As in many other European countries, the economy in Germany had been in recession since 2001, and unemployment was at a frighteningly high level. Admittedly, the Federal Republic of Germany had continued to enjoy considerable success with its exports, but the domestic economy, despite all the incentives and reforms, refused to take off. On 31 January 2005, there were five million out of work, a figure which had risen to 5.2 million by the end of February: but this included, for the first time, roughly 250,000 to 300,000 recipients of social security benefit who were classified as able to work. It was, however, the rapid rise above the five-million mark, not statistical nuances of this kind, which registered with the public. The opposition parties, quite naturally, revelled in all of this, and the standing of the Schröder government suffered accordingly. Wolfgang Clement, Minister for Economic and Social Affairs, was ridiculed as the "minister of announcements", Hans Eichel dismissed as a lightweight financial housekeeper, and even Gerhard Schröder was not left unscathed.

Moreover, there was the so-called visa affair – taken far too lightly by the Greens at first – in which a Foreign Ministry decree had eased the issue of visas to foreigners, and, particularly in the case of the Ukraine, had led to abuses. This became the excuse, mainly from the Union, for often unfair, malicious attacks and insinuations. Joschka Fischer was singled out for attack, with a systematic attempt being made to undermine his reputation. The opposition kept the affair on the boil with a Bundestag committee of investigation and considerable backing from quite a lot of the media.

From the beginning of 2005, the SPD once again began to drop in the polls. This was, in the main, a reaction to the dramatic unemployment figures, and also to the visa affair. But it also indicated growing doubts about the competence of the red-green government and its ability to take the country forward.

The first Landtag election of the year, in Schleswig-Holstein on 20 February 2005, was a litmus test. Despite the great popularity of Minister President Heide Simonis, the SPD plummeted from 43.1 per cent (in 2000) to 38.7 per cent, while the CDU went up from 35.2 per cent to 40.2 per cent, becoming the strongest single party. However, since the FDP, by comparison with 2000, dropped from 7.6 to 6.6 per cent, this was insufficient to give the previous opposition a ruling majority. The SPD and the Greens, who remained stagnant at 6.2 per cent, settled for a minority government with the cooperation of the South Schleswigian Electoral Association.[29]

Red-Green had pencilled in 17 March as a day of energetic action. Heide Simonis was supposedly going to be elected in Kiel, and in the Berlin Chancellery Gerhard Schröder and Joschka Fischer met the Union

---

29 The customary 5 per cent clause did not apply to the SSW, a party representing the Danish and Friesian minority. Its 3.7 per cent of the vote resulted in two seats, the SPD had 29, the Greens 4, the CDU 30, and the FDP 4 seats in the Landtag.

grandees Angela Merkel and Edmund Stoiber for top-level talks, the so-called jobs summit. Both events were expected to produce positive headlines. But on 17 March, Heide Simonis failed to win in each of the four electoral rounds, due to a deputy from her own camp refusing to vote for her.[30] With this, the career of the independently, and sometimes wilfully, minded powerhouse Heide Simonis came to a sudden and sad end. To sober observers of the German party landscape, this debacle was no surprise. But it came as a bitter blow for the red-green coalition at both state and national level. All that remained for the SPD in Schleswig-Holstein was the rocky path as junior partner in a Grand Coalition with the CDU. In April 2005, Peter Harry Carstensen (CDU) replaced Heide Simonis as Minister President.

The only remaining red-green coalition was in North Rhine-Westphalia under Peer Steinbrück. On 22 May, and after 39 years of SPD-led governments, the voters in this the most heavily populated state decided whether it would continue in power. The ruling camp's only advantage was its leading candidate, Minister President Peer Steinbrück, a man who, in contrast to the CDU's vacillating Jürgen Rüttgers, exuded solidity and competence. Overall, the SPD was lagging far behind in all the polls. The outcome was inevitable. By the night of the election on 22 May, the SPD was the big loser with 37.1 per cent, a drop of 5.7 percentage points. The Greens won 6.2 per cent. The CDU with 44.8 per cent (a gain of 7.7 per cent) were by far the largest parliamentary group, and with the FDP, who dropped to 6.2 per cent, they formed the next state government.

Schleswig-Holstein had been a bitter blow for the SPD, but North Rhine-Westphalia resembled a real disaster. The state on the Rhine and Ruhr, in which the SPD, after a long and arduous process, had gained the majority in 1966, had become the home and heartland of German social democracy. The election defeat, therefore, had not only personnel repercussions. Peer Steinbrück resigned. Hannelore Kraft took over the chairmanship of the parliamentary party in the Landtag from Edgar Moron, and after Harald Schartau's resignation, Jochen Dieckmann became party chairman at state level.[31] After almost forty years of uninterrupted SPD government, party and state politics, as well as the state administration, had often become closely interwoven. The SPD now no longer had recourse to state resources, and they had to get used to the unaccustomed role in opposition with a depleted organisation and personnel.

---

30   With 34 votes for Heide Simonis, and the same for the CDU candidate Peter Harry Carstensen, there was a stalemate.
31   See Vorwärts, June 2005, Vorwärts: Nordrhein-Westfalen, p. I and III.

With the loss of North Rhine-Westphalia, Red-Green lost its last stronghold in the states. Whereas in 1999 twelve of the sixteen states were governed by the SPD, there were now just five: in Brandenburg and Bremen in coalition with the CDU, in the Rhineland-Palatinate with the FDP, as well as in Berlin and Mecklenburg-Western Pomerania in collaboration with the PDS. Because of their coalition partners, the SPD no longer had any secure votes of its own in the Bundesrat, whereas the Union parties could rely on a more than comfortable majority (51 out of 69 votes). This meant that the red-green coalition's room for manoeuvre on domestic issues was extremely limited. A further difficulty in addition to the Union's blocking majority in the Bundesrat was also that Schröder did not want to let himself be pressurised by critics from within his own camp.

On the night of the election on 22 May 2005, Franz Müntefering as party leader, and Gerhard Schröder, announced that they were going to call early elections for autumn 2005 to enable the electorate to give their verdict on the government. For the party, this surprising move came almost completely out of the blue. On sober reflection, this step was not quite so surprising. A further agonising year in office, of muddling through and stagnation, would have certainly demotivated the SPD even more. In spite of often having to grit their teeth, the overwhelming majority of the party had generally been behind Schröder. There were more than a few, however, who were longing for a more specifically social democratic message.

When, in spring 2005, Franz Müntefering delivered his onslaught on capitalist excesses[32], he met with approval from many in the party who had been left troubled by the social cuts and took exception to the tough approach of many bosses and businesses. Amongst the majority of the population, too, this criticism was felt to be thoroughly justified. But for many it was seen as a transparent, tactical manoeuvre with the North Rhine-Westphalian Landtag elections in mind. The scorn expressed by many journalists and the media was not without effect. It meant that any really serious debate about the fateful consequences of purely egotistical financial interests, and the obligations of business with respect to the common good, was stifled.

The threatened demise of the red-green project in Berlin led to widespread disquiet within the SPD. Some feared for their offices, posts, and seats, others seemed almost paralysed. The official slogans "We will fight" and "We Social Democrats will win" seemed no more than whistling in the dark, and were not even able to persuade many of the weary comrades to get up off their backsides.

---

32 See, inter alia, Vorwärts, May 2005.

Shares rose at the prospect of a change of government in Berlin, and the Union continued to climb in the polls. According to Infratest-dimap, in June the CDU/CSU registered 48 per cent in response to the "Sunday question", the SPD a mere 28, the Greens 9, and the FDP 7 per cent. In July, the SPD fell even further behind, dropping to around 27 per cent.

The state of public finances was extremely grim, with prospects worsening. As a result of Hartz IV there were additional holes in the budget, which in May 2005 had been fixed at an expected ten billion euros. The debt interest alone ate up 14.4 per cent of the federal budget. It was becoming ever clearer that the Federal Republic of Germany would once again exceed the permitted deficit. Apart from the seasonal reduction in unemployment, down to 4.7 million in June, there was no sign of any tangible easing of the labour market. The number of people in work continued to drop, and, due to competition from cheap labour from the East, many German workers lost what they had considered to be secure jobs. The moving of jobs abroad by large German concerns operating in the global market continued, putting those working in the home market under severe pressure.

On 1 July 2005, Gerhard Schröder, as planned, lost the vote of confidence[33], and, on 21 July, after examining the legality of the situation, Federal President Horst Köhler called for new elections. This decision was approved on 25 August by the Federal Constitutional Court. The election campaign was short and, initially at least, produced no great surprises. The battle lines were clear: Black-Yellow under Chancellor candidate Angela Merkel with the expectation of emerging as winner on 18 September, and Red-Green who could only hope for a miracle. An unpredictable factor was the electoral alliance of PDS and WASG (Electoral Initiative Work and Social Justice) with their two prominent political personalities, Gregor Gysi and Oskar Lafontaine. These gifted and populist media stars were counting on winning as much of the protest vote as possible, with Lafontaine even fishing in right-wing waters with his xenophobic slogans. They fully accepted that they were weakening the SPD, and that a grouping might arise which would lead to a Grand Coalition.

After the decision had been made on early elections, the SPD attempted to lay more emphasis on the theme of social justice. Even though, in their election manifesto, they reaffirmed their belief in government policy and the reforms[34], and were once again going into the election with Gerhard Schröder, the tone of the campaign almost seemed to indicate that they

33 In the confidence vote, 151 deputies voted yes, 148 abstained, and 296 voted no.
34 The election manifesto, entitled "Trust in Germany", was published, inter alia, in Vorwärts, July 2005.

were preparing for the role of critical opposition. This was no way to convince people. But Gerhard Schröder refused to concede that the battle was already lost. In control, committed, and self-confident, he battled to preserve the respect he enjoyed as Chancellor, and to win over the voters. In direct comparison with his challenger, Angela Merkel, he seemed – and not just during the television duel on September 4 – more credible, competent and sympathetic. The fronts were reversed. The CDU/CSU made several mistakes, thereby revealing their ignorance. They seemed unsure of themselves, and antagonised working people with their neo-liberal ideas. The SPD got off the back foot, scoring points against their opponents particularly on tax policy and their balanced approach to social problems in the face of the "social coldness" of the Union and the FDP. From August on they rose steadily in the polls, until a few days before the election they were hovering between 32.5 and 35 per cent.[35]

On the night of the election on 18 September 2005, it was clear that there was a majority neither for Red-Green, nor for Black-Yellow. The SPD won 34.3 per cent, 4.2 points less than in 2002. But after their miserable position at the outset, they now celebrated this as a victory, and Gerhard Schröder as their shining hero. The Greens maintained their position with a respectable 8.1 per cent, while the populist Left Alliance/PDS managed to score as high as 8.7 per cent. The surprise winners, however, were the FDP who profited from the votes of some Union sympathisers and achieved 9.8 per cent. The Union parties, who had thought they would be certain winners having chalked up roughly 42 per cent in the opinion polls, suffered an unexpectedly severe setback. They won a mere 35.2 per cent, 3.3 per cent less than in 2002, and just 0.9 per cent more than the SPD. In terms of seats, with 225 as against 222 for the SPD, their advantage was even slimmer.[36]

The electors had cast their vote, but the result left it quite unclear who would now govern Germany: neither camp had a majority. The Left/PDS were in self-imposed isolation and had been rejected from the outset by both the SPD and the Greens as a possible coalition partner. The Liberals dismissed outright a "traffic-light coalition" of Red (SPD), Yellow (FDP), and Green (Alliance '90/Greens). As early as election night a new colour

---

[35] According to Forsa (12.9.05) they stood at 35 per cent, Infratest Dimap (8.9.05) at 34 per cent, Forschungsgruppe Wahlen (9.9.05) at 32.7 per cent, and Emnid (10.9.05) at 34.5 per cent. The CDU/CSU, on the other hand, were between 40.5 and 42 per cent. The Left/PDS were at roughly 8 per cent, with both the Greens and the FDP around 7 per cent.

[36] The death of a candidate in a Dresden constituency led to a by-election which brought the CDU one more seat.

combination did the rounds – Black (CDU/CSU), Yellow (FDP), Green (the Greens), the so-called "Jamaica coalition", named after the flag of that country. Numerically, a Grand Coalition of CDU/CSU and SPD was a possibility: and the two parties had cooperated once before with great success from 1966 to 1969. As a consequence of polarisation, however, there were enormous political, psychological, and personal obstacles in the way of an expedient alliance of this kind. Which way the scales would tip was, for the time being, anyone's guess. In the wake of this inconclusive election result it was going to be difficult to form a stable government capable of action.

With the office of Chancellor at stake, the power-political poker game immediately got underway. The self-confident, assertive incumbent Gerhard Schröder, as well as his somewhat battered challenger Angela Merkel, both laid claim to the post. She pointed to the narrow victory of the Union parties, the SPD countered with the argument that they were the strongest party ahead of the CDU who (without the 7.4 per cent for the independent CSU) had achieved only 27.8 per cent. Amidst this heated confrontation, it went almost unnoticed that both of the two largest parties had continued to lose ground. Their combined vote amounted to 69.8 per cent, with over 30 per cent of the electorate voting for the smaller parties. The three-party system in the Federal Republic which had been seemingly stable for so long, had, with the rise of the Greens, become a four-party system. With the Left/PDS there was now a fifth grouping in the Bundestag. The ability of the two largest parties to command allegiance and appeal to the voters was in decline, bringing about a shift in the traditional political system. The trust of citizens in the political class was being put severely to the test by this continuing lack of clarity.

High unemployment and financial cuts were behind the voters' loss of trust in the SPD. They were punished for government policies which were not always stringent enough, as well as for reforms which were the inevitable result of globalisation, financial squeeze, economic depression, and the dreadful state of the labour market. This was the understandable consequence of the pressures of being in government in difficult times, and of having to bear the heavy financial and social burdens of unification. The loss of respect for the government was mirrored in the situation of other European countries, where there was a similar loss of trust by many citizens in their particular governments. Seen in this light, the SPD could, in the European context, take some pride in the eminently respectable result it had achieved in the elections of 18 September.

Of even greater consequence, however, are the problems which for years have bedevilled the relationship of the citizens to politics. Closer contact between voters and their elected representatives is most likely to be found at local level. But even at this lower end of the democratic process, there are unmistakable signs of fault lines. It is often very difficult, particularly in the new states, to attract sufficient candidates for elected posts in the community. This is a clear symptom of the lack of interest in any active involvement in politics, a result of its dwindling attractiveness and credibility. It is even more in evidence, however, at the higher political and social level.

These are not, of course, problems specific just to the SPD and the red-green coalition during its period in office from 1998 to 2005: basically, they affect all parties and larger institutions such as the trade unions, associations, and the churches. In fact, they affect the entire political system. The decline in voter turnout is an indication of this. There has been a growing trend, particularly in the East, at most of the Landtag and local elections, and above all at the elections for the European Parliament, for voters to stay away. It has, moreover, been not only the unpolitical who have turned their backs on the parties in this way, but the well-informed and educated as well. This dissociation is a bitter loss to democratic culture.

The scepticism about politicians, the parties, and politics has grown to a frightening extent. There are many reasons for this. Not least is the devastating effect of the political scandals which surface with great regularity. It was disclosed in December 2004 that the CDU General Secretary and Merkel's close advisor, Laurenz Meyer, in addition to his politician's salary, was still being paid by his former employer, the electricity concern VEW/RWE.[37]

Following this, a number of further examples have emerged of politicians from all camps pursuing lucrative sidelines without having to do any actual work beyond straightforward lobbying. At a time when many citizens, and particularly the less well-off, have been subject to cuts and have had to make sacrifices, it has been inevitable that actual, as well as supposed, cases of politicians with their snouts in the trough have had a psychologically disastrous effect. But almost equally as bad has been the impact made by the insensitive behaviour of some managers and captains of industry who have been pocketing huge settlements and generous salary packages, while almost simultaneously expecting employees to accept wage cuts, longer working hours, and less job security. To old Joe Bloggs, "them up there" seemed to have lost all sense of responsibility towards employees, citizens, and the state.

---

37 He was finally forced to resign as General Secretary on 22.12.2005.

The apparent inability, despite every effort, to combat unemployment effectively and get the economy moving has undermined the respect for politicians and political parties. How limited the national room for manoeuvre has become, and how, in fact, restricted the state's effectiveness is, has been largely ignored or overlooked. Moreover, many citizens feel that decisions which they don't want, or of which they are afraid, are being made over their heads. Turkey's envisaged entry to the EU is one example of this, along with the French "Non" and the Dutch "Nee" to the European constitution (29 May and 1 June, respectively). This was a reflection not only of scepticism about Brussels bureaucracy and the expansion of the EU, but was also an expression of the reservations felt by many citizens about their political elites. The growing discrepancy between professional politicians who are striving for power and influence, and ordinary citizens who expect help, security, and hope for the future from politics is developing into a real problem for democracy, in Germany as well as in other European countries.

"Democracy needs the state" was the message to the SPD formulated by Franz Müntefering in his speech of 13 April 2005 in the Willy-Brandt-Haus in Berlin.[38] This was a reference primarily to the social obligations of the state, and spoke directly to the hearts of many in the party. The SPD also affirmed its commitment to a "strong and active state" in its election pledges. On the other hand, the deficiencies in fighting crime, about which many citizens quite rightly voiced their misgivings, as well as the increase in bureaucracy plaguing not just the world of business, played a somewhat minor role on this campaign agenda.[39] There is a gulf between the expectations made of a protective, helpful, and just state, and the desire for an individual life of one's own, which politics has difficulty in bridging.

When, in September 2002, the red-green coalition just managed to emerge as the winners of the federal election, serious challenges lay ahead. The German economy had fallen behind those of comparable countries, and tackling the consequences of globalisation, as well as pressing ahead with much-needed modernisation, proved difficult. The cuts the government introduced to the extensive network of social benefits affected mainly its own Social Democratic clientele. That alone was difficult for a party to swallow which, throughout its entire history, had devoted itself to the interests of working people. Furthermore, the individual measures were often introduced too suddenly, leading to bureaucratic errors and

38 See Der Spiegel, 14.5.2005, p. 25 f.
39 Otto Schily, however, did play a decisive role in his capacity as a "law-and-order" Minister of the Interior.

Franz Müntefering, SPD chairman 2004–2005

excesses. The average citizen found it hard to detect any promise for the future in all of this, or to see where things were going and what would be achieved. As the example of the Nordic countries shows, when presented with a recognisable, comprehensive, and clearly defined goal which can be demonstrated to be socially necessary and fair, people are willing to accept essential and painful cuts, particularly when they are seen to be successful.

The reform measures came too late to equip Germany rapidly for the future. Too many opportunities had been lost and postponed during the Kohl era, but the red-green coalition also wasted time in a process of *reculer pour mieux sauter*, first taking a backward step in order to then move forward. It is true that individual important projects were launched to control the burden of welfare expenditure, help the economy, and to stimulate personal initiative. This certainly took courage, and was a bitter pill for Social Democrats to swallow. But the measures to ease the labour market were slow to take effect, the economy stagnated instead of showing steady growth, and the pressing mountain of debt severely restricted the state's room for manoeuvre.

In the final years of his Chancellorship, Gerhard Schröder often seemed like a lone warrior who was trying to march ahead, but whose supporters were either reluctant, or refused, to follow him. This was reflected in the fact that the rampant growth of the federalist system, with an opposition which not only had a say, but also a *de facto* governing role, put a brake on things. And ultimately, when it came to the crunch, more than a few of those calling for reforms and a reduction in subsidies failed to go along with him. Many citizens were visibly losing faith in the competence of the red-green coalition and its ability to govern. In any functioning democratic system this signals time for a change. This mood was vigorously encouraged by a majority of the media and journalists, and was widely predicted by the opinion pollsters.

Changing governments is quite normal in a parliamentary democracy. The result of the general election of 18 September 2005, however, was inconclusive. With the country in urgent need of stable and effective government, the parties were now under an obligation. A lengthy wrangle over power and political instability would have further undermined the citizens' trust in politicians. It was not only Germany, but also the future of Europe which was at stake. The European project is in crisis. The European Union has to reform itself if the ancient continent is to be put on a free, prosperous, and just footing. In this, a powerful and effective social democracy is vital, to serve both as a corrective to neo-Liberalism and as the advocate of a social democracy of freedom and peace.

With the end of the red-green project the SPD was faced with a different political constellation. Alongside it, a new party had established itself – for the time being at least – which attracted mainly protest voters and the disaffected. This populist rival is a threat to the position which the Social Democrats have successfully held for so long as a left-wing party capable of integrating a wide spectrum of popular support. It now finds itself in the crucial middle ground, battling with the Union parties for approval, support, and voters. This is where it has to assert itself, and at the same time consolidate its traditional support amongst the labour force, if it is to seek, and be able once again, to lead a government in Germany. After seven years with their man, Gerhard Schröder, as Chancellor, and, as the leading party in government, of dictating policy, they must now reposition themselves in a changed political landscape. This will be a difficult act of adjustment.

It seemed as if the many bitter blows inflicted on the red-green alliance had left the SPD permanently drained and exhausted: only in the final sprint up to the elections did they recover their spirits. Amidst the euphoria of election night, Gerhard Schröder and his party seemed as one. But the harsh political realities demanded their price, for both the Social Democrats as well as the CDU/CSU. For neither of these adversaries was there a realistic possibility of joining forces with the smaller parties. Prior to the elections, the Union politicians in particular had rejected outright the possibility of an alliance between the SPD and the CDU/CSU. Now, however, reason and responsibility dictated that a coalition of the SPD and the Union was virtually inevitable.

Both sides, CDU/CSU and SPD, had to make enormous concessions to bring this about. Gerhard Schröder paved the way by renouncing his claim to the office of Chancellor[40], and, with a heavy heart, the SPD finally accepted the claim of the stronger CDU/CSU parliamentary group to the post of Federal Chancellor. With Angela Merkel, a woman and an East German occupied the Chancellor's office for the first time. In return, the SPD pressed their claim that the two coalition partners should be on an equal footing, and managed to secure eight of the fifteen specialist ministerial posts in the future government.[41] In effect, the Union largely abandoned the neo-liberal model of Angela Merkel, with the marriage of convenience between the two parties following the Gerhard Schröder legacy and its specific social democratic signature. In continuing to pursue the projects he had initiated with Agenda 2010, the Grand Coalition is set to bring the country further back on course, to consolidate the budget, and introduce the urgently needed reform of federalism. In foreign policy, too, continuity is the watchword.

Under the red-green coalition, Germany had made its mark as a power committed to peace and the avoidance of conflict, and which self-confidently played its part on the international stage. This was in keeping with SPD tradition. Since its very beginnings it had pledged itself to under-

40 He was formally released from the post on the 18.10.2005 when the new Bundestag sat for the first time. At the request of Federal President Köhler he remained in office in a caretaker capacity, pending the appointment of his successor.
41 Franz Müntefering was earmarked as Deputy Chancellor and Minister for Labour, Frank-Walter Steinmeier as Foreign Minister, Peer Steinbrück as Finance Minister, Sigmar Gabriel as Minister for the Environment, and Wolfgang Tiefensee as Transport Minister, along with also being responsible for Construction East. Brigitte Zypries (Justice), Ulla Schmidt (Health), and Heidemarie Wieczorek-Zeul (Development) would retain their posts in the Cabinet.

standing between nations and to a system of international mediation and security. The hope of peace gave rise to a purposeful peace policy. Under Willy Brandt the great task of reaching a settlement with Germany's Eastern neighbours was set in train, and continued by Helmut Schmidt. Brandt's vision of a "nation of good neighbours" was fulfilled, and the new and democratic Germany became an "asset in the securing of peace" (Helmut Schmidt). Under Gerhard Schröder's government, unified Germany took on greater international responsibility, including the participation of the Bundeswehr in military operations. But the priority was always the avoidance, or settling of conflict, and finding peaceful solutions.

Harsh historical experience has made this traditional concern of social democracy into what binds Europe together. It is now an integral part of the European heritage and identity. Social democracy and Europe are beacons of peaceful coexistence, understanding, and a particular way of maintaining peace and of reconciling freedom with social justice. The task of the SPD for the future will be to transcend the boundaries of the nation state and position itself much more firmly in the European context.

A constant preoccupation of German social democracy throughout its entire history has been freedom and democracy. Whereas in Western Europe the liberal bourgeoisie was the main protagonist in the battle for parliamentary democracy, the main burden in the struggle for democratic rights in Germany during the nineteenth and early twentieth centuries was borne by the labour movement. The paths of democratic socialists and Bolsheviks/Communists would later divide over the issues of freedom and democracy.

The SPD was the true constitutional party in the Weimar Republic (1918 to 1933), and had a crucial role in the construction and development of the Second German Republic. Willy Brandt's call to "venture more democracy" marked a move to pastures new, and the goal of a citizens' society. Given the present circumstances of the modern media democracies, the need for mature citizens who take responsibility for their own lives, and become involved in state and society, is greater than ever. The basic values of "freedom, justice, and solidarity" depend on people, not on a class or a collective. Paramount for social democracy are the rights and dignity of the individual, as well as respect for his or her freedom.

For Social Democrats, tolerance has, and always has had, its limits: with respect to National Socialism and Communism, for instance, or terrorist and extremist activities. Internal, as well as external, freedom and security are conditional on one another. Any free society must defend itself against those who threaten its very existence and trample on human rights. For social democracy this is not a departure from the goal of a civil society: it is a condition of it being achieved. It must, nevertheless, take great care that freedom does not suffer disproportionally in the necessary process of securing it.

Social democracy is associated most strongly with the goal of social justice. This is a common thread running through its entire history. Social Democrats wanted justice, not alms. In this they were putting their faith not only in the state, but also in solidarity and active self-help. Social democracy is about much more than the social state built up in the nineteenth and twentieth centuries. It goes far beyond this to encompass exerting a direct influence on the shaping of society from within, pluralism, and individuals, groups and associations taking responsibility for themselves.

The modern social state has been shaped and constructed largely by social democracy. It created a finely meshed social safety net to cope with unemployment, sickness, and need, and created a carefully worked-out pension scheme to provide an adequate income in old age. The system was based on the premise that it could be financed by steady economic growth and a balance between the generations. As a consequence, however, of high unemployment, a slow-moving economy, the pressure of globalisation, and a disproportionate increase in the number of the elderly, it has reached crisis point. Social justice remains a basic social concern: but the social state has to be reformed. It is a question of finding the right balance between self-responsibility, welfare provision, and solidarity, in order to ensure fairness and social justice for the future.

The road which the SPD has to take is a rocky one. The party has a difficult balancing act to perform which will require hard work and a steady step. In the course of its long history the SPD has overcome harsher tests than this, has suffered setbacks and recovered from them. Once more, and under changed conditions, it now must prove itself again. Since its beginnings, the party has, of course, changed from a primarily class party into a left-wing, pluralist *Volkspartei* in a democratic Germany. It had always committed itself to the goal of a democratic and just society, and stuck by this even in arduous times. These principles are not up for debate. What is crucial, is that, under changed circumstances, they now be put into social and political practice in a proper and balanced manner.

Our democratic system needs a great, responsible left-wing people's party as a corrective and alternative to the conservative-liberal camp. Social democracy, with its obligation to a noble inheritance, must both face up to the difficult tasks of the present, as well as tackle the shaping of the future with energy and skill. Germany, Europe, and the world need a German social democracy which is both self-confident and capable of resolute action.

Chronological Table

	1848
February	The *Manifesto of the Communist Party*, written by Karl Marx in collaboration with Friedrich Engels, appears.
Feb./March	Revolution in France, Germany, Austria, Hungary.
April	Workers' associations are founded in many cities.
28.8.–3.9.	A congress of German workers convenes in Berlin. The Brotherhood of Workers is founded under Stephan Born.

	1854
July	All workers' associations are dissolved following a Bundestag Law of Association.

1861

The prohibition of freedom of association is lifted in Saxony.

	1863
23.5.	The General Association of German Workers (ADAV) is founded. Ferdinand Lassalle is elected as its President for five years. The ADAV declares that its most important goal is "the establishment of universal, equal, and direct suffrage".

	1864
31.8.	Lassalle dies as a result of a duel.
28.9.	Founding of the International Workers' Association (the First International) in London.

	1866
19.8.	In collaboration with bourgeois democrats, August Bebel and Wilhelm Liebknecht found the Saxon People's Party.

	1867
12.2.	August Bebel, Wilhelm Liebknecht, and Reinhold Schraps are elected to the North German Reichstag.

1868

5.9. At the congress of the League of German Workers' Associations there is a majority vote to amalgamate with the International Workers' Association. There is support for the establishment of trade unions.

1869

7./8.8. Founding of the Social Democratic Workers' Party (SDAP) in Eisenach.

1871

March Revolt of the Paris Commune.

1875

22.–27.5. The "Lassalleans" and the "Eisenachers" merge at the party congress in Gotha to form the Socialist Workers' Party of Germany. The Gotha programme is approved.

1876

1.10. The first number of *Vorwärts*, the main organ of the Socialist Workers' Party, appears.

1878

30.7. In spite of electoral interference, the Socialist Workers' Party receives 437,158 votes, and 9 seats, in elections to the Reichstag.

19.10. Bismarck's "law against the dangerous activities of social democracy" (Anti-Socialist Law) is passed in the Reichstag by 221 votes to 149.

1880

20.–23.8. Congress of the Socialist Workers' Party in Wyden, Switzerland.

1889

14.–20.7. An international workers' congress designates the 1 May as the day of struggle for the eight-hour working day.

1890

25.1. The Reichstag rejects an extension of the Anti-Socialist Law.

20.2.	In the Reichstag elections, the SPD wins 1,427,000 votes, thereby becoming the numerically strongest party.
16./17.11.	Founding of the General Commission of German Trade Unions.

1891

16.–23.8.	Congress of the Second International.
14.20.–10.	Party congress in Erfurt. The Erfurt programme is approved.

1899

January	Bernstein publishes his book, *Presuppositions of Socialism and the Tasks for Social Democracy*.
9.–14.10.	Disputes about revisionism at the party congress in Hanover.

1903

13.–20.9.	Condemnation of revisionism at the party congress in Dresden.

1905

22.–27.5.	Debate about mass strikes at the trade-union congress. The propagation of the political mass strike is rejected.
17.–23.9.	At the SPD party congress in Jena the mass strike is approved only as a defensive measure.

1906

23.–29.9.	Continuation of the discussion about mass strikes at the Mannheim party congress. In the Mannheim Agreement the trade unions are granted a considerable measure of independence.

1912

12.1.	In the Reichstag elections, the SPD wins 34.8 per cent of the votes (4.25 million).

1913

13.8.	August Bebel dies in Switzerland.

1914

3.8.	The SPD parliamentary party in the Reichstag votes by 78 to 14 in favour of war credits.

4.8.	The SPD parliamentary party votes unanimously in the Reichstag in favour of the war-credits bill. The chairman Haase declares: "In its hour of danger, we will not leave the Fatherland in the lurch".
	1916
January	The International Group round Rosa Luxemburg and Karl Liebknecht; publication of the Spartacus letters.
24.3.	Split in the SPD parliamentary party, founding of the Social Democratic Working Group.
	1917
7.1.	Reich conference of the opposition; condemned by the party committee as a "special organisation".
6.–8.4.	The Independent Social Democratic Party (USPD) is founded.
	1918
January	Strikes, particularly in the armaments factories.
4.10.	Social Democrats join the government of Prince Max von Baden.
4.11.	A workers' and soldiers' council takes over political and military control in Kiel.
7./8.11.	The revolutionary uprising of workers, sailors, and soldiers spreads to all parts of Germany.
9.11.	Prince Max von Baden hands over the business of government to Friedrich Ebert. Scheidemann proclaims the Republic.
10.11.	Revolutionary government of the council of people's commissioners – a coalition of MSPD and USPD, Majority (Ebert, Scheidemann, Landsberg) and Independent Social Democrats (Haase, Dittmann, Barth). Executive council of the Berlin workers' and soldiers' councils.
12.11.	The council of people's commissioners proclaims "the realisation of the socialist programme".
16.–20.12.	Reich conference of the workers' and soldiers' councils. The councils vote to hold elections for a National Assembly, and call for immediate socialisation measures.
29.12.	Independent Socialists leave the council of people's commissioners.
30.12.	Founding of the German Communist Party.

1919

4.–13.1.	Fighting between revolutionary workers and soldiers and troops deployed by Ebert's government.
15.1.	Rosa Luxemburg and Karl Liebknecht are murdered.
19.1.	In the elections to the National Assembly, the SPD wins 37.9 per cent, the USPD 7.6 per cent of the votes.
11.2.	Ebert is elected Reich President.
13.2.	Scheidemann forms the first Weimar coalition government from the SPD, DDP, and the Centre Party.
10.–15.6.	SPD party congress in Weimar.
20.6.	After Scheidemann's resignation, Gustav Bauer (SPD) forms another coalition government with the Centre Party, later joined by the DDP.

1920

18.1.	The Works Committee Law is passed.
13.–17.3.	Kapp Putsch. A general strike called by the trade unions and the SPD forces Kapp to back down.
27.3.	After the resignation of Bauer's cabinet, Hermann Müller forms another government with the Centre Party and the DDP.
6.6.	In the Reichstag elections the SPD's share of the vote drops from 37.9 to 21.6 per cent, while that of the USPD goes up from 7.6 to 18.0 per cent.
12.–17.10.	At the USPD party congress in Halle, there is a majority in favour of accepting the 21 conditions for joining the Communist International. The result of the vote leads to a split in the USPD.
4.–7.12.	The left wing of the USPD merges with the KPD to form the United Communist Party of Germany.

1921

18.–24.9.	The SPD party congress in Görlitz adopts a new party programme.

1922

24.9.	The rump USPD reunites with the MSPD to form the United Social Democratic Party of Germany.

1923

January	The trade unions and the Social Democrats support the passive resistance to the occupation of the Ruhr.

1925
28.2. Death of Friedrich Ebert.
13.–18.9. A new programme is adopted at the SPD party congress in Heidelberg.

1928
20.5. Reichstag elections: SPD vote goes up to 29.8 per cent.
28.6. Hermann Müller forms a Grand Coalition government comprising the SPD, DDP, Centre Party, DVP, and the Bavarian People's Party.

1930
27.3. A planned change in unemployment benefit leads to the collapse of the Grand Coalition.
14.9. After the success of the NSDAP in the Reichstag elections the SPD decides to give its tacit support to the Brüning government.

1931
16.12. Founding of the "Iron Front" as a defence against the dangers of fascism. It comprises the SPD, ADGB, Reichsbanner, and workers' sports organisations.

1932
13.3. The SPD supports the election of Hindenburg as Reich president.
20.7. The government of Otto Braun in Prussia is deposed with the help of article 48.

1933
30.1. Hitler becomes Reich Chancellor.
23.3. The SPD in the Reichstag votes against the Enabling Law.
2.5. Occupation of the premises of the Free Trade Unions.
22.6. Banning of the SPD, the start of a wave of mass arrests.

1934
28.1. Prague manifesto of Sopade, "The Struggle and Goal of Revolutionary Socialism".

1941
19.3. Founding of the Union of German Socialist Organisations in Great Britain.

1945

19.4.	At a meeting between Kurt Schumacher and Social Democrats in Hanover it is decided to refound the SPD.
15.6.	Proclamation by the SPD central committee in Berlin under the chairmanship of Otto Grotewohl. He claims to represent the executive committee for the whole of Germany.
September	After the return of Erich Ollenhauer and Fritz Heine from exile, the "Schumacher Bureau" is constituted as the "Bureau for the Western Zones".
5.–7.10.	At the invitation of the "Schumacher Bureau", a conference of Social Democrat functionaries takes place in Wennigsen near Hanover.

1946

31.3.	In a ballot, 82 per cent of members of the SPD in the three Western sectors of Berlin vote against an immediate merger with the KPD.
21./22.4.	Founding congress of the Socialist Unity Party of Germany (SED) – the *Zwangsvereinigung* (forced merger).
9.–11.5.	SPD congress in Hanover. Schumacher is elected chairman, with Ollenhauer as first, and Willi Knothe (Frankfurt/Main) as second deputy chairman.

1947

Mai	The SPD group on the Economic Council for the United Economic Area decides to go into opposition.
29.6.–2.7.	SPD congress in Nuremberg adopts "Guidelines for the Construction of the German Republic" along with principles on economic policy.

1948

24.6.	Beginning of the Berlin Blockade by the Soviet Union. West Berlin is kept supplied by airlift.
1.9.	Constitution of the Parliamentary Council, with Konrad Adenauer being elected as its chairman, and Carlo Schmid becoming leader of the SPD parliamentary party.
11.–14.9.	SPD congress in Düsseldorf calls for the enactment of a statute of occupation as the legal basis for relations between the occupying powers and the Germans.

1949

8.5.	The Parliamentary Council approves the Basic Law, with the SPD voting in favour.
14.8.	Elections to the first Bundestag.
29./30.8.	The SPD executive approves guidelines for policy in the Bundestag (the 16 Dürkheim points).
31.8.	The SPD parliamentary party elects Schumacher as its first, Ollenhauer as its second, and Carlo Schmid as its third chairman. Adolf Arndt and Wilhelm Mellies become the party's business managers.
7.10.	Founding of the German Democratic Republic (GDR).

1950

26.4.	Beginning of the "Waldheim trials" in the GDR; by June, more than 3,400 convictions.
21.–25.5.	SPD congress in Hamburg calls for resistance to remilitarisation, and adopts a critical stance towards the Council of Europe, as well as the Schumann Plan.

1951

21.5.	Promulgation of the Coal and Steel Co-Determination Law.
30.6.–3.7.	The Socialist International is refounded in Frankfurt/Main. It approves a declaration of principle: the "Goals and Tasks of Democratic Socialism".

1952

20.8.	Death of Kurt Schumacher.
24.–28.9.	SPD congress in Dortmund approves a programme for action. Erich Ollenhauer is elected party chairman, with Wilhelm Mellies as his deputy.

1953

17.6.	National uprising in East Berlin and the GDR; strikes and demonstrations; uprising crushed by Soviet troops.
6.9.	Bundestag elections. Heavy defeat for the SPD gives rise to widespread discussion in the party.
29.9.	Death of Ernst Reuter.

1954

20.–24.7.	SPD party congress in Berlin approves changes and additions to the programme for action; a commission is set up under Willi Eichler to work out a Basic Programme.

1955

27.2. The Bundestag ratifies the Paris Treaties, with the SPD voting against.

14.5. Founding of the Warsaw Pact.

1956

7.7. The introduction of military service is approved by the Bundestag, with the SPD voting against.

10.–14.7. SPD party congress in Munich discusses problems arising from the second industrial revolution.

24.10. National uprising in Hungary against the Communist regime and the Soviets.

1957

19.5. The all-German People's Party decides to dissolve itself and recommends its members to join the SPD. Its chairman and chairwoman, Gustav Heinemann and Helene Wessel, stand as candidates for the SPD.

14.9. Bundestag elections.

4.10. First Soviet satellite "sputnik" sends shock waves throughout the West.

1958

18.–23.5. SPD party congress in Stuttgart resolves to change the organisation statute. A presidium elected by the executive committee replaces the existing "Bureau". Ollenhauer remains chairman, Waldemar von Knoeringen and Herbert Wehner are elected deputy chairmen. Willy Brandt becomes a member of the executive committee.

10.11. Khrushchev issues his ultimatum on Berlin.

1959

19.3. Publication of the SPD's "Plan for Germany".

13.–15.11. A special SPD party conference in Bad Godesberg approves the new Basic Programme.

1960

30.6. In the Bundestag, Herbert Wehner advocates a joint foreign policy between government and opposition on the basis of existing treaty obligations.

21.–25.11.	SPD party congress in Hanover. Willy Brandt is introduced as the SPD's Chancellorship candidate, and the "SPD team" for the elections is announced.

1961

28.4.	The SPD manifesto is announced.
13.8.	The GDR seals off West Berlin with barbed wire and barriers: building of the Berlin Wall.
17.9.	Bundestag elections.

1962

26.–30.5.	SPD party congress in Cologne. Willy Brandt is elected deputy party chairman along with Herbert Wehner.
October	Cuba crisis (deployment of Soviet missiles and US blockade); the *Spiegel*-Affair.

1963

12.5.	SPD rally in Hanover to celebrate the party's centenary. This is followed by events throughout the whole year in the Federal Republic.
15.7.	Speeches by Willy Brandt and Egon Bahr in Tutzing ("change through rapprochement").
14.12.	Death of Erich Ollenhauer.
17.12.	Signing of the first Berlin Passes Agreement.

1964

15./16.2.	Special party congress elects Willy Brandt as SPD chairman, with Fritz Erler and Herbert Wehner as deputy chairmen.
3.3.	Fritz Erler elected leader of the SPD parliamentary party.
23.–27.11.	SPD party congress in Karlsruhe. Willy Brandt presents his "government team".

1965

19.9.	Bundestag elections.

1966

18.3.–15.4.	The SPD executive replies to the SED's "Open Letters".
1.–5.6.	SPD party congress in Dortmund formulates a resolution on *Deutschlandpolitik* along with numerous others on the domestic political tasks facing a federal government of which the SPD would be a part.

10.7.	Landtag elections in North Rhine-Westphalia. With 49.5 per cent of the vote, the SPD outstrips the CDU for the first time in the largest federal state. The CDU/FDP coalition under Minister President Franz Meyers remains in power.
1.12.	Swearing in of the new Grand Coalition government. Willy Brandt becomes Foreign Minister and deputy to Federal Chancellor Kurt-Georg Kiesinger (CDU).
8.12.	After the fall of Meyers, Heinz Kühn (SPD) becomes Minister President of North Rhine-Westphalia and forms a coalition government with the FDP.

1967

22.2.	Death of Fritz Erler.
14.3.	Helmut Schmidt becomes leader of the SPD parliamentary party in the Bundestag.

1968

17.–21.3.	SPD party congress in Nuremberg discusses the party's activity in government. A new organisation statute is approved.
31.5.	Hans-Jürgen Wischnewski is appointed to the newly created office of SPD federal business manager.
21.8.	Invasion of Czechoslovakia by Warsaw Pact troops; end of the "Prague Spring".

1969

5.3.	Gustav Heinemann (SPD), with the votes of the FDP, is elected President by the Federal Convention.
16.–18.4.	Special SPD party congress in Bad Godesberg discusses the SPD manifesto.
28.9.	Bundestag elections.
October	Formation of the social-liberal coalition government under Chancellor Willy Brandt; Walter Scheel (FDP) becomes Foreign Minister and Deputy Chancellor; Herbert Wehner becomes leader of the SPD parliamentary party.
5./7.12.	Change of course at the *Jusos* (Young Socialists) federal congress in Munich.

1970

19.3.	Meeting of Willy Brandt and Willi Stoph in Erfurt.

11.–14.5.	SPD party congress in Saarbrücken charges the party executive with the setting up of commissions to work out suggestions for tax reforms, and to formulate a long-term programme for social and political action.
14.9.	The SPD executive welcomes the treaty with the Soviet Union signed on 12 August 1970.
7.12.	Signing of the Warsaw Treaty; Brandt kneels at the memorial to the Warsaw Ghetto.

1971

26.2.	The SPD executive publishes a declaration on the relationship between social democracy and Communism.
3.9.	Signing of the Four-Power Agreement on Berlin.
10.12.	Willy Brandt receives the Nobel Peace Prize in Oslo.

1972

24.1.	After the resignation of Wischnewski, the party executive elects Holger Börner as SPD party business manager.
27.4.	Brandt survives a CDU/CSU constructive vote of no-confidence.
June	Presentation of the "Draft for an economic and political Orientation Framework 1973–1985" ("Long-term Programme").
8.11.	Initialling of the Basic Treaty between the Federal Republic and the GDR.
19.11.	Bundestag elections. Formation of the second Brandt/Scheel government.

1973

10.–14.4.	SPD party congress in Hanover passes resolutions on the "Orientation Framework", on land law, and employees' profit sharing.
6.10.	Attack by Egypt and the Arab states on Israel (the Yom Kippur war) leads to an acute energy crisis in the industrial states, and to a general increase in the price of crude oil.

1974

6.5.	Willy Brandt resigns as Federal Chancellor. Helmut Schmidt becomes his successor on 16 May.
15.5.	Walter Scheel (FDP) is elected Federal President. Gustav Heinemann had declined to stand again.

1975

30.7./1.8. The final Conference on Security and Cooperation in Europe conference with the signing of the Helsinki Final Act.

11.–15.11. The SPD party congress in Mannheim approves almost unanimously Orientation Framework '85.

1976

18.3. The Bundestag ratifies the Co-determination Law which applies to all businesses with more than 2,000 employees.

3.10. Bundestag elections. The SPD loses its position as the strongest parliamentary group. The social-liberal government with Helmut Schmidt as Federal Chancellor remains in power.

22.11. Egon Bahr elected as SPD business manager. He takes over from Holger Börner who becomes Minister President in Hesse.

26.11. Willy Brandt becomes President of the Socialist International.

1977

28.9. Willy Brandt takes over the chairmanship of the Independent Commission on International Development Issues (North-South Commission).

15.–19.11. SPD party congress in Hamburg passes resolutions on energy policy, economic and employment policy, as well as on foreign policy and security issues.

1978

9.–10.12. Special SPD party congress in Cologne approves the manifesto and list of candidates for the European elections. It decides on the criteria for employment in the public sphere, rejecting *inter alia* making routine enquiries about candidates with the *Verfassungsschutz* (internal security agency).

1979

23.5. Karl Carstens (CDU) elected Federal President.

7.–10.6. In the first direct elections to the European Parliament the SPD wins 35 (one in Berlin) of the 81 mandates (three in Berlin) in the Federal Republic as a whole. The European Parliament has 410 seats in all.

3.–9.12. The SPD party congress in Berlin votes in favour of the social-liberal government's security and energy policy.

1980

11.5.	In the Landtag elections in North Rhine-Westphalia the SPD wins an absolute majority and is able to form a government on its own.
5.10.	The Bundestag elections broaden the basis of the social-liberal coalition. Helmut Schmidt remains Federal Chancellor, Hans-Dietrich Genscher his deputy.
12.12.	Peter Glotz is elected SPD party business manager. He succeeds Egon Bahr.

1981

23.1.	Hans-Jochen Vogel, the Federal Justice Minister, is elected Governing Mayor of Berlin.
10.10.	Mass peace-movement demonstration in Bonn.
11.–13.12.	Chancellor Helmut Schmidt attends inner-German summit conference in the GDR; talks with Erich Honecker at lake Werbellin and lake Mölln.
13.12.	Declaration of martial law in Poland.

1982

5.2.	In the Bundestag, Chancellor Schmidt asks for a vote of confidence and gets the unanimous backing of the SPD and FDP.
8.2.	The news magazine *Der Spiegel* reveals shady dealings in the trade union building concern "Neue Heimat".
19.–23.4.	The SPD party congress in Munich approves resolutions on unemployment. Willy Brandt is once again elected party chairman. As his deputies, Helmut Schmidt and Johannes Rau, who is new to the office.
17.6.	The FDP in Hesse decides in favour of a coalition with the CDU.
20.8.	The FDP chairman and Foreign Minister Hans-Dietrich Genscher writes about the necessity for a *Wende* (turnabout).
17.9.	Declaration by Chancellor Schmidt on the termination of the social-liberal coalition.
1.10.	With a constructive vote of no-confidence the Bundestag elects Helmut Kohl (CDU) as Chancellor.
8.–22.11.	Four Bundestag deputies resign from the FDP.

1983

21.1. The SPD election congress in Dortmund nominates Hans-Jochen Vogel as its Chancellorship candidate.

6.3. The SPD is defeated in the Bundestag elections. Helmut Kohl remains Chancellor, heading a coalition of the Union parties and the FDP.

8.3. Hans-Jochen Vogel is the new leader of the SPD parliamentary party in the Bundestag.

18./19.11. The special SPD party congress in Cologne rejects, with 14 votes against and three abstentions, the counter-arming with American medium-range missiles.

1984

17.–21.5. The SPD party congress in Essen charges the executive committee with the establishment of a commission to draw up a new Basic Programme. Willy Brandt re-elected as party chairman, with Johannes Rau as one of his deputies, and Hans-Jochen Vogel replacing Helmut Schmidt as the other.

23.5. Richard von Weizsäcker (CDU) is elected, with the help of the SPD vote, as the new Federal President.

17.6. The election in the Federal Republic to the European Parliament produces the following results: CDU/CSU 46.0; SPD 37.4; Greens 8.2; FDP 4.8 per cent.

1985

10.3. In the Landtag elections in the Saarland, the SPD wins an absolute majority with 49.2 per cent of the vote. Oskar Lafontaine becomes the first SPD Minister President in the Saarland. His cabinet is composed entirely of Social Democrats.

11.3. Mikhail Gorbachev is elected General Secretary of the Communist Party of the Soviet Union.

12.5. In the Landtag elections in North Rhine-Westphalia the SPD vote climbs to 52.1 per cent.

12.12. Formation in Hesse of an SPD/Greens coalition government.

15.12. The SPD executive nominate Johannes Rau as Chancellorship candidate.

1986

26.4. The most serious accident in the history of the peaceful use of atomic energy occurs at the nuclear reactor in the Ukrainian town of Chernobyl (USSR).

25.–29.8.	The SPD party congress resolves to phase out the use of nuclear energy.

1987

25.1.	The Bundestag elections produce a drop in votes for the SPD from 38.2 per cent to 37.0 per cent; the CDU/CSU-FDP coalition remains in power.
27.1.	Hans-Jochen Vogel once again becomes leader of the SPD parliamentary party.
23.3.	Willy Brandt resigns as SPD chairman.
5.4.	In the early Landtag elections in Hesse, the CDU becomes the strongest party.
14.6.	The special SPD party congress in Bonn elects Hans-Jochen Vogel as Willy Brandt's successor as party chairman. Oskar Lafontaine joins Johannes Rau as deputy chairman, and Anke Fuchs is the new party business manager.
27.8.	The joint paper "The Battle of the Ideologies and Common Security" produced by the SPD's Commission on Basic Values and the Academy of Social Sciences of the Central Committee of the SED is presented in East Berlin and Bonn.
7.–11.9.	Official state visit of Honecker to the Federal Republic.
13.9.	In the Landtag elections in Schleswig-Holstein, the SPD becomes the strongest party; the Barschel Affair.

1988

17.1.	Counter-demonstrators are detained during the Liebknecht/Luxemburg march in East Berlin; beginning of a wave of arrests and expatriations.
8.5.	In the Landtag elections in Schleswig-Holstein, the SPD wins an absolute majority.
31.5.	Björn Engholm is elected as the new Minister President of Schleswig-Holstein.
30.8.–2.9.	The SPD party congress in Münster, Westphalia, decides to implement a "women's quota". Hans-Jochen Vogel is elected party chairman, with Herta Däubler-Gmelin, Oskar Lafontaine, and Johannes Rau as his deputies.

1989

16.3.	Walter Momper (SPD) is elected as the new Governing Mayor of Berlin. He is supported by a coalition of SPD and the Alternative List (AL).

2.5.	Hungary begins dismantling the "Iron Curtain" along its border with Austria.
7.5.	Local elections in the GDR; independent observers uncover electoral fraud.
4.6.	Crushing of the movement for democracy in China; Tiananmen Square massacre.
12.–15.6.	Mikhail Gorbachev visits the Federal Republic.
18.6.	Elections to the European Parliament in the Federal Republic. Results in percentages: CDU/CSU 37.7; SPD 37.3; Greens 8.4; Republicans 7.1; FDP 5.6.
July/August	Growing exodus of GDR citizens fleeing via Hungary and West German embassies.
7.10.	Founding of the Social Democratic Party (SDP) in the GDR in Schwante (to the north of Berlin).
7.–9.10.	Huge demonstrations in East Berlin, Leipzig, Dresden, and other cities in the GDR.
18.10.	Erich Honecker resigns from all his offices. Egon Krenz becomes the new General Secretary of the SED.
4.11.	Mass demonstrations in East Berlin calling for reforms.
9.11.	Opening of the GDR borders with the Federal Republic. The end of the Wall greeted with indescribable elation.
18.–20.12.	SPD party congress in Berlin approves a new Basic Programme with the emphasis on ecological renewal of industrial society, social equality for women, shorter working hours, peace policy.

1990

19.1.	Death of Herbert Wehner.
28.1.	In the Landtag elections in the Saar, the SPD increases its majority from 49.2 per cent to 54.4 per cent.
22.–25.2.	The party congress of the East SPD in Leipzig approves a Basic Programme. Willy Brandt elected honorary chairman, Ibrahim Böhme elected chairman.
18.3.	The first free elections to the GDR *Volkskammer* (People's Chamber). Results in percentages: CDU 40.82; DSU (sister party of the CSU) 6.31; SPD 21.88; PDS (successor of the SED) 16.40; Liberals 5.28. Lothar de Maizière (CDU) becomes Minister President and head of a coalition government which also includes the SPD.
25.4.	Lafontaine is badly wounded in an attack by a mentally disturbed woman.

13.5.	In the Landtag elections in Lower Saxony, the SPD becomes the strongest party.
18.5.	Signing of the state treaty on German economic, currency, and social union.
10.6.	A special party congress of the East SPD in Halle elects Wolfgang Thierse as its new chairman.
1.7.	The currency union between the GDR and the Federal Republic comes into force.
31.8.	Signing of the *Einigungsvertrag* (unification treaty) between the Federal Republic and the GDR.
27.9.	Restoration of the unity of the SPD at the party congress in Berlin. Adoption of the Berlin Manifesto.
3.10.	Unification of Germany, with the GDR joining the Federal Republic in accordance with Basic Law Article 23.
14.10.	In the Landtag elections in the five new states, Brandenburg, Mecklenburg-Western Pomerania, Saxony-Anhalt, Saxony, and Thuringia, only in Brandenburg is the SPD the strongest party. The CDU victorious in the other states, in Saxony with an absolute majority. In the Landtag elections in Bavaria the SPD drops to 26 per cent.
1.11.	The Social Democrat Manfred Stolpe is elected as Brandenburg's first Minister President. He forms a coalition government made up of the SPD, FDP, and Alliance 90.
2.12.	All-German Bundestag elections. Results in percentages: CDU/CSU 43.8; SPD 33.5; FDP 11.0; Greens 3.9; PDS 2.4; Alliance 90/Greens 1.2.

1991

9.1.	Fruitless talks between the USA and Iraq on resolving the Gulf crisis.
15.1.	Expiry of the United Nations ultimatum calling for Iraq to withdraw from Kuwait.
17.1.	Start of the Gulf War.
5.4.	Hans Eichel (SPD) elected as Minister President of Hesse. Joschka Fischer (Greens) becomes Deputy Minister President, Minister for the Environment, and Bundesrat Minister.
21.4.	In the Rhineland-Palatinate Landtag elections the SPD becomes the strongest party. Rudolf Scharping (SPD) is elected Minister President on 21.5. This gives the SPD a majority in the Bundesrat.

28.–31.5.	SPD party congress in Bremen elects Björn Engholm as party chairman.
20.6.	The German Bundestag votes by 338 to 320 to make Berlin the seat of parliament and the federal government.
12.11.	Hans-Ulrich Klose beats Herta Däubler-Gmelin and Rudolf Dreßler in the election for the leadership of the SPD parliamentary party.
12.12.	Inge Wettig-Danielmeier, the chairwoman of the ASF, is elected SPD treasurer by the party executive. She officially takes up her new post on 14.1.1992.

1992

7.2.	Signing of the Maastricht Treaties on the founding of the European Union and the economic and currency union.
22.8.	Meeting behind closed doors on the Petersberg near Bonn of the leaders of the SPD and the SPD parliamentary group. The "Petersberg Resolutions" on asylum law and guidelines for the recognition of political refugees, as well as the deployment of the Bundeswehr within the framework of UNO.
14.9.	Willy Brandt resigns as chairman of the Socialist International: the SI congress in Berlin from 15.–17.9. elects Pierre Mauroy as his successor.
8.10.	Willy Brandt, SPD chairman from 1964 to 1987, and Federal Chancellor from 1969 to 1974, dies in Unkel after a long and serious illness.
16./17.11.	Special party congress in Bonn. In the approved motions put forward by the party leadership, the party expresses itself in favour of a change in the asylum law, and of an amendment to the constitution which would allow "blue-helmet" deployment of Bundeswehr troops (UNO resolutions).
2.12.	Ratification of the Maastricht Treaties.

1993

3.5.	Björn Engholm announces his resignation from the SPD chairmanship and as Minister President in Schleswig-Holstein. Johannes Rau becomes caretaker chairman.
19.5.	Election of Heide Simonis as Minister President of Schleswig-Holstein.
26.5.	The Bundestag approves the revision of the asylum law including the change to Article 16 of the Basic Law.

13.6.	In a poll of members about the future SPD party chairman, 40.3 per cent vote for Rudolf Scharping, 33.2 per cent for Gerhard Schröder, and 26.5 per cent for Heidemarie Wieczorek-Zeul.
25.6.	The special party congress in Essen elects Scharping as the new party chairman.
18.8.	Günter Verheugen takes over as party business manager (as successor to Karl-Heinz Blessing).
16.–19.11.	SPD party congress in Wiesbaden with resolutions on public safety, protection against criminality, combating right-wing extremism, and modernising the party: "SPD 2000". Scharping is confirmed as party chairman, with Herta Däubler-Gmelin, Oskar Lafontaine, Johannes Rau, Wolfgang Thierse, and Heidemarie Wieczorek-Zeul as his deputies.
1.11.	The Maastricht Treaties come into force; transformation of the European Community (EEC) into the European Union (EU).

1994

9.2.	The number of unemployed in Germany exceeds the four million mark.
13.3.	Landtag elections in Lower Saxony. The SPD with Gerhard Schröder as Minister President wins an absolute majority of the mandates with 44.3 per cent of the vote.
26./27.4.	Constitution of "SPD 60 plus" at its first federal congress in Mainz. Hans-Ulrich Klose is elected chairman.
13.6.	Elections to the European Parliament with losses for the SPD. The presidium declares that "the SPD has lost the European elections".
22.6.	SPD election party congress in Halle. 95.6 per cent of the delegates vote for Rudolf Scharping as Chancellorship candidate.
27.6.	Landtag elections in Saxony-Anhalt. The SPD gains 8 percentage points, the CDU loses 14.5.
22.7.	Reinhard Höppner is elected Minister President of Saxony-Anhalt. He forms a minority government composed of SPD and Alliance 90/Greens, which is given partial parliamentary backing by the PDS: the "Magdeburg Model".
8.9.	Jutta Limbach (SPD) is elected President of the Federal Constitutional Court.

11.9.	In the Landtag elections in Brandenburg, the SPD and Manfred Stolpe achieve a great victory with 54.1 per cent of the votes. The CDU and the PDS are almost dead level with 18.72 and 18.71 per cent respectively. In Saxony the SPD polls a mere 16.5 per cent. The CDU under Kurt Biedenkopf is able to defend its absolute majority there.
25.9.	In the Landtag elections in Bavaria, the SPD improves its standing to 26.1 per cent; the CSU retains its absolute majority with 52.8 per cent.
16.10.	Bundestag elections. The coalition achieves a narrow victory, with 41.5 per cent of the vote going to the CDU/CSU, and 6.9 per cent to the FDP. The SPD increases its vote to 36.4 per cent, the Greens poll 7.3, and the PDS 4.4 per cent. At Landtag elections taking place at the same time in Mecklenburg-Western Pomerania and Thuringia, the SPD polls in each case just 30 per cent. In the Saar, with 49.4 per cent, it wins a majority of the Landtag seats.
18.10.	Rudolf Scharping becomes leader of the parliamentary party in the Bundestag.
26.10.	Kurt Beck is elected Rudolf Scharping's successor as Minister President in Rhineland-Palatinate.

1995

26.3.	The Schengen Agreement comes into force. With this, the EU states, with some exceptions (Great Britain and Ireland), abolish border controls.
July	Massacre by Serb troops in Srebrenica of some 7,000 Muslims.
14.–17.11.	SPD party congress in Mannheim. After a battle for the candidacy with the existing chairman Rudolf Scharping, Oskar Lafontaine is elected new party chairman on 16.11. with 321 votes.

1996

24.3.	In the Landtag elections in Baden-Württemberg, the SPD wins only 25.1 per cent of the votes (1992: 29.4 per cent); the CDU wins 41.3 per cent.
21.4.	Reinhard Klimmt is elected chairman of the SPD in the Saar.
25.11.	Party congress of SPD youth in Cologne with the theme "Contract with the Future: new Chances for Youth".

1997

1.5.	Election victory for the Labour Party and Tony Blair in Great Britain.
1.6.	Election success for the French Socialists and Lionel Jospin.
12.11.	Ortwin Runde elected Mayor of Hamburg.

1998

January	The number of unemployed rises to 4.9 million, the highest figure in the history of the Federal Republic of Germany. In the new states, the unemployment level exceeds the 20-per-cent mark.
1.3.	In Lower Saxony, Gerhard Schröder and the SPD win an absolute majority in the Landtag with 47.9 per cent of the vote.
17.4.	SPD election party congress in Leipzig unanimously nominates Gerhard Schröder as Chancellorship candidate.
26.4.	In the Landtag election in Saxony-Anhalt the SPD becomes the strongest parliamentary group with 35.9 per cent.
27.5.	Wolfgang Clement is elected Johannes Rau's successor as Minister President of North Rhine-Westphalia.
27.9.	The SPD achieves a great victory in the Bundestag elections with 40.9 per cent of the vote. The CDU/CSU drops to 35.3 per cent, their worst result since 1949. The Greens become the third strongest party with 6.7 per cent, the FDP wins 6.2, the PDS 5.1 per cent.
25.10.	Special SPD party congress in Bonn.
27.10.	Gerhard Schröder is elected as the Federal Republic of Germany's new Chancellor.
3.11.	Harald Ringstorff forms an SPD and PDS coalition government in Mecklenburg-Western Pomerania.
10.11.	Chancellor Schröder's government statement. Reinhard Klimmt elected as Minister President in the Saar.

1999

| 1.1. | The euro is adopted as the common currency in eleven European countries. |
| 7.2. | In the Landtag election in Hesse, there is a slight increase in the SPD vote to 39.4 per cent. The CDU under Roland Koch, however, wins 43.4 per cent and forms a new government with the FDP. |

11.3.	Oskar Lafontaine resigns as Minister of Finance and SPD chairman.
24.3.	In the Kosovo conflict, NATO begins an air war against Yugoslavia. The deployment of Bundeswehr troops.
1.4.	Along with the re-regulation of 630-Deutschmark jobs, the first stage of tax reforms comes into force.
12.4.	Special SPD party congress in Bonn. Chancellor Gerhard Schröder is elected SPD chairman. Hans Eichel appointed Minister of Finance.
7.5.	New civil rights act approved by the Bundestag. To come into force on 1.1.2000.
23.5.	Johannes Rau elected Federal President by the Federal Convention; to take office on 1.7.1999.
13.6.	Elections to the European Parliament. The SPD achieves a mere 30.7 per cent, while the CDU/CSU makes large gains with 48.7 per cent.
5.9.	Landtag elections in the Saar and Brandenburg with losses for the SPD. The end of fourteen years of SPD government in the Saar. On 9.9. Reinhard Klimmt goes to Berlin as Minister of Transport. In Brandenburg, after the loss of his absolute majority, Manfred Stolpe finally forms a coalition with the CDU.
12.9.	Severe slump in the SPD vote in the Landtag elections in Thuringia; the CDU wins an absolute majority.
19.9.	Further SPD collapse in the Landtag elections in Saxony where the party secures only 10.7 per cent of the vote.
10.10.	In the elections to the Berlin Chamber of Deputies a further slump in the SPD vote, down now to 22.4 per cent.
7.–9.12.	SPD party congress in Berlin confirms Gerhard Schröder as chairman and gives its backing to the executive's policy on tax. Franz Müntefering elected as party business manager.
17.12.	Basic agreement on compensation for Nazi forced labour.

2000

27.2.	Landtag elections in Schleswig-Holstein. The SPD vote increases to 43.1 per cent. Continuation of the red-green coalition under Minister President Heide Simonis.
14.5.	In the Landtag elections in North Rhine-Westphalia the SPD achieves 42.8 per cent of the vote; strong gains by the FDP. In June Wolfgang Clement is once again elected Minister President.

14./15.6.	Chancellor Schröder and leading energy concerns come to an agreement about phasing out nuclear energy.
14.7.	Against the wishes of the CDU leadership tax reforms are passed by the Bundesrat with the help of some Union-led states.
25.7.	Provisional review by Chancellor Schröder of his government's policies to date.
17.8.	The auctioning-off of UMTS mobile phone licences produces 98.8 billion Deutschmarks.

2001

31.1.	The federal government applies to the Federal Constitutional Court for a ban on the right-wing extremist NPD. In March, both the Bundestag and the Bundesrat also submit proposals for a ban.
25.3.	In the Landtag elections in Rhineland-Palatinate the SPD vote under Kurt Beck climbs to 44.7 per cent. On 18.5. he is once again elected Minister President. In Baden-Württemberg under Ute Vogt the SPD makes clear gains (from 25.1 to 33.3 per cent); the CDU nevertheless remains the strongest party.
11.5.	The "Riester pension" is approved by the Bundestag.
16.6.	After Eberhard Diepgen (CDU) is voted out, the Berlin Chamber of Deputies elects Klaus Wowereit as Governing Mayor.
18.–22.8.	Contingents of NATO troops move into Macedonia with the task of collecting and destroying rebel weapons. The Bundestag approves, with 497 votes in favour, the deployment of Bundeswehr troops.
11.9.	Terrorist attacks on the World Trade Centre and the Pentagon by hijacked planes cost over 3,000 lives.
23.9.	In the city parliament elections in Hamburg, the SPD under Ortwin Runde makes some gains, but the Greens/Alternatives suffer losses. Ole von Beust (CDU) forms the new senate on 31.10. with the FDP and the right-wing populist Roland Schill.
7.10.	The USA begins air attacks on Afghanistan: Operation Enduring Freedom.
21.10.	In the elections to the Berlin Chamber of Deputies the SPD wins 29.7 per cent of the votes (22.4 in 1999), while the CDU suffers heavy losses (23.7 as opposed to 40.8 per

	cent). The PDS polls 22.6, the FDP 9.9, and the Greens 9.1 per cent.
16.11.	In the vote of confidence he requests, Chancellor Schröder receives 336 votes, two more than the Chancellor majority required. With this, the cabinet decision to make Bundeswehr soldiers available in case of terrorist attack is approved.
19.–22.11.	The SPD party congress in Nuremberg gives Chancellor Schröder its full support on all crucial issues. With 88.58 per cent of the vote he is confirmed as party chairman. In the vote for deputy chairmen Rudolf Scharping receives 58.78 per cent, a poor result.

2002

1.1.	The euro is introduced as legal currency in twelve European countries.
22.3.	With the votes of Manfred Stolpe (Brandenburg), the Bundesrat approves the immigration act.
21.4.	Landtag elections in Saxony-Anhalt. The SPD wins a mere 20.0 per cent of the vote (35.9 in 1998). With 37.6 per cent the CDU becomes the strongest party, the PDS takes 20.1 per cent, and the FDP 13.1 per cent.
August	Catastrophic flooding in eastern Germany.
22.9.	In the elections to the fifteenth German Bundestag, the number of constituencies is reduced from 328 to 299. The red-green coalition gains a narrow victory. The SPD gains 38.5 per cent of the votes, Alliance 90/Greens 8.6 per cent; the CDU/CSU get 38.5, the FDP 7.4 per cent. In Mecklenburg-Western Pomerania the SPD under Harald Ringstorff wins the Landtag elections.
17.10.	Constituent session of the Bundestag; re-election of Wolfgang Thierse as parliamentary President.
20.10.	SPD party congress in Berlin approves coalition treaty, Olaf Scholz becomes party business manager, succeeding Franz Müntefering.
22.10.	The Bundestag re-elects Gerhard Schröder as Chancellor by winning 305 of the 599 votes cast. New members of the cabinet are Wolfgang Clement as "super-Minister" for Economics and Labour, Brigitte Zypries (justice portfolio), Manfred Stolpe (transport, building, and East construction), and Renate Schmidt (children and families).

6.11.	Peer Steinbrück (SPD) is elected new Minister President of North Rhine-Westphalia by the Landtag.
18.12.	The Federal Constitutional Court declares the procedures surrounding the passing of the Immigration Law to be unconstitutional.

2003

21.1.	EU finance ministers institute proceedings against Germany over its budget deficit.
2.2.	The SPD suffers dramatic losses in the Landtag elections in Lower Saxony and Hesse. In Lower Saxony under Sigmar Gabriel they plummet to 33.4 per cent (as opposed to 47.9 per cent in 1998), in once "red Hesse" they drop to 29.1 per cent (39.4 per cent in 2003). The CDU with Roland Koch wins an absolute majority there, and in Lower Saxony under Christian Wulff they are the strongest party for the first time in 13 years.
14.3.	In a government statement, Chancellor Gerhard Schröder announces cuts in the benefits system and radical reforms: "Agenda 2010".
20.3.	Beginning of the Iraq war with air attacks by the USA.
9.4.	US forces reach the centre of Baghdad.
16.4.	The EU heads of state and government set 1 May 2004 as the date for the extension of the EU.
25.5.	In the elections to the city parliament in Bremen, the SPD, under its popular Mayor Henning Scherf, is able to maintain its share of the vote with 42.3 per cent (42.6 per cent in 1999), whereas its coalition partner the CDU plummets to 29.8 per cent.
1.6.	A special SPD party congress in Berlin approves with 90 per cent of the vote Gerhard Schröder's "Agenda 2010". Basic points of the reforms: unemployment pay limited to one year, unemployment and social security benefits are merged into "unemployment benefit II", relaxation for small firms of the law on wrongful dismissal for recent employees, a "sustainability factor" is added to the pension formula, the obligation to train under a master craftsman is lifted for many trades. Sickness benefit to be limited to 42 days, and retirement age raised in stages to 65.
10.7.	The draft for a European constitution is signed by the European convention.

21.7.	The federal government and the CDU/CSU reach agreement on a plan for health reform.
28.8.	Submission of the Rürup Commission's report on pensions, health and long-term care insurance.
21.9.	In the Landtag elections in Bavaria the SPD drops to a mere 19.6 per cent (28.7 per cent in 1998), and with 60.7 per cent of the votes the CSU has a two-thirds majority in the Landtag.
17.11.	Although Gerhard Schröder is confirmed as party leader at the SPD party congress in Bochum with 80 per cent of the votes, there is a critical mood amongst many of the delegates. Wolfgang Clement, for example, receives only 56.7 per cent in the vote for deputy leader, and party business manager Olaf Scholz is re-elected by a mere whisker with 52.6 per cent.

2004

29.2.	In the elections to the city parliament in Hamburg, Ole von Beust and the CDU win 47.2 per cent of the vote, and an absolute majority of seats; the SPD falls further behind with 30.5 per cent.
11.3.	Terrorist train bombings in Madrid kill 191 people.
21.3.	At a special SPD party congress in Berlin, Franz Müntefering is elected as new party chairman with 95.12 per cent of the vote. Klaus Uwe Benneter becomes the party's new business manager, with 360 votes in favour, 59 against, and 34 abstentions.
1.5.	The extension eastwards of the EU comes into force.
23.5.	Horst Köhler is elected as the new Federal President.
13.6.	With only 14.5 per cent at the Landtag elections in Thuringia the SPD makes considerable losses, and finds itself in third place; the CDU gets 43.3 per cent, and the PDS 26.1 per cent of the vote.
2.7.	The Bundestag approves the merging of unemployment and social security benefits, the so-called Hartz-IV Law.
5.9.	At the Landtag elections in the Saar, the SPD loses 13.6 percentage points, dropping back to 30.8 per cent of the vote.
19.9.	In the Landtag elections in Brandenburg and Saxony, both the SPD and the CDU suffer severe losses. In Brandenburg the SPD wins 31.9 per cent of the vote (39.3 per cent in

	1999), in Saxony a mere 9.8 per cent. With 9.2 per cent, the NPD wins seats in the Landtag.
26.9.	After the local elections in North Rhine-Westphalia, and despite considerable losses, the CDU is once again the strongest party throughout the state.
29.10.	Signing of the first EU constitution by the heads of state and government.
2.11.	George W. Bush beats his Democrat rival John F. Kerry in the US Presidential election.
17.11.	Negotiations on a thoroughgoing reform of federalism collapse after disputes over responsibility for educational policy.
26.12.	After a severe earthquake off the coast of Indonesia, a tidal wave causes devastation in the region. There are almost 300,000 dead.

2005

31.1.	The unemployment figures rise to over 5 million, and by the end of February to 5.2 million.
20.2.	At the Landtag election in Schleswig-Holstein, the SPD and Heide Simonis win just 38.7 per cent of the vote (43.1 per cent in 2000).
22.5.	At the Landtag elections in North Rhine-Westphalia, the SPD and Peer Steinbrück suffer heavy losses. They win only 37.1 per cent and lose power. Franz Müntefering and Gerhard Schröder announce that they are taking steps to call an early general election.
29.5.	In a referendum, the French reject the European constitution by a clear majority.
1.7.	Chancellor Schröder loses the vote of confidence in the Bundestag. This leaves the way open for fresh elections.
21.7.	Federal President Horst Köhler announces his decision in favour of fresh elections.
31.8.	SPD election party congress in Berlin.
4.9.	Television duel between Chancellor Schröder and his challenger Angela Merkel.
18.9.	The SPD suffers losses at the general election; they win 34.3 per cent of the vote. The CDU/CSU are marginally ahead with 35.2, the FDP win 9.8, the Greens 8.1, and the Electoral Alliance Democratic Left/PDS under the name Left/PDS 8.7 per cent of the vote.

Statistical Tables and Diagrams

1. SPD share of the vote and seats in the Reichstag 1871 to 1912 (in percentages)

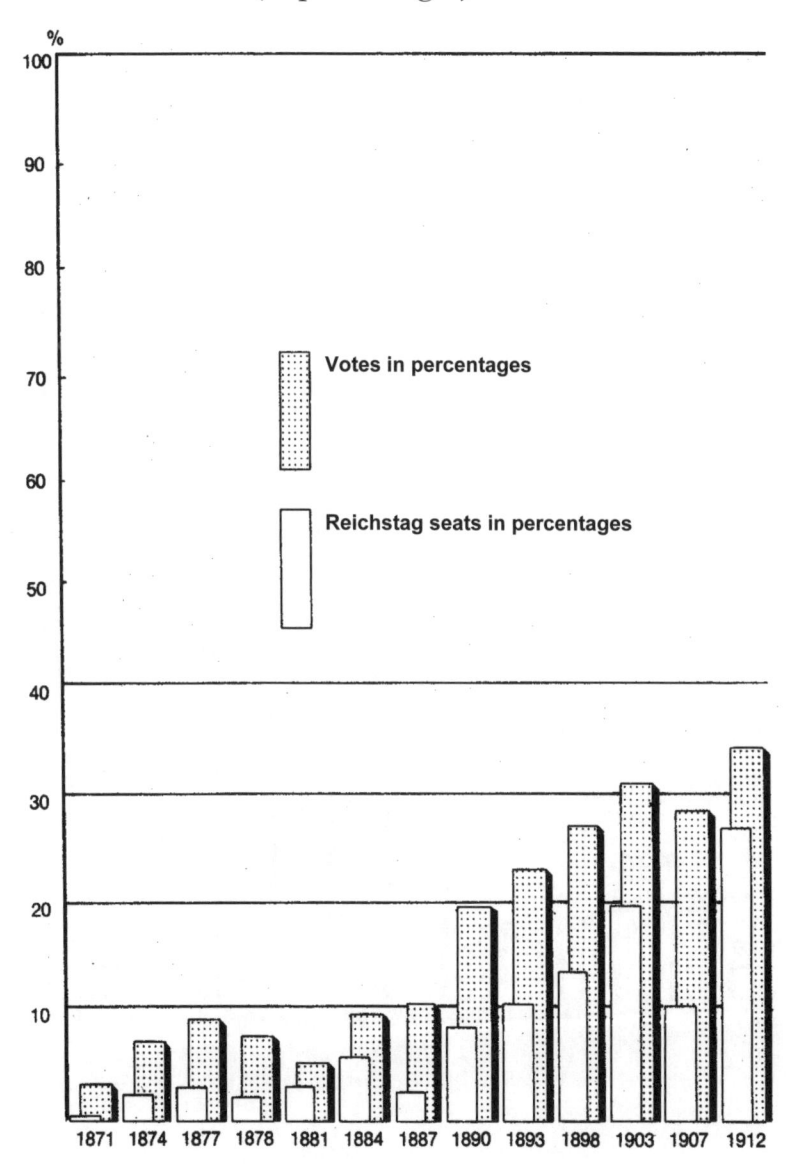

2. Votes and Reichstag seats for the SPD 1871 to 1912 (in absolute figures)

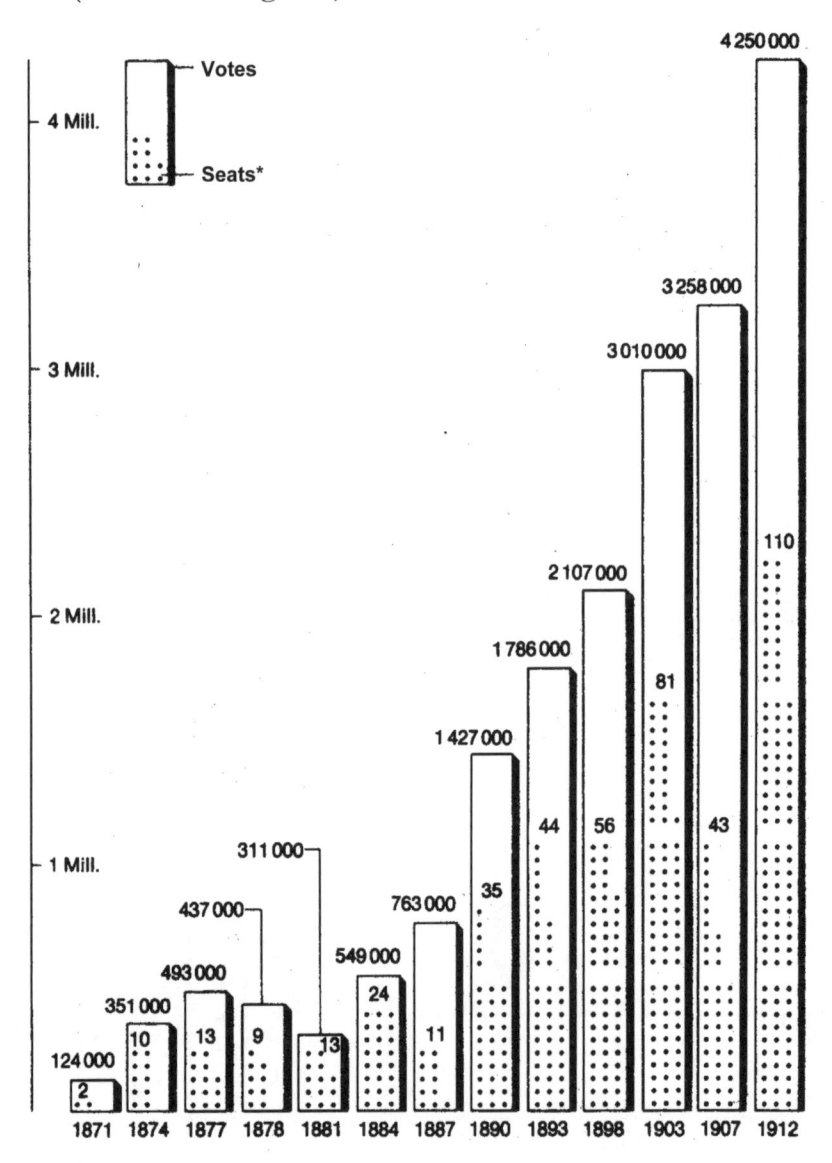

Year	Votes	Seats
1871	124 000	2
1874	351 000	10
1877	493 000	13
1878	437 000	9
1881	311 000	13
1884	549 000	24
1887	763 000	11
1890	1 427 000	35
1893	1 786 000	44
1898	2 107 000	56
1903	3 010 000	81
1907	3 258 000	43
1912	4 250 000	110

* out of a total of 397 seats overall; in 1871 there were only 382 seats

3. Reichstag elections 1919 to 1933

Chart showing the parties' share of the valid votes cast

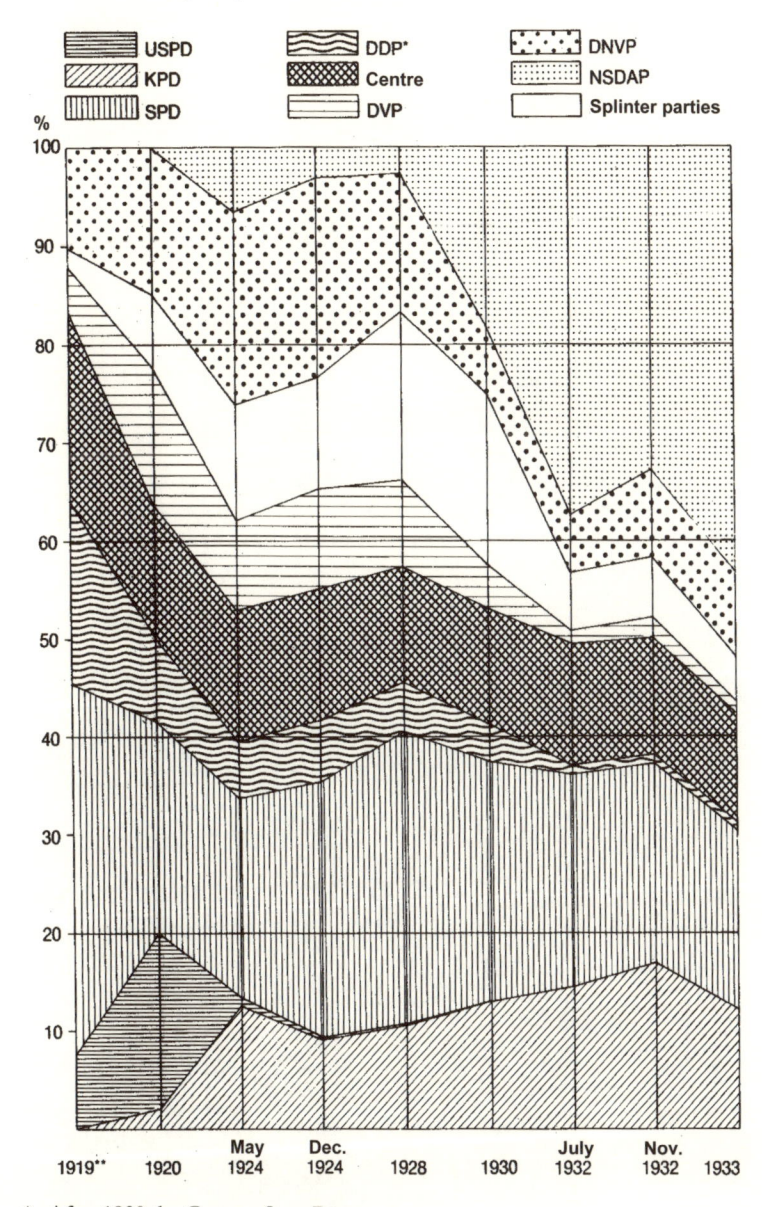

Legend:
- USPD
- KPD
- SPD
- DDP*
- Centre
- DVP
- DNVP
- NSDAP
- Splinter parties

X-axis: 1919**, 1920, May 1924, Dec. 1924, 1928, 1930, July 1932, Nov. 1932, 1933

* After 1930 the German State Party
** Elections to the National Assembly in 1919

4. Results of the Reichstag Elections 1919 to 1933 in %*

Party	Jan. 1919 (National Assembly)	June 1920	May 1924	Dec. 1924	May 1928	Sept. 1930	July 1932	Nov. 1932	March 1933
NSDAP	–	–	6,5	3,0	2,6	18,3	37,4	33,1	43,9
DNVP	10,3	15,1	19,5	20,5	14,2	7,0	5,9	8,5	8,0
Splinter**	1,6	7,4	11,8	11,2	17,0	17,8	5,9	5,9	4,3
DVP	4,4	13,9	9,2	10,1	8,7	4,5	1,2	1,9	1,1
Centre***	19,7	13,6	13,4	13,6	12,1	11,8	12,5	11,9	11,2
DDP	18,5	8,3	5,7	6,3	4,9	3,8	1,0	1,0	0,9
SPD	37,9	21,6	20,5	26,0	29,8	24,5	21,6	20,4	18,3
USPD	7,6	18,0	0,8	0,3	0,1	–	–	–	–
KPD	–	2,0	12,6	9,0	10,6	13,1	14,3	16,9	12,3

* According to statistics from the German Reich.
** Included under splinter parties are all parties which never received more than 5% of the vote in any of these elections.
*** Figures for 1919 include the Bavarian People's Party (BVP).

5. Percentage of the vote in Federal Elections 1949 to 2005

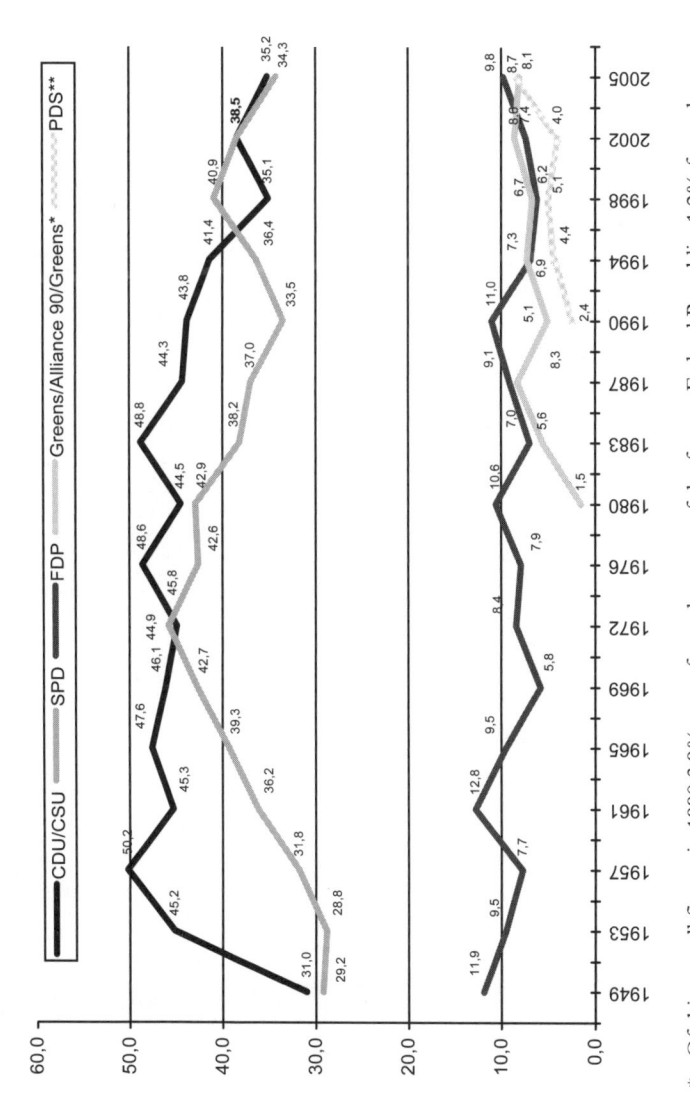

* Of this overall figure, in 1990 3.9% came from the states of the former Federal Republic, 1.2% from the new states.
** In the 2005 elections as the "Left/PDS".

6. The SPD in the Federal Elections 1949 to 2005

Federal Elections in %[1]

	14.8.49	6.9.53	15.9.57	17.9.61	19.9.65	28.9.69	19.11.72	3.10.76	5.10.80	6.3.83	25.1.87	2.12.90	16.10.94	27.9.98	22.9.02	18.9.05
Baden-Württemberg	23,9	23,0	25,8	32,1	33,0	36,5	38,9	36,6	37,2	31,1	29,3	29,1	30,7	35,6	33,5	30,1
Bavaria	22,7	23,3	26,4	30,1	33,1	34,6	37,8	32,8	32,7	28,9	27,0	26,7	29,6	34,4	26,1	25,5
Bremen	34,4	39,0	46,2	49,7	48,5	52,0	58,1	54,0	52,5	48,7	46,5	42,5	45,5	50,2	48,6	43,0
Hamburg	39,6	38,1	45,8	46,9	48,3	54,6	54,4	52,6	51,7	47,4	41,2	41,0	39,7	45,7	42,0	38,7
Hesse	32,1	33,7	38,0	42,8	45,7	48,2	48,5	45,7	46,4	41,6	38,7	38,0	37,2	41,6	39,7	35,7
Lower Saxony	33,4	30,1	32,8	38,7	39,8	43,8	48,1	45,7	46,9	41,3	41,4	38,4	40,6	49,4	47,8	43,2
North Rhine-Westphalia	31,4	31,9	33,5	37,3	42,6	46,8	50,4	46,9	46,8	42,8	43,2	41,2	43,1	46,9	43,0	40,0
Rhineland-Palatinate	28,6	27,2	30,4	33,5	36,7	40,1	44,9	41,7	42,8	38,4	37,1	36,1	39,4	41,3	38,2	34,6
Saarland[2]	–	–	25,1	33,5	39,8	39,9	47,9	46,1	48,3	43,8	43,5	51,2	48,8	52,4	46,0	33,3
Schleswig-Holstein	29,6	26,5	30,8	36,4	38,8	43,5	48,6	46,4	46,7	41,7	39,8	38,5	39,6	45,4	42,9	38,2
FRG (without Berlin)	29,2	28,8	31,8	36,2	39,3	42,7	45,8	42,6	42,9	38,2	37,0	35,7				
					People's Chamber elections						18.3.90					
Brandenburg	–	–	–	–	–	–	–	–	–	–	29,9	32,9	45,1	43,5	46,4	35,8
Mecklenburg West.-Pom.	–	–	–	–	–	–	–	–	–	–	23,4	26,6	28,8	35,3	41,7	31,7
Saxony	–	–	–	–	–	–	–	–	–	–	15,1	18,2	24,3	29,1	33,3	24,3
Saxony-Anhalt	–	–	–	–	–	–	–	–	–	–	23,7	24,7	33,4	38,1	43,2	32,7
Thuringia	–	–	–	–	–	–	–	–	–	–	17,5	21,9	30,2	34,5	39,9	29,8
Berlin	–	–	–	–	–	–	–	–	Election to the House of Deputies on 21.1.89		37,3	30,5	34,0	37,8	36,6	34,4
									Election to the City Council Assembly on 6.5.90		34,0					
Germany	–	–	–	–	–	–	–	–	–	–	–	33,5	36,4	40,9	38,5	34,3

1. As a percentage of valid votes (from 1953 of valid second votes).
2. The Saarland, after being returned to Germany, participated in federal elections for the first time in 1957.

Source: Publications of the Statistisches Bundesamt.

7. Income in Germany in three epochs – National income in Deutschmarks per inhabitant[1]

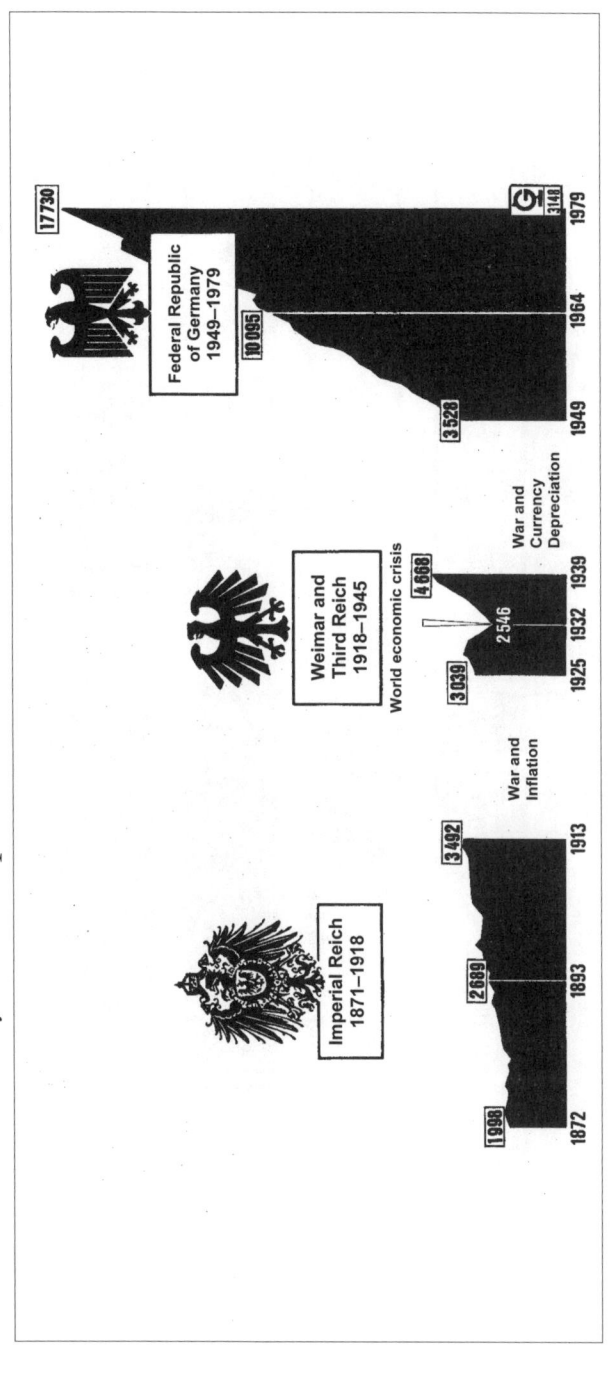

1. The national income per inhabitant developed after 1979 as follows: 1980: 18,656 DM, 1981: 19,248 DM, 1982: 19,850 DM, 1983: 20,941 DM, 1984: 22,179 DM, 1985: 23,270 DM, 1986: 24,719 DM, 1987: 25,661 DM, 1988: 26,878 DM, and 1989: 28,221 DM. For a better comparison, however, the rise in prices has to be included. From 1979 to 1989 it amounted *in toto* to 29.8 per cent. Calculated at 1989 prices, the national income per inhabitant in 1979 amounted to: 22,494 DM, in 1964 13,103 DM, 1949: 4,579 DM, 1939: 6,085 DM, 1932: 3,305 DM, 1925: 3,945 DM, 1913: 4,533 DM, 1893: 3,490 DM, and 1872: 2,593 DM. (Globus Kartendienst)

8. Changes in the world of work

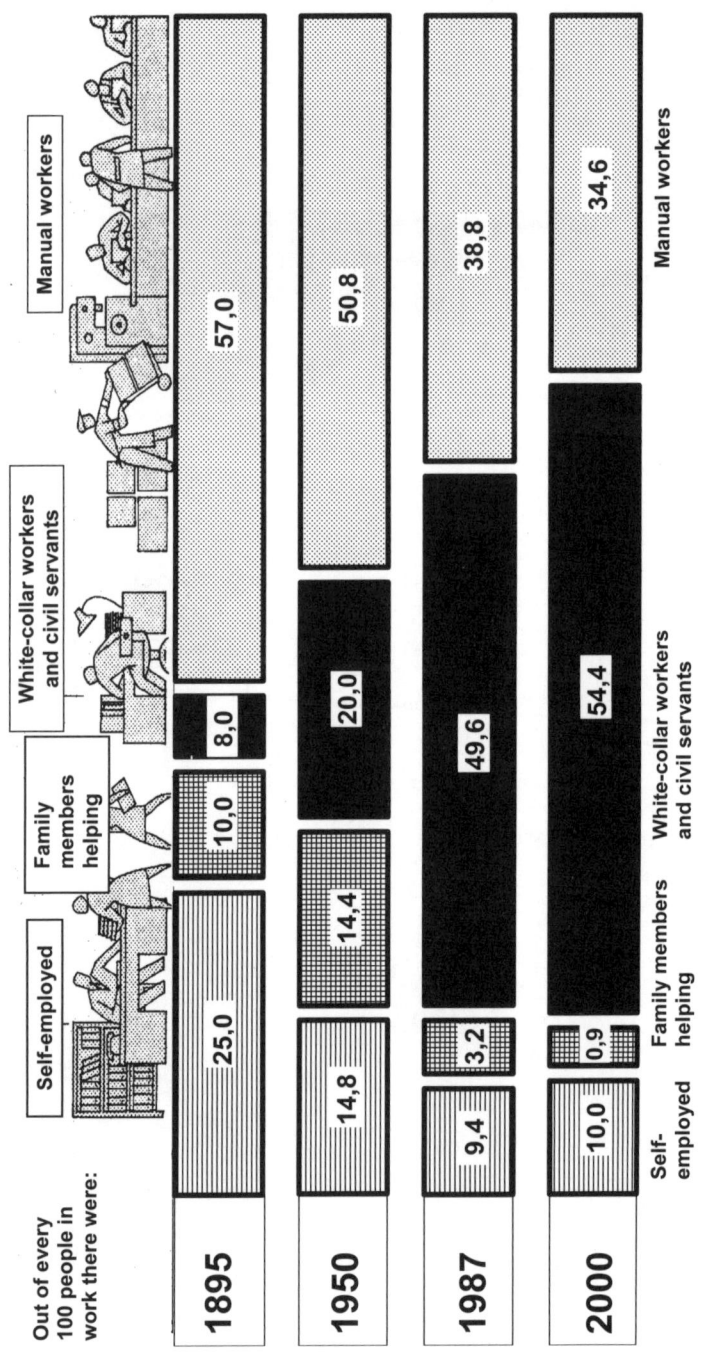

Out of every 100 people in work there were:

Year	Self-employed	Family members helping	White-collar workers and civil servants	Manual workers
1895	25,0	10,0	8,0	57,0
1950	14,8	14,4	20,0	50,8
1987	9,4	3,2	49,6	38,8
2000	10,0	0,9	54,4	34,6

Source: Publications of the Statistisches Bundesamt.

9. National weekly industrial wages and living costs 1871 to 1932 (Index 1913 = 100)

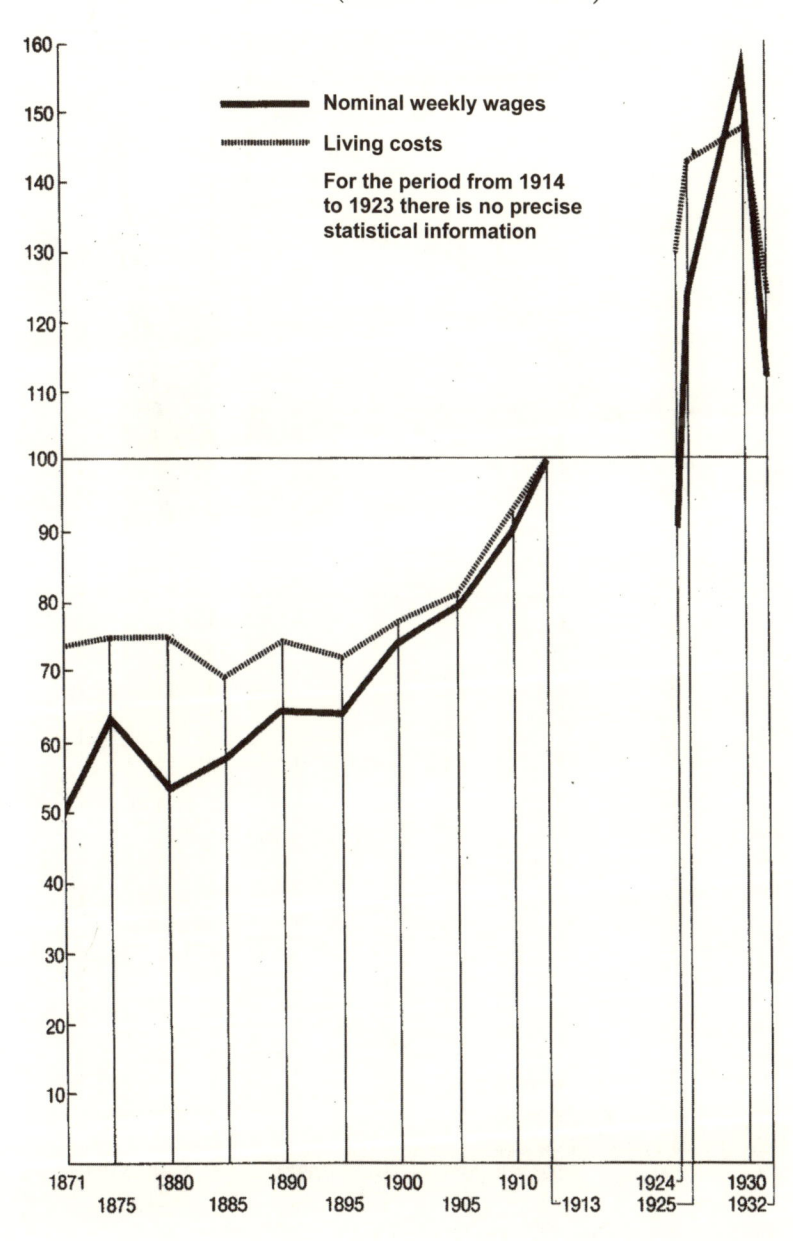

10. Real weekly industrial wages 1871 to 1932 (Index 1913 = 100)

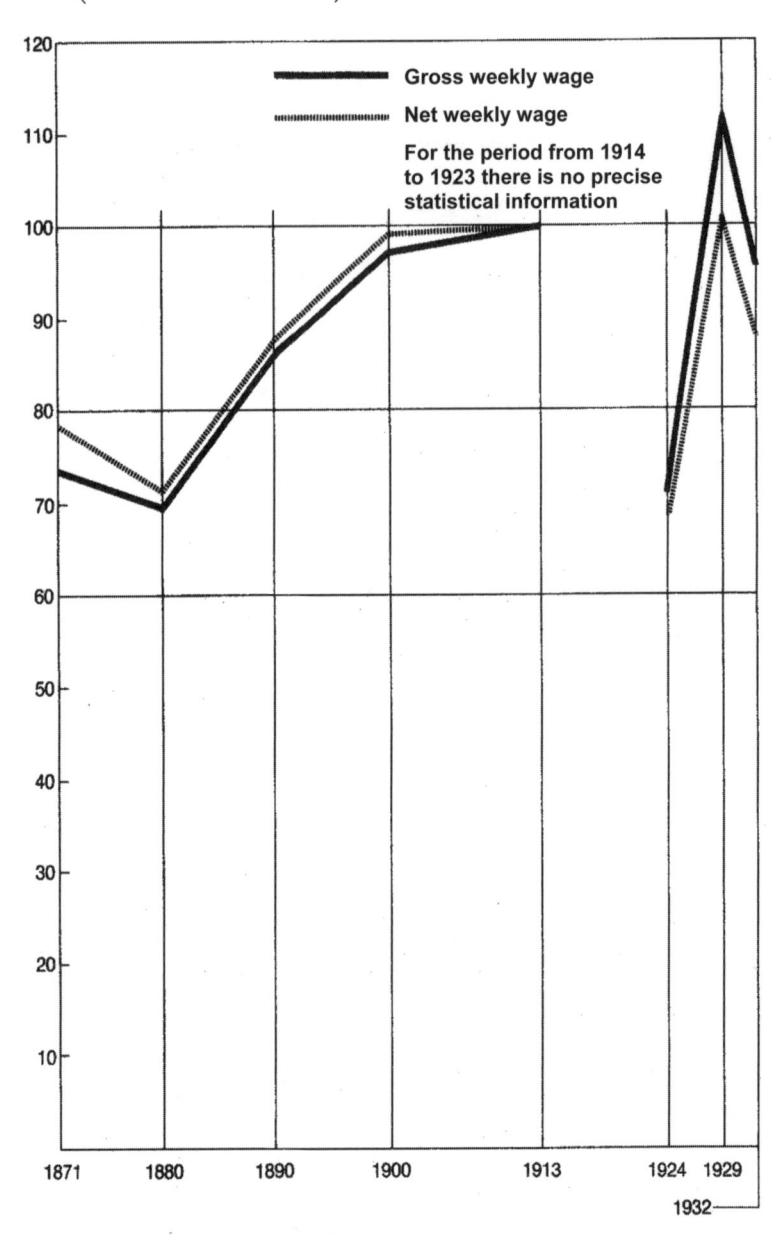

11. Numbers of unemployed 1919 to 1933 in thousands*

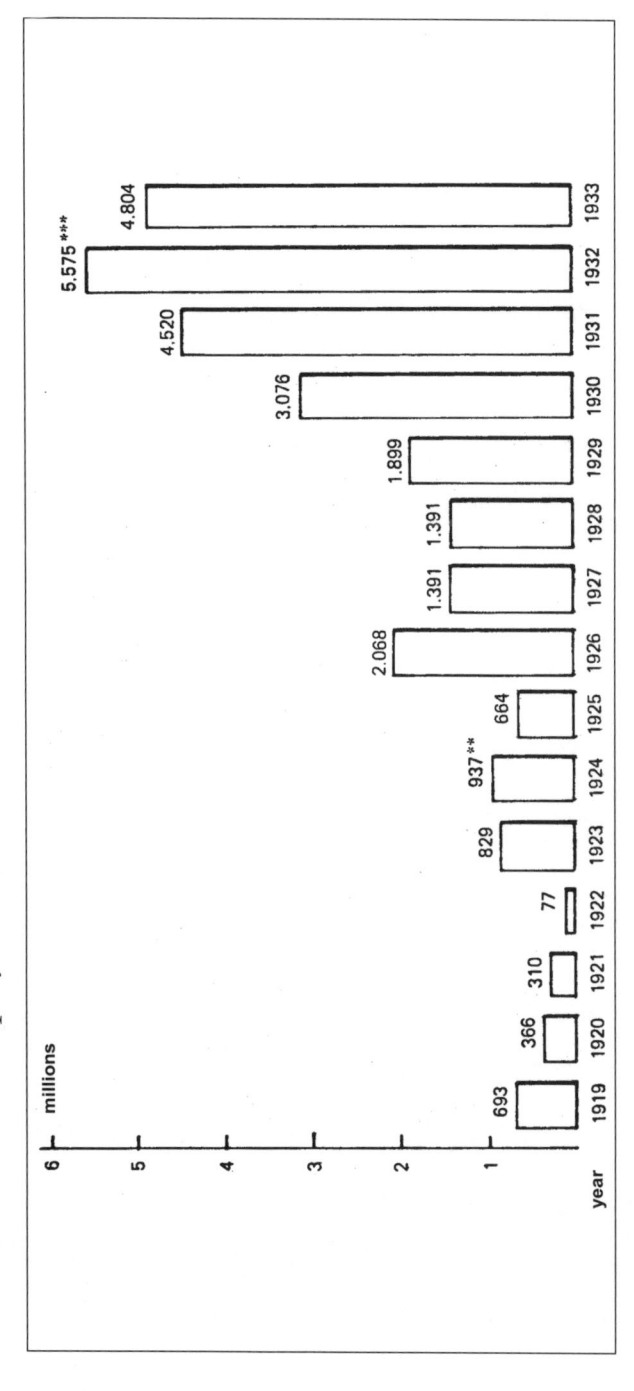

year	thousands
1919	693
1920	366
1921	310
1922	77
1923	829
1924	937**
1925	664
1926	2,068
1927	1,391
1928	1,391
1929	1,899
1930	3,076
1931	4,520
1932	5,575***
1933	4,804

* See Bry, Wages in Germany, pp. 325–329; in each case the annual average.
** 1924 saw a change in the way statistics were recorded. Up to 1923 only the main recipients of support were recorded, from 1924 the number of registered unemployed. The comparable figures under the old system are, for 1924 and 1925, 841,000 and 384,000 respectively.
*** The highest figure was recorded in February 1932 at 6,128,429.

12. Economic and social data 1950 to 1989

Year	Gross national product (real) DM billions[1]	Gross national product (real) annual change in %	Price index annual change in %	Wages and salaries[4] annual change gross[5]	Wages and salaries[4] annual change net[6]	Pensions annual rate of adjustment	Pensions net level[7]	Income from entrepreneurial activity and assets annual change in % gross	Income from entrepreneurial activity and assets annual change in % net	National debt (state budgets overall) in DM billions
1950	269,9	–	–6,1	–	–	–	–	–	–	20,6
1955	417,7	11,8	1,6	7,9	7,7	–	59,3[8]	15,8	20,9	40,9
1960	579,5 (731,7)[2]	8,8	1,5	9,4	8,0	5,9	56,2	13,9	13,0	52,2
1961	763,7	4,4	2,3	10,2	9,3	5,4	54,2	2,3	-0,4	56,6
1962	799,8	4,7	3,0	9,2	8,6	5,0	52,5	4,1	2,5	60,0
1963	821,8	2,8	2,9	6,1	5,7	6,6	53,0	2,6	2,0	66,7
1964	875,7	6,6	2,3	9,0	8,3	8,2	52,9	10,9	12,3	73,1
1965	922,7	5,4	3,3	9,1	9,9	9,4	52,7	7,1	9,7	83,0
1966	950,1	3,0	3,5	7,3	5,9	8,3	53,9	2,7	2,5	92,3
1967	949,4	-0,1	1,7	3,3	2,9	8,0	56,7	0,9	0,7	108,2
1968	1004,2	5,8	1,7	6,2	4,8	8,1	57,3	14,6	16,3	117,1
1969	1079,6	7,5	1,9	9,2	7,5	8,3	57,7	7,6	6,2	117,9
1970	1134,0	5,0	3,3	15,3	13,0	6,4	56,8	6,9	11,3	125,9
1971	1168,0	3,0	5,2	11,3	9,4	5,5	54,4	5,5	4,9	140,4
1972	1217,0	4,2	5,6	8,2	8,5	9,5	57,0	8,9	9,1	156,1
1973	1274,1	4,7	7,0	10,7	7,2	11,4	56,3	8,1	3,9	170,9
1974	1276,5	0,2	7,0	10,4	9,0	11,2	57,0	-0,5	-0,8	187,3
1975	1258,0	-1,4	6,0	6,1	6,4	11,1	59,0	3,1	5,4	256,4
1976	1328,2	5,6	4,3	6,4	3,8	11,0	62,8	15,9	15,4	296,7
1977	1363,4	2,7	3,7	6,5	5,3	9,9	65,6	4,6	-0,6	328,5
1978	1407,9	3,3	2,7	5,2	6,3	0,0	64,6	10,0	13,8	370,8
1979	1463,6	4,0	4,1	5,2	5,6	4,5	63,8	7,4	9,5	413,9
1980	1485,2	1,5	5,5	6,4	4,9	4,0	63,2	-1,9	-0,8	468,6
1981	1485,3	0,0	6,3	4,2	3,8	4,0	62,9	0,0	1,3	545,6
1982	1471,0	-1,0	5,2	3,3	2,1	5,8	64,6	5,5	5,7	614,8
1983	1498,9	1,9	3,3	3,0	2,0	5,6	64,5	13,8	17,7	671,7
1984	1548,1	3,3	2,4	2,9	1,7	3,4	65,2	10,6	11,4	717,5
1985	1578,1	1,9	2,0	2,8	1,5	3,0	65,1	6,2	5,0	760,2
1986	1614,7	2,3	-0,1	3,5	3,8	2,9	63,6	9,1	10,5	801,0
1987	1641,9	1,7	0,2	3,0	1,8	3,8	64,1	3,2	5,1	848,8
1988	1701,8	3,6	1,3	3,0	3,3	3,0	63,8	8,7	8,8	903,0
1989	1769,2	4,0	2,8	3,0	2,0	3,0	64,3	9,5	8,0	929,3

1. 1950, 1955, 1960 (first figure) without Saarland and Berlin. – 2. Up to 1960 in 1976 prices, from 1960 on (amount in brackets) in 1980 prices. – 3. 1952 to 1962 4-person employees household, from 1963 all private households. – 4. Per employee in work. – 5. Gross income from employment with employers' contributions deducted. – 6. With income tax and employees' actual contributions deducted. – 7. With 40 years insurance contributions as a percentage of annual remuneration. – 8. Net level for 1957; not until the pension reform legislation of 1957 was there an annual adjustment of pensions pegged to wages and income. – Source: *Statistisches Taschenbuch 1990. Arbeits- und Sozialstatistik*, published by the Bundesminister für Arbeit und Sozialordnung (Bonn 1990), tables 1.1, 1.10, 1.13, 1.14, 1.27, 7.9, 7.11, and 9.12.

13. Economic and social data 1990 to 2004

Year[1]	Gross national product (real) DM billions[2]	Gross national product annual change in %	Price index annual change in %	Wages and salaries gross[5]	Wages and salaries net	Pensions[3] (monthly) DM former Federal Republic	Pensions[3] (monthly) DM new states	Income from entrepreneurial activity and assets annual change in % gross	Income from entrepreneurial activity and assets annual change in % net	National debt (state budgets overall) in DM billions
1990	2543,9	+5,7	+2,7	+7,9	+10,7	1583	638	+11,2	+15,2	1048,8
1991	2668,1	+4,5	–	+8,2	+5,4	1657	–	+7,2	+6,3	–
1991	3369,0	–	+3,6	–	–	–	844	–	–	1165,5
1992	3440,7	+2,1	+4,6	+8,2	+6,5	1705	1063	+2,0	+1,9	1331,5
1993	3399,6	–1,0	+3,6	+2,6	+2,9	1780	1287	–3,3	–1,7	1497,2
1994	3449,6	+2,0	+2,7	+1,4	–0,4	1840	1380	+8,7	+11,9	1643,1
1995	3504,4	+1,7	+1,8	+3,2	+0,8	1849	1453	+5,6	+8,6	1974,1
1996	3536,5	+1,2	+1,4	+1,1	–0,5	1867	1535	+2,7	+2,3	2091,3
1997	3584,2	+1,6	+1,9	–0,2	–1,7	1898	1620	+4,1	+5,1	2188,7
1998	3650,7	+1,7	+0,9	+2,1	+2,3	1906	1635	+1,4	–0,7	2256,4
1999	3703,2	+2,0	+0,6	+3,0	+3,3	1932	1680	–1,4	–4,7	2313,9
2000	3815,5	+3,4	+2,0	+3,4	+4,0	1943	1690	–0,8	–4,4	2343,4
2001	3865,5	+1,0	+2,5	+2,1	+3,6	1980	1726	+3,3	+9,8	2354,6
	€ billions					€	€			in € billions
2002	1970,9	+0,6	+1,4	+0,8	+0,3	1034	908	+3,1	+5,1	1253,2
2003	1973,4	+0,7	+1,3	±0,0	–0,5	1045	919	+3,8	+4,5	1325,7
2004	2006,9	+1,7	+1,7	+0,3	+2,0	1045	919	+7,0	+6,6	1395,0[4]

1. To 1991 first line Federal Republic; from 1991 second line Germany.
2. To 1991 first line at 1991 prices; second line and subsequent years at 1995 prices.
3. Old age pensions in the pension scheme for workers and white-collar workers are for 40 years of insurance contributions.
4. Reference: Financial planning council of the Ministry for Finance.

Sources: Statistisches Taschenbuch 2001. Arbeits- und Sozialstatistik. Published by the Bundesminister für Arbeit und Sozialordnung (Bonn 2001), tables 1.1, 1.10, 1.13, 1.14, 1.27, 7.10, 1.10A, and 9.16, Statistisches Taschenbuch 2005. Arbeits- und Sozialstatistik. Published by the Bundesministerium für Gesundheit und Soziale Sicherung (Bonn 2005), tables 1.1, 1.10, 1.13, 1.14, 1.27, 7.10, 7.10A and 9.16.

14. The Development of the Labour Market 1950 to 2004

Year	Unemployed in 1000s[1]	Unemployed Quota[2]	Former Federal Republic
\multicolumn{4}{c}{Former Federal Republic}			
1950	1869	11,0	–
1955	1074	5,6	25
1960	271	1,3	3
1965	147	0,7	1
1970	149	0,7	10
1975	1074	4,7	773
1980	889	3,8	137
1981	1272	5,5	347
1982	1833	7,5	606
1983	2258	9,1	675
1984	2266	9,1	384
1985	2304	9,3	235
1986	2228	9,0	197
1987	2229	8,9	278
1988	2242	8,7	208
1989	2038	7,9	108
1990	1883	7,2	56
\multicolumn{4}{c}{Germany}			
1991	2602	7,3	1761
1992	2979	8,5	653
1993	3419	9,8	948
1994	3698	10,6	372
1995	3612	10,4	199
1996	3965	11,5	277
1997	4384	12,7	183
1998	4279	12,3	115
1999	4099	11,7	107
2000	3889	10,7	86
2001	3852	10,3	123
2002	4060	10,8	207
2003	4376	11,6	195
2004	4381	11,7	151

1 Annual average. – 2 As a percentage of people in work.

Sources: Statistisches Taschenbuch 1990. Arbeits- und Sozialstatistik. Published by the Bundesminister für Arbeit- und Sozialordnung (Bonn 1990), table 2.10, Statistisches Taschenbuch 2005. Arbeits- und Sozialstatistik. Published by the Bundesminister für Gesundheit und Soziale Sicherung (Bonn 2005), table 2.10.

Select Bibliography

No attempt has been made in this bibliography to draw up a list of the various and extensive SPD materials. The most important sources are the Social Democratic Party's yearbooks published by the SPD executive committee. Formerly annual publications, for more than a decade they have appeared as biennial volumes. The growing importance for the SPD of the Internet has meant that the yearbooks have diminished considerably in size. Equally indispensable are the proceedings of the SPD party conferences. Amongst works of reference, the annual volumes of the *Archiv der Gegenwart* are highly informative. Newspapers and magazines, along with the various information services provided by the SPD and the parliamentary party are, of course, an abundant source of information.

1. Bibliographies

Bibliographie zur Geschichte der deutschen Arbeiterbewegung, hrsg. von der Bibliothek des Archivs der sozialen Demokratie, Bonn-Bad Godesberg, I (1976) ff.

Dowe, Dieter: Bibliographie zur Geschichte der deutschen Arbeiterbewegung, sozialistischen und kommunistischen Bewegungen von den Anfängen bis 1863, 3. Aufl. unter Mitarbeit von Volker Mettig, Bonn 1981.

Emig, Dieter/Zimmermann, Rüdiger: Arbeiterbewegung in Deutschland. Ein Dissertationsverzeichnis, IWK, Jg. 13, H. 3., Berlin 1977.

Günther, Klaus/Schmitz, Kurt Thomas: SPD, KPD/DKP, DGB in den Westzonen und in der Bundesrepublik Deutschland 1945–1973. Eine Bibliographie, 2. Aufl. unter Mitarbeit von Volker Mettig, Bonn 1980.

Klotzbach, Kurt: Bibliographie zur Geschichte der deutschen Arbeiterbewegung 1914–1945, 3. Aufl. bearb. von Volker Mettig, Bonn 1981.

Steinberg, Hans-Josef: Die deutsche sozialistische Arbeiterbewegung bis 1914, Frankfurt/M.-New York 1979.

Tenfelde, Klaus/Ritter, Gerhard A.: Bibliographie zur Geschichte der deutschen Arbeiterbewegung 1863 bis 1914, Bonn 1981.

2. General Histories and Materials

Abendroth, Wolfgang: Aufstieg und Krise der deutschen Sozialdemokratie. Das Problem der Zweckentfremdung einer politischen Partei durch die Anpassungstendenzen von Institutionen an vorgegebene Machtverhältnisse, Frankfurt/M. 1964.

Braunthal, Julius: Geschichte der Internationale, 3 Bde., Hannover 1961/63/71, Neuauflage Berlin-Bonn 1978.

Dowe, Dieter/Klotzbach, Kurt (Hrsg.): Kämpfe – Krisen – Kompromisse. Kritische Beiträge zum 125jährigen Jubiläum der SPD, Bonn 1989.

Dowe, Dieter/Klotzbach, Kurt (Hrsg.): Programmatische Dokumente der deutschen Sozialdemokratie, 4., überarbeitete und aktualisierte Auflage, Bonn 2004.

Eckert, Georg (Hrsg.): 100 Jahre deutsche Sozialdemokratie, Hannover 1963.

Eichler, Willi: Hundert Jahre Sozialdemokratie. Hrsg. Vorstand der SPD, Bonn-Bielefeld [1963].

Fetscher, Iring/Grebing, Helga/Dill, Günther (Hrsg.): Der Sozialismus. Vom Klassenkampf zum Wohlfahrtsstaat. Text, Bilder, Dokumente, München 1968.

Freyberg, Jutta von/Fülberth, Georg/Harrer, Jürgen: Geschichte der deutschen Sozialdemokratie 1863- 1975, Köln 1975.

Grebing, Helga: Geschichte der deutschen Arbeiterbewegung, dtv-Taschenbuch Nr. 647, 10. Aufl., München 1980.

Grebing, Helga: Die deutsche Arbeiterbewegung zwischen Revolution, Reform und Etatismus, Mannheim 1993.

Groh, Dieter/Brandt, Peter: "Vaterlandslose Gesellen". Sozialdemokratie und Nation 1860–1990, München 1992.

Günsche, Karl-Ludwig/Lantermann, Klaus: Kleine Geschichte der Sozialistischen Internationale, Bonn 1977.

Institut für Marxismus-Leninismus beim ZK der SED (Hrsg.): Geschichte der deutschen Arbeiterbewegung, 8 Bde., Berlin (DDR) 1966.

Klönne, Arno: Die deutsche Arbeiterbewegung. Geschichte – Ziele – Wirkungen, unter Mitarbeit von Barbara Klaus und Karl Theodor Stiller, Düsseldorf-Köln 1980, Neuaufl. München 1989.

Kremendahl, Hans/Meyer, Thomas (Hrsg.): Sozialismus und Staat, 2 Bde., Kronberg/Ts. 1974.

Kuczynski, Jürgen: Die Geschichte der Lage der Arbeiter unter dem Kapitalismus, Bde. 1–21, Berlin (DDR) 1961 ff.

Kürbisch, Friedrich G. (Hrsg.): Sozialreportagen 1880 bis heute, 3 Bde., Bonn 1988.

Lehnert, Detlef: Sozialdemokratie zwischen Protestbewegung und Regierungspartei 1848 bis 1983, edition suhrkamp 1248, Frankfurt a. M. 1983.

Lern- und Arbeitsbuch deutsche Arbeiterbewegung. Darstellung – Chroniken – Dokumente. Hrsg. unter der Leitung von Thomas Meyer, Susanne Miller und Joachim Rohlfes, 2. ergänzte Aufl., 4 Bde., Bonn 1988.

Lexikon des Sozialismus. Hrsg. von Thomas Meyer, Karl-Heinz Klär, Susanne Miller, Klaus Novy und Heinz Timmermann, Köln 1986.

Lösche, Peter/Walter, Franz: Die SPD: Klassenpartei – Volkspartei – Quotenpartei. Zur Entwicklung der Sozialdemokratie von Weimar bis zur deutschen Vereinigung, Darmstadt 1992.

Lübke, Peter: Kommunismus und Sozialdemokratie. Eine Streitschrift, Berlin-Bonn 1978.

Mommsen, Hans (Hrsg.): Sozialdemokratie zwischen Klassenbewegung und Volkspartei, Fischer-Athenäum Taschenbuch, Frankfurt/M. 1974.

Mooser, Josef: Arbeiterleben in Deutschland 1900–1970. Klassenlagen, Kultur und Politik, Frankfurt/M. 1984.

Osterroth, Franz/Schuster, Dieter: Chronik der deutschen Sozialdemokratie, 3 Bde., neu bearbeitete und ergänzte Auflage, Bonn 2005.

Rovan, Joseph: Geschichte der deutschen Sozialdemokratie, Frankfurt/M. 1980.

Ruppert, Wolfgang: Fotogeschichte der deutschen Sozialdemokratie. Hrsg. von Willy Brandt, Berlin 1988.

Sassoon, Donald: One Hundred Years of Socialism. The West European Left in the Twentieth Century, London 1996.

Schadt, Jörg/Schmierer, Wolfgang (Hrsg.): Die SPD in Baden-Württemberg und ihre Geschichte. Von den Anfängen der Arbeiterbewegung bis heute, Stuttgart 1979.

Schmeitzner, Mike/Rudloff, Michael: Geschichte der Sozialdemokratie im Sächsischen Landtag. Darstellung und Dokumentation 1877–1997, Dresden 197.

Schneider, Michael: History of the German Trade Unions, 1. Aufl., Bonn 2005.

Schönhoven, Klaus: Die deutschen Gewerkschaften, Frankfurt/M. 1987.

Schumacher, Kurt: Der Kampf um den Staatsgedanken in der deutschen Sozialdemokratie, Urban-Taschenbuch Nr. 839, Stuttgart 1973.

Vom Sozialistengesetz zur Mitbestimmung. Zum 100. Geburtstag von Hans Böckler. Hrsg. Heinz Oskar Vetter, Redaktion Ulrich Borsdorf und Hans O. Hemmer, Köln 1975.

Vetter, Heinz Oskar (Hrsg.): Aus der Geschichte lernen – die Zukunft gestalten. Dreißig Jahre Deutscher Gewerkschaftsbund. Protokoll der wissenschaftlichen Konferenz zur Geschichte der Gewerkschaften vom 12. und 13. Oktober 1979 in München. Redaktion Ulrich Borsdorf und Hans O. Hemmer, Köln 1980.

Vorwärts 1876–1976. Ein Querschnitt in Faksimiles. Hrsg. von Günter Grunwald und Friedhelm Merz, eingel. von Heinz-Dietrich Fischer und Volker Schulze, 2. Aufl. Bonn 1980.

Walter, Franz: Die SPD. Vom Proletariat zur Neuen Mitte, Berlin 2002.

Weber, Hermann (Hrsg.): Der deutsche Kommunismus, Köln 1963.

Weber, Hermann (Hrsg.): Das Prinzip Links. Eine Dokumentation. Beiträge zur Diskussion des demokratischen Sozialismus in Deutschland 1847–1973, Hannover 1973.

Winkler, Heinrich August: Der lange Weg nach Westen. Bd. 1 Deutsche Geschichte vom Ende des alten Reiches bis zum Untergang der Weimarer Republik, Bd. 2 Deutsche Geschichte vom "Dritten Reich" bis zur Wiedervereinigung, 2. Aufl. München 2001.

3. Biographical Material

Adolph, Hans J. L.: Otto Wels und die Politik der deutschen Sozialdemokratie 1894–1939. Eine politische Biographie, Berlin 1971.

Albrecht, Willy: Kurt Schumacher, Reden – Schriften – Korrespondenzen 1945–1952, Berlin-Bonn 1985.

Albrecht, Richard: Der militante Sozialdemokrat. Carlo Mierendorff 1897 bis 1943. Eine Biographie, Bonn 1987.

Apel, Hans: Der Abstieg. Politisches Tagebuch 1978–1988, Stuttgart 1990.

Baader, Ottilie: Ein steiniger Weg. Lebenserinnerungen einer Sozialistin. Mit einer Einleitung von Marie Juchacz, 3. Aufl. (1. Aufl. 1921), Bonn 1979.

Bahr, Egon: Zu meiner Zeit, München 1996.

Bebel, August: Aus meinem Leben, 3 Teile, 1. Aufl. Stuttgart 1910–1914 (Neuaufl., Bonn 1986).

Besson, Waldemar: Friedrich Ebert – Verdienst und Grenze, Göttingen 1962.

Blumenberg, Werner: Kämpfer für die Freiheit, 3. Aufl. Berlin-Bonn 1977.

Born, Stephan: Erinnerungen eines Achtundvierzigers, hrsg. und eingeleitet von Hans J. Schütz, Berlin-Bonn 1978.

Brandt, Willy. Berliner Ausgabe. Hrsg. von Helga Grebing, Gregor Schöllgen und Heinrich August Winkler. Im Auftrag der Bundeskanzler-Willy-Brandt-Stiftung.

Bd. 1 Hitler ist nicht Deutschland, Bonn 2002.
Bd. 2 Zwei Vaterländer, Bonn 2000.
Bd. 3 Berlin bleibt frei, Bonn 2004.
Bd. 4 Auf dem Weg nach vorn, Bonn 2000.
Bd. 5 Die Partei der Freiheit, Bonn 2002.
Bd. 6 Ein Volk der guten Nachbarn, Bonn 2005.
Bd. 7 Mehr Demokratie wagen, Bonn 2001.
Bd. 9 Die Entspannung unzerstörbar machen, Bonn 2003.

Brandt, Willy: Erinnerungen, 3. Aufl., Frankfurt a. M. 1989.

Brandt, Willy: Links und frei. Mein Weg 1930–1950, Hamburg 1982.

Brandt, Willy: Über den Tag hinaus. Eine Zwischenbilanz, Hamburg 1974.

Brandt, Willy/Löwenthal, Richard: Ernst Reuter. Ein Leben für die Freiheit. Eine politische Biographie, München 1957.

Braun, Otto: Von Weimar zu Hitler, New York 1940.

Dowe, Dieter (Hrsg.): Kurt Schumacher und der "Neubau" der deutschen Sozialdemokratie nach 1945, Bonn, 1996.

Düding, Dieter: Heinz Kühn 1912–1992. Eine politische Biographie, Essen 2002.

Edinger, Lewis J.: Kurt Schumacher. Persönlichkeit und politisches Verhalten, Köln-Opladen 1967.

Ehmke, Horst: Mittendrin. Von der Großen Koalition zur Deutschen Einheit, Berlin 1994.

Eppler, Erhard: Das Schwerste ist Glaubwürdigkeit. Gespräche über ein Politikerleben mit Freimut Duve, rororo aktuell 4355, Reinbek bei Hamburg 1978.

Der Freiheit verpflichtet. Gedenkbuch der deutschen Sozialdemokratie im 20. Jahrhundert. Hrsg. vom Vorstand der SPD, Marburg 2000.

Friedrich Ebert. 1871–1925. Mit einem einführenden Aufsatz von Peter-Christian Witt, 2. Aufl., Bonn 1980.

Gilcher-Holthey, Ingrid: Das Mandat des Intellektuellen. Karl Kautsky und die Sozialdemokratie, Berlin 1986.

Glotz, Peter: Die Innenausstattung der Macht. Politisches Tagebuch 1976–1978, München 1979.

Harpprecht, Klaus: Willy Brandt. Porträt und Selbstporträt, München 1970.

Hirsch, Helmut: August Bebel. Sein Leben in Dokumenten, Reden und Schriften, Berlin 1968.

Hirsch, Helmut: Friedrich Engels, rowohlts monographien Nr. 142, Reinbek 1968.

Hoegner, Wilhelm: Flucht vor Hitler. Erinnerungen an die Kapitulation der ersten deutschen Republik 1933, München 1977.

Hoegner, Wilhelm: Der schwierige Außenseiter, München 1959.

Huber, Antje (Hrsg.): Verdient die Nachtigall Lob, wenn sie singt? Frauen in der Politik. Die Sozialdemokratinnen, Stuttgart-Herford 1984.

Kaisen, Wilhelm: Meine Arbeit, mein Leben. München 1967.

Keil, Wilhelm: Erlebnisse eines Sozialdemokraten, 2 Bde., Stuttgart 1947/48.

König, Rudolf/Soell, Hartmut/Weber, Hermann (Hrsg.): Friedrich Ebert und seine Zeit. Bilanz und Perspektiven der Forschung, München 1990.

Krause-Burger, Sibylle: Helmut Schmidt. Aus der Nähe gesehen, Düsseldorf-Wien 1980.

Kühn, Heinz: Aufbau und Bewährung. Die Jahre 1945 bis 1978, Hamburg 1981.

Kühn, Heinz: Bekenntnisse und Standpunkte. Mit einem Vorwort von Willy Brandt, Bonn 1977.

Kühn, Heinz: Widerstand und Emigration. Die Jahre 1928–1945, Hamburg 1980.

Kürbisch, Friedrich G. (Hrsg.): Wir lebten nie wie Kinder. Ein Lesebuch, 2. Aufl., Bonn 1980.

Lassalle, Ferdinand: Reden und Schriften, hrsg. von Friedrich Jenaczek, dtv-Taschenbuch Nr. 676, München 1970.

Leber, Julius: Ein Mann geht seinen Weg. Schriften Reden, Briefe, hrsg. von seinen Freunden, Berlin 1952.

Leber, Julius: Schriften, Reden, Briefe, hrsg. von Dorothea Beck u. Wilfried F. Schoeller, mit einem Vorwort von Willy Brandt und einer Gedenkrede von Golo Mann, München 1976.

Leipart, Theodor: Carl Legien. Ein Gedenkbuch, Berlin 1929.

Lemke-Müller, Sabine: Ethischer Sozialismus und soziale Demokratie. Der politische Weg Willi Eichlers vom ISK zur SPD, Bonn 1988.

Leugers-Scherzberg, August H.: Die Wandlungen des Herbert Wehner. Von der Volksfront zur Großen Koalition, Berlin-München 2002.

Lösche, Peter/Scholing, Michael/Walter, Franz (Hrsg.): Vor dem Vergessen bewahren. Lebenswege Weimarer Sozialdemokraten, Berlin 1988.

Maehl, W. H.: August Bebel. Shadow Emperor of the German Workers, Philadelphia 1980.

Mayer, Gustav: Friedrich Engels. Eine Biographie, 2 Bde., Haag 1934, Neudruck Köln 1971.

Mehringer, Hartmut: Waldemar von Knoeringen. Eine politische Biographie, München-London-New York 1989.

Merseburger, Peter: Der schwierige Deutsche. Kurt Schumacher. Eine Biographie, Stuttgart 1995.

Meyer, Thomas: Bernsteins konstruktiver Sozialismus. Eduard Bernsteins Beitrag zur Theorie des Sozialismus, Berlin-Bonn 1977.

Möller, Alex: Genosse Generaldirektor, München 1978.

Na'aman, Shlomo: Lassalle, 2. Aufl., Köln-Berlin l971.

Nettl, J. Peter: Rosa Luxemburg, 2. Aufl., Köln-Berlin 1968.

Nicolaevsky, Boris/Maenchen-Helfen, Otto: Karl Marx. Eine Biographie, 3. Aufl., Berlin-Bonn 1976.

Osterroth, Franz: Biographisches Lexikon des Sozialismus, Hannover 1960.

Scheidemann, Philipp: Memoiren eines Sozialdemokraten, 1. und 2. Teil, Dresden 1930.

Schmid, Carlo: Erinnerungen, Bern-München-Wien 1979.

Schmidt, Helmut: Die Deutschen und ihre Nachbarn, Berlin 1990.

Schmidt, Helmut: Menschen und Mächte, Berlin 1987

Schöllgen, Gregor: Willy Brandt. Die Biographie, Berlin-München 2001.

Scholz, Arno/Oschilewski, Walther G. (Hrsg.): Turmwächter der Demokratie. Ein Lebensbild von Kurt Schumacher, 3 Bde., Berlin 1952 ff.

Schulze, Hagen: Otto Braun oder Preußens demokratische Sendung. Eine Biographie, Frankfurt a.M. 1977

Seebacher-Brandt, Brigitte: August Bebel. Künder und Kärrner, 2. Aufl., Berlin-Bonn 1988.

Seebacher-Brandt, Brigitte: Ollenhauer. Biedermann und Patriot, Berlin-Bonn 1984.

Severing, Carl: Mein Lebensweg, 2 Bde., Köln 1950.

Soell, Hartmut: Fritz Erler. Eine politische Biographie, 2 Bde., Berlin-Bonn-Bad Godesberg 1976.

Stern, Carola: Willy Brandt in Selbstzeugnissen und Bilddokumenten, rowohlts monographien Nr. 232, Reinbek 1975.

Uexküll, Gösta von: Ferdinand Lassalle, rowohlts monographien Nr. 212, Reinbek 1974.

Vogel, Hans-Jochen: Nachsichten. Meine Bonner und Berliner Jahre, München/Zürich 1996.

Wachenheim, Hedwig: Vom Großbürgertum zur Sozialdemokratie. Memoiren einer Reformistin, Berlin 1973.

Weber, Petra: Carlo Schmid 1896- 1979. Eine Biographie, München 1996.

Wehner, Herbert: Zeugnis (Hrsg. Gerhard Jahn), Köln 1982.

Wischnewski, Hans Jürgen: Mit Leidenschaft und Augenmaß. In Mogadischu und Anderswo. Politische Memoiren, München 1989.

Witt, Peter Christian: Friedrich Ebert. Parteiführer, Reichskanzler, Volksbeauftragter, Reichspräsident, 2. Aufl., Bonn 1988.

Wolff, Jeannette: Mit Bibel und Bebel. Ein Gedenkbuch (hrsg. von Hans Lamm) Bonn 1980.

4. From the Beginnings to 1945

Die Allgemeine Deutsche Arbeiterverbrüderung 1848–1850. Dokumente des Zentralkomitees für die deutschen Arbeiter in Leipzig. Bearb. und eingel. von Horst Schlechte, Weimar 1979.

Bajohr, Stefan: Die Hälfte der Fabrik. Geschichte der Frauenarbeit in Deutschland 1914 bis 1945, Marburg 1979.

Balser, Frolinde: Sozial-Demokratie 1848/49–1863. Die erste deutsche Arbeiterorganisation "Allgemeine Arbeiterverbrüderung" nach der Revolution, (Industrielle Welt 2), 2 Bde., Stuttgart 1962.

Bebel, August: Die Frau und der Sozialismus. Mit einem einleitenden Vorwort von Eduard Bernstein. Neusatz nach der Jubiläumsausgabe von 1929, Bonn 1980.

Bernstein, Eduard: Die Voraussetzungen des Sozialismus und die Aufgaben der Sozialdemokratie, 7. Aufl., Berlin-Bonn 1977.

Bernstein, Eduard: Texte zum Revisionismus. Ausgewählt, eingeleitet und kommentiert von Horst Heimann, Bonn 1976.

Bieber, Hans-Joachim: Gewerkschaften in Krieg und Revolution. Arbeiterbewegung, Industrie, Staat und Militär in Deutschland 1914–1920, Teil I und II, Hamburg 1981.

Birker, Karl: Die deutschen Arbeiterbildungsvereine 1840–1870, Berlin 1973.

Boll, Friedhelm: Frieden ohne Revolution? Friedensstrategie der deutschen Sozialdemokratie vom Erfurter Programm 1891 bis zur Revolution 1918, Bonn 1980.

Braun, Lily: Die Frauenfrage. Ihre geschichtliche Entwicklung und ihre wirtschaftliche Seite. Mit einer Einleitung von Beatrix Wrede-Bouvier, (1. Aufl. 1901), Bonn 1979.

Breitman, Richard: German Socialism and Weimar Democracy, Chapel Hill 1981.

Bry, Gerhard: Wages in Germany 1871–1945. A study by the National Bureau of Economic Research, New York (Princeton University Press), Princeton 1960.

Conze, Werner/Groh, Dieter: Die Arbeiterbewegung in der nationalen Bewegung. Die deutsche Sozialdemokratie vor, während und nach der Reichsgründung, (Industrielle Welt 6), Stuttgart 1966.

Drechsler, Hanno: Die Sozialistische Arbeiterpartei Deutschlands (SAPD), Meisenheim a. Gl. 1965.

Edinger, Lewis L.: Sozialdemokratie und Nationalsozialismus. Der Parteivorstand der SPD im Exil 1933–1945, Hannover-Frankfurt/M. 1960.

Feldman, Gerald D.: Armee, Industrie und Arbeiterschaft in Deutschland 1914 bis 1918, Berlin-Bonn 1985.

Fischer, Benno: Theoriediskussion der SPD in der Weimarer Republik, Frankfurt/M.-Bern-New York 1987.

Foitzik, Jan: Zwischen den Fronten. Zur Politik, Organisation und Funktion linker politischer Kleinorganisationen im Widerstand 1933 bis 1939/40 unter besonderer Berücksichtigung des Exils, Bonn 1986.

Friedrich-Ebert-Stiftung (Hrsg.): Widerstand und Exil der deutschen Arbeiterbewegung 1933–1945, Bonn 1982.

Fricke, Dieter: Die deutsche Arbeiterbewegung 1869–1914. Ein Handbuch über ihre Organisation und Tätigkeit im Klassenkampf, Berlin (DDR) 1976.

Fromm, Erich: Arbeiter und Angestellte am Vorabend des Dritten Reiches. Eine sozialpsychologische Untersuchung, bearb. und hrsg. von Wolfgang Bonß, Stuttgart 1980.

Fülberth, Georg/Harrer, Jürgen: Die deutsche Sozialdemokratie 1890–1933, Darmstadt und Neuwied 1974.

Geary, Dick: Arbeiterprotest und Arbeiterbewegung in Europa 1848–1939, München 1983.

Die geheimen Deutschlandberichte der SPD 1934–1940, 7 Bde., Frankfurt/M. 1980.

Grasmann, Peter: Sozialdemokraten gegen Hitler 1933–1945, Reihe "Geschichte und Staat", Bd. 196/197, München-Wien 1976.

Grebing, Helga: Arbeiterbewegung. Sozialer Protest und kollektive Interessenvertretung bis 1914, München 1985.

Groh, Dieter: Negative Integration und revolutionärer Attentismus. Die deutsche Sozialdemokratie am Vorabend des 1. Weltkrieges, Frankfurt/M.-Berlin 1973.

Guttsman, W.L.: The German Social Democratic Party 1895–1933, London 1981.

Heimann, Horst/Meyer, Thomas (Hrsg.): Reformsozialismus und Sozialdemokratie. Zur Theoriediskussion des Demokratischen Sozialismus in der Weimarer Republik, Bonn 1982.

Heupel, Eberhard: Reformismus und Krise. Zur Theorie und Praxis von SPD, ADGB und AfA-Bund in der Weltwirtschaftskrise 1929–1932/33, Frankfurt/M.-New York 1981.

Hohorst, Gerd/Kocka, Jürgen/Ritter, Gerhard A.: Sozialgeschichtliches Arbeitsbuch. Materialien zur Statistik des Kaiserreichs 1870–1914, München 1975.

Hunt, Richard N.: German Social Democracy 1918–1933, New Haven-London 1964.

Jantke, Carl: Der Vierte Stand. Die gestaltenden Kräfte der deutschen Arbeiterbewegung im XIX. Jahrhundert, Freiburg 1955.

Kastning, Alfred: Die deutsche Sozialdemokratie zwischen Koalition und Opposition 1919–1923, Paderborn 1970.

Kocka, Jürgen: Arbeitsverhältnisse und Arbeiterexistenzen. Grundlagen der Klassenbildung im 19. Jahrhundert, Berlin-Bonn 1990.

Kocka, Jürgen (Hrsg.): Europäische Arbeiterbewegungen im 19. Jahrhundert. Deutschland, Österreich, England und Frankreich im Vergleich, Göttingen 1983.

Kocka, Jürgen: Lohnarbeit und Klassenbildung. Arbeiter und Arbeiterbewegung in Deutschland 1800–1875, Berlin-Bonn 1983.

Kocka, Jürgen: Weder Stand noch Klasse. Unterschichten um 1800, Berlin-Bonn 1990.

Langewiesche, Dieter/Schönhoven, Klaus (Hrsg.): Arbeiter in Deutschland. Studien zur Lebensweise der Arbeiterschaft im Zeitalter der Industrialisierung, Königstein/Ts. 1980.

Lehnert, Detlef: Reform und Revolution in den Strategiediskussionen der klassischen Sozialdemokratie. Zur Geschichte der deutschen Arbeiterbewegung bis zum Ausbruch des 1. Weltkrieges, Bonn 1977.

Levenstein, Adolf: Die Arbeiterfrage. Mit besonderer Berücksichtigung der sozialpsychologischen Seite des modernen Großbetriebes und der psychologischen Einwirkungen auf die Arbeiter, München 1912.

Link, Werner: Die Geschichte des Internationalen Jugendbundes (IJB) und des Internationalen Sozialistischen Kampfbundes (ISK), Meisenheim a. Gl. 1964.

Löwenthal, Richard/von zur Mühlen, Patrik (Hrsg.): Widerstand und Verweigerung in Deutschland 1933 bis 1945, Berlin-Bonn 1984.

Luthardt, Wolfgang (Hrsg.): Sozialdemokratische Arbeiterbewegung und Weimarer Republik. Materialien zur gesellschaftlichen Entwicklung 1927–1933, 2 Bde., Frankfurt a. M. 1978.

Luxemburg, Rosa: Schriften zur Theorie der Spontaneität, rowohlt klassiker Nr. 249, Reinbek 1970.

Matthias, Erich: Kautsky und der Kautskyanismus. Die Funktion der Ideologie in der deutschen Sozialdemokratie vor dem ersten Weltkrieg, in: Marxismus-Studien 2, Tübingen [1957].

Matthias, Erich: Sozialdemokratie und Nation. Ein Beitrag zur Ideengeschichte der sozialdemokratischen Emigration in der Prager Zeit des Parteivorstandes 1933–1938, Stuttgart 1952.

Matthias, Erich/Morsey, Rudolf (Hrsg.): Das Ende der Parteien 1933, Athenäum/Droste Taschenbücher, Düsseldorf-Königstein/Ts. 1979.

Mehring, Franz: Geschichte der deutschen Sozialdemokratie, 4 Bde., 10. Aufl., Stuttgart 1921, (Neudruck 2 Bde., Berlin [DDR] 1960).

Miller, Susanne: Die Bürde der Macht. Die deutsche Sozialdemokratie 1918–1920, Düsseldorf 1978.

Miller, Susanne: Burgfrieden und Klassenkampf. Die deutsche Sozialdemokratie im Ersten Weltkrieg, Düsseldorf 1974.

Miller, Susanne: Das Problem der Freiheit im Sozialismus. Freiheit, Staat und Revolution in der Programmatik der Sozialdemokratie von Lassalle bis zum Revisionismusstreit, 5. Aufl., Berlin-Bonn 1977.

Mit dem Gesicht nach Deutschland. Eine Dokumentation über die sozialdemokratische Emigration, hrsg. von Erich Matthias, bearb. von Werner Link, Düsseldorf 1968.

Mommsen, Hans (Hrsg.): Arbeiterbewegung und industrieller Wandel. Studien zu gewerkschaftlichen Organisationsproblemen im Reich und an der Ruhr, Wuppertal 1980.

Morgan, David W.: The Socialist Left and the German Revolution. A History of the German Independent Social Democratic Party 1917–1922, Ithaca und London 1975.
Mühlen, Patrik von zur: "Schlagt Hitler an der Saar!" Abstimmungskampf, Emigration und Widerstand im Saargebiet 1933–1945, Bonn 1979.
Neumann, Sigmund: Die Parteien der Weimarer Republik, hrsg. von Karl Dietrich Bracher, Urban-Taschenbuch Nr. 175, 3. Aufl. 1973.
Nichols, Anthony/Matthias, Erich: German Democracy and the Triumph of Hitler. Essays in Recent German History, London 1971.
Offermann, Toni: Arbeiterbewegung und liberales Bürgertum in Deutschland 1850–1963, Bonn 1979.
Petzina, Dietmar/Abelhauser, Werner/Faust, Anselm: Sozialgeschichtliches Arbeitsbuch, Band III: Materialien zur Statistik des deutschen Reiches 1914–1945, München 1978.
Potthoff, Heinrich: Freie Gewerkschaften 1918 bis 1933. Der Allgemeine Deutsche Gewerkschaftsbund in der Weimarer Republik, Düsseldorf 1987.
Potthoff, Heinrich: Gewerkschaften und Politik zwischen Revolution und Inflation, Düsseldorf 1979.
Potthoff, Heinrich/Weber, Hermann (Bearb.): Die SPD-Fraktion in der Nationalversammlung 1919–1920, Düsseldorf 1989.
Prager, Eugen: Geschichte der USPD. Entstehung und Entwicklung der Unabhängigen Sozialdemokratischen Partei Deutschlands, Berlin 1922, (Neudruck unter dem Titel: Das Gebot der Stunde. Geschichte der USPD, Berlin-Bonn 1980).
Pytha, Wolfram: Gegen Hitler und für die Republik. Die Auseinandersetzung der deutschen Sozialdemokratie mit der NSDAP in der Weimarer Republik, Düsseldorf 1989.
Die Regierung der Volksbeauftragten 1918/19, eingel. von Erich Matthias, bearb. von Susanne Miller unter Mitwirkung von Heinrich Potthoff, 2 Bde., Düsseldorf 1969.
Die Reichstagsfraktion der deutschen Sozialdemokratie 1898 bis 1918, bearb. von Erich Matthias und Eberhard Pikart, 2 Bde., Düsseldorf 1966.
Ritter, Gerhard A.: Die Arbeiterbewegung im Wilhelminischen Reich. Die Sozialdemokratische Partei und die Freien Gewerkschaften 1890–1900, 2. Aufl., Berlin 1963.
Ritter, Gerhard A.: Staat, Arbeiterschaft und Arbeiterbewegung in Deutschland. Vom Vormärz bis zum Ende der Weimarer Republik, Berlin-Bonn 1982.
Ritter, Gerhard A./Miller, Susanne: Die deutsche Revolution 1918–1919, Dokumente, 2. erw. und überarb. Aufl., Hamburg 1975.
Ritter, Gerhard A./Tenfelde, Klaus: Arbeiter im Deutschen Kaiserreich 1871 bis 1914, Bonn 1991.
Röder, Werner: Die deutschen sozialistischen Exilgruppen in Großbritannien. Ein Beitrag zur Geschichte des Widerstandes gegen den Nationalsozialismus, 2. Aufl., Bonn-Bad Godesberg 1973.

Rosenberg, Arthur: Entstehung und Geschichte der Weimarer Republik, Neuaufl., Frankfurt/M.1955.

Rüden, Peter von (Hrsg.): Beiträge zur Kulturgeschichte der deutschen Arbeiterbewegung 1848–1918, Frankfurt/M. 1979.

Rüden, Peter von/Koszyk, Kurt (Hrsg.): Dokumente und Materialien zur Kulturgeschichte der deutschen Arbeiterbewegung 1848–1918, Frankfurt/M. 1979.

Saage, Richard (Hrsg.): Solidargemeinschaft und Klassenkampf. Politische Konzeptionen der Sozialdemokratie zwischen den Weltkriegen, Frankfurt 1986.

Schorske, Carl E.: Die große Spaltung. Die deutsche Sozialdemokratie 1905–1917, Berlin 1981 (engl. Ausgabe 1955).

Schneider, Michael: Unterm Hakenkreuz. Arbeiter und Arbeiterbewegung 1933 bis 1939, Bonn 1999.

Schraepler, Ernst: Handwerkerbünde und Arbeitervereine 1830–1853, Berlin-New York 1972.

Stampfer, Friedrich: Die vierzehn Jahre der ersten deutschen Republik, 3. Aufl. Hamburg [1953].

Stearns, Peter N.: Arbeiterleben, Industriearbeit und Alltag in Europa 1890–1914, Frankfurt-New York 1980.

Steinberg, Hans-Josef: Sozialismus und deutsche Sozialdemokratie. Zur Ideologie der Partei vor dem 1. Weltkrieg, 5. Aufl., Berlin-Bonn 1979.

Stephan, Cora: Genossen, wir dürfen uns nicht von der Geduld hinreißen lassen. Aus der Urgeschichte der Sozialdemokratie 1862–1878, Frankfurt a.M. 1977.

Tenfelde, Klaus/Schönhoven, Klaus/Schneider, Michael/Peukert, Detlef J. K.: Geschichte der deutschen Gewerkschaften. Von den Anfängen bis 1945, Köln 1987.

Varain, Heinz Josef: Freie Gewerkschaften, Sozialdemokratie und Staat. Die Politik der Generalkommission unter der Führung Carl Legiens (1890–1920), Düsseldorf 1956.

Wachenheim, Hedwig: Die deutsche Arbeiterbewegung 1844–1914, Köln-Opladen 1967.

Walter, Franz: Jungsozialisten in der Weimarer Republik, Göttingen 1983.

Weber, Hermann: Kommunismus in Deutschland 1918–1945, Darmstadt 1983.

Weisenborn, Günther (Hrsg.): Der lautlose Aufstand. Bericht über die Widerstandsbewegung des deutschen Volkes 1933–1945, 2. Aufl. Hamburg 1954.

Weißbuch der deutschen Opposition gegen die Hitlerdiktatur, hrsg. vom Vorstand der Sozialdemokratischen Partei, London 1946.

Welskopp, Thomas: Das Banner der Brüderlichkeit. Die deutsche Sozialdemokratie vom Vormärz bis zum Sozialistengesetz, Bonn 2000.

Wickert, Christl: Unsere Erwählten. Sozialdemokratische Frauen im Deutschen Reichstag und im Preußischen Landtag 1919 bis 1933, Göttingen 1986.

Widerstand und Exil 1933–1945 (Schriftenreihe der Bundeszentrale für politische Bildung, Bd. 223), Bonn 1985.

Widerstand, Verfolgung und Emigration, hrsg. vom Forschungsinstitut der Friedrich-Ebert-Stiftung, Bad Godesberg 1967

Winkler, Heinrich-August: Von der Revolution zur Stabilisierung. Arbeiter und Arbeiterbewegung in der Weimarer Republik 1918 bis 1924, 2. Aufl., Berlin-Bonn 1985.

Winkler, Heinrich-August: Der Schein der Normalität. Arbeiter und Arbeiterbewegung in der Weimarer Republik 1924 bis 1930, Berlin-Bonn 1985, 2. Aufl. 1990.

Winkler, Heinrich-August: Der Weg in die Katastrophe. Arbeiter und Arbeiterbewegung in der Weimarer Republik 1930 bis 1933, Berlin-Bonn 1987, 2. Aufl. 1990.

Wunderer, Hartmann: Arbeitervereine und Arbeiterparteien. Kultur- und Massenorganisationen in der Arbeiterbewegung (1890–1933), Frankfurt/M.-New York 1980.

5. *After 1945*

Albrecht, Willi (Hrsg.): Die SPD unter Kurt Schumacher und Erich Ollenhauer 1946–1963. Sitzungsprotokolle der Spitzengremien, Bde. 1 und 2, Bonn 1999/2003.

Ashkenasi, Abraham: Reformpartei und Außenpolitik. Die Außenpolitik der SPD, Berlin-Bonn-Köln-Opladen 1968.

Baring, Arnulf in Zusammenarbeit mit Görtemaker, Martin: Machtwechsel. Die Ära Brandt/Scheel, Stuttgart 1982.

Beier, Gerhard: SPD Hessen-Chronik 1945–1988, Bonn 1989.

Bender, Peter: Die Ostpolitik Willy Brandts oder die Kunst des Selbstverständlichen, rororo aktuell Nr. 1548, Reinbek 1972.

Bender, Peter: Die "Neue Ostpolitik" und ihre Folgen: Vom Mauerbau bis zur Vereinigung, München 1995.

Benz, Wolfgang (Hrsg.): Die Bundesrepublik Deutschland. Geschichte in drei Bänden, Frankfurt/M. 1983.

Bickerich, Wolfram (Hrsg.): Die 13 Jahre. Bilanz der sozialliberalen Koalition. Spiegelbuch, Reinbek bei Hamburg 1982.

Blessing, Karl-Heinz (Hrsg.): SPD 2000. Die Modernisierung der SPD, Marburg/Berlin 1993.

Bölling, Klaus: Die letzten 30 Tage des Kanzlers Helmut Schmidt. Ein Tagebuch. Spiegelbuch, Reinbek bei Hamburg 1982.

Bouvier, Beatrix: Ausgeschaltet! Sozialdemokraten in der Sowjetischen Besatzungszone und in der DDR 1945–1953, Bonn, 1996.

Bouvier, Beatrix W.: Zwischen Godesberg und Großer Koalition. Der Weg der SPD in die Regierungsverantwortung, Bonn 1990.

Bracher, Karl Dietrich/Eschenburg, Theodor/Fest, Joachim C./Jäckel, Eberhard (Hrsg.): Geschichte der Bundesrepublik Deutschland, 5 Bde., Stuttgart-Wiesbaden 1981–1987.

Brakelmann, Günter: Abschied vom Unverbindlichen. Gedanken eines Christen zum demokratischen Sozialismus, Gütersloh 1976.

Brandt, Willy: Friedenspolitik in Europa, Frankfurt/M. 1968.

Brandt, Willy: Frieden. Reden und Schriften, Bonn-Bad Godesberg 1971.

Brandt, Willy: "... was zusammengehört". Reden zu Deutschland, Bonn 1990.

Brandt, Willy/Kreisky, Bruno/Palme, Olof: Briefe und Gespräche 1972–1975, Frankfurt/M.-Köln 1975.

Brandt, Willy/Schmidt, Helmut: Deutschland 1976 – zwei Sozialdemokraten im Gespräch. Gesprächsführung Jürgen Kellermeier, rororo aktuell Nr. 4008, Reinbek 1976.

Braunthal, Gerard: The West German Social Democrats 1969–1982. Profile of a party in power, Boulder (USA) 1983.

Deist, Heinrich: Wirtschaft von morgen. Hrsg. von Gerhard Stümpfig, 2. Aufl., Berlin-Bonn 1973.

Dowe, Dieter (Hrsg.): Von der Bürgerbewegung zur Partei. Die Gründung der Sozialdemokratie in der DDR, Bonn 1993.

Dübber, Ulrich: Die deutsche Sozialdemokratie nach 1945, in: Aus Politik und Zeitgeschichte. Beilage zur Wochenzeitung Das Parlament, B 21/63, 22.5.1963.

Ehmke, Horst (Hrsg.): Perspektiven. Sozialdemokratische Politik im Übergang zu den Siebziger Jahren. Erläutert von 21 Sozialdemokraten, rororo aktuell Nr. 1205, Reinbek 1969.

Ehmke, Horst: Politik als Herausforderung, 2 Bde., Karlsruhe 1974/79.

Ehrenberg, Herbert/Fuchs, Anke: Sozialstaat und Freiheit. Von der Zukunft des Sozialstaats, Frankfurt/M. 1980.

Eichler, Willi: Weltanschauung und Politik. Reden und Aufsätze. Hrsg. und eingel. von Gerhard Weisser, unter Mitwirkung von Susanne Miller, Bruno Friedrich, Klaus Helfer, Franklin Schultheiss, Frankfurt/M. 1967.

Eichler, Willi: Zur Einführung in den demokratischen Sozialismus, Bonn-Bad Godesberg, 2. Aufl. 1973.

Enquete-Kommission Aufarbeitung von Geschichte und Folgen der SED-Diktatur in Deutschland (12. Wahlperiode des Deutschen Bundestages), hrsg. vom Deutschen Bundestag), Neun Bände in 18 Teilbänden, Baden-Baden/Frankfurt a.M. 1995.

Eppler, Erhard: Ende oder Wende?, Stuttgart-Berlin-Köln-Mainz 1975.

Eppler, Erhard: Plattform für eine neue Mehrheit. Ein Kommentar zum Berliner Programm der SPD, Bonn 1990.

Erler, Fritz: Demokratie in Deutschland, Stuttgart 1965.

Erler, Fritz: Politik für Deutschland. Mit einem Vorwort von Willy Brandt. Hrsg. und eingel. von Wolfgang Gaebler, Stuttgart 1968.

Faulenbach, Bernd/Potthoff, Heinrich (Hrsg.): Die deutsche Sozialdemokratie und die Umwälzung 1989/90, Essen 2001.

Faulenbach, Bernd/Potthoff, Heinrich (Hrsg.): Sozialdemokraten und Kommunisten nach Nationalsozialismus und Krieg. Zur historischen Einordnung der Zwangsvereinigung, Essen 1998.

Flohr, Heiner/Lompe, Klaus/Neumann, Lothar F. (Hrsg.): Freiheitlicher Sozialismus – Beiträge zu seinem heutigen Selbstverständnis, 2. Aufl. Bonn-Bad Godesberg 1973.
Garton Ash, Timothy: Im Namen Europas. Deutschland und der geteilte Kontinent, München/Wien 1993.
Gerster, Florian/Stobbe, Friedrich (Hrsg.): Die linke Mitte heute, Bonn 1990.
Glotz, Peter: Die Beweglichkeit des Tankers, München 1982.
Glotz, Peter: Der Weg der Sozialdemokratie. Der historische Auftrag des Reformismus, Wien-München-Zürich 1975.
Grabbe, Hans-Jürgen: Unionsparteien, Sozialdemokratie und Vereinigte Staaten von Amerika 1945–1966, Düsseldorf 1983.
Grebing, Helga (Hrsg.): Entscheidung für die SPD. Briefe und Aufzeichnungen linker Sozialisten 1944–1948, München 1984.
Grebing, Helga u. a. (Hrsg.): Die Nachkriegsentwicklung in Westdeutschland 1945–1949, 2 Bde., Stuttgart 1980.
Grosser, Alfred: Geschichte Deutschlands seit 1945. Überarbeitete Fassung des Bandes Deutschlandbilanz, 5. Aufl., München 1977.
Günther, Klaus: Sozialdemokratie und Demokratie 1946–1966. Die SPD und das Problem der Verschränkung innerparteilicher und bundesrepublikanischer Demokratie. Bonn 1979.
Heimann, Horst: Theoriediskussion in der SPD. Ergebnisse und Perspektiven, Frankfurt/M.-Köln 1975.
Heimann, Siegfried: Die SPD in den neunziger Jahren, in: Werner Süß (Hrsg.), Die Bundesrepublik in den 90er Jahren, Leverkusen 2002.
Hemmer, Hans-Otto/Schmitz, Kurt Thomas (Hrsg.): Geschichte der Gewerkschaften in der Bundesrepublik Deutschland, Köln 1990.
Herles, Helmut: Machtverlust oder das Ende der Ära Brandt, Stuttgart 1983.
Historische Kommission beim Parteivorstand der SPD (Hrsg.): Von der SDP zur SPD, Bonn 1992.
Jäger, Wolfgang: Die Überwindung der Teilung. Der innerdeutsche Prozess der Vereinigung 1989/90, Stuttgart 1998.
Jarausch, Konrad: Die unverhoffte Einheit 1989- 1990, Frankfurt a.M. 1995.
Jung, Matthias/Roth, Dieter: Wer zu spät geht, den bestraft der Wähler. Eine Analyse der Bundestagswahl 1998, in: Aus Politik und Zeitgeschichte B 53/98.
Kaack, Heino: Geschichte und Struktur des deutschen Parteiensystems, Opladen 1971.
Kaden, Albrecht: Einheit oder Freiheit. Die Wiedergründung der SPD 1945/46, 3. Aufl., Berlin-Bonn 1990.
Kielmannsegg, Peter Graf: Nach der Katastrophe. Eine Geschichte des geteilten Deutschlands, Berlin 2000.
Kleßmann, Christoph: Die doppelte Staatsgründung. Deutsche Geschichte 1945–1955. 4. Aufl., Göttingen-Bonn 1986.
Kleßmann, Christoph: Zwei Staaten, eine Nation. Deutsche Geschichte 1955–1970, Göttingen-Bonn 1988.

Klotzbach, Kurt: Der Weg zur Staatspartei. Programmatik, praktische Politik und Organisation der deutschen Sozialdemokratie 1945 bis 1965, Berlin-Bonn 1982 (Nachdruck 1996).

Korte, Karl-Rudolf, Deutschlandpolitik in Helmut Kohls Kanzlerschaft. Regierungsstil und Entscheidungen 1982–1989, Stuttgart 1998.

Koschnick, Hans (Hrsg.): Der Abschied vom Extremistenbeschluß. Mit Beiträgen von Hans Koschnick, Erich Küchenhoff, Hans-Jürgen Schimke, Martin Kriele und Ernst-Wolfgang Böckenförde und einer Dokumentation, 2. Aufl., Bonn 1979.

Lafontaine, Oskar: Die Gesellschaft der Zukunft. Reformpolitik in einer veränderten Welt, Hamburg 1988.

Lafontaine, Oskar: Das Herz schlägt links, München 1999.

Lösche, Peter: Die SPD nach Mannheim. Strukturprobleme und aktuelle Entwicklung, in: Aus Politik und Zeitgeschichte B 6/96.

Löwenthal, Richard (Paul Sering): Jenseits des Kapitalismus. Ein Beitrag zur sozialistischen Neuorientierung. Mit einer ausführlichen Einführung: Nach 30 Jahren, 3. Aufl., Bonn 1978.

Löwke, Udo F.: Für den Fall, daß ... Die Haltung der SPD zur Wehrfrage 1949–1955, Hannover 1969.

Lompe, Klaus/Neumann, Lothar (Hrsg.): Willi Eichlers Beiträge zum demokratischen Sozialismus. Eine Auswahl aus dem Werk, Berlin-Bonn 1979.

Lührs, Georg/Sarrazin, Thilo u. a. (Hrsg.): Kritischer Rationalismus und Sozialdemokratie. Mit einem Vorwort von Helmut Schmidt, 2 Bde., Bonn 1975/76.

Malycha, Andreas: Auf dem Weg zur SED. Die Sozialdemokratie und die Bildung einer Einheitspartei in den Ländern der SBZ. Eine Quellenedition, Bonn 1995.

Marßolek, Inge/Potthoff, Heinrich: Durchbruch zum modernen Deutschland? Die Sozialdemokratie in der Regierungsverantwortung 1966–1982, Essen 1995.

Meyer, Thomas: Demokratischer Sozialismus. Eine Einführung, Bonn 1982.

Meyer, Thomas (Hrsg.): Demokratischer Sozialismus. Geistige Grundlagen und Wege in die Zukunft, München-Wien 1980.

Meyer, Thomas: Grundwerte und Wissenschaft im Demokratischen Sozialismus, Berlin-Bonn 1979.

Meyer, Thomas: Soziale Demokratie und Globalisierung. Eine europäische Perspektive, Bonn 2002.

Meyer, Thomas: Die Transformation der Sozialdemokratie. Eine Partei auf dem Weg ins 21. Jahrhundert, Bonn 1998.

Meyer, Thomas/Scherer, Klaus-Jürgen/Zöpel, Christoph: Parteien in der Defensive? Plädoyer für die Öffnung der Volkspartei, Köln 1994.

Miller, Susanne/Ristau, Malte (Hrsg.): Erben deutscher Geschichte. DDR-BRD: Protokolle einer historischen Begegnung, Reinbek bei Hamburg 1988.

Moraw, Frank: Die Parole der "Einheit" und die Sozialdemokratie. Zur parteiorganisatorischen und gesellschaftspolitischen Orientierung der SPD in der Periode der Illegalität und in der ersten Phase der Nachkriegszeit 1933–1948, 2. Aufl., Bonn 1990.

Morsey, Rudolf: Die Bundesrepublik Deutschland. Entstehung und Entwicklung bis 1969, München 1987.

Moseleit, Klaus: Die "Zweite" Phase der Entspannungspolitik der SPD 1983–1989. Eine Analyse ihrer Entstehungsgeschichte, Entwicklung und der konzeptionellen Ansätze, Frankfurt a.M. 1991.

Narr, Wolf-Dieter: CDU-SPD. Programm und Praxis seit 1945, Stuttgart-Berlin-Köln-Mainz 1966.

Narr, Wolf-Dieter/Scheer, Hermann/Spöri, Dieter: SPD – Staatspartei oder Reformpartei?, München 1976.

Narr, Wolf-Dieter/Thränhardt, Dietrich (Hrsg.): Die Bundesrepublik Deutschland. Entstehung, Entwicklung, Struktur, Königstein 1978.

Neubert, Ehrhart: Geschichte der Opposition in der DDR 1949–1989, Berlin 1995.

Oertzen, Peter von/Ehmke, Horst/Ehrenberg, Herbert (Hrsg.): Orientierungsrahmen '85. Text und Diskussion. Bearbeitet von Heiner Lindner, 3. Aufl., Bonn-Bad Godesberg 1979.

Ott, Erich: Die Wirtschaftskonzeption der SPD nach 1945, Marburg 1978.

Paterson, William E./Schmitz, Kurt Th. (Hrsg.): Sozialdemokratische Parteien in Europa, Bonn 1979.

Pirker, Theo: Die SPD nach Hitler. Die Geschichte der Sozialdemokratischen Partei Deutschlands 1945–1954, München 1965.

Potthoff, Heinrich: Bonn und Ost-Berlin 1969–1982. Dialog auf höchster Ebene und vertrauliche Kanäle. Darstellung und Dokumente, Bonn 1997.

Potthoff, Heinrich: Die "Koalition der Vernunft". Deutschlandpolitik in den 80er Jahren, München 1995.

Potthoff, Heinrich: Im Schatten der Mauer. Deutschlandpolitik 1961 bis 1990, Berlin 1999.

Rexin, Manfred: Die SPD in Ost-Berlin 1946–1961. Mit Beiträgen von Siegfried Heimann und Horst Hoffke, Berlin 1989.

Roth, Wolfgang: Humane Wirtschaftspolitik. Die sozialdemokratische Alternative, Köln 1982.

Sarcinelli, Ullrich: Das Staatsverständnis der SPD. Ein Beitrag zur Analyse des sozialdemokratischen Staatsverständnisses auf der Grundlage der SPD-Programm- und Grundsatzdiskussion in den Jahren 1969 bis 1975, Königstein 1979.

Scharpf, Fritz: Sozialdemokratische Krisenpolitik in Europa. Das "Modell Deutschland" im Vergleich, Frankfurt/M. 1987.

Schellenger jr., Harold Kurt: The SPD in the Bonn Republic. A Socialist Party modernizes, Den Haag 1968.

Schlei, Marie/Wagner, Joachim: Freiheit – Gerechtigkeit – Solidarität. Grundwerte und praktische Politik, m. e. Vorwort von Helmut Schmidt, Bonn 1976.

Schmidt, Helmut: Freiheit verantworten, Düsseldorf-Wien 1983.

Schmidt, Helmut: Kontinuität und Konzentration, 2. erw. Auflage, Bonn-Bad Godesberg 1976.

Schmollinger, Horst W./Müller, Peter: Zwischenbilanz. 10 Jahre sozialliberale Politik 1969–1979, Hannover 1980.

Schneider, Michael: Demokratie in Gefahr? Der Konflikt um die Notstandsgesetze. Sozialdemokratie, Gewerkschaften und intellektueller Protest (1958–1968), Bonn 1966.

Schönhoven, Klaus: Wendejahre. Die Sozialdemokratie in der Zeit der Großen Koalition 1966–1969, Bonn 2004.

Schröder, Klaus, unter Mitarbeit von Steffen Alisch: Der SED-Staat. Geschichte und Strukturen der DDR, München 1998.

Schütz, Klaus: Die Sozialdemokratie im Nachkriegsdeutschland, in: Parteien in der Bundesrepublik. Studien zur Entwicklung der deutschen Parteien bis zur Bundestagswahl 1953, Stuttgart-Düsseldorf 1955.

Schumacher, Kurt/Ollenhauer, Erich/Brandt, Willy: Der Auftrag des demokratischen Sozialismus, Bonn-Bad Godesberg, 2. Aufl. 1973.

Schwan, Alexander/Schwan, Gesine: Sozialdemokratie und Marxismus. Zum Spannungsverhältnis von Godesberger Programm und marxistischer Theorie, Hamburg 1974.

Schwan, Gesine: Sozialismus in der Demokratie? Theorie einer konsequent sozialdemokratischen Politik, Stuttgart-Berlin-Köln-Mainz 1982.

Sozialpolitik nach 1945. Geschichte und Analysen, hrsg. von Reinhart Bartholomäi, Wolfgang Bodenbender, Hardo Henkel, Renate Hüttel, Bonn 1977.

Die SPD-Fraktion im Deutschen Bundestag. Sitzungsprotokolle. 1949–1957, bearbeitet von Petra Weber, 2 Bde.; 1957–1961, bearbeitet von Wolfgang Hölscher; 1961–1966, bearbeitet von Heinrich Potthoff, 2 Bde., Düsseldorf 1993.

Staritz, Dieter: Geschichte der DDR, Frankfurt/M. 1984.

Steffen, Joachim: Krisenmanagement oder Politik?, rororo aktuell Nr. 1826, Reinbek 1974.

Steinbach, Peter: Sozialdemokratie und Verfassungsordnung, Leverkusen 1980.

Steininger, Rolf: Deutschland und die Sozialistische Internationale nach dem Zweiten Weltkrieg. Die deutsche Frage, die Internationale und das Problem der Wiederaufnahme der SPD auf den internationalen sozialistischen Konferenzen bis 1951, unter besonderer Berücksichtigung der Labour Party. Darstellung und Dokumentation, Bonn 1979.

Stephan, Dieter: Jungsozialisten: Stabilisierung nach langer Krise? Theorie und Politik 1969–1979. Eine Bilanz, 2. Aufl., Bonn 1980.

Strasser, Johano: Grenzen des Sozialstaats? Soziale Sicherung in der Wachstumskrise, Köln-Frankfurt 1979.

Strasser, Johano/Traube, Klaus: Die Zukunft des Fortschritts. Der Sozialismus und die Krise des Industrialismus, Bonn 1981.

Stöss, Richard/Niedermayer, Oskar: Zwischen Anpassung und Profilierung. Die SPD an der Schwelle zum neuen Jahrhundert, in: Aus Politik und Zeitgeschichte B 5/2000.

Vogel, Hans-Joachim/Ruhnau, Heinz/Buschfort, Hermann u. a.: Godesberg und die Gegenwart. Ein Beitrag zur innerparteilichen Diskussion über Inhalte und Methoden sozialdemokratischer Politik, Bonn-Bad Godesberg 1975.

Vogtmeier, Andreas: Egon Bahr und die deutsche Frage. Zur Entwicklung der Ost- und Deutschlandpolitik vom Kriegsende bis zur Vereinigung, Bonn 1996.

Walter, Franz: Die SPD nach der deutschen Vereinigung – Partei in der Krise oder bereit zur Regierungsübernahme?, in: Zeitschrift für Parlamentsfragen, Heft 1/95.

Weber, Hermann: DDR. Grundriß der Geschichte 1945–1976, Hannover 1976.

Wehner, Herbert: Wandel und Bewährung. Ausgewählte Reden und Schriften 1930–1967. Hrsg. von Hans-Werner Graf Finckenstein und Gerhard Jahn. Mit einer Einleitung von Günter Gaus, Berlin-Hannover 1968.

Wehner, Herbert/Friedrich, Bruno/Nau, Alfred: Parteiorganisation, Theorie und Praxis der deutschen Sozialdemokratie, Bonn-Bad Godesberg 1969.

Werner, Emil: Im Dienst der Demokratie. Die bayerische Sozialdemokratie nach der Wiedergründung 1945, München 1982.

Wilke, Lothar: Die Sicherheitspolitik der SPD 1956–1966. Zwischen Wiedervereinigungs- und Bündnisorientierung, Bonn 1977.

Winkler, Heinrich August (Hrsg.): Politische Weichenstellungen im Nachkriegsdeutschland 1945 bis 1953, Göttingen 1979.

Index

Abbe, Ernst 57
Adenauer, Konrad 179, 186 f., 189–191, 193–195, 203–207, 217, 267, 271, 296, 301, 431
Adler, Victor 70
Agartz, Victor 175
Albrecht, Ernst 258, 289
Altmann, Rüdiger 300
Angst, Heinrich 70
Apel, Hans 234, 277, 298
Arndt, Adolf 166, 175, 189, 197, 432
Arndt, Klaus Dieter 228
Arnim, Hans Herbert von 278, 281
Ashkenasi, Abraham 204
Audorf, Jakob 30
Auer, Ignaz 39, 47
Auerbach, Walter 155
Aufhäuser, Siegfried 138, 149, 152
Axen, Hermann 289 f.

Bahr, Egon 217, 234, 237 f., 240, 246, 264, 283, 289 f., 315, 319, 335, 351, 434, 437 f.
Baker, James 323
Bakunin, Michail 33
Barbe, Angelika 313, 323
Barschel, Uwe 294–298, 344, 440
Barth, Emil 79 f., 88, 428
Barzel, Rainer C. 219–221
Bauer, Gustav 76, 94, 100, 103, 429

Bauer, Otto 200
Baum, Gerhart 266
Bebel, August 13, 32, 35–37, 39 f., 42, 44–46, 58, 63–65, 67–71, 73–75, 132, 292, 425, 427
Becher, Johannes R. 320
Beck, Kurt 386, 408, 445, 448
Bell, Johannes 94
Benneter, Klaus Uwe 239, 408, 451
Bergmann, Christine 366
Bernstein, Eduard 47, 50, 62 f., 67, 73, 427
Bethmann Hollweg, Theobald von 72
Beust, Ole von 408, 448, 451
Biedenkopf, Kurt 337, 445
Birthler, Marianne 309
Bismarck, Otto von 28, 35, 37 f., 42 f., 45 f., 56 f., 426
Blair, Tony 367 f., 371, 398, 446
Blessing, Karl-Heinz 342, 444
Blüm, Norbert 363
Blumenberg, Werner 141
Bodewig, Kurt 375
Böchel, Karl 152
Böhme, Ibrahim 313, 323–325, 441
Bölling, Klaus 252
Börner, Holger 237, 251, 286, 293, 436 f.
Bohm-Schuch, Clara 139
Borchert, Jochen 363
Born, Stephan 18, 25–27, 425
Bosch, Robert 57

Bracke, Wilhelm 39
Brandt, Willy 83, 129, 166, 175, 191, 193, 197, 200 f., 203–205, 207, 209–211, 215–220, 222–227, 229–233, 240 f., 246, 248 f., 256, 264, 266 f., 272, 274, 282 f., 287, 288, 290–293, 295 f., 299, 302 f., 308 f., 314, 316, 318–321, 324, 326–328, 332, 335, 343, 349–352, 356, 423, 433–441, 443
Brauer, Max 153, 191, 200, 203
Braun, Otto 115 f., 123 f., 127 f., 132 f., 138, 430
Breitscheid, Rudolf 135, 138, 153 f.
Brezhnev, Leonid 246
Brill, Hermann 146
Brockdorff-Rantzau, Ulrich von 86, 100
Brüning, Heinrich 123, 125–129, 432
Brundert, Willi 259
Büchner, Georg 21
Bulmahn, Edelgard 366, 399
Buschfort, Hermann 228
Bush, George W. 398 f., 404, 452

Carstens, Karl 221, 251, 273, 437
Carstens, Manfred
Carstensen, Peter Harry 413
Carter, Jimmy 263
Chamberlain, Neville 152
Chirac, Jacques 398
Churchill, Winston 154 f., 157
Clement, Wolfgang 290, 292, 326, 343, 363, 374 f., 386, 399, 403, 407 f., 412, 446 f., 449, 451

Coppik, Manfred 245
Crispien, Artur 138
Christoffersen, Chris 309
Crummenerl, Siegmund 138, 149
Cuno, Wilhelm 107

Däubler-Gmelin, Herta 298, 343, 365, 367, 399, 440, 443 f.
Däumig, Ernst 81, 84, 87, 98
Dahrendorf, Gustav 146
Dahrendorf, Ralf 354
Daladier, Edouard 153
Darwin, Charles
David, Eduard 94
Deist, Heinrich 197, 203
Derossi, Carl 39
Dettling, Warnfried 373
Dieckmann, Bärbel 409
Dieckmann, Jochen 413
Diepgen, Eberhard 448
Dietzgen, Joseph 39
Dißmann, Robert 99
Ditfurth, Christian von 350
Dittmann, Wilhelm 79 f., 84, 138, 428
Döhling, Gerd 313
Dohnanyi, Klaus von 216, 234, 332
Dreesbach, August 39
Dregger, Alfred 295
Dreßler, Rudolf 341–343, 443
Dübber, Ulrich 182
Duesterberg, Theodor 125

Eberhard, Fritz 184
Ebert, Friedrich 74 f., 79–81, 84–86, 89, 93, 95, 103, 108, 116, 428–430
Ehmke, Horst 220, 228, 234, 277, 305, 326

Ehrenberg, Herbert 228
Ehrhardt, Hermann 103
Eichel, Hans 333, 367, 372 f., 377, 399, 412, 442, 447
Eichler, Willi 155, 166, 175, 197 f., 432
Eisner, Kurt 73, 78, 88, 95
Engels, Friedrich 18, 21–25, 28 f., 31 f., 37, 40, 49–52, 58 f., 64 f., 69, 73, 425
Engholm, Björn 295–297, 304, 319, 333, 336 f., 342, 344 f., 408, 440, 443
Eppelmann, Rainer 311, 350
Eppler, Erhard 228 f., 246, 254, 294, 303, 311, 332, 335, 338, 366, 378, 380
Erhard, Ludwig 181–183, 187 f., 195, 207, 209
Erler, Fritz 142, 166, 194–197, 201–203, 207, 225, 434 f.
Ertl, Josef 215
Erzberger, Matthias 76 f., 92–94 f.

Faulenbach, Bernd 349
Fehrenbach, Konstantin 106
Fichter, Tilman 316
Filbinger, Hans 235
Fimmen, Edo 143
Fischer, Joschka 286, 293, 333, 335, 366, 378 f., 380, 391, 397–399, 412, 442
Fischer, Richard 73
Flick, Friedrich Karl 278–280
Foch, Ferdinand 92
Focke, Katharina 220
Fourier, Charles 21
Franco y Bahamonde, Francisco 153, 351
Frank, Karl 152

Frank, Ludwig 67
Franke, Egon 245
Freisler, Roland 144, 154
Frick, Wilhelm (NSDAP) 138 f.
Frick, Wilhelm (SPD) 39
Friderichs, Hans 220
Friedrich Wilhelm IV.
Fritzsche, Friedrich Wilhelm 29, 39, 42
Fröhlich, August 108
Frohme, Karl 39
Fuchs, Anke 293, 440
Fukuyama, Francis 307, 353
Funke, Karl-Heinz 366, 376

Gabriel, Sigmar 375, 385, 407–409, 422, 450
Gansel, Norbert 316
Gareis, Karl 95
Gaulle, Charles de 393
Geib, August 39
Geißler, Heiner 280
Genscher, Hans-Dietrich 215, 233, 236, 242, 249–252, 256, 273, 276, 291, 294, 298, 318, 345, 438
Gerlach, Paul 138
Gerster, Florian 392
Geßler, Otto 100
Geyer, Curt 98
Giddens, Anthony 371
Giscard d'Estaing, Valéry 234
Glogowski, Gerhard 375, 385
Glotz, Peter 229, 287, 293, 303, 368, 393, 438
Goebbels, Joseph 134, 298
Goerdeler, Carl 147
Göring, Hermann 126
Gollancz, Victor 154
Gorbachev Mikhail, 288 f., 298, 307 f., 439, 441

Gottfurcht, Hans 155 f.
Gotthelf, Herta 197
Grass, Günter 320
Greulich, Hermann 70
Grillenberger, Carl 39
Groener, Wilhelm 85, 94
Gromyko, Andrei 217
Grotewohl, Otto, 167 f., 174, 431
Grottkau, Paul 39
Grzesinski, Albert 115, 132 f., 138, 153
Gscheidle, Kurt 234
Guillaume, Günter 224
Gumbel, Emil 95
Guttenberg, Karl Theodor von und zu 206
Gutzeit, Martin 312 f.
Gysi, Gregor 415

Haase, Hugo 69, 71 f., 74 f., 79–81, 84, 95, 98, 428
Habermann, Max 147
Habermas, Jürgen 335
Haenisch, Konrad 73
Hänsch, Klaus 353
Haffner, Sebastian 139
Hansen, Karl-Heinz 245
Hardie, J. Keir 70
Hartmann, Georg Wilhelm 39
Hartz, Peter 403
Hasenclever, Wilhelm 39
Hasselmann, Wilhelm 39, 46
Hatzfeldt, Sophie von 29
Haubach, Theodor 131, 146, 148, 173
Hauff, Volker 300
Hauptmann, Gerhart 19
Heim, Georg 89
Heine, Fritz 156, 171 f., 197, 431

Heine, Wolfgang 104
Heinemann, Gustav 213 f., 219, 224, 233, 370, 433, 435 f.
Henke, Klaus-Dietmar 167
Henßler, Fritz 176
Hertz, Paul 138, 149, 152
Herwegh, Georg 30
Herzog, Roman 346
Hildebrandt, Regine 333 f.
Hilferding, Rudolf 99, 113, 115, 138, 154
Hilpert, Werner 147
Hilsberg, Stephan 313, 324
Hindenburg, Paul von 77, 85, 93 f., 116, 123–126, 129, 133, 136, 430
Hintze, Peter 350, 362
Hirsch, Max 36
Hirsch, Paul 115
Hitler, Adolf 14, 106, 108, 120, 124–126, 129, 135 f., 138–141, 143–145, 149 f., 152–157, 160, 173, 176, 399, 430
Hoegner, Wilhelm 128, 174
Höltermann, Karl 133
Höppner, Reinhard 362, 386, 444
Hofmann, Gunter 335
Hombach, Bodo 290, 366 f., 369
Honecker, Erich 221 f., 246, 276, 283 f., 288, 290, 295, 308, 310 f., 316, 351, 438, 440 f.
Horn, General von 20
Hugenberg, Alfred 120 f., 124
Huntington, Samuel 352 f.
Hupka, Herbert 219
Hussein, Saddam 334, 398

Immerfall, Stefan 384

Jahn, Hans 143
Jaksch, Wenzel 152, 203
Jarausch, Konrad 320
Jarres, Karl 116
Jaruzelski, Wojciech 246, 309
Jaurès, Jean 70
Jenninger, Philipp 297
Jogiches, Leo 95
Jospin, Lionel 371, 446
Junker, Karin 340

Kahr, Gustav von 108
Kaisen, Wilhelm 174, 186, 191, 200
Kaiser, Jakob 147
Kamilli, Karl-August 324
Kampffmeyer, Paul 59
Kant, Immanuel 129
Kapell, August 39
Kapell, Otto 39
Kapp, Wolfgang 100, 102–105, 429
Kasimier, Helmut 258
Katz, Rudolf 153
Kautsky, Karl 37, 47, 50, 52, 58, 63 f., 88, 113
Keil, Wilhelm 115, 127
Kennedy, John F. 204 f.
Kerry, John F. 452
Ketteler, Wilhelm Emmanuel von 40 f.
Keynes, John-Maynard 250
Khrushev, Nikita 194, 202 f., 433
Kiep, Walther Leisler 280, 374
Kiesinger, Kurt Georg 209 f., 435
Kinkel, Klaus 363
Kirdorf, Emil 57
Kirchner, Johanna 154

Klimmt, Reinhard 370, 375, 385, 445–447
Klose, Hans-Ulrich 291, 343, 443 f.
Klühs, Franz 141
Kluncker, Heinz 222
Knoeringen, Waldemar von 152, 156, 175, 197, 433
Knothe, Willi 431
Koch, Roland 367, 446, 450
Koch-Weser, Erich 108
Köhler, Horst 409, 415, 422, 451 f.
Köster, Adolf 100
Kohl, Helmut 221, 236, 242, 248, 256, 271–273, 275–277, 279–283, 288, 291, 293, 296–298, 300 f., 306, 308, 311 f., 317–328, 330–333, 343 f., 346 f., 350, 352 f., 356–365, 370, 373 f., 376, 384, 390, 393, 401, 420, 438 f.
Kolping, Adolf 40 f.
Kopf, Hinrich Wilhelm 200
Koschnick, Hans 237, 332
Kraft, Hannelore 413
Krahnstöver, Anni 181
Krenz, Egon 316, 441
Kriedemann, Herbert 171, 181
Kronawitter, Georg 300
Krone, Heinrich 204
Krupp, Alfred 57
Krzeminski, Adam 368
Kubel, Alfred 258
Kühn, Heinz 211, 435
Künast, Renate 376, 399
Künstler, Franz 133
Kuhl, C. J. 39
Kummernuss, Adolph 143

Lafontaine, Oskar 246, 254 f.,
    282, 286 f., 290–293, 295, 303–
    305, 316, 320 f., 324–328, 331 f.,
    334, 343–346, 348 f., 357–
    362, 365–368, 370, 372, 390,
    410, 415, 439–441, 444–447
Lambertz, Werner 221
Lambsdorff, Otto Graf 250 f.,
    253, 255 f.
Landauer, Gustav 95
Landsberg, Otto 80, 84, 428
Lassalle, Ferdinand 15, 18, 28–
    32, 35, 37, 39 f., 73, 92, 152,
    172, 425
Leber, Georg 215
Leber, Julius 106, 131 f., 137,
    146–148, 173
Ledebour, Georg 79
Legien, Carl 62, 102 f.
Leipart, Theodor 102, 133, 138
Lenin, Wladimir Iljitsch 14, 88,
    97, 157, 160
Lensch, Paul 73
Leuschner, Wilhelm 146–148
Leussink, Hans 215
Levi, Paul 84, 98
Lewy, Gustav 28
Liebknecht, Karl 67, 69, 71 f.,
    74, 79, 84 f., 95, 97, 311,
    428 f., 440
Liebknecht, Wilhelm 13, 32,
    35 f., 38–40, 42, 61, 425
Limbach, Jutta 341, 444
Li Peng 313
Löbe, Paul 115, 139, 145, 191
Lösche, Peter 271, 303 f., 340
Löwenheim (Miles), Walter 142,
    155
Löwenthal, Richard (Paul Sering)
    142, 152, 155, 229, 249, 264,
    272

Ludendorff, Erich 77, 93, 108
Lücke, Paul 206
Lüdemann, Hermann 186
Lütje, Uwe 280
Lüttwitz, Walter von 103
Luxemburg, Rosa 67, 73 f., 83–
    85, 95, 97, 311, 428 f., 440

Maas, Heiko, 385
Machnig, Matthias 372, 385
MacMillan, Harold 205
Mahlein, Leonhard 245
Maihofer, Werner 266 f.
Maizière, Lothar de 325, 441
Mann, Thomas 393
Marshall, George C. 183
Marx, Karl 18, 21–25, 27–29,
    31–33, 35–40, 42, 47, 49 f.,
    52, 56, 59, 64, 69, 73, 92, 425
Marx, Wilhelm 116
Mathiopoulos, Margarita 292
Matschie, Christoph 385
Matthäus-Maier, Ingrid 257,
    298, 324, 341
Matthöfer, Hans 166, 234, 287,
    291
Maurer, Ulrich 303 f.
Mauroy, Pierre 443
Max von Baden 76, 79, 428
Mazzini, Guiseppe 33
Meckel, Markus 309, 312 f., 321,
    323, 325, 350
Mehring, Franz 67
Mellies, Wilhelm 181, 432
Menzel, Walter 184
Merkel, Angela 341, 376, 398,
    409 f., 413, 415–418, 422,
    452
Merseburger, Peter 178
Merz, Friedrich 376, 410
Meyer, Laurenz 376, 418

Meyer, Thomas 381 f.
Meyers, Franz 211, 435
Middleton, James 154
Mielke, Erich 224
Mierendorff, Carlo 131, 146, 148, 173
Miller, Susanne 71, 186, 349
Milosevic, Slobodan 353, 379
Mischnick, Wolfgang 222
Mitterrand, François 175, 353
Modrow, Hans 322 f.
Möllemann, Jürgen 375
Möller, Alex 201, 203, 207, 215, 219
Möller, Walter 259
Momper, Walter 299 f., 315, 318, 440
Monnet, Jean 190
Moron, Edgar 413
Most, Johann 39, 46
Motteler, Julius 39
Müller, Günther 219
Müller, Hermann 94, 100, 104–106, 117, 119, 121–123, 127, 225, 429 f.
Müller, Peter 370
Müller, Richard 84
Müller, Werner 366
Munkelt, Peter 405
Müntefering, Franz 348, 358, 363, 366, 372, 388, 399, 402, 405, 408, 410 f., 414, 419 f., 422, 447, 449, 451 f.
Mussolini, Benito 153

Nahles, Andrea 409
Napoleon III. 32, 42
Nau, Alfred 171
Nelson, Leonard 129
Neumann, Franz 170, 204
Niedermayer, Oskar 369

Noack, Arndt 313
Nölting, Erik 175
Noske, Gustav 82, 84 f., 87, 100, 104

Oertzen, Peter von 166, 228, 303
Oeser, Rudolf 104
Ollenhauer, Erich 138, 149, 156, 167, 171 f., 179, 187, 190, 195–197, 201 f., 207, 431–434
Ott, Jochen 385
Owen, Robert 21

Paasche, Hans 95
Palme, Olof 283
Papen, Franz von 122–124, 126 f., 129, 133 f.
Pfeiffer, Anton 296
Pinochet, Augusto 246, 351
Pirker, Theo 186
Platzeck, Matthias 409
Polenz, Ruprecht 376
Preuß, Hugo 89
Proudhon, Pierre-Joseph 21
Putzrath, Heinz 349

Rackow, Heinrich 39
Radbruch, Gustav 95
Rapp, Heinz 229
Rathenau, Walther 95
Rau, Johannes 243, 254, 273, 287–291, 293, 295, 298, 311, 318, 322, 326, 332 f., 343 f., 346 f., 351, 363, 370, 375, 378, 409, 438–440, 443 f., 446 f.
Ravens, Karl 258
Reagan, Ronald 246, 263, 275, 288

Reiche, Steffen 316
Reichwein, Adolf 146–148
Reimer, Otto 39
Reinhardt, Walther 103
Renger, Annemarie 220, 249, 251
Reuter, Ernst 183, 186, 191, 200, 204, 432
Rexin, Manfred 316
Richter, Willi 203
Riester, Walter 366, 382, 387, 399, 448
Ringstorff, Harald 386, 409, 446, 449
Rinner, Erich 150
Rinser, Luise 286
Röhm, Ernst 125
Rohde, Helmut 234, 341
Rommel, Manfred 300
Roosevelt, Franklin D. 154, 157
Rosenfeld, Kurt 129
Roth, Wolfgang 324
Rühe, Volker 363
Rühle, Otto 72
Rüttgers, Jürgen 413
Ruhnau, Heinz 228
Rumsfeld, Donald 398
Runde, Ortwin 446, 448

Saefkow, Anton 143
Saint-Simon, Claude Henry de Rovroy 21
Schabowski, Günter 317
Schäuble, Wolfgang 290, 360, 376
Schalck-Golodkowski, Alexander 276
Scharping, Rudolf 304, 333 f., 342, 345–349, 354, 357 f., 366, 371, 378 f., 391, 399, 405, 442, 444 f., 449
Schartau, Harald 413

Scheel, Walter 215 f., 233, 435 f.
Scheidemann, Philipp 74–76, 79–81, 84, 86, 92–94, 100, 102, 138, 428 f.
Scherf, Henning 407, 450
Schevenels, Walter 146
Schill, Roland 386, 448
Schiller, Karl 175, 188, 201, 207, 210, 215, 219
Schily, Otto 280, 365 f., 383, 399, 419
Schleicher, Kurt von 123–127
Schleußer, Heinz 375
Schleyer, Hanns Martin 237
Schliestedt, Heinrich 155
Schmid, Carlo 166, 175, 185, 190, 195 f., 203, 431 f.
Schmidt, Helmut 166, 197, 201, 207, 214 f., 219 f., 223–225, 227, 230, 233–238, 240, 242–246, 248 f., 252–257, 262–264, 266 f., 271–277, 282 f., 287, 295, 300, 308 f., 316, 331, 333, 335, 343, 423, 435–439
Schmidt, Renate 399, 449
Schmidt, Ulla 376, 399 f., 422
Schmude, Jürgen 251, 311
Schoeler, Andreas von 257
Schöllgen, Gregor 204
Schönhoven, Klaus 402
Schönhuber, Franz 301
Schoettle, Erwin 152, 156, 175
Scholz, Ernst 119
Scholz, Olaf 399, 405, 408, 449, 451
Schorlemmer, Friedrich 311
Schraps, Reinhold 425
Schreiner, Ottmar 372
Schröder, Gerhard (CDU) 209, 211, 213

Schröder, Gerhard (SPD) 13, 17, 286, 289, 290, 295, 304, 319, 325–327, 334, 338, 340, 345 f., 348, 354, 357, 359–366, 368–374, 376–378, 380–383, 385–387, 390 f., 392, 394, 397–401, 403 f., 406–408, 410–412, 414–417, 421–423, 444, 446–452
Schroeder, Louise 200
Schröder, Richard 325
Schuchardt, Helga 257 f.
Schüler, Manfred 369
Schütz, Klaus 189
Schulz, Klaus-Peter 219
Schulze-Delitzsch, Hermann 30, 40
Schumacher, Kurt 131, 138, 145–147, 165, 167–175, 178 f., 181–183, 185–187, 189–191, 431 f.
Schuman, Robert 190
Schwarz, Gesine 409
Schwarz, Hans-Peter 178
Schweitzer, Jean Baptist von 28, 37 f., 42
Seebacher-Brandt, Brigitte 350 f.
Seeckt, Hans von 103, 107
Seehofer, Horst 410
Seger, Gerhart 144, 149, 153
Seiters, Rudolf 316
Seldte, Franz 124
Serke, Jürgen
Seume, Franz 219
Severing, Carl 105, 115, 132–134, 137
Seydewitz, Max 129
Sielaff, Horst 311
Simonis, Heide 341, 357, 375, 386, 409, 412 f., 443, 447, 452
Sollmann, Wilhelm 137, 152

Späth, Lothar 300
Spöri, Dieter 303 f., 338
Stalin, Josef 14, 126 f., 143, 157, 160, 191 f.
Stampfer, Friedrich 138, 149 f., 153
Stauffenberg, Claus Schenk von 148
Stein, Lorenz von 21
Steinbrück, Peer 399, 408, 413, 422, 450, 452
Steiner, Julius 219, 222
Steinhoff, Fritz 203
Steinmeier, Frank-Walter 369, 422
Stiegler, Ludwig 405
Stinnes, Hugo 107, 110
Stöss, Richard 369
Stoiber, Edmund 387, 391, 397 f., 402, 407, 413
Stollmann, Jost 366
Stolpe, Manfred 333 f., 338, 344, 370, 386, 392, 399, 442, 445, 447, 449
Stoltenberg, Gerhard 300
Stoph, Willi 217, 317, 435
Strauß, Franz Josef 206, 210, 220, 235, 240, 242 f., 276, 295, 297
Stresemann, Gustav 86, 107 f., 117, 121
Strobel, Käte 203
Ströbel, Heinrich 129
Struck, Peter 366, 399, 405
Stumm-Halberg, Carl Ferdinand von 57
Suhr, Otto 204

Tarnow, Fritz 155
Tessendorf, Ernst Christian 38
Teufel, Erwin 410

Thälmann, Ernst 116, 125, 127
Thape, Ernst 146
Thierse, Wolfgang 299, 327 f., 332, 365, 442, 444, 449
Tiefensee, Wolfgang 409, 422
Tölcke, Carl Wilhelm 39 f.
Traube, Klaus 267
Trittin, Jürgen 366, 399
Tüttenberg, Achim 337

Ulbricht, Walter 168, 192, 205
Ulrich, Karl 115

Vahlteich, Julius 29, 39
Vaillant, Edouard 70
Vansittart, Robert 157
Veit, Hermann 176
Verheugen, Günter 257, 345, 348, 444
Vogel, Bernhard 295, 297
Vogel, Hans 138, 149, 156, 167, 172
Vogel, Hans-Jochen 220, 228, 266, 273–277, 282, 284, 287, 291–293, 295, 297–301, 303, 305, 311, 316–318, 320, 326–328, 332, 343, 349, 351, 438–440
Vogt, Ute 385, 448
Voigt, Karsten D. 315, 351
Vollmar, Georg von 44, 58 f., 62 f., 197

Wachenheim, Hedwig 153
Wagner, Leo 219
Waigel, Theodor 300, 382
Walesa, Lech 309
Wallmann, Walter 259
Walster, August 39
Walter, Franz 135, 170, 203, 271, 303 f., 340, 390

Wehner, Herbert 166, 175, 194, 196 f., 202 f., 206 f., 215, 220–222, 225 f., 240, 246, 256, 271, 276, 283, 309, 350 f., 433–435, 441
Weisskirchen, Gerd 311, 316
Weitling, Wilhelm 21, 27
Weizsäcker, Carl-Friedrich von 302
Weizsäcker, Richard von 274, 286, 295, 298, 439
Wels, Otto 101, 103–105, 133, 137 f., 140, 149
Wentz, Martin 299
Wessel, Helene 433
Westarp, Kuno Graf von 107, 121
Westerwelle, Guido 339, 397
Wettig-Danielmeier, Inge 298, 340, 443
Weyrauch, Horst 280
Wichern, Johann Heinrich 39
Wieczorek-Zeul, Heidi 345, 366, 399, 422, 444
Wienand, Karl 222
Wilhelm I. 43
Wilhelm II. 78
Wirth, Joseph 107
Wischnewski, Hans-Jürgen 252, 287, 435 f.
Wissell, Rudolf 82, 84, 118
Wolf, Markus 224
Wolf, Walter 147
Wowereit, Klaus 386, 409, 448
Wulff, Christian 407, 450

Zeigner, Erich 108
Zetkin, Clara 98
Zinn, Georg August 200, 203
Zinoviev, Grigori 99
Zörgiebel, Karl 126
Zypries, Brigitte 399, 422, 449

Bildnachweise

Archiv der sozialen Demokratie, pages 16, 37, 43, 51, 59, 64, 85, 117, 138, 160, 188, 210, 213, 227, 290, 333, 339, 358, 385, 412

Barbara Klemm, pages 236, 305

dpa, pages 70, 180, 263, 310, 350, 391

WAZ-Zeichnung, Klaus Pielert, page 268

Jupp und Marc Darchinger, pages 316, 324, 348

Lothar Kucharz, page 354

Sepp Spiegl, page 361

bonn-sequenz, Hans Windeck, page 367

Notes on the Authors

Heinrich Potthoff, PhD, born in 1938, historian. Until 1991 research work for the Commission on Parliamentarianism; until 2003 deputy chairman of the Historical Commission of the SPD. Author of numerous books on contemporary history, particularly on the history of the labour movement; inter alia, Freie Gewerkschaften 1918-1933 (1987), Die SPD-Fraktion im Deutschen Bundestag 1962-1966 (1991), and on all-German relations, inter alia, Bonn und Ost-Berlin 1969-1982. Dialog auf höchster Ebene und vertrauliche Kanäle (1997), Im Schatten der Mauer. Deutschlandpolitik 1961 bis 1990 (1999). Lives in Königswinter as a freelance historian and writer.

Professor Susanne Miller, PhD, born 1915. Exile in England 1938-1946; employee with the SPD executive committee in Bonn 1952-1960; adviser to the Committee on Parliamentarianism 1964-1978; since 1996 chairperson for the Working Group on Persecuted Social Democrats. Numerous publications on the history of social democracy and the international labour movement: inter alia, Das Problem der Freiheit im Sozialismus (1964), Burgfrieden und Klassenkampf (1974), Die Bürde der Macht (1978). She lives in Bonn and is an active commentator on politics and contemporary history.